PENGUIN BOOKS

SIX ENCOUNTERS WITH

Elizabeth Brown Pryor (1951–2015) was an award-winning historian who also served as a senior officer in the American Foreign Service. She was the author of the biography *Clara Barton, Professional Angel* and of *Reading the Man: A Portrait of Robert E. Lee Through His Private Letters*, which won the 2008 Lincoln Prize, the Jefferson Davis Award, the Richard B. Harwell Book Award, and the Richard Slatten Award.

* * *

Praise for *Six Encounters with Lincoln*

"At a moment when questions about the efficacy of government are on everybody's lips, this book eerily reflects some of today's key issues. . . . A different Lincoln inhabits the pages of *Six Encounters with Lincoln*. Here we meet the skilled raconteur whose tales promote vacillation, and whose humor disguises costly indecision and delay. . . . Fascinating reading on its own terms, *Six Encounters with Lincoln* nevertheless confronts readers with startlingly relevant questions. . . . The notion that democracy involves compromises resonates today."
—*The New York Times Book Review*

"Pryor's Lincoln is a man of excessive ambition, handicapped by strange looks and profound social awkwardness, whose pragmatism often contradicts his loftier ideals. . . . Pryor is particularly adept at conveying the impossibility of Lincoln's task: to represent a profoundly fractured country in which, as one of Lincoln's friends put it, 'the eyes of the whole nation will be upon you while unfortunately the ears of one half of it will be closed to anything you say.'" —*The Wall Street Journal*

"This history aims at deconstructing Lincoln's mythic reputation as the Great Emancipator to arrive at a more nuanced view. . . . Pryor paints a provocative historical portrait while testing common assumptions about an American icon."
—*The New Yorker*

"Provocative . . . Trenchant analysis and graceful writing . . . Pryor found six overlooked episodes that reveal Lincoln's character, his fallibility, and the awesome task he confronted, at times with mixed success. With them she seeks to replace the 'mirage' that Lincoln has become with a living, breathing politician."
—*The Christian Science Monitor*

"[An] extraordinary book . . . Pryor carefully examines Lincoln's interactions with little-known contemporaries, which provides a new and illuminating way of looking at his life and his presidency." —*The National Book Review*

"Deeply researched, telling moments in the life of arguably the most written-about man in history . . . Gets beyond the hagiographic portrayals of Lincoln, allowing rare glimpses of the man as vulnerable, clumsy, inarticulate, and very human. . . . Kudos to Pryor for offering readers something fresh about our six-teenth president—no small feat." —*Kirkus Reviews* (starred review)

"Will cinch Pryor's legacy as a creative scholar . . . What makes the encounters particularly fascinating is that the participants recorded them at the time, so they remain uncolored by the sentimentality of post-assassination remembrance. . . . Pryor's impressive final book will be of great appeal to Lincoln aficionados." —*Publishers Weekly*

"In her meticulously researched study of these little-known but arresting encoun-ters with Lincoln, Elizabeth Brown Pryor teases out their meaning with cool dis-crimination, sensitivity, and a vivid pen. She exposes a human president—sometimes blundering, graceless, socially awkward, obstinate, intolerant—struggling to cope in time of war with the fluid messiness of democratic government. Iconoclastic, unsentimental, and hard-headed, this is a brilliant work that is bound to provoke animated scholarly discussion." —Richard Carwardine, author of *Lincoln: A Life of Purpose and Power*

"A daring, provocative, and exceptionally important book that convincingly challenges many of the assumptions on which Abraham Lincoln's greatness is based. Elizabeth Brown Pryor examines Lincoln's often startling behavior in heretofore little-known but highly revealing encounters, and from them she ex-pertly weaves a larger narrative of his fitful progress as the beleaguered leader of a nation at war. The research is prodigious, the writing graceful and assured. I highly recommend *Six Encounters with Lincoln* to readers seeking a truly fresh perspective on the sixteenth president and believe it to be one of the most signifi-cant works on Lincoln of this generation." —Peter Cozzens, author of *The Earth Is Weeping: The Epic Story of the Indian Wars for the American West*

Six Encounters with Lincoln

A President Confronts Democracy and Its Demons

ELIZABETH
BROWN PRYOR

PENGUIN BOOKS

PENGUIN BOOKS

An imprint of Penguin Random House LLC

375 Hudson Street
New York, New York 10014
penguin.com

First published in the United States of America by Viking Penguin,
an imprint of Penguin Random House LLC, 2017
Published in Penguin Books 2018

ISBN 9780143111238 (paperback)

THE LIBRARY OF CONGRESS HAS CATALOGED THE HARDCOVER EDITION AS FOLLOWS:
Names: Pryor, Elizabeth Brown, author.
Title: Six encounters with Lincoln : a president confronts democracy and its
demons / Elizabeth Brown Pryor.
Description: New York, New York : Viking, 2017. | Includes bibliographical
references and index.
Identifiers: LCCN 2016042837 (print) | LCCN 2017001615 (ebook) | ISBN
9780670025909 (hardcover) | ISBN 9780735222793 (e-book)
Subjects: LCSH: Lincoln, Abraham, 1809–1865—Anecdotes. | Presidents—United
States—Anecdotes. | Lincoln, Abraham, 1809–1865—Miscellanea. |
Presidents—United States—Miscellanea.
Classification: LCC E457.15 .P93 2017 (print) | LCC E457.15 (ebook) | DDC
973.7092—dc23
LC record available at https://lccn.loc.gov/2016042837

Printed in the United States of America
1 3 5 7 9 10 8 6 4 2

Set in Adobe Garamond Pro
Designed by Alissa Rose Theodor

Contents

Foreword

My sister Elizabeth Brown Pryor tragically lost her life on April 13, 2015. A manic-depressive driver, who thought that he could fly his car, was trying to "taxi" down a quiet city street in Richmond, Virginia, when he rear-ended her beloved Audi TT at 107 miles per hour. She was instantly killed. She left behind two completed manuscripts: one for this book and another for an article, " 'The Grand Old Duke of York': How Abraham Lincoln Lost the Confidence of His Military Command," which will be published separately.

I remember her sheer elation the previous January, when she called me in London to announce that she had finally finished *Six Encounters with Lincoln*. It had been a long, slow gestation that had begun with a chance discovery in 2008. The day that she received the Lincoln Prize for *Reading the Man: A Portrait of Robert E. Lee Through His Private Letters,* she had spent the morning doing research at the New-York Historical Society. When she arrived back at the flat where we were staying to change for dinner (into my new Armani jacket), she was ecstatic. Not in anticipation of receiving such a singular honor—although she was, of course, delighted to receive it—but because she had just discovered an unpublished drawing of Abraham Lincoln sketched in a letter written home during the Civil War. As she put it, "There sits Abraham Lincoln, with a familiarity almost unimaginable today, legs folded and tall hat in place, looking for all the world like a cricket perched on the nation's front porch."

What had been a brief encounter in 1862 between the President and one of his military guards turned out to be not only a fascinating tale, but a springboard for investigating a neglected but significant aspect of Lincoln's administration. Over the next seven years Elizabeth submerged herself in the letters, diaries, and newspaper articles of the 1860s, carefully piecing together six episodes that explored Lincoln's difficulty in managing a republic. Her own quarter-century career in the State Department gave her a unique perspective on how slowly the wheels of government turn and how our Founding Fathers' insistence on a balance of power could cause the cogs of those wheels to lock in an unwelcome impasse. Few other Civil War historians can marry personal experience with scholarly insight in such a compelling way. She served as the foreign affairs adviser to both houses of Congress and so had an insider's view of the government at work. When we read her criticism of Lincoln as commander in chief, we should remember that she was once the chief U.S. spokesperson for NATO and had earlier been deeply involved with Bosnia, serving in Sarajevo at the time of the siege. She experienced firsthand the importance of military discipline when one was under fire, and she understood that rank matters. As she was fond of saying, she had lived "real-time" history. It was her unique ability to tie the various threads of her life experience together and reflect upon the lessons she had learned that allowed her to render such a vivid picture of nineteenth-century American history. As one critic put it, "The sheer power of [her] language is as inspiring as a great painting."

When I found the manuscript of *Six Encounters with Lincoln* after her death, the text, footnotes, and bibliography were virtually ready for publication. She had meticulously highlighted in yellow any quotations or page numbers that needed to be rechecked. Only the preface was missing. I undertook the task of checking the notes, quotations, and bibliography, but what appears in the following pages is completely her work in her words. She had ordered four or five photographs, but left no list of illustrations. I knew only that she had once told me that she wanted "a lot of pictures." Luckily, since I am an art historian, ordering photographs is one thing I know how to do and my major contribution to this book was deciding what should be illustrated and where it should be placed within the text.

Elizabeth and I and our sister, Peggy, grew up listening to my mother's tales of the Civil War with rapt attention. Not that Mother herself had been around then, but as a child she had spent hours sitting on the front porch in Terre Haute, Indiana, listening to the tales of her great-grandfather John Jackson Kenley. Grandpa Kenley, who according to family lore had lived to the ripe old age of 104 (his military records, however, show him to have been 96 at his death in 1938), had been a foot soldier in the Twenty-Fourth Indiana Regiment. He saw action at the battles of Shiloh, Corinth, Vicksburg, and Mobile as well as the occupation of New Orleans. The house was full of Civil War "heirlooms," including the walnut bookcase made for his wedding in

1863, the fork from his mess kit, and a pile of letters, one of which Elizabeth quotes in this book. Yet as she often said, it was not the "stuff" that got her hooked on the Civil War, but Mother's storytelling ability. "History" after all means "story" and Mother was able to make it seem very real to the three of us. Mother died just four months after Elizabeth, but for seven years she had been able to follow the progress of the book from beginning to end, listening to the chapters as they were written. She was inordinately proud that her middle daughter was just as good a storyteller as she was.

On a road trip, Elizabeth retraced the Lincoln family's journey from Virginia to Kentucky to southern Indiana; the same trip that the Kenley family had made in the early years of the nineteenth century. I remember her excitement at finding the gravesite of Grandpa Kenley's mother, who had died as the family passed through the bluegrass country of Kentucky. In her eyes Lincoln's history and our history were to some extent inextricably bound. Her trip to what she inevitably referred to as the dreaded CTZ, that is to you and me the Central Time Zone, was tainted only by the lack of three-star Michelin restaurants. For two months she was forced to subsist on a diet of monkey chow, which in her parlance meant Subway sandwiches, chocolate-covered cranberries, and Diet Dr Pepper. The upside, however, was that she saw firsthand the furniture made by Lincoln's father and found new insights into the Rail-splitter's boyhood.

In the preface to her book on Robert E. Lee, Elizabeth paid me the compliment of saying that my work as an art historian had inspired her to look deep into the letters of Lee and place them within a larger historical context. "When an expert points out the factors that influenced the artist, how he or she mixed the paint and chose the colors, where the subject was found and what is behind the iconography, the painting becomes something more than it was. In the same way, interpreting Lee's letters for the reader lends them context and heightens their value." I would like to return that compliment now. I learned from her that "retread history" is never good enough. No matter how compelling another author's arguments might be, it is imperative that one return to the original sources, judging them for their own merit. Too often the yellow varnish applied so thickly by scholars to enhance a story simply obscures the truth. Elizabeth would remind me that there was so little in Lincoln's own words about his feelings that we were beholden to the observations of those around him. But she would warn me that Renaissance scholars like myself, who must often rely on the secondhand accounts of Giorgio Vasari, should be at once both grateful and skeptical of such observations. As a historian, she would say, you have no greater tool than your skepticism.

Even as a child, Elizabeth had an unquenchable thirst for knowing the facts. Shortly before my mother's death, I spent an afternoon talking to her about Elizabeth. When I asked what she remembered most about her middle daughter, she said without hesitation, "She was always standing at the kitchen counter looking things up in the encyclopedia." One often finds the phrase "meticulously researched" in reviews of her books, but from an early age she felt compelled to rummage for answers, to seek out hidden gems and to search for the truth. As a mature historian she never ceased exploring new topics with the same inquisitiveness, although the stakes became higher and the process harder. For *Clara Barton, Professional Angel,* she had some sixty-five thousand autobiographical documents, so many that she felt that at times she took on the role of editor as much as author. With Robert E. Lee, when she was led into doubt, contradiction, or subterfuge, she had his own words to quote and ponder as she laid out his life story. But with Lincoln, she was plunged into incertitude and became reliant on writers such as Dennis Hanks and William Herndon to supply interpretations of his character. Unsatisfied with these well-trawled sources, Elizabeth became something of a ferret, unearthing new nuggets of information in the most unlikely and far-flung places. The Museum of English Rural Life at the University of Reading in Great Britain springs to mind, but that was only one of some fifty libraries and archives that she worked in while researching this book. With a fine-tooth comb, she sifted through more than 350 unpublished collections of family papers and diaries. This was in addition to the sizable number of letters, memoirs, and chronicles that have already seen print, like those of Hanks and Herndon. "Leave no stone unturned" might well have been her mantra. As these pages show, she truly believed that one account or eyewitness report was never enough to prove a point. For each chapter of *Six Encounters with Lincoln* the evidence she presents is overwhelming—carefully crafted bricks piled one atop another until the wall is so high and impenetrable that we are obliged to stop and reevaluate every preconceived notion we hold of Lincoln.

I did not find a list of acknowledgments. I know that she had a fellowship from the Huntington Library and spent a good deal of time working at the Abraham Lincoln Presidential Library, Harvard University, the Virginia Historical Society, and, of course, the Library of Congress. But for me to create a list of the people I know she would have thanked or to thank only those who helped me as I finished work on her manuscript would be invidious. I would ask only that one day when you pull this book from the shelf that you will remember the question that you answered at the information desk, the heated debate you had over lunch, the glass of wine you shared at the end of day or the laughter over dinner, and know that she was profoundly grateful for your help, for your insights, for your friendship, and for your love.

Beverly Louise Brown
London, April 2016

Note to the Reader

The quotations from primary sources, including letters, diary entries, books, and journals, have been transcribed without changing the spelling, capitalization, or punctuation. Any edits are noted with brackets or ellipses.

Introduction

> We shall not cease from exploration
> And the end of all our exploring
> Will be to arrive where we started
> And know the place for the first time
>
> —T. S. ELIOT, "LITTLE GIDDING," V,
> *FOUR QUARTETS* (1943)

To look again with open eyes at a subject we think we know is never straightforward. All the more so when the figure has reached the mythic status of Abraham Lincoln. What more can be said about our sixteenth president that we do not already know? So much has been written, and overwritten, and written over that it seems nearly impossible to find a new nugget of truth to offer. Lincoln is an American icon, whose shadow hangs over every president as the quintessential paradigm of high-caliber leadership in a moment of great moral crisis. President Theodore Roosevelt kept a picture of him over the mantelpiece in his office, and when he was confronted by some matter of conflicting rights, he confided "that I would look up at that splendid face and try and imagine him in my place and try to figure out what he would do in the circumstances."[1] Yet, in truth, we know less of what Lincoln actually was and stood for than what we hope he embodied. He is one of the most malleable figures in American history. Depending on how you read him, he was either maddeningly simplistic or elusively complex. His fame follows from his dogged ability to be the determined and patient tortoise to the harebrained Fire-Eaters surrounding him and from the handful of eloquently written expressions of the agony at hand. Rarely were the latter appreciated in their day nor did they have much contemporary sway, but they—along with his martyr's death—have propelled him into a special category of American heroes.

Six Encounters with Lincoln is an invitation to rethink our presumptions about Abraham Lincoln. It is an unorthodox and provocative look at the Lincoln presidency, although it did not start out that way. The book began as a simple collection of intriguing stories about a man who himself prized story-telling. The anecdotes were good ones—mostly unknown and all unexplored, involving characters as diverse as Robert E. Lee, Chief Little Crow, Susan B. Anthony, and an old Confederate with a menacing stick in his hand named Duff Green. The backstories were even better, astonishingly so in fact, revealing Lincoln in a way that put the color-enhanced tinsel of his acclaim in a new, more garish light. Each tale describes a meeting between the sixteenth president and his constituents—plebeian or prominent—revealing his opinions and character in surprising ways. Simply to have found new Lincoln material, especially anecdotes that help us peer into dusty corners, is something to celebrate. On the most basic level, these incidents are cracking good stories, showing Lincoln in all his quirky greatness. But each tale also provides a springboard for delving into significant aspects of Lincoln's administration that have been neglected or previously unknown. Every one of these stories causes us to ponder our preconceptions about Lincoln. The episodes are also connected by a number of common threads, so that in the end the yarn I wanted to spin has re-formed itself into a web.

First and foremost, the stories illustrate the difficulty of managing a republic and creating a presidency. In all of these situations we watch Lincoln struggle to define his administration's priorities, while resisting the attempts of others to wrest the initiative from him. The democratic "demons" evoked in the subtitle are not just the political devils Lincoln battled in his ambitious exercise of power—though that could be said to have fully demonized America. They arise from the contradictions inherent in self-government, forming the darker side of our bright republican currency. Among the phantoms that plagued Lincoln's administration were greed; impatience; the ignorance of the public; the need to manage a large army while subordinating it to the popular will; the structural dysfunction of the American government, guaranteed by Founding Fathers who were suspicious of any authority that might be too efficient; and constant demands from competing sectors of the population—sectors with little in common save their appetite for dominance. Every chief magistrate struggles with this reality, but Lincoln confronted it in the rawest possible context: a nation at war with itself.

Throughout his presidency Lincoln struggled with the very nature of democracy, not only its definitions and traditions but its momentum and fluidity, that irksome capacity to change swiftly like a flash flood in the mountains. He wrestled with the very people who made up so vibrant a community, grappling with their clamorous diversity, their impatience, their outspoken opinions, and above all their demands. Every leader of a republic faces a similar challenge. As President Bill Clinton so aptly put it, "[Y]ou come in with your agenda and vision, and the fact is, whether you want it or not, ultimately a lot of the legacy for Presidents is how they handle the hand they were dealt."[2] We see this in high relief with Lincoln, who both responded to and helped shape a new way of looking at democratic inclusion, not necessarily because he wanted to but because he had to.

The devil in democracy is that it cannot help being itself. It provides a fierce and constant debate; a cacophony of opinions; a minefield of stubborn wills and terrible egos. Within the great truth—the supremacy of the people—there are a myriad of small truths all vying for respect and often at odds with one another. In Lincoln's day the greatest of these was contradiction between the ideal of democracy and the prevailing views on the treatment of Indians and slavery. As the Emancipation Proclamation went into effect, voices rang out in dissent, describing a paralyzed legislative body swayed by the "infernal machinations" of Mr. Lincoln. "Congress keeps in awe the reckless and unscrupulous Administration, as, according to the pious belief of medieval times, holy water awed the devil."[3]

The 1860s was an era of highly individualistic democracy, when all citizens believed they could petition the nation's leader for rights, privileges, or direct support. At times it seemed the whole, unwieldy nation was at the President's doorstep, selling an opinion or begging a favor. Those watching today will remember another slim lawyer from Illinois, who worked to keep true to himself and his policies in the midst of national malaise, and appreciate just how overwhelmingly personal is the job of the president and how difficult it is to address the relentless democratic demands. In the episodes presented here, we see how Lincoln must *design* his presidency in a hundred daily ways and as he tries to satisfy players as diverse as Julia Ward Howe and John Ross, chief of the Cherokee Nation.

The stories also remind us that Lincoln's republic was a government of, by, and for *only some* of the people. It was not just the black population that was excluded, but Native Americans, women, whole categories of immigrants, and even many white males. It may have been, as Lincoln pronounced it, the "last best hope on earth"—but *"hope"* is the operable word here: *hope* of inclusion and pluralism; *hope* for equal rights and opportunities. It was not an ideal reached during Lincoln's lifetime. He surely started—in important ways—the momentum toward a broader democracy, but his vision proved myopic in many instances. Democracy after all is a slippery concept. Lincoln was certainly enthusiastic about the liberty he had embraced—the liberty to reinvent himself; the liberty to move and sway with perceived opportunities; the liberty to try to grow; and even the liberty to fail and try again. That democracy and the idea of true equality were different concepts. While Indians, women, and Negroes might be equals in social niceties or as Lincoln said "in the right to eat the bread . . . which his own hand earns," they remained unequal in political rights, social mobility, and opportunity. Lincoln moves to eliminate slavery only when it is a medium to end the war; no matter how eloquently he proclaims it to be a universal wrong. For all his promotion of a society where all men might rise, he raises no platform for better education or universal suffrage.[4]

Interestingly, these encounters also give us a sense of the difficulty Lincoln sometimes had in communicating. The eloquence of his formal writing and his delightful, whimsical humor have, to some degree, obscured the inelegance of his everyday interactions. He disliked spontaneous discussion with people who might misinterpret him. He seemed to be most comfortable when he could project his thoughts through parables or from a written script. In *Six Encounters with Lincoln* we observe him standing gracelessly mute at his first review of the Army; swearing precipitously at a young soldier on the White House portico; alternately pontificating or talking pidgin English to Indian chiefs; simply avoiding most interaction with women; and in a state of chronic miscommunication with Southerners. The episodes remind us of the human psyche's contrariness; of how even the most sensitive intellect can be clumsy or obstinate or intolerant.

Lincoln is not always shown at his best in these six episodes. As the eyewitnesses make clear, in *his* day "Honest Abe" was not looked upon as the savior of the nation. Instead he was largely viewed as a well-meaning bumbler, a curious and earnest man, but not the leader needed in a national crisis. In each chapter of this book we have multiple protagonists who question Lincoln's wisdom. Even many of his closest allies believed the war was won despite, rather than because of, his efforts. Today we may be tempted to dismiss this as the poor ability of lesser mortals to appreciate the greatness before them. But the blindness is perhaps ours, not theirs. Speaking of the Irish revolutionary martyr Roger Casement, Mario Vargas Llosa noted that his multifaceted personality will never be totally acknowledged: "There will always be a reluctance to accept this complexity which is the complexity of human nature. We are not perfect, and that is not tolerable in our heroes."[5]

Americans have had the same trouble. We are willing to tolerate little personal quirks: George Washington's false teeth, for example, or Thomas Jefferson's philandering. We can accept the lovable foibles in Lincoln: his unruly shock of hair or strange gargoyle of a face; his unrealized ambitions in local politics; his problematic marriage; and his smutty, smirking jokes. But questioning his aspiration to lead a country in turmoil, without the barest qualifications; suggesting that he blundered through military labyrinths with all the agility of an angered buffalo, while thousands of people died; accepting that his fundamental racism accompanied his clear distaste for slavery; and acknowledging that as the consummate politician he often cheerfully compromised his principles for favor or party or expediency—these have been taboo subjects for more than a century. They are issues that need to be revisited and rethought if we are going to understand our past with a modicum of honesty.

We cannot do this if our only point of reference is a face staring up in a thousand handfuls of pocket change or down from the magisterial Lincoln Memorial. Over the years, Lincoln's image has been polished and embellished to add luster to a political party and a set of ethical precepts that he himself did not espouse. It is a kind of mirage shimmering in the water in the road before us, promising more than is actually there. What appeared to his fellow citizens at the time was considerably more concrete, and I have at every instance tried to rely on their words, written in real time. I am less interested in the historical shadows cast by well-meaning memorialists and more interested in actions and outcomes, which are all that we can with veracity assess. For this we must rely on the Johnny-on-the-spot reporters, chroniclers of the moment, diarists, and letter writers.

This testimony is far from complete. Lincoln is largely absent as a voice, because his own writings are sparse, uneven, and largely dull. Even with nine volumes of closely spaced transcripts, the cache is disappointing for those who want to feel the spirit of the man. Most of his writings are limited in subject matter (political scheming and business of the day), and exhibit jumbled thought patterns and syntax. God knows you do not read most of them for the prose. They are filled with countless small acts of accidental violence to the English language. They lack the tone, style, verse, and veracity of Lincoln at his best. Only later in his career did he learn to express himself in sharp, succinct prose, the fineness and brevity of which had the power to dazzle. Much of the earlier writing is so self-contradictory or measured against political advantage that it is difficult to know what he stood for outside of his enormous ambition for elected office. It is a paper-thin personality that emerges, the flimsiest of characters, without the satisfying girth of a well-formed man. It is too bad that Lincoln did not record more of his thoughts and observations, because it really would be interesting to know, for example, what he thought of the women's movement burgeoning around him. Because on so many issues Lincoln does not share his thoughts, it is open season for those who wish to interpret him.

What we know—or think we do—about Lincoln, and what gives him fascination, all comes from other people. We see him secondhand, through the eyes of friends or enemies and secretaries, who presume to speak for him or of him from authority. Some of those wrote as he lived; some knew him well and respected and liked him. But far more wrote after his tragic assassination, when vice turned to virtue and his legacy seemed unique to all. His famous words were often placed in his mouth by others, for their own purposes. It is the chroniclers who supply the wry, entertaining, and astute oral pyrotechnics that we have come to associate with Lincoln. Some of what they tell us about the man is verifiable, but far more is sullied by the mystic chords of memory.

I have been intrigued by many points of view, but persuaded only by those of people who knew Lincoln and wrote in real time. The six narratives in *this book* are based on firsthand accounts—no tainted memoirs or heroic post-assassination recollections. I discovered these sources while doing research on topics other than Lincoln—on Clara Barton's relation with the women's rights activist Frances Dana Gage, for example, or why the Cherokee fought for the Confederacy. The fact that the documents were in unexpected places and far-flung locations is perhaps why they have escaped the notice of generations of Civil War scholars. In several of the stories, the new information is so striking that it might be worthy of its own monograph. One could explore all of the themes here at length: our loss of Lincoln through mythology; the way he tackled the conundrum of American democracy; and the troubling way that his endearing quirkiness has obscured questions about whether his governance was effective. However, the goal of this particular work is to present the six chapters as an interlinked series of episodes.

The strength of the eyewitnesses is that they knew and worked with Lincoln, and wrote as they were living through the nightmare of civil war. Listening to their voices helps us avoid projecting our perfect knowledge of what did happen—both triumph and tragedy—on our assessment of the war's outcome. They force us to ask what are apparently unmentionable questions: whether the war could have been ended sooner or less bloodily or with better consequences under a different president. "Whatever sacrifices his vacillations may have cost the people, those vacillations will now be forgiven," noted one astute observer on the night Lincoln died. Predicting the onslaught of praise-laden works that would appear for the next century and a half, he added: "The murderer's bullet opens to him immortality."[6]

It did not take long for the petrification of immortality to set in. By the 1880s Lincoln's halo was so brightly polished that the orator Robert G. Ingersoll could lament that "[h]undreds of people are now engaged in smoothing out the lines in Lincoln's face—forcing all features to the common mold—so that he may be known, not as he really was, but according to their poor standard, as he should have been." As the literary scholar Stephen Greenblatt has noted, we want to cling to vivid symbols, the memorable images that have captured our collective imagination. This is why it is so difficult to even suggest that Abraham Lincoln might have been something less than the mythologers have told us. But to fetishize Lincoln is only to demean him by pretending that he was something that he was not. It should be enough to praise his *personal* achievement in rising from a humble backwoods beginning to make a mark in the world and to celebrate his quest for greater knowledge and higher understanding. The pride of being something more than you were expected to be is part and parcel of the American dream. What he had already achieved by 1858 was notable enough.[7]

The historian Douglas L. Wilson has written about Lincoln's pathway between two worlds as a young man.[8] He undoubtedly took this journey, consciously and unconsciously—blazing not only a trail for himself, but for generations of aspiring Americans. But one of the troubling aspects of Lincoln is that throughout his career he is less a man of principle than of political expediency. Early on he shuns his idol Henry Clay for the presidency when it appears that his party may falter with Clay's candidacy. In 1836 he denounces the disenfranchisement of tax paying (or mocks it as a possibility). In any case, he never makes a move to alleviate this democratic paradox. By comparison, in his years as president, he had to open up new roads, shaking off long-held prejudices as he created innovative ways of progressing. I see him throughout his presidency, probing the darkness—extending his long fingers into the unknown—for his situation was perilous and his role unprecedented. Reaching into the void he would have had nothing to turn to, neither his lawyerlike instinct for precedent nor the smooth bonhomie of his familiar political machine. At times he did have limited support from long-standing friends, but suspicion often filled the air. His presidency was forged not only by quiet thought and weighty consultation, but also by the constant pressure to respond to the demands of the day. We watch him react or at times overreact to those who sought him out, men—

struck by his awkwardness and shrewdness—who made up the chain of experience that ultimately gave him insight.

Lincoln's trajectory from farm boy to president has been likened to the parable of the mustard seed (Mark 4:26–32), in which large things grew from small beginnings. Well-meaning scholars have tried to rationalize his self-contradictory statements into a kind of Lincolnian unified field theory, by saying he "grew" over time or was "big enough to change" as he thoughtfully honed his policies. Yet growing on the job is just another way of saying that he was always playing catch-up—he was behind, not before the curve. Learning on the job is always laudable and might have been fine if the times had been less perilous. It would have been acceptable in a Martin Van Buren or William Henry Harrison presidency and perhaps that is what Lincoln envisioned—a job of patronage, posturing, and party politics. But with a close reading of the political trends of the time, it simply looks like he was expedient, finding the most popular path and following it. This does not make him a moral compass for the nation, especially at a time of war when the consequences were greater and every stumbling step could and did lead to a corpse. In war, the price for "growing" was death.

We err in assuming the war had to take the course it did and that Lincoln's heroism lay in the tenacity to see the nation through the labyrinth of terror. Lincoln himself takes this line in his Second Inaugural Address, writing as if the war, the loss, the devastating calamity had nothing to do with him—"and the war came"—it all took place in the passive tense.[9] But we cannot say for certain how someone else might have galvanized, rather than divided, the nation, or quickened the end of the war. There is no apparent alternative, although that is not particularly important given the unlikely examples of great war-leaders such as Winston Churchill or Harry S. Truman. Who might have had a better touch cannot be retrospectively predicted. What we do know is that at many junctures the war might have been managed differently. Many serious options for change in policy, personnel, and partisan appeal were presented to Lincoln—options he chose not to take. By his own admission, he lurched and stumbled through much of the crisis, learning on the job. What we do know for certain are the catastrophic consequences of the outcome. But what we like about him is that he tried so very hard to do his best. What we must question is whether in doing *his* best, he did the best for the country.

Abraham Lincoln's lasting legacy is the ability to inspire us to be better selves and to do better for our country. We should not underestimate the power of this but nor should we confuse this inspiration with a call to imitate his style of governing. There is much that Lincoln deserves credit for. First and foremost is cementing the concept of majority rule—the disappointed and disgruntled should not simply take their ball and go home, but stay and tough it out, make their case, fight and persuade their way back to power. The emancipation question is more problematic, but certainly he deserves praise for political courage. He hewed a line that made the difficult possible and won at least noisy acquiescence from opponents. It was not a purely humanitarian gesture, however, as Lincoln's response to Horace Greeley's open letter in the *New York Tribune*, which was published in the *Daily National Intelligencer* on August 20, 1862, makes clear. As a speechwriter Lincoln's hand became ever surer, but his words—which have so much resonance today—fell flat when they were uttered. The initial response to the Gettysburg Address was decidedly muted. Lincoln was not a crusader. His saving grace is that he upheld a system that allowed for change even when he was not its champion.

When you look through a peephole into the past, you hope for a clear view, but more often than not what you get is a kaleidoscope vision. Little pieces, multifaceted and multicolored, that fit together to make a knowable pattern—not completely knowable because we are looking from afar—yet recognizable and describable. It is not a seamless, unified, or perfectly delineated vision. Looking through the peephole, we have to strain to see clearly and to gain as wide a view as possible. The six episodes presented here offer a changing pattern of images. Some shapes and colors appear in every frame, yet each one is different. The challenge is to adjust our view—to rethink—so as to make sense of them all. As we swivel our kaleidoscope, the Lincoln whom we find at the end may not be the Lincoln whom we wanted to find at the beginning. When we are aware of greatness we want to hear about it over and over again, but greatness does not mean perfection. It is the quirky note in the symphony, the brilliantly odd step in the ballet, the misplaced word in the awe-inspiring sentence that keeps our heroes human, interesting, and bright. Abraham Lincoln is like this, in that his very fallibility punctuates his moments of greatness.

In 1876 Frederick Douglass, speaking at a ceremony to dedicate the Freedmen's Monument in Washington, D.C., declared that there was nothing new to say about Abraham Lincoln. "His personal traits and public acts are better known to the American people than those of any other man of his age."[10] Yet thousands of books later, we still have important insights to relate. And America's yearning to know its sixteenth president seems not to have abated.

President Lincoln at the foot of Colonel Elmer Ellsworth's coffin,
detail of drawing on page 40

1

A WARY HANDSHAKE

O f course it was a dismal day. The sky was as leaden as the national mood. Washington, D.C., had suffered incessant storms that winter, and on March 12, 1861, the roads were sticky with mud from the latest squall. Nervous residents could not help comparing the gloomy weather to the turbulent politics threatening the country. Seven Southern states had left the Union since the election of Abraham Lincoln, forming a new Confederate States of America. The outgoing Buchanan administration had only halfheartedly defended federal property against the secessionists, and efforts to find a peaceful resolution to the crisis were faltering. Now it appeared that the new government was following the same uncertain path. "We are a weak, divided, disgraced people, unable to maintain our national existence," the Republican magnate George Templeton Strong wrote in alarm. The *New York Herald* agreed. It was a "deplorable state of affairs," complained its editors. "All joy, all hope, is fled."[1]

Against this dreary backdrop a curious apparition appeared about midday. At the stolid, neoclassical War Department a large group of military officers in full-dress uniform was assembling, their gold-crested buttons and vivid sashes piercing the dull light. Falling into two columns, they lined up behind Secretary of War Simon Cameron and Lieutenant General Winfield Scott, the Army's venerable chieftain. In perfect formation, they marched to the Executive Mansion along the tree-lined footpath that connected the two buildings. At the door Scott himself solemnly rang the bell. The United States Army had come to call on its new commander in chief.[2]

By one count, seventy-eight men paraded into the East Room. Such a large group overfilled the space and they began to snake around the perimeter in an undulating line. The officers were resplendent in dark blue frock coats, tall patent leather boots, gilt scabbards, and black-plumed hats. Set against the shabby yellow wall covering of the "nation's parlor," their presence was all the more splendid. It was a "spectacular exhibition," noted one of the company; another observer thought he had "never seen an equal number of such fine-looking men in uniform." They stood at attention, kid-gloved fingers lightly pressing the stripes of their trousers, silently awaiting the President. After a few moments, Lincoln entered, accompanied by several cabinet members. Some officers had been influenced by newspaper accounts to expect an afternoon of jesting, and now they were surprised. The man before them was as clumsy as his descriptions, but his face was deadly serious.[3]

The East Room of the White House, c. 1861–65
WHITE HOUSE COLLECTION

The new president had good reason to be grave. Since taking the oath of office on March 4, he had been confronted with multiple crises, sometimes on an hourly basis. Two days into the job, Lincoln learned that the Confederate

Congress had called out 100,000 troops to protect its territory. The attorney general and the secretary of war had just informed him that there was no legal way to stop the shipments of arms reportedly being rushed to Charleston, New Orleans, and nearby Baltimore. Samuel Cooper, a New Yorker who had served for a decade as adjutant general of the Army, left his post on March 6 and headed straight for the Confederate capital—taking with him detailed knowledge of personnel, matériel, and federal intentions. On March 11 the rebel government adopted a constitution containing elaborate legal justifications for a separate nation. A delegation from that "nation" was in Washington at the moment, under instruction to establish "diplomatic ties." Humiliation was in the air, as federal institutions unraveled and Southern sympathizers sniggered over everything from congressional defections to the disappearance of patent files. Worse yet, the country was broke. When Buchanan's treasury secretary Howell Cobb followed his native state of Georgia out of the Union, he left the nation bankrupt.[4]

Most pressing was the question of whether to withdraw United States forces from Fort Sumter in Charleston harbor. This crisis had been transferred to Lincoln just hours after his inauguration. Since his election, occupation of the fortress had been an emotional flashpoint: a contest between the South's angry belief that it was no longer governed by consent and Northern determination to protect Union prerogatives and Union property. On March 5 the War Department received a letter from the officer in charge of the garrison, Major Robert Anderson, stating that provisions were nearly exhausted and that Confederate leaders were blockading the harbor, forcing a showdown. Lincoln would have to reinforce the fort or retreat, with all the symbolism that implied.[5]

The news came as a shock, for Lincoln had wanted to move slowly, to buy time, allay passions, and reassure nervous Unionists south of the Mason-Dixon Line. As president-elect he had tried to downplay the crisis, terming it "artificial" and claiming there was "nothing going wrong." Once he realized that something was going terribly wrong, and that matters had moved beyond cool reflection, he hoped the separatist fervor would burn itself out. His deliberative political style would prove a handicap, as every day the situation in Charleston became more perilous. While Lincoln temporized, South Carolina strengthened its defenses. Anderson told his superiors he needed twenty thousand soldiers to defend the fort, a number larger than the entire standing army. Now he impatiently awaited the President's reply. "I thought the policy of this new admins. would have been developed by this time," he complained the day before the Army reception, adding that Lincoln's promise to "put the foot down firmly" against secession appeared easier said than done.[6] In fact, the President was getting a swift lesson in the difference between a campaigner's offhand remarks and the grim responsibility of actually leading the nation through perilous times. The dilemma had paralyzed his predecessor—though Buchanan later claimed he had stood ready to support Anderson, if only he had been asked. No matter how meek—or even traitorous—Buchanan's inaction seemed, Lincoln now found himself hesitating in just the same manner. "Is it possible that Mr. Lincoln is getting scared[?]" wrote an influential Illinoisan. "I know the responsibility is grate; But for god sake . . . I don't want to bequeath this damnable question to any posterity."[7]

The Sumter situation was particularly tricky, for it was not just a question of defending a fort or robustly exerting executive authority. It was coupled with an urgent need to keep those slave states that straddled North and South in the Union. These "border states" included Missouri, the President's native Kentucky, and the entire region surrounding the nation's capital. Of these, Virginia was most significant, not only because of its proximity to Washington, but in terms of size, industrial output, and prestige. Maryland, whose communication lines linked the government to the rest of the nation, was also of critical importance. The ties that attached these states to the Union were fraying in March 1861, and their leaders made clear that any "coercion" against the South would result in those bonds being cut completely.

The tension between these two issues—the need to restore confidence in the border states, yet firmly uphold federal laws and national dignity—had, in fact, been a theme of Lincoln's inaugural address. That had been a tense day, the proceedings clouded by rumors of Confederate insurrection or attempted assassination. General Scott had summoned all his imposing powers to ensure the new president's safety, calling up hundreds of troops to guard the Capitol grounds and personally commanding the sharpshooters placed on adjacent roofs. Lincoln was not yet master of simple, compelling statements, and his long message attempted to placate hostility on all sides, while conceding nothing. Despite an emotional appeal to the shared history that bound together the American people, the laboriously crafted address received a mixed response, both North and South. "Never did an oracle, in its most evasive response, receive so many, and such various interpretations, as did the President's inaugural," observed the *New York Times*.[8] Within the military it sparked general dismay. "Mr Lincolns inaugural came to day," wrote an officer named William T. H. Brooks, who was stationed in Texas. "If it can appease or quiet the troubled waters it must bear a different interpretation from what I can give it." At Fort Sumter, officers saw little in the speech to resolve either their dilemma or the nation's. "We have just received the inaugural and from it we derive no hope at all that there will be any peaceful settlement," wrote Assistant Surgeon Samuel Wylie Crawford, despairing that "so many qualifications" in the President's words would undermine the address's impact. Soldiers wanted to hear a simple declaration of intent, but this speech smacked of equivocation. "A steel hand in a soft glove" was how Major Samuel Heintzelman described it, a few days before stepping into the East Room to greet the President. "I fear it will lead to Civil War."[9]

The Sumter issue pressed on Lincoln to the point that he was physically ill, losing sleep and suffering chronic headaches. Before the end of that tempestuous March, his wife reported he had keeled over from worry and fatigue. One of his aides referred to those days as "the terrible furnace time," when public anxiety was stoked to the limit, and old patterns of governing melted away in the political fire. Lincoln wanted desperately to avoid appearing as stymied as Buchanan yet found himself unable to formulate a decisive policy. He later told Orville Hickman Browning, a Republican ally, that all the "troubles and anxieties of his life had not equaled" those he faced during the Sumter crisis.[10]

II

Lincoln was suffering from these intense pressures as he faced his finely arrayed officers, but there were other reasons for his distraction. He was new to this world of official events and was not particularly comfortable with the military. At his first levee, three days previous, an invitee noted how the President had gracelessly received the public in oversized white gloves "with much the same air & movement as if he were mauling rails." Military niceties particularly confounded him. On March 8 he had hosted a similar group of naval officers, with an embarrassing outcome. Participants remarked that Lincoln was confused by the imposing ceremony, interrupting formal introductions several times to chat with casual visitors or sign papers. Before the end of the reception he abruptly ran off, leaving the officers to stand uncomfortably at attention while he searched for his wife, who wanted to see the display of gold braid. When a senior officer made a handsome speech, pledging allegiance to the beleaguered Union, Lincoln dismayed the company by not responding. "The interview was not at all calculated to impress us . . . and there

were many remarks made about the President's gaucherie, far from comple-
mentary to him," noted a naval man.[11]

Despite his discomfort among the officers, Lincoln was not without military experience. In 1832 he volunteered with the Illinois militia when it was
called out to combat the Sauk and Fox Indians. Those tribes, led by Black
Hawk, had been tricked into moving from their ancestral lands but decided to
fight for their territory.[12] The Army was ultimately victorious against Black
Hawk, but the campaign was a badly directed affair, marked by undersup-
plied troops, slipshod skirmishing, and missed opportunities. Lincoln saw little combat, though he did have enduring memories of camp deprivation and
the unsavory burial of mutilated corpses. It was not, he later remarked, a war
"calculated to make great heroes of men engaged in it."[13]

The Black Hawk War also offered Lincoln his only opportunity to command soldiers. He was selected captain of his first company, an honor that gave
him lasting pride. A number of his men remembered him as fair, frank, and
companionable. His record of real leadership was more problematic. Accounts
mention several situations in which he could not control his troops, who strag-
gled, pillaged, and were sometimes unable to march on account of drunkenness. Captain Lincoln himself was disciplined for recklessly shooting off his
gun. Called to organize a field formation for the minor purpose of crossing a
fence, he could not command forcefully enough to direct his soldiers through
the narrow gate. In his next company Lincoln was not elected captain. His
difficulties reflected the unprofessional tone of the whole campaign, but they
also foreshadowed problems he would have as commander in chief.[14]

Lincoln experienced army life at its worst during the Black Hawk War,
but that was only part of his martial malaise. He shared the popular mistrust
of a standing armed force, whose starched and steely-eyed commanders
seemed a throwback to the hated feudal powers of Europe. As a congressman
during the Mexican War he also spoke disparagingly of the military tradition
of valor, calling it "an attractive rainbow, that rises in showers of blood—that
serpent's eye, that charms to destroy." He again scorned the armed forces
during an address to Whig supporters in 1852. Lincoln was then promoting
Winfield Scott for the presidency, yet he ridiculed the high-blown military
imagery that dominated the campaign. Recalling a local muster day, he
mocked the pretension of militia leaders, exaggerating their uniform into "a
paste-board cocked hat . . . about the length of an ox yoke . . . [and] five
pounds of cod-fish for epaulets." He went so far as to assign the citizen-
warriors a cutting motto: "We'll fight till we run, and we'll run till we die."

Although he was agile in political circles, which relied on popularity and personal ties for success, Lincoln was never really at ease with military culture, or embraced its heritage of discipline and battlefield gallantry.[15]

Now, in the East Room, he uncertainly faced officers whose epaulets were not of codfish, but richly embroidered with gold and silver thread: emblems that in their eyes signified pride and sacrifice and honor. These were the very qualities the President would desperately need as the nation careened into war. If Lincoln appreciated the tradition and service represented by the martial decorations, however, he most certainly failed to communicate it to the men standing at attention.

At least part of Lincoln's discomfort stemmed from his newly acquired role as head of the armed forces. Among the Constitution's more problematic clauses is the single sentence that establishes the president as commander in chief of the Army and Navy. This stipulation is at once all-encompassing and vague; granting full responsibility, yet unspecific on the actual exercise of authority. Although the president is not part of the military establishment, he retains ultimate command, including selection of leaders, direction of institutional structures, and the authority to pardon. In the twentieth century, the clause was interpreted to give the president every power a supreme leader is allowed in international law, but this had yet to be recognized in 1861.

Lincoln could look to several predecessors who had interpreted their military function broadly. George Washington did not hesitate to order an extraordinary armed operation during the 1794 Whiskey Rebellion. When federal prerogatives were challenged, he skillfully avoided real strife by displaying military might, yet limiting the action. Four decades later, Andrew Jackson's stern threat of force silenced states' righters when they attempted to nullify national law. James K. Polk, a strong and decisive wartime president, used the Army as a tool to implement his political goals. Devising an invasion of Mexico for the thinly veiled purpose of acquiring territory, he stretched the executive role by avoiding a congressional declaration of war, as well as by taking a hands-on approach to questions of strategy and command. The unwavering military stance of his successor, Zachary Taylor—which made no concessions at all to those threatening the federal authority—deflected the crisis of 1849–1850 by convincing the opposition that he would never back down. As a congressman, Lincoln protested what he saw as unauthorized use of the military by Democrats like Jackson and Polk.[16]

In the early days of 1861 Lincoln had little desire to follow these examples or to flex his military muscles. His ambitions for the presidency had been imagined differently: an opportunity to preside over party and patronage and to put a few domestic policies in place. Although he would greatly expand presidential war powers, Lincoln arrived in office without a blueprint for doing so. He executed an abrupt about-face, however, when he ordered significant belligerent measures within a few weeks, many of them of questionable legal status. (With Congress out of session, among other things he increased the size of the regular army, ordered a blockade of Southern ports, seized suspicious individuals without warrant, and funded it all with unauthorized sums from the Treasury.) Lincoln later maintained that extraordinary times demanded extraordinary measures, making the case with enough conviction that Congress then upheld him. Ironically, he also justified the actions by invoking the very presidents he had previously criticized. When the wisdom of resupplying Fort Sumter was questioned, he retorted, "[Y]ou would have me break my oath and surrender the Government without a blow. There is no Washington in that—no Jackson in that—no manhood nor honor in that." The tension between presidential prerogative and shared constitutional authority over matters of war, coupled with the anomaly of a civilian leading professional soldiers, would challenge Lincoln for the next four years. [17]

III

Lincoln entered the East Room flanked by Simon Cameron, his war secretary of one day. Cameron was a wiry, silver-haired man in his early sixties, with a thunderous, jutting brow. He was a famous wheeler-dealer from the Keystone State—Scott liked to say that Cameron "carried Pennsylvania in his breeches pocket"—with a reputation for being more shrewd than honest. Although the new secretary had served as a state militia officer in the 1820s, and was given the honorific title "general," he seemed more like one of Lincoln's pasteboard warriors than a real soldier. Cameron himself admitted he knew nothing about military matters and had been appointed because of his talent for backroom bargaining. Lincoln was warned from many corners not to undermine presidential credibility by such an appointment, and, indeed, he vacillated about putting the Pennsylvanian in the cabinet. "The country believes him not only *unprincipled,* but *corrupt* [and] *intellectually* incompetent for the proper discharge of the duties of a Cabinet officer," Lincoln's close associate

George C. Fogg cautioned. "Besides, he has indulged in expressions of contempt for you personally, which should render his official connection . . . an impossibility." But Lincoln was beholden to Cameron for support during the nomination process and thought he would have a quarrel on his hands if he did not give him an office. In the end, Lincoln bowed to partisanship, making a selection more political than principled.[18]

Among those offended by Cameron were the regular officers, who had watched his shady dealings while he was an Indian agent in the 1830s. "It appeared to me a simple absurdity that a man of his noted reputation as a *pec*ulator, not merely a *spec*ulator, could really be advanced to a high position in the government," wrote a brigadier general who refused to serve under the man. The appointment was especially irritating because there were clearly more compelling candidates for the post. One of the best, Judge Joseph Holt, had already impressed the nation by his performance as secretary of war in the final months of the Buchanan administration. As a Kentuckian, he had been under intense pressure from his family to join the Confederate cause yet had never faltered, either in questions of personal integrity or in his ability to deflect crisis. The *New York Tribune* asserted that Unionists were more indebted to Holt "for arresting the progress of treason than to all other men." Similar accolades came from the seceding states, where Holt's "firm, manly, patriotic, and wise administration of the War Department" convinced many that

Simon Cameron, secretary of war,
photograph by Mathew Brady, c. 1861
LIBRARY OF CONGRESS

retaining him would do much to appease the exasperated South. Holt was probably in the East Room that March 12, for Lincoln had summoned him just prior to the reception. The contrast between his studious, deferential manner and that of the hawk-eyed Cameron could not have been sharper.[19]

As the naysayers predicted, Cameron's appointment proved most unfortunate. The secretary of war snubbed the rest of the cabinet, often failing to attend meetings, and handed out key military contracts through his pals in

Pennsylvania, circumventing normal procedures. Before the disastrous first battle at Bull Run in July 1861, the War Department seemed to move in slow motion, only backhandedly preparing for combat. The result was a terrible waste in lives and money that alienated both regular officers and volunteers. Although Cameron would later try to defend his actions, saying he faced unprecedented "dangers and difficulties" and oversaw a military structure simultaneously disintegrating and mushrooming, his ineptitude became ever more injurious. By October 1861 John Nicolay, Lincoln's private secretary, would write: "Cameron utterly ignorant and regardless of the course of things; selfish and openly discourteous to the President, Obnoxious to the Country; Incapable either of organizing details or conceiving and advising general plans." Still, Lincoln kept him on. The military preparedness of the nation limped along until Cameron crossed the President politically—by preempting him on the formation of an African American army regiment—and was exposed by Republican congressman Henry Dawes for plundering the Treasury. Only then was he eased out.[20]

The selection of Simon Cameron for what was arguably the most critical position in the administration raised questions among officers about just how well Lincoln understood the gravity of the nation's situation. His appointment seemed insulting; an indication that politics, not military concerns, took priority at this pivotal juncture. In addition, Cameron not only irritated the South but proved so weak that Confederate leaders were encouraged to break openly with the administration. Indeed, in the early weeks of the crisis it almost seemed that Lincoln wanted to dismiss the importance of national defense. When he met with William Tecumseh Sherman a few days after his inauguration, the President was so dismissive of the need for trained soldiers that the offended Sherman swore he would not serve him. "If this be the Rule," Sherman told his brother, a Republican senator from Ohio, "Mr. Lincoln must expect all National men to slide out of his service, and the want of appreciation of fidelity . . . will lead to the betrayal of his army & navy." Lincoln's apparent disdain for the regular forces was already being whispered through the ranks, demoralizing men just when their services were taking on increasing importance.[21]

Entering the East Room alongside Lincoln and Cameron was the officer who had formed this army, and now stood ready to introduce it to the President. Lieutenant General Winfield Scott was seventy-four years old, born on a farm outside Petersburg, Virginia, just before the Constitution was written. A colossus of a man, Scott had an imposing physique that dwarfed the sinewy Lincoln. He was thought by some to favor Southern ways and Southern men, but most of the public saw only his decades of commitment to the nascent United States. Scott had been a young lion in the poorly managed War of 1812; then went on to lead a stunning set of victories during the Mexican conflict, taking risks and executing maneuvers that profoundly influenced protégés such as Robert E. Lee. His masterpiece, however, was the formation of a highly trained, strictly disciplined, and modernly administered military force.[22]

In the early 1820s, Scott joined with Secretary of War John C. Calhoun and West Point Superintendent Sylvanus Thayer to persuade skeptical Americans that a permanent corps of professionally trained troops would pose no threat to their society. Instead of representing armed oppression, they argued, these men would guard the peace and provide a model of leadership for the entire nation. To codify his beliefs, Scott wrote a manual called *General Regulations for the Army; or, Military Institutes,* which contained rules for everything from the proper salute to standardized procurement forms. It ensured that military leaders would take no liberties with their authority, but literally do everything "by the book." In addition, a West Point education stressed *national* service, encouraging soldiers to identify with the whole country, rather than promote sectional interests. Despite setbacks, the creation of this skilled cadre had been a brilliant success. By the 1850s the United

General Winfield Scott,
photograph by Mathew Brady, c. 1861
NATIONAL ARCHIVES

States Army was recognized internationally for its accomplishments, and its leader was considered one of the world's finest field commanders. As he aged, however, the brilliant Scott had taken on the characteristics of a puffed-up martinet, becoming pompous, inflexible, and gouty. Those who observed him in the winter of 1861 differed on whether he alone had wit enough to stem the crisis, or simply blocked the way of those who did.[23]

Scott had never before met the new chief executive, though they shared an old Whig Party background. In the 1860 race, Scott favored John Bell, the Constitutional Union Party candidate, but saw little to fear in the Republican victory. He tried to calm those who believed Lincoln meant to challenge existing laws or bully the South. Despite his Virginia background, Scott was dedicated to the federal government and opposed to the principle of secession. Indeed, he thought the menacing rhetoric of Charleston hotheads was ridiculous. "I know your little South Carolina," he scornfully told the wife of one of that state's senators. "I lived there once. It is about as big as Long Island, and two-thirds of the population are negroes. Are you mad?" Even before the November poll, the general wrote a lengthy essay on the national crisis, sending it to Buchanan, as well as political allies among Virginia Unionists. When a Republican confidant called on the old warhorse, he recorded that Scott believed Lincoln to be an honest politician and questioned only whether he was "a *firm* man."[24]

Scott had a habit of overstepping his military authority to offer sweeping political analyses and unsolicited advice to his presidents. Though well intended, their format was often rambling and the tone presumptuous. He had gotten into trouble with past leaders such as Polk for blurring the lines between martial expertise and political meddling. The "Views" he expressed in October 1860 followed this pattern. In them, he advised a public expression of conciliation to the secessionists, backed by a clear commitment to the use of force—specifically, the reinforcement of all military facilities in the Southern states. By these means Scott hoped that "all dangers and difficulties will pass away without leaving a scar or a painful recollection behind." But his "Views" were roundly ignored, both before and after the election. In late December he again urged the secretary of war to strengthen fortifications while there was still time, complaining that inaction not only endangered the Union but was causing him to sleep poorly. He worried too about Lincoln's reticence during this period, feeling that both the outgoing and incoming administrations were playing into Southern hands by allowing them to preach, plan, and prepare war. The president-elect's *"silence,"* Scott warned, "may be fatal."[25]

IV

At the White House, Scott began to introduce the blue-coated men, who were moving toward the President in rank order. Emotions in the room were volatile, yet the officers' faces were trained to impassivity, and Lincoln had no idea what thoughts were forming under those patent-leather visors. Neither could the military men fathom his feelings. The issues were too complex to discuss on such an occasion and few speeches were made. Not knowing how to salute as per Scott's regulations, the President pumped hands; but the unease was too palpable to dispel with a cordial greeting. The room, recalled several, was strangely quiet.[26]

As Scott called out the names, Lincoln may have noticed something striking about this group. Newspapers had commented on the inflated number of officers on duty in Washington during the inauguration, but the line moving slowly toward the chief executive was strangely short. In fact, the small cadre was sadly indicative of the country's modest defenses. George Washington's sage advice—that "to be prepared for war is one of the most effectual means of preserving peace"—had seldom been taken to heart. Over the years, the same mistrust of a standing army that Lincoln expressed had led congressmen to reduce the size of the officer corps, cutting military budgets arbitrarily, and sometimes indulging in open ridicule. As a result there were only 1,100 officers and some 15,000 men in the regular army in early 1861. This slim force had to guard a continental nation of thirty million inhabitants, one that was more or less at perpetual war with Native Americans, border ruffians, and foreign adventurers. James Buchanan maintained that his failure to hold the southernmost forts was due to the inadequacy of forces— that at best he could spare only 500 men to respond to urgent situations. Even though the fifteenth president's statesmanship was open to question, his understanding of the scanty resources available to him was not.

In theory this skeletal force was to be fleshed out by a three-million-strong militia, but this was something of a chimera. Fragmented geographically and controlled by local officials, the state militias were generally disorganized and undisciplined, scarcely fit for emergencies. At best, most were outfitted for duty at ceremonial "muster days," like the one Lincoln had mocked, or drilled to adorn funeral parades. The striking ineptitude of the militia in the War of 1812, or in debacle-prone contests like the Black Hawk War, had not dispelled popular fantasies about the nobility of "citizen-soldiers," however. Nor had the splendid performance of the regular army in Mexico inspired robust congressional support. The army budget already stood at its lowest point in years, when, on the very precipice of crisis in December 1860, the Senate called for an inquiry into how it could be further reduced. Atop this shaky foundation, Scott's achievement in maintaining professionalism and morale was little short of remarkable.[27]

The aged appearance of many officers added to dismay about the under-sized force. The entire army was led by only five generals, whose average age was over seventy. Two of these—Scott and Quartermaster General Joseph E. Johnston—faced the President that day, as did a half dozen colonels, who nearly outpaced the generals in years. Most of them manned administrative departments—and some had been at the same desk for decades. The number of promotions was strictly regulated by Congress, so that no one could move up unless a position was vacated. Since there were no annuities, no one re-tired. The result was an organization clogged at the top with men past their prime, shored up by frustrated subordinates. "The vegetables," one wag termed them. "Few die and none retire" was another popular witticism. An assistant adjutant general made a "conjectural calculation" that in the prevailing cir-cumstances it would take an incoming lieutenant fifty-eight years to reach the level of colonel. All of this fostered a smoldering resentment among enterpris-ing officers, who chafed at their enforced obeisance to the hierarchical reli-quary and yearned for greater opportunities.

That March 12, Lincoln was introduced to Colonel George Gibson, the Commissary Department's nominal head, who had held that post since 1818 and was now completely unequal to its duties. Farther down the line stood his assistant, an infirm lieutenant colonel named Joseph P. Taylor, who was just as advanced in years and just as incapable of responding to the exigencies of war. Surgeon General Thomas Lawson, who had been in the Army since 1809 and kept a dictatorial hold on his post for twenty-five years, also doddered past Lincoln. His duties were performed by a subordinate for a few more weeks—then Lawson figuratively dropped in the saddle. Henry K. Craig, whose white hair and strikingly red face provoked ridicule, had served in the Ordnance Bureau for thirty years and controlled its affairs for a decade. Despite shock-ing reports of arms transfers from the bureau to the South in early 1861, Craig was clinging to his post, citing "seniority" as justification. His case was typi-cal: virtually all of these worn-out men genuinely believed that decades of staff service equated with professionalism, and, if open to bureaucratic changes in theory, they resisted them in practice. The War Department had been func-tioning for years on the strength of red tape, neatly tied up by lower-ranking aides, whose loyalty—and ambition—kept the bureaus running. More than one person observed that no one at the War Department, with the possible exception of Scott, seemed fitted for the responsibilities of the moment, let alone those of the age.[28]

Lincoln was inheriting a miniature army, wizened at the top and stifled throughout the ranks. Yet these were not toy soldiers. Among them were some of the finest field officers in the world, as well as pioneers of military arts. West Point was not only the earliest but the best center of scientific education in the United States. Its graduates had presided over the techno-revolutionary marvels of the last four decades, developing superior weaponry, redirecting water routes, and engineering roadways that linked the vast expanses of the continent. Many defined themselves as *scientists* rather than *soldiers*. Chief Engineer Joseph Totten, an accomplished chemist near the head of the receiving line, had invented a novel type of cement to fortify coastal installations against the pounding tides. William Buell Franklin, a captain, also about to meet the President, was at the moment supervising construction of a new Capitol dome, an engineering marvel with great symbolic significance for the fractured nation. A few paces ahead of him stood Captain Montgomery Meigs. A gifted engineer, Meigs already coupled his notable eccentricity (he ate milk toast with cucumbers and French dressing for breakfast) with technical genius and artistic sensibility. He had conceived and constructed the Washington Aqueduct, a beautiful structure that encompassed the world's grandest stone arch. His magnificent Pension Office Building, with its carved frieze of Union soldiers marching toward infinity, was still in the future, but Meigs's talents already stood out in high relief.[29]

In addition, many officers had won laurels in the Mexican War and viewed the looming threat of combat with far greater understanding than their fellow citizens. Despite its political sins, that war had been a tour de force for the regular army and the Navy. They had fought the larger Mexican Army on its own territory, outmaneuvering the enemy on punishing terrain by what General Scott liked to call "head-work." Many of the men standing before Lincoln had received two or three "brevet" promotions for their valor— which in the absence of genuine advancement gave them rank and recognition. Under Scott's direction, American forces then occupied Mexico with a generosity to the conquered nation that was unheard of at the time, inventing the concept of a just peace. Scott himself had faced down the world's skeptics. Even the Duke of Wellington, who had raised his eyebrows at Scott's bold drive toward Mexico City, finally admitted: "His campaign is unsurpassed in military annals. He is the greatest living soldier."[30]

The officers of the United States Army had no reason to apologize as they stood before their new president. They were better educated than he was, and more poised and polished to boot. Posted all over the continent, they knew intimately the challenges of the wild and sprawling country. They were also politically sophisticated, having suffered the consequences of self-serving officials who sacrificed national interests for party or privilege; and they had witnessed a great deal more of war's violent reality than Abraham Lincoln could imagine.

They were, moreover, entirely aware of these advantages.

One would like to think the commander in chief had been briefed about the condition of his army before he was introduced, but this kind of staff work was never a strength of the Lincoln White House, and especially not in these early days. Nonetheless, he probably knew enough to realize that, despite its gloss, the military fabric was unraveling. For one thing, the Army was out of funds. In 1860 Congress had seen fit to appropriate no greater monies than it received in 1808, though America's population had quadrupled, and its territory nearly doubled. The situation was particularly acute because Buchanan's headstrong, incompetent war secretary, John B. Floyd (Holt had served for only the final months of the administration), had taken no action to ready his department for conflict. Outgoing Treasury chief Howell Cobb had meanwhile done his best to exhaust the coffers before departing, and the armed forces had not been funded in months. From Washington Territory to Santa Fe, supplies, provisions, and pay were in short supply—or nonexistent. "We are all out here in a state of great anxiety as to our future, the Paymasters have no money, the QMaster [quartermaster] has none, & the Commissary but little," complained a still loyal, but anxious, soldier named Cadmus Wilcox from his western post. A visitor to Fort Washington, guarding the Potomac River approach to the capital, was stunned to see how shabbily it was maintained and how thinly manned. When Scott was broached on the fort's condition, he retorted that a few weeks earlier it "might have been taken by a bottle of whiskey. The whole garrison consisted of an old Irish pensioner." In the Navy the state of affairs was equally lamentable. Arriving at his new post in early March, Secretary of the Navy Gideon Welles found near disarray: "No one can realize the confusion and utterly deplorable condition of things that then existed in naval administration," he recalled. Over at the War Department, Cameron discovered that they were virtually devoid of munitions, and that Massachusetts senator Henry Wilson (who would later take a spirited pro-army stance as head of the Military Affairs Committee) was proposing to save money by allocating outmoded smoothbore weapons to the forces. "These arms were good enough to fight the Mexican War with," Wilson calmly asserted.[31]

As it happened, ordnance was a particularly sensitive point with the Army at that moment. Congress had underfunded munitions for decades, and though there were shops and machines enough to produce 40,000 stands of arms a year, appropriations were too small to turn out more than 18,000. Even this scant supply became the subject of a scandal when outgoing war secretary Floyd was accused of allowing large numbers of arms to be sold to firms that later transferred them to arsenals in the South. Actually, Floyd—a reluctant secessionist—had not directly sold federal weapons to state agents. He had, however, instituted practices that made old armaments available to militias, and new production methods open to copy by nongovernmental manufacturers. Nonetheless, an incensed Northern public believed the worst, and the credibility of the Army as a whole suffered. Several fine officers, notably General John E. Wool and Major Alfred Mordecai, were stunned to find their reputations under fire when they carried out Floyd's orders to furnish the weapons. Mordecai, one of the most respected men in the service, was particularly suspect since he had close family ties in North Carolina and Virginia. The "chafe of public affairs" he experienced during the arsenal questioning influenced Mordecai's decision to resign from the Army, though he later declined to fight for either side.[32]

V

The munitions scandal fueled worries that Southerners in the Army were tacitly keeping their old commissions, while actively working on behalf of the seceding states. And, indeed, some were playing this double game. Captain Bernard Bee, a South Carolinian, sent a remarkable letter to Virginian Henry Heth, describing his clandestine activities among the companies at Fort Laramie in Nebraska Territory. He was encouraging sympathetic officers to keep their units intact, Bee confided, then to march them southward, bringing "all they can with them." He requested that Heth call on Jefferson Davis to affirm that if a state seceded, its native sons would be absolved of any previously sworn loyalty oaths. Such an assurance, noted Bee, would "aid me in bringing men and material South." In a like spirit, Quartermaster General Joseph E. Johnston was using his office to explore transportation projects that would benefit the expanding Southern territories. He proposed his ideas to none other than George B. McClellan, a former army officer and railroad executive with pro-slavery sympathies, with whom he had dreamed similar dreams in the 1850s. Others, like former United States marshal Ben McCulloch, were actively conspiring with the secessionists, both politically and militarily. Two weeks before Lincoln's inauguration, McCulloch played a key role in forcing another Southern officer, General David E. Twiggs, to surrender federal troops and property under his command in Texas.[33]

The Twiggs incident—and the mistrust it had fostered—was uppermost on everyone's mind that afternoon at the Executive Mansion. A native of Georgia, Twiggs had given distinguished service in every American conflict since 1812 and had been honored by Congress for his role in the Mexican War. One of the septuagenarians who populated the higher ranks of the service, he had been ill for a year when, on December 13, 1860, he took over the Department of Texas from Lieutenant Colonel Robert E. Lee, who was acting in his absence. Sensing the drift toward disunion, Twiggs wrote the same day to Scott for instructions. Scott replied that at this critical moment all decisions were political, and that he too was unable to get a clear idea of President Buchanan's intent.

Twiggs wrote four more times to Washington, candidly stating that a crisis was brewing, and that he did not want personally to be responsible for starting a fratricidal war. He pointed out the difficulties of defending a department that included 10 percent of the Army's assets, but was spread over a thousand miles of rough territory. He told Washington that Sam Houston, Texas's Unionist governor, had warned him of the secessionists' plan to commandeer federal property. Houston was trying to work out a sub-rosa arrangement to keep the Army in Texas, but Twiggs admitted to the governor that he had no instructions on how to respond to such a request. He then dutifully relayed the entire correspondence to headquarters.

Completely cut off, and convinced that "coercion" would not help the situation, Twiggs asked to be relieved of command before Lincoln's inauguration. The request was granted, but communication delays meant the order did not reach him until after the Texas convention had voted for disunion. At that point, Twiggs was forced to conduct negotiations with a junta of secessionist politicians and Ben McCulloch's unruly band of Texas Rangers—without support from Washington. Unnerved, the general waffled rather than readying his men for a counterchallenge; and in the end he capitulated. Twiggs did try to arrange the most "honorable" deal he could without resorting to an armed confrontation: ordnance and arsenals, including the symbolic Alamo, were turned over to the rebels, but he secured safe passage out of the state for his troops. (That there was considerable pressure to take captives is clear from

McCulloch's records, for he angrily wrote that to let the soldiers go was "an insult to the commissioners and the people of the State.") Nevertheless, Twiggs's surrender shocked the North, deepening the shadow of suspicion over the Army.[34]

In one of his last acts as president, Buchanan cashiered Twiggs, without court-martial. It was an unprecedented move, and officers debated whether they had been more betrayed by Twiggs or the authorities in Washington. William T. H. Brooks, who would become a Union general, told his father during the withdrawal from Texas that Twiggs had been treated high-handedly. "We got the news about Gen Twiggs being struck from [the] rolls of the Army by todays mail—It is an exhibition of very petty spite to call him a coward," Brooks protested, adding that few people understood the difficulty of their situation. Nonetheless, he acknowledged, military men were in "a most humblifying situation, placed so by his act—We don't go out exactly as prisoners of war but it is the next thing to it." Edward Hartz, another West Point man serving under Twiggs, was incensed by the general's actions but thought the furor over the Lone Star State was ridiculous. He considered Texas worthless, Hartz declared: "[She] has never brought anything into the Union but . . . her quarrels and her debts." Twiggs, thinking he had taken all proper measures, was stunned by Buchanan's dismissal, and for the rest of his life wrote threatening letters in a shaky hand to the ex-president. "This was personal, and I shall treat it as such, not through the papers but in person," he warned Buchanan. "So prepare yourself. I am well assured that public opinion will sanction *any course* I may take with you." A few weeks later, he joined the Confederate forces.[35]

Those standing before Lincoln in the East Room were still reeling from the incident. Most felt little charity toward Twiggs. Major Samuel Heintzelman asserted that no officer should ever relinquish arms under his control, and that Twiggs's actions were treasonous. Lieutenant Colonel Lee, just arrived from San Antonio, took pains to assure colleagues that, had he continued in command, the secessionists would not have gotten "the arms from [his] troops without fighting for them." It seemed the whole officer corps was mourning the loss of its integrity. Crusty old General John Wool spoke for many, mincing no words. "Twiggs has proved himself worse than an hundred Benedict Arnolds," he thundered. "It was rumoured last evening that he had been shot. The news is too good to be believed. A greater villain never existed."[36]

The Twiggs affair stunned the regular officers, but his was not the only early defection from their ranks. Adjutant General Samuel Cooper's sudden departure, a few days before the Army's introduction to the new president, had rubbed salt into the wound left by Twiggs. Cooper was married to a Virginian—indeed, the sister of pro-slavery senator James Murray Mason—and these ties had overridden his own New York heritage. He could no longer "dissemble" on a daily basis, Cooper told the one comrade who dared write him for an explanation; and he had decided he would "at least, have the consolation to feel that I shall go down to my . . . resting place without self reproach." Others were leaving in an equally painful manner. Future Confederate general Ambrose P. Hill, then a lieutenant assigned to a coastal survey team, pointedly requested that his resignation be accepted before the sixteenth president's inauguration. His demand was honored. There was also a gap in the blue-coated line where Mississippian John Withers, a much admired assistant adjutant general, usually stood. His resignation was accepted on March 1, and his duties turned over to a co-worker, Captain Julius P. Garesché, who now moved forward to meet Abraham Lincoln.[37]

Garesché was a dark, serious man whose amiability masked a fiery temperament that some linked to his Cuban heritage. He was greatly distressed by the resignations of Cooper and Withers, both of whom he liked. The departure of his boss was all the more disturbing because Garesché's two brothers were Southern sympathizers, then under suspicion in St. Louis. Captain Garesché shared his siblings' fear of slave insurrection, which his family had experienced in the Caribbean, but he was intensely loyal to the Union. With his superiors gone, Garesché was now assigned to keep the Army's official register. There was a pot of bloodred ink on his table, and a straightedge ruler beside it. As withdrawals arrived in the adjutant general's office, Garesché drew thick scarlet lines across each departing soldier's name, fully aware that if they were deserters in his eyes, they were heroes to others. By May 1861 the toll of resignations would encompass more than a third of the regular officers, and the pages of the roster grew into a crimson-blotched omen of the carnage to come. Garesché's grisly end seems also to have been foretold in the stained pages. He had embraced a charismatic brand of Catholicism, which induced a premonition of sudden, violent death in battle. Just as he prophesied, Garesché fell "in a cloud of blood" in his first field assignment, when a cannonball blew off his head during the December 1862 action at Stones River, Tennessee.[38]

As Garesché's roster became ever more blotted, many were outraged that these resignations were being countenanced at all. The military academies had

taught that officers should give equal allegiance to all elected authorities, regardless of their political leanings. This was what distinguished democratic
armed forces from those led by tyrants, who demanded personal fealty. Every
military man had sworn an oath to defend the United States against "all opposers, whatsoever," and desertion of the old flag mocked this premise. To
some it appeared that by accepting the resignations, rather than treating them
as treasonous, the administration was deliberately furnishing the South with a
well-organized force, tailor-made to protect its interests. Naval captain Samuel F. Du Pont "spoke out plainly" against those who he believed served two
masters and chafed at the demoralization the departures caused. "The Department should not have accepted a single resignation," he wrote passionately, "if
a brother of mine could have been of the number, I should never wish to see
his face again." In fact, Navy Secretary Welles ultimately decided it was impolitic to ignore the flight to rebellion. After the action at Fort Sumter, naval
officers were stricken from the rolls if they resigned and then took up arms for
the South. Many considered this dismissal the most painful event of their
lives, and some spent a lifetime trying to reestablish their honorable status.[39]

But at the War Department Cameron took a different tactic, obligingly
consenting to all resignations. In a few weeks the pace of defections was so
brisk that the department actually began sending out *form letters,* approving,
without question, the relinquishment of commissions. Remarkably, those letters were signed "respectfully, Your obedient servant" by the secretary. Much
of the public looked askance at this, calling for loyalty oaths to be administered to the remaining officers or demanding that those who resigned be ap-
prehended and tried. Navy lieutenant David Dixon Porter was one of many
who thought that anyone resigning just as the nation faced a critical test
should be imprisoned. As commander in chief, Lincoln could have halted the
easy approval of resignations, of course, by establishing a uniform policy
among all the armed forces or by placing disloyal officers under military arrest
for the safety of the country. He could also have proposed that defections of
this kind constituted treason. But in early 1861 Lincoln's mind was bent on
calming emotions, not heightening them, and he took no action. As a result,
the United States Army and Navy evaporated before him.[40]

Officers who remained in service found their long habits of cooperation
severely tested as they faced the "new, supreme, untried, cursed grief" of
guessing who might next abandon Old Glory. Welles and Cameron both
noted when taking up their duties that the air was poisonous with doubt and
distrust. Military men found their easy familiarity so strained that they "grad-

ually receded from that frank communion which is apt to exist between offi-cers of the same service" or sometimes exploded into open quarrels. Assistant Adjutant General Dabney Maury, anxiously waiting news at a frontier post, remarked that even socializing was highly orchestrated so that men on oppo-site sides of the debate would not have to meet. Margaret McLean, who on March 12 floated into the East Room with Mary Lincoln to view the resplendent gathering, must have been reminded of a re-ception a few weeks earlier where she had watched officers play guessing games about who would stay with the old army and who would go. McLean was the daughter of an erect, somber man near the head of the reviewing line, Colonel Edwin Sumner, who would serve the Union, though without particular dis-tinction. She was also the wife of a Virginia secessionist, Captain Eugene McLean, who stood at at-tention farther down the ranks.[41]

Collegiality was swiftly eroding, and the uniformed men mourned its loss. "The breaking up of the associations of a life time . . . ; the abandon-ment of high positions . . . ; the crushing out of hopes, aspira-tions, plans, friendships & all the prospects of life that we have so carefully originated, cherished and digested; all these come to us with a force that none other of our Countrymen feels or can feel," mused a devastated officer named Henry Wayne, who had been decorated for gallantry during the Mexican War but felt he must side with his fellow Georgians. Beyond dashed ambitions and broken relationships there were more serious consequences. In the rough-and-

The Army form letter of resignation for
J. E. B. Stuart, May 16, 1861

tumble of field life, where isolation was common, and pay, promotion, and reinforcement uncertain, shared hardships had forged ties that allowed the military to function with cohesion and resolve. "All its venerated customs of service and its immutable regulations, its mathematical tactics and rigid discipline, its cherished history and sacred legends, its unyielding esprit . . . [were] to be swallowed up and diffused," lamented a Northern officer. As traditions began to crumble, so did the confidence and mettle of the forces.[42]

Some of the men in the East Room were attempting to shore up their institution by rekindling the old camaraderie. Captain William Farrar ("Baldy") Smith was one who spent a good deal of the secession winter trying to persuade Southern-leaning colleagues to remain loyal to the United States. But many officers lashed out at the political wrangling they believed responsible for the nation's predicament. Lieutenant Custis Lee, the youngest of the three Lee family members greeting Lincoln that day, had sorrowfully broached this with his Ohio comrade James B. McPherson just as the crisis began. "You know Mac that I am not much of a politician; and have a great disinclination for the dirty business . . . but have been obliged to read and see a great deal in reference to it recently; and must say that I hardly know what to think of the signs of the political times." In the election Lee, like Winfield Scott, had supported John Bell, but he thought fears of the new Republican administration were overblown. Yet he was pessimistic about the ability of politicians to manage the emergency. "I have heretofore thought them harmless; but they have finally succeeded in bringing the country to the verge of dissolution, if not to the fact," he glumly remarked. As if in echo, General Wool poured out his rage to Republican Party boss Thurlow Weed: "Treason, imbecility, and intrigue rule the hour!"[43]

Custis Lee and Wool, like most of their compatriots, had kept aloof from political shenanigans. Many army men, including Scott, actually refused to vote because they felt the role of the military was to act with equal loyalty under all governments. There were those who tried to pull political strings, of course, hoping for place or promotion, or liked to hobnob with elected officials and talk the talk of national strategy. But among the West Pointers it had been a point of pride to shun parochialism or undue partisanship. Julius Garesché, for example, leaned toward the Democrats, but never acted on his beliefs since "it was not considered a proper thing for an Officer to take a prominent position in party discussion or to pronounce any decided opinion on the subject." Now, to their dismay, some were directly blaming the Republicans for a platform that had inflamed the country. In Texas, Edward Hartz pointed at Lincoln as author of "the unholiest of unholy wars ever instituted," all for the sake of "so many miserable negroes." The men were tired of listening to the President's "wing flaps & crowings," complained an officer at Jefferson Barracks in the border state of Missouri: they wanted Lincoln to *act*. At Fort Sumter, the garrison was appalled to find itself being held responsible for a predicament caused by partisan bellowing and administrative bungling. As the situation worsened, tempers and rhetoric were dangerously inflamed. "The truth is *we are the government* at present," Assistant Surgeon Samuel Crawford wrote hotly to his brother from Charleston harbor. "It rests upon the points of our swords."[44]

If the officers mistrusted their untried commander in chief, Lincoln was equally chary of the men in uniform. He was all too aware of the irregularities at various arsenals, the disaffection of senior officers, and incidents such as the one at Pensacola, Florida, where two naval men surrendered the United States Navy Yard to the rebels, then calmly resumed their duties, this time for the Confederacy. Before he arrived in Washington, Lincoln had begun to inquire about the loyalty of military men surrounding him. He was concerned about Fort Sumter's commander, Kentuckian Robert Anderson, and made a point of soliciting Joseph Holt's opinion on the subject. Even venerable General Wool thought he might be distrusted by the president-elect, and took the unusual step of officially proclaiming his unswerving devotion to the United States.[45]

Lincoln was particularly nervous about Winfield Scott and had him checked out more than once before they met. When Scott ran for president in 1852, Lincoln had both campaigned and voted for him, and now, in the midst of turmoil, he badly wanted to rely on the seasoned lieutenant general. In reality, Scott was so firm in his national allegiance that he lashed out at overtures from Confederate officials, as well as at critics who believed his taste for Virginia ham smacked of disloyalty. When Kentucky senator John J. Crittenden wired to ask the general's intentions, he sent back a curt reply: "I have not changed. I have had no thought of changing. I am for the Union. Winfield Scott." But in the days following the inauguration, Scott had also sent a series of disturbingly contradictory messages to the Executive Mansion on the critical issue of Fort Sumter, bouncing between opinions in a way that seemed erratic, if not duplicitous. It tarnished Lincoln's bright hopes for a collaborative administration, feeding instead the President's inclination toward secrecy and maneuver.[46]

Scott initially thought he and his men could ward off catastrophe if only the civil authorities would allow him. "Gen Scott told Brother John [naval officer John Rodgers] today that he 'believed he could save the country if *they* would let him,'" an officer's wife named "Nannie" Rodgers Macomb confided to Montgomery Meigs in early 1861. Scott had seen this situation before, during the nullification crisis of 1832, when Andrew Jackson quietly dispatched him to South Carolina with orders to strengthen military facilities while avoiding overtly provocative actions. Scott was not opposed to using force: he told another naval man that "there were worse things than bloodshed & he didn't mind shedding a little if it would preserve the Union, it was a good country & worth preserving." But his 1832 experience proved a false model during the secession winter. Emotions had grown rawer in the ensuing decades, and prospects in the slave states brighter. Moreover, although Scott had strongly recommended in late 1860 that federal forts in the South be strengthened, he now believed the rebels had been allowed so much leeway that Charleston and other key spots were well fortified. The time for showboating was over.[47]

Nine days before the reception Scott penned these thoughts to incoming secretary of state William Seward. Indicating that the moment for a swift rebuke to the secessionists had passed, he mapped out four options for the crisis-gripped administration: conciliation with the rebels; calculated inaction; military aggression; or peaceful acceptance of disunion. Fort Sumter had no military importance, he argued, and it could be abandoned without sacrificing the larger political point. When Lincoln directed him on March 5 to reinforce all United States military establishments, the general dragged his feet, and the instruction had to be underscored with a written command. Then, the day before the meeting in the East Room, with the secretary of war's concurrence, Scott actually ordered Major Anderson to withdraw from Sumter—an order that had to be rescinded by Lincoln. He caused further doubts by handing the President a paper the next day—possibly at the reception—advising that to hold Sumter would be continuously to reinforce it, making confrontation inevitable.[48]

Scott's messages jolted the cabinet and angered Lincoln, but in fact the government was also at odds with itself. When he entered the East Room on March 12, the President had come directly from a meeting with an old Washington guru, Francis P. Blair, who bluntly told him that "the surrender of Fort Sumter was virtually a surrender of the Union." Some cabinet members had gone further, devising a secret plan to resupply the garrison with coastal survey vessels—an arrangement that was ultimately deemed impractical, and of which Lincoln may have been unaware. At the same time, Seward, in agree-ment with Scott, was hatching schemes to placate the secessionists. The Presi-dent was receiving conflicting advice from all over the country, some urging him to abandon the polarizing stronghold, while others stated it was impera-tive he stand his ground. Meanwhile, Unionist leaders in border states were begging for a clear policy that would strengthen their hands, and Northerners were beginning to panic. "Is Democracy a Failure?" the usually sympathetic *New York Times* asked in a biting editorial that month. The Union could only survive, it maintained, through a radical reform of its structure and purpose. "Are we great enough for it—are we capable of it?" asked the *Times* editors. "One thing is, at least, certain, face it we must."[49]

VI

L incoln struggled over Sumter's defense, but most of the officers in the East Room agreed with Scott. Several had been involved in the developing events, and all were sobered by the prospect of waging war over an insignifi-cant, half-built fortification that lacked the capacity to defend anything, in-cluding itself. (One ordnance expert concluded that guns placed at the fort could not reach a single target in Charleston and that any firing would be "ex-ceedingly wild at such an elevation and non-effective.") Captain Fitz-John Por-ter, who was sent to assess the situation the previous autumn, had recommended the garrison's command be turned over to Anderson, whose Southern creden-tials might placate the local population. The change of command had already taken place when Major Don Carlos Buell, a colleague of Porter who was now standing about midway up the blue line facing Lincoln, arrived to consult with Anderson about the situation in December 1860. Buell had strict orders to avoid confrontation. He interpreted these liberally, by helping orchestrate a clandestine movement of the vulnerable federal force from Fort Moultrie to the more secure Sumter. That action, engineered in the dark of Christmas night, only enraged South Carolinians. When Governor Francis Pickens took imme-diate measures to fortify the harbor, war began to look unavoidable.[50]

Short of stature, but long on martial savvy, Buell was thought by some to have a greater grasp of the deteriorating situation than any man in the Army. By the time Lincoln met the elegant major on March 12, he almost certainly knew of Buell's actions in Charleston and may also have heard that Buell had Southern family connections. Perhaps this is why the President failed to consult him, for it is striking that as Lincoln formulated his strategy, he conferred with neither Porter nor Buell, the two men in Washington with the greatest firsthand understanding of Anderson's predicament. Instead he sent a new team to Charleston, which included a midrank navy man, but no army officer, and the burly Ward Hill Lamon, a former law partner whom Lincoln came to use as a kind of White House bouncer. Lamon confused the situation by stepping completely outside his brief to converse unofficially with Pickens and to inform both the governor and Major Anderson—erroneously—that the fort would soon be evacuated. Sumter's force viewed this expedition, led by a man who "had never been in a small boat nor in a Fort before," with scorn; and Pickens angrily concluded he had been willfully misled. It was an ominous preview of Lincoln's pattern of shunning professional military expertise to rely on amateurs with whom he had personal ties. Uncertain as he was, these were the only men the President felt he could count on.[51]

Part of Lincoln's problem was that he had listened to gossip from the military men around him. All of it was unsolicited and much of it self-serving, but in his ignorance of personalities and procedures he had rather gullibly swallowed these accounts. Even before the election, some officers had sent Lincoln lengthy descriptions of supposed betrayal in the Army. These astonishing letters went well beyond the boundaries of the military's crisp code of conduct. Lincoln's files held furtive notes from lieutenants, captains, and disgruntled majors, and even one toadying message from the venerable Colonel Sumner. Scott was also guilty of stretching his prerogative in this fashion, but he was the leading general in a crisis-stricken nation, with some justification for directly addressing his future commander. A few of the men aired their long-held grievances; many were fawning or openly currying favor. All were far outside established military regulations, which prohibited unauthorized communication with government officials and required formal messages to go through hierarchical channels.

Major David Hunter, in a letter marked "Private and Confidential," took it upon himself to warn Lincoln in October 1860 of Southern officers' "most certainly demented" views on slavery. Posted to isolated Fort Leavenworth in Kansas, he was well out of the informational loop, yet he ominously predicted that the Army and Navy might cooperate in a coup d'état when the new president entered office. For good measure he recommended himself for a generalship. In an extraordinary seven-page letter, Captain John Pope slammed those who had "embarrassed" the government in its hour of need and were now rewarded for their "treachery" by secessionist authorities. He also took the opportunity to assure Lincoln of his personal fidelity, as well as to remind the president-elect that he was a son of Illinois. Captain George W. Hazzard went further, naming names of those he thought disloyal, including his superior officer—a breach of etiquette that would have been grounds for a court-martial had the letter been intercepted. Lieutenant Colonel Erasmus Keyes, an aide in Scott's office, laid bare his long-festering grudge against Southern colleagues and boldly suggested a few candidates for secretary of war.[52]

Had Lincoln better understood the importance of discretion and hierarchy for a functional army, he would have forwarded these effusions to the War Department with an order that the practice be halted. Instead, he not only absorbed the extracurricular tales but embraced the storytellers. Sumner, Hunter, Hazzard, and Pope were all invited to accompany him when he traveled from Springfield to the inauguration, and Keyes became an early favorite, charged with confidential missions pertaining to Fort Sumter. Ostensibly the officers were invited in order to protect the president-elect, but they appear to have been rarely called upon for this duty. Instead, they took full advantage of their proximity to Republican nabobs to express ex officio opinions and lobby for posi-

Colonel Elmer Ellsworth's Chicago Zouaves, pencil, by Alfred R. Waud, 1861

tion. These were probably the first "military briefings" Lincoln experienced and their influence was pronounced. The hearsay heightened fears of disloyalty by those not sharing his party allegiance and reinforced his predilection for trusting personal allies, rather than the structures of government. His willingness to accept unauthorized information even before he had any authority, and to embrace those acting outside the system, signaled the start of the President's unfortunate mingling of informal political ways with the military's stricter means.[53]

As if to underscore the point, a diminutive twenty-three-year-old named Elmer Ellsworth was also invited on the train trip. Ellsworth, a Lincoln enthusiast who had helped in the election, was besotted by military lore. He had put together a drill team of Chicago cadets loosely based on French Zouave companies in North Africa, including their colorful dress of embroidered jackets and loose pantaloons. The company toured Northern cities, entertaining crowds with marching formations and acrobatic stunts. After Lincoln's election Ellsworth hastily mustered a group, composed mainly of New York City firemen, to defend the capital. When the newly formed Eleventh New York Infantry marched into Washington, the troop received a personal welcome from Lincoln. Ellsworth styled himself their colonel, but he was a parade-ground warrior, ignorant of combat. Nonetheless, one of Lincoln's first official acts was to nominate Ellsworth for two inappropriately high posts in the War Department. Attorney General Edward Bates advised the President that he did not have the power to do this, and concerned Republicans warned it presaged a "reign of mediocrity and imbecility"; nonetheless, Lincoln remonstrated that he was "pressed to death for time and don't pretend to know anything of military matters," ordering Bates to "fix the thing up so that I shan't be treading on anybody's toes." The ludicrousness of this was not lost on the nervous nation. "Old Scott is to resign in favor

DEATH OF COL. ELLSWORTH.

The Death of Col. Ellsworth,
hand-colored lithograph, Currier & Ives, 1861
LIBRARY OF CONGRESS

of Col. Ellsworth," teased humorist Artemus Ward. "Col. Ellsworth is only thirteen years of age."[54]

Scott was seriously worried about the boasting Ellsworth, whose "hard set" of men had trashed their quarters in the Capitol and terrorized townspeople. Lincoln, too, cautioned Ellsworth on the "great delicacy" of the situation, saying he wanted nothing done that might alienate still loyal Virginians. Their concerns turned out to be justified.[55] A few weeks after the bombardment of Fort Sumter, the flamboyant "colonel" circumvented orders by wrenching a rebel flag from atop a Virginia hotel—a reckless, amateurish act that cost him his life. Ellsworth's compatriots—"wild with rage"—nearly burned down the town. His body was taken to the White House and laid in state in the East Room, where a mournful president sat in silence at his feet as military officers stood at command. The nation pronounced Ellsworth a martyr, but the undisciplined move actually exacerbated tensions at a sensitive moment, something Lincoln acknowledged.[56]

Colonel Elmer Ellsworth Lies in State in the East Room, pencil, by Alfred R. Waud, May 25, 1861. The people shown are numbered as follows: 1. General Winfield Scott; 2–3. general officers; 4. Edwin Sumner; 5. reporters; 6. President Abraham Lincoln; 7. William Henry Seward; 8. officers; 9. Reverend Smith Pyne.

Ellsworth was probably not at the reception on March 12, for he was a militia man, outside the regular army. However, the President's other new favorites—Sumner, Hunter, Hazzard, and Pope—were among the company. The rest of the officers were largely unfamiliar to Lincoln. He knew Scott, of course, and had glimpsed men like Colonel Charles Stone, who was called to Washington to organize local volunteers guarding the inauguration. One of the few Lincoln had previously met was Lieutenant Colonel Robert E. Lee, standing about a third of the way down the line. They had served together as "managers" for President Zachary Taylor's 1849 inaugural ball, in a day when both men embraced Whig principles. Lincoln was a congressman at the time and Lee, a kinsman of Taylor, had just returned with honors from the Mexican War. While it is doubtful that Lincoln and Lee knew each other well, they must have had at least a passing acquaintance.[57]

The lanky president and booming Scott aside, Lee was arguably the most striking figure in the East Room. His commanding presence had been noted since he was a West Point cadet, and his magnetism included social charms as compelling as his military skill. Lee enjoyed a reputation for cool bravery, most recently showcased in his near perfect operation against John Brown's insurrection at Harpers Ferry. This was not the silver-bearded figure so familiar to generations of Americans, but a man of matinee-idol looks, with curling black hair, a neat mustache, and an easy, "brilliant" smile. He was a particular favorite of Scott, with whom he had fought in Mexico. It was a mutual admiration that caused some chatter within the officer corps. In Scott's eyes "even God had to spit on his hands when he made Bob Lee," sarcastically com-

Robert E. Lee,
retouched photograph by
Mathew Brady, c. 1859
LIBRARY OF CONGRESS

mented one colleague.[58] The general had called Lee home from Texas in February, and it was widely rumored that he would be given a prominent position.

Promotion was not on Lee's mind at this time, however. In March 1861 he was as troubled as Lincoln at the idea of dismantling the nation. Like the President and Joseph Holt, he saw disunion as a recipe for weakness, and he worried "whether we are to continue as a united powerful & prosperous nation, or to be divided into separate communities, feeble at home, powerless abroad, wrangling, quarreling, fighting & destroying each other." Friends reported that the normally unflappable Lee openly wept when he heard Texas had seceded. Now he was pressed by the weight of conflicting allegiance: to his state, his profession, his political principles—and to his cruelly divided family.[59]

The intricate network of relatives shared by Lee and his wife, Mary Custis Lee—a great-granddaughter of Martha Washington—was nearly unparalleled in its proud service to Virginia. They had also been instrumental in creating a strong and secure central government for the United States. Lee's own father, Revolutionary War hero Light-Horse Harry Lee, had fought for Virginia's ratification of the Constitution, championing the opening "We the People" against those who wanted the more ambiguous "We the States." Most of Lee's relatives from his own generation opposed disunion and many were actively working to restore the old compact. The day before Lincoln's reception, Williams Carter Wickham, whose mother was Lee's first cousin, wrote a plaintive note to Scott, begging him to do all in his power to aid Virginia conservatives who were fighting secession. A brother-in-law, William Marshall, was a Republican stalwart who had been recommended for attorney general in the Lincoln cabinet. Marshall's wife, Anne Lee Marshall, never spoke to her brother again after Lee made his fateful decision to join the South. Even Lee's immediate family was Unionist. A daughter reported that when Lee told his wife and children he had resigned from the United States Army, the pronouncement was so distressing that they faced him in stunned silence. Yet a brother, Charles Carter Lee, was a fanatical sectionalist, and some of the younger family members were eager to mark themselves with distinction in the rebellion. The schism in the Lee family was evident in the lineup before Lincoln, for in addition to the troubled lieutenant colonel, the group included his cousin, Major John Fitzgerald Lee, then judge advocate of the Army, and Robert E. Lee's eldest son, Custis, both of whom were leaning against disunion. Major Lee would retain his post, and his brother, Samuel Phillips Lee, a senior naval officer, served the Union throughout the war.[60]

Fellow officers noted Lee's worried demeanor, and his writings from the time reveal acute anxiety. He believed secession was a radical action, only to be considered as a last resort. Lee also thought that if the country broke down into conflict it would be "long & desperate," waged with a bitterness that would prevent any side from truly winning. Although an apologist for slavery, he did not believe the institution merited destroying the republic. "While I wish to do what is right," he declared in a moment of intense confliction, "I am unwilling to do what is not, either at the bidding of the South or the North." Like other Southern officers, he was probably receiving overtures from the Confederate government. Some of these were comparatively dazzling to men who had languished for decades in midgrade posts. Lee himself had spent thirty-two years rising from lieutenant to his present rank—and that was considered a meteoric ascent. Still, between him and a brigadier's command stood nineteen colonels, three senior lieutenant colonels, and four others whose commissions were dated the same day as his. At this moment, however, Lee was not seduced by a general's stars; he still thought salvation lay in keeping his state in the old constitutional pact. "I am particularly anxious that Virginia should keep right," he told his daughter. "I would wish that she might be able . . . to save the Union." Nonetheless, when Virginia Unionists pressed him to take an active part in thwarting secession, Lee declined. Instead, he clung to the hope that somehow it would all come right in the end.[61]

Lincoln shared Lee's belief that Virginia's muscle might slam the door against further dissolution. He had actively courted that state's interests since his election, and its leaders had eagerly consulted with him. According to a number of accounts, Lincoln twice went so far as to promise delegates from Richmond he would give up Fort Sumter if they would adjourn the secession convention then under way. This was the kind of quiet deal he liked to broker, by which everyone might benefit, and where fingerprints were hard to trace. He also fell back on familiar habits of dispensing political favors, believing that the more positions he offered the Old Dominion, the more fealty he could buy. When a Virginian wrote to secure a position for his son, the President advised his postmaster general: "I think Virginia should be heard, in such cases." Later assessments showed that piecemeal patronage was probably not the best way to win over the state, but at the time Lincoln thought it might halt the flood of defections.[62]

We do not know what, if anything, the new president and Lee said to each other on March 12, or in what way they may have impressed each other. But it was against the backdrop of wooing Virginia that Lincoln promoted Lee to full colonel, just four days after the reception. He still had a nagging mistrust of Southern officials, and evidently some effort was made to ascertain Lee's intentions. Scott was reportedly questioned by Cameron on the subject. "He is true as steel, sir," was the general's reply, "true as steel!" Twiggs's dismissal had resulted in an unusual opening in the general officer ranks, and Lincoln gave Edwin Sumner the brigadier's position. This was a logical choice, since Sumner had long been a colonel, and it was widely accepted. But Lee's promotion was outside the mandated system, in which advancement was strictly by seniority. Lincoln vaulted him over at least seven other men (by some counts fifteen) to give him a colonel's commission. Although Lee accepted the post, it was indicative of the Army's malaise that he obscured this promotion and even hid it from his wife and son.[63]

Did Lincoln misread Lee's heart when he placed such confidence in him, including promotion outside normal military protocol? The President's knowledge of this man was shallow, but on trusted authority he believed Lee was against secession and devoted to the Union. In March 1861 Lee and Lincoln were both clinging to the same driftwood dreams of national cohesion, a cohesion that hinged on Virginia's resolve. However, in addition to cementing relations with the Old Dominion, it appears Lincoln may have had a special operation in mind for Colonel Lee.

In an attempt to forestall total disaster, Lincoln was courting several departing states besides Virginia. Chief among these was Texas. His hope for the Lone Star State centered on Sam Houston, the staunchly Unionist governor. Houston was no Republican, but he publicly rejected the idea that Lincoln's election presented a real danger to Southern interests. Nonetheless, he sensed danger, and within weeks requested that federal forces stationed in his state be united for "home protection" with the famed Texas Rangers; and that every possible measure be taken to avoid the "madness and fanaticism" of civil war. It was this fear that had caused the governor to forewarn Twiggs of the secessionists' intentions. Despite Houston's fiery assertion that "the Demons of anarchy must be put down and destroyed," by Lincoln's inauguration Texans had already voted to leave the Union and were on the verge of joining forces with the Confederacy.[64]

In the early days of March, Lincoln concocted a desperate plan to rebind Texas to his cause by sending military support to Houston. Apparently two different missions were dispatched. Frederick W. Lander, an astute army officer whose hide had been toughened by years of western duty, and who was acquainted with Houston, was recruited by Seward on March 10 to lead the first excursion. Lander received orders to travel to Austin with a proposal that Lincoln would supply an impressive force to help Houston keep Texas in the Union. Accounts of the offer vary: Houston stated a few months later that he was promised 70,000 men—a striking suggestion from a commander in chief who could not summon even 1,000 troops to defend his capital. Others who joined Houston during the discussion of Lincoln's offer recalled equally fantastic figures of 50,000 or 100,000 men. A few days later, Scott went so far as to sign orders halting the retreat of troops leaving Texas after the Twiggs upheaval. Instead, he proposed they be entrenched to create a nuclear fighting force, which would be expanded from headquarters.

Houston evidently remarked to friends that had he been younger he might have chanced the plan. Instead, he reluctantly requested that all federal forces be withdrawn as soon as possible, rather than precipitate a crisis that would devastate his state. His hand was more or less forced—Houston had been confronted by Texas secessionists before Lander's arrival, and he had refused to take an oath of loyalty to the Confederacy. As a result, he was drummed out of office on March 16. There is evidence that a second offer from Lincoln arrived just as Houston was moving out of the State House. It was met by the deposed governor with murmurings that it was, unfortunately, "too late." In the end, reports of Lincoln's correspondence with Houston became public and played into the secessionists' hands, heightening tensions.[65]

Part of the proposal was that the troops would be adequately led, by someone Houston trusted. Lander did not want the position; and another likely contender, Colonel Albert Sidney Johnston, who had served for years in Texas and had considerable command capability, was strongly suspected of unfaithfulness because of his Southern ties. Johnston, in fact, was brokenhearted over the disintegration of the country and had courageously managed sensitive ports and arsenals in California against pro-secessionist forces. "I have heard foolish talk about an attempt to seize the strongholds under my charge," he told Southern sympathizers. "Knowing this, I have prepared for emergencies, and will defend the property of the United States with every resource at my command, and with the last drop of blood in my body." Lincoln, however, would irregularly relieve Johnston a few days after Lander's departure, virtually pushing the undecided colonel into the arms of the South—a move the President later regretted and tried, unsuccessfully, to walk back.[66] It therefore seems probable that Lee was in mind for the imagined Texas expedition. He had been promoted to lead the First Cavalry, which was stationed in the West, and he had a good deal of prior experience in Texas, having been posted there three times. The Second Cavalry, which he had formerly led, was still a presence on the ground. In addition, Lee had acquitted himself well as acting head of the Army's Department of Texas, winning Houston's respect. Whatever fantasies of massive battalions were being dreamed in the White House, few men could have commanded the force with as much on-the-ground knowledge and authority as Lee.[67]

VII

Robert E. Lee was ultimately offered a larger role, as head of the federal army called up by Lincoln in mid-April. In an iconic decision, he overrode family concerns and the traditions of the service to refuse that post and join forces with the South. Wrenching as it was, Lee's dilemma was only one of dozens percolating in the tense East Room on March 12. Another protégé of Winfield Scott, Virginian Lunsford Lindsay Lomax, fourth-generation scion in a line of distinguished professional soldiers, stood with the lieutenants at the far end of the room. Already a proven fighter during the border unrest in "bleeding Kansas," Lomax had been called to the capital for special duty guarding the President. When Lomax weighed his prospects a few weeks later, he described himself as "almost suicidal." Near him in line stood one of the most talented mapmakers in the Army, a whiz kid named Charles Read Collins. Collins hailed from Pennsylvania; nonetheless, he was wrestling with his sympathy for Southern concerns. He spent a few disappointing months amid the Union command, then fled to the Confederate Army, where he won great respect before being killed on the field in 1864. Meanwhile, one of his close friends from the military academy was taking a different stance. Alfred Mordecai Jr. was suffering fallout from suspicion of his father's arms transfers; but though a Virginian, he angrily pointed to the South as the "cause of the disruption of the country, of the unhappiness of my entire family, and of producing such a change in the prospects for my own fortune that I have become embittered towards it." Shunning his father's example, and ignoring pressure from relatives, Mordecai refused to resign. He fought to the end under the Stars and Stripes, rising to the rank of lieutenant colonel.[68]

One of Mordecai's sisters understood his perspective: "for any officer who had been educated at West Point to fight against the United States," she wrote, "it seems . . . like stabbing his own mother with the sword she put in his hand for her defence." Quartermaster General Joseph E. Johnston, standing with noble bearing at the head of Scott's column, was feeling just that piercing pain. It is impossible to know if Lincoln recognized the anguish behind Johnston's official demeanor that day, but those who saw him about this time commented that Johnston was so distracted he did not answer when spoken to, and that he often paced his rooms in an agony of contemplation. Like so many, Johnston had Revolutionary antecedents; he was a nephew of Patrick Henry, and his father had fought in Light-Horse Harry Lee's legion. Peter Johnston, his brother, was a member of the Virginia secession convention, fighting hard with the Unionist camp, and decrying the underhanded stratagems used by Fire-Eaters to force secession. In a letter that was probably delivered the day of the reception, Peter counseled his brother to avoid any hasty action: "there is no reason now for your resignation—so hold on, and wait the course of events, *without saying what you may hereafter do.*"[69]

Johnston was skeptical about both slavery and secession, but he was also receiving invitations from the Confederate government and worrying that he would lose opportunities if he waited too long to make a move. Financial considerations were among the issues before him—at age fifty-four he had no other professional prospects and he could not afford to be unemployed. (This was a concern for many officers. Robert E. Lee confronted it, and the whole military establishment was still reeling from the death of a navy man, Captain George Tilton, who, when faced with secession, a rebellious son, and large debts, resolved his dilemma by shooting himself between the eyes on the day his home state, Florida, joined the Confederacy.) When Johnston finally resigned, a few days after Virginia's secession, he was escorted from the secretary of war's office in a state of collapse, sputtering desperately about the horror of raising his hand against the land that had educated and honored him.[70]

Abraham Lincoln never sympathized with the agony of men like Lee and Johnston, who had sworn allegiance to their country, yet felt they could not hold it above obligations to family and community. For him the questions were more straightforward. The President saw no advantage in a rebellious compact that undermined the great democratic experiment; besides, these men had willingly taken loyalty oaths, binding them to protect the United States. He was particularly chagrined about Lee, whose early "ambiguity" and ultimate "disloyalty" he later cited as justification for suspending the writ of habeas corpus. Lincoln showed an uncharacteristic vengefulness toward Lee for the rest of his life. However, none of the officers in the East Room review disappointed him as much as the showy Lieutenant Colonel John Bankhead Magruder, who paraded before the President in the "gorgeous" military trappings he had recently brought home from Europe.[71]

Magruder's personal history was similar to that of several fellow officers. A native Virginian, he was brevetted for gallantry in the Mexican War, and called to Washington by Scott to augment the forces there. He had just arrived on March 10, but Lincoln already knew him slightly, for Magruder led a unit that guarded the White House. Lincoln came to like this man, whose flamboyance appealed to his love of theater, and who could skillfully converse on the perils facing the nation. Somehow, in those early spring weeks, the

President got the impression that Magruder would follow Scott's example and remain loyal to the Union flag. Indeed, in his fondness for the officer, Lincoln began to view him as an ally.

Had his staff done its homework, the President would have known this was unlikely. Magruder had been an old-line Whig, but switched his allegiance to the Democratic Party in 1856, when John C. Frémont was nominated as the first "black Republican" candidate. Magruder had already published letters describing his abhorrence of the "leprous" abolitionists, as well as his belief that they were willfully destroying the country. His determination to follow the lead of his state—*"where I belong"*—had also been made public. Magruder seems to have walked a careful line during the edgy days of March 1861, avoiding any future commitments, but assuring army superiors that as long as he was still a commissioned officer he would apply himself diligently. He proved true to his word, impressing observers with his confident leadership and charismatic charm. "Magruder's cavalry command . . . is composed of fine, hardy-looking, well-drilled men," approved the *Washington Evening Star,* two weeks after the army reception, "and is regarded as one of the most efficient in the service."[72]

The rifts in the Lee, Johnston, and Mordecai clans were painful, but few men faced family conflicts as dramatic as Magruder's. His older brother, Captain George A. Magruder, was the third-ranking officer in the United States Navy. The popular and respected head of the Hydrographic Bureau, Captain Magruder hoped fervently for the restoration of the Union. Nonetheless, he vowed that if his state seceded he would leave the country rather than fight a fratricidal war. This is exactly what he did, departing with his family for England shortly after the commencement of hostilities, and never returning. Another brother, Allan Bowie Magruder, was a prominent attorney in the nation's capital. He was also a close friend of William Seward, and through him won the President's trust. The confidence went so far that Lincoln used Allan Magruder as a secret envoy to Richmond, to lobby on behalf of keeping the Old Dominion in the Union. Like his brothers, however, Allan Magruder was caught between two worlds, neither of which completely pleased him. As tensions mounted he continued to serve the administration, but with growing discomfort. He later resigned and joined Confederate forces in Virginia—until this too left him conflicted and he returned to Washington in a state of uneasy neutrality.[73]

However ambivalent, John Bankhead Magruder was cagey enough to convince Lincoln he would faithfully serve him no matter how events developed. The President was taken by surprise, therefore, when he learned during the Sumter crisis that Magruder had said his farewells at a Washington soiree, then dramatically galloped south across the Potomac Long Bridge, his cape flying behind him. It was not a rash act: it took Magruder four days to resign after Virginia's secession, and he called it "the most unhappy moment of my life." Lincoln was astonished when told of the theatrical exit. "Three days ago, Magruder had been in his room making the loudest protestations of undying devotion to the Union," John Hay, Lincoln's private secretary, confided to his diary. "This canker of secession has wonderfully demoralized the Army." The desertions also greatly affected Lincoln. He later recounted to several people how much these episodes upset him. Talking with General Samuel Sturgis as they reviewed troops in late 1862, the President described the particular sting of Magruder's exit. At "the very moment he was making to me these protestations of loyalty and devotion," Lincoln mused,

> he must have had his mind fully made up to leave; and it seemed the more wanton and cruel in him because he knew that I had implicit confidence in his integrity. The fact is, when I learned that he had gone over to the enemy and I had been so completely deceived in him, my confidence was shaken in everybody, and I hardly knew who to trust any more.[74]

VIII

The President's introduction to his army was but a brief interlude in the frantic first weeks of his term, yet it cast a long shadow. The reception was "little calculated to inspire hope and confidence," wrote one of those present, and a sense of foreboding lingered long after the encounter. It jolted Lincoln into understanding that if he commenced war it would be with a graying, dilapidated military force, and it raised the specter of disloyalty—even treason—in his midst. The queasy realization that he might have to rely on men who were unknown to him—and perhaps unworthy—would persist long afterward, coloring his decisions. The officers were also left with strong impressions. The awkward new White House denizen did not impress them and, in the wake of the Twiggs and Cooper defections, the officers were increasingly wary of one another. The air was heavy with mistrust, foretelling difficulties the Army would face over the next four years within its ranks, and with its commander in chief.[75]

To uniformed men, the most striking impression Lincoln left was his woeful lack of "presence." The statuesque officers noted the stooped shoulders, the shuffling gait, and the wandering attention with dismay. The President lacked what Samuel Du Pont succinctly termed "dress and address," without which, noted the naval captain, one could not hope to influence the armed forces. Such indifference to form was not just disappointing, but alarming to men who sensed what loomed before them. Dignified presentation was important for these warriors, whose erect bearing and cool decision making formed part of their psychological weaponry. In their world, careful attention to detail sometimes meant the difference between life and death. "The first essential for military authority lies in the power of command,—a power which it is useless to analyze, for it is felt instinctively, and it is seen in its results," observed Thomas Wentworth Higginson, a colonel of volunteers. "It is hardly too much to say, that, in the military, if one has this power, all else becomes secondary; and it is perfectly safe to say that without it all other gifts are useless." To such eyes, Lincoln looked unfit, unkempt, and unready.[76]

The undignified image grated to the point that open letters were addressed to Lincoln begging him to pay attention to the decorum that was so important to military morale. A few weeks after the reception, Robert Colby, a prominent New York Republican, frankly advised the commander in chief that soldiers were writing letters home, ridiculing him. Lincoln could not address even simple military issues, they complained, and his figure sagged ludicrously when reviewing troops. Sometimes he brought his wife and children along and "straddled off" after them, or told jokes while they stood at attention. "These things dont sound well at all—The influence is bad here," Colby advised,

. . . and you, though you were autocrat, can never be popular with the army unless you try your best . . . and your manner is full as important as your talk—A lawyer in his office can put his feet on a table higher than his head if he wishes to, but he cant come any such performance as Commander in Chief of the Armies of the United States in their presence—There he must pretend to be a soldier even if he don't know any thing of tattoos at all—You had better let some officer put you through a few dress parades in your leisure moments if you can get any, and get some military habit on you so you shall feel natural among military men—Don't let people call you a goose on these *very, very* important relations to the army—[77]

Lincoln made an effort to understand the unfamiliar regulations, studying General Henry Halleck's *Elements of Military Art and Science* and talking shop with officers at the War Department and the Washington Navy Yard. But ultimately the President found that martial bearing was not something to be learned like a grammar lesson. His informal attitude continued at reviews, levees, and tattoos for the duration of his presidency.[78] Nor did the careworn face, so beloved by latter-day admirers, rally sympathy within his command. Those who respected Ulysses S. Grant, for instance, commented on his unflappability, even under fire. "He is everywhere on the battle field, the coolest and most impertable man I ever saw," remarked one observer. By contrast, officers who met Lincoln wrote that he looked "quite paralyzed and wilted down," or "as if he would soon go to kingdomcome . . . there is not in the ranks of this army a more miserable looking man than old Abe." Lincoln openly expressed his apprehensions, plaintively asking advisers what he should do, sometimes "wringing his hands and whining" that "nobody can imagine what influences are brought to bear on me." Such uncertainty at the top of the hierarchical chain can infect an army, stifling nerve and zeal. For the next four years, the commander in chief would struggle to project authority, never really understanding how spit and polish instilled confidence. Ultimately, as he would confess to John Hay, Lincoln could not get the armed forces to follow him at all.[79]

The impression that Lincoln was not in full control tempted a number of senior advisers to take liberties with their positions. Men like Hunter, Sumner, and Keyes had already begun to manipulate the President before he took office, and cabinet officials soon followed suit. Cameron liberally gave positions to cronies and approved questionable procurement deals, adding to the mistrust of Lincoln. Seward conspired with General Scott, pursuing unauthorized negotiations with Confederate leaders, which misled several, and clouded the already threatening atmosphere. When he saw the President falter, Seward boldly offered to take the reins, until Lincoln made it clear to his secretary of state that he would remain in charge. Postmaster General Montgomery Blair went so far as to correspond with former presidents, complaining that Lincoln was incapable of taking strong action, as well as disorganized. Alarmed at what seemed to be a dangerous leadership vacuum, Franklin Pierce proposed that the five "retired" presidents form a rump ruling committee until Lincoln could be replaced. All this put further pressure on the chief executive, who craved time and clarity, but was beset by an ever louder cacophony of voices. Still, he took no action to regularize the chain of command. The result was a great deal of ad hochery, as well as badly confused communications.[80]

Part of the problem was that Lincoln himself was undisciplined. His office was a disorganized den of loose papers, unscreened visitors, and, if we are to believe his secretary, chaotic decision making. "He was extremely unmethodical," Hay testified. "He would break through every Regulation as fast as it was made." A dozen highly regarded military men urged him to establish a war council, or at least take on a military attaché who could advise the administration and coordinate operations. The President always sidestepped this suggestion, claiming aides would interfere with his freedom of movement and become "an uncompensating incumbrance." Instead he wrote orders himself, countermanded decisions, or sent mixed messages, without informing senior leaders—then wondered why his commands were not carried out. "The truth is, we must adopt a systematic, scientific warfare," worried one of Lincoln's most seasoned generals. "I feel anxious about . . . the want of *system* which seems to pervade our operations."[81]

What Lincoln seems not to have understood in these early days, and what he never fully grasped during the war, was the stark difference between the backroom caucuses and private arrangements he managed so well and the immense importance of structure and clarity in the military. Large groups of armed men become mobs if not taught to respect rules that maintain order. Discipline is especially critical in the chaos of battle, when senses are confused by the smoke and roar of death's machinery. The President's style, formed in the frontier political tradition, was one of intuition, maneuver, and the play-off of personalities and power grids to form alliances and thwart enemies—just the opposite of a military culture based on regulations, obedience, and control. "War is not a town meeting to be ruled by the ayes and nays," exclaimed a colonel, who, though admiring Lincoln, increasingly lost heart at the President's poor grasp of military system. When the commander in chief began blurring lines of authority, listening to tattletales, and offering patronage to officers as if they were party operatives, he was undermining the finely honed cohesion that enabled an army to operate effectively on a killing field. His role was to buttress military resources from the top, and foster the proud traditions that had given

American soldiers and sailors such success. Instead—however unwittingly—Lincoln was tearing through the very fabric of command.[82]

The haphazard management showed itself most clearly in Lincoln's attempt to relieve Fort Sumter. Just days after the army reception, Lincoln allowed Seward to lead him into an unorthodox effort to support the beleaguered garrison. The President thought he could strike a clever psychological compromise by resupplying the starving garrison with provisions rather than sending weapons, while simultaneously reinforcing the armaments of Fort Pickens in Florida. That concession was unlikely to relieve Anderson's situation or placate the fire-breathers' powerful emotions, but Lincoln hoped it would buy him more time. The woeful organization of the expedition, however, sealed its doom. Instead of coordinating a professional joint operation, Seward, who had no business meddling in military affairs, recruited an army captain and a navy lieutenant to devise a high-risk venture. Scott was not consulted, nor were the navy and war secretaries. During the episode, the President and secretary of state ("amateur strategists in March, 1861, if ever there were such," in Montgomery Meigs's view) signed questionable orders before reading them, laid aside previously agreed plans without apprising officers who had been instructed to execute them, and had ships and men reassigned without the commanders' knowledge. Poor weather hampered the operation, but its failure was already assured by capricious direction and the lack of a united purpose. Lincoln then spoiled any hope that the vessels could secretly resupply Sumter by informing Governor Pickens that he had ordered the expedition. Pickens immediately demanded that the fort be abandoned either voluntarily or by force. A few hours after Confederates began firing, Anderson and his men surrendered.

Southern hotheads, who already construed Lincoln's hesitation as cowardice, crowed even louder over his apparent incompetence. The President reluctantly admitted some responsibility, telling the man tapped to lead the ill-fated expedition, Captain Gustavus Fox, that it was all an "accident, for which you were in no wise responsible, and possibly I, to some extent was." But those who observed the confusion knew precisely where the blame lay. A political confidant surveyed the wreckage and remarked wanly that Lincoln "blew his trumpet before he had a sword to draw—and now he can't get his sword & is likely to lose his trumpet." Years later, key players in the debacle, including Welles, Scott, and Fox, were still sputtering over the insultingly amateurish plan and the humiliating failure of Fort Sumter's attempted resupply.[83]

Lincoln's approach to managing military affairs would have consequences for army and navy operations far beyond the immediate problems caused by the Sumter expedition, however. His tolerance of actions outside normal channels, as well as his encouragement of freelancing by men not authorized to conduct operations, hampered military effectiveness for the duration of the war. Not only Seward but Treasury Secretary Salmon P. Chase carried on correspondence with leading generals, who whinged, begged favors, or questioned strategy, all outside the established chain of command. Lincoln frequently circumvented cabinet members and commanding officers to consult whomever he pleased, at any rank, ignoring both branch of service and seniority. In 1864 Grant was astonished to find troops still being assigned without his authorization; when he inquired at headquarters, he was informed that "things are some times done very strangely here" and that the President himself was sending orders "over and around every body"—something the military bureaucracy deemed "a ruinous policy." Experienced soldiers saw this as something beyond a breach of etiquette or an affront to officers' rank or pride. It undercut the authority of men who needed absolute control in desperate situations, setting in place a culture of chaotic management and disregard for discipline that persisted to the end of the war.[84]

Thus the seeds of chronic disobedience, which would so plague the Union Army, were planted in Lincoln's earliest military meetings. If the commander in chief was ignoring hierarchy, established procedure, and customary courtesy, and rewarding unregulated behavior, the path was cleared for irregular actions at every level. The once highly disciplined officers began openly promoting themselves, publicly disagreeing with policy, and conniving against their superiors. Men like George Hazzard now wrote to the White House, the captain declaring his supervisor at Fort McHenry unfit for the job and recommending himself as replacement. When chastised by Scott, Hazzard announced "it was none of his business who I wrote to." In another of many instances, Brigadier General William Nelson took the opportunity to undercut the Army of West Tennessee's leadership. "Gen'l Grant I say XXX XXXX," he bellowed from the page. "Consider it said." Some told tales to department heads or even took them to the press, whispering dangerous revelations and undercutting much needed esprit. David Hunter went so far as to write directly to "the Titular President of the so-called Confederate States," accusing Jefferson Davis of fighting for a cause "Satan . . . was contending for when he was cast into hell," and proclaiming policies that were entirely unauthorized by Washington. Lincoln did nothing to rein in such practices, and uncontrolled behavior spilled into field operations. "Law and rank, and usage, are apparently lost sight of," General Samuel Curtis warned the President from Missouri, "and lead to insubordination and extravigance which would ruin any country or cause." When men ran from their formations at Bull Run; when officers thwarted one another, sometimes willfully undermining important campaigns; when Army and Navy failed to coordinate, or masses of troops were missing from battle; when General George B. McClellan (who returned to the Army after Fort Sumter) crassly denounced the President with no threat of reprisal, they were all only following the lax example set at the Executive Mansion. The military maxim—that performance below is but a reflection of the top—was as operable during the Civil War as it is today.[85]

Scott tried to stop the practice of corresponding directly with senior politicians by putting out a general order forbidding contact outside the chain of command, but officers such as McClellan simply ignored him. Faced with such blatant breaches of discipline, Scott remonstrated. "Has then senior, no corrective power over a junior officer in case of such persistent neglect and disobedience?" he pointedly asked Simon Cameron. The lack of compliance was particularly grating to the lieutenant general since his *General Regulations* had created the mold from which these soldiers were made, and he staunchly believed that battlefield success stemmed from order, obedience, and accountability. This was never truer than in the crisis of 1861. Scott felt personally insulted, but his real concern was that sloppy practices were encouraging the enemy. Yet the problem was not vested in Scott—it spoke to the complete absence of military procedure on all levels. "It is now evident, that the Admin[istration] has no system—no subordination—no unity—no accountability—no coordination," worried Attorney General Edward Bates a few months later. Unable to find a workable remedy, Scott tried twice to resign over the issue of White House–sanctioned insubordination, before he was finally retired in November 1861.[86]

The firm discipline Scott desired never materialized. Something in Lincoln shrank from exercising crisp authority, and his erratic leadership often led directly to battlefield losses. "I am sure he sees and feels the wrong done," Bates observed, "but cannot pluck up the spirit to redress the evil, much less to punish the wrong-doers." It was the "hazard" of his good nature, wrote one observer; the fallibility of "a man irresolute but of kind intentions"; the debility of one "always disposed to mitigate punishment, and to grant favors." Officers came to understand that Lincoln was far more comfortable in negotiable political dealings than in the absolute world of professional killing. But they also knew that during combat his laxity was lethal. Lincoln grasped the theory of discipline, wrote one, but lacked the courage to apply it. Patience, compromise, and tolerance, he concluded, might be "the marks of a great soul, but not of a great soldier."[87]

IX

W hile army professionals worried over eroding discipline, the stark reality for Lincoln was that he would soon have to rely on an army he did not know and did not trust. This was already unnervingly evident at the army and navy receptions, where the blue lines were marked by glaring gaps. The waves of defection began soon hitting the administration with full force: officers with sensitive knowledge fled southward by the dozens; every Southern midshipman at the Naval Academy resigned; militiamen called up to defend Washington refused to join regular forces to protect the President. The disappointment Lincoln felt at the departure of Lee, Johnston, and Magruder only strengthened his instinct to trust no one outside his political persuasion. Insecurity and fear of disloyalty, so palpable in these early days, colored his selection of officers throughout the war.[88]

Winfield Scott had arranged his cadre in rank order for the commander in chief's first review, but it was not clear that Lincoln understood how carefully the lineup had been organized, or how important seniority was to men whose chance to move forward sometimes rested on the precise *hour* of their tenure. The parade of incompetent septuagenarians who saluted the President cannot have improved his respect for the military's rigid promotion protocols. Halfway through the war, he would admit being surprised by the officers' sensitivity to rank, or to the way that commands were decided. "Truth to speak, I do not appreciate this matter of rank on paper, as you officers do," he told General William S. Rosecrans. He was accustomed to forming liaisons based on personal trust and partisan loyalty, and adroitly keeping rivals at bay by leavening the whole with a few sympathetic representatives from opposing camps. That formula had worked well for him in Illinois, and now, in the most difficult test of his life, he naturally gravitated toward it.[89]

It was not just Elmer Ellsworth or Robert E. Lee whom Lincoln singled out for unusual appointments in those early spring days, but several men in the adjutant general's office and, significantly, an officer further down the line, Captain Montgomery Meigs. Meigs's case was at once unusual and telling. He was known as an innovative engineer but also as a man who was willing to buck authority. Lincoln may not have noticed him at the White House reception, but two weeks later Meigs was tapped, along with Navy lieutenant David Dixon Porter, to formulate and lead the ill-fated resupply mission to Fort Sumter. Meigs knew the action was unconventional but also saw opportunity in it, and he risked the ire of General Scott to follow Seward's shaky plans. Despite the dismal outcome of the operation, the President felt a growing bond with Meigs. Only a few weeks after they met, Lincoln gushed about Meigs's "masculine intellect, learning and experience of the right sort," and then jumped the captain up four grades, appointing him quartermaster general of the Union Army after Joseph Johnston resigned.[90]

Quartermaster General
Montgomery C. Meigs,
carte de visite, March 1861
LIBRARY OF CONGRESS

As it turned out, this would be one of Lincoln's best appointments. Meigs was an outstanding quartermaster general, careful of resources, and adroit enough to develop sophisticated systems to supply the Union's growing military machine. The President allowed him to manage his bureau without interference; nonetheless, Meigs's diary indicates he made a point of keeping a good distance from presidential intrigues. In 1861, however, regular officers were appalled at Meigs's appointment, for Lincoln had pushed aside several deserving men to fill the slot, including an irate William Tecumseh Sherman. Interestingly, Sherman was among those who believed more junior officers should be scouted out for promotion. But Lincoln's methodology, which ignored rank and meritorious service to reward men considered courtiers—as Meigs was—reinforced Sherman's already negative impression that the President was undermining army loyalty by the way he exercised his prerogatives.[91]

If all of Lincoln's unorthodox appointments had all been as fortuitous as Meigs's, perhaps assertions that he pioneered a new system of flexibility and meritocracy could be justified.[92] But his record of promoting men who were untried—or tried and found wanting—did not improve with the years. Edward Baker, a Republican friend, with limited know-how and a reputation for heedlessness, directed an inexpert assault at Ball's Bluff, Virginia, in October

1861. Baker lost his life and a thousand men, buoying the Confederate sense of invincibility at a critical moment, and opening the way for intensive congressional involvement in military affairs. John A. Dahlgren, an officer Lincoln liked to chat with at the Washington Navy Yard, pressed the President to advance him from ordnance work to command during the critical 1863 Charleston campaign. Lincoln acquiesced, despite the navy secretary's opposition and Dahlgren's comic-opera tendency to seasickness. When Dahlgren could not subordinate his lust for laurels to teamwork, army-navy tactical maneuvers broke down, scuttling the opportunity to take the city. Lincoln also continued to support those practicing the "glib and oily art" of flattery, such as John Pope and Joseph Hooker. Lincoln knew these arrogant men were not respected by the Army, but appointed them anyway—and they handed him humiliating defeats. It rankled officers who had been decorated for valor or had superior experience to be forced to carry out orders from such men. "How must these poor fellows feel who have had Dahlgren put over their heads," Admiral David Farragut lamented on hearing of that unfortunate appointment. "It is, in my opinion, a great perversion . . . [to] give him the rank of admiral over . . . men who have been fighting for their country ever since the commencement of the war." Some, like Julius Garesché, thought the commissions not just awkward but actually illegal. He turned down a promotion rather than be forced to serve under a less qualified Lincoln appointee.[93]

Some of Lincoln's selections were good men placed in the wrong position, for miscasting was a consistent problem. Even though Lincoln managed to dislodge Cameron from the War Department after nine debilitating months, his replacement by the abrasive, militarily inexperienced Edwin Stanton, as well as the recent appointment of nervous Henry Halleck to the rank of full major general, only added to the Army's alienation. The majority of the disappointing appointments were political, meant to placate critics or the radicals in Congress, or given as favors to personal friends. Among them was Nathaniel Banks, a competent politician who might have been a credible staff officer but was given a field command, where his talent was conspicuously lacking. The final accounting sheet for Banks was particularly grim: disasters in two theaters of war, hugely wasted resources, and thousands of deaths—all leading to diminished public confidence. Similar failures occurred with partisan generals such as John C. Frémont, Franz Sigel, Benjamin F. Butler, and John A.

McClernand. One of Lincoln's Illinois allies, McClernand was singled out by the assistant secretary of war for his "repeated disobedience of important orders—his general insubordination, disposition, and his palpable incompetency for the duties of the position." Nonetheless, the President backed away from relieving him. McClernand's case illustrated how Lincoln evolved a sliding scale of judging officers, generally favoring party fealty over performance. It was understandable that there was a higher set of expectations for the professionals, but the chief executive showed disproportionate impatience with West Point men while giving his political appointees far too many chances after they had demonstrated dangerous incompetence in the field. George B. McClellan's roller-coaster ride as general in chief was a particular conundrum. There may have been good reasons for relieving the overcautious general, but it unsettled the nation to see him retained after crass insubordination and dismissed after success. Fighting men were even more perplexed.[94]

The administration, in explaining the dispiriting string of failures, claimed that the field of available men was a poor one. "Military genius is not as plenty as blackberries in our army," wrote John Nicolay. In fact, Lincoln continued to show an unnerving ability to pluck the green, the overripe, or the spoiled from the bush, as he had with Sumner, Pope, Hunter, and Ellsworth. Many good field officers were underutilized; many promising men were overlooked. As Lincoln's interference in field operations increased, some fine soldiers—including Frederick Lander, Phil Kearny, and John Reynolds—refused commands because they would not subordinate their expertise to misguided direction from Washington. "I fear," wrote Sherman, "that we are approaching that stage . . . when no man of principle will accept command under our Government."[95] Other excellent men, like Brigadier General James A. Garfield, were recalled from the field to serve political purposes. (This scheme backfired when Garfield, who had been persuaded to take a seat in Congress, began to feel disdain for what he termed the "stupidity and weakness" of Lincoln's war leadership and proceeded to vote against the President's platform on every issue.) Other proven soldiers were passed over because of their Southern roots or their support for the Democratic Party. Virginian George Thomas was held back, although in 1861 he trod the difficult path Lincoln hoped Lee and Magruder would take. (While he steadfastly served the Union, Thomas's family disowned him, ultimately asking him to change his name.) Democrat Alpheus Williams never received appropriate recognition, even after impressively pinch-hitting as corps commander at Second Bull

Run and Antietam. Feisty Baldy Smith, who watched Lincoln with wide eyes at the March 12 reception, was shunned because of his support for the unpopular McClellan, losing his corps command but not his zeal to serve. All these men were strongly committed to the Union cause, for much the same reasons as Lincoln, and had no intention of undermining military operations. "I am with no party that does not insist upon a rigorous and intelligent prosecution of the war, till the Gov't is entirely successful, and the cause of the trouble is eradicated," insisted Smith. His loyal service after demotion proved his assertion.[96]

Lincoln tried to explain to several generals the difficulties of simultaneously waging a shooting war and a public opinion campaign, asking them to understand the need to balance competing political and military necessities. This was a legitimate concern; indeed, it is always an issue in a democracy. What the President never fully accepted, however, was that party affiliation did not equate with loyalty; nor did he understand that professionally trained soldiers took pride in obeying civil authorities regardless of political viewpoint. As a result he never subordinated his party skirmishes to the larger battle—a habit that many believed lengthened the war. When pressed about his appointments, Lincoln admitted he preferred political affinity to military knowledge, yet he could not point to any notable success from his choices. Halleck was often blamed for the partisan promotions, but he actually disapproved of them. "The waste of money and demoralization of the Army by having incompetent and corrupt politicians in nearly all military offices, high and low," he complained, "has almost ruined the Army, and . . . will soon ruin the country." Indeed, the dismal procession of battlefield failures brought on by these appointments disappointed public hopes and badly affected armed service morale. It was victory—and an end to negligent killing—that was needed to create national unity, not patronage.[97]

The equilibrium the White House sought between Republican interests and military expertise proved elusive throughout the war. The final balance sheet showed that little advantage was gained by favoring party men. And in the end it was not politico-generals who would win the contest for Lincoln. Instead, victory would finally be secured by the men standing at attention in the East Room, and their comrades from the old army.[98]

X

After about an hour, the President left the army reception, in some relief. Perhaps the most striking aspect of the event was how clearly he did not want to be there. Leading the military—as a figurehead or otherwise—was not the kind of executive power that had captured his imagination. War was menacing on that March afternoon—and it now appeared he might fail to avoid armed conflict, something he wanted badly to do.

Lincoln would chafe throughout his term at the role that had been thrust upon him, candidly telling aides, generals, and even reporters that he did not want the responsibility. When he was unable to contain the conflict, he responded by expanding his role, but there was rarely any ego in it, simply a sense of desperation, as, never knowing whom to trust, the beleaguered president fell back on his own imperfect instincts. Many have credited him with improving his skills and, finally, learning to entrust more to the professionals and stay out of their way. But however laudable his self-education, it also meant he was forever catching up. Terrible tragedies occurred and thousands lost their lives in the time it took Lincoln to comprehend strategy and tactics, discipline and military protocol, staffing and morale; and to back away from his unfortunate experiments with hands-on direction of the war.[99]

Few encounters have been as tense as that ceremonial occasion on March 12, 1861. Every man in the room had something at stake, not only of principle but of personal fortune. Officers were watching the disintegration of a country they had served despite danger and deprivation. Their proud profession was self-destructing, its enriching camaraderie shattered. They faced the specter of broken families and communities, financial distress, and wrenching doubts about the meaning of loyalty and patriotism. Lincoln was watching the approach of fratricidal war, for which he would be held personally responsible. Presiding over these early military reviews as commander in chief was like stepping onto alien territory—a place he did not understand and did not really want to be. Although he strove to improve his credentials, as well as to comprehend the horrific reality of battle, Lincoln would never fully grasp the warrior's culture or become comfortable with his part in it. He did not have the military stature of a Washington or a Jackson, nor the steely confidence needed to send men swiftly and surely into deadly contests. The war effort would suffer as a result. The qualities for which the sixteenth president would be admired—horror at violence, forbearance, and a talent for compromise—

may have been notable political assets, or the signs of a sensitive spirit, but they were not the hallmarks of a great chieftain.

Abraham Lincoln sighed in relief as he walked out of the claustrophobic East Room. His army command waited at attention as he left the room: shoulders square; faces passive; breaths held in check.

No one would exhale for a very long time.

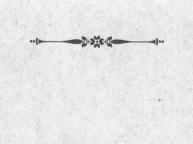

Lincoln Raises the Flag at the White House, detail of drawing on page 66

2

PFUNNY PFACE

The President was hurrying across the South Lawn of the White House. Abraham Lincoln's strides were long and loping, but his face was pensive. It was a fine day in late June 1861, and he looked forward to inaugurating a new Marine bandstand. The young soldiers had tacked together a makeshift marquee to stage their performances and a crowd stood in festive anticipation on the close-cut grass. Lincoln liked martial tunes and the gaiety that surrounded such occasions. His task that afternoon was an enjoyable one: to run the Stars and Stripes up the new flagpole, giving a much needed morale boost to the worried nation.[1]

Lincoln proceeded through a crowd of uniformed soldiers on the lawn. The Marine detachment was there, of course, but so were band members from the Twelfth New York Regiment, and an honor guard from the Third U.S. Infantry Regiment. These were not the first military men the President had met that day, however. He had just left a tense discussion with his senior commanders, a debate over the steps needed to end the rebellion quickly. General Irwin McDowell was recommending a swift movement against rebel forces at Manassas Junction, some twenty miles from Washington. General Winfield Scott disagreed with the plan, maintaining that the troops were undisciplined, unready, and unfit for battle. Instead he advocated a choking blockade on the Mississippi, a lengthier process, but one Scott felt would more effectively subdue the Confederacy. Lincoln and some cabinet members shook their heads at these slow campaign proposals. The Northern public wanted to avenge the April 12 insult at Fort Sumter, wanted to teach the impertinent rebels a swift lesson. The Southern boys were just as green as the Yanks, Lincoln reasoned, and the country was growing impatient. As in so many instances, the commander in chief looked first to political considerations to shape battle strategy. The nation's mood called for action.[2]

The President was still pondering this as he walked into the sunshine with Secretary of State William Seward and Generals Scott and Joseph Mansfield. He was also preoccupied by the message he would deliver to Congress in a few days. Like the public, the legislators wanted an explanation for the slow military response. Moreover, Lincoln would have to defend the unparalleled—indeed possibly illegal—measures he had authorized in the first months of his presidency. In the heat of the moment Lincoln had taken on exceptional powers, justifying them through his authority as commander in chief and the constitutional responsibility to see that the laws were faithfully executed. Without statutory authorization he had approved actions that ranged from suspending the writ of habeas corpus in several places and arresting persons who were "represented to him" as prospective traitors, to increasing the Army well beyond its authorized size. Lincoln was an attorney who respected the law and he thought these unusual moves were warranted by the crisis. Nonetheless, they were irregular. The bright bunting and trilling melodies on the South Lawn would be rendered meaningless if Lincoln's extraordinary acts undermined the values they symbolized.[3]

Lincoln Raises the Flag at the White House, pencil, by Alfred R. Waud, June 29, 1861
LIBRARY OF CONGRESS

An observer that day noticed Lincoln's "abstract and serious eyes" and sensed that the President had "withdrawn to an inner sanctuary of thought." The onlooker remarked something else as well: some part of Lincoln was sizing up the situation, cannily regarding the flagpole and the arrangements, and trying to figure out how he was going to get that "heap of stuff through the hole at the top of the partition." The marquee looked something like a carelessly constructed circus tent, with the mast running through a small opening at the top, allowing barely enough room for the standard to squeeze through. The flag itself was a ceremonial one, taken from the war steamer USS *Thomas Freeborn,* which two days before had been engaged in a naval skirmish at Mathias Point, Virginia. The rebels had won the day, harvesting the first naval death of the war by repulsing the Union ships and killing the Potomac flotilla's commander. Not only were these associations sobering, but the flag was immense. Measuring nearly seven by nine feet, it was far too large and heavy for the unstable new flagstaff.[4]

The President certainly wanted the ceremony to go off well. Reverend Smith Pyne from St. John's Church across Lafayette Square had been invited to give the invocation, and the regimental brass was already sounding the national anthem's opening stanza. In previous months, at similar events, Lincoln had given stirring tributes to the banner and all it represented. He had told audiences that he considered it his sacred duty to maintain "every star and stripe of the glorious flag," and that he had pondered the original thirteen stars, what they meant, and how the field had expanded to thirty-four. Each new star on the flag, he noted, "has given additional prosperity and happiness to this country." His sentiments were echoed on postal envelopes, which patriotically declared "Not a Star Must Fall." At an emotional post office opening, the chief executive had spoken about the honor of raising the flag, how it had "hung rather languidly about the staff" until "a glorious breeze soon came and caused it to float as it should." Lincoln concluded with the hope "that the same breeze is swelling the glorious ensign throught [*sic*] the whole nation."[5]

So the band played, and the Reverend Pyne prayed, and Lincoln stepped forward to hoist the Stars and Stripes above the rickety gazebo. Then, the very problem he had feared materialized in the most mortifying fashion. As he pulled on the cording, the huge flag caught between the pavilion and the pole and "stuck so fast that the President had to tug away with all his strength." Lincoln's powerful arms did manage to raise the ungainly material, but when Old Glory appeared above the crowd, "lo! the upper stripe and 4 of the stars were

"Not a Star Must Fall," Civil War
envelope, c. 1861–62
WARREN E. SAWYER PAPERS,
THE HUNTINGTON LIBRARY

torn off & dangling [from] the rest of the flag." One witness thought five stars had flown off; another believed the entire flag had been shredded. It was painfully reminiscent of satirist Artemus Ward's recent commentary in the new humor magazine *Vanity Fair:* "Feller sitterzens . . . the black devil of disunion is trooly here, starein us all squarely in the face! . . . Shall the star-spangled Banner be cut up into dishcloths?"[6]

Lincoln also tried to make light of the mishap. A few days later, at a similar ceremony before the Treasury Building, he remarked that he understood his job was to hoist the banner "which, if there be no fault in the machinery, I will do." Once raised, he added, the people would have to do their part to keep the national standard afloat. But even the President's closest friends, who had gathered on the White House lawn for a jolly evening concert, were unsettled by the implications of the ripped flag, representing as it did the rent condition of the Union, and Lincoln's inability to mend the tattered nation. "A bad omen, as all thought," noted Benjamin French, his loyal commissioner for public buildings. "A bad augury," echoed the *Chicago Tribune,* adding that the damaged flag did not show the half of it, as eleven states had actually been torn from Union. Superstition and inference weighed heavily on the spectators. The discomfort was only relieved when a plucky Marine advised the President that he should not worry too much about the dangling stars. "Never mind," said the serviceman, "we can sew 'em on again."[7]

One of the striking things about the flag-raising tale is that it is so little known. This is surprising, since the documentation is excellent and the story itself both humorous and haunting. Its symbolism is so pronounced that it might well have become a venerable part of the patriotic canon. Yet it is not one of the stock anecdotes about Lincoln. Perhaps this has been conscious—the image of a president wrenching apart the nation's flag just as his country embarks on fratricidal war is too unsettling to be the stuff of popular lore. It may have been suppressed at the time by administration-friendly publications such as the *Daily National Intelligencer,* which declined to mention the incident in its coverage, noting instead that the "evening was pleasant and every thing passed off happily." The story has been edited out of later publications as well: Commissioner French's eyewitness account was not included in printed collections of his papers, and modern biographers have ignored the incident. Nevertheless, it is a tale worth telling, not only for its ominous overtones, but because it is exactly the kind of portentous yarn that Lincoln himself liked to spin.[8]

Recollections of Lincoln, particularly those that appeared after his assassination, are notably unreliable and frequently at odds with accounts written as events unfolded. Dimness of memory, grief, and self-conscious attempts to sanctify the "martyr-president" all undermine their historical value. Mary Todd Lincoln noted this soon after her husband's death: "There are some very good persons, who are inclined to magnify conversations & incidents, connected with their slight acquaintance, with this great & good man." But one characteristic clearly impressed nearly everyone who had even the briefest contact with Lincoln, and there is such a critical mass of similar accounts that they must be taken seriously. That was his great fondness for storytelling, and the way that he used his skill as a raconteur to enhance both his personal and political power.[9]

People remembered Lincoln trading yarns with cronies in Indiana and Illinois, amusing fellow politicos in the Capitol's back rooms, joking with soldiers in the field, or breaking up cabinet meetings to read from his favorite humorists. These are among the most endearing images of the sixteenth president, the delightful human element that has created a rapport across the centuries. At certain points in his presidency, Lincoln became almost a caricature of himself in this regard, yet his penchant for wit and parable, for the apt reply or saucy joke, was so natural that whatever ulterior purposes his tales served, they seem to have been grounded in a genuine love of laughter.

Men particularly liked Abe's stories, and liked the fact that they tickled the teller as much as the listener. "He is [of] a gay & lively disposition, laughs & smiles a great deal & shows to most advantage at such times," wrote John Henry Brown, an artist who traveled to Springfield in 1860 and regretted that he could not depict this effervescence in the campaign portrait he was painting. In anticipation of a good laugh, Lincoln apparently became oblivious to expected social composure. He liked to rub his trouser leg with delight or run his fingers through his bristly black hair until it stood out in all directions; and when the punch line came, he would double up until "his body shook all over with gleeful emotion" and "drawing his knees, with his arms around them, up to his very face," he would let out a jagged eruption of high-pitched laughter.[10]

As remarkable as these gyrations were, what impressed Lincoln's audiences most was the transformation of his face when he turned to jesting. The normally coarse features, the air of aloofness or distraction, the sadness that suffused his countenance, would soften when he looked up "with his peculiar smile and eye-twinkle" to recall a story. Noah Brooks, a newspaperman who spent a good deal of time with the President, wrote that "[f]ew men ever passed from grave to gay with the facility that characterized him," and a military confidant described how his "small eyes, though partly closed, emitted infectious rays of fun." Even his less admiring contemporaries, like the journalist and legislator Donn Piatt, who described Lincoln's face as "dull, heavy, and repellent," acknowledged that it "brightened like a lit lantern when animated." (The winning smile may in fact have been a gap-toothed, jack-o'-lantern grin, for we know that Lincoln had at least twice submitted to the dentist's pliers.) He had a peculiar habit, as well, of screwing up his face and wrinkling his nose, then screaming with laughter until, as a loyal Republican visitor noted, the President resembled a wild animal—an "affinity with the tapir and other pachyderms." Still, the transformation was beguiling. As funny as the jokes were, it was Lincoln's way of sharing them, his "unfeigned enjoyment," that made them memorable. "There was a zest and bouquet about his stories when narrated by himself that could not be translated or transcribed," remembered one friend. "The story may be retold literally, every word, period and comma, but the real humor perished with Lincoln."[11]

Some believed Abe Lincoln inherited the storytelling gift from his father, indeed thought Thomas Lincoln outshone his son in this respect. Wherever it was acquired, it soon became a defining part of the long-limbed Midwesterner's character. Like so many other aspects of Lincoln, we know of it largely through secondhand information, for, interestingly, it does not permeate his own writings. There is little amusing in the papers that have been left to us—most are wooden documents, often clumsily written, unless highly polished for political purposes. As a younger man, he experimented with satire, publishing some barbed opinion pieces in local papers, or occasionally producing a ribald poem or pointed commentary for a public statement. Sometimes these got him into trouble. In 1842, for example, he went overboard in his lampoon of a rival politician named Shields, landing with an awkward challenge to a duel. Lincoln's wit was evident at that event as well, however, for when he was allowed the choice of weapons he demanded "cavalry broadswords of the largest size" brandished from a narrow plank, rendering the encounter as ridiculous as possible. Many of these early mockeries seem adolescent—a kind of rustic gasconade—and Lincoln had largely dropped them by the time he became a serious contender for national office. By then the smart aleck in him had matured into a wryer, more sophisticated wit. There is very little levity in the papers of his presidency, though he occasionally lapsed into sarcasm when exasperated with his generals. Scornful remarks like the one to George McClellan—"if you don't want to use the army I should like to borrow it for a while"—only diminished respect for him in military circles, however, and this kind of taunting letter also became rarer as the years went on.[12]

Instead, Lincoln's legacy of fun has come to us through the oral tradition. Abe's listeners fondly remembered the yarns told from atop stumps or around a smoky fire, and repeated them to others. Many of the jokes seem to have lost their context or punch after so many decades, but some are still delightfully fresh. Most of them came from Lincoln's experience among country folk, and even after years in the spotlight, he still relied on blustering preachers, unscrupulous millers, or hogs mired in mud to make his point. He wove many strands together in his tales—fables, allegories, and stories grounded in metaphor—but always with an ear for homely phrases and an eye to the familiar scenes of life. "He had a marvelous relish for everything of that sort," recalled an Illinois acquaintance. "He always maintained stoutly that the best stories originated . . . in the rural districts." Lincoln was not above the social prejudices of his region, and mercilessly mimicked Irishmen, Dutchmen, and African Americans in many a gag line. He knew the cadence of frontier speech—the lingo of flatboat men and Yankee peddlers and Negro minstrels—and used their expressive language to portray the logical illogic of the unschooled. Lincoln also relished the absurd, in speech and in simile. "No one could ever use the term fac simile in his presence, without his adding 'sick family,'" stated a colleague from Lincoln's circuit-riding days. Sometimes he coined unique words or novel phrases to give life to a particular character or idea. Meddlesome people he called "interruptuous"; those who were easily

duped were "dupenance." Albert B. Chandler, a young man who kept a journal while working at the War Department telegraph office, noted how peculiar names and alliterations caught the President's eye, and how he would
repeat them over and over until they were fixed in his mind. One night Lincoln laughed with the boys over an invention that used a trapdoor to rob a
chicken of its newly laid egg, inducing her to produce another. Its title—"The
Double Patent Back-Action Hen Persuader"—set him rocking on the legs of
his chair.[13]

Lincoln also liked to deflate the self-important or highly placed. Likening them to ignorant (if shrewd) hicks was a handy way to accomplish this.
He compared his cabinet members to skunks or pumpkins, and rival Democrats to a squirrel hunter shooting in desperation at a louse dangling before his
gun sight. When pressured by adversarial religious sects, Lincoln regaled his
cabinet with tales of a Presbyterian minister who denounced Universalists for
believing that *all* men could be saved. "We brethren," fumed the Presbyterian,
"*we* look for better things." In 1863, after the long preparation for bombard-
ing Charleston ended in a fizzle, Lincoln reproached Admiral Samuel Du
Pont by telling him he felt like a hungry man who had been made to stand
through a very long grace, only to be served a miserable plate of soup. And the
chief executive dismissed Treasury Secretary Salmon Chase's ambitions to
take over the presidency as just like a "horsefly on the neck of a ploughhorse—
which kept him lively about his work."[14]

Lincoln appears to have been a natural raconteur, but his performances
were not entirely spontaneous. Several friends remarked on the conscious effort he made to hone his comic skills, both to tickle the audience and to
sharpen his points. One remembered that Lincoln quickly sized up his listeners, brought out new and appropriate material, and never "vexed the dull ears
of a drowsy man by thrice-told tales." An army officer claimed the President
explained his method for holding attention by saying that there were two ways
to tell a story. "If you have an auditor who has the time and is inclined to listen," explained Lincoln, "lengthen it out, pour it out slowly as if from a jug. If
you have a poor listener, hasten it, shorten it, shoot it out of a pop-gun." There
is nothing particularly insightful about this observation: every good comedian
knows that gauging an audience is the secret to packing a punch. Lincoln's
delightfully expressive language, however, makes it a memorable anecdote.
Apparently, the President also chose the timing of his routines and balked at
performing on demand. When a New Yorker visiting the presidential summer
retreat begged for "one of your good stories," he was chastened by Lincoln's

curt refusal, and the remark that his stories were not a carnival act, but a useful way of directing discussion.[15]

During Lincoln's lifetime, a number of books appeared with titles like *Old Abe's Joker* (1863) or *Old Abe's Jokes* (1864). They purportedly contained original Lincoln material, but most of their contents were actually tired, recycled jests. A journalist named Alexander McClure, who claimed to have an intimate relationship with the President, later produced an anthology of Lincoln's stories, but few can authoritatively be traced to him. One historian who made a detailed study of bons mots attributed to Lincoln found that many had been circulating literally for centuries, but that "Old Abe" had a knack for shaping their context and making them his own. Lincoln himself told Noah Brooks that only about one-sixth of the stories credited to him had actually been his invention. "I don't make the stories mine by telling them," he said, laughing. "I am only a retail dealer."[16]

It seems clear, however, that Lincoln actively looked for new stories. His compatriots in Illinois remembered that he keenly took in every comical episode or bizarre name, and loved to collect gossip at local fairs or minstrel shows. The jokes that can be authentically attributed to him show that he picked up material wherever he found it: in the literature of the day, or from political cartoons and offhand remarks. Some said that he kept a file of the best ones in his desk. A general who traveled with Lincoln was amused to see the lanky executive sprawl across the deck of a boat to cut an absurd article out of a newspaper and then read it with great glee to every member of the party. A New York politician told how the President held up a White House receiving line for an apparently intimate conversation with one attendee. When the tête-à-tête ended, a curious crowd pressed the man for details and learned that he had shared an anecdote a few days before "and the President, having forgotten the point, had arrested the movement of three thousand guests in order to get it on the spot."[17]

What seems to have been truly original were Lincoln's clever quips, the one-liners that gave him a reputation for shrewdness and quick repartee. These witticisms were widely replayed and admired at the time, and still please us today. Take, for example, the remark that he could not execute those who ran from battle because it "would frighten the poor devils too terribly to shoot them," or his comment that trying to get the Army of the Potomac to move was "jes like *shovlin' fleas!*" When a captain was court-martialed for voyeurism, Lincoln could not resist playing on the name of Count Piper, the Swedish ambassador to Washington, with a double pun: the guilty officer, he told John

Hay, "should be elevated to the peerage . . . with the title of Count Peeper." Then there is his wonderful retort to Senator Benjamin F. Wade, who stormed the White House in the tense days of 1862, barking that the President was leading the country to Hell, and that in fact they were within a mile of it at that very moment. "Yes," Lincoln replied, thoughtfully gazing out the window, "it is just one mile to the Capitol." It was this kind of delicious tidbit that launched Lincoln into the enduring pantheon of American wits, alongside Benjamin Franklin, Mark Twain, and Will Rogers.[18]

Some of Lincoln's sayings and aphorisms were simple country corn, but a great number were also smutty. The witnesses are too many to doubt that Lincoln relished lewd scenes and double entendres. Illinois friends remarked that he had "a Great passion For dirty Stories," that his mind "ran to filthy stories—that a story had not fun in it unless it was dirty," and that "the great majority of Lincolns stories were very nasty indeed." A fellow lawyer claimed that when he once asked why Lincoln did not collect his anecdotes and compile a book, Lincoln drew himself up and replied, "Such a book would Stink like a thousand privies." When the writer Nathaniel Hawthorne visited the White House in July 1862, he recorded conversations that "smack of the frontier freedom, and would not always bear repetition in a drawing-room." (Hawthorne cut them from his article for the *Atlantic Monthly*.) Walt Whitman apologized to friends in 1863 for Lincoln's crudeness by saying that "underneath his outside smutched mannerism, and stories from third-class country barrooms," there was some practical wisdom. Hugh McCulloch, Lincoln's last treasury secretary, was another who allowed that "the stories were not such as would be listened to with pleasure by very refined ears, but they were exceedingly funny."[19]

Some of the ribald stories have been left to us. Most seem sadly juvenile, filled as they are with outhouse pranks, vomiting drunks, sexual high jinks, and bare behinds. Few are ennobled by illuminating insights or memorable lines, and, at least in the retelling, hardly elevate Lincoln to the level of a backwoods Chaucer. At best they contain some simple, clever puns. "How is a woman like a barrel?" ran one Lincoln ditty from the age of coopers and crinolines. "You have to raise the hoops before you put the head in." Another story circulated by Lincoln told how the great Revolutionary hero Ethan Allen traveled to England, where many Britons made fun of the Americans. One day they hung a picture of George Washington in a "Back house" where Allen would see it. When he made no comment, they finally asked if he had recognized the likeness. Allen replied that he thought it very appropriate for Englishmen to see it there because "their [*sic*] is Nothing that Will Make an Englishman Shit So quick as the Sight of Genl Washington." Another moment of indelicacy was recorded at the War Department, where one night the President sat reading a stack of telegrams. When he came to the bottom of the pile he announced: "Well, I guess I have got down to the raisins." Puzzled, the telegraph operators asked what he meant. He explained that a little girl he knew, having eaten too large a share of treats filled with raisins, became violently sick. After "an exhausting siege of throwing up, she gave an exclamation of satisfaction that the end of her trouble was near, for she had 'got down to the raisins.'"[20]

Leonard Swett, who concerned himself with the sixteenth president's reputation, was among those who winced at such lore, but he proposed that there was no vulgarity in Lincoln's character, only the desire to make his point. "It was the wit he was after—the pure jewel, and he would pick it up out of the mud or dirt just as readily as he would from a parlor table." Historians of the apologist school have also sometimes downplayed the off-color jokes, feeling they might interfere with the heroic portrayal of their subject. (Biographer David Herbert Donald was among those who regretted that some of the rougher tales had been lost through prudery.) But scatological jokes only appeal to a certain kind of jester, and scrubbing Lincoln to the point of one-dimensionality cannot take the salt from his skin. Lincoln's stories were never of the tittering, parlor variety but were made for a thigh slap and a guffaw. Indeed, much of the pungency in his rural style came from its earthiness.[21]

Whether silly, spicy, or sage, Lincoln's jokes served several purposes for him. The most straightforward, of course, was to indulge his fondness for a chuckle. It was not just that he wanted an audience—though it is clear that he craved that too. What seemed to animate him was the tonic of hilarity. He felt a "deep satisfaction expressed in the ha ha," one admiring friend attested. Both before and during his time in public office he went to music halls and minstrel shows, treated visitors to juicy bits from his favorite comic stories, and surrounded himself with others who liked to laugh. His secretary John Hay recorded a wonderful scene of the President wandering the halls at midnight dressed only in nightclothes ("his short shirt hanging about his long legs &

setting out behind like the tail feathers of an enormous ostrich") in order to recite an inane poem. Lincoln indulged the antics of his children, attended their magic lantern shows (they sent him complimentary tickets), and was vastly amused by a cabin they built on the White House roof, dubbed the "Ship of State." He was merry at receptions, and visitors recalled hearing a good deal of laughter coming from his cabinet rooms. He even bantered while being shampooed. He had a strong sense of the ridiculous, and on occasion relaxed by inviting Tom Thumb or "Hermann the Prestidigitateur" to perform after dinner, liking the ludicrous spectacles, and taking part in the performances. In these situations, wrote an administration official, the beleaguered president looked "natural & easy. He is Old Abe & nothing else."[22]

Many have thought that Lincoln's pursuit of laughter was a much needed antidote to his introspective, melancholy disposition. The swift change in his countenance, from shadow to sunshine, argues for this, as do the observations of long-standing friends, who saw how his moods would shift rapidly within a single day. His closest confidant, Joshua Speed, maintained that telling tales was "necessary to his very existence," replacing any desire to escape with drink or dice. Longtime law partner William H. Herndon agreed. An eccentric man, Herndon was nonetheless in a position to observe Lincoln at close range. He quoted his partner as saying that if "it were not for these stories—jokes—jests I should die: they give vent—all the vents of my moods & gloom." Herndon's curious assessment was that Lincoln was naturally slow-moving and slow-thinking; he needed stimulation not only to chase depression but to increase the flow of blood to the brain and awaken his full productive power. Assistant Secretary of War Charles A. Dana echoed these thoughts, though in less peculiar terms, stating that the "safety and sanity" of the President's intelligence were maintained through the outlet of humor.[23]

Those studying Lincoln's moods have indeed found dangerous dips and erratic behavior, particularly in his younger days. But the dynamics of his psyche have remained elusive. Lincoln, as always, tells us next to nothing—his writings offer little illuminating introspection and few clues about the trials and tensions of his life. Some intriguing studies have concluded that Lincoln's changeable disposition was the consequence of childhood losses. Others refer to an abnormal homeostasis. Several of Lincoln's associates related that he took "blue mass" pills, a common remedy of the era for many disorders, and one group of modern doctors has proposed that he suffered mercury poisoning as a result. The medication was concocted from almost pure mercury, in dangerous doses, and could have caused Lincoln's explosive laughter and unrestrained outbursts of temper, as well as the insomnia, memory loss, and neurological instability that seem to have plagued him. There is no clinical evidence, however, and only shaky historic grounds for any authoritative analysis of Lincoln's "mercurial" nature. Whatever the cause, sadness and mirth seem inextricably linked in the man. His jokes often pointed up the absurdity of fretting over trivial concerns, or the frivolity of human vanity, and how such disproportion may lead to a wasted life. Perhaps it was this classic overlap of comedy and tragedy, pride and futility, that gave his humor such force.[24]

Whatever psychological benefits joking had for Lincoln, his storytelling was also a powerful social tool. On the most basic level it made him popular. Community acceptance was important on the rough frontier—a dangerous place where goodwill was crucial for survival, not to mention success. Abe Lincoln was a strange young man there: he looked odd, and he seemed to disdain the pleasures of the local boys. He disliked hunting, drinking, or smoking; shied away from chasing girls; and, as he got older, increasingly made himself a curiosity by climbing trees to read a geometry book or a worn copy of Shakespeare. It was fortunate for Lincoln that he was as physically impressive as he was: those loose-jointed limbs were deceptively strong, and once the hardscrabble crowd figured out that he could outrun, -jump, and -wrestle them, they treated him with respect. But comedy was what made Abe's company desirable. He was fun and irreverent, and the fellows would gather in little knots to hear him perform. No matter how ludicrous he became, no matter if he wobbled on the line of good taste, his dignity never suffered. He may have been a clown, but he was admired, not reviled. When Lincoln's career interests grew, his good-natured banter became important for cementing professional friendships. Every politician both craves and needs popularity, and comedy was the way Lincoln first attracted a crowd.[25]

Humor also gave Lincoln power. It was not just the power to command applause, but the ability to control a situation. As a laboring man he could undermine a strict foreman by luring the field hands from their work for some jesting; as an attorney he influenced decisions in the courtroom—sometimes thwarting justice—by suggesting a droll analogy to the case at hand. His aptitude for homey phrasing that plainspoken jurors could understand earned him a fine reputation for summing up a case, as did his ability to think on his feet. Nor was he above using stagecraft to gain his point. A fellow circuit lawyer described the way Lincoln swayed one jury when there was a seemingly airtight case against his client.

He picked up . . . a paper, from the table. Scrutinizing it closely, and without having uttered a word, he broke out into a loud, long, peculiar laugh, accompanied by his most wonderfully funny facial expression. There was never anything like the laugh or the expression. A comedian might well pay thousands of dollars to learn them. It was magnetic. The whole audience grinned. He laid the paper down slowly, took off his cravat, again picked up the paper, looked at it again, and repeated the laugh. It was contagious. . . . He then deliberately took off his vest, showing his one yarn suspender, took up the paper, again looked at it, and again indulged in his own loud, peculiar laugh. . . . Judge Woodson, the jury and the whole audience could hold themselves no longer, and broke out into a long, loud, continued roar; all this before Lincoln had ever uttered a word.

Needless to say, the prosecution's case was completely destroyed, though apparently Lincoln took care that the damages paid were fair.[26]

Lincoln also manipulated his personal conversations by the timing and tenor of his jokes. He could end an interview, sidestep an argument, deflect tension, or buy time for reflection—all by announcing that something "reminded him of a little story." The astute people around the President understood that he had the last word, that he was leaving them laughing, but they were helpless against his prowess. William Howard Russell, a skeptical British observer of the American scene, attended a dinner soon after Lincoln's first inauguration at which Attorney General Edward Bates began a diatribe against a minor political appointee. Lincoln quashed the impending quarrel by raising a chuckle with "some bold west-country anecdote," and while the company was laughing he beat a quiet retreat "in the cloud of merriment produced by his joke." Pennsylvania Republican Titian J. Coffey was another who admired Lincoln's ability to stage-manage a situation. "The skill and success with which Mr. Lincoln would dispose of an embarrassing question or avoid premature committal to a policy advocated by others is well known," he commented. "He knew how to send applicants away in good humor even when they failed to extract the desired response." Longtime friend and bodyguard Ward Hill Lamon called the jokes "labor-saving contrivances," whose purpose was to expose a fallacy or disarm an opponent.[27]

He also knew how to make his point without belaboring it. As Lincoln's stature grew, he told his stories less to tickle the funny bone than to drive home an argument. His repertoire came to resemble a set of illustrative fables that could clarify issues or persuade detractors. Aphorisms and apologues became a kind of shorthand for him, helping, as Lincoln reportedly told one visitor, to "avoid a long and useless discussion . . . or a laborious explanation." As a raconteur, for example, he could subtly voice his sympathy for those who quaked under battle fire by telling the story of a private who advised his captain that he had as "brave a *heart* as Julius Caesar ever had; but some how or other, whenever danger approaches, my cowardly *legs* will run away with it." (The commander in chief's leniency toward "leg cases" became famous during the conflict.) When Lincoln compared the problem of slavery to a venomous snake in bed with a child—a terrible danger, but one that must be handled with skill and caution—it was an analogy that every prairie family could understand.[28]

However calculated the effort, Lincoln's effect was clearly very real. He had the knack most coveted by political comedians: first to make his audience laugh—and then to make them think. Even those who sparred with the Lincoln administration understood his gift for winning a debate with a telling phrase. George McClellan, 1861: The President's stories "were as usual very pertinent & some pretty good. . . . he is never at a loss for a story apropos of any known subject or incident." Horace Greeley, 1864: "President Lincoln . . . has had no predecessor, who surpassed him in that rare quality, the ability to make a statement which appeals at once, and irresistibly." Congressman Henry Dawes, a radical Republican: "He was a storyteller, not for the story's sake, but for the use he could put them to, to clinch an argument, to show up an absurdity as in a looking glass, or to make plain an impossibility." Dawes once sought the President's advice about circumventing a knotty political problem. Lincoln replied with a parable. "You were a farmer's boy and held [a] plow, I guess," he said. "What did you do when you ran against a stump, drive through and smash everything, or plow around it?" That was all he said, noted the congressman—and that was enough.[29]

This kind of Lincoln lore seems to indicate that the President profited by a mild approach and soft political invective. However, though he quoted Shakespeare's warning about the "power to hurt"—how a withering remark could ultimately wither the critic—he did not always heed the caution. Lincoln could, and did, use his verbal agility to crush opponents, as well as to buttress his arguments. At times his attack was savage. He sometimes used sophisticated logic to undermine an argument, but he could also descend into personal assaults, even when the victim was not present to defend himself. This was particularly true in Lincoln's younger days, when he took on some of the most prominent men in his region, undercutting them on the stump and in the local press, and leaving their reputations in question. For example, Lincoln confronted a celebrated local preacher, Methodist circuit rider Peter Cartwright, not with measured argument but with caustic newspaper attacks, which unjustly accused him of hypocritical acts. Cartwright fought back, but Lincoln, who had hidden behind a pseudonym, escaped relatively unscathed. In another notable case, Lincoln challenged a rival politician named Jesse B. Thomas, employing all his powers of smirking enfilade fire, until his opponent publicly dissolved in tears. The episode, which came to be known as the "Skinning of Thomas," was something of a cautionary moment; even Lincoln understood that he had overstepped the mark, and took some care afterward to avoid handing up total humiliation.[30]

Despite his attempts at self-restraint, however, lawyer Lincoln was, in the words of Judge David Davis, "hurtful in denunciation, and merciless in castigation." He continued to jab at political adversaries, especially pompous or preening men, referring to them as "dogs," *"caged and toothless"* lions, or "little great men." According to one loyal retainer, Lincoln even boasted of his "hits" when he thought he had got the best of a situation. Stephen A. Douglas cringed when encountering the sneering Lincoln during their famous debates: Abe Lincoln's reasoning could be got around, Douglas maintained, but "every one of his stories seems like a whack upon my back. . . . [W]hen he begins to tell a story, I feel that I am to be overmatched." The desire to undercut his opponents, by fair means or foul, was part of Lincoln's inordinate ambition, his unflagging desire to win. It came as handily to him as a half nelson had in the years when wrestling defined his local dominance. Some of this urge to lead by belittling continued into his presidency, when he took delight in deflating the egos of his cabinet and generals, sometimes ungenerously. "Mr. Lincoln," wrote his ever admiring secretary John Nicolay, "seems always to have been as adroit in answering a fool according to his folly as in silencing the follies of men who consider themselves wise."[31]

Thus, for Lincoln, humor was an important weapon, sometimes with a razor-sharp point. At times, it was also a refuge. Lincoln was an intensely self-absorbed person, private and protective. He was not good at small talk and had trouble forming deep bonds. His law partner thought he drew a defensive circle around himself, meant to ward off the curious and shelter him from unnecessary conversation. The comedic act was part of this. It gave Abe a way to connect with people without truly revealing himself. He would "laugh and smile and yet you could see . . . that Lincoln's soul was not present," Herndon wrote. Lincoln's political ally Leonard Swett thought so too. "He always told enough only of his plans and purposes to induce the belief that he communicated all, yet he reserved enough to have communicated nothing." Martinette Hardin, the sister of Lincoln's fellow Whig legislator John Hardin, recalled that Lincoln was often mute in genuine discussions, or that he did not respond at all until he could interject a little joke. Moreover, Lincoln's stories were also prefaced with a kind of disclaimer—that he had heard them from someone else, or read them somewhere—which distanced him from the barbs or bawdiness of the laugh line. Lincoln defended his silence, once saying that although he was a taciturn man, it was more unusual "to find a man who can hold his tongue than to find one who cannot." Nonetheless, his joshing precluded dialogue, making much of his interaction one-sided. Engaging tales and set-piece routines let Lincoln control a conversation, without truly interacting.[32]

Storytelling also provided him with a script. The popular impression today is that Lincoln was a master of both beautiful prose and inspired conversation. He worked dutifully at the English language and became a fine writer, but this, like his compelling dramatic talents, was not spontaneous—it was a skill he practiced and honed, one requiring prodigious application and constant revision. All the available evidence during his lifetime shows him to be an awkward conversationalist, with a poor grasp of grammar and elegant expression. He was largely at a loss when he had to speak extemporaneously. Even Lincoln's admirers saw him as a "country clodhopper . . . always stiff and unhappy in his off-hand remarks," or praised his political insights while acknowledging his sad lack of grammar. "I wish he would leave off making *little* speeches," faithful retainer Benjamin French remarked. "He has not the gift of language, though he may have of *western gab*." Two fellow party men noted that he was "not a successful impromptu speaker," that he was "often perplexed to give proper expression to his ideas; first, because he was not master of the English language; and secondly because there were, in the vast store of words, so few that contained the exact coloring, power, and shape of his ideas." John Hay, whose veneration for his chief knew few bounds, squirmed after reading the "hideously bad rhetoric" and indecorous language of a pivotal presidential letter and even accused his boss of uncommon dexterity at "snaking a sophism out of its hole."[33]

What is remarkable is not that Lincoln lacked communications skills, but that he came so far from such a shaky base. Well aware of his shortcomings, he avoided off-the-cuff remarks and apparently wrote down and committed to memory any appropriate phrases that might serve him. Noah Brooks remembered him struggling to avoid improper or overly quaint phrases. Finding Lincoln laboring at his desk over a manuscript, Brooks was surprised to hear the President say that he had to be "mighty careful" when addressing the nation. He had once used the expression "turned tail and ran," Lincoln said, which outraged some Bostonians, and he had resolved to give no more unrehearsed speeches. He reiterated this at a fair held in February 1864 to benefit the United States Sanitary Commission. After noting that "a little fraud" had been perpetrated by not telling him he was expected to speak, Lincoln sidestepped the matter by noting that it "was very difficult to say sensible things" and that he had better keep quiet or both he and the country might be in trouble. Even in his penultimate speech, a response to a serenade celebrating Union victory, he made the embarrassing admission that he had nothing to say on the great occasion. The set-piece stories and quips he perfected offered him a sturdy safety net to avoid this discomfort in both formal and informal discussion.[34]

At times the fund of jokes also provided a shield against those who would make the President himself the object of fun. Humor helped him ward off criticism before it bruised too deeply, as well as maintain much needed perspective. He was a natural target for lampooning—if ever a human seemed formed for ridicule, it was Abraham Lincoln. His unusual height would have been enough to cause comment, but added to this was "the loose, careless, awkward rigging" of his frame; the stooped, shuffling walk; and a shock of coarse, unruly black hair that one amused citizen likened to "an abandoned stubble field." The prominent nose was clownishly tipped in glowing red. His face had an unfortunate simian cast: more than one observer thought that a president who "grinned like a baboon" was a disgrace to the nation. He paid little attention to his dress and this only increased the opportunities to scoff. Lincoln routinely greeted guests of all rank in scruffy carpet slippers and rumpled suits. One soldier who met the commander in chief thought his clothing was the dirtiest he had ever seen. Another visitor compared him to a shabby undertaker, and when Nathaniel Hawthorne came to call, he was startled to encounter the nation's highest official in "a rusty black frock-coat and pantaloons, unbrushed, and worn so faithfully that the suit had adapted itself to the curves and angularities of his figure, and had grown to be an outer skin of the man." What saved the President from being completely ludicrous were his utter lack of pretension, a winning twinkle in his eye, and an ability to impress guests with his sincerity. Hawthorne saw this, and it overrode his surprise at a hairdo that had apparently seen neither brush nor comb that morning; so did a young James A. Garfield, who recognized Lincoln's peculiar power to impress men with his candor and direct gaze. George Templeton Strong spoke for many when he confided to his diary: "He is a barbarian, Scythian, yahoo, or gorilla, in respect of outside polish . . . but a most sensible, straightforward, honest old codger."[35]

Lincoln learned to "whistle off" those who snickered at his appearance or to preempt them with self-mockery. Laughing took the sting from his detractors, overcoming their taunts with an aura of good-humored self-acceptance. An Illinoisan who met Lincoln in 1858 noted that he was just as gangly as reported, but his sharp eyes made it clear that "if a man should insult him he would laugh at him and shame him out of it sooner than to fight him." When Stephen Douglas tried to gain advantage in the 1858 senatorial election by pointing up his distinguished national reputation, Lincoln admitted that there was not much in *his* "poor, lean, lank, face" that was

presidential. He then adroitly linked Douglas's "round, jolly, fruitful" countenance to greed, patronage, and corruption. Lincoln also poked fun at his own ungainly figure on horseback, chortled over satirical pieces that pictured him vowing "to split 3 million rails afore night," and borrowed laugh lines from scornful cartoonists such as the one who pictured him as "Shaky" in *Vanity Fair.* One wonderful anecdote claimed that when a rival accused Lincoln of being two-faced, he responded: "If I had another face do you think I would wear this one?" Alas!— like so much Lincoln lore—this story is probably apocryphal. More credible is the wisecrack the President made after he contracted a mild form of small-

"Shaky," wood engraving, *Vanity Fair,*
June 9, 1860

pox in 1863: "There is one consolation about the matter. . . . [I]t cannot in the least disfigure me!"[36]

Lincoln effectively shrugged off remarks about his eccentric physique, but he disliked being made to look ridiculous, and he had a pronounced sensitivity to serious criticism. Acquaintances found him "touchy" when his self-esteem was tried: he was "keenly sensitive to his failures and it would not do to mention them in his presence." When he could not dismiss a slight, he sometimes struck back fiercely. His first foray into satire was a smarty-pants piece of verse that cast doubt on the virility of some local cronies who had chosen not to invite him to a wedding. Lincoln's early public writings are filled with unconstrained language denouncing the "fabrication and falsehood" of his rivals or deriding them as "not more foolish and contradictory than they are ludicrous and amusing." The president-elect was embarrassed in 1861 when detractors branded him a coward for surreptitiously entering Washington in order to circumvent threats on his life. That mortification may have caused him to take unwise risks thereafter. Nor was he laughing when Maryland senator Reverdy Johnson questioned his policies toward Unionists in Louisiana, or when he was squeezed by a Christian committee on emancipation, or when his old friend Carl Schurz bluntly criticized the way the war was being handled. Lincoln lashed out at these men, saying that he had been "*very ungenerously attacked*" and that he mistrusted "the *wisdom* if not the *sincerity* of friends, who would hold my hands while my enemies stab me"; he also accused the press of maligning him. "You think I could do better; therefore you blame me already. I think I could not do better; therefore I blame you for blaming me," he petulantly retorted. In Schurz's case Lincoln tried to backtrack, making light of the outburst by slapping his knee with a loud laugh and saying, "Didn't I give it hard to you in my letter? Didn't I?" But Schurz had already picked up the "undertone of impatience, of irritation"

"Honest old Abe on the Stump, Springfield, 1858";
"Honest old Abe on the Stump, at the ratification Meeting of Presidential Nominations, Springfield 1860," lithograph
LIBRARY OF CONGRESS

and recognized how defensive the President had become. Herman Haupt, an army engineer whom Lincoln esteemed highly, witnessed a similar explosion when a member of the Joint Committee on the Conduct of the War frankly told the President how dissatisfied the military was with his leadership. "Stop right there!" the commander in chief shouted, drawing a hand across his chest. "Not another word! I am full, brim full up to here." It is striking that so many similar outbursts were recorded, since Lincoln also liked to preach a philosophy that advised self-control and the avoidance of "personal contention," and at times took pains to avoid confrontation. Such explosions help us understand how vulnerable Lincoln could be, how fragile he was under the armor of bonhomie. It appears that the man who had "skinned Thomas" had a thin skin himself.[37]

Wordplay is part of the comedian's genius, but another important element is timing. After Lincoln's death many noted with admiration how perfectly pitched his taglines could be. Unfortunately, just because a witticism is apt does not always make it appropriate. During his lifetime the President faced significant criticism for his near addiction to joking, and for the way it interrupted real dialogue or showed insensitivity to the severity of the nation's crisis. He reverted to flippancy too easily when the business at hand was somber, and he jested with people who were not well acquainted with him, and consequently liable to misunderstand his levity. As early as 1839, his Illinois constituency showed concern for his "assumed clownishness," advising Lincoln to give up the "game of buffoonery," which not only lacked dignity but failed to persuade an audience of his points. In 1861 a British journalist was dismayed to find Lincoln, his legs sprawled over the railing of a veranda, "letting off" one of his jokes to federal officers in the field, apparently oblivious to a menacing Confederate flag waving in the near distance. Military men also frowned at their commander's inexplicable mirth. William Thompson Lusk, a captain with the New York Highlanders (and a man willing to support Lincoln), was greatly offended in the wake of 1862's disastrous Virginia campaigns. "The men are handed over to be butchered—to die on inglorious fields," he protested. "Lying reports are written. . . . Old Abe makes a joke." The Army was willing to fight, he mourned, but "the brains, the brains—we have no brains to use the arms and limbs and eager hearts with cunning." A fellow officer echoed the sentiment. "What is to become of us with such a weak man at the head of our government, be he ever so honest?" he queried. "One who . . . turns off things of the most vital interest with a joke?" A Southerner who beseeched Lincoln to take measures to protect Unionists caught in the Confederacy listened patiently while the President trotted out a string of stories. Then he responded candidly:

> Mr. Lincoln, this to me, sir is the most serious and all absorbing subject that has ever engaged my attention as a public man. I deprecate and look with horror upon a fratricidal war. I look to the injury that it is to do, not only to my own section—that I know is . . . desolated and drenched in blood—but I look to the injury it is to do to humanity itself, and I appeal to you, apart from these jests, to lend us your aid and countenance in averting a calamity like that.

As Confederate momentum remained unchecked, the Polish-born writer Adam Gurowski acidly summed up the situation: "And so Davis is making history and Lincoln is telling stories."[38]

Among those most annoyed by Lincoln's perpetual joshing were senior members of his government. McClellan, of course, thought anecdotes told by the "Gorilla" were "ever unworthy of one holding his high position." Salmon Chase was also offended by the constant banter when "danger was too imminent & the occasion too serious for jokes"—as it was during a midnight discussion of desperate reinforcement operations at Nashville in September 1863. Secretary of War Stanton and Senator Henry Wilson simply abhorred the stories, and Stanton, particularly, was not above showing his anger to the President, his staff, or the military brass. Stanton had hoped when he took office that there would be "no jokes or trivialities" and that the contest would be taken in "dead earnest." He was to be disappointed. Benjamin French, despite his fondness for the man, had to admit that Lincoln's judgment and timing were often astonishingly poor. After Confederate general Jubal Early made a daring raid on Washington in July 1864, pointing up the impotence of Union intelligence and defensive strategy, French went round to his chief's office to express alarm. He was regaled with a long Lincolnian story that compared a yokel who thought he saw a wolf's tail with the Union Army, now so far in the rear of the Confederates "that it is doubtful if they will even get sight [of] their tails." French got "mad & came away disgusted." The President showed so little concern for beating the rebels, noted French, that he was jeopardizing the welfare of the country.[39]

II

To a large degree Abraham Lincoln was able to overcome his curious physical appearance and clumsy perpetual joking through his sympathetic nature. But this personal touch was only felt by the small number of people with whom he actually had contact. The vast majority of the nation knew their chief magistrate through partisan broadsides, or newspaper accounts, some of which were little more than printed hearsay. And by the 1860s elected officials were publicly commented on more than ever before. Americans were not shy about expressing their opinion of a president's fitness for office, whether justified by firsthand knowledge or not.

Lincoln's tenure coincided with the rise of photography, and the boost it gave to the cult of political personality. He was the most photographed president to date, and it appears he liked to have his portrait taken. Unfortunately, the camera did not love him. The sharp imagery of the glass plate prints showed every detail of his gaunt face, unruly mane, and tortured necktie. The warts were literally there, and the benevolent expression lost, in all but a handful of pictures. In addition, his flapping appendages and western gaucherie were simply meant for caricature. It was also the golden age of lithography, and the illustrated papers had a field day, in the North as well as the South. Because they could narrate a great deal with a few sketchy lines, using sarcasm or allegory to distill complex emotions or policies, cartoons held a dispro-

Abraham Lincoln, photograph by
Alexander Gardner, February 5, 1863
LIBRARY OF CONGRESS

portionate influence. They became as emblematic as the Capitol dome, creating stereotypes more potent than a slogan. Moreover, with the telegraph and mails well established, the reach of these images was vast and immediate. The entire nation was able to share an impression or a chuckle at Washington foibles in real time, forming a collective consciousness that could be either unifying or highly divisive. The *New York Herald* recognized that technology and the popular press had combined to make Lincoln an "eccentric addition" to the gallery of prominent men, for "it is only in the present age of steam, telegraphs and prying newspaper reporters, that a subject so eminent . . . could have been placed under the eternal microscope of critical examination." It was no longer possible to cover up an unfortunate moment like the misbegotten flag raising—it zipped across the wires in an instant.[40]

Political satire had, of course, existed for centuries. After all, Machiavelli delighted in exposing the wiles of power-hungry princes, whose professions of goodwill were in absurd contrast to their private ambitions. But political humor had become particularly forceful in the United States, where the most scathing remarks went unpunished, and where growing literacy created a wide audience. By the mid-nineteenth century, poking fun at the nation's leadership had grown to be a fine art. The paradox between presidential celebrity and its bossy bed partner, the rule of law, was simply too good to pass up. In addition, the colorful trappings of each polling season smacked of farce, nearly begging for a sardonic spree. The campaign of 1840, in which Lincoln participated, was an excellent example. It was almost devoid of substance, the goal of each party being simply to win the spoils of office for itself—and the log-cabin origins of William Henry "Tippecanoe" Harrison, invented by early image makers, were in preposterous juxtaposition to his genteel upbringing. By the time of Lincoln's election, the spoofs were more fearless and more widespread. The inevitable clumsiness of self-rule and the perpetual cycle of political mischief were kept on prominent display, warning the public not to take its rulers too seriously. In London's *Punch,* the comic-strip version of Lincoln, outfitted in striped pants and a star-spangled vest, became confused at times with Uncle Sam (who grew a beard when Abe did), but the image was not meant to elevate the President. Instead, it mocked his inability to hold the Union together.[41]

In a sense Lincoln was the first true media president, though Buchanan had come in for some impressive drubbing during the last days of his administration. Lincoln's sensitivity about off-the-cuff remarks, and their possible misinterpretation, is one indication that he recognized the burgeoning power of the fourth estate. Another is the way he and Republican leaders took concrete measures to appease newspapermen. Joseph Medill, the influential editor of the *Chicago Tribune,* for example, advised Lincoln after his 1860 nomination that the party would want to mollify "his Satanic Majesty" James Gordon Bennett, publisher of the critical *New York Herald*. Bennett's "affirmative help is not of great consequence," Medill cautioned, "but he is powerful for mischief." Medill thought Bennett, who longed for social status, could be bought by a White House invitation or two. It proved not to be so. Like several other prominent journalists, Bennett remained true to the Union, but not necessarily to administration policies. In 1863 Lincoln was still trying, in his words, to "humor" the *Herald* by giving its reporters advance copies of documents or special access. As time went on, his "management" of the press would edge perilously close to state censorship.[42]

THE LATEST FROM AMERICA;
Or, the New York "Eye-Duster," to be taken Every Day.

"The Latest from America; Or, the New York 'Eye-Duster,' to be taken Every Day," wood engraving by John Tenniel, *Punch,* July 26, 1862

Lincoln understood that, for the president, public commentary was one of democracy's more fiery trials. Citizens cherished their right to heckle their leader—to deride not only his policies but his personal traits. The playful slap at authority was a kind of leveling exercise. It stripped down the powerful by implying that their leadership was a hilarious sham that could be knocked away by jeers as easily as by violence. "Democracy," H. L. Mencken would write, "is the art and science of running the circus from the monkey cage." It was this, the vaudeville of republican government, that made parody such a forceful expression of popular will.[43]

The freedom to complain publicly had long been one of the hallowed distinctions between authoritarian regimes and elected government, but this did not necessarily make it more comfortable. Lincoln was greatly distressed, for example, by a cartoon *Harper's Weekly* ran after the Union debacle of De-

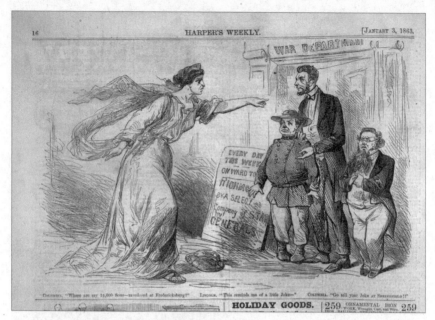

"Columbia: 'Where are my 15,000 Sons—murdered at Fredericksburg?' Lincoln: 'This reminds me of a little Joke—'," wood engraving, *Harper's Weekly*, January 3, 1863

cember 1862, which showed "Columbia" asking the President, "Where are my 15,000 Sons—murdered at Fredericksburg?" and Lincoln replying, "This reminds me of a little joke—" He did not guffaw at the *New York Herald*'s February 19, 1864, editorial, which began, "President Lincoln is a joke incarnate. His election was a very sorry joke. The idea that such a man as he should be the President of such a country is a very ridiculous joke." He found the *New York World*'s semifictitious account of his request for saucy songs during a trip to the Antietam battlefield so mortifying that he could not bear to look at it. The story was not entirely true, though accounts by officers present attest that the President rode through the battlefield in an ambulance, listening to aides sing childhood ditties and "grinning out of the windows like a baboon," and that he later shared smutty stories at the mess table. Lincoln wrote a reply for the songster's signature, maintaining that the revelry had taken place off the field and not at his request, but the piece was widely replayed by the opposition press, and the damage had been done.[44]

Lincoln did not relish being the brunt of jokes, but as the highest elected official in the land, he could not just counteract the satire with a clever retort or belittle the humorists who criticized him. Others could do this, however, and he was fortunate to have surrogates who could lightheartedly scoff at the scoffers. Nothing was sacred to the era's comic writers, including the sentimental trappings of patriotism and battlefield glory. Artists made a travesty of democratic virtues by mingling them with the gore of war, and they contrasted the nation's noblest aspirations with the haplessness of its leaders. The pundits might castigate Lincoln for escaping through laughter, but the public appreciated that the horrors surrounding them could be relieved by a little hilarity, and irreverent newspapers, books, and jokes circulated quickly.[45]

The President himself liked to read popular rags such as *Pfunny Pfellow,* as well as columns in local papers that ran mock editorials on military matters. "An order has been issued by the Secretary of the Navy prohibiting sailors from using, hence forth, the expression 'shiver my timbers,' which is no longer applicable now that wooden war ships are doomed to extinction," ran one lampoon. Given the popularity of ironclads, the piece continued, Secretary Welles was proposing the phrase "Flummux my rivets." Lincoln was particularly drawn to *Vanity Fair,* whose self-proclaimed goal was the castigation of secessionists, shady contractors, and "flagitious politicians." "Union and the Constitution is our motto," they boasted. "A Rod in [a] Pickle for all who Deserve it, and a word in aid of all who need and are worthy of it." Until it closed in July 1863, *Vanity Fair*'s editors made free with a wide variety of leaders, taking aim at everyone from Winfield Scott to Henry Ward Beecher. They treated Confederates like irritating relations who should be ignored, while robustly criticizing excessive abolitionists, political hacks posing as generals, and anyone else who hindered the foot soldier. Lincoln underwent some ribbing as well. He was pictured as a silly man who traded on poor witticisms and impotent public statements while doing little to end the conflict. Ran one ditty:

> *We have found a way*
> *At the present day*
> *To fix the affairs of the nation.*
> *The magic pill*
> *For every ill*
> *Is—issue a Proclamation!*

For the most part, however, *Vanity Fair* cut the President a good deal of slack, and forcefully nipped at administration foes, relieving some pressure from the government. Lincoln mentioned to at least one acquaintance that the magazine's pointed reviews were "very helpful to him."[46]

Whatever their political benefit, the President liked the satirists because they gave him an excuse to chuckle away his fatigue or irritation. Lincoln was especially tickled by the writings of longtime *Vanity Fair* editor Charles Farrar Browne, who became indistinguishable from his fictional creation "Artemus Ward." Browne was a professional journalist who took his role as critic seriously; he saw his writings as a correction against the excesses of the era. The "shaft of ridicule," he noted, "has done more than the cloth-yard arrows of solid argument in defending the truth." Yet his pseudonymous persona Artemus Ward was pure burlesque. An itinerant carnival barker, Ward traveled around the country with an exhibition consisting of "three moral bares," a kangaroo, and a wax model of George Washington. Ward's travels allowed him to observe, with canny accuracy, the social curiosities of the era, from unorthodox religious cults to the burgeoning women's movement. Browne's ear for dialect was extraordinary, whether he parodied the "flatulence" of a pompous local sheriff or the malapropisms of a clodhopper quoting Shakespeare. The writings are peppered with Ward's particular sagacity, such as his comment on the virtues of thrift: "By attendin strickly to bizniss I've amarsed a handsum Pittance." This use of wacky misspellings, bombastic speechifying, and gross exaggeration gave the writings a distinct sense of absurdity. "People laugh at me more because of my eccentric sentences than on account of the subject-matter in them," Browne once noted. Still, Artemus Ward's sympathy was always for the small-town citizen, and he pointed up, as did Lincoln, the shrewd pragmatism of frontier folk. In his story "The Draft in Baldinsville," Ward roasted draft dodgers as well as prattling politicians who intoned the need to fight while remaining safely at home. "War meetin's is very nice in their way, but they don't keep Stonewall Jackson from comin' over to Maryland and helpin' himself to the fattest beef critters. What we want is more cider and less talk," opined Ward. The writings were something more than a send-up of bucolic simpletons. They made a plea for common sense and moderation that proved an antidote to the fanaticism of the war.[47]

It is not surprising that Charles Farrar Browne had such an appeal for Lincoln, for they shared a number of traits. Both were awkward and ambling, noted for their ill-fitting trousers and unruly hair. Both were sometimes given to morbid introspection, cracking jokes to chase depression. Both cared passionately about language; they popularized stories and expressions that have survived for many generations, influencing the growth of a characteristic American humor. Politically they were further apart, with Browne reflecting the more conservative and pro-slavery leanings of Midwestern Democrats. At best he gave lukewarm support to the sixteenth president's program. When *Vanity Fair* published Ward's story of a fictional meeting with Lincoln and several cabinet members in April 1862, it poked fun at both the style and ineffectiveness of the war leaders, and the magazine consistently pushed for a return to older interpretations of the Constitution. Still, Browne and Lincoln shared an animosity toward draft evaders and the radicals in Congress, and the President found Ward's send-up of provincialism to be instructive as well as amusing.[48]

Lincoln liked to pull a copy of Artemus Ward's *His Book* out of his pocket to read passages aloud. He thought the mildly blasphemous "High Handed Outrage at Utica" particularly funny, though that episode seems to have lost its pungency over time. He regaled his cabinet with an interpretive reading of the piece on September 22, 1862, just before announcing his decision to publish the Emancipation Proclamation, a juxtaposition of gravity and mirth that greatly annoyed Edwin Stanton. Lincoln's penchant for these comedic routines became known outside Washington, and in 1863 the *New York Herald* published an editorial called "Artemus Ward and the President," which claimed the performances were meant to convulse the cabinet with laughter so that they would agree to whatever Lincoln proposed. "We scarcely know which most to admire, the simplicity, the sublimity or the success of the idea." Most descriptions of the President's readings, however, give the impression that he simply enjoyed sharing a good story, whether it was his or borrowed from someone else.[49]

The presidential office also held the writings of Robert Henry Newell, a New York journalist who used his pen to highlight the more ludicrous side of the military situation. It is interesting that Lincoln appeared to enjoy Newell's work, for they were not closely allied politically, and Newell had little admiration for those wielding power. He opened his first commentary with the words "Though you find me in Washington now, I was born of respectable parents, and gave every indication . . . of coming to something better than this." On virtually the same day, Newell inaugurated his character Orpheus C. Kerr—whose name was a play on "office seeker"—in a drawing sent to Lincoln's secretary of state. Showing a harried official sorting through piles of petitions for office, it pointedly reproached administration spoilsmen. Newell was a highly educated man who shunned the use of dialect and sprinkled his columns with literary allusions, but he had a keen eye for paradox and the affectations of those wielding power. He disliked equally abolitionists, antiwar Democrats, the arrogance of the South, and the wasteful incompetence of civilian and military leaders. He once described Lincoln as bowing "like a graceful door-hinge," and expressed bemusement at the President's near obsessive penchant for long anecdotes. He was not personally hostile, however, and seems to have gained some respect for the chief executive over time. Nonetheless, Newell was one of the most effective and biting satirists of the administration. George Templeton Strong thought the Orpheus C. Kerr papers the "most brilliant product of the war," likened them to champagne, and pronounced their author a "genius of the Rabelaisian type."[50]

Lincoln's interest in the adventures of Orpheus C. Kerr is all the more intriguing because Newell's main thrust was antimilitaristic, and he dared poke fun at the nearly untouchable embarrassment of the Army of the Potomac. He took a steely-eyed view of the war, shunning popular romanticism, and the empty bravado of the battlefield. The majority of Newell's stories involved Kerr's service with the hapless "Mackeral Brigade" of the "Army of Accomac," a unit known for its "remarkable retrograde advances." Most of the brigade's actions centered on efforts to cross a puddle-sized body of water called Duck Lake in order to capture a two-house burg named "Paris." It was an amphibious operation, with the Navy patrolling the lake in an ironclad, rigged up from a converted stove, whose front grate came unhinged in violent action. Experiments with pontoon bridges and novel weapons constantly backfired. Across Duck Lake, the rebels constructed massive batteries and rival ironclads in plain sight of the Union men, and occasionally the two sides went fishing together. For those familiar with the disappointing progress in the Eastern Theater during 1862 and 1863, the stories are a wonderful take on the imbecilities of the campaign, and only a hilarious hairline from the truth. Perhaps this is also what caught Lincoln's eye. He was wildly frustrated by the operations of the Army of the Potomac, with its seemingly irrelevant movements and inexplicable failures. Perhaps a mordant presidential cackle over the Mackeral Brigade forestalled an explosion of another kind. Pinning the failure on military ineptitude may also have soothingly removed any discomfort about Lincoln's own responsibility for the debacles in Virginia and Charleston harbor, which Kerr only thinly disguised.[51]

Orpheus C. Kerr offered a laugh at the Army's expense and Artemus Ward set up the arrogance of petty officials and small-time hucksters. But arguably no one filled Lincoln with more glee than David Ross Locke's fabulous character Petroleum Vesuvius Nasby.

Vesuvius Nasby erupted onto the scene in April 1862, in one of Locke's regular columns for an Ohio newspaper. A preposterous bucolic preacher, who lived at "Confederit X. Roads," he liked to remain lubricated with the whiskey he called "koncentratid kontentment" and was opposed to "methodis, Presyterin, Luthrin, Brethrin, and other hetrodox churches." Like Charles Farrar Browne, Locke used cacography and tortured common sense in his caricature, in this case a spoof of the Copperheads—as those who opposed the war were popularly known. Nasby parroted their racial prejudice and blustered over the evils of conscription, which the antiwar party used as a rallying point against Lincoln. The commentary was scathing, whether it roasted outspoken critic Clement Vallandigham ("The trooth is, Vallandigum . . . hez tongue, without discreshun. . . ."), Democratic journals ("The Noo York Illustratid Flapdoodle"), or the lame excuses of draft dodgers ("I am bald-headid, and hev bein obliged to wear a wig these 22 years"). Nasby's sermons were delivered in a pseudo-trenchant style that purported to show a principled abhorrence of fratricidal war, but Locke's stinging wit exposed these attitudes as nothing more than ignorance and bigotry.[52]

Like other humorists, Locke had a day job as an editor. He wrote serious political commentary against the mismanagement of the Union effort, as well as the "masked secessionists who go about grinning at every reverse." But nothing matched the reach or genius of Petroleum V. Nasby's uncouth voice. Locke was aware that his satire influenced the public more profoundly than his straightforward reporting. Objectivity was not his goal, nor was pure humor. Having personally experienced the disruption of his neighborhood by antiwar politics, as well as religious divisions that were altogether too similar to Nasby's "Church uv the Noo Dispensashun," he determined to speak out strongly. "I have simply exaggerated error in politics, love, and religion," he told a friend, "until the people saw those errors and rose up against them."[53]

Lincoln greatly admired Locke's inventive turns of phrase, and reportedly once told him that "for the genius to write these things I would gladly give up my office." It was said that the President read the *Nasby Papers* more than he did the Bible, and his worn copy, now in the Library of Congress, attests to his faithful perusal. Lincoln pulled Nasby from his pocket as often as he did Artemus Ward's *His Book,* sometimes interrupting serious strategy sessions to regale his cabinet with the latest exploits from Confederit X. Roads. Massachusetts senator Charles Sumner was surprised to find Lincoln in March 1865 so engaged with Locke's writings that he set aside other business to "initiate" Sumner into their hilarity. The senator thought it a "delight to see him surrender so completely to the fascination," but was concerned that Lincoln kept a group of legislators waiting more than twenty minutes while he recited Nasby's pseudo-wisdom.[54]

Lincoln's partiality for Nasby reflected something more than frivolity. The nation's leader recognized that Locke had handed him a salve against the bruises of rough and ready democracy—indeed, a cunning restraint against an unschooled public's right to jeer at authority. Locke played havoc with the pretensions of armchair critics and shrewdly undermined the credibility of the naysayers. Hypocritical preachers, pompous journalists, and self-righteous politicians were felled with the nib of his pen. Petroleum V.'s naïve assessments, his blunt, Swiftian japery, and his unerring eye for paradox became an unofficial machine for administration efforts to suppress the opposition. Although Edwin Stanton evidently dubbed Locke's humor "the God damned trash of a silly mountebank," in the end it may have been more effective at stifling criticism than the sterner measures devised by Lincoln's administration. Locke's writings were a "constant and welcome ally," Sumner admitted. "Unquestionably they were among the influences and agencies by which disloyalty in all its forms was exposed, and public opinion assured on the right side."[55]

III

As outlandish as Locke's writings were, they were not more pungent than some of the genuine protests that found their way onto Lincoln's desk. His letter bag carried many a semiliterate assault on administration policies, some of them just as pithy as the sermons preached by Petroleum V. Nasby. One correspondent, who signed himself only as "SNB," allowed that "it would be a most gratifying thing to The majority of this nation if the Bowells of the Earth or Hell it Self . . . would open their Bowells & Engulph the whole damned Abolition administration for their damned Hypocracy the[y] are only decieving themselves and not God." In case the point had not been strongly enough expressed, SNB signed off saying, "So good by you damn old abolition negroe thiefing Scoundril." Not to be outdone, a Chicago man admonished the President: "Mr. Abe Lincoln . . . if you don't Resign we are go-

ing to put a spider in your dumpling and play the Devil with you." Exercising
the American right to speak his mind, this correspondent then veered into
colorful obscenity. From the pulpit and in the press, Lincoln was demeaned as
"a flat-boat tyrant" or denounced for having a mind that attracted vulgarity as
"*mange* to dogs or *meazles* to swine." One particularly cheeky editor, Marcus
M. Pomeroy, of the *La Crosse* [Wisc.] *Democrat,* wrote a contemptuous epithet
for Lincoln in August 1864:

> **Beneath this turf the widow-maker lies**
> **Little in everything, except in size.**[56]

Pomeroy liked to gloat over his snide phraseology, but his disgruntlement
was grounded in serious concerns. He was, in fact, equally disgusted with extremists on all sides, whom he thought had brought on the war for political
purposes. At the same time, he was genuinely shocked by the casualties and
the license of the conflict. After seeing a pile of crude coffins on the wharf at
St. Louis, Pomeroy dryly noted that it rather took the poetry out of military
gold braid. As it happened, his views differed little from those of David Ross
Locke, who wrote that his own satiric voyage had been launched when war
shattered the economy in his Ohio hometown and siphoned its young men off
to battle. Where the Pomeroys and Lockes diverged was over the legitimacy of
the war itself, not the methods Lincoln was employing to win it. In his serious
editorials, Locke did not hesitate to complain of the administration's ineptitude, but as a racial egalitarian and social reformist, he saw a moral purpose in
the contest that overshadowed the messiness of its waging.[57]

Nasby's relentless racism—"a holsum prejoodis agin evrything black"—
is perhaps the most defining aspect of Locke's stories. In exaggerating fears of
"amagamashun" and economic competition, and peppering his writings with
the offensive term "nigger," Locke was taking specific aim at the Copperheads'
resistance to emancipation and the use of black soldiers in the Union Army.
An English visitor to Philadelphia was surprised to find open antipathy to the
Emancipation Proclamation in the North, and to learn that many who opposed secession did not necessarily object to slavery, even seeing it as commer-
cially advantageous. "I thought that outside Carolina I sh[oul]d never hear
such sentiments," he confided to a relative. It was also a source of disgruntlement within the Army, especially among officers. Not every "Peace Democrat" was pro-slavery, but most were staunchly conservative; reluctant to
meddle with the Constitution's property guarantees or to embrace a multira-

cial society. After Lincoln announced his Emancipation Proclamation, their resistance increased.[58]

The antiwar Democrats were also opposed to conscription, particularly if the point of fighting was to free the slaves, and they resented the provost marshals and other measures that President Lincoln and War Secretary Stanton put in place to enforce the draft. Conscription was a new phenomenon, and a source of discomfort for wide swaths of American society. It was resisted in the South (where it was pioneered) as well as the North. Copperheads saw the provisions as unfair to the poor, who could not afford to pay for substitutes, as well as a usurpation of the state prerogative to raise militia forces. New York governor Horatio Seymour worried that this "lottery for life" was being enacted without proper safeguards for impartiality, and in opposition to the needs of his state, which could not even man the forts within its borders. In addition, he questioned the draft's constitutionality and asked that its legality be judged before he enforced it. (Lincoln did not disagree on the legal principle, but pleaded that time and necessity forbade such a review.) For the Copperheads, conscription foreshadowed increasing government interference with individual freedom. It was also a potent sign that Lincoln's foundering war strategy was discouraging volunteerism. William Havemeyer, the former mayor of New York City who made a serious effort to shore up flagging civilian morale, joined others in pointedly telling the President that the "dissatisfaction with the management of the War, which makes volunteering impossible," was likely to make conscription ineffectual as well. "Half a Million More Men for the Shambles—The Want of Brains Must Be Made Up by Numbers," read the headline of an opposition paper in Pennsylvania after a call-up in 1864. Irritation with the draft opened other sores, many of them economic. Conscription led to labor shortages and was widely suspected of fostering corruption in the Army, the government, and the business community. It added to dismay over the slow pace of commercial activity, which had been hampered by tariffs, as well as the closure of Southern markets and Mississippi River traffic. The production of paper money—the "greenbacks" that floated the cost of the war—also deflated pocketbooks. As the price of gold soared, the Peace Democrats became stronger and more vocal.[59]

Many of these issues were political, and indeed party rivalry was the backdrop to much of the controversy over Copperhead activities. The mid-nineteenth century was an intensely partisan era, with well-defined factions and strong organizations at all levels. The Democrats had commanded national power for decades, but the splintering of their support—and consequent defeat in the 1860 election—left them scrambling to reassert their influence. They also held a deep ideological resentment of the Republican Party, which they viewed as the source of the nation's divisions. They used all the traditional tools of the opposition to undermine their rivals: slogans, symbols, provocative editorials, and bellicose carping on contentious points, whether petty or profound. The Republicans fought back, of course. As early as July 1861 they had coined the word "Copperhead," meant to liken their opponents to vicious snakes. The Democrats tried to make the epithet a virtue—copperhead was also the nickname of the penny that sported a picture of Lady Liberty on one side—but the reptilian image stuck. Almost as ubiquitous was the Republican habit of defining any difference of opinion as "treason." "The fact is the . . . opposers of the administration are doing us more damage now, than the traitors of the South," a concerned citizen told Congressman Henry Dawes in 1863. For some, the terms "Peace Democrat" and "domestic traitor" became interchangeable. "Internal treason extends over this country like a diabolical net," brayed the ever emphatic Adam Gurowski. "A defender of slavery, a Copperhead, and a traitor, differ so little from each other, that a microscope magnifying ten thousand times would not disclose the difference."[60]

In their concern for partisan loyalty and the unity of the war effort, Republican zealots made little distinction between honest dissent and evil intent. They saw Southern sympathizers in every Washington bureau, and intrigue at every peace rally. "Secret" organizations with names like the Sons of Liberty or the Knights of the Golden Circle were said not only to be encouraging the South but to have large memberships and subversive plans. Nervous citizens bombarded the administration—at some points on a daily basis—with rumors about blood oaths and murderous pacts. Alarmists reported that Copperhead associations were raising rival militia companies or were planning to liberate the Confederate prisoners held by the Union. In June 1864 William Rosecrans, commander of the Department of Missouri, urgently telegraphed Washington, claiming that a massive conspiracy to overthrow the government was afoot, under the direction of the Order of American Knights. Lincoln took it seriously enough that he sent John Hay to investigate the matter, but ultimately concluded that Rosecrans's panic had more to do with military rivalries and a desire for enhanced resources than any real danger to the nation. The President's take on the societies was that they were just another political faction—albeit characterized by "malice" and "puerility."[61]

Lincoln probably called it right. Many of the fears of subversive associations were greatly exaggerated—in some cases brilliantly—by Republican propagandists. A few ambitious plots to disrupt Northern harmony were uncovered, and some communities were genuinely terrorized by their threats. In most instances, however, the societies appear to have been little more than a showcase for bravado and bullying. Union general Samuel Heintzelman mockingly dismissed one parading group as nothing but a specimen of "unterrified, unwashed Democracy." No highly organized network of these groups was established, nor was any coordinated plan for aiding the rebels ever uncovered. In a number of cases, the Democratic Party even backed away from the organizations or played a restraining role.[62]

It is tempting to see the societies' actions as slightly ridiculous, something akin to Orpheus Kerr's farcical tales of provincial "war-meetins." Still the impact of the antiwar protesters cannot be completely ignored. Most dissent came from Democrats, and in some instances it resulted in organized resistance against conscription or the enrollment of black troops. The New York draft riot of July 1863 was the most visible of these disruptions. This was not an idle scare, but a full-blown uprising, the largest civil disturbance in American history, with scores of victims and ugly racial and social overtones. It left war leaders on edge, concerned that the antidraft movement would spread like an epidemic. Small-town intrigue was also used to whip up disgruntlement and further partisan ends. When the great-great-grandfather of this writer, John Jackson Kenley, was on furlough from the Twenty-Fourth Indiana Regiment in 1863, his wedding was interrupted by a hissing mob that asserted there were "butternuts"—another term for some Copperheads—in the bridal cake. A brawl ensued, the purpose of which was to prevent his return to the Army (it was unsuccessful). Viewing the escalation of such incidents, one Republican stalwart thought Indiana was on the verge of an internal war that would cause the streets of Indianapolis to run with blood. In neighboring Illinois, a constitutional convention dominated by the Democracy (as Democrats liked to term themselves) tried to strip the Republican governor of any meaningful power, again unsuccessfully, though not without ramifications. Observant Southern leaders monitored these protests, hoping they might undermine the Union effort and give the Confederacy an opening to sue for peace on its own terms. Robert E. Lee's excursions into Union territory in 1862 and 1863 were partly based on the hope that he could exploit Northern divisions, though in the end his bold moves only rallied the Yankees to their own defense.[63]

Some Copperheads *were* viciously partisan and a few truly dedicated to interrupting the military campaigns. Others—like *La Crosse* [Wisc.] *Democrat* editor Pomeroy and Clement L. Vallandigham, an Ohio congressman whose spirited oratory directly challenged the Republican platform—had personal ambitions and outsized egos. However, a great number of Peace Democrats sincerely believed that the nation had split unnecessarily, that fratricidal war was not only abhorrent but actually sinful, and that the appalling loss of life resulted from the recklessness and incompetence of the Lincoln administration. Many protesters retained their loyalty even while voicing their concerns. For example, an outspoken critic of the war named William B. Pratt noted in his diary how he constantly irritated the "war Republicans." But he also referred to Union soldiers as "our Army," and, as a town supervisor in Prattsburgh, New York, worked to make sure the area met its conscription quota. Charles Mason, a distinguished jurist and former chief of the Patent Office, watched with dismay as the years brought increasing disruption of civil liberties, along with grotesque casualty lists. His diary is a day-by-day lesson in disaffection, as he was transformed from a willing helper of the administration to a disgruntled observer of the chaos and waste it produced. Within the military, the disparity between commitment to the war effort and allegiance to Lincoln's policies was particularly clear. "The support of the war is a very distinct thing from the support of the President," wrote an officer with the Army of the Potomac. "The more I think of it the more angry I am with the government for placing in such a dilemma good citizens like myself."[64]

Preachers from many denominations also criticized the government for its ethical stance and absolutism. "Instead of feeding your people with 'the bread of life,' you feed them with blood and gunpowder," intoned one pastor. Some of these admonitions came from the more conservative sects, which cited scripture to justify slavery and opposed the employment of African American soldiers. Often their words were only slightly different from Reverend Nasby's forays into the "aposssel biznis." But many of the most urgent sermons came in response to excessive Republican war rhetoric, such as the assertion by one Methodist parson that his party would put down the rebellion even "if in doing so, we have to exterminate from God's green earth every living human being south of Mason and Dixon's line." Stunned, peace-promoting ministers maintained that they, not Lincoln, held the moral high ground.[65]

Copperhead righteousness reached its apogee in protests against Lincoln's stance on constitutional rights. Within weeks of taking office, he began using his executive power to curb the authority of courts, suppress "disloyal" news-papers, establish martial law, and suspend the writ of habeas corpus. Oppo-nents professed outrage that the President was undercutting essential freedoms that had long been associated with America's guardianship of liberty. "He is tearing down our institutions daily, and seems to comprehend the magnitude of his work . . . no more than the rat does which is at work upon the timbers of the strong and beautiful ship," railed one critic. Although Lincoln respected the Constitution, and at one time had been leery of altering its provisions, as president he began to view it less as a sacred philosophical framework and more as a flexible tool to help him govern. Explaining this to Congress was, in fact, one of his concerns on the day he unwittingly mangled the Stars and Stripes. But his arguments did not sway everyone, and even those in his own party raised their voices. "Our Presdt is now dictator, Imperator—what you will," protested Charles Sumner, "but how vain to have the power of a God if not to use it God-like."[66]

Habeas corpus, the only fundamental right specifically protected by the original Constitution, was considered the basic guarantee against arbitrary imprisonment or unlawful exercise of power. Its suspension was an especially sensitive issue. David Ross Locke caught its importance to the American psy-che when he sardonically noted that a "tyrannikle President hez taken our old habis corpusses from us, and persistently refuses to furnish us new wuns," or advised, with tongue only half in cheek: "I kin find no constitooshnal warrant for half what is bein dun. I am in favor uv a war for the Union ez it used to was, and the Constitooshn ez I'd like to hev it." No matter how much Lincoln enjoyed the fictitious exploits of Petroleum V., he did not see the activities of Peace Democrats as a laughing matter. His main concern seems to have been with those who hampered the prosecution of the war, and many whose rights were abridged were draft dodgers or leaders who encouraged them. It was not a perfect balance, however, and plenty of politics was mixed with the legiti-mate attempt to promote recruitment and bolster army morale. Lincoln justi-fied his actions by citing provisions that gave him extraordinary powers in times of rebellion or by the authority granted him as commander in chief. He also made skillful use of public statements to explain his unusual exercise of authority. Copperhead anticonscription campaigns, for example, were undermined by eloquently upholding the rights of "simple soldier boys" against those who maliciously enticed them to run from duty. The President rejected the notion that his wartime measures would create a precedent for future tyranny by maintaining that his crackdowns were akin to giving medicine to a sick man, which could be stopped when the ailment was cured. And he taunted opponents of the U.S. Colored Troops by saying: "You say you will not fight to free negroes. Some of them seem willing to fight for you."[67]

As nimble as the words were, Lincoln's curtailment of civil liberties was, and still is, controversial. Some of the early arrests went unnoticed, or were executed with a sleight of hand from the administration that indicated its desire to downplay the measures. However, when a national suspension of habeas corpus went into effect in September 1862 (unfortunately timed just a few days before the controversial Emancipation Proclamation was issued), there was widespread dismay, as well as suspicion that Lincoln was forcing his contentious policies on a public that no longer had the right to protest. The Connecticut Assembly sent a formal resolution decrying "the unjustifiable interference with the liberty of our citizens." Pennsylvania's chief justice handed down a powerful opinion in February 1863, arguing that fundamental rights could not be overturned because of a rebellion: "The very purpose of the law is to set a rule that may remain fixed and immovable among the disturbances of society, and that shall be the standard of judging them." Objection was particularly strong to the imposition of military authority in places where civil structures were still intact, a practice that grew during the conflict. For some, suspension of the writ and like actions simply pointed up the ineffectiveness of the administration. "There was no necessity for them," wrote an exasperated soldier, "and their appearance indicates cowardice in the government in addition to its other weaknesses." Another officer, who loyally served for three years, asked a comrade, "Do you not think it would have been better for Abraham to have worked less for expediency and have done what was constitutional and right, would not honesty have been a better policy than those crooked ways by which he sought to cheat his own conscience and that of the North?" Attorney General Edward Bates carefully upheld the need to maintain public safety, but he also cautioned the President about overuse of arbitrary arrests, usurping the power of the courts, and curtailing freedom of speech, especially the right to remain silent rather than vocally support the President. "We may regret his lukewarmness," Bates wrote of one case, "but no man has a right to dictate the measure of another man's zeal & activity."[68]

To sensible Republicans, the great concern of such crackdowns was that they might give the Democrats a pretext for their disgruntlement—which indeed they did. Instead of silencing the dissent, curbs on free speech offered the Copperheads a great rallying cry, which helped overcome the party's weakness in its early antiwar protests. The more the President constrained his opponents, the more ammunition he handed them. When the only paper in Baltimore that opposed Lincoln's 1864 reelection was forcibly closed, for example, the chief executive received wide-ranging cries of foul play, with even highly partisan Republicans cautioning him that "the stopage of the paper in Baltimore and the refusal to see the Editor will hurt us more than we can gain by stoping it." The worst of it was that the policies also gave the South a justification for rebelling against usurpation of authority by the "Tyrant Lincoln." "What a sad state their political affairs must be in if they cant bear comment!" exclaimed one Louisianan. "O Free America! You who uphold free people, free speech, free everything what a foul blot of despotism rests on a once spotless name!" A careful observer in the Confederate War Department came to the same conclusion. "But how can it be possible for the people of the North to submit to martial law?" he queried. "The government which directs and enforces so obnoxious a tyranny cannot be sure of its stability."[69]

IV

According to Noah Brooks, who covered the White House for the *Sacramento Bee,* Lincoln relished a Nasby lampoon of Copperhead protests against black enlistment in the Union Army. The President liked to recite it "with great effect," to point up the contradictions in Democratic statements on that issue. Ironically, inconsistency was one of the chief flaws with Lincoln's own way of managing the opposition. The questionable legality of measures taken by his government was made more uncomfortable by the unevenness of their application, as well as by the way political motives so often trumped principle. Without any uniform code, and with a great deal of latitude left to the generals who oversaw military districts, punitive measures were frequently based more on personal impulse than on established procedure.[70]

Administration handling of press criticism bordered on the capricious—perhaps surprisingly so, given the media's ability to defend itself publicly. In Maryland, a Christian newspaper that castigated both abolitionists and secessionists was shut down because its masthead listed Richmond among its distribution points. Officials were annoyed by some of the paper's factual accounts of plundering by Union troops, but no one could ever explain what law had been broken by its editor. In New Orleans, the famed *Picayune* had remained guarded in its coverage but was finally closed because of a "series of little pin thrusts" at the commanding politico-general, Nathaniel Banks. "It was more from frequent irritation," a foreign observer remarked, "than from any fear of mischief that the paper was stopped." In 1864 two opposition papers, the *New York World* and *Journal of Commerce,* were shuttered after they unsuspectingly ran a false announcement of another call for troops, which had been put on the wires by the Associated Press. Despite reassurances from the New York provost marshal that the real culprits had been detained, and the fact that the announcement held some truth (the administration was in fact on the verge of announcing another draft), Lincoln approved the closures. When protests arrived from around the country, he had to backtrack once more, suffering months of editorial criticism. Treatment of newspapers in Missouri, Kentucky, and other border states was particularly chaotic. Some tabloids that slammed the actions of the government remained open, while serious publications were closed for reporting facts. Papers loyal to Lincoln's centrist policies were sometimes shut down by Republican secret societies—for those too existed—who ironically labeled them "Copperhead" propaganda.[71]

Of course, no one protested this more vociferously than the press itself. Journalism of the day was far from uniformly responsible, but it forcefully championed free speech and the right to unrestricted information. As early as July 1861, William Howard Russell noted that Lincoln's acts were casting a shadow over the grand reputation of the Constitution. "The freedom of the press, as I take it, does not include the right to publish news hostile to the cause of the country in which it is published," he complained. Some newspapermen simply found ways around the censorship, but others courageously fought it. The Baltimore journalist whose McClellan-leaning newspaper was closed in 1864 sent multiple messages to Washington contending that citizens had been deprived "of the means of deciding intelligently upon the questions at issue," making "the so called election a mockery." Lincoln did not respond. In Pennsylvania several editors battled restrictions to the point of endangering themselves physically. One, Franklin Weirick, owner of the minuscule *Selinsgrove Times,* wrote impudent editorials that were remarkably similar to the parodies so beloved by Lincoln. When he exposed the fact that soldiers had been stationed at strategic locations during the midterm election of 1862 to make sure Republicans carried some doubtful districts, he was threatened with lynching. Hoisted onto a barrel by the local party faithful, he spent the day with a noose around his neck, until he muttered "three cheers for the Union." Impervious to the consequences, Weirick subsequently ran a headline announcing he was "Unshaken by the Frowns of Unprincipled Demagogues, Unintimidated by the Clamours of the Rabble and the Threats of Insolent Mobs."[72]

The inconsistent handling of the press revealed Lincoln's overall ambivalence about handling the "unofficial war" waged by noncombatants and irregular "guerrilla" forces, particularly in the fragile border states. His options in these places were not good. Leniency as a policy encouraged license; ruthlessness caused more resistance. Lincoln's 1863 letters to leaders in Missouri show he understood the danger of spiraling violence, yet his administration frequently allowed—or cast a blind eye to—harsh measures to maintain control. In Maryland, a Kent County judge named Richard Carmichael was bodily torn from a courtroom for protesting the suspension of habeas corpus. He was beaten with rifles until blood flowed and incarcerated for eight months, without disloyalty being either charged or proved. In several states, stationing troops at polling places—theoretically to prevent disruption—was sanctioned, as were ballot requirements that fell outside state laws. Often there was no proper supervision, resulting in widespread reports of voter intimidation. "Fraud added to force" was how one jurist described the measures. Citizens loudly protested, as did officials such as Maryland governor Augustus Bradford, who was gingerly supporting his state's adherence to the Union, while resisting the federal government's erratic military occupation. He rather pointedly called out Lincoln's ignorance of the applicable statutes and noted that the troop presence only served to alienate Unionists. The President, however, chose to view border state dissenters as guilty until proven innocent. He rather huffily dismissed one group of petitioners, saying the Democrats could manage their affairs their way and he would manage his side his own way. Although he pledged to look into several violations, no robust action by the government was forthcoming.[73]

Missouri—where peaceful protests alternated with vicious guerrilla raids, some of them sponsored directly by the Confederates—was an even more delicate case. There the administration wavered between underestimating the danger and sudden, brutal suppression of opposition activities, including unauthorized arrests and confiscation of property. A parade of generals was dispatched to control events; however, many of them also exercised questionable authority. John C. Frémont's extra-legal attempt to seize and liberate slaves in the district in 1861 was followed by John Schofield's arbitrary displacement of entire communities and William Rosecrans's inexplicable order requiring that the oath of allegiance be administered before anyone could attend church. ("Not only is this order wrong in principle, I can say unhesitatingly there is for it not the slightest political necessity," complained one pastor.) Lincoln tried to advise Schofield to act judiciously and to avoid alienating the public, and General in Chief Henry Halleck drew up a code of military conduct for dealing with insurgent activity. But no one in the Lincoln government, including the President, strictly enforced it.[74]

The situation in the Show Me State was worsened by disarray in neighboring Kansas, which was deteriorating into what one observer called "a carnival of crime." In 1863 the Kansas legislature had declared rebel sympathizers to be "outside the law." Although there was little real evidence of Copperhead activity, marauding bands such as the "Jayhawkers" were allowed to settle old scores under the protection of this edict because of their relationship to the Republican Party. When the head of the Army's Department of the Frontier, General James G. Blunt, moved to crack down on lawlessness and enforce public order, he was recalled. Lincoln tried to insert himself in the Kansas mess, sorting personal animosities from professional misconduct, but ultimately had no more success establishing clear guidelines for civil procedure or military administration than he had in Missouri. The best alternative to martial law he could suggest, late in the war, was to hold town meetings, which he rather optimistically thought would be guided by "memory and honor and Christian Charity."[75]

Lincoln's friends were concerned about this kind of inconsistency and so advised him. "The necessity for some *uniform* order on the question of arrests, [and] the suppression and exclusion of disloyal papers from military departments, appears so necessary, that I hope such an order as all loyal men can approve and defend may after full and free consultation be adopted," pleaded James M. Ashley, a Republican from Ohio. "The people ask and pray the Administration to give them *plain* and *positive* directions for their own government and for the government of their military officers." Ashley was particularly concerned about the way a directive from General Ambrose Burnside, head of the Department of Ohio, had been imposed, and its confusing consequences.

Issued on April 13, 1863, General Orders No. 38 stated that the "habit of declaring sympathy for the enemy will not be allowed in this department," and that those not complying would be immediately arrested or banished to Confederate territory. The order had been issued without the permission of Lincoln or Stanton—which was already enough to raise eyebrows—and the administration was caught in an embarrassing position as Burnside proceeded to implement it. At first the President expressed "firm support" for Burnside's action, even when his general nabbed the highly visible Copperhead spokesman Clement Vallandigham for challenging his order. "Valiant Val," as he was known to his supporters, had been an annoyance to the administration since the outset of the conflict, but Burnside's treatment of him soon threatened to create a backlash and launch Vallandigham into martyrdom. Although Ohio was a loyal state where the civil courts were still operating, Burnside tried Vallandigham by military commission, which sentenced him to imprisonment for the duration of the war. Lincoln rather deftly overruled the incarceration, calling Vallandigham's pro-Southern bluff by forcing him into exile beyond Union lines. The notion of a prominent Copperhead slithering his way through Confederate society almost seemed like one of the President's little jokes. The ensuing adventure, with Valiant Val wandering the halls of Richmond (which proved to be less receptive than he had imagined), then escaping to Canada and finding his way back to his homeland to run for governor of Ohio, became a kind of popular sideshow, not unlike the spectacles of Artemus Ward's traveling carnival. Lincoln monitored it as well, with a keen eye for any political ramifications. Noting that Vallandigham was getting more publicity than ever, the President did not protest when his Copperhead foe slipped back into the country. Vallandigham's violent rhetoric, Lincoln shrewdly noted, might benefit the Union by causing significant portions of the Democratic Party to back away.[76]

The Vallandigham escapade was coupled with an awkward administration flip-flop over the closure of the *Chicago Times*. The *Times'* Democratic editor, Wilber F. Storey, unapologetically ran opinion pieces quoting disgruntled Union troops, and asserting that conscripts would be "sacrificed uselessly if the imbecile management that has distinguished the conduct of the war hitherto continues." Such inflammatory statements caused Burnside to close the paper on June 1, 1863. Two days later, prominent Chicago business and political leaders, concerned about collateral damage at the next election, demanded that the order be rescinded. A near vaudevillian to-and-fro ensued. Caught within the political vise that so often squeezed the pulp out of princi-

"The Great American WHAT IS IT? Chased by Copperheads," lithograph
by E. W. T. Nicholas, 1863
LIBRARY OF CONGRESS

ple, Lincoln first ordered War Secretary Stanton to revoke the suppression order. On receiving another petition, this time from Republican worthies who desired that the *Chicago Times* be kept closed, Lincoln again backtracked. He advised Stanton to reverse the order once more, putting the censorship back in force—but to do it slowly. So, in that telegraphic age, a mule-mail order was sent, which arrived too late to go into effect until the Army had destroyed every copy of the paper and Storey was in open defiance. Watching the spectacle, Navy Secretary Gideon Welles—who had little sympathy for anyone claiming protection from a government that person was trying to undermine—lamented that "without absolute necessity" military officers were "disregard[ing] those great principles on which our government and institutions rest." In the end, the *Times* was closed for only a few days, and continued its editorial protest throughout the war.[77]

Supporters might term such inconsistency an admirable "flexibility," but this kind of irresolution, and seeming lack of executive control, opened Lincoln up to derision that went far beyond mockery of his goofy appearance. The ever caustic Chauncey C. Burr, editor of the antiwar magazine *The Old Guard,* for example, reworked *Macbeth,* the President's favorite play, with warlocks Seward, Stanton, and Chase tossing the remnants of liberty into their toxic caldron. The scene features Seward advising the grinning president:

Make a charm of powerful trouble,
Make the hell-broth boil and bubble;
The Habeas Corpus *put it in,*
It is the charm by which we'll win. . . .
Put in FreeSpeech; boil freeman's tongue,
In the negro's odor flung;
Nor let free-press the cauldron 'scape. . . .

When Lincoln tells the trio they have done well, and asks when they shall meet again, Stanton replies, "When the hurly-burly's done, / And our battles *are not* won." In its own way, this satire was as clever as anything devised by the pro-Republican pundits, and its bite had a similar galvanizing effect on the opposition. In another jibe at dubious federal efforts to "manage" dissent, *Vanity Fair* ran a cartoon of Lincoln trying to keep a locomotive labeled "Union"

on track by burning up timber labeled "democracy." Even the President's staunch supporters became discouraged, not just by the war's grim progression, but by the state of free government. "The great experiment of democracy may be destined to fail . . . in disastrous explosion and general chaos," wrote a despondent Republican, who questioned whether Lincoln was "strong enough to manage so large and populous an asylum." Indeed, he queried, was anyone? "Satan seems superintendent *de facto* just now."[78]

Even the humorists who kept Lincoln's spirits afloat joined the heckling chorus. When clothed in

"Keep on the Track!," wood engraving, *Vanity Fair,*
November 22, 1862

solemn editorial garb, David Ross Locke was consistently critical, questioning the chief executive's military judgment and his sensitivity to public opinion, and especially his stance on civil liberties. Nor did Locke hesitate to unloose Nasby in protest. In "An Interview with the President," written during the height of the suspensions, Nasby challenged the "goriller" to "Restore to us our habis corpuses, as good ez new. Arrest no more men, wimmin, and children for opinyun's saik." Although the piece also ridiculed "Valandigum" and his followers, Locke's censure was real, and he ended it in the tone of a Shakespearean sage: "Linkin, scorn not my words. I hev sed. Adoo." Orpheus C. Kerr also mocked restrictions that were loosely termed "military necessity" by having a fictitious congressman, "Mr. Chunky" of New Hampshire, question whether it was true that *every* man in McDowell's army had been imprisoned on suspicion of being secessionist. "If so," admonished Chunky, "he would warn the Administration that it was cherishing a viper which would sting it." The Copperheads, he cautioned, were not the only poisonous politics the President was handling.[79]

A year after the blowup over General Orders No. 38, Lincoln was asked to justify those who had protested the *Chicago Times* suppression. In his response the President admitted that he was "embarrassed with the question about what was due the military service on the one hand, and the Liberty of the Press on the other." The tension between the need for national security and the defense of cherished rights was precisely the thorny problem he faced. It represented the inherent contradiction in a republic, where liberty is fundamental, but its protection must sometimes be upheld at the cost of absolute freedom, and where leadership is expected to be both forthright and constrained. Lincoln was not the first president to sacrifice perfect freedom for national safety, or to further his political aims by loosely interpreting the Constitution. Washington, John Adams, Jefferson, and Polk—not to mention the feisty Jackson—had all taken measures that stretched constitutional principles when they believed the nation was in peril. The Supreme Court did not meaningfully challenge Lincoln's actions, though his attorney general feared it might, and Congress legitimized many of the administration's restrictive measures, albeit sometimes grudgingly. This was not enough to justify an erosion of liberty, however, and Lincoln also knew he must square his policies with national ideals and public expectations.[80]

Lincoln wrestled with the conundrum throughout 1863 and 1864. He never fully resolved it. He allowed that irregularities had been practiced and that he had "not the power or the right" to interfere if citizens chose not to uphold his government. He also conceded that nothing justified suspension of civil authority except military necessity, and that that was being imperfectly interpreted. Part of the issue, he noted, had also to do with the concept of liberty itself, which was open to many interpretations. He recognized that Americans were in need of a cogent definition, but in practice every faction was defining "freedom" for itself. Lincoln's operating principle was that he could not fully protect the Constitution if it meant losing the nation. As was his habit, he used logic and an everyday analogy to make his point. A limb, he wrote, must sometimes be amputated to save a life; "but a life is never wisely given to save a limb." As chief executive, Lincoln urged the nation to take a longer view, submitting that his "small" mistakes paled beside the great work before them.[81]

Lincoln also argued that because events threatened to spiral out of control, he had to anticipate trouble, or try to forestall it, rather than wait for it to develop. A solitary anticonscription rally might quickly transform itself into a full-scale uprising, or encourage guerrilla action. He thus became greatly angered when state judges began to release protesters held without charge, waving aside cabinet members who advised him that states had long had the power to issue their own writs. In Lincoln's eyes it was all a "formed plan of the democratic copperheads, deliberately acted out to defeat the Govt., and aid the enemy." When a group of Democrats led by New York congressman Erastus Corning questioned the integrity of his legal constraints, Lincoln responded that allowing complete liberty of speech would only allow internal enemies to "keep on foot . . . spies, informers, supplyers, and aiders and abettors of their cause." He stressed the need for vigilance and caution, and once more lambasted those who remained mute in the national crisis, or who spoke ambiguously, qualifying their support "with 'buts,' and 'ifs,' and 'ands.'" The President had been fooled once, during the secession winter, when he underestimated the audacity of the Southern Fire-Eaters, and overestimated the loyalty of men such as John Magruder and Robert E. Lee. Even if mistakes might be made, he had no intention of being called out again in such apparent naïveté.[82]

This was the administration's strongest public statement against Copperhead machinations. It was widely reprinted and greeted enthusiastically among supporters, who admired the President's skillful argument and catchy phrasing. Yet it did not persuade everyone. Corning and his cohorts questioned Lincoln's implication that personal integrity would prevent any abuse of power, noting that the President ignored the danger of precedent for a less scrupulous leader. They accused him of jumping to the conclusion "at a single bound" that "there is no liberty under the Constitution which does not depend on the gracious indulgence of the Executive only." The skeptics also questioned Lincoln's assertion—as had Attorney General Edward Bates—that those who remained silent, or qualified their support for the war, were disloyal. "We think that men may be rightfully silent if they so choose," ran the retort; "as to the 'buts' and 'ifs' and 'ands,' these are Saxon words and belong to the vocabulary of freemen."[83]

It is easy to conclude that the sixteenth president erred on the side of repression, overreacting in situations that were never really threatening, and failing to set a uniform standard for dealing with opposition. If, as he conceded, he had not the right to constrain the public, he had nonetheless taken the liberty to do it. The constitutional questions particularly stand out because of the contrast between Lincoln's lofty rhetoric about cherished freedoms, and the rough way he allowed those freedoms to be handled. This must have bothered Lincoln as well, for he mused "whether any government, not *too* strong for the liberties of its people, can be strong *enough* to maintain its own existence, in great emergencies." Gideon Welles, who also pondering these questions in June 1864, insightfully described the dilemma. Lincoln, he noted, was being

blamed for not being more energetic and because he is despotic in the same breath. He is censured for being too mild and gentle towards the Rebels and for being tyrannical and intolerant. There is no doubt he has a difficult part to perform in order to satisfy all and to do right.

This war is extraordinary in all its aspects and phases and no man was prepared to meet them. . . . I have often thought that greater severity might well be exercised, and yet it would tend to barbarism.[84]

Here then was the rub. Striking the right balance has always been one of the critical tests of a democracy, which must find the strength to uphold its values under even the severest pressure. The First Amendment was particularly frustrating in this regard for leaders trying to maintain security in wartime, because within the privilege of free expression lies the unintended consequence of a sometimes reckless cacophony of voices. Shrill or disruptive debate can also dent the nation's determination, and this was another of Lincoln's concerns. Although military officers frequently criticized the administration's policies, common soldiers by and large detested the Copperheads. They resented those who disrupted recruitment or showed disrespect for the dangers of the field. If anything, they wanted to see the Peace Democrats treated more harshly than they were. "If Vallandigham should come here and talk the way he does in Congress the Soldiers would kill him," asserted a sergeant fighting in Virginia. A similar piece of advice came to the President from the western front: "instead of suspending the writ of *habeas corpus* he should suspend the necks of those who prate so violently against its suspension." Lincoln's strongest civilian proponents concurred. It was impossible for him to ignore these groups, which formed the very backbone of his support.[85]

History would show that the Copperheads posed less of a menace than Lincoln feared. They were able to neither defeat him through constitutional processes nor overturn the policies—conscription, emancipation, and militarism—they so hated. Although they discouraged army recruitment, and their bellicose statements embarrassed the government, few truly seditious actions can be proven. Whether the opposition's ineffectiveness was due to Lincoln's restrictions or the threat was never that grave to begin with is difficult to gauge from the available sources. Those studying the Copperheads closely have concluded, however, that most of their activities were within the boundaries of a loyal minority, and that they acted as an important guardian of civil liberties during the war. Although he made some sporadic efforts to have meaningful dialogue with his opponents, Lincoln never found a way to interact effectively with them, and it is hard to know exactly what he so feared. He undoubtedly wanted to avoid any further fissures in Northern unity, for he saw that the Union might founder as much from internal disruption as from the defiance of the South. But even this does not explain Lincoln's nervous reaction. Perhaps his sensitivity to criticism was pricked, the same vulnerability that caused him to don the armor of japery. Perhaps it was his ambitious ego that balked at the censure. If so, it is all the more interesting because he was a partisan's partisan, and many of his nemeses were acting from his own political script, furthering their party, and stumping for votes.[86]

The tragedy was that the one thing that could have broken the opposition and galvanized the country was swift military victory. Repression of dissent, mandatory conscription, and even Lincoln's inspiring rhetoric could not rally the North as battlefield success would have. The Confederate government understood this: it sustained a remarkable degree of cohesion, until the rebel army's increasing defeats left its public bewildered and dispirited. But military command was not Lincoln's genius, and decisive victory was exactly what he could not give the country, no matter how badly he wanted it. The President was constantly reminded of this from 1861 on: his mailbag brought the message from well-wishers as well as detractors. A three-year veteran warned that the nation was on the verge of a civil crisis which was directly linked to "the great necessity of properly guiding our military operations." "I am sorry to say," he continued, "we have much . . . to complain of *from lack of competency.*" One Democrat who tried to work with Lincoln, Maryland's Reverdy Johnson, observed that the President's oppressive policies could not counter the "lack of a successful result of the contest while he is commander in chief of the army and navy. . . . This must be arrested, or the country will be ruined." Even personal friends shook their heads. The Democrats were gaining points, a Patent Office examiner named Horatio Nelson Taft wrote in his diary, but that did not "indicate disloyalty to the Union, it is more like an expression of want of confidence in . . . those in power for their inefficiency and blunders. A few Victories will put the matter all right." From Bull Run on, Lincoln confronted the nation's sinking morale, seemingly helpless to reverse it by the one measure that would have silenced the criticism.[87]

Perhaps it was because he could make so few inroads against the Copperheads that he laughed heartily at them through the inspired works of the humorists. It was a kind of gratifying retribution to belittle them, to cast them down in hilarious scorn, when sterner measures failed. It allowed the President a sense of moral superiority, by validating his belief that the war was being prosecuted for ends larger than an Orpheus C. Kerr could ever appreciate. And it gave Lincoln something more. He could so easily have been a citizen of the Confederit X. Roads; he had, indeed, been born to that world. A letter sent to Lincoln in 1864 by a kinsman, asking in muddled Nasby-esque syntax "whot is to cunm," painfully points out the semiliterate life he might have led. Yet he had escaped, and by his own exertions. Despite his rustic mannerisms, Abraham Lincoln no longer reflected the provincialism, or bigotry, of the susceptible masses. Awkward and crude he might be, but he was no yokel. There was satisfaction in that—and justifiably so.[88]

V

A few weeks after Lincoln's death, the *New York World* published a mournful article entitled "The Empty White House." The piece is remarkable for a number of reasons. The *World* was one of the most critical news media during the Lincoln administration. Its editor, Manton Marble, had not balked at fabricating stories or writing editorials that were harmful to the Union cause or to the President. One fellow journalist termed Marble the "most malignant, the most brutal, the most false and scurrilous of all the assailants of the President and of the Republican party." (It was Marble who had embellished the hurtful story of ribald songs being sung over the graves at Antietam.) However, the letter filed from Washington on May 14, 1865, that Marble printed, spoke of Lincoln in sorrowful language, casting the country's loss in tragic terms. It was a complete reversal for the journal, and indicative of the radical reshuffling of opinion that followed the assassination. The *World*'s candid assessment of Lincoln's performance would no longer sell, and even Marble's heart was not cold enough to dissect the previous four years or speculate on the late president's chances for success at reconstruction. No longer catering to a partisan audience, and caught up in the national trauma of war and public murder, Marble, like so many others, played to the sentimentality of the moment, and did an about-face.[89]

One of the war's leading reporters, George Alfred Townsend, had filed the letter with the *New York World* after wandering with John Hay through the somber Executive Mansion. Mary Lincoln had not yet left the premises, but the family's belongings were being sorted and packed. "They are taking away Mr. Lincoln's private effects," Townsend wrote, as he watched young Tad Lincoln run through the rooms, dressed in mourning, "and the emptiness of the place, on this sunny Sunday, revives that feeling of desolation from which the land has scarce recovered." Entering Lincoln's office, he noted battle maps still pinned to the wall, campaign markings scribbled on them. Untidy mounds of paper covered every surface; old law books jammed the shelves. Townsend noticed something else and, going to a table, picked up some dog-eared copies of Artemus Ward and Orpheus C. Kerr. They were apparently untouched since Lincoln left the room for an evening of merriment at Ford's Theater. Hay remarked how the satirists had cheered up the President between moments of labor. "Their tenure here," wrote Townsend, "bears out the popular verdict of his partiality for a good joke."

They walked to the window and looked out over scenes Lincoln had viewed when contemplating the division of the nation: the silvery gash of the Potomac, slicing North from South; Arlington, Robert E. Lee's home, so close, yet a world away in the Virginia hills; the Capitol, newly crowned with a sculpture of "Armed Freedom." Then Hay and Townsend gazed down at the South Lawn's grassy expanse, where the little Marine bandstand that Lincoln inaugurated still stood. The flag flying there had all its stars and stripes intact now, but it drooped, as in mourning. The clumsy moment in 1861 was long forgotten; left behind were myriad other stories, humorous and heartbreaking, and a chill foreboding that the nation must brace for new challenges. As in 1861, the flag's meaning floated in limbo. It no long radiated a simple pride of place nor waved with the excited huzzahs of victory. Now it was the pity of war that was caught in the downcast folds—the pity of 750,000 dirges echoing from once merry bandstands—and of a leader slain while laughing at a farce.[90]

Sergeant Lucien P. Waters in the uniform of Scott's 900,
carte de visite, c. 1862
NATIONAL ARCHIVES

3

TWO EMANCIPATORS MEET

On the day he met Abraham Lincoln, Sergeant Lucien P. Waters was fed up.[1] He was fed up with the suffocating summer heat, which to his Northern sensibilities felt close to 120 degrees. He was fed up with the Union's frustrated advances in Virginia, which left his men demoralized and his horses exhausted. Most of all he was fed up with the fact that more than a year into the conflict the country's noblest goals were far from being met. The South was still in rebellion, the slaves were still in bondage, and thousands of patriotic young men were mired in a war that seemed to be waged for little more than naked belligerence. "War for the sake of war is hellish," Waters confided to his family, voicing his fear that a nation dedicated to true liberty was fast fading from view. In August 1862 Sergeant Waters decided he would run these thoughts by the President—and when he did so he left us a remarkable sketch of a leader under pressure.[2]

Lucien Parkhurst Waters was twenty-four years old when he joined a New York cavalry regiment in the spring of 1862. The youngest son in a Presbyterian preacher's large family, he was working in Yonkers as a supervisory mechanic when the war broke out. Service records describe Waters as five feet six inches tall, of fair complexion, with hazel eyes and sandy hair, though a wartime carte de visite shows him sporting dark curls. Waters described himself as possessing "a *loving & earnest heart* . . . an ordinary education, & a *practical* knowledge of several trades & departments of business, having of late had charge of quite a number of men."[3] He was also an unhesitating Republican who used stationery with a beardless "Honest Abe" adorning the letterhead. Fiercely opposed to slavery, Waters originally hoped to serve his country by going to the Sea Islands of South Carolina to teach African Americans who were under the protection of the occupying Union Army.[4]

Instead, a charismatic colonel named James B. Swain persuaded Waters to join the regiment he was just forming. Swain was working at the behest of Assistant Secretary of War Thomas A. Scott, and the 890 men he enlisted came to be known as "Scott's 900." Initially they were attached directly to the First U.S. Cavalry, but were later redesignated the Eleventh New York Volunteer Cavalry. In early 1862 Swain was on the lookout for sharp men because he understood that they would be assigned as special forces. Scott wanted this regiment to scout, to surprise and intercept civilians aiding the rebels, and to disrupt irregular behavior by Union troops. As part of Washington's defense system, they were to act generally as the eyes and ears of the government. "Were the secret history of the regiment written," Swain later recalled, "even those most intimate with its Colonel would be astonished at the extent and character of the secret service he was detailed to perform."[5]

Lucien Waters was attracted by the promise of adventure and by the opportunity to strike a personal blow against slavery. Accordingly, on March 28, 1862, he was mustered in for three years, with the rank of private. A month later he was promoted to sergeant of Company G, a position that entitled him to bed and board and seventeen dollars per month. Dressed in new blue uniforms, with yellow blouses, Scott's 900 appeared a dashing outfit when it left in early May on what Waters called their "patriotic pilgrimage to the Land of Freedom."[6] They were assigned to a comparatively luxurious post in Washington on Meridian Hill named after their colonel's wife, whose maiden name was Relief. Lucien's letters from Camp Relief contain the typical soldier's complaints about food and the confinement of camp life. He hated "those damp stinking barracks," he told his folks, and acquired an interest in vegetarianism after encountering some sutlers who were apparently selling pies made of rat meat. He also found that having direct responsibility for "the whole company or portions of it, as the case may be," was not light work. The long days were crowded with supervising drills, looking after the soldiers' health, maintaining proper conditions in the stables, and ensuring day to day—sometimes minute by minute—discipline. "My duties crowd so Thick upon me," Waters told his parents, adding that he spent more time breaking up fights than patrolling.[7]

One thing Waters did not grouse about was the quality of the horses. The regiment had unusually fine steeds, with Company G riding spirited iron grays. There was a reason for this privilege: not only was Scott's 900 charged with maintaining peace along the Potomac, it was made part of the escort for President Lincoln. A group of five or six men sometimes guarded the White House carriageway, or rode at the President's side as he made calls around town, but their particular duty was to accompany him when he traveled to and from his summer home, three miles from the White House. Rumors of assassination had followed Lincoln from the time he was elected and the danger only increased as rebel actions grew bolder during the warm days of 1862. Lincoln's friends thought the dark, wooded road up to the cottage was a likely path to misadventure and had persuaded the Army to provide some protection. The long-stirruped president, surrounded by his little knot of soldiers— sabers drawn and accoutrements clanking—became a familiar Washington sight in the morning and late evening. Walt Whitman recorded that he frequently saw them pass and thought them more somber than ceremonious. Others who noticed the slow-trotting procession that summer were amused by its unassuming appearance: "I have seldom witnessed a more ludicrous sight than our worthy Chief Magistrate presented on horseback," wrote one New York soldier. "It did seem as though every moment the Presidential limbs would become entangled with those of the horse he rode. . . . That arm with which he drew the rein, in its angles and position, resembled the hind leg of a grasshopper."[8]

Since the day Lincoln had arrived unannounced at the capital, ridiculously dressed in mock disguise, he had been embarrassed by rumors that he was fearful in public. Now he chafed under his guard and sometimes sneaked away early to avoid its company. He lobbied steadily for the unit's disbandment, grumbling about it to anyone who would listen. "I do not believe that the President was ever more annoyed by anything than by the espionage that was necessarily maintained almost constantly over his movements," recalled a member of the regiment. "Nearly every day we were made aware of his feelings upon the matter." Lincoln reportedly told one acquaintance that the guard made so much clatter he could not carry on a conversation with his wife and that he "was more afraid of being shot by the accidental discharge of one of their carbines or revolvers, than of any attempt upon his life." But what he really hated about the escort was the conspicuousness of it, the inconvenience, and the intrusion on his privacy.[9]

Lincoln may have resented the presence of his bodyguards, but for the most part he was genial and companionable with the cavalrymen. The unit was entertained by what they termed his "oddities" and impressed by his unpretentious and polite conversation. Lucien Waters reported that the President bowed solemnly and awkwardly to the troops as he rode by, and others recalled that occasionally he would come into camp and chat with the men, sometimes even sharing their simple supper. They in turn took advantage of their unusual access. The escort's bivouac was so close to the first family's cottage that their boisterous talk could be heard from the veranda. Lincoln would rise and ask them to lower the racket and when he did so they would pepper him with complaints of poor equipment and inedible rations. He apparently took their words seriously. One guard thought the commander in chief went so far as to address every one of their grievances, and told how he had once ripped apart a pair of shoddy socks with his powerful hands and stuffed them into his pocket to use in a protest to the War Department. "The great man, bending beneath the weight of the Republic and its gigantic war, found time amid all his cares to be just to the common soldier," he wrote in amazement.[10]

In addition to protecting the President, Scott's 900 was ordered to keep an eye on the activities of Southern sympathizers who lived near Washington. Those who sided with the Confederacy were spiriting supplies into Virginia, secretly establishing rebel militia units, and passing information to Jefferson Davis's army. Company G drew duty in both Maryland and northern Virginia, where it broke up local recruiting rings, patrolled polling places, and intercepted smuggled goods. Waters confided to his parents that the work was "attended with a great deal of hazard" and demanded a clear head, since the unit was frequently accosted by hostile civilians as well as rogue "secesh" raiding parties. He likened the citizenry of southern Maryland to "starving wolves" who grew bolder as they edged toward desperation. At night the patrols faced particular danger. The contact was frequently violent, especially because Scott's 900 preferred to fight with sabers, implying close hand-to-hand combat. After one fierce skirmish, Waters wrote of a sickening field hospital, located by a stream that had become "so coloured & mixed with the blood from the wounds & amputations" that the horses refused to drink from it. A comrade admitted that because of the use of sabers, some of the men had become "horribly disfigured."[11]

Like many army units in slaveholding territory, Scott's 900 attracted African Americans who hoped to find a safe haven within the Union lines. From the early days of the war, an unofficial policy of sheltering these runaways arose. Dubbed "contraband of war" by General Benjamin Butler, who accepted some of the earliest refugees into his camp at Fort Monroe, Virginia, the fugitives were employed as laborers or simply followed the Army for protection. Initially, the practice had been largely ad hoc, with each commander forming his own procedures, and some taking pains to return the refugees to their owners. With the Confiscation Act of August 1861, however, Congress officially sanctioned the forfeiture of any property—including slaves—being

Contrabands Escaping, pencil, by Edwin Forbes, May 29, 1864
LIBRARY OF CONGRESS

used for Confederate military purposes. By the time Waters entered the ranks, the guidelines had been strengthened. On March 13, 1862, Lincoln signed a bill that created a uniform policy for dealing with runaways and prohibited military officers from returning them to bondage.[12]

Colonel Swain clearly approved of the orders and "liberated" more than a dozen slaves only a few weeks after his outfit went on duty, setting them to work as military servants. Some men in his regiment took the policy a step further, by taunting neighboring slaveholders about inhumane treatment, threatening the owners with "confiscation" if they did not cooperate, and sometimes encouraging the blacks to run away. Lucien described the scene when one slave, fleeing from "the rankest sort of secessionist," escaped into their camp and was hunted down by the master. After hiding the runaway in a weedy lot, he wrote, "we gave [the planter] 'particular rate' in regard to his slave & in regard to his enlightenment &c. . . . The boys swore by all they held sacred that he should never take the darkey out of camp. He quailed & said he was a loyal citizen. It was too late to play that game."[13]

As can be imagined, not every slave fared as well as this man. Once in Yankee camps, the contraband had a variety of experiences. Colonel Willis A. Gorman of the First Minnesota protected every black person who came within his jurisdiction, declaring he would not "be at all displeased to see the whole slave population run away." Some, like General Joseph K. Mansfield, went further, instituting extraordinary measures to encourage those who ran from the "tirents and wicked men" of the South.[14] Many Northern soldiers, however, used their charges in a manner that differed little from the bondage the slaves were fleeing, working them harshly for meager food and clothing, or treating them as court jesters who would sing, dance, or have head-butting contests for the amusement of the troops. Both Waters and one of his comrades from Company F noted that this was the case in their camp, where the men would "throw the darkies up in blankets" for fun or steal from the refugees. Although Colonel Swain was sympathetic to the slaves, it infuriated Waters that in the colonel's absence Company G's captain made a point of contacting masters to retrieve the runaways who came within their lines.[15]

Swain and other liberal officers thought they were doing the commander in chief's bidding by depriving slaveholders of property that could aid the Confederacy and encouraging the slaves to self-liberate. Actually, at this point, Lincoln's policy was to refrain from intimidating slave owners or encouraging runaways. Indeed, Lincoln thought the constitutional soundness of the Confiscation Act dubious. The eradication of slavery had not been his prime war goal, and although his attitude toward manumission was evolving in important ways during this period, his convictions lagged far behind those of committed abolitionists. Deeply concerned about alienating the loyal slave states of Delaware, Kentucky, Maryland, and Missouri, he had only reluctantly allowed the Confiscation Act to become law. In addition, slavery had just recently been outlawed in the District of Columbia, increasing tensions in the crucial area surrounding the nation's capital. The need to keep the border states in the Union and the pro-South Democrats at least superficially calm was thus pitted against Lincoln's impatience to end the war. By the summer of 1862 the chief executive had finally come to the conclusion that robbing the rebels of a key part of their labor force (not to mention the psychological blow of a mass defection of their "faithful" servants) could hasten the end of the conflict. However, for both political and practical reasons he drew the line at enticing slaves to escape. On July 1, he told Illinois senator Orville Hickman Browning that although he had agreed to protect runaways and employ them in the Union cause, "no inducements are to be held out to them to come into our lines for they come now faster than we can provide for them and are becoming an embarrassment to the government."[16]

Unaware of these views, Lucien Waters seized the moment to work toward his ideal of *an honorable peace or none at all.* His view of slavery's menace was far less equivocal than the President's. In his mind there was only one reason for the war: the righting of a grave humanitarian wrong. If Lincoln favored calculated pragmatism to address America's contradiction between freedom and bondage, Lucien oozed passion. He had abhorred slavery from afar; when he encountered its reality he was disgusted. He witnessed beatings, figures misshapen from overwork, and nearly white children, unacknowledged by their planter fathers, who were kept in servitude. Riding through several plantations near Port Tobacco, Maryland, Waters told his parents he believed God frowned on the nation while it indulged in the *"damnable stinky curse of protecting the institution of Slavery!"* and that his own resolve to fight for a true land of liberty was doubled. "The issues are becoming sharper," he exclaimed, "& it behooves the people of the North to awake from their supiness [*sic*] to save, what I hope in the future we may call 'great freedom's land,' but which at present does not answer to that name."[17]

Frustrated by what he believed was near sinful inaction in the face of a national moral crisis, Sergeant Waters decided to move on the issue personally. For many of his compatriots, emancipation was a secondary war goal, but from the beginning of the conflict Waters had known that he was fighting for freedom. He fervently believed in liberation for the individual bondman, but also in liberation of the country from the political straitjacket of slavery. Unable to see swift movement in his government's policies, Waters became a kind of self-appointed emancipator, seeking out slaves he could help. He told his parents that he wished he could "divide myself into four able bodied soldiers to do battle for the cause" and thought that in his zeal he might at least do the work of two men. Invoking the words of abolitionist preacher Henry Ward Beecher, he proclaimed that if the Lincoln administration would not move on the issue, he at least had the use of his "wits & legs." Shocked that "incompetency & tretchery" characterized many government officials, Lucien vowed that he would "labor & suffer alone with The Thought That my *motive* was right." Within weeks, he could tell his brother James that his name had spread like wildfire from plantation to plantation as a harbinger of freedom for the slaves.[18]

Using secret paths and hideaways known to the bondmen, Waters encouraged many to run away, smuggling some to Washington aboard U.S. gunboats that plied the Potomac River. He wrote false passes, told tall stories to slaveholders, and collaborated with like-minded sailors to conceal his freedom seekers. In one instance Waters helped a runaway fashion a halter from a grape vine when the owner, fearful that his property would flee, denied him the use of leather equipment. Another time he went six miles on foot to tell some fugitives about the presence of a boat nearby, secreting them in the marshes as they waited to be taken aboard. The sergeant also tried to protect the contraband in camp against the robberies and humiliations some of his men inflicted on them. Perhaps most remarkably, he was a rare example of a white man who defended the African Americans' innate ability and noted their strong human ties to family and friends. At a time when Lincoln was still questioning whether blacks could live effectively among whites, Waters scribbled this notation on the back of a letter written him by a grateful escapee: "This letter should show that 'niggers' are not so stupid as is so commonly claimed. It also shows by its many requests to friends left behind them in bondage that one's work is not ended with simply getting the parties into freedom—for they have those they love as their lives which they leave behind them."[19]

Among the black people, Waters became known as the "bobolition Sergeant," but among whites he gained a reputation for being a "damned abolitionist." He admitted that the local planters would as soon shoot him as a dog and intended to do so if they caught him. His midnight rescue operations were conducted behind the backs of both his captain and the captain of transport. Waters did not mince words in their company, however, and stoutly told his parents that he would "fawn on no man, neither do I play the sycophant to any superior officer & for the sake of his good will & pleasure *sacrifice my manhood* by hiding my true sentiments. . . . NO! By all that is true & holy, my *manhood is not for sale.*" Believing that in this war there was only one "great object each man should have in view," he continued to risk the ire of plantation lords and his authorities, conducting his freelance manumissions to the very end of the struggle. By the summer of 1862 Waters was luring dozens at a time away from their masters. "My hand is in at stealing darkies," he confessed. "I have traveled on foot & on horse & have brought & protected them to Camp secretly. . . . My name is without a mistake, a terror to the planters, & a talisman of good to the slave. The first they enquire for is Sgt. Waters & he never proves untrue to them."[20]

Lucien Waters had taken morality and the law into his own hands.

Waters mistakenly thought he was pursuing his Moses-like mission with the blessing—indeed, under the orders—of the commander he called "Uncle Abe."[21] So it was not for approbation that he sought an interview with the President. Rather, his plan was to get Lincoln's approval for a furlough. Waters called it a discharge, though it was meant to be temporary—the idea was that he would go on a recruiting expedition in New York, sign up twenty men for his regiment, and gain a lieutenancy by doing so. The matter was small, and the moment unpropitious, but Lucien was an impatient young man and despite the doubts of his colonel, he wanted to press forward. By the time sergeant and commander in chief met, both men had been under weeks of pressure; they were as flammable as dry tinder. The meeting that Waters recorded was, therefore, a startling one.[22]

Waters appears to have waylaid the President sometime during the second week of August 1862, for he described the encounter to his brother on August 12, but made no mention of it in letters of July 31 or August 5. He intercepted Lincoln on the portico of the White House and handed over his request for a temporary discharge. Lincoln, who virtually never turned a petitioner away—and certainly not a blue-clad soldier—took the paper and unceremoniously plopped down on the floor of the portico, leaning back against a column, his knees drawn up "as high as his head."[23] It was his characteristic pose, awkward but engagingly unself-conscious—the essence of a man without pretense. There are many accounts of the lanky Midwesterner lounging in this way, or balanced uncomfortably on the chairs that never seemed to fit him. Friends, family, and strangers commented on the way Lincoln's legs would swing across chair arms or how he would tell stories in his office, "reaching out with his long arms to draw his knees up almost to his face." Others remarked on how his feet and legs wandered all over the floor in front of him, until guests "had serious apprehensions that they would go through the wall into the next room."[24]

Waters was amused enough that he drew a sketch of the President for his brother. It is just a little scribbled cartoon, but it wonderfully captures the informality of the scene. There sits Abraham Lincoln, with a familiarity almost unimaginable today, legs folded and tall hat in place, looking for all the world like a cricket perched on the nation's front porch. And Waters put himself in the drawing too, replete with dress hat and saber, striking a daring pose. It might have been a whimsical moment, but then Lincoln rather spoiled the magic. Before he bothered to read the sergeant's request, he turned up his head and remarked moodily that the paper had "probably something to do with 'The damned or Eternal *niggar, niggar.*'"[25]

"That spoke volumes to me," Waters glumly remarked, and in retelling the story he placed two exclamation marks after Lincoln's words. He viewed it as proof that the chief executive was under the "insiduous & snaky influences" of Washington's many Southern sympathizers, the same influences that had

Lucien P. Waters's sketch of Lincoln on the porch of the White House, August 12, 1862
NEW-YORK HISTORICAL SOCIETY

kept slavery alive for decades. Lincoln had no idea, of course, of Waters's political leanings—was unaware of his freelance emancipations—and that makes his outburst the more intriguing. (Had the President known of Waters's activities, there might have been additional expletives flying across the portico. One of the most powerful recollections ever written of an enraged Lincoln came from a military officer who had lured Maryland slaves to join the Union Army. The chastised officer "did not care to recall the words of Mr. Lincoln.") As it was, Lucien was offended enough and admitted to his brother that he would have liked to give the President "a 'right smart' talking to." But mindful that he had approached Lincoln to ask a favor, he kept his opinions to himself.[26]

Contemporary readers will likely share Waters's surprise and disappointment. Did Lincoln, known for his eloquence and his marks of respect to African Americans, speak this way? Why did he assume the issue was about slavery before he had even read the cavalryman's petition? Did the soldier perhaps make up or embellish the story to impress his brother?

The evidence suggests that the encounter took place just as Waters described it. Waters is a highly credible source—a staunch Republican who had not only voted for Lincoln but sympathetically observed him firsthand. All of his letters show that he prized candor, almost to the point of recklessness, and that he was willing to stand courageously behind his beliefs and his words. We also know that a certain coarseness was a feature of Lincoln's character and that he could be brusque and sarcastic, especially when he was displeased or under pressure. One friend recalled that generally Lincoln had a very good nature, though "at times, when he was roused, a very high temper. . . . [I]t would break out sometimes—and at those times it didn't take much to make him whip a man." In addition, accounts of Lincoln's outbursts during times of stress show that he used the word "nigger" in connection with serious political issues, not just in colorful stories. For example, Edward Lillie Pierce, a dedicated educator of ex-slaves, told of an 1862 interview at which the President "did not behave well. He talked about 'The itching to get niggers into our lines.' His son was very ill and quite likely that had something to do with his temper at the time. I never met him again, and as I remember did not care to."[27]

And by August 1862, Lincoln himself admitted he was so overwhelmed that he was more or less living day to day. The Peninsula campaign of George McClellan had ended in disaster during the appalling Seven Days' battles; in the West progress was stalled; the public mood was explosive. White House aides noted that their boss had grown "sensitive and even irritable," especially on the subject of slavery's future. That summer the President snapped at a Union officer who came to ask him for permission to bring his wife's body from the South, and when he later apologized, Lincoln acknowledged that he was "utterly tired out" and had become "savage as a wildcat." Horace Maynard, a Southern congressman who had remained in Washington, advised Senator Andrew Johnson, his fellow Tennesseean and Unionist, that Lincoln had expressed "himself gratified in the highest degree that you do not . . . raise any 'nigger' issues to bother him." Another conversation, nearly identical to the one with Waters, took place around the same time, when Connecticut governor William A. Buckingham made a call to present a petition from antislavery activists in his state. Before Buckingham could speak, Lincoln said "abruptly, and as if irritated by the subject: 'Governor, I suppose what your people want is more nigger.'" Lincoln evidently changed to a more conciliatory tone when he saw that Buckingham was startled, but his initial reaction had its impact.[28]

The source of Lincoln's discomfort was his own confliction over the seemingly irresolvable problem of emancipation. He was as troubled by the bondmen's plight as Lucien Waters, but was disinclined to approve the kind of precipitous acts his young sergeant favored. Lincoln had long felt a moral repugnance at slavery, but he had a competing attachment for the Constitution, which set the United States apart from all other nations in the great experiment of democracy. That document specified that the federal government should not interfere with the prerogatives of the states—and slavery was one of those prerogatives. Lincoln's formula for the elimination of the offensive institution was to persuade the states to relinquish it themselves, gradually, and with compensation. He hesitated to move too quickly lest he outpace public opinion or alienate the border states, whose fragile support was essential. "I hope I have God on my side, but I must have Kentucky," he is famously reported to have quipped. Provocative exploits like those of Sergeant Waters were exactly what he feared might push Unionist slaveholders toward secession.[29]

Lincoln wanted to move on the slavery issue, but he wanted to move cautiously and deliberately. No perfectionist, he preferred to embrace the art of the possible in his politics. He did not like risky actions, and he likened the destruction of slavery to the removal of an irritating wen (or cyst) on a man's back. Although the sufferer may have wished the growth had never occurred, Lincoln observed, it was another thing to have the surgeon remove it in a dangerous operation. He also understood the value of careful timing. Leonard Swett, one of his most trusted political confidants, remarked that Lincoln was not one to hurry an issue; rather, he preferred to get himself into the right place to act, and wait for an opportune moment.[30] The President himself described his anxiety over abolition as if he were a farmer waiting for pears to mature in a frustratingly slow season. "Let him attempt to *force* the process, and he may spoil both fruit and tree," he noted. "But let him patiently *wait,* and the ripe pear at length falls into his lap!"[31]

Many of those benefiting from historical hindsight have viewed Lincoln's desire to move gingerly on the issue of slavery as wise—if frustrating to those anxious for a quick end to the institution. He had a keen appreciation of the difficulty most people have in accepting great change, and he knew that no matter how prudent the course, emancipation, either as a moral policy or as a military tool, was a revolutionary act. Like all experimental weapons it had the advantage of novelty—but also the liability of being untried and therefore the potential to backfire. After all, what he was searching for was a lasting resolution to the nation's troubles, not an additional source of division. As one longtime political observer noted, as radical as he might be as to *ends,* he was ever conservative as to *means.*[32]

Here then was Lincoln's dilemma in that stifling summer of 1862: how to satisfy the diverse components of the Union on a subject so volatile it had brought on war itself.

Lincoln's cautionary notes were like a plaintive oboe among the tubas. Dedicated citizens like Lucien Waters, who were exasperated that the President did not act swiftly to right a monstrous wrong, were quick to express their chagrin. Abolitionist Wendell Phillips thought the Illinoisan a "huckster" whose antislavery principles did not go much beyond those of most Southerners. Senator Charles Sumner badgered him every few weeks, promoting the idea that emancipation was necessary to win the war. Horace Greeley, the feisty editor of the *New York Tribune,* loudly proclaimed similar views as did "preachers, politicians, newspaper writers and cranks who virtually dogged his footsteps, demanding that he should 'free the slaves.'"[33] Union generals got ahead of him, trying to jump-start liberation in their military districts, and had to be reined in. African American voices were also heard within the din. On August 1, 1862, a group of freedmen gathered in front of the White House for a prayer meeting. "One old chap with voice like a gong prayed with hands uplifted," recalled a witness. "'O Lord command the sun & moon to stand still while your Joshua Abraham Lincoln fights the battle of freedom.'"[34]

At the same time, the White House was attuned to nervous rumblings from those who wanted slavery left *out* of the conflict, either to avoid societal upheaval or for constitutional reasons. Some were slaveholding Union men who warned the President not to "make slaves freemen, but to prevent free men from being made slaves." Lincoln's own best friend, Joshua Speed, was among them. His advice was to stay clear of state laws—such as those in his native Kentucky—that actually forbade manumission. And not all the critics came from Dixie. There was a robust set of Yankees who made considerable money either directly or indirectly from slavery, or who otherwise sympathized with the South. As Lincoln pondered the question of liberation and the dislocations it might cause, Washington's *Daily National Intelligencer* served up a daily dish of news about riots perpetrated against free black laborers in Ohio, St. Louis, and Brooklyn—reports that can only have reinforced the chief executive's concerns about a post-emancipation society.[35]

Then there was the Congress. For six months it had been closely monitoring the administration's performance through the Joint Committee on the Conduct of the War. Its secret hearings, occasional leaks to the press, and brash statements challenged executive and military authority, to Lincoln's annoyance. The Joint Committee was also in the antislavery vanguard and heavily influenced congressional actions on the matter. Seizing the initiative, it launched a spirited debate over whether slavery should be abolished, and who had the right to do so. Men like Senator Charles Sumner asserted in strong language that there was "not a single weapon in [war's] terrible arsenal, which Congress may not grasp"—and, indeed, Congress had already grasped a good many. (Not everyone was in agreement with this proactive stance: Orville Browning, for example, had some animated discussions with the President on this theme just about the time Lucien Waters showed up on the White House steps. Senator Browning argued that to talk of proclamations and confiscation schemes was to usurp powers that were not meant to be given to the federal government and that could not be sustained.) The legislature had pushed the edges of its authority by passing bills that forbade slavery in the District of Columbia and United States territories, and by closing a treaty with Great Britain for suppression of the slave trade. While Lincoln was not necessarily opposed to these acts, he disliked the heedlessness with which some measures were approved, as well as the power plays by Congress. "Sumner thinks he runs me," he sarcastically told a friend.[36]

His allies feared that allowing the legislature to take such a lead suggested serious weakness in the commander in chief. Deliberations turned as warm as the weather, peaking over a second Confiscation Act, which Congress passed in July 1862. That act stated that any slave who was owned by a disloyal master and took refuge behind Union lines would be considered a captive of war and set free. Whether the slave had been used as a tool for the Confederate war effort was no longer the criterion for manumission. Several cabinet members, as well as legislators like Browning, thought Lincoln should veto the act. Indeed Browning saw it as a watershed in his presidency. "I said to him that he had reached the culminating point in his administration," the senator confided to his diary, "and his course upon this bill was to determine whether he was to control the abolitionists and radicals, or whether they were to control him." Angered at the idea of being bullied by Congress, Lincoln sent a peevish note to Capitol Hill demanding that certain qualifying provisions be included in the second Confiscation Act. He also sent the draft veto message he would publish were the provisions not included—gaining the point, if not the whole match.[37]

Lincoln's pique with the Congress was further evidence of his foul mood that summer, for as a general rule he had tried to work cooperatively with the legislature. Matters were exacerbated by the way some cabinet members, as well as other officials, were trying to outmaneuver him to score their own points. Browning was not satisfied by merely arguing with the chief executive about the second Confiscation Act; he began working with Attorney General Edward Bates to force Lincoln's hand on the veto. Cabinet officers were speaking directly to generals on the sensitive subject of military emancipation, even advising them to go around the President's orders and formulate their own policies on the ground. Petitioners wrote to Treasury Secretary Salmon Chase and other counselors rather than approach the President openly. Several cabinet officials did not hesitate to advocate practices that had not been cleared by their boss.[38]

It seemed as though Lincoln's management of his government, his army, and even his own party was foundering. Leonard Swett recalled meeting with him that August and being shown a dispiriting bundle of letters from *New York Tribune* reporter Charles Dana, reformist Robert Dale Owen, and others. The gist of their message was that the administration was composed of "a set of 'wooden heads' who were doing nothing and telling the country to go to the dogs." Senator John Sherman (brother of General William Tecumseh Sherman) was another who despaired of Lincoln's executive ability. Writing from his home state of Ohio, he expressed the deep discontent of the public over the course of the war. "Oh God, how I feel what a blessing it would be, if in this hour of peril we had a strong firm hand at the head of affairs—who would use boldly all the powers of his office to put down this rebellion. . . . If we fail my conviction is that history will rest the awful responsibility upon Mr Lincoln—[not] for want of patriotism but for want of nerve—"[39]

These critics were known to hold views that differed from the President, but they were not unthinking men. Indeed Owen's open letter to Stanton of July 23, a remarkably cogent and polished statement of Lincoln's options regarding slavery as a war tool, was thought by Swett to outshine the President's own ruminations on the subject. The fact was, even Lincoln's most loyal supporters were alarmed. He himself acknowledged his responsibility for the leadership crisis in a speech to the Union Meeting of Washington on August 6. "If the military commanders in the field cannot be successful, not only the Secretary of War, but myself for the time being the master of them both, cannot be but failures."[40]

And looming in the background were the awful consequences of a false step: more obscene death lists—an exhausted and shattered nation—the terrible judgment of history. Lincoln was all too aware of this. His campaign biographer, John L. Scripps, had written him a candid note, beseeching him to understand that the success of free institutions was in his hands. "*You must either make yourself the grand central figure of our American history* for all time to come, or your name will go down to posterity as one who . . . proved himself unequal to the grand trust," he cried. When the celebrated historian George Bancroft similarly remarked that Lincoln's leadership had come at a moment that would be remembered by all peoples, and that no outcome would be acceptable that did not include some redress of the slave issue, the President soberly responded that these matters were very much on his mind. It argued, he said, for clear judgment—and caution.[41]

Under pressure from all sides, Lincoln likened himself to the great aerialist Charles Blondin, who had crossed the thundering chasm of Niagara Falls on a tightrope. Imagine, he said, that all the riches of the United States—its wealth and welfare, fine achievements, democratic dignity, past traditions, and future hopes—were strapped to Blondin's back as he made the perilous crossing. Would it be helpful, he dryly asked, to have the public screaming "Blondin, a step to the right! Blondin, a step to the left!" as he tiptoed across the void? No, he concluded, it would be better to remain silent, to hold all comment but prayerful petition, until he safely reached the other side.[42]

THE COMING MAN'S PRESIDENTIAL CAREER, à la BLONDIN.

"The Coming Man's Presidential Career, à la Blondin," wood engraving, *Harper's Weekly,* August 25, 1860

Critics might complain that the presidential aerial act was "elephant-like" and that his slowness across the precipice was "marked with blood and disasters." Still, in a remarkable show of fortitude, Lincoln did not lose his footing. Instead, he used his political finesse to form a policy that satisfied his own complex requirements and could be made to satisfy those of his diverse constituency. Although Lucien Waters and most of America did not yet know it, by midsummer he had decided to use his powers as commander in chief to release a military proclamation that would free the slaves of defiant Southerners and enlist their services for the Union Army. Such an order would preserve the authority of the executive branch without overtly defying either the Congress or the Constitution. It would also avoid punishing Unionist slaveholders, or too directly threatening the border states. In addition, it would provide much needed manpower to the Union service and demoralize the Confederate public. In short, it would buttress the President's shaky authority, giving him the lead on both emancipation and the conduct of the war.[43]

It was, in some ways, a tardy move, reflecting actions that had already been occurring spontaneously, and political views that were more prescient than Lincoln's own. (Lucien Waters had needed no such proclamation to give life to the principles he held sacred; he simply acted out his beliefs.) Nonetheless, the proclamation would also stretch the public imagination in unforeseen ways, offering a more concrete goal for the war than the status quo ante of 1860, bravely embracing a new kind of societal "progress," and challenging the oxidizing precepts of the slave-owning community. Although Lincoln's proclamation would also generate invective and fear, it was couched in terms that checked a mass rejection of its principles. Its cunning lay in a formulation that made it at least marginally acceptable to the majority of citizens. Many people looked back in later years and realized that it was this ability to inch along the narrow lane to consensus—to steer "the great balance-wheel"—that defined Lincoln's political skill.[44]

This delicate course, melding military authority with popular opinion, was not original to Lincoln, nor did he embrace it easily. Prominent antislavery men such as the Boston preacher William E. Channing had been promoting it since the 1830s and some of those around the President, including Generals John C. Frémont and David Hunter, had tested the waters months beforehand by decreeing liberation in their military districts. Even though Lincoln overturned their diktats, those efforts helped crystallize the idea of using a military justification for a groundbreaking societal act. That rationale was beautifully set forward by Robert Dale Owen, who noted that it was a long accepted principle that the government could appropriate property in times of peril to further the common good; and given the shocking spillage of treasury and blood there was no reason to hesitate. Chase was for it, and even cautious Browning thought that slaves should be seized in order to rob the rebels of advantages in labor and morale. But Lincoln had preferred to stick to his long trodden path of gradual, compensated manumission, and to avoid provoking further hostility in slaveholding regions.[45]

Finally, in early July, with the Union Army in crisis, it became clear that new military muscle needed to be bared. The public was in an uproar: John Nicolay, a White House secretary, complained that he "heard more croaking" in those days than any time since the war began, and that it was coming from all social classes. The pressure was heightened by reports—true or not—that McClellan was about to defy the commander in chief by freeing the slaves under his jurisdiction, and that "the President would not dare to interfere with the order." Lincoln made one last unsuccessful effort to push gradual emancipation, then seriously pondered the course of "military expediency" his counselors had proposed. His favorite Kentuckians were also softening their opposition to liberating and arming blacks, and this may have influenced his change of heart. Recognizing that "we had about played our last card, and must change our tactics, or lose the game!" he began at least mentally to draft a proclamation. Newspapers speculated that the move was afoot, cutting through the stagnant air with rumors that border state slave interests might no longer trump humanity and national unity.[46]

On July 13 Lincoln told several cabinet members he now felt it was essential that the slaves be freed or the country itself would be indefinitely bound by the chains of war. By the time he called his cabinet together a week later to discuss the new policy, the President had written a draft proclamation. On reading the paper aloud, he again met with a frustrating variety of opinion. Secretary of War Edwin Stanton and Attorney General Bates gave their immediate and hearty approval. Chase remained largely silent, though he confided to a friend that "these measures, if all of them are adopted will decide everything." Postmaster General Montgomery Blair sent a disapproving letter that ran to nine pages. The comments that had the most resonance for Lincoln, however, were those of Secretary of State William Seward, who wanted to be perfectly sure the citizens would accept this radical action. For although the proclamation was carefully characterized as a measure that would help win the war, and stopped short of universal manumission (critics would complain that it left more than 800,000 souls in bondage), few doubted that the decision would "loose the wheel" on the emancipation movement, propelling it forward with new momentum. Lincoln agreed that such a daring political move, made while the war news was so dismal, might appear to be the "last shriek, on the retreat." So for the remaining months of summer, amid the

The First Reading of the Emancipation Proclamation, engraving after Francis B. Carpenter's 1864 painting. [From left to right: Edwin M. Stanton, secretary of war; Salmon P. Chase, secretary of the treasury; President Abraham Lincoln; Gideon Welles, secretary of the navy; Caleb B. Smith, secretary of the interior; William H. Seward, secretary of state; Montgomery Blair, postmaster general; Edward Bates, attorney general.]
LIBRARY OF CONGRESS

oppressive national malaise, he kept quiet about the proclamation. Tensely gauging public opinion, he waited for victory.[47]

If Lincoln had already determined his course toward emancipation, why would he make such an easily misconstrued remark to Lucien Waters a few weeks later? Most likely he was still testing the strength of popular support. One of the reasons he rarely turned away petitioners like Waters was that it helped him to hear their views. Immersion in the throngs became what Lincoln later called his "public opinion baths." It was a way, in the days before pollsters, that he could unofficially gauge the effect of the war on the national psyche. A shrewd judge of the popular will, Lincoln did not believe widely held views could be disregarded and once wrote that there was no higher consideration in a democracy than the force of public sentiment. With it, he maintained, "nothing can fail; without it nothing can succeed." It was *molding* popular perception, he noted, that was the test of the politician.[48]

The difficulty of leading public opinion, however, was one of his greatest frustrations. It was also a deep source of criticism. There were plenty of people, including loyal allies, who questioned the President's judgment in exhausting his time and temper with the petty concerns of persons "proper and improper" who jostled through his anteroom. His awestruck young secretaries, as well as Senator Henry Wilson, were among those who tried to dissuade him or redirect his schedule to more official business. Lincoln himself expressed annoyance with the crowds, and admitted his bone weariness. Still, he discouraged anything that kept the masses away.[49]

The teasing question was (and is now) whether his hands-on democracy was actually persuading anyone—whether it was at all effective in shaping the popular will. Adam Gurowski, a grudgingly respected Washington gadfly, doubted it, and said so in his usual unrestrained verbiage: "Mr. Lincoln never did anything in advance of the people's wish, never showed any prescience. Lincoln acts when the popular wave is so high that he can stand it no more or when the gases of public exasperation rise . . . powerfully and strike his nose." It was not just blowhards like Gurowski who were worried. Attorney General Bates thought the President's "amiable weakness" allowed him to be co-opted and darkly noted in his diary that public opinion was "always a manufactured article" and that weak men allowed their enemies to control public opinion against them, but strong men created popularity for themselves. A War Department official commented that Lincoln never rose *above* the people and was strong just so long as he led only in the direction they wanted to follow. From Massachusetts a concerned woman expressed herself plainly about this to Salmon Chase, stating that in the "mazes" of the slavery issue she hoped "neither you nor Mr. Lincoln would wait for the popular voice but would *lead* it by definite actions." Emancipation was indeed a labyrinth and Lincoln was still feeling his way through it.[50]

His public opinion "baths" were probably inadequate to the challenge. (Historian David Donald called them "retail, rather than wholesale, tactics to shape public opinion.") However, tradition and geography had given him few overt ways to reach the populace directly. Speechifying was not thought seemly, and even his messages to Congress were read aloud by the chamber clerks, with the pithy bits lost in their drone. Newspapers were unreliable and highly local. The only one with any pretense to national scope, the *New York Tribune,* was edited by the capricious Horace Greeley, who was hardly a trusted ally. It was not that Lincoln was unwilling to use a politician's tools to prod his constituents. No prude, he did not hesitate to be manipulative, elusive, or downright disingenuous when it served his purpose of swaying public sentiment. He knew when to be coy and at the time he met Sergeant Waters he thought it prudent to mask his intentions. The President was in fact unwilling to reveal his hand even to favored cronies at that sensitive moment, let alone confide in an unfamiliar cavalryman. The last thing he wanted to do was feed the relentless Washington rumor mill by letting his emancipation plan out piecemeal.[51]

Instead he was looking to shape a platform that could be widely accepted in the spirit of national interest. To consolidate support he often floated positions that rose above parochialism to a larger ideal that could be embraced by everyone. Sometimes he did it through his cornpone parables, and sometimes by directly challenging his interlocutors to view a situation from his perspective. He used this latter ploy a few days before he encountered Lucien Waters. When Cuthbert Bullitt, the U.S. marshal for Louisiana, passed on complaints that the administration's contraband policies were disadvantageous for Unionist slaveholders in the federally occupied portion of the state, the President retorted: "What would you do in my position? . . . Would you give up the contest leaving any available means unapplied?" Then, in a masterly argument, he subordinated all other interests to the prime goal. Everything he did, Lincoln protested, was done for one reason: to uphold the Union. "The truth is, that what is done, and omitted, about the slaves, is done and omitted on the same military necessity. . . . I shall not do *more* than I can, and I shall do *all* I can to save the government, which is my sworn duty as well as my personal inclination." To give the message a longer reach, he showed it to friends, who were impressed at his unfettered determination to protect the government.[52]

A few weeks later, Lincoln hit upon an even more effective way to manipulate the national viewpoint when he published a public letter in response to a particularly critical *New York Tribune* piece by Horace Greeley. Printed first in the *Daily Intelligencer* and then across the country, it gained immediate currency. In it he once more placed the country's integrity above all other considerations and clearly stated that any form of emancipation was simply a tool for preserving the Union. Understanding that much of the citizenry needed justification for an action as bold as liberating the slaves, Lincoln made the one argument with which most everyone could agree.[53]

There was yet another public issue stifling the air when Lucien Waters appeared uninvited on the White House portico. As an observant abolitionist pointed out, Lincoln dreaded "the magnitude of the social question" and wondered whether the slaves could be freed without rending the nation's civil fabric. The President had long been concerned about this and spoke openly about the perils of "amalgamation." For that reason he advocated colonization, by which liberated blacks would be removed to another country. He had a pronounced interest in this program, which on some occasions he dubbed "deportation" and on others characterized as "voluntary." It seems to have stemmed from the early days of his political career, when colonization had been promoted by his hero, Henry Clay. "I cannot make it better known than it already is, that I strongly favor colonization," Lincoln declared a few weeks before signing the Emancipation Proclamation. He maintained his enthusiasm for resettling freedmen at least until mid-1864, by which time several actual attempts at the project had ended in disappointment, if not disaster. It was indicative of Lincoln's compartmentalized beliefs about African Americans, in that while he genuinely believed that slavery was wrong, and that "the man who made the corn should eat the corn," he also resisted the ideal of real equality in a color-blind society. It also reflected his conservative nature—he was a man of his time and a cautious one too—and his dislike of sudden change. Moreover, the President knew that most white Americans agreed with him and were fearful of black customs and competition. He was skating on thin constitutional ice in his advocacy of emancipation and felt that if his decision to "proclaim" liberation was to be accepted, it must come with a social outlet rather than a threat.[54]

Two days after Waters penned his account of their tête-à-tête, Lincoln met with a group of African American leaders and proposed that after liberation all blacks should relocate to another country. There was little dialogue at this session. Lincoln read from a prewritten paper that, while attempting courtesy, was brutal in its paternalistic directness. He once again reiterated his belief that the differences between the races were too vast to be overcome, and that this unpleasant fact had to be accepted. "I cannot alter it if I would," were his words. While recognizing that blacks had suffered greatly, he seemed to blame them not just for white discomfort, but for causing the war, apparently forgetting that Africans had been involuntary immigrants to America, and that blacks had not originated the conflict—slavery had. He then threw out the question of whether his audience would not join him in promoting emigration, painting a picture of a new chance in a new land. The former slaves should embrace a revolutionary spirit akin to George Washington's and make a gesture benefiting everyone—one that would help them shed the discrimination of white Americans. Unfortunately, the situation he described (he had Central America in mind) did not mesh with information at his command, which had given a grim description of fetid air and filthy corruption in the proposed new homeland.[55]

Some have viewed the meeting at least in part as a public performance, meant to reassure nervous Northerners that they might not have to absorb the freedmen. That a journalist was present, and a story carried around the country the next day by the Associated Press, points to this. But Lincoln's decades of support for the issue and his eagerness to put the theory into practice in 1863 and 1864 argue against a stage-managed act. Indeed, it appears that in his mind, emancipation could not be justified without a program of removing the freed people. Nor is its unseemliness merely a symptom of present-day sensibilities. In 1862 most African American leaders, as well as progressives, thought the meeting more than unfortunate. "How much better would be a manly protest against prejudice against color!—and a wise effort to give freemen homes in America!" Treasury Secretary Chase exclaimed to his diary the next day. Frederick Douglass was so offended by reports of the encounter that he viewed them as proof of Lincoln's "contempt for Negroes and canting hypocrisy" and fourteen years later still chafed at the memory. A wide variety of newspapers, including the very ones Lincoln may have been trying to influence, protested against its impracticality as well as its inhumanity. "Mr. Lincoln draws pleasing pictures of the prosperity which the exiles may enjoy in their new home, and earnestly urges them to give one more proof of their regard for the white man by getting out of his way," the popular *Harper's Weekly* snidely opined.[56]

Lucien Waters, who abhorred the biases that underpinned slavery, was in agreement with *Harper's*. More idealistic than Lincoln, he fought the war as much to shackle prejudice as to liberate the bondman. The contrast between his view of emancipation and that of his commander is noteworthy. Waters made it his business to smuggle slaves through the swamps of Maryland to a life free of coercion, but he also carried their testimony—precious in its rarity—through the bayous of bigotry, to prove their worthiness as citizens. Refusing to limit himself to liberating African Americans, he chronicled their abuse by former masters, voluntarily sending in reports on the treatment of the contraband. Even when his regiment faced horrible decimation during bitter and fruitless combat in Louisiana and he plaintively wrote that it required "all the philosophy & fortitude" of his character to keep going, Lucien knew he was fighting for universal values, not just military advantage. "The glorious cause for which I contend, consoles me for all suffering & sacrifices," he maintained. "I thank God that I am counted worthy to be one of the number who are appointed to sustain the hopes of humanity in freedom & equality of rights."[57]

Ultimately, Lincoln would also embrace a more inclusive doctrine, but not until the opposition of Latin American nations, the dearth of colonization volunteers, and a tragic experiment near Haiti proved his "solution" unworkable. The need to absorb the former slaves, particularly those who had fought for their freedom, would force the President to change and adapt—to take a leap in the dark by accepting that inevitably American society would become multiracial. The social dislocation he hoped to avert was, in fact, unavoidable.[58]

No wonder, then, that the chief executive whom Sergeant Waters encountered was in a testy mood. The critical deliberations of that overheated summer and the necessity to keep mum; to wait and hope and meanwhile absorb criticism; to be disingenuous when he prized candor; to endlessly explain himself—all this weighed on Lincoln and caused him to snarl in frustration. With pressure from every side and slavery on his mind, it is not surprising that he assumed Waters's business would add another noisy opinion to the cacophony around him. Lincoln's rude comment may also have been an attempt to evade the troublesome issue of slavery altogether, by closing the conversation before it began. But why the choice of words, the offensive expletive about the "Eternal *niggar*"?

The record is clear that "nigger"—and its second cousin "cuffee"—were part of Lincoln's private as well as public vocabulary. The body of evidence from those who knew him is so great that there can be little doubt that he used the coarse epithets in anecdotes and stories. He hugely enjoyed David Ross Locke's satirical *Nasby Papers,* featuring the eponymous poor white preacher who spouted pearls of wisdom such as "Niggers was ordained 2 be bondmen from the very day Noah took a overdose uv the Great Happyfier."[59] Journalists who attended Lincoln's speeches during the 1850s reported him frequently evoking the word, though it is not always apparent how much of this was the speaker and how much the scribe. It is notable, however, that many of these reports were corrected by Lincoln himself, who may have sometimes eliminated the attention-grabbing pejorative.[60]

After he entered the White House, Lincoln evidently thought better of using such language in his presidential statements, though racial epithets are frequently quoted in his private conversations. In later years, friends and admirers, including historians, tried to explain away his crude usage, some on the grounds that it was just an innocent way of provoking mirth, others that the greatness of his soul overrode any vulgarity of voice. Still others remarked that the unpleasant words should be covered up since the public simply did not want to know this side of Lincoln's character.[61]

There is no question that the word "nigger" was a derogatory term during Lincoln's lifetime, not considered a part of a gentleman's speech. As early as the 1760s, writers noted that words like "Negur" were used by the "vulgar and illiberal" to demean their subjects. By 1837 a visitor to the United States commented that "'Nigger' is an opprobrious term employed to impose contempt upon [blacks] as an inferior race." Years before abolitionist William Seward became Lincoln's secretary of state, he was reportedly so offended by the extensive use of the expression by Senator Stephen Douglas that he once berated him by saying, "Douglas, no man who spells Negro with two gs will ever be elected President of the United States."[62] In one instance Lincoln apparently tried to explain his choice of the word "cuffee" by saying that he was a Southerner by birth "and in our section that term is applied without any idea of an offensive nature." But, if crude, Lincoln was not naïve, and if this anecdote is true, it argues more for the ubiquity of racial slurring than the President's unlikely ignorance of its denigrating tone. For while it is true that the use of such words was widespread (even Senator Benjamin Wade, an aggressive critic of Lincoln's slow move toward emancipation, called Washington a "god-forsaken Nigger rid[d]en place"), one is hard-pressed to explain it away as a term of regional slang. Indeed dismissing the degrading connotation of the words itself makes an uncomfortable statement.[63]

Like all profanity, "nigger" was meant to show the speaker's irreverence and shock his audience. The fact that Lincoln seemed to use such words in anger or under pressure underscores his understanding that these were expletives, chosen to demean the object of discussion or emphasize his irritation. In addition to the recollections of his minstrel-style stories, there are private tales like that of Waters, in which he blurts out the remark in annoyance, using it to put off his interlocutor. In every one of these incidents, the statement was abrupt and the emphasis ugly. Indeed, if alienating his audience was Lincoln's goal, he surely succeeded.[64]

In public speaking, grabbing attention seems to be what Lincoln frequently wanted to achieve by using such a loaded expression. He had more than a little of the thespian in him and was a gifted writer: he knew the value of words. Without excusing the crudeness of his choice, it is evident he often said it when he wanted to mock those who used the term without irony—in other words, to belittle the belittlers. Lincoln regularly called on sarcasm to make his sharpest points. Earnest and eloquent speech sometimes fell flat with the masses, and what better way to point up the vulgarity of the bigot than by parroting his words? And Lincoln was an accomplished mimic. Many of his references to "niggers" were in speeches lampooning Stephen Douglas for his fable of the Negro and the crocodile, in which black folks were said to be to the white man as reptiles were to Africans. The joke was on Douglas in these performances, not on the blacks. Interestingly, Lincoln was just as capable of cruelly imitating pompous New Englanders as he was Southern racists. In one hilarious impersonation, he caught the exact tone of a Democrat who was trying to blame a shoe factory strike on the conflict over slavery: "I cannot dawt thot this strike is the thresult of the onforchunit wahfar brought aboat boy this sucktional controvussy!"[65]

Lincoln's use of such pejorative speech also points up the power of environment on even the largest intellect. There is no reason to doubt his assertion that he believed slavery was intrinsically wrong and that he could not remember a time he did not feel so.[66] Casually referring to "niggers" reflected cultural boorishness rather than naked hypocrisy. Americans had woven such an intricate pattern of racial relationships, such a set of conflicting principles and interactions, that few escaped the contradictions. Robert E. Lee, for example, was never known to have uttered the word "nigger" and thought such language beneath him; yet he treated the slaves under his control with harsh disdain. When Lincoln slipped into coarse speech, or guffawed over Reverend Nasby's preposterous pronouncements, he was reflecting a way of acting he had absorbed almost by osmosis, not necessarily a politically motivated code of conduct. Indeed, given his impoverished frontier upbringing, it is striking that he did not let prejudice prevail more often.[67]

It is also notable that Lincoln never used the word "nigger" in letters or official texts, and rarely in serious extemporaneous speech. Perhaps he simply thought it inappropriate for more formal writing. But he also understood the difference between the transience of mere talk and the lasting quality of the written word. Casual words, as Lincoln's friend Joshua Speed once reminded him, are "forgotten . . . passed by—not noticed in a private conversation—but once put your words in writing and they Stand as a living & eternal Monument against you."[68]

Whatever Lincoln's motives, his language failed to impress Lucien Waters, who viewed it as the unbecoming statement of a man still enchained by the influences of the Slavocracy. Waters did not chastise the President, however, though he was chafing to do so. The sergeant had observed the exhausted leader at close range, knew that he had scarcely a moment to relax, realizing as well that the demands of war and America's diverse constituency made every decision hard and contradictory. Moreover, Waters had an object to achieve with his petition—he wanted that furlough. As he told his brother, he therefore kept "a close mouth."[69]

And what of his petition? Did Lincoln grant Waters his leave? It appears not. The timing was disastrous, because one of the many questions vexing Lincoln was how to invigorate his military machine. The Union Army was suffering stalemate in the West and before Charleston, and it was outmaneuvered by Robert E. Lee in Virginia. Losses in recent battles had been stunning. The size of the Confederate force before Washington was a subject of anxious discussion, with rebel strength greatly exaggerated. By early August the President had approved a change of command and a controversial draft of 300,000 men, with serious penalties for those trying to dodge their responsibility. The new influx of green soldiers would need supervision. Colonel Swain had warned Waters that the army chiefs were looking to keep seasoned men, so his plan was therefore unlikely to be approved. Swain had his ear to the ground. The commander in chief himself valued the veteran units and said that "one recruit into an old regiment is nearly . . . . equal in value to two in a new one." Under such circumstances, Lincoln could ill afford to indulge one officer's self-serving schemes. Indeed, a senior officer in the War Department witnessed the chief executive brush away another soldier from Scott's 900 during a similar petition for personal favors. "Now, my man, go away, *go away!*" he cried out. "I cannot meddle in your case. I could as easily bail out the Potomac River with a teaspoon as attend to all the details of the army." In the end, military records show that Waters served throughout the war without a single day of furlough.[70]

An acquaintance of Lincoln once remarked that he was "an artful man." Lucien Waters could not have guessed on that August day the extent to which "Uncle Abe" was practicing his art, balancing on the cusp of history. Although it was a brief exchange, Waters glimpsed the President in all his complexity: the crude backwoodsman; the harried public servant; the dedicated champion of American-brand democracy, who passionately believed that the people must have access to power; the hardheaded politician; the gangly, near gargoyle of a man. Waters thought perhaps he should have taken Lincoln to task for his crass speech but was astute enough to perceive the great pressure under which he was laboring, and ultimately rationalized and forgave the outburst. What is remarkable is the directness and confidence with which these men

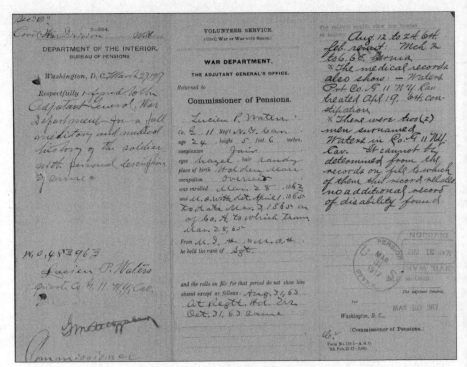

Service record of Lucien P. Waters
NATIONAL ARCHIVES

faced each other. Lincoln did not hesitate to listen to the concerns of a common citizen, and Lucien showed no fear in the presence of the nation's leader.

The differing brands of emancipation favored by Abraham Lincoln and Lucien Waters are what make their brief encounter so compelling. Waters, more impatient and optimistic, showed his dedication through actions, not fine words. Convinced that Americans could and should embrace the freedmen, he was loath to shunt them into a separate future. His war was one of unwavering conviction. When he saw that the government would not instantly eradicate the hated institution of slavery, Waters simply moved to remedy the situation himself. Lincoln was without question the more hesitant liberator. His views were cautious and pragmatic, and more skeptical about both African American potential and his nation's capacity for racial absorption. To uphold the law, he was willing to promote political practices that he personally abhorred. Caught within a dynamic that he could not control, Lincoln was forced to evolve his thinking over time, as facts proved his assumptions wrong and popular clamor made his divisive policies obsolete. But the stakes were also higher for Lincoln. As a sitting president, bound by law and tradition, and entangled in an epic societal transformation, he could not just mount his iron-gray steed and single-handedly entice slaves to freedom like an idealistic sergeant. He accomplished the great work of emancipation, but without the zeal of Waters and his political counterparts, who pushed him until his views more closely reflected the absolutism he had once shunned. In the end, probably both perspectives were needed to clear the awful stench of slavery from the land.

It is too bad that Waters did not enjoy a richer dialogue with his president, for they had much in common. At heart both were distressed by the festering sore of slavery; both wanted to lance the boil. Both cherished a belief in democracy's innate practicality and goodness. In their short conversation they were living out the fundamental principles of the republic: that in a nation *of* the people the dialogue between governor and governed is essential; that where all men might rise there can be no pretense—no undue deference from a simple sergeant; no arrogance or intimidation from his commander. Waters belonged to an outfit charged with protecting the President, but Lincoln understood instinctively that he must not be too protected, lest he become isolated—an island of power without a public causeway to keep him honest and responsive and relevant.

When Lucien Waters described his meeting with Abraham Lincoln, he only meant to give his brother a little picture of an eccentric leader in an unguarded moment. What he left us was a lasting sketch of direct democracy, in all its roughness and grandeur.

Abraham Lincoln's commitment to emancipation and, ultimately, a more equitable place for blacks in American democracy grew over time. He never embraced the idea of perfect equality among the races, but he did drop his more blatant prejudices, including his public support for colonization. He was at first noncommittal about the Thirteenth Amendment to the Constitution, which abolished slavery forever from all parts of the United States, but later helped to promote its passage through the House of Representatives. He signed the measure, sending it to the states for ratification, on February 1, 1865. He began work that would redefine the meaning of citizenship and won the respect of many African Americans, including Frederick Douglass, who had criticized him throughout the emancipation summer. We do not know, however, what his vision for a postwar society would have been, for it is impossible to ascertain from the contradictory documents left to us after his assassination on April 14, 1865.[71]

Lucien Waters continued to serve with the Eleventh New York Cavalry until 1865. After several years of lobbying, in 1864 Colonel James B. Swain finally succeeded in having the men of Scott's 900 transferred to the field. Their new assignment was to scout and interrupt "disloyal" behavior, first in Louisiana, and later in Tennessee and Arkansas. It was punishing work amid a hostile citizenry. Aggressive fighters making lightning raids, such as Nathan Bedford Forrest, challenged the regiment, as did the harsh climate. Sickness took its toll as well: Scott's 900 lost an astonishing 819 men to disease, at least in part due to the incompetence of Union Army doctors. Waters wrote bitterly of the deprivations suffered by the men. Nevertheless, he was determined to persist in his fight for "the priceless legacy of human freedom which the future imperatively demand[s] of us." He also continued to work on behalf of the freedmen, helping many to escape the lingering burdens of servitude and writing about the disgraceful treatment blacks received at the hands of their former masters. It was perhaps an indication of the hardship the regiment suffered that Waters left the army on March 28, 1865, just weeks before the end of the war and exactly three years to the day from his initial appointment.

After he was mustered out, Waters returned to his fiancée, Mary G. Smith, and his career in Brooklyn. He planned to be married in late May 1866. When Lucien failed to appear at the wedding, his bride tracked him down at his brother's house and discovered he had suffered a stroke, falling in the street just after purchasing a wedding ring. Mary and Lucien were married as he lay in bed. He died a few days later, on June 10, 1866.[72]

Following is the text of Lucien Waters's letter to his brother Lemuel Waters of August 12, 1862, with its original punctuation and grammar.

Camp Relief "Scotts 900"
Washington D.C. Aug 12 '62

Very dear Bro. Lemuel & Family:

> *I have only a few moments in which to answer your two very kind missives, lately received from New York & The Catskill. You will excuse me if I do not as extensively reply to your patriotic & metaphysical suggestions as The importance of The Themes would seem to demand. I am not in The best of*

health These days, & having very arduous tasks to perform in keeping my Co. straight in The absence [of] my superior officer, I have not time to devote to any Thought on any subject disconnected with my duties or even to read The news of The day. After The duties of the day are over, I try to keep awake by The Camp fire & Think over The past with its many pleasing recollections, to Think of the gigantic issues which are growing out of This nations present convulsions, & Throes to rid itself of its many hellish corruptions, & to plant my feet on The only ground on which I have ever cared to stand; & That is to labor & suffer alone with The Thought That my motive *was* right *& Though The issue was not as sharp & desisive as The more advanced & patriotic minds would have it, & Though incompetency & tretchery characterized The heads of The government, yet I try to draw a balm from our present ills, & trust The* all-wise *controller of events to so shape our reverses as to awake The* canelle[73] *of America, to Their rights & The rights of Africa's trodden race. I would here rehearse a conversation which I had with President Lincoln as I presented a petition for him to sign in conjunction with my Col. for my discharge from The Army. He in his characteristic style but not in a very dignified manner, took the said petition & sitting down on The marble pavement of The portico of The White House with his back against one of The south pillars, & with his feet drawn close up under him Thereby elevating his Knees as high as his head, [picture drawn here] turned his head up & said that it had probably something to do with "The damned or Eternal* niggar, niggar."!!. *That spoke volumes to me as to the influences by which he was constantly surrounded, & which influences are the same as have for the past Thirty years made slaves to The aristocratic minds of the South, of every Executive who has occupied a place at the head of the nation.*

A man has much to contend with, that would keep pure where such insiduous & snaky influences are constantly brought to bear. I should have given him a "right smart" talking to had I not an object to gain. For policies sake I for once kept a close mouth, & not through fear. With all respect for his office, I should like to have given him a dressing down as father sometimes says. I pity the man from my heart for he is nearly worked to death. His private hours are scarcely kept sacred to his repose & comfort, & he may have been vexed & tormented with a hundred that very day who were trying to worm something out of the government for their own personal agrandiziment. Charity, Charity should be our watch word as well as the keen acumen of criticism.

Please to write soon & send me "on tick" a few more postage stamps, as mine were all stolen the other day with quite a number of valuable receipts. I will agree to send on letters until our next pay day, if you will pay the postage, my money being all spent for little additional articles for my comfort & protection which were absolutely necessary & for fruit & vegetables & milk which I had bought previous to pay day & for which I was in debt. You cannot rightly appreciate my condition unless you are here to see & experience. Our Co. is greatly fatigued with the night scouting which we have had to do of late in the Old Dominion. I cannot stop to begin to tell for it would be an agrivation to commence & not finish. I trust I may get a permit to go north & recruit for a 2d Lieutenancy, & if I do, rest assured that I shall try & put on an old woman's gassifing hat & talk and twaddle from sun rise until sun set. Much I know of interest but as you see from the beautiful composition & writing cannot now stop to relate (You cannot write a letter as quick if you should try.) I hope I may not be as much hurried next time. The Stable calls have sounded & I must see that my men attend to their horses.

You do not know what hot weather is up your way. We have to drill in the sun when it is at 120° & 101° in the coolest shade & where it is the most sheltered.

Love to all
Your loving brother Lucien

Write soon it gives me great pleasure to hear from you & to receive your papers. They are about the only reading I have except those papers which Bro. James is kind enough to send. Don't neglect the poor Soldier, for he craves reading matter as well as those [at] home, though at all times he has not the time to read. Lucien

John Ross, daguerreotype, c. 1850

4

OF FATHERS AND SONS

John Ross did not look like a storybook Indian: he wore no paint or feathers, and his expressive voice neither whooped nor grunted. Nonetheless, he was chief of the Cherokee, one of the largest and most resourceful tribes in North America. On September 11, 1862, he arrived at the White House, dressed in the fine clothes he enjoyed, a top hat crowning his brow. He was an old hand at this Washington game. For more than thirty years Ross had been parlaying with presidents, Supreme Court justices, and congressmen to uphold his people's rights against an ever encroaching white tide. Now he had come once more to speak with the "Great Father," as many Native Americans called the President. Ross was better educated than the man he was about to meet; had been in public office longer; and was more financially secure. As head of a sovereign nation he had important business with Abraham Lincoln, and he was anxious to get to work.[1]

Ross's skill as a leader was honed during a turbulent period in Cherokee history. Born in 1790 to a Scottish father and half-Native mother, he was raised bilingually, studying both sacred Cherokee traditions and Enlightenment principles. Ross—or Guwisguwi ("A rare bird")—was drawn to politics, and by age thirty his talents were well recognized. In 1827 he was elected president of a convention that drew up the first codified tribal statutes in North America. Modeled after the United States Constitution, it featured three clearly defined branches of government, with a principal chief who was elected every four years. During the same period, the Cherokee established newspapers, a rigorous school system, and profitable businesses. A "syllabary" was developed by the genius named Sequoyah—a rare instance of nonliterate people inventing a system of writing. After its publication, literacy among the Cherokee surpassed that of their white neighbors. In 1828 Ross was elected the first principal chief of this energetic nation.

Ross's priority was to protect the Cherokees' fertile territory, which bordered on Georgia and Tennessee. Land lust had begun to squeeze the area's "Five Civilized Tribes," and President Andrew Jackson strongly supported white demands for open settlement. Lobbying relentlessly for peaceful relations, Ross hired William Wirt, a noted attorney, to represent his people before the law. John Marshall's Supreme Court ruled in favor of the Cherokee, defining them in *Worcester v. Georgia* as a sovereign nation, and guaranteeing them protection on their land. But the iron-willed president and Georgia officials defied the rulings, demanding that the Indians be moved west of the Mississippi. "John Marshall has made his decision; now let him enforce it!" Jackson reportedly exclaimed. "Build a fire under them. When it gets hot enough, they'll go."[2]

Under pressure, the Cherokee themselves began to differ on their best course. Ross, with his faith in the law, could not believe they would be forced to leave. Others, sensing their options would only diminish, advised negotiating an agreement before they were dispossessed altogether. Three prominent men challenged Ross: John Ridge, Major Ridge, and Elias Boudinot, the brilliant editor of the *Cherokee Phoenix*. Boudinot's brother, Stand Watie, a lawyer and an entrepreneur, joined them to make a potent opposition. Against Ross's will, these men signed the Treaty of New Echota in 1835, which granted the Cherokee a homeland on the southwestern plains, protection, and annuities if they relinquished their ancestral lands. Under the treaty terms, the U.S. Army escorted the tribe on a forced march, thousands of miles, to "Indian Territory" (present-day Oklahoma). This "Trail of Tears" was a logistical and psychological horror that cost a third of the Cherokee their lives. John Ross lost his wife, Quatie, as well as substantial property, in the catastrophe.[3]

Still chief of the nation, Ross remained resilient, establishing successful businesses and working to unite his exhausted people. Factionalism was his main concern. Tensions with the pro-treaty bloc had heightened after the Ridges and Boudinot were murdered by men loyal to Ross—though apparently without his knowledge. Watie's rivalry was sharpened by anger over his brother's death, as well as financial interests in developing the new land. Important differences of opinion also existed about what defined their nation—whether it was bound by traditional kinship relations; or by laws and institutions that would include those of mixed-blood and non-Cherokee backgrounds. In addition, there were frictions with the "Old Settlers"—tribes removed to Indian Territory prior to the Cherokees' arrival, including the Chickasaw, Choctaw, Creek, and Seminole.

For two decades Ross struggled to strengthen the national structures he thought underpinned Cherokee success and to renew his people's vitality. By the outbreak of the Civil War, he had succeeded to a remarkable degree. Jealousies were muted, at least on the surface. Watie and Ross cooperated in council meetings; schools and churches were created; democratic institutions rebounded under the roof of a handsome capitol building; agriculture and husbandry flourished as they had hoped. Progressive in his views, Ross introduced humane prison sentences and built seminaries for girls as well as boys. The chief and his new wife built a large house called Rose Hill, owned fifty slaves, and led a life befitting the head of a proud nation. A Cherokee man described this era of peace and comparable plenty, on the eve of war. He longed "to hear the cows lowing the hogs squealing and see the nice garden and the yard with roses in the waving wheat and stately corn growing," he told his family, "and be conscious that there was no one in want."[4]

In 1862 John Ross was a slight, silver-haired septuagenarian, but in attainments and renown he stood as high as Abraham Lincoln. There were many similarities between the two men that might have created a sympathetic bond. Both had been born outside the easy paths of success but had risen through talent, pluck, and opportunism. Both believed fervently in education as a refining influence on society. Ross's gift for the elegant phrase at times rivaled the President's, and he shared Lincoln's understanding of how shrewd words could shape political ends. Each expressed a profound dedication to democratic government and an understanding that compromise and unity were its essential underpinnings. Ross did not consider himself a vassal of the United States, but he admired its institutions, and deftly interwove them with native traditions of negotiation and consensus building—a style that resembled Lincoln's own way of governing.[5]

As the country splintered over Lincoln's election, Ross viewed the situation with concern. "If the good people of these United States duly appreciate the blessings of liberty they enjoy," he told his wife, they "should choose some great & good conservative Patriotic Man . . . under the Banner of *the Union* and *Constitution*." His vote would have been cast for the Constitutional Unionist John Bell, not Lincoln. Ross was wary of the Republicans—wary, as a slaveholder, of their policy against the institution's expansion; and nervous about William Seward's claim that the territory south of Kansas should be "vacated" by the Five Nations. Ross was also only too aware of the fragile geographic position of the Cherokee, surrounded as they were by Kansans, who were engaged in a violent internal struggle over slavery, and Texans, who were already blustering about disunion. Hoping to maintain neutrality, he shunned zealous secessionists, as well as "Abolitionism, Freesoilers, and northern Mountebanks."[6]

Ross admitted that the Cherokees' Southern roots and slave property fostered greater cultural affinity with the secessionists, but he also recognized he was bound by treaties with the United States that theoretically safeguarded his people. "'The Stars and Stripes' though an emblem of superior power, is also the Shield of [Cherokee] protection. They all know that Flag—many of them have fought beneath it," he wrote defiantly to a newspaperman who had "hissed" about the pro-slavery sympathies of "savages." "But," Ross added, "if ambition, passion and prejudice blindly and wickedly destroy it . . . they will go where their institutions and their geographical position place them." Although he deeply regretted the conflict, Ross made it clear his main concern was to prevent outside interference in Cherokee affairs. A group of Texans, sent to woo the chief, found him "diplomatic and cautious," and noted he agreed with Lincoln's refusal to consider the Union dissolved. Declining to join either side, Ross advised the Cherokee to refrain from partisan speeches or provocative activities that might incite a fratricidal war.[7]

But the strategy of neutrality failed. A convergence of events tested Ross's impartiality and ruptured the tenuous cooperation among tribal members. With the onset of war, Lincoln declined to supply the protection the Cherokee had been promised, instead removing federal troops from the borders of Indian Territory. It proved an unfortunate policy. Not only did the President's action break treaty obligations, leaving Ross and his fellow chieftains vulnerable to rebel incursions, it closed the Union's best route for infiltrating Texas, while allowing the Confederates to penetrate toward Kansas. Indian agents in the vicinity—many of them holdovers from the Buchanan era—aided the unrest by openly supporting the South, sometimes causing drunken demonstrations. (Lincoln claimed it was impossible to get new men into place, but the accounts of eager politicians and speculators show they had little trouble moving into the area.)[8] Factionalism among the Five Nations also played a decisive role in undermining neutrality. The Choctaw and Chickasaw were committed to slavery and unequivocally for the South; the Seminole were fervently antislavery, but comparatively weak; Creeks and Cherokees were divided among themselves. Also opposing Ross's policy were Stand Watie's followers, who were largely slave owners and solidly pro-South. They saw opportunity within shaky tribal politics, as well as benefits in doing business with a Confederacy anxious to make concessions. Feeling that Ross's National

Party had for years "had its foot upon our necks," Watie tried to force a confrontation by attempting to raise the Confederate flag in Tahlequah, the Cherokee capital. Some 150 "armed and painted" neutralists halted the demonstration, but Confederate leaders quickly capitalized on the divisions.[9]

Using an effective carrot-and-stick policy, Jefferson Davis posted the belligerent General Ben McCulloch in the region while sending a smooth-talking envoy, Albert Pike, to negotiate with the tribes. Pike offered the Cherokee a nearly irresistible deal. It included everything they had been trying to obtain from the United States for more than a dozen years, including armed protection; unrestricted title, and perpetual possession of their country; payment of $500,000 for lands bordering Kansas that were destabilized by squatters and outlaws; Confederate assumption of annuities; and a delegate seat in the Confederate House of Representatives. Pike considered Ross a smart, decisive leader, but he was able to shake the chief's determination by threatening to make a direct agreement with Watie. Correctly surmising that Watie had everything to gain by a tribal split and backed by the strong presence of Confederate soldiers, Pike wedged apart the unity Ross had wrought with so much difficulty.[10]

Ross tried to rally the Five Nations, or persuade them to form a coalition, but by the summer of 1861, the other tribes had formed alliances with the South—and Watie was leading a regiment in their support. Surrounded on three sides by hostile forces, abandoned by the federal government, and troubled by a string of Union defeats, including a bloodbath at nearby Wilson's Creek in Missouri, Ross suspected Confederate leaders were about to forcibly end his neutrality. Federal agents finally impressed Washington with the gravity of the situation, but the administration fumbled arrangements until it was too late. On August 21, 1861, Ross called together four thousand tribesmen and appealed in eloquent language to their long history of honor and cohesion. As he had throughout his career, Ross deferred to what he believed was the best interest of the Cherokee; and, to the surprise of his audience, ended his speech by announcing an alliance with the Confederacy. "We are in the situation of a man standing alone upon a low, naked spot of ground, with the water rising rapidly all around him," Ross poignantly declared. "If he remains where he is, his only alternative is to be swept away and perish. The tide carries by him, in its mad course, a drifting log. . . . By seizing hold of it he has a chance for his life." Advising the equally divided Creeks to follow his lead, Ross signed Pike's treaty on October 7. "The Cherokee People stand upon new ground," Ross told his nation. "Let us hope that the clouds which overspread the Land will be dispersed and that we shall prosper as we have never before done."[11]

It had been the most pragmatic of decisions, born of a need to survive. But Ross's hope for peace and Indian unity was quickly disappointed. The Cherokee raised two regiments for the Confederate Army, one under Stand Watie and another led by men who had supported Ross. However, Opothle Yohola, the neighboring Creek leader, was strongly pro-Union. Convinced his tribe would be massacred by Southern forces, he took flight to Union lines in Kansas, joined by some of the loyal Cherokee. He was pursued by rebel Colonel Douglas H. Cooper, with an army that included soldiers from all five tribes— a grim realization of the fratricidal war Ross had worked to avoid. After a series of short, but bloody battles, Cooper took hold of Indian Territory. Thousands of Cherokees fled to Kansas, living in desperate conditions and exacerbating tensions in the area. It also soon became evident that Southern leaders were unwilling or unable to uphold their rosy treaty promises. Annuities were rarely forthcoming. Native regiments were undermanned, under-supplied, and unprepared to guard Indian Territory. Confederate agents were scattered or distracted by military matters. Internal quarrels led to inaction in Richmond, as well as the dismissal of Pike, whom the Indians had trusted. Ross urgently reminded Jefferson Davis of his treaty responsibilities, as well as the federal threat on the Kansas border, and asked for means of self-defense. He received no response.[12]

Agents and military officers reported the volatility to Washington, asserting that most Native Americans under Confederate control would prefer to be aligned with the Union. But the cabinet hesitated to intervene, especially after hearing an account of Watie's exceptional performance at the Battle of Pea Ridge, including some exaggerated rumors involving mutilated prisoners. Lincoln led the vacillation. He was under "hard pressure" from political patrons, but tried to order the creation of a "snug, sober column" to keep peace. He dispatched and recalled men in such confusing fashion, however, that officers such as General James Lane, who simultaneously served as a senator from Kansas, and General David Hunter only quarreled over rank or worked against one another. When Lincoln twice more reversed plans, Hunter refused all cooperation, and Lane openly ignored the commander in chief's orders, complaining he had been publicly humiliated by that "d—d liar, demagogue, and scoundrel" in the White House. Not until June 1862 was a

Union force finally dispatched to the area; and it was July before federal troops were able to reestablish their authority.[13]

Meanwhile the plight of the refugees had become frightful. An army surgeon reported seeing hundreds lying naked in the snow, without blankets or food. According to one report, seven hundred Creeks and Cherokees froze to death in a few days. William Coffin, the superintendent of Indian affairs for Kansas, begged for assistance: the "destitution, misery, and suffering amongst them," he wrote, "is beyond the power of my pen to portray." The fate of Ross and his followers became yet more precarious as they fell victim to both armies in the to-and-fro contest. In late summer 1862 Chief Ross was "arrested" and removed to the protection of the Union line, accompanied by his family and the Cherokee archives. Many of his followers also defected, assured by federal officers that they would be given immunity as long as they ceased all guerrilla activities and promoted peace. A large number not only laid down their Confederate arms but joined the Union forces.[14]

In Kansas, Ross claimed that most Cherokee had never really abandoned their loyalty to the United States. The treaties signed with the Confederate government, he argued, were only a desperate response to dire circumstances. Most who met him took him at his word. They advised Ross to discuss his case in Washington, arming him with supportive letters of introduction to the president. General James Blunt, appointed commander of the Department of Kansas after the Lane-Hunter debacle, represented Ross as "a man of candor and frankness upon whose representations you can rely." He also backed Ross's assertion that he had aligned with the South only after the United States failed to meet its treaty obligations. Mark Delahay, a Republican collaborator, reminded Lincoln that despite their brief flirtation with the rebels, Cherokee warriors would be valuable to the Union cause. Indeed, maintained Delahay, the volatility along the border and the refugee problem could not be solved without their help.[15]

But Lincoln already knew about the situation and was unconvinced. When he raised the issue with the cabinet, he advocated a hard policy of invading Indian Territory with a force of white and black soldiers and repossessing it from the tribes. Assistant Secretary of the Interior John P. Usher, whose portfolio included Indian affairs, objected. He proposed that it would be better to deal "indulgently with deluded natives," win their goodwill, and at the same time impress them with the immense power of the federal government. Most other secretaries concurred, and the President reluctantly dropped his proposed offensive against the Cherokee.[16]

When John Ross crossed the White House vestibule on September 11, 1862, Lincoln met him coolly. He was still uncertain about the chief's sincerity, and leery of making concessions to a man who shifted his allegiance under pressure. The President's skepticism is interesting, for he was himself struggling to steer his ship through a crisis, and relying on practical expedients to keep it afloat. If anyone understood the difficulties of clinging to ideals in the midst of a clamorous civil war (or to the legal instruments that protected them), he did. Just a few weeks before, he had succinctly expressed his belief that absolutist principles were subordinate to the larger good of national survival. If he could save the Union by abolishing slavery, he would do it, Lincoln had told the *New York Tribune;* but if it could only be saved by retaining the institution he would do that instead—whichever worked best. By the time of Ross's interview, the President had circumvented the law on issues ranging from increasing the size of the Army to spending unappropriated Treasury funds, and was only days away from reversing his oft repeated pledge not to meddle with slavery in states where it already existed. But the similarity of Ross's circumstances eluded Lincoln, and he dismissed the chief with a lawyerly request that he put his thoughts in writing.[17]

Ross wrote at length, reciting the pressures that had pushed him toward the Confederacy, stressing that at the first opportunity his nation had again "rallied spontaneously" to the Union cause. Complete restoration of U.S.-Cherokee relations had been thwarted only by the untimely withdrawal of federal troops from Indian Territory, he noted, which left his people prey to rebel depredations. He asked for the reinstatement of exiting treaties, as well as the safeguards they promised, and for a proclamation listing assurances he said Lincoln had given during their interview. Lincoln answered noncommittally that he had decided nothing definite, but would look into the matter. If the Cherokee remained loyal, the President would provide "all the protection which can be given them consistently with the duty of the government to the whole country."[18]

In the following weeks, Ross met Lincoln again and talked several times with William P. Dole, the capable commissioner of Indian affairs. Dole was persuaded enough of Ross's position that he publicly admitted the administration had erred—first by creating uncertainty over slavery's future, and then by abandoning Indian Territory. He allowed that in the absence of federal support, it was understandable the tribes had "quietly submitted to the condition of affairs by which they were surrounded." In addition, Ross petitioned Secretary of War Edwin Stanton to make Indian Territory a military district, with sufficient troops to protect life and property, or to allow loyal Cherokee to form a "Home Guard" under Union auspices. Lincoln also followed up, querying Interior Secretary Caleb B. Smith about Cherokee relations and proposing that a unit under the command of General Samuel Curtis be used to guard Indian Territory. But in putting the plan into force, Lincoln was still hesitant, and he requested Curtis's opinion rather than sending an order. Curtis replied that the troops "available" in the southwest were too scanty to spare; in any case, he doubted that occupying the area would be of much use. Once again, no action was taken to relieve the tribes.[19]

Meanwhile, in Ross's absence from the region, Stand Watie was made principal Cherokee chief, and the territory became a pawn of rival groups. Already "despoiled" by Confederate soldiers (some of them Watie's men), the tribes now faced equally unscrupulous federals. General Blunt's intention to return the refugees to their homes seemed well meaning, but, in reality, his own men were robbing them, and the territory was increasingly dangerous. "These Vandals have entered our houses, insulted the weak and unprotected— and stripped them of every last thing they possess," wrote an eyewitness. Government agents reportedly joined in the plunder, and the plight of the starving refugees became increasingly horrific. By year's end, wrote an observer, the camps had become "literally a graveyard." The Cherokee wanted to continue supporting the Union and to return to their self-sufficient ways, a blue-clad soldier observed, but the "cruel and disappointing" lack of assistance was undermining their loyalty.[20]

II

John Ross was not the first Native American Lincoln met at the White House, nor the last. Chiefs often came to Washington, either on their own volition or at the behest of agents or politicians. Usually one party or other hoped to gain concessions. The government wanted the cessation of hostilities, treaty amendments, or the acquisition of more land, while tribal leaders petitioned for the fulfillment of agreements already in effect, larger annuities, or an end to the epidemic of swindling. Dressed in traditional finery, the chiefs inevitably drew attention, sometimes inspiring artists and writers to record their stories and appearance. Not everyone was pleased with the commotion these visits aroused. Many tribal leaders did not particularly enjoy being gaped at, and whites who felt they had suffered at Native hands thought the notoriety unseemly. "The Red Lake Indians create a sensation here as a deputation of Indians always do," complained Minnesota editor Jane Swisshelm in 1864. "The popular sympathy of Washington is in favor of Red men and Rebels, and individuals of either class are apt to be feted."[21]

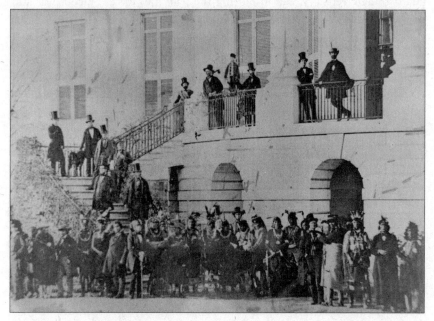

Native Americans on the steps of the White House, photograph, c. 1861–65
LIBRARY OF CONGRESS

The Lincolns began receiving Native American representatives just weeks after their first inauguration. Some of these visits seem to have been social— Mary Lincoln invited a Seneca woman to sing at a reception in early April 1861 and accepted invitations to other concerts of indigenous music. The President amused three Potawatomi delegates that same month, when he tried out the few Native words he knew, then addressed them in childlike English. "Where live now? When go back Iowa?" Lincoln awkwardly inquired, apparently oblivious to the Potawatomi spokesman's "very exceptional" English. Chippewa, Osage, Delaware, Sioux, and Winnebago chiefs entered the Executive Mansion, as well as representatives of western tribes.

Some, like John Ross, stayed in Washington for long periods, conducting in-depth negotiations.[22]

Southern Plains delegation at the White House, photograph, March 27, 1863. [In the front row left to right: War Bonnet, Standing Water, Lean Bear, and Yellow Buffalo. In the center at the back, J. G. Nicolay, President Lincoln's private secretary, and on the extreme right, Mary Todd Lincoln.]
LIBRARY OF CONGRESS

The most heralded White House meeting took place on March 27, 1863. More than a dozen chiefs were present, representing the Cheyenne, Kiowa, Arapaho, Comanche, and Apache peoples, whose hunting grounds covered vast areas of the southwestern plains. The visit had a formal agenda—to press the chiefs to amend treaties from the early 1850s that had allowed the United States to build roads, depots, and military posts guarding emigrant routes. With the discovery of gold and silver in Colorado and Nevada years later, those routes had become increasingly crowded, and the government wanted more Indian land. But the treaties had already squeezed the tribes onto ever diminishing tracts, a provision that was misunderstood by some chiefs, and unacceptable to others. The Cheyenne and Arapaho, who had already adapted to a buffalo-centered existence after being pushed out of the eastern woodlands, found the idea of living in a constricted space with limited grassland particularly repugnant. Claiming that they had been bribed to sign the original treaties, several chiefs simply refused to honor them, or to sign further documents. Others actively resisted abandoning their hunting culture. As white settlement mounted, Native American frustration also rose, and hostilities increased. Settlers blamed the Indians for loss of livestock and for terrifying attacks on their forts and cabins, while the tribesmen accused the newcomers of stealing ponies, deflowering their women, spreading disease, and encouraging drunkenness. By bringing the chiefs to Washington, the Lincoln administration hoped to win new agreements that would place the Indians on reserves that were smaller and farther from whites, and limit their movements by controlling where they could obtain goods and receive annuities.[23]

The business at hand was serious and the tribal leaders took it seriously, arriving in ceremonial attire. Photographs taken at the encounter show them wearing supple garments of buckskin or cloth, the sleeves and trousers intricately embroidered with beads. Several chiefs carried a staff of office, decorated with fur or trophies; a few sported feather headdresses and some wore soft hats, fastened with memorial pins. No bare-breasted "savages" were present, and, despite later reports, their bodies were unpainted. A journalist for the *Washington Morning Chronicle* saw "hard and cruel lines in their faces," but noted they were "evidently men of intelligence and force of character." The solemnity of the occasion was undercut by the presence of a large crowd, invited by the Lincolns to view the proceedings. Diplomats from three continents had been summoned to the East Room, as well as society grandees, cabinet officials, and newspapermen. The First Lady joined the gathering, as did Miss Kate Chase, the treasury secretary's fashionable daughter. "I am in a tremendous hurry as *we* are all going to the President's in ½ an hour to see the *wild* Indians," Benjamin French, the commissioner of buildings, wrote excitedly. For many invitees this was a rare moment. Native Americans had been uncommon on the Eastern Seaboard for more than half a century; and some knew of them only through the romantic literature of James Fenimore Cooper. Others had formed their opinions from more lurid tales of marauding bands on the frontier.[24]

As the chiefs entered the room, the crowd pressed them so tightly that the throng had to be physically held back. Nonetheless, it was reported, the visitors "maintained the dignity or stolidity of aspect characteristic of 'the stoics of the woods'" and appeared unimpressed by the trappings of the White House. They were seated on the floor along one side of the room, where the guests could better see them. Commissioner Dole introduced the chiefs one by one to the President: Lean Bear, War Bonnet, and Standing Water of the Colorado Cheyenne; Yellow Buffalo, Lone Wolf, Yellow Wolf, White Bull, and Little Heart from the Kiowa tribe; Arapaho chiefs Spotted Wolf and Nevah; Comanche leaders Pricked Forehead and Ten Bears; Poor Bear of the Apaches; and a Caddo principal chief called Jacob. While the crowd jostled rudely for the best view, Lincoln invited the chiefs to speak. Just what they said and how much they understood of the meeting is unclear, for only one interpreter had been provided for men speaking several different dialects. (Indeed, one witness later noted that the translator interpreted every speech identically.) The crowd tittered when Lean Bear, nervous before an audience, had to prop himself against a chair; Lincoln checked their laughter, but himself joined in when another earnest speech was translated as a petition for "many sausages." One tribal leader candidly remarked that his only request was that the "Great Father" send them home as soon as possible.[25]

Lincoln then addressed the group, apparently extemporaneously. His speech pointed up the differences between white and red men: the "big wig-wams" of the whites; their greater population; their evident prosperity. He advised the chiefs that this was because Europeans cultivated the land, living on agricultural products rather than wild game. The President avoided pre-scribing a course for the Indians but admitted he saw no viable path for them but to adopt the ways of white men. Lincoln went on to assert that a Euro-American aversion to war aided their success: "we are not so much disposed to fight and kill one another as our red brethren." This was a rather astonishing statement, coming as it did after decades of foreign and Indian wars, and in the midst of brutal civil strife. There were settlers who broke treaties, or whose actions were reprehensible, continued Lincoln, but the chiefs would under-stand that "it is not always possible for any father to have his children do pre-cisely as he wishes them to do." The lecture concluded with a geography lesson from Joseph Henry of the Smithsonian Institution that explained the forma-tion of the American continent, and talked of "canoes shoved by steam" that traveled around the globe. One observer thought Lincoln had admirably adapted "his ideas, his images, and his diction" to those whom he addressed. Others in the crowd found the message patronizing and suggested that "he was blending with the advice a little chaffing."[26]

Lincoln ended the ceremony by giving each chief a peace medal to wear on his breast and an American flag. These, he explained, were more than me-mentos; they were a pledge of federal protection. As he left the room, the President dryly quipped to a reporter that it was the first delegation he had recently met "which did not volunteer some advice about the conduct of the war." After he left, a photo shoot was held in the conservatory, where guests, including Lincoln's young secretaries, vied for a spot in the groupings. John Nicolay later had his photograph made into a stereopticon show, and John Hay dined out on witty stories of the visit. The Indians observed it all "with becoming gravity."[27]

It was the most succinct statement of cultural values and Indian policy that Lincoln would ever make, and an ominous one for the Native Americans. But the sobering message was lost in the White House spectacle, smacking as it did of Phineas T. Barnum's circus—indeed, literally so. The great showman heard of the visit, and paid "a pretty liberal outlay of money" to bring the chiefs to New York. Such excursions were not unheard of—chiefs were often taken to major cities to see and be seen, as well as to be impressed with the scale of the white man's empire. When an Indian agent told Barnum the chiefs would go to his American Museum only if visitors appeared to be paying homage, Barnum set up an elaborate ruse to convince them that the customers were not there to gawk, but to honor them. Barnum was a longtime Indian hater who felt no hesitation about exhibiting Native American leaders alongside armless women and two-headed monkeys, but he gave his display a further twist. While the chiefs sat onstage, without benefit of translation, Barnum described their characteristics in sensational terms. Patting them familiarly and smiling unctuously, he led them to believe he was singing their praises. He had a particular dislike for the Kiowa chieftain Yellow Buffalo, who he believed was responsible for the death of a white family. "This little Indian, ladies and gentlemen is Yellow Bear," Barnum began his deprecating monologue, starting with a misnomer, who "has tortured to death poor, unprotected women, murdered their husbands, brained their helpless little ones; and he would gladly do the same to you." Giving Yellow Buffalo a stroke on the hand, he had the chief bow to the audience, as if to admit the ringmaster's words were just. At length the chiefs discovered the game and, highly offended that people had been charged money to insult them, refused to appear again. Their "wild, flashing eyes were anything but agreeable," Barnum later recalled. "Indeed, I hardly felt safe in their presence."[28]

The Native American spectacles continued throughout the Lincoln years, to the embarrassment of some invitees. But most viewed the display as P. T. Barnum did: a kind of freak show, blending "barbarian" Indian ways and picturesque artifacts. Despite their disdain and fear, Euro-Americans were fascinated by the tribes. At the White House, Nicolay collected Indian lore and studied the "simplicity & superstition" of Native spiritual beliefs, all the while publishing articles that criticized "their idleness, their filth, their savage instincts and traditions." His conclusion was that indigenous peoples possessed "none of the beauty which the refining emotions of love, generosity, pity, or moral courage lend to . . . civilized man and woman." Renowned scientist Louis Agassiz hoped to study this "natural man," soliciting the War Department for the bodies of "one or two handsome fellows" who had died in federal prisons,

as well as the severed heads of several others. He included a recipe for em-
balming fluid with his request. Hay was also eager to collect artifacts. When
his compatriot Nicolay was on a western assignment, he asked for a pair of
beaded slippers—if, he joked, Nicolay's hide had not already been made into a
"festive tomtom." Lincoln too liked the feathers and the finery: he was sent a
handsome pair of quillwork moccasins and slipped them on with a grin. Observing the scene, Hay asked Nicolay whether he thought the exquisite crafts-
manship might persuade their boss against appointing a "peculating" man as
the tribe's agent. "I fear not, my boy," Hay concluded. "I fear not."[29]

Exactly what Lincoln's intentions were toward Native Americans is not
entirely clear. As in so many instances, his writings show ambivalence and his
words do not always match his actions. Certainly, his remarks to the Plains
delegation reflected the standard platitudes and paternalistic tone of the day.
As the Great Father, he did not hesitate to expound the Euro-American worldview, as if to ignorant children. Nor did he envision a future when different
races might respectfully share the land. "That portion of the earth's surface
which is owned and inhabited by the people of the United States, is well
adapted to the home of one national family; and it is not well adapted for two
or more," the President had told Congress just a few months earlier. Yet the
idea of educating, Christianizing, and settling the Indians on agricultural
lands was considered enlightened at the time. Many believed that obliterating
the ancient ways would not only remove the threat to white advancement but
benefit Native peoples. In hoping to acculturate the Indians there was at least
a small recognition of their humanity—though they were easily reduced to
subhuman stereotypes when it became morally or economically convenient to
do so. Some of Lincoln's fellow Whigs had sympathized with the plight of
Native Americans—notably, John Quincy Adams, who avowed that Indian
policies were "among the heinous sins of this nation"—but many did so only
when it was useful as a partisan tool. Lincoln's political model, Henry Clay,
for example, liked to thump Andrew Jackson for his callous removal policies,
even though a few years earlier Clay had declared that the "Indians' disappearance from the human family will be no great loss to the world." Only
rarely did whites spend enough time in Native communities to respect the
cultures. Sam Houston, George Thomas, General Ethan Allen Hitchcock,
and a handful of missionaries were among the very few, and, in the end, even
they acquiesced to policies that corralled the tribes. The rest of the country
simply thought the Indians should be exterminated.[30]

Lincoln's lecture to the chiefs expressed several of his strongest convictions. He had long believed that tilling the soil was an indispensable route to economic independence, for poor whites as well as people of color. He enthusiastically supported the Homestead Act, which he thought would give "every man . . . the means and opportunity of benefitting his condition." He also believed in the redeeming value of work—a pointed message for Native peoples, whose hunting culture was widely considered a lazy man's life. "*Useless labour*" was the same as idleness, Lincoln once commented; and "*idleness* would speedily result in universal *ruin*." Upward mobility, self-definition, and the value of a helping governmental hand were themes Lincoln reiterated many times. He saw successful citizens as "miners" who exploited resources for public benefit and criticized the "indians and Mexican greasers" who had "trodden upon and overlooked" the continent's mineral riches. To Lincoln's mind, using technological knowledge to tame the daunting expanse of North America meant progress and prosperity.

In addition, the power of education was almost a credo with him: a sacred obligation to harness the wisdom of the past and apply it to the future. His personal story was a testament to America's promise of a fluid society: if he believed in anything, it was the ability to rise through individual will and the application of knowledge. "Degraded" was the word he used to describe cultures that did not possess written records or depended on oral tradition to transmit knowledge—an intriguing statement from a man who made many of his most salient points as a raconteur. Adaptability was another of Lincoln's keys to success on the ever expanding geographical and intellectual frontiers of American society. Indian adoption of white ways was simply one more sign of social mobility. For Native American culture to remain static was to resist the dynamic nature of the time; it was contrary not only to enterprise and advancement but to the moral worth they embodied.[31]

Many of these assertions stemmed from Whig and Republican ideas about the nature of "progress" and the unstoppable trajectory of the country's development. Americans' abiding belief in the perfectibility of man was also at play here. Lincoln's call for Indians to "adapt or die" reflected his faith in the power of opportunity—a power he believed was embodied in the Declaration of Independence. Lincoln focused attention on this revered document in the years leading to his presidential election, reinterpreting it in many ways. In the promise of "life, liberty, and the pursuit of happiness," he saw freedom of movement, the latitude to invent and reinvent oneself, and the chance to rise through ambition and energy. It was this that led him to defend the slave's right to "eat the bread without the leave of anybody else, which his own hand earns," and to admit (at least tacitly) that the guarantees expressed in the Declaration should be extended beyond the realm of white males. "As a nation, we began by declaring that *'all men are created equal.'* We now practically read it 'all men are created equal, *except negroes,'*" he told his friend Joshua Speed, adding that he feared the nativist Know-Nothing party would like it to read "'all men are created equal, except negroes *and foreigners and catholics.'*" Lincoln never specifically included Native Americans in mankind's inalienable rights, but he hinted at it when Stephen Douglas goaded him on citizenship for "negroes, Indians and other inferior races" during the last of their famous debates. The leaders of the American Revolution, Lincoln retorted, "intended to include all men. . . . They meant to set up a standard maxim for free society . . . [for] all people, of all colors, everywhere."[32]

Yet, significantly, he never grappled with the contradiction between his ethnocentric vision of the Indians' future and the right of self-determination. For Lincoln, there was no reason Native Americans should not flourish, as long as they did so on white men's terms. The liberty to pursue a destiny different from the invaders of their continent, and to fashion a way of life unique to themselves, was not the bargain that was offered. What was offered was that they abandon any habit that seemed offensive or strange to whites, that they accept limitations on their movements, and that the value of land be viewed from the settlers' perspective. But the Indians were reluctant to abandon their traditions and worldview, which were fundamentally at odds with Lincoln's scenario. It is difficult to generalize, for nearly six hundred distinct cultures existed among Native peoples, but much of their belief embraced a concept of inhabiting, but not disrupting the land; a delicate balance between harvesting Earth's resources and leaving them undisturbed; and a commitment to ensuring bounty for the next generation. Although they could, and did, manipulate nature, they were not convinced that bending the landscape to man's will was either ethical or profitable.

For many tribes, the land itself was sacred, imbued with spiritual qualities. As the home and resting place of their ancestors, it was filled with a power that was to be respected in its own right. Acquisition was not the route to status or well-being in these societies, nor did they prize individual gain over collective good. Lincoln's concept of civilization as a community of diligent miners, exploiting nature for personal benefit, was fundamentally at odds with Native credos, as was his belief in the value of private land ownership and settled communities. In fact, farming was considered an inferior profession by many Native Americans, and toiling at any hard labor was thought demeaning. Alexis de Tocqueville observed in the early 1830s that Indians compared "the farmer to the cow who plows a furrow, and in each of our arts he perceives nothing but the work of slaves." That Indians lived on far rawer terms than many of their white counterparts is clear. That they could be ruthless is also evident: brutalities committed by Native Americans rivaled all the atrocities visited in return by whites. But their resistance to European ways, overcome in most cases only by violence against them, also bespoke pride, as well as contentment with their heritage and lifestyle. "We do not own this," the Lakota said of the grand American expanses, "we only borrow it from our children."[33]

The cultural friction was intensified by a sliding scale of expectations on the part of the whites. Whatever their loftily stated goals, that scale was pegged to self-interest. The original idea of "removing" tribes from European settlements had foreseen them as permanent residents west of the Mississippi River, but by the time Lincoln entered office, whites coveted that land too and intended to cajole, chase, or cheat the Indians to obtain it. This included the rich territory owned by John Ross's tribe, which had—strikingly—lived up to every expectation of "civilization" set out in Lincoln's culturally bound dictums, including conversion to Christianity and the establishment of a written language. None of this exempted them from the insatiable hunger of industrialists, railroad speculators, and ambitious farmers, and much of the tension that led to Cherokee defection in 1861 centered around encroachments on their property. Ownership of Indian Territory was supposedly guaranteed by treaty, but Americans of all persuasions had already dismissed the idea of Indian entitlements. The word "enough" did not exist in the vocabulary of ambition.

Republicans as well as Democrats were complicit in this—as they were in placing the blame squarely on Native Americans. Indians were frequently referred to as demons who undermined development—"Satans of the forest," "devils in the path," "evil forces that pollute the ways of the righteous." Yet Indians were not the worm in the democratic apple. The worm in the apple was the cankerous American tendency toward avarice, which turned opportunity into opportunism and allowed greed to be rationalized under the guise of progress. That complication—that the other side of Liberty's coin was etched with License—riddled the whole national saga, but was particularly true in regard to Native Americans. The entire white relation to indigenous peoples was based on the presumption that might—political, financial, or firepower—made right. Lincoln cleverly reversed this in his 1860 address at the Cooper Institute (now known as The Cooper Union), avowing that "right makes might"—but with the Indians he either could not determine what was right or subordinated it to political expedient. It was telling that Native Americans, who were disbarred from legal representation, unleashed much of their violence defending themselves against encroachments on their property. Their issues were the very ones Lincoln the lawyer had fought to protect for his clients: the right not to be swindled, rightful recognition of established boundaries and legally protected lands, and freedom of movement. The similarity between American values and Indian interests never registered with the sixteenth president, or with most other white people. In the end, Lincoln's defense of American opportunity would be distorted by the sham nobility of "progress." But for those hungrily eyeing Indian holdings, it reflected little more than appetite.[34]

III

Prior to taking office, the President had had few personal encounters with Native Americans. Indians were a legendary part of the pioneer experience, but by the time of Lincoln's birth, in 1809, most had been driven from the Ohio River Valley. The southern part of Indiana, where he spent his youth, had been home to the Iroquois, who kept it as a hunting preserve, leaving it relatively empty. The last organized Indian resistance against white encroachment in the area ended with Tecumseh's defeat in 1813. By the time the Lincolns moved to Spencer County five years later, the local Delaware and Miami peoples had ceded their lands and moved westward.[35]

Although he had little direct experience with Indians, young Abraham was influenced by the vivid tales he heard from his family. Most impressive was a grisly story of his grandfather's death at the hand of an Indian, and the near kidnapping of his father. Accounts differ, but many sources indicate that shortly after moving to Kentucky the elder Lincoln—also named Abraham—was killed while working in the fields, and six-year-old Thomas, playing nearby, was snatched up by the assailant. The eldest son, Mordecai, watching the scene from their house, shot the murderer, who dropped Thomas. In recounting the story, Lincoln emphasized that his grandfather's death had not been in a battle or fair fight but was the result of Native American "stealth." There were other tales as well. One involved his mother's dearest girlhood friend, who was taken captive when a raiding party killed her father but was later miraculously released. Another story told how a family living near the Lincolns in Spencer County, Indiana, had been heartlessly butchered by the last few Shawnees in the area—and vividly described the rough justice a vigilante group meted out to the Native men afterward. Both accounts were true. Later in life Lincoln would also hear his wife's fund of Indian lore, including the killing of Mary Todd's great-uncle during a battle with Miami and Chickasaw warriors, and how another relative was forced to run a Shawnee gauntlet and nearly lost his scalp.[36]

Such stories fed the sharp nighttime fear of the wilderness. Lincoln remembered the warnings of Indian treachery as vividly as he recalled the scream of the panther. Exaggerated or not, the tales instilled an understanding of the high stakes of survival on the frontier, and the need to subdue "wild" men if civilization was to triumph. It was also the way myth and mistrust were spread. Herman Melville, who so often had his finger on the quixotic American pulse, expressed the power of such oral traditions in *The Confidence-Man*. On the frontier, Melville wrote, a father thought it best

> not to mince matters . . . but to tell the boy pretty plainly what an Indian is, and what he must expect from him . . . histories of Indian lying, Indian theft, Indian double-dealing, Indian fraud and perfidy, Indian want of conscience, Indian bloodthirstiness, Indian diabolism. . . . The instinct of antipathy against an Indian grows in the backwoodsman with the sense of good and bad, right and wrong.[37]

The elder Abraham Lincoln's death was, in fact, more than just an adventure story: his relatives believed it had signaled a downward spiral in the fortunes of the Lincoln clan. The family typified the restless pioneers of the late eighteenth century, migrating over the years from Massachusetts to Pennsylvania, and then settling for a time in Virginia before making the trek into Kentucky around 1782. They seem to have been scrappy fortune seekers, eager to improve their lot, and willing to take on the wilderness challenge of wild beasts and violent men. (As a presidential candidate, Lincoln stated his family included some peace-loving Quakers, but, if so, they were ties by marriage.) In all their settlements the Lincolns owned substantial acreage and held positions of responsibility. There is also considerable evidence that some family members were slaveholders. Abraham senior possessed several thousand acres of fine Kentucky bluegrass and was instrumental in building the fort near which he was killed. He died intestate, and under Kentucky law the property was inherited by his eldest son, who built a handsome house with a Palladian window and fine woodwork, which still stands in Washington County.[38]

Court records indicate that that heir, Mordecai Lincoln, provided his younger brother Thomas with the opportunity to learn a trade—cabinetmaking and carpentry—and the education needed to practice it. Mordecai probably also helped his brother acquire his first property, for which Thomas paid cash. Official documents suggest that Thomas, like other Lincolns, was a respected member of the community: a landowner and stock raiser, with enough income to hold a memorable wedding, pay his debts, and make loans to his neighbors. His son, however, grew up with the impression that Thomas had been disadvantaged, becoming a "wandering, laboring boy" who attained no more education than to "bungling sign his name." Thomas's signature in court records and other documents belies this, showing a clear, practiced hand, until late in life. Neighbors noted that Thomas Lincoln's cabinetry was "sound as a trout," and the pieces left to us are marked by carvings, inlays, and fine proportions, indicating mathematical expertise and an appreciation of artistic trends. By Lincoln's boyhood, his father may have already suffered the eye injury that would undermine his ambition, and which perhaps accounts for the "bungled" writing. The sixteenth president's knowledge of family history was not perfect—the date he gives for his grandfather's murder is in error, as is the Quaker lineage. Perhaps he was simply misinformed. But Lincoln showed a consistent tendency to overstate the level of his father's poverty, and at times seems even to have scorned his own background. It may have been a matter of good politics—grassroots origins appealed to his audiences, as they do to contemporary voters. In his earliest known political address, Lincoln described himself as being from the "most humble walks of life," just as he later attached a fictional impoverished background to Henry Clay for the benefit of a Whig audience.[39]

Still, despite exaggeration, there is no question that Abraham Lincoln was raised on the frontier, in log houses that seem impossibly cramped to present-day eyes, and that as a boy he wore hide breeches, which shrank to his calves as they met sun and rain and his own phenomenal growth. Lincoln's aspirations also outgrew his environment. Southern Indiana was not a place noted for its ambition. Had settlers followed the Iroquois example, they would have shunned its poor soil, unhealthy situation, and limited potential. Lincoln's father believed he was bettering himself by moving across the Ohio to an area free from the competition of skilled slaves, and surveyed in a more regulated manner. (In Kentucky he had lost a series of property suits because of the archaic landowning patterns inherited from Virginia law.) But Thomas seems also to have made some poor decisions in Indiana—for example, following the advice of his kin to settle in a dense forest, difficult to cultivate, rather than in a town that could support his trade. There were good decisions as well, notably marrying two supportive women and establishing a community reputation for decency, generosity, and side-splitting storytelling. Thomas Lincoln was the man called on to settle disputes at the Little Pigeon Creek Baptist Church, chosen to serve on the school committee, and always willing to take out-of-luck relatives into his modest home. He was certainly not "shiftless" or "poor white trash," as some have claimed. He was a landholder and possessed the qualities necessary for success on the frontier: optimism, physical strength, and resilience.[40]

But the neighborhood Thomas Lincoln chose was far from markets or cultural centers and offered little inspiration for betterment. Those studying the region have found it was a highly egalitarian society, where landownership was the sole measure of status. There was no strong impetus to acquire worldly goods or compete with neighbors. The settlers were not lazy or improvident, but neither were they drawn by the lure of high wages or opportunities for profit. A cousin who came to live with the Lincolns remarked that the family was "like the other people in that country. None of them worked to get ahead. They wasn't no market for nothing unless you took it across two or three states." Another relative reinforced the image of Thomas Lincoln as a "man who took the world Easy—did not possess much Envy. He never thought that gold was God." When in 1830 Thomas Lincoln left Indiana for Illinois, he was evidently able to sell off hundreds of bushels of corn and scores of hogs— a far cry from subsistence farming. Still, his land dealings lost him money, and he was never able to retrieve the promise of his more prosperous ancestors. To his mind, the trouble had all started with the Indians.[41]

Some have portrayed Thomas Lincoln as a petty household tyrant, lording over his talented son like a slave driver, and a few reminiscences do paint him in that fashion. The majority, however, speak of him as did cousin John Hanks: "he was a good quiet citizen, moral habits, had a good sound judgement, a kind Husband and Father Even and good disposition was lively and cherfull." Thomas seems to have been a typical father of the era, schooled in eighteenth-century notions of the patriarchal family. Life on the frontier was difficult, and most men believed their role was to ensure survival and instill habits that would enable their children to face hardship. Sons and daughters were expected to bow to their parents' wishes and contribute to the economic welfare of the family. This was serious business, and strong words and occasional whippings would have been normal in that rough-and-ready society. The idea of the household head as a companionable guide through life's vicissitudes, or as the indulgent spoiler of a child-centered family—the "spare the rod" style favored by Abraham Lincoln with his own unruly boys—would not come into vogue for several decades, when middle-class ease allowed such indulgence. Lincoln himself denied feeling he was in bondage—but neither did he want to duplicate his father's life. This too seems normal: that a sixteen-year-old chafed under parental authority and longed to pocket his own earnings is hardly revelatory. From Thomas Lincoln's perspective, his son, no matter how talented, was not shaping up to be of much assistance on the farm, or to help him in old age—important sociological considerations in that time and place. Abe was apt to drop chores to study a book; and he was also something of a smart aleck, correcting his less educated father in front of others and even contradicting visitors. One kinsman recalled that "the worst trouble with Abe was when people was talking if they said something that wasn't right Abe would up & tell them so. Uncle Tom had a hard time to break him of this." There may have also been competition between father and son, both of whom were powerfully built and relished an appreciative audience. It is easy to imagine Thomas's annoyance when he "was telling how any thing happened and if he didnt get it just right or left out anything, Abe would but[t] in right there and correct it." According to several stories, Abe also challenged his teachers, and finally dropped out of his catch-as-catch-can schooling because he felt he had surpassed the master—which he may have done. Thomas still pushed him to learn "cipherin"—which his son later ridiculed—because he hoped to set the boy up in his own craft of cabinetmaking. Evidently Abe showed no interest in the trade; though there are two surviving pieces of furniture said to have been made by him.[42]

Later in life, Abraham showed Thomas little of the respect generally considered due the older generation. He did not assist on the farm, though his father was lame and blind, and offered only meager financial assistance, even with his law practice flourishing. As an older man, Thomas Lincoln expressed modest pride and affection for his son, despite their spotty interaction. Stories of Lincoln's refusal to visit his father's deathbed in 1851 are exaggerated, however. He had come quickly the previous year, at some expense and difficulty, when he received a letter advising that Thomas was dying and crying for his son in a manner "truly Heart Rendering." But his father recovered. At the time of Thomas's final illness, Mary Todd Lincoln was also unwell; in addition, it may have seemed just another false alarm. Unfortunately, the farewell letter penned by Abraham is quite callously worded. There is little to indicate whether Lincoln resented his parents or was embarrassed by them, or whether he only wanted to retreat to his self-created world. One thing, however, was certain: he did not want to continue the downward slide that had begun with an Indian attack on his namesake.[43]

Lincoln's most direct Indian experience came in his early twenties, when he joined the militia to fight against Black Hawk (Ma-ka-tai-me-she-kia-kiak), the Sauk leader. The Black Hawk War was the culmination of a decades-long misunderstanding between the tribes and ambitious frontiersmen in the Old Northwest. The Sauk and Fox, along with their neighbors the Winnebago and Miami, had been pushed ever westward, ultimately agreeing in 1804 to cede their homeland east of the Mississippi and move across the river. They had been residents of the area for some eight thousand years, subsisting much as the Lincolns and their neighbors did, by a combination of corn farming and hunting. According to some accounts, in the early 1800s they were so successful in the fur trade that they sold up to $60,000 worth of pelts annually. Sauk and Fox territory also included a productive lead mine, which Indians as well as whites valued. The treaty negotiation was tense and murky, with the usual difficulties of translation and cultural interpretation, which contributed to misunderstanding about boundaries, as well as the land's use after its transfer. Article 7 stated that as long as the tracts remained property of the United States "the said tribes shall enjoy the privilege of living and hunting upon them." Chiefs who agreed to the sale believed this meant that they would have perpetual use of the land, which included their ancestral burying grounds and other hallowed places.[44]

The concept of selling land itself was foreign to the Sauk and Fox culture. Black Hawk stated this clearly the following year: "My reason teaches me that *land cannot be sold.* The Great Spirit gave it to his children to live upon, and cultivate . . . and so long as they occupy and cultivate it, they have the right to the soil. . . . Nothing can be sold but such things as can be carried away." Moreover, the documents had little meaning for the chiefs. They were unable to read them to start with; but, in any case, paper agreements were not part of the Sauk tradition of honor. When Edmund P. Gaines, the general in charge of Indian relations for that region, spoke with Quash-ma-quilly (Jumping Fish) about the treaty, the Sauk spokesman said he was told his people had been released from the arrangement. Asked for legal proof of this, he replied: "I am a red skin & do not use paper at a talk, but my words are in my heart, & I do not forget what has been said."[45]

The federal government saw it differently. Under pressure from settlers who coveted the mines and fertile river lands, they began selling the property in 1829. For a time the tribes coexisted with whites in uneasy proximity. The pioneers became increasingly anxious, however, as frictions between the Sauk and Fox and their rivals, the Sioux, filled the night air with war cries, making movement dangerous. One local scout overheard Black Hawk warning against the loss of ancestral forests, as well as complaining that costly government goods were being shipped to the Sioux. "Shall the treasures of the pale-faces reach their destination?" the scout heard Black Hawk cry. ("A fierce and thrilling shout" was the only answer to his question.) In 1831 a settler remarked that tensions were not just setting nerves on edge, but retarding emigration. Rumors of an Indian war, he noted, excited "as much dread among the frontier settlers, as does the howling of wolves among sheep."⁴⁶

Over the next year the unrest grew, as Black Hawk moved many hundreds of Native families to an area around Rock River, not far from the lead mines. The sixty-five-year-old warrior was not strictly a chief—indeed, many of his own tribe saw him as a chronic malcontent and troublemaker. Keokuk, head of the Sauk, a shrewd and pragmatic man, was among those who tried to dissuade Black Hawk. But the Hawk and his followers were heavily influenced by a spiritual leader called The Prophet, who believed that the purity of native traditions needed to be revived. Under his influence, the clan determined to plant corn annually on their ancient territory. Black Hawk's motive was in many ways idealistic: even the army men sent to restrain him were impressed by his sincerity. When Black Hawk spoke of "the tie he held most dear on earth," recorded one officer, "on . . . his fine face there was a deep-seated grief and humiliation that no one could witness unmoved." The Sauk leader ignored official warnings to leave. Complaints from farmers began to escalate— including some from men who were themselves illegal squatters. "You cannot imagine the anoyance," wrote one. "The citizens of some of the counties made no crops last year, & can make none this year. Business of every kind is che[cked]. . . . Horses & cattle &c &c are every day stolen and the whole country is kept in a constant state of alarm." Black Hawk refuted the charges, vowing he had done nothing beyond peacefully growing corn on inherited lands. But when he crossed the river again in April 1832, Illinois governor John Reynolds declared it an "invasion" and called out the militia.⁴⁷

Abraham Lincoln joined several thousand young men in answering the governor's call. His motivation remains uncertain. He was an itinerant worker at the time, living far from Rock River, without property to protect. Perhaps he felt some latent vengeance for his grandfather's death; perhaps, as a friend suggested, he was stirred to action by the local "Patriock Boys," who had signed up to "Defend the frontier settlers . . . from the Savages tomihock and Skelping Knife." Another acquaintance said Lincoln left the impression the campaign was largely a "holiday affair and chicken-stealing expedition." He was mustered into the Fourth Volunteer Regiment in late April 1832.[48]

Lincoln's company consisted of sixty-nine local men, a rough lot by all accounts. A traveler who saw the volunteers described them as "unkempt and unshaved, wearing shirts of dark calico"; and a fellow militiaman called the band "the hardest set of men he ever saw." Like the others, Lincoln had no arms of his own and was issued a smoothbore flintlock rifle. Emotions ran high. Many had given up their spring plowing and hopes for a good crop to wage the war. Few had sympathy with Native concerns. "I wish some of your Presyters folks was here that was so troubled about the Indians being hurt," one wrote, alluding to the Presbyterian reputation for compassion toward Native Americans, "they wood sing another song." All were ready for a fight, Lincoln included. A comrade recalled that he "often expressed a desire to get into an engagement" and wondered how the hardscrabble boys would "meet Powder & Lead."[49]

Lincoln was elected captain of the company, something he later remembered with pride. His selection may have been due to his physical prowess— he could beat almost everyone at racing, jumping, or wrestling, and he took on any bully who threatened his crowd. Some of the men claimed the volunteers idolized their captain and would follow him anywhere. The circumstances of the election, however, were questionable and recollections vary. The men all spoke of Lincoln without rancor, but some suggested he was "indolent and vulgar" and had been chosen to spite another candidate, or because of his reputation for laxity. Discipline was, in fact, a serious problem with all the volunteer companies. Crisp commands and orderly camps were rare. Captain Lincoln's authority followed this pattern. Reportedly, his men responded to commands by saying "Go to the devil, sir!" or broke into whiskey barrels and drank until they were unfit to march. At times they were so rowdy that they could not be directed even to cross a fence. Lincoln was punished for his laxity, as he was for excitedly shooting off his gun without authorization. But he was far from alone in his want of authority. Another officer in the battalion reported there was no effort to drill troops, that they obeyed or disobeyed as they pleased, and sarcastically concluded: "this way men may grow grey in service without becoming soldiers." The problems mirrored the disorganization of the campaign as a whole, which included a chronic lack of coordination between the untrained volunteers and regular troops. Colonel Zachary Taylor, one of the senior officers, described it as simply "a tissue of blunders, miserably managed from start to finish."[50]

Lincoln's tenure as captain was short. After thirty days the conflict was largely contained and his regiment was disbanded. He apparently told his law partner that he reenlisted because he was out of work and had nothing better to do. He was again mustered in, this time by Lieutenant Robert Anderson, who would later gain fame as Fort Sumter's commanding officer. (Anderson was one of several latter-day luminaries who took part in the 1832 war. Others included Albert Sidney Johnston, Jefferson Davis, and Winfield Scott.) In his two subsequent tours Lincoln was not reelected captain and joined the units as a private. He was initially part of Elijah Iles's Mounted Rangers, which was formed in response to a call for horse troops that could chase the elusive Indians more effectively. When that unit also disbanded, Lincoln was attached to Captain Jacob Early's Free Spy Company. Formed for reconnaissance work, the unit was elite and autonomous, taking orders directly from the commanding general, drawing no guard or other duties, and receiving a larger allowance of rations.[51]

In all this, Lincoln saw few hostile Indians and virtually no action. The campaign consisted largely of pursuing Black Hawk's warriors around the northwest corner of Illinois, trying to block their raids on forts and settlements. At this they succeeded badly. In one instance they passed through an area where two hundred Fox lay in wait, without suspecting them; two days later they discovered to their horror that local white settlements had been burned and the terrified survivors were huddled in a stockade. Time and again they were outmaneuvered by their Native opponents, arriving too late to assist local residents. As Lincoln would later write, it was not a war "calculated to make great heroes of men engaged in it." Due to mismanagement, the green volunteers were futilely marched long distances on the double-quick, while supply trains lagged far behind. Lincoln later recalled the absurdity of the organization, as well as the hardships, admitting that he was often hungry. It was "the quintessence of folly," one of Lincoln's compatriots in the Fourth Regiment reported. "No doubt Gen. Black Hawk was much amused and not a little edified in the arts military by his civilized and *scientific* enemies."[52]

Participants remarked that it was fortunate the full chaos of their organization was not known to the Indians, or the militia might easily have been slaughtered. Lincoln was present in the aftermath of one disorderly disaster, an engagement known as Stillman's Run, which appears to have made a lasting impression. In mid-May, Black Hawk, believing he was outnumbered and despairing of hoped-for support from the outside, apparently sent a group of three men under a white flag to negotiate with the state troops. Either missing the flag—or mistrusting its sincerity—the militia imprisoned the braves and fired on another group that approached. Outraged, Black Hawk then attacked the camp at dusk and, to his surprise, routed the much larger force with a small band. The militia had been drinking, and virtually no discipline had been maintained in the battle. It was a "disgraceful affair," Taylor reported, with settlers fleeing in terror, and the army missing a perfect chance to force Black Hawk back across the river "without there being a gun fired." The Sauk and Fox warriors suffered few casualties, but twelve militiamen were killed. The Fourth Regiment arrived the next morning, finding the mutilated bodies still on the field. Lincoln later gave a vivid description of the scene to a reporter, recalling the revulsion of seeing hacked and scalped men, and how the reddish early morning sun bathed everything in a bloody light. Others verified the grisly scene, describing headless corpses, and shallow graves dug with hatchets and hands, in the absence of proper equipment. Lincoln was part of that burial detail. It was, as he said, "frightful."[53]

Finally, in midsummer, Black Hawk's braves were cornered on the Wisconsin border at the Battle of Bad Axe. From start to finish the campaign had been a debacle. Begun as a protest against the duplicity of the treaty process, it ended with death and defeat for the Sauk and Fox. For the white settlers it devolved into a panic, fostering fear, economic loss, and the spread of cholera, which was brought to the area by the regular troops. Lewis Cass, the secretary of war, vowed to make an example of Black Hawk and his followers. He advocated humane treatment for the leaders—they were more valuable as hostages than dead. But the tribes had now lost their bargaining power and they were swiftly banished so far to the west that another attempt to return could never be made. The full tragedy was that the Sauk and Fox, although beset by intertribal rivalries, had made their peace with white expansion, feeling it was better to adapt than engage in endless confrontation. "I cannot be persuaded that the Indians crossed our border with any hostile intention beyond that of raising corn for their subsistence," wrote one of the more circumspect members of the Fourth Regiment, "and whilst I freely grant that this was an infraction of the treaty of Rock Island . . . the manner in which we have attempted to repel it was as unwise and injudicious as the result has proved disastrous and inglorious." Ironically, in many ways the shady practices and inflationary ways of the land speculators posed a greater threat to settlers than did the impoverished Indians. But the presumption of the whites, with their open disdain of

Native American ways, and their insatiable taste for resources, provoked a deadly conflict where one need not have occurred.[54]

To the end Black Hawk believed that the land of his ancestors was worth holding and his tribe's honor worth defending. In a dignified speech, he told his jailers he was proud to have fought those who despised him and would rest in peace for having attempted to save his nation. After a few months he was released, and, in a curious reversal of fortune, was sent on a mission to the Eastern Seaboard, along with his eldest son and The Prophet. Journalists interviewed the warrior; he sat for portraits and was paraded before "Great Father" Andrew Jackson, in much the same manner as the Plains chiefs during Lincoln's time. Assessing the huge cities and the government's power, Black Hawk had the last, apocalyptic word. "I see the strength of the white man," he told a reporter. "They are many, very many. The Indians are but few. They are not cowards, they are brave. But they are few."[55]

Wabokieshiek (known as The Prophet), Black Hawk in European dress, and his son Nasheaskuk, oil on canvas, by James Westhall Ford, 1833
LIBRARY OF VIRGINIA

IV

How much Abraham Lincoln reflected on his Black Hawk War experience is not known—generally he deprecated the conflict and his role in it. But the same tragic cycle of fraud, displacement, and retribution continued to spin uncontrollably during his presidency. He certainly had a similar conflict in mind when John Ross walked into his office in September 1862. An eruption of violence by the Dakota and Ojibway peoples of Minnesota a few days earlier had created panic, and a demand for government action. Ross protested that the Cherokee had nothing to do with the Minnesota crisis and that relations should be based solely on the provisions of his own treaty. Nonetheless, pressures created by the Dakota may well have influenced Lincoln's ambivalence about the situation in Indian Territory.[56]

The Dakota, particularly the group known as the Santee Sioux, were a people of decided personality. Missionaries described a lively culture with a sophisticated calendar of ceremonial games, music, and dancing. The Sioux were "naturally reverent," wrote one minister, with a language that contained no profane words. They lived a stable, semiagricultural life, growing crops and hunting buffalo and other game. They were also known for their tall, merciless braves, who were feared by other Indians as well as by whites. The common frontier sign for the tribe was a hand drawn sharply across the throat. The Dakota's ferocious fighting ability had allowed them to dominate the upper plains for centuries, but they were rivaled by their bitter enemies the Ojibway (or Chippewa), a distinctive linguistic and cultural group. In 1851 the Dakota agreed to cede some 24 million acres of land to the United States, for the usual consideration of annuities, gifts, and protection. The new treaty confined the tribe to a narrow, 150-mile-long strip on the Minnesota River. In 1858 this treaty was amended—a hard bargain that allowed government roads and forts on the property; penalized the Dakota for destructive acts; and forbade alcohol. Neither side strictly upheld its provisions.[57]

With the rush of settlers to the area came increased efforts to acculturate Native Americans to white ways. Attempts to develop settled agricultural communities and instill habits of European dress and religion had some success. However, despite the efforts of sympathetic missionaries such as Episcopal bishop Henry Whipple, many Sioux felt the superimposed values were at odds both spiritually and materially with their way of life. The "civilizing" process created significant tensions between those who became farmers and leaned toward white society, and the majority of tribespeople, who wished to retain their traditional culture. As Sioux chief Big Eagle (Waŋbdí Tháŋka) explained, farming was considered women's work, beneath the dignity of a brave; and the "cut-hairs"— those who adopted the ways of the settlers—were mistrusted. Nor were the motives of the missionaries and federal agents benign. There was obvious arrogance in assuming white ways were superior, but the government also meant to undermine traditional social structures and diminish native cohesion. "The theory, in substance, was to break up the community system among the Sioux; weaken and destroy their tribal relations; individualize them by giving each a separate home and having them subsist by industry," admitted Thomas J. Galbraith, an inexperienced businessman whom Lincoln appointed as the Dakota agent. Internal tribal conflict grew, and several antiwhite leaders were selected for chiefdom a few months before the uprising. Control over their increasingly restless people collapsed. Attacks on farmer Indians increased, and war drums were heard in the night.[58]

Yet the most immediate reason for the violence was the Dakota's chronic mistreatment by government agents and traders. The habit of appointing officials with few qualifications—save ambition and political connections—had long been established, but it reached a crescendo under Lincoln's administration. Situated in remote locations and holding large quantities of cash, the agencies had many opportunities for malfeasance. Agents misrepresented available funds, colluded with traders, and absconded with gold sent for tribal annuities. Some openly solicited the aid of the Bureau of Indian Affairs to do so. Galbraith cynically remarked that "the *biggest* swindle" pleased the bureau best, "if they but have a *share* in [it]." A few weeks later five thousand dollars was found missing from his agency. In the months preceding the outbreak, Chippewa chief Hole-in-the-Day (Bug-o-na-ghe-zhisk), an educated man and accomplished leader, conducted his own investigation into fraudulent behavior against his tribe. He found records that stated he had been given twice the monies he actually received, and he traced the corruption to senior Republicans. Traders also exploited the Indians' different understanding of loans and property by advancing large amounts of food, clothing, and other goods against annuities, which many chiefs believed was a generous gift. When they called in the debts, the Indians, who kept no books, and could not go to court, were unable to dispute them. "There was always trouble over the credit," Big Eagle stated. In addition, traders encouraged the Native American thirst for whiskey, despite its express prohibition in the 1858 treaty. Seven months before hostilities began, George E. Day, a commissioner sent by Dole to look into corruption, wrote Lincoln personally to report that the situation was reaching a breaking point. The Sioux and other chiefs requested their "Great Father" be told "of many wrongs they had suffered from the Gov Agents and especially *Traders* the *greatest Curse* of the Indians and the *Curse* of the *nation*," he declared. When Day traced the fraud to congressmen and Lincoln appointees, he was recalled.[59]

Bishop Whipple chimed in two months later, pleading with the President to address conditions before a tragedy occurred. "The United States has virtually left the Indian without protection," he wrote. "Thefts, murders and rapes are common and no one pays more attention to them than if they were swine." Rape was a particular source of anger for the Dakota. Their own culture prized sexual fidelity: as one observer wrote, the "women are so chaste, that . . . certain death follows any breach of the marriage tie." Officials, merchants, and soldiers had an ugly history of abusing tribal women, either through brutal violation, or by "marrying" them, then abandoning the "wives" when they became inconvenient. In addition to the psychological and physical cruelty involved, the production of so many mixed-race children destroyed the kinship lines that were the basis of Dakota society. Henry Sibley and Alexander Ramsey, both governors of Minnesota, as well as Henry M. Rice, a trader turned senator, were among those believed to have illegitimate children of Dakota blood. James Lynd, an agency clerk, deserted his Indian wife and child in late 1862; his murder was one of the actions that triggered the Minnesota conflict. Even John Hay bantered to Nicolay with sly vulgarity about having a dalliance in the bushes with an Indian maiden for "two bits."[60]

The government had decades of experience with the Indian system's corruption, yet its excesses only seemed to multiply. Lincoln passed over the warnings, referring the matter to subordinates. In early 1862 he approved the appointment of another callous politico, Clark Thompson, to serve with Galbraith as agent to the Santee Sioux. Both men proved unpopular, as well as unequal to the sensitive conditions. By that summer, when thousands of Dakota arrived at the Yellow Medicine Agency to collect their annuities, the atmosphere was volatile. Crops had failed the previous season, and some Dakota were subsisting on little but roots and acorns. The annuities were delayed, partly because of a debate over whether they should be paid in gold, as stipulated in the treaty, or in new, war-driven greenbacks, and partly to give agents time to "riddle" the books and take their cut. Tempers flared. The Dakota were nervous and needy, an Indian Bureau inspector told Lincoln, and outraged at the "insulting taunts of the Agents," one of whom told them if they were hungry they must eat grass or "'their own—excrement' (I soften the word)." By mid-August, when four Sioux teenagers killed a white family, in what was evidently an isolated incident, the atmosphere was primed for an explosion.[61]

The Dakota were divided on whether to escalate the violence, and their newly elected chief, Little Crow (Čhetáŋ Wakhúwa Máni), was especially skeptical about the wisdom of a war party. But his braves were exasperated, and, fearing revenge for the murders in any case, Little Crow acquiesced. The next day he led a surprise attack on the Lower Sioux Agency. Among those killed was Andrew Myrick, the agent who had rudely counseled the Indians on their dietary possibilities: he was found with grass and excrement stuffed in his mouth. White inhabitants panicked, fearing a massacre while so many men were absent in the Union Army. Unprepared for the conflict, the settlers nonetheless staged a valiant defense, sometimes with improvised weapons.

LITTLE CROW,

Little Crow, Sioux chief and leader of the Indian massacre in Minnesota, photograph, 1862
LIBRARY OF CONGRESS

At undermanned Fort Ridgely the Dakota were pushed back, as they were in New Ulm, where a good deal of burning and looting took place. Governor Ramsey telegraphed Washington that widespread slaughter was under way; others reported that half the settlers had flown. There were rumors that Confederates had fueled the unrest to harass the North with a "fire in the rear," though no proof was ever found. Nevertheless, popular cartoons depicted Jefferson Davis swearing in Indians as part of his "Scalping Bureau" and there was a widespread fear that there might be a coordinated uprising by all the Plains tribes.[62]

Accounts of Indian savagery filled newspaper columns and officials' ears. Governor Ramsey reported lurid stories of "Infants hewn into bloody strips of flesh, or nailed alive to door posts to linger out their little life in mortal agony . . . young girls . . . outraged by their brutal ravishers, till death ended their shame." John Nicolay, dispatched by Lincoln to assess the situation, could not refrain from describing nights made "hideous with fiendish yells and horrid music of their war dances." Most of these stories were exaggerated,

132   VANITY FAIR.

THE TERRIBLE CHIEF "HOLE-IN-THE-DAY;"
TAKING THE OATH OF OFFICE FROM PRESIDENT DAVIS, AS HEAD OF THE SCALPING BUREAU.

"The Terrible Chief 'Hole-in-the-Day'; Taking the
oath of office from President Davis, as Head of the
Scalping Bureau,"
wood engraving, *Vanity Fair,*
September 13, 1862

but the reality was grim enough. Many frontiersmen and -women who had nothing to do with swindling the tribes were murdered, including some who had worked to coexist peaceably. Atrocities did take place, particularly at the hands of Red Middle Voice and his followers, who specialized in hacking off the limbs of their victims and leaving them to bleed to death. Settlers in isolated communities were especially vulnerable, and much of the violence took place outside pitched battles. Most Native American leaders, including Little Crow, did not approve of such behavior—killing legitimate enemies in combat was considered a noble obligation, but slaughtering civilians was thought cowardly. Some tribal members refused to fight at all, and others guarded and protected whites with whom they had associated. With his followers fragmented, and the war's momentum spoiling his advantage of stealth and surprise, Little Crow was defeated at the Battle of Wood Lake in late September. By Lincoln's estimate, eight hundred whites had been killed, though this figure is now believed to be an overstatement.[63]

A volley of complaints arrived in the President's office from terrorized Minnesotans who wanted the tribes eradicated or removed completely from their state. "Exterminate the wild beasts and make peace with the devil and all his host sooner than with these red-jawed tigers whose fangs are dripping with the blood of the innocent!" thundered Jane Swisshelm, editor of the *St. Cloud* [Minn.] *Democrat.* "Get ready . . . and be sure they are shot dead, *dead,* DEAD, DEAD!" Survivors warned Lincoln that leniency would only allow the Indians to "dance around their war fires" boasting that "we *dared* not punish them."

State legislators pressed the cabinet for revenge, pushing so hard that Navy Secretary Gideon Welles thought they "were but slightly removed from the barbarians they would execute." Religious groups and some scrupulous officials also wrote to the White House, arguing for a radical remake of the system that had launched this disaster. Bishop Whipple traveled to Washington, an official Episcopal condemnation of Lincoln's actions in hand, as well as a six-point plan for reform. Like others, he blamed federal policies for "dragging the savage down to a brutishness unknown to his fathers, it has brought a harvest of blood to our own door." When he met with cavalier treatment by officials, Whipple publicly railed against the "lack of statesmen," and called for some wisdom, beyond small-minded politicians who could only "talk and bluster."[64]

Caught in the crossfire, Lincoln sent Dole and Nicolay, as well as Assistant Secretary of the Interior John Usher, to assess the situation. They helped deflect tensions with Hole-in-the-Day, whose complaints had never been addressed, and reported that although a genuine tragedy had occurred, local accounts of the carnage were exaggerated. Usher wrote a balanced assessment, criticizing the Sioux for recklessness and barbarity, but laying equal blame on the malicious actions of agents, and a pitiless system that had made tribes dependent, then left them with "the impression they had been abandoned." The President chose to respond more to white fears than calls for reform. He approved a significant militarization of Indian affairs, one that would come to define the government's future interaction with Native peoples. At its head, Lincoln placed General John Pope, an avowed foe of the red man, who had disappointed the nation at Second Bull Run and needed reassignment. Pope heightened tensions, peppering the War Department with excited messages ("Universal panic prevails along the whole frontier"), and requesting men, supplies, and approval for a prolonged campaign to exterminate all Plains tribes, whether or not they had participated in the violence.[65]

The tug-of-war between retribution and reform reached a straining point with the popular clamor to execute those thought to have led the uprising. A military commission condemned some three hundred to be hanged, and Pope and General Henry Sibley, who were charged with keeping peace, requested authorization to carry out the punishment. The "trials" had been little more than a sham, averaging only a few minutes per case, and lacking in solid evidence. Objections arose from whites who claimed to have been saved by friendly Dakota, some of whom were on the execution list, but Pope warned that if the sentences were not fulfilled, a posse of Minnesota citizens would rise up and slaughter the prisoners. Lincoln tried to duck the decision, asking

Judge Advocate Joseph Holt whether he could delegate the responsibility to a subordinate. When the judge replied that clemency could only be granted by the President, Lincoln followed Dole's recommendation to study the accusations seriously—and then execute only key leaders. Dole and his office did a careful assessment and Lincoln again bowed to their judgment, ordering a stay of execution for all but thirty-nine men, who were believed to be the ringleaders. Included on the death list were those who had led massacres, as opposed to fighting battles, and Indians thought to have raped white women—though only two cases of this could be credibly proved. There was also a question whether the Native Americans should be treated as prisoners of war, rather than criminals, under the laws of military justice. It was a fine line, as Lincoln noted, between acting "with so much clemency as to encourage another outbreak on the one hand" and avoiding "real cruelty on the other." Many Minnesotans were outraged at the pardons and vowed to take private revenge. Nonetheless, when thirty-nine Dakota were hanged on December 26, 1862, it was the largest mass execution in American history.[66]

Dole had wanted to steer a course toward justice, and Lincoln, despite the outcry against him, also believed the administration's decision was fair. "I could not hang men for votes," he told Governor Ramsey, who protested the decision. However, the President had made a bargain on the executions, and it was not a lenient one. In return for clemency, he agreed to dispossess the Dakota of lands, annuities, self-governance, and freedom of movement. The cost of the fracas was paid by the Treasury, but those warriors who had not been hanged remained in captivity, without specific charges. Among them were several who were praised for their aid to the whites, and forty-nine who had been acquitted but never released. Lincoln's comment to the governor's query about their fate was that it was an "unpleasant subject" that he would deal with later. During the next few years, sixty-seven Dakota would die in prison under unspeakable conditions. Big Eagle, who had been singled out for his role in saving white lives, was incarcerated for years, and even when Lincoln finally ordered his release, the request was ignored for some time. Had he imagined his treatment in that penitentiary, the chief later stated, he would never have given up. "I had surrendered in good faith, knowing that many of the whites were acquainted with me and that I had not been a murderer," he protested.[67]

In March 1863 a removal bill was passed by Congress that exiled the Dakota outside the boundaries of any state. Most of the dispossessed were farmer Indians who had helped white captives during the uprising. The Winnebago, who had taken no part in the conflict, were also deported. Some cabinet members saw through the elaborate justification for this, questioning Pope's actions. "The Winnebagoes have good land which white men want and mean to have," Welles remarked in his diary. After weeks of deprivation and forced transport, the Native Americans were deposited on the Crow Creek reservation, a harsh spot known to be inhospitable for agriculture. Lacking water, food, and even the most basic shelter, and left without guns and horses that would allow them to hunt, the Dakota faced "a desert as to location, starvation as to condition." For a while the federal troops fed them a concoction of gruel, offal, and dead mules, but by spring, the Indians were dying in large numbers. The following winter it was reported that they were "now [at] *midwinter* so universally naked, that one half of them positively cannot get out of their tents . . . the young and old and feeble, are *actually freezing to death.*" The women were particularly vulnerable. Sibley's diary speaks of soldiers "wild as deer," and how he had "the greatest difficulty keeping the men from the Indian women when the camps are close together." He expressed hope that their intercourse was consensual, but that was unlikely, given the circumstances. An inhabitant at Crow Creek recorded that the reservation girls were pressed to attend dances "gotten up by white men" that were "a disgrace to humanity." There was testimony of similar behavior at Davenport, Iowa, where the prisoners were being held. There the squaws were systematically sexually assaulted, sometimes by gangs. Reportedly, some were used for target practice. Lincoln, who had made such a nicety of searching for violators of white women, took no action to control his own men's predilection for rape.[68]

As conditions worsened at Crow Creek, some of the tribesmen were allowed to wander in search of food, and others were again relocated, to somewhat better lands on the Omaha reservation. But further deprivation came about as a result of hostility between the Winnebago and other tribes. The War Department's rivalry with the Indian Bureau, as well as Pope's belief that the Native peoples should be under strict military control, caused more hardship. Under the severe regime, Indians were forbidden activities that "whites do without censure," including playing sports, holding hunts, and enjoying traditional festivals. At the same time, agents, traders, and soldiers continued to promote the use of alcohol, harass the women, and make "general trouble." A proposal made by Dole in early 1865, that "friendly" Dakota be allotted tillable eighty-acre plots, was turned down as being unacceptable to white Minnesotans. A local missionary wrote the epilogue on Lincoln administration policy for the Dakota: "Exhorted to abandon hunting, and with no means or encouragement to open farms, no education to any trade, merely subsisted and played with by the Government, hundreds of Indians are fast becoming mere beggars, and their children growing up without knowledge of any honest or manly way of obtaining a livelihood." When several chiefs begged assistance to change the situation, he remarked: "They are like men praying for life."[69]

V

One reason Hole-in-the-Day was outraged was that several attempts had been made to impress Chippewa men into the Union Army. There were rumors that whites had enlisted a group of mixed-bloods after plying them with drink, and Hole-in-the-Day swore there would be trouble if any more braves were taken. At the Crow Creek reservation, the Winnebago were also told their "useless" men might be drafted. This was not official policy—Dole had, in fact, resisted conscripting Indians, who were generally not American citizens and thus ineligible. But Lincoln had just called for 600,000 more men, substitutes were needed for those avoiding service, and there were bounties to be had. The tribes were well aware of the white man's war and found it somewhat duplicitous that United States representatives should counsel them to avoid intertribal fighting while they themselves were engaged in a deadly fratricidal conflict. Sioux agent Galbraith reported to Washington that "when I have upbraided them for going to war with their hereditary enemies, the Chippewas, have they replied to me thus: Our Great Father, we know, has always told us it was wrong to make war; now he is making war and killing a great many; how is this?"[70]

Nonetheless, some twenty thousand Native Americans did participate in the war, often with distinction. The Union was initially reluctant to take on Indian fighters, despite their reputation as fine warriors. Iroquois leaders met resistance when they began to recruit, and there was particular reluctance for the idea of commissioning Indian officers. Ely S. Parker (Hasanoanda, later known as Donehogawa), who as a lieutenant colonel served as adjutant to General Ulysses S. Grant, was initially rebuffed when he tried to sign up in his native New York. He was finally forced to move to Pennsylvania to be accepted in the Army. Ultimately he was brevetted brigadier general in 1867. John Ross's offer to form a cavalry unit from his expert horsemen was also lukewarmly received by Lincoln, who continued to view Cherokee loyalty

General Ulysses S. Grant and his staff, with Ely S. Parker seated on the left,
carte de visite by John Adams Whipple, c. 1865–74
COURTESY OF SPECIAL COLLECTIONS, FINE ARTS LIBRARY, HARVARD UNIVERSITY

with skepticism. When General James Blunt, on the remote western flank of the war, suggested enlisting the help of friendly tribesmen to counter Confederate incursions, he was curtly told that "it was not the policy of our government to fight high-toned southern gentlemen, with Indians." The *Detroit Free Press* also scorned the idea of such recruits, saying a move by the state legislature to arm and equip a regiment of Native Americans "cannot be too strongly reprobated." After the Dakota outbreak, there were rumors that tribesmen in Wisconsin were looking for excuses to arm themselves and infiltrate settled areas. Others feared that white soldiers would balk at serving alongside Native men or would be sabotaged by them. For many, the "wild men of the forest" seemed dangerous enough without handing them government weapons.[71]

By early 1862, however, the demands of war were severely testing the Union, and prejudice took a backseat to augmenting the army. In March of that year, Dole finally wrote Parker to say that although he would not draft Native Americans, he was grateful for volunteers, paving the way for Parker to raise a Seneca regiment. Indian outfits became increasingly common as the war went on. The units participated in some of the fiercest engagements of the war, including at Fair Oaks, on the Chattanooga campaign, in the worst fighting at Spotsylvania, and with Sherman on his March to the Sea.

Pamunkey Indians in Virginia volunteered as scouts and gunboat pilots on the tricky Chesapeake river ways. A Cherokee and Creek "Union Brigade" was formed that took over much of the defense needed in Indian Territory, participating in significant engagements at Locust Grove and Honey Springs. Ross's son James was a member of this brigade; he was captured by the Confederates and died in prison. Particularly notable was Company K of the First Michigan Sharpshooters, made up of elite marksmen from the Ojibway tribe. Rallying under their mascot—a large, live eagle—they were at the front of the action, taking punishing casualties and inflicting them as well. During the desperate fighting in the Wilderness, one of the company, Daniel Mwa-ke-we-naw, single-handedly killed thirty-two rebels, a number of them officers. At the Petersburg Crater, the unit was praised for its "great coolness," despite its many casualties. "Some of them were mortally wounded," reported an onlooker, "and clustering together, covered their heads with their blouses, chanted a death song—and died." Fifteen members of Company K were captured and sent to Andersonville Prison, where at least seven perished. Native Americans also joined the Navy. Iroquois sailor William Jones, for example, worked on the USS *Rhode Island* during the assault on Fort Fisher, and made journal notes about his struggle to adapt to the language and culture of his white comrades.[72]

For the most part, the performance of Native American troops earned praise. In Kansas, General Blunt thought the Cherokee and Creek men performed "excellent service for the Union cause." William Dole officially commended the role of Wisconsin's Menominee tribe, reporting that they made "brave and enduring soldiers, coming easily under discipline." A member of Company K was recommended for the Medal of Honor for his valor at Petersburg. Some soldiers remarked on differences in fighting style. "Indians were good skirmishers, but didn't like the open country or pitched battle," wrote one, seeming to imply that they preferred silent tracking or irregular action. However, the actions of the Company K seem to belie that idea, as do tactical manuals of the day, which gave skirmishers a formidable role, one in the forefront of the killing field. Yet, despite noteworthy participation under fire, resentments about Indian forces smoldered on both sides. The color prejudice that plagued black troops also affected Native American soldiers, who suffered taunts and ostracism from their Union comrades, along with lower pay. Confederate soldiers felt insulted facing Native troops, just as they disliked fighting against African Americans. In some instances, such as at the Crater, Indian soldiers were purposely slaughtered when captured by the rebels. Many men were also suspicious of what they saw as "sly" habits of stalking or subterfuge. Elisha Stockwell Jr., a white volunteer in the Fourteenth Wisconsin, wrote at Kennesaw Mountain of the way Indians of Company F could sneak up on the enemy without being seen or heard, and how one captured rebel protested the "unfairness" of this ploy. From the Indian point of view, the white style of warfare—with men exposed, in gigantic, fruitless struggles—was laughably unproductive. Chief Hole-in-the-Day personally advised Lincoln of this. "All no good," he said, according to Nicolay's transcription; "give me fifty thousand men, I fix 'em." He would hunt rebels as he hunted Sioux, he told the President, in ambush or with sudden, swift surprise. "Somebody," the chief concluded, "would have been hurt."[73]

Clearly, Native Americans performed well in combat, but what inspired them to volunteer? Whatever the merits of the Union cause, this was not a country that had shown them either generosity or respect. At bottom, most tribes wanted to protect themselves, and sometimes this influenced their actions. The Cherokee, for example, had briefly aligned with the Confederacy because of concern about their status as an independent nation. Treaty obligations also came into play: the Cherokee, as well as the Menominee and other tribes, were bound by agreements to aid the United States, something John Ross took seriously. Some Indian leaders hoped to parlay wartime participation into a better position in treaty negotiations, or to use it as leverage to have white squatters removed from their land. Others were sincerely antislavery. "To be driven to the man-market for sale is, we think, a rank offense before the Great Spirit, and a foul blot on the Grand Republic," an Odawa man wrote in 1862. Despite the fact that many Cherokee, including Ross, were slaveholders, that tribe also formally abolished the practice after the Emancipation Proclamation was issued. In some instances, there was a financial motivation. The need to support families was an issue for the Ottawa men of Company K, who, after being forced to cede land to the government, became increasingly desperate when drought and insects spoiled their crops. The tribal destitution is startlingly clear in a remarkable photo of Mohicans of the Stockbridge-Munsee band, which shows them being sworn into the Union Army dressed, literally, in rags. For men such as these, enlistment bounties were a tangible incentive. Native American traditions also played a role in mobilizing soldiers. Indian braves had a long history of battlefield courage, and in many tribal societies manhood could only be truly proven in war.[74]

Mohican Indians of the Stockbridge-Munsee band
being sworn into the Union Army,
photograph by Thomas Bigford, 1861
WISCONSIN HISTORICAL SOCIETY

The rationale was clearer for those who allied themselves with the South. Indeed, nearly four times as many Native Americans fought with the Confederacy as joined Union forces. For some, the proximity of Southern white communities made them natural allies, particularly among those who defended slavery. Six chiefs in the Wichita Agency wrote early in the conflict that they were of "one heart" with Texans and their institutions and pledged to join their fight against "the cold weather people." In South Carolina, the Catawba had been forced to vacate most of their land by 1861, and were dependent on local white society for work, goods, and liquor. Facing necessity, and attracted by adventure and potential glory, they joined the Confederates, becoming one of the most committed of the Indian contingents. In addition, Native Americans and Southern whites frequently shared the belief that nationhood was based on kinship and racial identification rather than legal or administrative structures. The Confederate government sweetened the deal with advantageous treaties and the promise of respect. Among the Five Nations, internal political motives also influenced alliances with the South. Stand Watie, while sympathizing with Confederate aspirations and views on slavery, created a platform for his "Southern Rights" Party that was far different from the official Confederate line; for him, fighting against the Union was largely a pretext for the larger goal of undermining John Ross. In the disarray following Ross's flight to Washington, when Watie was made chief, he was, for a time, successful in his bid for power. But he was unable to maintain unity within his nation, and as the war progressed, Cherokee commitment to a coalition with the South wavered.[75]

Jefferson Davis had begun with a good game plan for Native American relations, but as time went on trust was eroded by Confederate malfeasance and neglect. Although Watie and others volunteered to fight with the rebel army, for example, some Indians were dragooned into the service. Many were sent to coastal fortifications around the Cape Fear River, where they were essentially treated as slaves, working in deep water even in winter, without proper food or clothing. Some eastern Choctaw were forced against their will to fight—until they deserted en masse during the Vicksburg campaign. The more enthusiastic troops faced suspicion from ranking officers, particularly after reports of scalping—largely disproved—came from some battlefields. After this, Watie and his regiment were confined to protecting Indian Territory. Unprofessional practices created additional mistrust between Native American forces and Richmond officials. Albert Pike, who had so successfully brokered treaties with the Five Nations, continued to favor Indian units but was frustrated by the confiscation of arms, rations, and supplies designated for them. He protested vigorously to Davis, stating that arbitrarily changing policies—always to the detriment of the Native men—left them "weary, disheartened, disgusted, plundered at every turn," and unable to fight with a will. Other officers complained of antiquated or defective armaments, arguing that the Indian regiments would have been quite effective if properly supplied. Habitually late pay—or no pay at all—was another complication. By summer 1863 Creek chief Moty Kanard was pleading with the white "Father" in Richmond to "aid and effectually assist his distressed and sinking children," who had been left "with few exceptions, unarmed, most of the time without ammunition; bareheaded, barefooted, without bread, and body in rags." Watie also wrote to Confederate officials, in elegant language, protesting the "lethargy and procrastination" of officers in the West, whose "lack of spirit, inactivity, and apparent cowardice" kept them from defeating Union forces. Davis and General Edmund Kirby Smith responded with soothing words, but their policies essentially did not change.[76]

The Confederate government thus created a kind of circular dilemma for itself, since Indian absenteeism increased in proportion to the army's malfeasance. This was particularly true after battles such as the July 1863 confrontation at Honey Springs, where Confederate forces were defeated as much by inadequate equipment as by Union prowess. The "general Spirit of dissatisfaction and desertion became contagious," wrote a Cherokee participant, "and . . . what could we do against an enemy three times our number better armed and equipped than we were? I suppose we could have made a sacrifice of ourselves . . . but I don't Think the occasion required it." After such scenes, some regular officers scorned the dependability and effectiveness of Native American troops. "The Indians come and go at will, or nearly so. Their whims and caprices have been pandered to until it is impossible to put any reliance in them," General William Steele advised Richmond. Concerned that he might be blamed for the setback, Steele asserted that "the policy of raising brigades of Indian troops will only result in an increased expenditure of public money without an adequate increase of the fighting strength."[77]

Despite widespread nervousness about their constancy, many Native American outfits gave valuable service to the South. Watie was among the disenchanted after Honey Springs, calling the Confederate coalition a "useless and expensive pageant; an object for the success of our enemies and the shame of our friends." Still, he did not want to give up—and indeed, he did not. He had unusual soldierly ability, which he harnessed in a series of guerrilla campaigns that destabilized Union forces. Northern opponents saw Watie as unpredictable and ruthless, particularly after reports that his horsemen systematically slaughtered African American forces, including wounded men. But he was heralded by Confederates for "the brilliancy and completeness" of actions such as the capture of major Union supply trains at Cabin Creek in late 1864. Promoted to brigadier a few months later, Watie was the last Southern general to lay down arms, not leaving the field until June 23, 1865. As it happened, the final Confederate legion to surrender east of the Mississippi was also led by a Cherokee. William Holland Thomas (Wil-Usdi) had put together a formidable force of several hundred warriors, who served as spies and sentinels in high country, blocking Union incursions into the mountains. They continued to stymie their foes for six weeks after the defeat of Robert E. Lee.[78]

VI

While Stand Watie was threatening Ross's authority and Cherokees were suffering devastation by two armies, the chief faced yet another challenge. This was the proposed removal of an unrelated tribe—the Delaware—into Indian Territory. The crisis resulted from the frantic competition for land that followed Kansan statehood in 1860. After Kansas was opened to white settlement in 1854, it had become a hotly contested area. None of its five million acres were public—all were tied to intricate treaties that forbade the sale of property or its use for industrial development. Squatters as well as speculators chafed at this. They smelled opportunity when the 1860 Republican platform called for construction of a transcontinental railroad to the Pacific coast and a homesteading policy that encouraged white landholding. A New York firm was one of many that lobbied Lincoln to support railroad growth, avowing it would bring "the productive wealth of free labor [and] . . . the riches & fruits of mineral and pastoral enterprise." Lincoln endorsed these policies enthusiastically. By the time of his inauguration, the lust to exploit western riches had grown into a freewheeling grab after acreage and railroad rights and a scramble to position men for power and profit. In the case of the Delaware, the President was personally involved in a murky affair that led to their displacement.[79]

Among those betting on expansion was a group of prominent Republicans in eastern Kansas. The consortium included Thomas Ewing Jr., a well-known politician and General Sherman's brother-in-law; James Lane, who would later serve as one of Kansas's first senators; and Governor Charles Robinson. In 1857 they contracted surveys for the Leavenworth, Pawnee and Western Railroad (LP&W), which proposed linking Leavenworth with Fort Riley to the west. The obstacle in their path was a rich tract owned by the Delaware. By the 1850s a good many schemes had been devised to dupe Native Americans, but the backers of the LP&W developed a new ruse. The terms of the Delaware's treaty with the federal government stated that all tribal interactions should be conducted by Washington, which theoretically would protect Indian rights. The LP&W, however, began to negotiate directly with the chiefs, giving federal watchdogs promises or paybacks to remain silent. In 1860 they made a bold move by concluding an unofficial agreement to buy several hundred thousand acres of prime land, which they hoped to incorporate into an amended treaty. Their goal was something more than merely acquiring a right of way for the new railroad—they also wanted surplus acreage that could be sold to finance the construction of the tracks, and used as collateral to raise more capital. Samuel Pomeroy, a Republican who would become one of Kansas's senators upon statehood, was against the sale, saying it defrauded the tribe; but the real reason was that he was heavily invested in a rival rail line. Nonetheless, Ewing's group quietly slid the amended treaty through Congress, and President Buchanan signed it in August 1860.[80]

By the time Lincoln took office, an opposition had formed, with lawyers and interpreters claiming that tribal leaders had been willfully misled, plied with liquor, or threatened with a loss of annuities if they did not sign the amendment. In May 1861 the LP&W was close to a dream deal: acquisition of nearly 224,000 acres at $1.25 per acre, paid for by a mortgage on the excess land they expected to sell. This was a rock-bottom rate, based on a large-parcel sale under closed bid, and the Delaware, who had been advised that at a public auction their best property could fetch up to $50 an acre, were wary. Had the treaty been enforced as written, it did contain guarantees for the Delaware, including designated tracts for tribespeople, a provision that they would retain title until the line was built, royalties for valuable timberland, and an understanding that they would remain on the land. Both opponents and supporters of the treaty lobbied Lincoln hard as the complicated transaction was completed. In the early summer of 1861 Ewing traveled to Washington to try to seal the deal.[81]

Lincoln was brought in to mediate the disagreement. He told one investor that he was against swindling the Indians, which may have been the case. But others recounted—only hours after the meetings—that his real concerns were negative publicity and alienating the powerful congressional lobby that opposed the new treaty. Nonetheless, he finally acquiesced, optimistically stating that the agreement would benefit the country, as well as protect the Delaware, because the government would hold their land rights in bonds. Yet Lincoln also personally agreed to let the LP&W execute the bonds for $286,742—secured by the huge tract they were allowed to keep in reserve—without laying out a penny. In so doing, the President tacitly admitted that the Delaware's holdings had been undervalued, and that the 123,000 acres which the company was now free to sell or mortgage to other parties were worth at least the amount placed by appraisers on the original 223,996 acres. Lincoln thought the arrangement would be square if the new provisions could be incorporated in a revised treaty, which the tribe could approve or reject before it was sent to the Senate. He selected Commissioner Dole to carry out the mission, and by late summer Dole had succeeded in gaining the chiefs' consent. Tribal leaders trustingly declared they were signing the new treaty because "they believed their Great Father to be a good man, and would do justice by his red children."[82]

The chiefs' concurrence gave a veneer of legitimacy to a one-sided bargain. Yet, it was here, under the veil of "consent," that the real fraud was revealed. For in implementing the agreement, the discrepancy between stated policy and actual intention became crystal clear. As a former railroad lawyer, familiar with property values and legal instruments, Lincoln understood this. Months later, he admitted he was uncomfortable about the arrangement, saying he was "down on all such matters, that there had been so much said about cheating the *Poor* Indians &c &c." But he agreed to see it through on the basis of "personal considerations" with his political crony Mark Delahay, who was also a Kansan. Thomas Ewing Jr. exposed the true situation in the elation of his letters home. "I am on the high road to fortune," he announced to his sister; and to his father he gloated that they had paid nothing, guaranteed only $1.25 an acre, and felt "assured of being able to sell 15.000 to 20.000 of the best land this fall at about $7.00."[83] Corruption continued as administration officials got kickbacks from the arrangement. Interior Assistant Secretary John Usher, who had initially represented the Delaware, switched sides when Indian pickings began to look slim. He then gave legal counsel to the LP&W, undermining the integrity of his office. He also handed notes for land to lobbyists, as well as to the comptroller of the currency, General James Blunt, and John Nicolay. In the long, muddy debate over treaty ratification, Pomeroy, Delahay, Governor Robinson, and a double-dealing translator named Charles Johnnycake all received positions, stock, or parcels of land—sometimes comprising thousands of acres. [84]

The LP&W never sent any money to the Delaware. When the first payment came due, the road was not yet begun, so the company was not obliged to forward any cash. Construction was hindered by difficulties of wartime financing, endless lawsuits over prime routes, and Lincoln's decision to designate Omaha, rather than eastern Kansas, as the eastern starting point for the transcontinental road. In the end, only a few miles of the LP&W were ever built. Although the 1861 treaty stated that ceded land would be forfeited if the railroad was not completed "in reasonable time," the Delaware never regained their property. Before the treaty was even ratified, the LP&W began selling the land, poaching on Delaware timber reserves, and expelling tribespeople. Rather than enforce the provision for restoring ceded land, Lincoln proposed deporting the Delaware to Indian Territory. The removal ignored cultural and kinship differences between the tribes, as well as treaty assurances to both the Delaware and the Cherokee pertaining to sole and perpetual possession of their tracts. Ross, ever the statesman, offered a generous deal, by which the Delaware would share educational institutions, have use—though not ownership—of communal land, and enjoy all the protections of the Cherokee constitution. But settlement of another tribe among his people was the beginning of Ross's worst nightmare. This was not just a legal violation, or the theft of land, but the loss of identity: an ominous erosion of the proud and distinct Cherokee heritage.[85]

Corruption created conflict and weakened the government's hand in dealing with complex Indian matters. It also undermined the very goals Republicans were trying to promote. In his 1864 report to Congress, Lincoln spoke of his concern for Indian welfare, but it was framed within a call to close the territorial gap between the Atlantic and Pacific states and to secure western riches for white entrepreneurs. In actuality, insider deals worked against the populist principles of the Homestead Act. Lincoln had supported that act as a kind of safety valve "so that every poor man may have a home," but, as passed, it applied only to public property—that already held by the government. Private agreements like the one brokered by the LP&W allowed prime land to become the booty of corporations and speculators. Settlers, both legitimate and squatting, were ineligible to start homesteads on the property and unable to compete at auction with the inflated land prices. The government was also outbid. Lincoln believed—or at least stated—that encouraging railway development and the access it provided would advance emigration. But speculators, and the complicated transfer of titles, so tied up the land that it could not be settled. In the end, railroads themselves proved a mixed economic blessing. Despite the justification of wartime necessity, few lines were constructed during the conflict, yet the companies received vast tracts and important mineral rights for the routes they proposed. This culminated in the Pacific Railway Act of 1864, which granted a whopping 12,800 acres for each *projected* mile of track—offering far more incentive to *plan* lines than to build them.

The railroads that were proposed often did not link together, because the more mileage a circuitous route took, the more profitable it was to the investors. With virtually no governmental regulation and a shaky loan structure, the game became one of personal profit, masquerading as public advantage.[86]

By December 1862 even Lincoln was fed up with the nefarious doings of the system, telling a Republican backer he was "greatly mortified at the manner that Indian affairs has been conducted in Minnesota and Kansas," and hinting there was to be a clean sweep of the Bureau of Indian Affairs. But the broom was never applied, and the pattern of questionable deal making and corrupt administration continued. As with the Delaware, disadvantageous treaties with the Ottawa, Kickapoo, Potawatomi, and others were negotiated directly with holding companies under coercive circumstances—and then "railroaded" through the Senate ratification process. Lincoln's mailbag was filled with complaints about the agents appointed by his government, a record of such incessant chicanery it could be taken for slapstick, if the consequences had not been so terrible. Some Indian superintendents literally begged to be sent representatives with "clean hands and pure hearts," but most agents continued to be appointed because of political connections or personal favoritism. Old friends from the Black Hawk War, unemployed cronies from New Salem, the Illinois town where Lincoln had lived in his twenties, and the President's personal doctor all made the grade, though he drew the line at commissioning his nearly illiterate stepbrother. From Oregon, New Mexico, Colorado, and Utah came stories of agents paying annuities in worthless scrip, abusing Native women, or working Native Americans as slaves.[87] Both contemporary observers and careful scholars have concluded that corruption and politicization of the Indian system reached its zenith during Lincoln's presidency. The result, complained frontier folk, was that hostilities had actually escalated, making their life "intolerable" under his administration. One missionary calculated that tribal antipathy to whites increased tenfold in the 1860s. It was, wrote another, "a blunder and a crime."[88]

William Dole was only too aware of the system's shortcomings and sincerely hoped to reform it. A friend of the president from their days on the Eighth Judicial Circuit, Dole had little experience, but he had a zest for learning, and was more honest than most. His purposefulness compensated in part for the inertia of Caleb B. Smith, the administration's initial secretary of the interior, and Assistant Secretary Usher's compromised activities. Moreover, he had a concrete Indian policy. Like Lincoln, Dole believed the Native Americans' best hope for survival was to adopt a settled agricultural existence. He was optimistic about the prospects for this, citing in an early report that it was "a demonstrated fact that Indians are capable of attaining a high degree of civilization." He was also candid about the responsibility for bloodshed, pointing the finger straight at whites. In many cases, Dole noted, reservations were entirely surrounded by settlers, and Native Americans were subjected to constant swindling and encroachments. "If a white man does them an injury, redress is often beyond their reach," Dole reported to Congress. "If one of their number commits a crime, punishment is sure and swift, and oftentimes is visited upon the whole tribe." His remedy was the establishment of smaller, more easily protected reservations, with better educational facilities, amalgamated tribes, and restrictions on white entry. In Dole's eyes this would mark clear boundaries between the worlds of red and white men. Ultimately the plan would rob Native peoples of yet more territory, autonomy, and identity, but Dole was convinced it was both practical and humane. He persuaded the President, who endorsed it in his annual message to Congress in 1862.[89]

VII

Not everyone agreed with this comparatively benign program. The Army was among the factions that sympathized with more radical views. For decades military men had been responsible for frontier security, and some officers had spent their entire careers fighting Indians. Many thought the military should be handling Native American affairs, and a rivalry between the War and Interior Departments arose over the issue. Most soldiers believed that only raw power would compel the Indians to give up their "savage" ways. When Robert E. Lee was sent to patrol the Comanche in the late 1850s, for example, he justified his punishing raids as "the only corrective they understand, & the only way in which they can be taught to keep within their own limits." General Samuel Curtis, commanding the Department of Kansas, agreed that this was the most effective method of bringing the Indians "to terms." "I abhor the style," he wrote, but admitted that "the popular cry of settlers and soldiers on the frontier favors an indiscriminate slaughter, which is very difficult to restrain." John Pope sent a group of searing letters to the War Department, proposing the tribes be forced to abandon their way of life by putting them under strict martial control. Pope was no supporter of the system as it stood, which he believed goaded the Indians into retribution. But he also believed that, like "maniacs or wild beasts," they could be "tamed" only by force. He advocated moving the tribes far from white areas and restraining their movement by prohibiting horses and other trappings of nomadic life. Under Pope's plan there would be no treaties, no annuities, and no firearms: the Indians would have to labor on white terms to survive.[90]

In 1863 an amalgam of Dole's and Pope's theories was implemented in New Mexico Territory by General James H. "Jimmy" Carleton. Historically the area's trail routes had been troubled by periodic ambushes, but by the time Carleton arrived these had greatly diminished. Destitute Apaches still lived by plunder, but their neighbors, the Navajo, had developed an economy based on herding and trade in their finely woven blankets. "They are said to be intelligent and industrious, and their manufactures . . . in their neatness and finish, go far to prove this," reported a military man in 1850. Nonetheless, the Army thought that "forbearance exercised towards the Navajos would be mistaken humanity; and the blood of our own citizens would be the fruits of it." Carleton, who ruled his department with near dictatorial force, imposed a harsh removal policy on the Apache, Navajo, and other regional tribes. "The purpose now is never to relax the application of force with a people that can no more be trusted than you can trust the wolves that run through their mountains," he reported to Washington. Theoretically the campaign was meant to separate peaceful from warring factions, but the real goal was to capture the tribes' rich livestock holdings and orchard lands, as well as to open the area to prospecting. Carleton employed a reluctant Kit Carson to break up the Indian communities, ordering the murder of all male tribesmen, a scorched-earth policy, and no negotiation. Under instruction, Carson seized or destroyed stock, crops, and homes, leaving the starving tribes with little will to resist, especially as winter set in. In January 1864, in a final act of self-defense the Navajo faced Carson at Canyon de Chelly, where they were beaten back, largely by the use of howitzers. The eight thousand destitute and demoralized survivors were forced on a three-hundred-mile march to a remote reservation called Bosque Redondo, already populated by Mescalero Apache, who had been their sworn enemy for centuries.[91]

Carleton optimistically predicted the Navajo would become a "happy and contented people," and that under the sympathetic direction of missionaries a successful agricultural society would be developed at the reservation. It was not to be. The experiment was thwarted by drought, destructive insects, and the broken spirit of the tribes. Navajo agent Michael Steck protested to Washington, but Dole would not overrule the military and the removals continued. The cruelty of the "Long Walk" became a point of harrowing memory to the Navajo, but in official eyes Carleton's ruthlessness had paid off. Harassment diminished along routes like the Santa Fe Trail, and with nearly three-quarters of the tribal population displaced, the Indians were kept from menacing white development. New Mexicans hailed Carleton as a hero.[92]

Thus the pattern continued through the Civil War years. Anxious to maintain tenuous telegraphic and postal links to Pacific states, and concerned that western resources be kept firmly under Union control, the Lincoln administration instructed the Army to maintain order in the West, giving it a great deal of latitude in doing so. In places like Bear River in Washington Territory, provocations on both sides ended in full-scale operations by federal forces. At Bear River, the Shoshone, whose land was being invaded and food supply destroyed by settlers, were nearly reduced to beggary. A series of raids by Indian teenagers triggered retaliatory action in January 1863, during which the under-armed Shoshones were killed by the hundreds. In the frenzy of battle, army men apparently lost control, and appalling atrocities followed. It was the largest mass killing in the long, sad chronicle of white-Indian relations, yet the incident went largely unnoticed. But soon, in November 1864, this relentless cycle of raid and reprisal reached such an extreme that lawmakers were finally forced to take note.[93]

In Colorado Territory, disgruntlement over treaty amendments—which had brought the Plains chiefs to see Lincoln in 1863—heightened as the full impact of the arrangements was felt. John Nicolay, sent to assess the situation, gazed at the small, scruffy tracts assigned to hunting tribes and forecast trouble. Some Indian groups were refusing to recognize the new boundaries, now less than a twelfth of their former holdings. A group of Cheyenne and Lakota braves, known as "Dog Soldiers," considered its members openly at war. They were stealing livestock, attacking supply trains, and sometimes murdering pioneer families. Tempers flared, particularly when the victims' scalped bodies were put on public display. But other leaders, such as Lean Bear and Black Kettle of the Northern Cheyenne, and Nevah of the Arapaho, had come to believe that conflict with the white man was unproductive and signaled their desire to cooperate. The new territorial governor, John Evans, took a hard line against the marauders, doubting the chiefs' profession of peace. Governor Evans's policy, as he succinctly noted, was "to exterminate the Indians . . . and that seemed to be quite a popular notion too." His request for permission to call out the militia was endorsed by Lincoln, and, in the spring of 1864, soldiers began destroying Indian settlements. During one raid, Lean Bear emerged from his tipi signaling friendly intentions and was shot dead—with President Lincoln's protective medal around his neck. Fearing coordinated retaliation by several tribes, or an uprising instigated by the Confederacy, Evans declared all-out war on the Indians. With War Secretary Stanton's blessing, he authorized vigilante groups to attack Native camps and keep the plunder. His actions were backed by General Samuel Curtis, who was similarly determined to rid the plains of Indian "mischief."[94]

Among those leading the militia forces was Colonel John Chivington of the Union Volunteers. A Methodist minister by profession, he had taken an extremist view of frontier conflicts, famously stating: "I have come to kill Indians, and I believe it is right and honorable to use any means under God's heaven to kill Indians." Evans agreed, adding that "the only way to fight Indians is to fight them as they fight us; if they scalp and mutilate the bodies we must do the same." With land disputes becoming increasingly problematic, prices rising, and settlers nervous, Evans felt under pressure to act. The upcoming fall elections also influenced him. As a founder of the Republican Party in Illinois and a longtime Lincoln crony, Evans was eager to secure the territory solidly for his faction, and he had his eye on a potential Senate seat. Chivington, too, had political ambitions, along with dreams of frontier fame. In a final effort to offer protection to friendly tribes, Evans directed them to take refuge near U.S. forts. But the orders were miscarried, and Black Kettle was told to return to a distant winter camp near Sand Creek. With most braves away on the annual buffalo hunt, the settlement was left largely defenseless—populated by women, elderly men, and children.[95]

With the term of his troops about to expire, and his own commission exhausted, Chivington took a parting shot at the Indians. He marched 675 men several hundred miles to Sand Creek, mountain howitzers in tow. Ignoring the Dog Soldiers and other hostile bands, Chivington instead surprised Black Kettle's peaceful camp at sunrise on November 29. Believing there had been a mistake, the chief is said to have hoisted the American flag over his tipi, along with a white banner. The militia, fired by Chivington's vengeful Old Testament language, nonetheless launched a full-scale attack. The few braves present were poorly armed, and Chivington's men had cut loose their horses, so they were forced to wage a "running fight" against a line of rifle and artillery fire. One soldier noted in his diary that the Indians "were peppered with gun ball and grape most effectually, slaying them by the hundred." Most of the Cheyenne fled in terror; others were slaughtered as they huddled under the Stars and

Stripes. Statistics vary, but 135 to 200 were killed, two-thirds of them women and children. The atrocities that took place in the wake of battle became notorious. Even allowing for exaggeration, testified one officer, "the recital is sickening." Children's heads were dashed against rocks; fingers and ears amputated for their jewelry; both male and female bodies grossly mutilated. Eyewitnesses reported that women's genitals were cut off and worn as trophies; another soldier spoke of scrotums being made into tobacco pouches. The local press lauded the raid, boasting that "Colorado soldiers have again covered themselves with glory." Chivington claimed he had faced twice his number and killed 800 bloodthirsty heathens. "Posterity will speak of me as the great Indian fighter," he bragged. "I have eclipsed Kit Carson." He dismissed the tales of savagery as lies told by jealous rivals. Cheyenne and Arapaho chiefs, who had heard Great Father Lincoln's vow of protection, could only express dismay. How could it be, asked one, that a man they thought so powerful "was unable to constrain his white people as well as control red people."[96]

Chivington's actions were popular in Colorado, but elsewhere reports of the massacre were met with horror. A few weeks later, Congress called for an investigation. Over the next months representatives interviewed dozens of witnesses, sent a delegation to examine Indian conditions in both New Mexico and Colorado, and published their findings in a five-hundred-page report. They did not mince words when describing Chivington's excesses. "Wearing the uniform of the United States, which should be the emblem of justice and humanity," sputtered Senator Benjamin Wade, "he deliberately planned and executed a foul and dastardly massacre which would have disgraced the veriest savage among those who were the victims of his cruelty." The War Department, hoping to justify its soldiers' actions, also sent a representative to assess the campaign. General Alexander McCook, a veteran of Indian wars in the Southwest, traveled to Colorado, confident that he was unburdened by any "mawkish sentimentality" toward Native Americans. He found the hostilities at Sand Creek "the most cold-blooded, revolting, diabolical atrocity ever conceived by man or devil." Chivington's attack on peaceful tribes and his failure to chase rogue bands, reported McCook, added poltroonery to his barbarity. Some of those who testified before the Joint Committee on the Conduct of the War were murdered in Colorado streets, yet when newspapers began carrying the salacious details, there was a public cry for reform.[97]

Abraham Lincoln did not respond to the Sand Creek massacre. The congressional investigation was still ongoing when he was assassinated, and he had been loath to withdraw Evans, Dole, or Curtis from power. He told his doctor, Anson Henry, that he did not want to chastise allies. "The thing that troubles me most," Lincoln said, was not the gross injustice done to Indians, but that he disliked "the idea of removing Mr Dole who has been a faithful and devoted personal & political friend." (Andrew Johnson would quickly dismiss Dole and Evans, collapsing their national ambitions, though Evans retained influence in Colorado.) As for Black Kettle, he was one of the few who escaped Chivington's slaughter, but he was left profoundly disillusioned. "I once thought that I was the only man that persevered to be the friend of the white man," he said in August 1865. "My shame is as big as the earth."[98]

VIII

On several occasions during his term, Lincoln called for "remodeling" the Indian system. Acknowledging its woeful state, he noted that "our imperative duty to these wards of the government demand our anxious and constant attention to their material well-being." Henry Whipple found the President an attentive listener when he called at the White House in 1864 to describe the desperate condition of the Dakota and Winnebago. The bishop was disappointed, however, when Lincoln made no promises and ushered him out with a story about a plantation owner who had a monkey capable of picking cotton faster than a slave. The problem was that it took two overseers to watch the monkey, said the chief executive, concluding: "This Indian business needs ten honest men to watch one Indian Agent." According to a thirdhand account, Lincoln reportedly also said the "rascality" of the agents affected him "until I felt it to my boots," and vowed he would make sure the Indian system was restructured. But, if the account is true, he was never shaken into action. Public antipathy to the Indians also influenced Lincoln, who was particularly concerned with popular opinion. Editor Jane Swisshelm found people so bored and frustrated by "the hopeless medley of Indian perplexities" that everyone just passed on the responsibility to someone else, "Congress throwing it on the President and the President waiting for the people." Secretary Stanton spoke candidly on this point when Whipple tried to enlist his help. He refused to see the bishop, instead sending him a message saying: "the government never redresses a wrong until the people demand it. When he reaches the heart of the people, the Indians will be saved." Lincoln's lack of administrative skill also contributed to the impasse; he never got the habit of effectively juggling the multiple concerns that make up the portfolio of every president. Those apologizing for his failure to curb inhumane practices have contended he could not be expected to deal with extraneous issues under the heavy pressure of war. But this argument would be more persuasive if Lincoln had not spent such a remarkable amount of time in his anteroom, focusing on people and policies of little consequence, or at the War Department, worrying over issues that would have been better delegated.[99]

There is little reason to doubt the sincerity of Lincoln's belief that he was promoting Indian welfare by pressing them to adopt white ways. Yet for all the well-meaning pronouncements about "civilizing" Native Americans, there was little relish for incorporating acculturated red men into American society. The Lincoln administration continually allowed hostile actions against tribes that had clearly moved toward its vision of a settled existence. The Delaware, victims of the LP&W scandal, were described by Dole as "much further advanced in civilization than I had been led to suppose," dressing like Europeans and living on well-cultivated farms. The Santee Sioux had also largely accommodated to whites before the 1862 swindle at their agency. The Navajo, as well as Black Kettle and Lean Bear, had reluctantly acquiesced to a nearly complete forfeiture of their property, and were promoting peace when their people were slaughtered. The successful amalgamation of white and traditional culture by the Cherokee was neither recognized nor protected, and they too were dispossessed for white advantage. Far from welcoming educated Native Americans, most people preferred to keep them in malleable ignorance. A missionary commented that nobody in the country "cares one straw" for assimilating the Native population, "and very few would care to have them different or better than they now are." As John Ross was tragically to find, clothes and customs were not the problem, for white attitudes were shaped by something cruder: those twin incubi of American idealism—race and greed. As a congressman succinctly noted, "the vineyard was coveted and the vineyard was to be had."[100]

Ross was disappointed when he left Lincoln's office for the last time. Dismay turned to despair as his people—so proud of their accomplishments, so sure of their path—were forced into a chattel relationship with the United States. Suspicion of the Cherokees' Confederate connections had grown with Stand Watie's aggressive warfare, and Ross did not help his case by lobbying Dole for a large government expense account. The administration increasingly saw Indian Territory as a necessary outlet for the troubles in Kansas, and it soon became convenient to ignore treaty agreements altogether. Ross, understanding exactly what opening his territory to whites and other tribes would mean, began bargaining for a new treaty, designed to end the long practice of official abuse. He demanded a onetime settlement on price and boundaries, the right to grant trading licenses and approve entry onto Cherokee lands, and a congressional delegation equal to that of other territories. That he did so with a high degree of professionalism was not appreciated—an Indian who understood his rights and could legally defend them was not what most whites wanted to see. When a new treaty was forthcoming, it read very differently from Ross's proposal. Instead of rectifying the litany of wrongs, it punished the Cherokee for their support of the South by diminishing their lands and undercutting their institutions. A year after war's end, they too had become desperate and dependent; physically and emotionally starved. With nothing left of his life's work, within a few months John Ross died, brokenhearted.[101]

By almost any measure, the Lincoln administration was catastrophic for Native Americans. The Civil War caused tribal divisions and destruction of their holdings. The advance of the railroad and the voracious quest for land and minerals decimated hunting grounds, squeezing tribes into ever more restricted circumstances. Militarization of Indian policy laid the groundwork for the armed defeat of Native peoples in the coming decades. The miserable reservations onto which they were herded became places of physical deprivation and spiritual death. In his zeal for the advance of white culture, Lincoln would scarcely have named destruction of the Indians as a hidden political goal. Yet it was not a case of good intentions leading to unexpected consequences. The consequence Lincoln *desired* was to clear these people from the pathway to what he considered "progress" for his own tribe. Native Americans had no real place in his plan. There are indications that the sixteenth president wanted to be fair—his clemency in the Dakota execution, for example, was followed by the pardon of Shoshone chief Pocatello after the Bear River massacre. But it was "fairness" based on unfair assumptions. This was recognized in his own day, in debates that flourished around him. One need only look at congressional discussions about broken treaties, corrupt agents, and the ethics of forcing tribes into starvation to see that the morality play was unfolding before Lincoln's eyes. John Nicolay's on-the-ground reports, observations from his close friends in Indian agencies, Whipple's imploring remarks, and the continued pleas of his frustrated commissioner of Indian affairs make it hard to believe the sixteenth president was unaware his nation was moving inexorably toward the destruction of a people.[102]

The tragedy of Lincoln's policies is most poignant when placed within the lustrous framework of his reputation as a defender of human rights. To speak as eloquently as he did of values embodied in the Declaration of Independence is to be accountable to those values: they cannot be donned and discarded for convenience. Yet one of the defining paradoxes of Lincoln's term as president is the gap between his nobly expressed intent and his failure to take robust action to sustain those ideals. On one occasion he rhetorically included Indians in the grand principles of self-definition and security from tyranny, but in practice Lincoln never applied these "inalienable rights" to Native peoples. The power of self-determination was not extended to them, nor was the liberty of self-expression. He maintained that "if there is any one thing that can be proved to be the will of God" it was "the proposition that whatever any one man earns with his hands and by the sweat of his brow, he shall enjoy in peace"; but the Indians' right to hunt and thrive unmolested on their ancient lands was never practically upheld. Instead, the policies of his administration rolled over the prairie like tumbleweeds, depositing seeds of avarice and exclusion and choking out conscience, until the country was at the brink of genocide. Lincoln claimed to revere universal truths, but acting on white self-interest, Lincoln's relation to Native Americans reminds us that a finely turned phrase and a ready laugh do not a humanitarian make.[103]

THE STRONG WOMEN'S LEAGUE.

WHAT between Dr. DIO LEWIS's system of parlor gymnastics,

"The Strong Women's League," wood engraving, *Vanity Fair*, May 30, 1863

5

HELL-CATS

Heads turned when a woman with soft eyes and brown curls entered the Executive Mansion, quiet as a small bird. It was a familiar face to most of those present, as it was to much of the world. Her work had been greatly acclaimed, setting abolitionists to beaming and slaves to cheering, but Harriet Beecher Stowe was a self-effacing woman, who maintained the credit should rightfully go to God. "I merely did his dictation," she protested. The only person who did not recognize the author of *Uncle Tom's Cabin* when she arrived on December 2, 1862, was Abraham Lincoln. Senator Henry Wilson had given her a spirited introduction, but the President was not listening, and the name slipped by him.[1]

Stowe was not surprised. She did not like this man, who ignored her letters and looked about distractedly; moreover she was distressed over the conduct of the war, which she thought slow and indecisive. She viewed the conflict in moral terms—a war about rescuing an oppressed people from unspeakable cruelty—not constitutional niceties. A few weeks earlier, when Lincoln publicly declared he would keep every slave in bondage if that was the only way to save the Union, Stowe had shot back her own views. "My paramount object in this struggle is to set at liberty them that are bruised, and *not* either to save or destroy the Union," she wrote, parodying the President's style. "What I do in favor of the Union, I do because it helps to free the oppressed; what I forbear, I forbear because it does not help to free the oppressed."[2]

It had been difficult for the author of *Uncle Tom's Cabin* to arrange this meeting. Her remarkable reputation had not been enough to secure the appointment. She had to finagle it through political contacts like Wilson and even lower herself to cajole the First Lady into an invitation, even though she viewed Mary Lincoln with some scorn. But Stowe had an object in mind and she persevered. She was anxious to know if the pre-liminary Emancipation Proc-lamation Lincoln had issued in September would prove "a reality & a substance, not a fizzle out at the little end of the horn." She did not expect much from the President, who she feared was a "well-meaning imbecile." But she did want one thing: reassur-ance that the proclamation would not come to an "impo-tent conclusion," and that she could use it with her British contacts to leverage support for the Union. Whatever she expected, however, Stowe could not have imagined the scene that took place.[3]

For the President sham-bled in, "a rough scrubby—black-brown withered—dull

Harriet Beecher Stowe, daguerreotype
by J. D. Wells, 1852
SCHLESINGER LIBRARY, HARVARD UNIVERSITY

eyed object . . . I can give you no idea of the shock." He did nothing to open conversation after Wilson left the room, but sat by the fire, moodily staring at Stowe, her sister Isabella, and daughter Hattie.[4] Although Mrs. Stowe was known as a "delightful" conversationalist, she was shy in such situations, and they remained in awkward silence until Isabella offered some small talk about "the charming open wood fire," and "at last Mr. Lincoln—was 'reminded of a man out west.' . . ." Stowe matched the President's story with one of her own and, the ice broken, finally got the guarantee she wanted. Lincoln would "stand up to his proclamation," she reported, and would not allow the nervous border states to block the way. "I have noted the thing as a glorious expec-tancy!" Stowe rejoiced, and went off to drink tea with Mrs. Lincoln. The un-friendly presidential manner and the chatter of his wife ("an old goose & a gobbler at that")—not to mention the rusty tin pans lying around the office ("much worse than those Eddie [her brother] is accustomed to feed his chickens from")—made the whole experience seem a bit surreal. The three ladies returned to their hotel and, barely able to contain themselves, "perfectly screamed and held our sides while we relieved ourselves of the pent up laughter that had almost been the cause of death." It was not, they noted, Lincoln's jokes that caused their hilarity.[5]

Mrs. Jane Swisshelm sat in the President's anteroom, eyes alert, patience strained to the limit. A longtime editor, she had an opinion on everyone in that town of little-big men, and swished her skirts through court and Congress with ease. The delicate beauty of her youth was still apparent in her late forties, making her sharp political judgments unsettling to some. Worse, she could trim a pretty bonnet and make a tasty biscuit, blurring the lines of domestic and public spheres that defined gender roles of the day. Men were afraid of Jane Swisshelm. She broke barriers wherever she traveled: she had been the first woman to take a seat in the congressional reporters' gallery, shed her husband when he became disagreeable, and stood down the opposition while her printing press was being burned in St. Cloud, Minnesota. When opponents taunted her about "unfeminine activities," she spit back retorts that hit squarely below the belt:

Jane Grey Swisshelm, carte de visite by Joel Emmons Whitney, c. 1865
NATIONAL PORTRAIT GALLERY

You say—and you are witty—That I—and tis a pity—
Of manhood lack but dress;
But you lack manliness,
A body clean and new,
A soul within it, too.
Nature must change her plan
Ere you can be a man.[6]

Swisshelm believed that women had not only the right but an obligation to influence issues of the day. She thought it a moral imperative to tackle the world's wrongs and overturn societal prejudice. Women might be disenfranchised, she maintained, but they could write, lecture, petition, and lobby—and nothing less than their own welfare was at stake. The "life, liberty, and happiness of woman depends on the policy of her own country," Swisshelm asserted in an early editorial, and females must help form those policies. As an accomplished orator she brooked no compromise, argued unrelentingly, and, as one critic noted, was "disagreeably witty." She would make a perfect martyr, concluded an adversary, "for she would risk the stake any time for the privilege of the last word." The ink might flow acrid from her pen, but it had helped Abraham Lincoln win votes in Minnesota, where she was considered the "Mother of Republicanism." Now, in January 1863, Swisshelm had come to Washington on an official mission to persuade the chief executive to take strong action against the Sioux Indians. She meant to be heard.[7]

Lincoln did not hear her. He was busy with other matters; he was overbooked; he could not be persuaded. After three attempts to gain a private interview, Swisshelm was advised to see him at a reception, but, as she remarked, if the President would not seriously discuss her concerns, she had little interest in a grip-and-grin meeting at a crowded levee. It was "useless to see Mr. Lincoln on the business which brought me to Washington," she concluded, "and I did not care to see him on any other. He had proved an obstructionist . . . and I felt no respect for him." Convinced the President was stumbling through his job, "without any comprehensive plan" and "getting deeper and deeper into the mire," she instead called on Edwin Stanton, an old friend from her days as an editor in Pittsburgh. Not until she had gained her object in other ways would she finally go through a receiving line and shake the President's hand.[8]

Talented, temperamental Anna Dickinson appeared on the political horizon in 1861 "like a meteor," Elizabeth Cady Stanton would write, "as if born for the eventful times in which she lived." A young, lithe Philadelphian, Dickinson had grown up with the rising abolition movement—and with the Quaker assumption that women could and should speak their minds. While still in her teens she began to agitate in antislavery and feminist causes; as the national crisis heightened, she waded into political topics as well. She made some early faux pas, bashing popular figures such as General George McClellan, a mistake that resulted in dismissal from her job at the United States Mint, but once she found her ground, her confidence soared. Veteran abolitionist William Lloyd Garrison arranged a series of lectures for the twenty-year-old; and when Wendell Phillips requested that she substitute for him at a Boston rally, afterward embracing Dickinson with tears in his eyes, her reputation gained national status.[9]

By 1863 Dickinson had become something of a phenomenon. She had youth, natural presence, and an undaunted spirit. She spoke without notes, and her rich contralto voice was said to have the mesmerizing power of a spiritual medium. One critic who saw Dickinson pacing the stage compared her to a tigress in a cage: if any-thing, he wrote, "her look was more fierce, her bearing more majestic, and her wrath more terrific." Min-gling argument, pathos, and invec-tive in her talks, she created an oratorical style whose power was compared to Demosthenes and Joan of Arc. Dickinson spoke be-fore thousands at New York's Coo-per Institute; and in the run-up to the 1863 elections Republican offi-cials in four states organized mass meetings starring Dickinson. All were close races that were critical for Lincoln's war policies. In these campaigns Dickinson was not asked to address reform-minded women or argue social issues, but to sway male voters—a most un-usual circumstance at the time.

Anna E. Dickinson, photograph, c. 1855–65
LIBRARY OF CONGRESS

One Connecticut official, who admitted his initial skepticism, conceded that Dickinson "had not spoken ten minutes before all prejudices were dispelled . . . ; sixty minutes and she held fifteen hundred people breathless with admiration . . . ; two hours and she had raised her entire audience to a pitch of enthusiasm which was perfectly irresistible." Every candidate she supported won.[10]

Dickinson was happy to stump for Republicans, but her real interest was in the plight of slaves, freedmen, and the U.S. Colored Troops. She was frustrated with Lincoln, who, she believed, gave only lip service to the cause of emancipation, and angered when the President overturned proclamations by Generals John Frémont and David Hunter that liberated slaves in their military districts. "Abraham Lincoln," Dickinson fumed, "had made such an Ass of himself for the Slave Powers to ride" that he was stifling army recruitment and demoralizing the nation. Mollified somewhat by the Emancipation Proclamation but still concerned that nothing was being done to help ex-slaves thrive as free men, she took the stage with antislavery luminaries like Frederick Douglass to attack the administration's lackluster policies and halfway measures.[11]

At the zenith of her career, Dickinson was invited by one hundred members of Congress to speak in the Capitol, the first woman so honored. On January 16, 1864, escorted by Vice President Hannibal Hamlin and the Speaker of the House, Dickinson stepped onto a platform in the Hall of Representatives to address the nation's leaders on "The Perils of the Hour." The audience saw a "slim waisted girl with curls cut short as if for school," wrote an army officer who was present, "eyes black with the mirthfulness of a child, save when they blaze with the passions of a prophetess, holding spell bound . . . two thousand politicians, statesmen and soldiers!" Dickinson challenged Copperheads, railed against the perfidy of secession, and praised the nobility of Union troops. Her most impassioned language, however, was reserved for Lincoln's recently announced reconstruction policy, which showed generosity to former slaveholders and promised nothing for the freedmen. "Let no man prate of compromise," she thundered. "There is no arm of compromise long enough to stretch over . . . the mound of fallen heroes, to shake hands with their murderers." Her words were undiluted, even when Lincoln and his wife entered the room. The President sat with head bowed while she denounced his actions and was too abashed to speak when called to the podium. It was a sensitive moment, for the Republicans had not yet nominated their candidate for the November presidential election. A congressman sympathetic to Dickinson's viewpoint remarked that the address was "full of beautiful things and brilliant consecutions"—but it was "very sharp. I should as soon have a chest of joiner's tools for a wife."[12]

Dickinson's remarkable performance was capped by a surprise finale. After roundly censuring Lincoln, she suddenly changed direction and gave a stirring endorsement for his reelection. The war had been a people's war, she cried, and it must be guided by a man of the people. There was much to lament, but also much left to do; and the man to do it was Lincoln. Just why Dickinson chose to alter her tone so completely is unclear. Historians have speculated that she may have been embarrassed by Lincoln's presence, or that she was counseled to soften her message. Perhaps she instinctively knew she needed an upbeat ending for the largely Republican audience. If so, she got the response she desired. The rousing conclusion brought forth "volleys of cheers" and a personal greeting afterward from the President. "You have conquered Washington," wrote an admirer, "you have taken the capital."[13]

Dickinson immediately regretted the endorsement. Three days later, at an interview arranged though Pennsylvania representative William D. Kelley, she renewed tensions with Lincoln. Their conversation centered on efforts to implement his reconstruction plan in Louisiana. It had been hastily pushed through and threatened to leave many freedmen in a state of quasi-slavery. According to Dickinson, she told the President this was "all wrong." She was also offended by his soiled shirt and stockings, his "old coat out at the elbows, which looked as if he had . . . used it for a pen wiper," and became impatient when Lincoln tried to change the subject with the ubiquitous "that reminds me of a little story." "I didn't come to hear stories," snapped Dickinson. Three months later there was another meeting, at which both parties apparently tried to make amends, with Dickinson offering a semiapology and Lincoln declaring he would rather "have her on his side . . . than any twenty men in the field." But there was no agreement on reconstruction policy, which Dickinson had hoped to influence. When Lincoln closed the conversation by saying if abolitionists wanted him to lead, "let them get out of the way and let me lead," Dickinson vowed: "I have spoken my last word to President Lincoln."[14]

Dickinson publicly complained about the unfortunate encounters, and Kelley—himself in need of party approval at the time—admonished her. The congressman gave a modified version of events, in which a more cordial Lincoln essentially ignored the triumphant rhetorician and Dickinson remained demurely quiet. Dickinson was known to be excitable, and her self-assurance may have turned to overconfidence in these meetings. That she may have over-reacted is entirely possible. Yet nothing in her account was at variance with depictions by myriad male visitors who also witnessed Lincoln's shabby attire, dependence on homely tale-telling, and reluctance to take advice. When Dickinson began to belittle the President on the campaign trail, however, matters became more serious. All agreed that the meteoric ascent of America's Joan of Arc had lost its trajectory and was shooting dangerously into uncharted space.[15]

Clara Barton had been marching in lockstep with Abraham Lincoln since the beginning of his administration. One of the earliest women employed by the government, during the 1850s she had surpassed male colleagues at the Patent Office in quality and quantity of work. Nonetheless, when James Buchanan assumed the presidency, Barton was accused of being a "Black Republican" and summarily dismissed. After the votes were tallied for Lincoln, she was brought back, praising the new chief executive and bemusedly stating she had returned to Washington to "watch the play." The play proved far more dramatic than Barton imagined. Within months she found herself in a wartime capital, chafing to contribute to the fight. "I cannot rest satisfied," she wrote to a friend; "it is little one woman can do, still I crave the privilege of doing that."[16]

By the time she took a seat in the President's waiting room in February 1865, Barton had "done" a great deal. One of the earliest people to recognize the insufficiency of Union medical arrangements, she not only collected supplies but went to hospitals and camps to distribute them personally. Many women labored at the front, but only a handful were actually on the battlefield, under fire, as was Barton. On fields like Antietam, Fredericksburg, and Fort Wagner she extracted bullets, braved firestorms that shot away portions of her skirt, and bound amputated limbs under artillery bombardment. "I am told that she seemed on such occasions totaly insensible to danger," an administration confidant remarked. She also instructed recently freed slaves, turned her rooms into a vast warehouse for medical goods, and fought to obtain proper food and treatment for the wounded. "The patriot blood of my fathers was warm in my veins," she stated, by way of explanation. By war's end the name Clara Barton was recognized in households across the North. Already she was known popularly as the "angel of the battlefield."[17]

Clara Barton, photograph, c. 1865
LIBRARY OF CONGRESS

Moreover, she had championed not just the common soldier but Lincoln himself, defending his policies when few wartime workers would do so. "I grant that our Government has made mistakes, sore ones too in some instances," Barton candidly told New York editor Thaddeus Meighan from the siege of Charleston, "but we shall never strengthen their hands, or incite their patriotism by deserting and upbraiding them." She claimed to have no political motive (*"as I am* merely a *soldier,* and *not a statesman,* I shall make no attempt at discussing *political* points"), but her attitudes marched forward at the same pace as the President's. "Who am I going to vote for?" Barton taunted her skeptical feminist friend Frances Dana Gage in 1864. "Why I thought for president Lincoln, to be sure. I *have* been voting for him for the last three years." He had not assessed the situation clearly at the opening of the war, she admitted, and had stumbled badly in military affairs, but Barton still stood by her man. She would support whomever the Republicans nominated, she told

Gage, but she hoped the "care worn face" that had become "very dear" to her would again head the presidential roster.[18]

Now Barton was seated for the third day in Lincoln's vestibule, hoping to offer him one more service. She was a striking figure at age forty-three. Her face was not beautiful, but strong-featured and full of character. Her gray-tinged black hair, specially dressed that day by a friend, was tied back in a tasseled silk net; her hands were nervous in the new gloves she had bought for the occasion.[19] The war was nearing its end and, again sensing a need she could fill, Barton wanted to propose a program to catalog "missing" soldiers. There had been no system of identification, no detailed prison rosters, and nearly two hundred thousand graves were unmarked. On the home front, where thousands of households waited nervously to hear a familiar footstep, it was an anxious issue. Barton hoped to interview men returning from Southern prisons who might remember a missing comrade's fate and to compile lists for official records. The War Department had embraced the project, and Barton sent a formal petition to Lincoln, summoning her most influential contacts to endorse it. Massachusetts congressman William Washburn penned a strong letter recommending Barton as "one of the most useful devoted *valuable* ladies in the country," and General Ethan Allen Hitchcock, who was in charge of prisoner exchange, also tried to catch Lincoln's attention. Even powerful Senator Henry Wilson, who often consulted Barton on military matters, wrote the President, advising that "Miss Barton calls on you for a business object and I hope you will grant my request. It will cost nothing. She has given three years to the cause of our soldiers and is worthy of *entire* confidence."[20] Yet here she was waiting *again* at the White House, turned away by the guards. Bitterly disappointed, Barton left, succumbing to tears in the privacy of her rooms. "I . . . do not feel it my duty to bring myself to public mortification in order to do a public charity," she crossly concluded.[21] Nonetheless, she borrowed some courage as well as a fur coat from a fellow war worker and tried the White House door the next day. Once more she was not admitted. In the end, Lincoln delegated the issue to General Hitchcock. Considering this an authorization, Hitchcock approved the plan.[22]

Miss Barton was never received by the President.

These stories show Lincoln in an impatient mood, annoyed with petitions and the high-pitched public criticism that forms part of every presidential brief. There may have been genuine reasons for the unfriendly reception these women received at the White House. Lincoln was irritated after Republican defeats in the election of November 1862 when Stowe met him, and not particularly receptive to charges of inaction; Swisshelm was seen as something of a harpy, swooping in to whip the President into stronger action against the Sioux, just when he wanted to back away from the situation; Dickinson had publicly denounced his policies in sarcastic terms. But . . . Clara Barton? That snub is harder to understand, given her fame, and her staunch loyalty to Lincoln.

The same discouraging note was sounded in a long string of encounters with other women. Anna Ella Carroll, a widely respected pamphleteer who had written powerful pieces that helped keep Maryland in the Union, was turned away with an explosive presidential laugh when she sought the pay promised for her work. She was then mortified to find Lincoln had openly ridiculed her to other influential men.[23] Mary Livermore and Jane Hoge, who collected a half million dollars for medical stores while directing the Western Sanitary Commission, called for words of encouragement but found Lincoln's reception so "dispiriting" that it "cost those of us who belonged to the Northwest a night's sleep." Julia Ward Howe, author of "Battle Hymn of the Republic"—essentially the Union Army's anthem—was treated "perfunctorily" by the President, and rudely overlooked as he spoke to her escort, Governor John Andrew.[24] Mary Abigail Dodge, whose writings under the pseudonym Gail Hamilton bolstered home-front morale after a string of military disasters, was unable to get an appointment with either Lincoln or his wife when she called to offer her services. Cordelia Harvey, widow of a Wisconsin governor who had been killed at the front, and herself a hospital worker, was also roughly treated. She tried to gain approval for a convalescent facility behind the battle lines, only to meet with a scowl and a "snap" from Lincoln that she was presuming "to know more than I do." (In fact, Harvey did know considerably more than Lincoln about hospital conditions. She persevered, but persuaded him only after she raised the issue of soldier votes in the Midwest.)[25] A Quaker activist met with similar testiness. When she entered a plea for immediate emancipation, counseling the President to fulfill the Lord's design, he responded with "ill-subdued impatience." "Has the Friend finished?" he asked testily. Lincoln then retorted that if God had instructions for him, He would give His advice personally, not through a lady.[26]

And so the progression of discomfiting stories continued, forming a clear and consistent pattern. Indeed, the intriguing question is not *whether* Abraham Lincoln rebuffed the leading women of his day, but *why* he did so.

II

Lincoln's professional reputation rose at a time when women were beginning to gain a voice and a purpose in the political world. In the early days of the republic, it was believed women's role in democratic development lay in educating their children to support patriotic ideals. In the decades after the Revolution, the rise of evangelical religion encouraged women to support causes that softened the harsher edges of society, such as temperance, or school and asylum reform. As it became more acceptable for women to take a public part in such movements, the line was blurred between their "legitimate" role in domestic matters and participation in the male "sphere" of civic affairs. When the first female antislavery society was founded in Boston in 1833, for example, charter members feared losing their reputations, so strong was the bias against women's involvement. Four years later there were seventy-seven similar societies. Such organizations offered an increasing opportunity for women to contribute, teaching managerial skills as well as methods of pressuring the government. Charity leaders wrote bylaws, ran meetings, and through acts of incorporation were able to raise money, invest funds, or bring lawsuits—all activities that were prohibited to married women. At the same time, women were reshaping their outlook. They no longer saw worldly affairs solely through the prism of relationships to men but relied on their own views and trusted their own competence.[27]

The election of 1840 proved a watershed for women's direct participation in the political pageant. The Whigs, hoping to portray themselves as the more honorable party, believed they could downplay vulgar "male" motives (like greed and ambition) by harnessing female "purity" to elevate the tone of their platform. Understanding the value of public theater, Whigs enlisted women as moral standard-bearers to write tracts, present banners, and join parades. Ladies did not hesitate to become allegories of virtue, riding in white gowns atop floats dedicated to "Liberty and William Henry Harrison" or pinning bright partisan buttons to their bodices. Slogans such as "Calhoun, Tecumseh, Cass or Van / With the LADIES' aid we'll beat the whole clan" or—later—"The girls Link on to Lincoln" helped push Whig and Republican candidates across the victory line. Democrats, who preferred to keep women at a pristine distance from rough political arenas, reluctantly followed suit.[28]

All this was a far cry from male-dominated political rituals that had featured drinking, acrimonious debate, and symbolic "pole-raisings." (The last was a particular craze in Lincoln's Springfield district, where rival parties cut huge tree trunks, then compared the length of their "poles" and competed to see who could raise them most rapidly—with the obvious corollary that the quicker the pole was erected, the more potent the candidate.)[29] Once women were given a role, they proved an asset. Their presence at rallies was not only morally uplifting but subliminally erotic, as evidenced in excited descriptions of "exquisitely moulded arms" and "bounding bosoms." Lincoln, who was a spirited campaigner in the 1840 contest, must have been aware of this trend, for women played an active part in his home state. Mary Todd, whom he was courting, was among the enthusiasts. "This fall I became quite a *politician,*" she confided to a friend, "rather an unladylike profession, yet at such a *crisis,* whose heart could remain untouched?" By 1844 women were an accepted feature of electioneering, and Henry Clay could declare: "I hope the day will never come when American ladies will be indifferent to the fate and fortunes of our common country, nor fail . . . to demonstrate their patriotic solicitude."[30]

Many early feminists were allied to the antislavery movement and gravitated naturally to the Republican Party, which most nearly expressed their views after the demise of the Whigs. Women were present at the creation of the party at Ripon, Wisconsin, in 1854, and were eagerly sought to grace serenades and speeches. When the Republicans nominated John C. Frémont for president in 1856, reform-minded women made strong statements on his behalf. Frémont's dashing looks, reputation as a western trailblazer, and outspoken opposition to slavery reflected many female hopes for the country's future. He was all the more attractive since his wife, Jesse Benton Frémont (also known as Jessie), was conspicuous in the campaign. Jesse Frémont, a scion of Missouri's influential Benton family, was a hardheaded political broker in her own right and the power behind her husband's compelling public image. "Isn't it pleasant to have a *woman* spontaneously recognized as a moral influence in public affairs?" enthused Lydia Maria Child, an early advocate of abolition and women's rights. "What a shame that *women* can't vote! We'd carry 'our Jessie' into the White House on our shoulders, *wouldn't* we?"[31]

Women were in fact moving exactly in the direction Child indicated—from moral influence to an aspiration for true political rights. The emphasis on changing society through good works was giving way to a call for legal reforms, especially against practices that denied women control over their property, their labor, and their children. Early political organizers, including Elizabeth Cady Stanton and Lucretia Mott, who spearheaded the first women's rights conference at Seneca Falls, New York, in 1848, wanted concrete legislation that would overturn decades of officially mandated subordination.

Increasingly, they were willing to make themselves unpopular to fight for it. By the time of Lincoln's presidency, they could point to some real gains. The New York State Earnings Act of 1860 gave a woman the right to sue and to retain wages in her own name. Twenty-nine of the thirty-five states had passed some kind of legislation granting married women control of their prenuptial property by 1865. Women were writing tracts under their own names or taking the public platform without apology. Their words sometimes carried great weight. Anna Ella Carroll, who essentially wrote the textbook on presidential war powers and influenced several antebellum elections, could attest to this. So could Harriet Beecher Stowe, whose views held such power that people confused *Uncle Tom's Cabin* with a government document. Petticoats in a parade no longer gratified women: they wanted a voice and a way of making it heard. "The speculative has in all things yielded to the practical," commented "Isola" to the women's rights journal *Una* in 1852. "In this sense, moral suasion is moral balderdash."[32]

What such women wanted was to turn the dynamic inside out. Instead of inspiring men to reach a superior feminine moral standard, they wanted an equal chance to fix those standards politically. As they grew bolder, "strongminded women" (a popular and not altogether flattering term for advocates of liberal reform and female rights) expanded their scope of action. They spoke out for better education, for dress reform, for the ability to choose a profession—and to be paid for their work. Increasingly, they also demanded the ballot, without which, many thought, they could never truly be part of the democratic community. Crusaders like Sarah Smith Martyn, who founded the New York Female Moral Reform Society in the 1830s, came to believe that disenfranchising women underlay *the whole enormous structure of evil* which . . . must be removed before the regeneration of the world can take place."[33]

If the ballot was essential, it was also maddeningly elusive. Yet what had once been unthinkable was now at least discussable. Three weeks before Lincoln gave his celebrated 1860 address at New York's Cooper Institute, Henry Ward Beecher—Stowe's brother—stunned the same house with a rousing speech on "Women's Influence in Politics." In it he further blurred the boundaries of gender-based spheres. Political rights would not detract from a woman's role as moral guardian, he argued, but would make her an even richer asset at home. "Whatever makes her . . . a larger-minded actor, a deeper-thoughted observer, a more potent writer or teacher," the Brooklyn-based clergyman declared, "makes her . . . a better wife and mother." Beecher advocated giving women the vote and also encouraged them to hold public office. The body politic, he argued, would be strengthened by contributions from both men and women, for their interests were one. Indeed, his plea was for *men,* who were robbed of a better society by limiting women's involvement. The ideas were bold, but just as striking was the speaker and his forum. Beecher was a known reformer, but he was also a Protestant minister, popular with the middle class. His words had a power and reach enjoyed by few others in America. Once he spoke out, the quest for a female role in national politics entered the mainstream.[34]

Progressives like Henry Ward Beecher might uphold female aspirations, but many people looked askance at women's public visibility. It ruffled sensibilities to see ladies give impassioned speeches, and it bred fears that orderly societal relations were about to be upended. Pioneering women were sometimes viewed as curiosities, or simply ignored, but many people considered them meddling misfits. When well-regarded activist Caroline Healey Dall lectured on "Women's Rights Under the Law," a prominent Harvard scientist, Josiah Parsons Cooke, likened it to "hen-crowing," and accused her of trying to "annihilate marriage." He was all for open discussion, Cooke concluded, but "when obscenities constitute the material of a lecture, it is time for the police to interfere." Antislavery champion Charles Sumner was generally an ally of women; nevertheless, he discouraged Julia Ward Howe from publicly reading her essays. ("I did not expect your sympathy in this undertaking," complained Howe. "But I do feel that I have cast too much 'love oil' on your head for you to throw cold water on mine.") Others simply thought the movement and its leaders ridiculous. Feminists were a subspecies afflicted with "Gynaekokracy," opined a journalist from Geneva, New York, "bold, unblushing, flippant, unfeminine and bad imitators of men." Petroleum V. Nasby and Artemus Ward both roasted feminists, liberally using terms like "she-devils" to describe them. *Vanity Fair* ran cartoons showing beefy activists boisterously bullying boys and prodding the President.[35] Women were also nervous about the burgeoning feminist movement and many took care not to associate too closely with it. Mary Lincoln joined others who denied they were "strong-minded," declaring she had a "terror" of that breed. Nonetheless, she viewed herself as a ringside adviser to her husband and admitted she thought it wrong to withhold "a word fitly spoken . . . in due season."[36]

Just what Lincoln thought about women's growing political involvement is difficult to know with certainty. He was not particularly keen on political pageantry of any form, preferring behind-the-scenes strategizing with a few collaborators to flashy, emotion-laden spectacles. "I think too much reliance is placed in noisy demonstrations," he stated. "They excite prejudice and close the avenues to sober reason."[37] As a young man Lincoln once declared he favored sharing government with everyone who helped bear its burdens: "Consequently I go for admitting all whites to the right of suffrage, who pay taxes or bear arms (by no means excluding females)." Some have seen this as a clear statement of support for women's rights. Others have found it an ironic, even sarcastic comment, since women did not join the militia in 1836, and only a few held property in their own name, making them taxpayers.[38]

"A Fit for the 'Ladies' League,'" wood engraving,
Vanity Fair, May 30, 1863

While living in New Salem, Lincoln belonged to a debating society that discussed whether women should be educated and have voting rights, but his opinion on these issues is not recorded. On the stump, he cautioned against the danger of curbing freedoms for one group in order to elevate another, but when he invoked the principles of the Declaration of Independence or asked rhetorically, "Who shall say, 'I am the superior, and you are the inferior?'" he was discussing male prerogatives and did not include women in the discussion. His law partner William Herndon claimed Lincoln's innate sense of justice made him uncomfortable denying privileges to others that he personally enjoyed, and that he "often" said women were the "other and better half of man" and entitled to full rights. Lincoln did not publicly support this, said Herndon, for he felt the moment had not yet come to put it before the people. These comments were written nearly half a century after the two men shared an office in Springfield, however, and Herndon's quirkiness makes him a problematic source. In any case, if Lincoln believed women deserved greater civil liberties, he never acted on it in any way.[39]

There *is* evidence that Lincoln defended women skillfully in his years as a trial lawyer, particularly in cases of sexual violation. In his first public defense, a young woman brought suit against a seducer who refused to marry her. Lincoln won his client a substantial award by arguing that a man's soiled reputation could be "washed" clean, while a shamed woman was like a broken bottle that could never be mended. In other cases, Lincoln successfully advocated child support for unwed mothers, won damages for a woman raped by her father, and prosecuted the violator of a seven-year-old girl, persuading the jury to sentence him to eighteen years in prison. Once in the White House, he seems to have been favorably disposed to loyal women who were in need or who had been directly wronged. The President responded positively to widows and to those who appeared helpless. He also showed sympathy to families of slain U.S. Colored Troops, understanding that the South's refusal to recognize black marriages denied wives many rights, including pensions. In these cases Lincoln could play the traditional male role of protector and generous benefactor. Women clamoring for position, promoting reform, or proposing better ways to manage the war, no matter how constructive, found a far less receptive hearing. These were not supplicants, but *demandeurs,* who challenged him with both their ideas and their expectations. The parade of forthright females rebuffed in the presidential office indicates a great deal of ambivalence on Lincoln's part about ladies who sought something more than a patronizing dispensation of favors.[40]

III

Lincoln's discomfort with accomplished women also reflected his innate malaise around the fair sex. The origins of this are puzzling, for in early life he had positive relationships with his mother, stepmother, and older sister Sally. Nancy Hanks Lincoln was by every account a woman of intelligence, industry, and kindness. An in-law recalled that "she was a brilliant woman—a woman of great good sense and Modesty. . . . Tho[ma]s Lincoln & his wife were really happy in Each others presence—loved one another." Others remembered the President's mother as tenderhearted, but marked by sadness.[41] Some said Abe, with his dark hair, hazel-gray eyes, and sharp features, took after her physically as well as temperamentally. It is uncertain whether she was literate, but at least one account has Lincoln stating that "[a]ll that I am or hope ever to be I get from my Mother." Whether Nancy Lincoln resembled the "angel mother" concocted by later artistic imagination is more doubtful. Women aged quickly on the frontier, and her son's only description mentioned a "want of teeth" and "weather-beaten appearance in general." It was commonly acknowledged that her death in 1818 was a calamity for the family and a sorrow in the community.[42]

After Nancy Lincoln's burial, the household was run by Abe's sister Sarah—known as Sally—who was two years older than her brother. Sally took after her father physically and was a bright child: "a gentle Kind, smart—shrewd—social, intelligent woman—She was quick & strong minded," stated a neighbor.[43] Abraham was disturbed when Sally married Aaron Grigsby at age nineteen, believing Grigsby treated her badly. He made his displeasure clear enough that the Grigsbys did not invite him to a double family wedding. Lincoln's response was to pen a scathing poem called "Book of Chronicles," long remembered in the community as a "good—sharp—cutting" satire about a mix-up of bridal chambers, featuring pointed barbs about the masculinity of the male Grigsbys. The "Chronicles" heightened tensions among the in-laws and resulted in a fistfight—the neighborhood's standard way of resolving differences. William Grigsby, who offered the fight, refused to take on the much larger Lincoln, and John Johnston, Lincoln's stepbrother, was substituted. When the contest started going against Johnston, Lincoln stepped in and thrashed Grigsby. Sally died in childbirth after little more than a year of marriage, and Abe was said to have been devastated.[44]

The anchor in Lincoln's youth was his stepmother, Sarah Bush Johnston Lincoln, a woman who impressed Herndon as rising "high above her surroundings." Thomas Lincoln had known her before his marriage to Nancy Hanks, and he returned to Kentucky to wed Sarah about a year after Nancy's death. A widow with three children, Sarah was described as tall, handsome, and "straight as an Indian." A photograph taken later in life shows a woman with large, pale-colored eyes and regular features, her face framed in a ruffled cap. She was practical and unflappable, a good choice "to tie to," as one neighbor remarked, and equal to the work of raising five children in a frontier cabin. Sarah arrived in Indiana with a wagonload of furniture and a few books, set to washing the children until they "looked more human," and proved to be a sympathetic parent. She thought Abe a good, obedient boy, encouraged his reading, and was proud of his success. She later said that "his mind & mine . . .

seemed to run together—move in the same channel."[45] Lincoln appears to have felt more affection for his stepmother than for his father, and took some trouble to provide for her in later life. Unfortunately, some of the funds were apparently siphoned off by other family members, and they ceased altogether after Lincoln was assassinated. Sarah Lincoln, who had not wanted her stepson to be president, mourned his death, spending her final years in poverty and loneliness.[46]

Sarah Bush Johnston Lincoln, photograph by
H. R. Martin, c. 1865
CHICAGO HISTORY MUSEUM

There were shadows behind these bright relationships, however. Lincoln's mother and sister both died when he was comparatively young. For a child, the death of a parent is a seminal experience and can have significant emotional consequences, often lasting a lifetime. We do not know exactly how these tragedies affected young Abraham, and there is no clinical evidence, but some have postulated that the early losses were responsible for his enduring melancholy. They may have also caused him to beware of emotional attachments to women, attachments that might end abruptly, through no fault of his own.[47] Lincoln sympathized with a young girl whose father died in battle, saying that though sorrow comes to all, "to the young it comes with bitterest agony, because it takes them unawares." He memorized a poem by Scottish poet William Knox called "Mortality," which spoke of a girl, alive with beauty and pleasure, who was erased from the Earth "like a swift-fleeting meteor." Lincoln spoke of his reverence for this poem ("I would give all I am worth, and go in debt, to be able to write so fine a piece as I think that is") in the same breath as the memory of a trip he made in 1844 to the graves of his mother and sister. On that visit he mourned anew the "things decayed and loved ones lost" and felt keenly his helplessness against mortality.[48]

Other clouds hung over these relations, having to do with sexuality. Sister Sally had died in childbirth. Lincoln may have viewed this as the wages of passion, or blamed it on her husband's lust. His mother's reputation also seemed smudged with uncertainty. Herndon reported that Lincoln told him his mother was a bastard, the illegitimate child of Lucy Hanks and a well-off Virginia planter, and that Abe believed he had inherited superior traits from this man. There may have been some truth to the story, for Lucy Hanks was charged with fornication in Mercer County, Kentucky, and no wedding certificate was ever found for her. Herndon believed this caused Lincoln to feel he was different from other men, feeding his self-absorption and depression. There were rumors about the chastity of Nancy Hanks Lincoln as well. Several acquaintances speculated that she had had relations with neighbors, and that her son was perhaps not fathered by Thomas. (Cousin Dennis Hanks denied this; and Lincoln's fellow circuit rider Henry Whitney pointed out that Thomas and Nancy Lincoln had been married before Abraham's birth, making his legitimacy presumptive in law.) Whether true or not, such gossip may have disturbed the sensitive boy, causing him to mistrust sexual instincts or feel that the consequences of lovemaking were grave and intimidating.[49]

Lincoln's odd looks and eccentric personality also fed his nervousness around the opposite sex. He formed friendships with sympathetic older ladies or the wives of his friends, but many witnesses remembered his discomfort around girls his own age. Some put this down to shyness; others thought he disdained girls as "too frivolous."[50] He could boast the standard attainments of frontier boys and was a fine athlete, but his outsized limbs, craggy features, and uncontrollable hair were made for mockery. An acquaintance from Lincoln's Indiana years remembered that all the young ladies made fun of him, sometimes to his face. He appeared to join in the laughter and tried to spend time with the girls, "but no sir-ee, they'd give him the mitten every time." His self-consciousness may have been sharpened by his stepbrother's popularity. The smooth-talking Johnston was "mighty good lookin' and awful takin'," one woman recalled, while Abe "wus so quiet and awkward and so awful homely" that the girls shunned him. At times Lincoln joined them in self-deprecation, admitting that "if any woman, old or young, ever thought there was any peculiar charm in this distinguished specimen . . . I have, as yet been so unfortunate as not to have discovered it." During the 1860 campaign, he reportedly quipped that it was lucky for him women could not vote, because his portraits would have defeated him.[51]

Lincoln's peculiar looks were matched by his chronic social clumsiness.

He had perfected an easy affability with the boys but clammed up in mixed company. Friends described a man who retreated into bashful silence when he could not avoid women, or introduced himself by shifting uncomfortably from foot to foot, making bizarre gestures, and proclaiming, "I don't know how to talk to ladies!" Lincoln's sister-in-law recalled that he did not have the knack of polite parlor talk, and Mary Owens, a young woman who kept company with him in 1836, wrote that he was too self-absorbed to offer the little attentions that "make up the great chain of womans happiness." She recounted how once, when crossing a dangerous stream together on horseback, he showed no concern for her safety, and said he reckoned she could take care of herself. Owens thought this kind of careless comment sprang from a want of training rather than intentional rudeness.[52] Most likely, it was a symptom of Lincoln's habitual distraction, for both his mothers—from whom he might have absorbed some etiquette—were considered uncommonly decorous in their frontier community. In addition, Lincoln did not help himself by playing the buffoon in social situations. More than one person remembered him cutting up at barn raisings and corn shuckings, drawing his pals into a corner to tell crude stories until the girls complained he was "smashing up things generally." Rather than quit, he would perform stunts to ruin the party. "Abe would go to all the dances in the country but would not dance, would get to one side . . . and tell jokes & funny stories & . . . turn handsprings and stand flat footed and lean backwards until his head would touch floor or ground, and a great many other athletic performances." If Lincoln felt an adolescent triumph in these antics, they did not endear him to the girls.[53]

Perhaps Lincoln broke up dances and relished smutty jokes as a defense against his fear of sexuality—fear that he was unattractive, or of the consequences of normal male-female interaction. His courting history was certainly rocky. He saw several young women while living in New Salem and Springfield, including Mary Owens and a girl named Sarah Rickard. These relations were not easy, with Lincoln inept at flirtation and alternating between angst-ridden fantasies and self-recrimination. "Perhaps any other man would know enough without further information," Lincoln wrote to a woman who was anxious to resolve their uncertain relationship, "but I consider it *my* peculiar right to plead ignorance, and your bounden duty to allow the plea." It is a striking sentence, indicative of his self-centered tone as a suitor. (In one such letter he uses the word "I" twenty-six times in thirty-seven lines, and throws all responsibility for the relationship onto the lady.) Yet, perhaps nagged by the specter of his sister's abuse, Lincoln also stated that he wanted badly to do right by women. He was not entirely sure what that meant and the dilemma made him hesitant. The unhappy outcome of several of these relations (Rickard reportedly "flung him high & dry," and Owens also ultimately rejected him) cannot have bolstered his confidence.[54]

Lincoln's most intense relationship appears to have been with Anne Rutledge, the daughter of an innkeeper in New Salem. By all accounts Anne (pronounced "Annie," according to her sister) was a nice-looking girl, not overly intellectual, but sympathetic. There is evidence that Anne and Abraham enjoyed a close rapport, but the extent of the relationship is unclear. Anne was engaged to another man—which was perhaps part of the attraction for Lincoln, who was clearly most comfortable with safe, unavailable women. When Anne died of a fever, Lincoln's grief was extreme enough to excite local comment, and his friends "feared that reason would desert the throne." The legend of their ill-starred romance was inflated by Herndon, who later claimed that Rutledge was Lincoln's true love, and her death a blow from which he never recovered. The most credible comments on the relationship were made by Anne's sister Sarah, who, on reading a newspaper account of the affair, denied most of the rumors, including stories that Lincoln and Anne were engaged. "She came to her mind a little before she died & called for Lincoln," recalled Sarah, "then they were left in the room alone & no one ever knew what they said she died soon after that. . . . There was not any of that *kissing* between them & there is a lot more there that is not true at all." But there is no doubt that Lincoln was deeply affected by his friend's death. The whole affair must have reinforced his sense that loving was a high-risk business.[55]

Some writers have interpreted Lincoln's discomfort around women as a sign of uncertainty about his masculinity, suggesting he was "undersexed," or possibly homosexual or bisexual. They cite his clumsiness in female company, his fumbling attempts at forging relationships, and his fear when faced with the possibility of a real attachment. They also look at the close camaraderie Lincoln shared with men—his strong friendship with Joshua Speed, and his evident fondness for young courtiers such as Nicolay and Hay, as well as for the flashy drillmaster Elmer Ellsworth. There was also gossip about the President's close relation with a guard officer at his summer residence. Sometime in 1862 Lincoln did take a shine to Captain David Derickson, and the friendship was so widely known that it appeared as part of the regimental history of the

150th Pennsylvania volunteers. Drawing room chitchat included reports that Derickson sat at table with Lincoln when Mary was absent and even shared the presidential bed. Sleeping habits were much more casual in that era of overcrowded conditions and lower standards of privacy, however, so that a sexual implication was not necessarily self-evident, especially as it was talked about so openly. When Washington insider Virginia Woodbury Fox recorded the hearsay in her diary, she remarked: "What stuff!"[56]

In that era of prudery, the salacious revelations may have had more to do with Derickson's access to privy information or ability to angle for position than any illicit acts. That all of Lincoln's favorites were actively heterosexual also argues against the theory of closet liaisons. A more likely scenario, particularly once Lincoln became president, is the one seen in every White House: a powerful man, isolated by position, and anxious to maintain his authority, finding it easier to interact with low-level aides who openly admire him, than with competitive men who might benefit from a too candid discussion. Lincoln's young companions arguably tickled his ego more than his physical fancy.

Whatever smoldered behind the rumors, there is abundant evidence of Lincoln's heterosexuality. His political ally David Davis wrote that he was "a Man of strong passion for woman," whose conscience kept him from seducing girls. Herndon seconded this, noting that Lincoln had "terribly strong passions for women—could scarcely keep his hands off them." Lincoln told him that after Anne Rutledge's death he fell into some of the seamier habits of the local lads and feared he had contracted syphilis from a casual tryst. Herndon also said that from the time Lincoln came to Springfield in 1837, he and Joshua Speed were "quite *familiar*—to go no further—with the women." Speed was a well-known ladies' man who sometimes helped set up assignations for his friend and, along with other "old rats" in the area, liked sexual gossip. Lincoln apparently shunned this kind of disrespectful talk. His friends commented that, if anything, his moral standards were liberal. His idea was "that a woman had the same right to play with her tail that a man had and no more nor less," including the right to stray from the marriage vow if she chose. But Lincoln did not want to dabble in extramarital affairs, and when tempted, used his strong will to "put out the fires of his terrible passion."[57]

Within the context of his day, Lincoln was also considered a "manly" man. This is particularly interesting since so much Lincoln lore glorifies traits usually considered feminine. After his assassination, and well into the twenty-first century, the sixteenth president was praised for his tenderness toward children and animals, his dislike of bloodshed, his kindness and avoidance of confrontation, and his love of "right" over "might." He did indeed embody some of these things, some of the time. But they were not necessarily considered womanly characteristics in his day. The rough masculinity of the Jackson era prized physical power, rugged individualism, and a willingness to fight with the fists for dignity, power, or survival. Lincoln, whose love of book learning, absentminded ways, and outlandish appearance distinguished him from other frontiersmen, was fortunate in having inherited his father's two outstanding traits: a powerful, athletic body, and a gift for storytelling. Thomas Lincoln had been obliged to prove himself by sheer physicality— winning neighborhood respect when he clobbered the local bully at a Kentucky tavern—much as his son took on the Grigsbys to defend his sister. In both cases, the lion of the territory was the most powerful slugger. As a kinsman noted, no one ever again tested Thomas's "manhood in personal combat," and this allowed him to become the mediator in community disputes. His son's strength also earned him the right to make peace, rather than continually fight other males.[58]

But as midcentury approached, Lincoln consciously moved away from the cruder male stereotypes, embracing a new sensibility about masculinity that was sweeping the nation's middle class. Restraint, self-reliance, and financial success were now considered the measure of a man; family concerns were his legitimate "sphere" as much as a woman's; and real power came from directed energy and self-control. Maleness was not defined as a set of physical attributes, like muscularity, but as a series of actions. A true man *achieved*, rising in society and assessing masculinity by his economic standing vis-à-vis other men. De Tocqueville noticed this obsession to "get ahead," seeing the American male as "restless in the midst of abundance"—forever glancing over a shoulder to gauge his comparative advantage. During this period, Lincoln stopped viewing himself as an axe-swinging, arm-wrestling strongman of rural districts and began identifying with the Whig Party's professional men and bourgeois aspirations. He was especially taken by Whig leader Henry Clay. Although a Virginia aristocrat, Clay adopted the persona "Harry of the West" to promote the virtues of "self-made men," a term he coined in 1832. To rise through "patient and diligent labor," argued Clay, was to be a man worthy of the highest esteem. The conceit worked well for Lincoln, whose desire for betterment and earnest application to learning would become the stuff of national myth.

Interestingly, it was this generation of men who so neatly defined the concept of separate spheres for the sexes, the better to demark success in the male world. At the same time, their philosophy softened gender boundaries, so that men might also be admired for child rearing or their interest in culture. Mixed messages formed part of this credo and contributed to the anxiety de Tocqueville recognized in aspiring Americans, as well as the sexual confusion manifested by young men like Lincoln.[59]

IV

As he rose in society, Lincoln wanted to associate with women of a better class. Thus Mary Todd enters the stage. Lincoln evidently met the vivacious Kentuckian during the Tippecanoe campaign of 1840, when she and her friends were among the young women enjoying the excitement. Plump, bright-eyed Mary was one of sixteen children in a prosperous plantation family with important connections throughout the Ohio Valley. Her sister Elizabeth had married into the prominent Edwards family of Illinois, and when Mary visited them in 1839, she was a popular addition to Springfield society. Well-educated and an enthusiastic Whig, Miss Todd had supped with Lincoln's hero Henry Clay, and she enjoyed parlor politics and flirtatious repartee. She was also ambitious. Mary told more than one person that she intended to marry a man who would become president. Lincoln caught her eye.[60]

The two corresponded, planned group outings, and occasionally met, probably at the Edwards home. Twenty-one-year-old Mary was described as the "very creature of excitement," and her sister recalled that Lincoln was often struck dumb in her company. Their backgrounds were strikingly different and Mary's family thought Lincoln an unsuitable match. Still, the two had similarities. Both had lost mothers at a young age; both enjoyed reading and reciting poetry and were obsessed by politics. Yet whatever fascination Lincoln felt for Mary Todd in 1840, by the following year he had either rethought the friendship or possibly was smitten by another visitor, the bewitching Matilda Edwards. Even Mary admitted she had never seen a lovelier girl than Matilda, who stole several Springfield hearts during her stay. Mary apparently tried to keep Lincoln's interest by playing her many beaux off one another, but according to later accounts, he broke off the relationship in an awkward interview.[61]

What happened next is not entirely clear. Lincoln sank into a deep depression, which he called "the hypo," making him "the most miserable man

Abraham and Mary Todd Lincoln,
daguerreotypes by Nicolas H. Shepard, c. 1846
LIBRARY OF CONGRESS

living." On Mary's side there was self-accusation, perhaps for playing too fast and loose with her suitors. Ultimately some friends intervened and a rapprochement followed. The two wed on November 4, 1842. Acquaintances speculated that Mary was the more interested party, and that Lincoln struggled with his sense of honor for having led her on. Others thought Lincoln's insecurity left him doubting his ability to make a woman happy. There was also talk that he was selling his soul to gain the patronage of Mary's powerful family. In any case, Joshua Speed was not "entirely satisfied" that his friend's "*heart* was going with his hand."[62] Historians have wondered if a sexual element was not present, compelling the couple to marry quickly. The wedding did take place in haste, under arrangements that were unseemly for the elite Edwards family, and particularly for Mary, who loved parties, finery, and attention. Robert Todd Lincoln was born almost nine months to the day from the Lincolns' marriage; but even had the couple enjoyed premarital relations, Mary could not possibly have known with certainty that she was pregnant. (Abraham was unsure too. The following March he told Speed he could not "say, exactly yet" if Speed would have "a namesake at our house.") Both bride and groom were silent about their decision to wed, except for Abraham's cryptic comment that his marriage was a "source of profound wonderment."[63]

The relationship between a man and a woman is among the most basic and ancient of conflicts; each contains some element of mystery, as well as tension. The inner workings of the Lincoln marriage are particularly opaque, for scanty evidence of it survives. Mary sentimentally spoke of her husband's "dear loving letters," but only a few remain today. Perhaps she or their son Robert destroyed them; perhaps there were never more than a handful to begin with. Herndon thought his law partner wrote "fewer social letters—& even political ones" than any man he knew, and Lincoln admitted he avoided writing letters to women, "as a business which I do not understand." The correspondence that does exist is kind and confiding, full of pets and plans and the domestic details that make up every life. The rest of what we know is secondhand, often relayed decades after the fact, making it exceedingly hard to sort the marital wheat from the chaff.[64]

The impression given in many recollections is that of an uneasy marriage between two difficult partners, whose tastes and inclinations sometimes clashed. Lincoln was moody and aloof, slovenly and coarse, careless and over-indulgent with their four sons. He retreated into himself, whereas his extroverted wife looked for companionship and comfort—which she did not always receive. She was from a well-heeled home and she expected to live with a certain gentility. Lincoln's muddy boots, unschooled table manners, and informal habits sorely tried her. Mary was often left alone, to feel vulnerable and unprotected while her husband rode the court circuit, or swapped stories in male-only back rooms. She was also apt to scold and demand, and many friends recounted ugly bouts of henpecking. Lincoln often ignored or laughed at this, which was perhaps an impolitic response. Nonetheless, his compatriots tended to think he was the long-sufferer. The frictions are illustrated by an instance when Lincoln harnessed himself like a horse to the baby carriage and, lost in thought, allowed the buggy to overturn and pitch the child— "kicking and squalling"—into the gutter. He did not notice and trotted on, but Mary flew from the house, full of fright and fury. Her husband ran off "with great celerity," without waiting to face her stormy protest. Whether they fought it out or toughed it out in these situations is impossible to know; but a separation was clearly never in order. A cousin thought they were mismatched, but overlooked each other's foibles and appreciated the values that lay beneath. Herndon, who was not an admirer of the marriage, concluded that "when all is known the world will divide between Mr. Lincoln and Mrs. Lincoln its censure."[65]

There were also bright sides to the relationship. Mary was volatile and thin-skinned, yet she was "a delightful conversationalist, and well-informed on all the subjects of the day." Lincoln had brought large debts to the marriage and in the early years she was game enough to live (and give birth) in a tavern. Mary epitomized devotion to a wife's circumscribed sphere, in which home life was bound by the man's expectations and career. Her husband was loyal and hardworking and intellectually stimulating, with serious prospects of becoming a leader in the state, if not the nation. What Abraham and Mary shared was the sum of these worlds: pleasure in their growing sons and searing sorrow at the death of Eddie, the second eldest; a comfortable life; excitement in their future prospects. Moreover, their political ambitions meshed. Mary was not only politically astute but enormously proud of "Mr. Lincoln" and protective of his interests. She encouraged him to dream large. He, in turn, took her advice seriously. There is also evidence that they enjoyed their companionship. Having looked forward to time alone when he arrived in Washington as a congressman, Lincoln almost immediately missed his wife. "I hate to stay in this old room by myself," he admitted; a few months later, he encouraged Mary to "come along, and that as *soon* as possible." After the ballots were counted on that fateful November night in 1860, the first person the president-elect ran to tell was his wife. "Mary, Mary!" he cried out, "we are elected!"[66]

The election would affect a great deal, including Lincoln's family relations. From the beginning it was a controversial win, and the president-elect and his wife became targets for those wanting to diminish the Republican triumph. The nation's deteriorating stability, a strenuous (and often criticized) whistle-stop trip to Washington, and threats of assassination did not lessen the tension. Nor was the situation helped by both Lincolns' naïve expectations of the presidency. Republican insiders doubted the president-elect knew how to conduct himself in his new position and feared he and his wife would become objects of fun. Both Lincolns showed strain under these pressures.[67]

The White House was the prize they had worked for all their lives, but from the start the Lincolns were uncomfortable there. The transition from obscurity to First Lady had been abrupt for Mrs. Lincoln. She had envisaged herself as a grand hostess and was unprepared for either criticism or national crisis. Now the spotlight was trained on her without mercy. "Her smiles and her frowns become a matter of consequence to the whole American world," observed journalist William Howard Russell. "If she but drive down Pennsylvania Avenue, the electric wire thrills the news to every hamlet in the Union." Her dress, her manners, and, most of all, her political maneuvering were soon talked about. Mary first overstepped her position by spending large sums for furnishing the White House, without thought to either regulations or discretion. The Executive Mansion undoubtedly needed renovation, but it infuriated Lincoln to find her buying "flub dubs for this damned old house" while soldiers suffered.[68] Mrs. Lincoln also sent unwise letters to major political figures, in which she censured generals and cabinet members, tried to influence appointments, or promoted Kentucky-bred horses for the cavalry. (There are indications that she was quite effective in her lobbying: Washington insiders stated that "she always *succeeds*," and men of prominence like *New York Herald* owner James Gordon Bennett and Senator Charles Sumner courted her for access and information.) She was also vulnerable to intriguers like Henry "Chevalier" Wikoff, a professional rogue notorious for leaking information and angling for personal gain. Such men sometimes led Mrs. Lincoln into verbal indiscretion. If the motive was to help her husband, the impression it left accomplished the opposite.[69]

There were many who knew and admired Mary Lincoln, finding her, as did Commissioner of Grounds Benjamin French, "a smart, intelligent woman" who "bore herself well and bravely & looked Queenly." George Bancroft, a renowned historian and a Democrat, was similarly "entranced" by the First Lady, whom he thought "a fair counterpart to Mr Lincoln's brains." General John Sedgwick noted how she visited his corps hospital "giving little comforts to the sick, without any display or ostentation." Indeed, the dichotomy between those judging from afar, such as a catty diarist named Maria Lydig Daly, who concluded Mrs. Lincoln was little more than "a vulgar, shoddy, contractor's wife," and those who actually knew her is striking. But the damage had been early done and only worsened under the pressure of war. Mary Lincoln's intrigues were whispered about both North and South, with the truth sometimes embellished. Some thought she was passing along state secrets, either through foolhardiness or from lingering Southern sympathy. Her relatives were slaveholders and three Todd brothers and a brother-in-law were enrolled in the Confederate Army, sparking "dark insinuations against her . . . Union principles, and honesty." A British journalist observed that "the poor lady is loyal as steel to her family and to Lincoln the first, but she . . . has permitted her society to be infested by men who would not be received in any respectable private house." The First Lady's image had become so distorted that no number of admiring comments could bring it back into focus.[70]

And the missteps continued. There were rounds of receptions that Mary must have envisioned in the Dolley Madison mode—elegant levees at which opponents could meet and ideas be exchanged. Her husband hated these events but did nothing to prevent them. The fact that the Executive Mansion was used to present evenings of conjuring tricks by "Hermann the Prestidig-itateur" or Barnum-like displays of Tom Thumb and his bride did not elevate the reputation of either Lincoln. The unfortunate optic reached its apogee when the Lincolns gave a lavish and ill-timed ball on February 5, 1862. Re-freshments included more than a ton of turkeys, pheasants, and venison, as well as spun-sugar confections in the shape of nymphs and a fully gunned Fort Sumter. Such a wartime spectacle was unseemly to say the least, and it caused a backlash in both press and political circles. "A dancing-party given at the time the nation is in the agonies of civil war!" exclaimed Henry Dawes, a Republican congressman already critical of corruption in Lincoln's admin-istration. "With equal propriety might a man make a ball with a corpse in his house!" Even staunch supporters boycotted the affair. The questions now were not about the First Lady's overspending but the President's judgment.[71]

"Grand presidential party at the White House, Washington, Wednesday evening, February 5th," wood engraving,
Frank Leslie's Illustrated Newspaper, February 22, 1862

Family tensions came to a head with the illness of Willie Lincoln during that ill-fated dance. By many accounts he was the most likable, and perhaps the most promising, of their boys. He and younger brother Tad had caught typhoid fever, and, despite their parents' desperate ministrations, Willie began to succumb as the party roared below. Both Lincolns were devastated. Nicolay recalled how the President came to his room in tears; a nurse brought in to help recorded his nightlong vigils at Tad's bedside. Indeed, the tragedy may have affected his stability. Under constant pressure from the slow advance of the war, he now made a series of extremely poor military decisions, with serious consequences. Still, he had the distraction of official business and constant company, while his wife lay in a darkened room, falling prey to self-reproach, as well as to anxiety for her sons. Although Tad recovered, eleven-year-old Willie died at five in the afternoon on February 20 in the carved rosewood bed, now known as the Lincoln Bed. Mary, already suffering from isolation and public criticism, sank to new levels of despair. Friends came to help, and she tried to relieve her mind by dabbling in spiritualism, but her once coveted position now seemed a "mockery."[72]

Perhaps she took morphine as well, for it was a popular remedy for a variety of physical and psychic ailments. More than one person thought the drug detached Mary's mind from reality. Misfortunes only multiplied, as several Todd men fighting for the Confederacy were killed in horrible battles like Shiloh, Vicksburg, and Chickamauga. These were losses she could not mourn publicly, and "like a barrier of granite" they estranged the First Lady from her family. One sister, the widow of Southern general Benjamin Helm, came to visit; but the press was quick to resent the presence of a rebel officer's wife in the White House, and Mrs. Helm soon retreated. Once Mary was cut off from sympathy and blasted as "the scape-goat for both North and South," a close acquaintance remarked: "I do not believe her mind ever fully recovered its poise."[73]

The double burden of grief and public pressure formed a gulf in the Lincolns' marital relations. There is evidence that both partners tried to console each other but were handicapped by the wartime

Lincoln's Midnight Thinky,
pencil, by Charles W. Reed, c. 1862

244 Six Encounters with Lincoln

situation and their own divergent personalities. "Sister has always a cheerful word and a smile for Mr. Lincoln, who seems thin and care-worn and seeing her sorrowful would add to his care," Mrs. Helm noted in her diary, and the President tried to find medical help and kindly friends to soothe his wife's misery. Despondent, Lincoln became recklessly oblivious to his personal safety, complaining that the war was destroying him, and wandering alone at night without a guard. "I often meet Mr. Lincoln in the streets," wrote State Department translator Adam Gurowski. "Poor man . . . ! [His] looks are those of a man whose nights are sleepless, and whose days are comfortless."[74] Lincoln's imprudent outings filled his wife with fear, as did the idea that his draft-age son, Robert, might also be lost to the conflict. She became increasingly erratic, her clandestine correspondence more frequent, and swings of emotion more pronounced. Many of the President's colleagues had not particularly liked Mary Lincoln in Springfield; now they viewed her as a dangerous interloper, incautious in her words and actions. Secretaries called her the "Hell-Cat," and Republicans worried she was revealing sensitive information to the opposition. Her imperiousness was also noted. Although Mary could be exceedingly gracious, she often demanded special prerogatives. She also appears to have been jealous of her husband's time and imagined he gave attention to other ladies. At a military review toward the close of the war, Mrs. Lincoln raised a fuss when an officer's good-looking wife rode alongside the President, causing her to fear the young woman would be mistaken for the First Lady. The episode was much magnified by Adam Badeau, an aide to General Ulysses S. Grant, raising more eyebrows. Grant's wife, Julia, who was present, later tamped it down, describing it as awkward but not a major scene. Still, it was indicative of Mary Lincoln's volubility during these years, and her dangerous flirtation with unreality.[75]

In her anxiety, Mary fell into a pattern of frantic economizing, alternating with compulsive overspending. Gossips thought she starved her husband, or lowered the tone of the White House by grazing cows and goats on the lawn. Actually she tried to persuade the President to eat and sleep more regularly and orchestrated their summer moves to the Soldiers' Home, where the breezes and political pressures blew cooler. At the same time, she made eye-popping purchases, "ransacking" jewelers and dry goods stores, inviting criticism of her self-indulgence. The First Lady was undoubtedly the prey of sharp-eyed merchants in Washington and New York; and the problems were compounded by Lincoln's inattention to household finance. However, this kind of aberrant behavior also bespoke her fear of destitution and desire to escape through compulsive spending. After her eldest son, Robert, joined the Army the wild splurges increased. Toward the end of the war, Mary bought eighty-four pairs of kid gloves and $3,200 worth of jewelry within a few weeks. Some believed she had also begun to steal objects. At the time of Lincoln's death, she was $25,000 in debt—as much as his yearly salary.[76]

More grief would come to Mary Todd Lincoln, as each of her worst nightmares came true: her husband murdered before her eyes; her kin and eldest son estranged; Tad succumbing to death while in his teens; and the horrid specter of poverty slowly tightening its grasp. Her eyes, once universally described as "sparkling," became dull with the inability to absorb more disaster. Yet her descent into darkness, destructive as it was to her family and to herself, was never malicious. To read her life's correspondence, with its shattering chain of sorrows, is to be moved more to pity than to disdain.[77]

V

It is unclear whether Mary Lincoln's strong personality influenced her husband's reticence toward forceful women—if so, he never stated it in so many words. But that he disliked women with confident ideas or pointed demands is too well documented to doubt. His secretaries noted that he thought it an "unpleasant and irksome thing" for a lady to arrive on "business," when she could have made her requests through a male emissary. Even noted women like Barton, Howe, and Elizabeth Cady Stanton were unwelcome at the White House without an escort, and often it took a congressman or other luminary to gain them access. This was in stark contrast to the "open door" policy of the presidential office, in which, theoretically, anyone could enter and speak his piece. ("Nobody ever wanted to see the President who did not," claimed William Seward, "there was never a man so accessible to all sorts of proper and improper persons.") Despite his attempts to discourage female callers, Lincoln complained he was "constantly beset by women of all sorts, high and low, pretty and ugly, modest and the other sort."[78] Letters also regularly arrived from prominent women, on themes that included deporting freed slaves (Anna Ella Carroll), women's right to government jobs (Lydia Sayer Hasbrouck, editor of *Sybil*, a feminist magazine), and the President's failure to rally the country's "moral enthusiasm" (Lydia Maria Child). For the most part, the notes were left unacknowledged. When Mary Livermore wrote to request Lincoln's participation in a fair being organized to animate Northern esprit and attract Union dollars, he did not respond until prodded by a Chicago politico, Isaac Arnold. Even constructive suggestions seem to have been taken as censure. Lincoln disliked criticism from men as well as women, but something about the commentary of female activists seemed to have particularly grated on his nerves.[79]

Lincoln was also annoyed by the nearly ceaseless parade of women who arrived to promote the interests of their menfolk. Some were angling for promotions, others for release from prison or from military service altogether, and some for political position. Their tactics ranged from bluster and belligerence to weeping and prayerful entreaty. A few cases touched the President's sympathetic nerve, for many women had truly suffered during the war, experiencing overwhelming personal loss, and sometimes economic devastation. "So many women . . . in these days, have their hearts wrung with sorrow, and want a scapegoat to bear the wrongs which have been the cause of it! And who can bear them better than the President?" asked journalist Lois Bryan Adams. "Who, they ask, is more responsible?" Some wives and daughters became unreasonable, demanding Lincoln overrule his generals, or that he dispense special privileges. Apologists have claimed he was uniformly kind and patient with female supplicants, but, in fact, he often angrily rebuffed the more aggressive, particularly those grumbling about hardships faced by pro-South families. His impatience is clear in a note sent to John Nicolay about a woman seeking a brigadier generalship for her husband. "She is a saucy woman," complained the President, "and I am afraid she will keep tormenting till I may have to do it."[80] More than one lady tried to gain favor by appealing to Lincoln's vanity. An acquaintance claimed the chief executive told him of a woman who came to his office soliciting a job for "somebody supposed to be her husband." She bent so close to the President that he thought she intended to embrace him. Then, Lincoln said, "indignation came to my relief, and drawing myself back . . . I gave her the proper sort of a look and said: 'Mrs.——, you are very pretty, and its very tempting, BUT I WON'T." Petitioners also inundated the White House with letters—pleading, insistent, or chastising. "I know you are harassed, by half the women in the country, seeking one favor or another and often feel tempted to throw every feminine letter into the waste basket," sympathized Lincoln's friend Jane Speed. She then begged to have her son be transferred from the field to a soft job in the paymaster's department.[81]

Lincoln had brought it all on himself, of course, through his belief that the public should be granted such extraordinary access. But he never found the knack for handling his feminine constituency. His innate discomfort around women left him not knowing how to deny unwelcome requests firmly without provoking tears or causing offense. The social tools Lincoln had honed were ones that smoothed his path in the male sphere—logic and cool taciturnity to control situations, or humor to disarm opponents and leave them laughing. Seward thought this ability "a cunning that was genius," but with women—even those who were politically attuned—the practical jokes and clubroom banter fell flat. They did not like the earthy stories, and they generally wanted action, not words, as proof of leadership. Moreover, he was often plainly rude.[82]

Over the years Lincoln had taught himself many things—from grammar to geometry—but he had never bothered to master the etiquette so valued by mannered society. An assistant treasury secretary acknowledged that Lincoln was not "overburdened" with civility, "and his manners were any thing but acceptable to the fair sex." The wife of a favorite aide was alarmed that he made faces and "threw himself around *promiscuously*" when in their company. In another instance, visitors to the White House were stunned when Lincoln remained seated while a woman standing near him spoke to him earnestly. "After a while he arose and drew up another chair, as she supposed with the intention of offering it to her. Nothing of the sort. He stretched out his own long legs upon it." (Told he was the worst-bred man the company had ever seen, Lincoln had the good humor to agree.) In the best cases, such as with the Stowe party, accomplished ladies left his company in gales of laughter, simply thinking him ludicrous. With women like Anna Dickinson, his dismissive attitude was taken as an insult, inviting contempt for his inelegant conduct. These ladies had *expectations*. If Lincoln was going to lead the country without their consent at the polls, he should at least act the part.[83]

The most difficult encounters were with women who had connections to men leading the war effort. They brought complaints about Lincoln's policies or his personal treatment of generals, and their confidence was often matched by their insistence. Among the more notable was Ellen Ewing Sherman, who arrived to tackle the chief executive on January 29, 1862. William Tecumseh Sherman had been so frustrated by his "impossible" command in Kentucky ("thirty thousand raw recruits . . . armed with the old European muskets that *McClellan had rejected*" to guard three hundred miles of mountainous terrain) that he had spectacularly vented his temper. Some labeled him "insane" and the War Department quickly accepted Sherman's resignation. His wife immediately took charge, harnessing support from her prominent father, political broker Thomas Ewing, as well as Sherman's brother John, a Republican senator from Ohio. She marched to the White House with her father and pointedly asked Lincoln why her husband had been left "to be reviled & ridiculed and calumniated & scouted as a madman" by jealous officials, while the war stagnated and the President did nothing. She demanded that Sherman's name be cleared and that he be restored to an appropriate position. Lincoln took one look at the powerful Ewing-Sherman front before him and capitulated on the spot, professing ignorance of the situation (though the Kentucky plans had come directly from him), and proclaiming himself eager for Sherman's promotion. It was, Ellen Sherman told her husband, a "most satisfactory interview."[84]

Jesse Benton Frémont, carte de visite
by Mathew Brady, c. 1860
COURTESY OF SPECIAL COLLECTIONS, FINE ARTS LI-
BRARY, HARVARD UNIVERSITY

Another talked-about encounter involved Jesse Benton Frémont. Like Ellen Sherman, Frémont had a distinguished political pedigree through her father, Thomas Hart Benton. She also had long experience dealing directly with high-level officials, including presidents. Her political activism went beyond Mary Lincoln's armchair politicking to embrace a joint presidential campaign with her husband in 1856. In 1861 John C. Frémont was a general, commanding the volatile Missouri district. It quickly became apparent that he was less capable, both politically and administratively, than his legendary status suggested. At the same time, another powerful family, the Blairs, whose eldest son was Lincoln's postmaster general, was waging a struggle for influence in Missouri. They secretly tried to recruit Jesse Frémont as an informant, hoping to form a coalition through which they would divide power in the state. She refused the offer. On August

30, with conditions deteriorating, General Frémont issued an order that, among other things, liberated the slaves of traitorous owners in his district. Abolitionists applauded the move, but Lincoln questioned it. He was worried that the proclamation might alarm slaveholding Union states like Kentucky; and also noted it was at odds with laws passed a few weeks earlier. When the President asked Frémont to rescind the emancipation clause, Jesse boarded the night train for Washington.[85]

According to her account, Frémont had to sit up two nights on the train, arriving at Willard's Hotel on September 10, exhausted and soiled from the journey. Undaunted, she immediately sent a note to the White House, time-dated 8:00 p.m., asking when she might have an interview, either that evening or the next day. She received a one-word reply—"Now." Even though her baggage had not yet been delivered, she contacted a prominent judge to escort her and hurried to the Executive Mansion. This was a familiar place, where she had always been treated as family, noted Frémont, and "with all the old confidence of the past, I went forward now." She was received in the Red Room, but the tone of the President's greeting jarred her. It was midnight by this time, and Lincoln barely acknowledged her; nor did he offer a seat. The weary Mrs. Frémont drew up a chair nonetheless. She handed the chief executive a letter from her husband, and added her own arguments in favor of the proclamation, stressing that it would encourage badly needed European support for the Union. "You are quite a female politician," the President remarked with a disapproving glance. "I felt the sneering tone," stated Frémont, "and saw there was a foregone decision against all listening." She then described a tirade, during which Lincoln expounded on the disadvantages of her husband's order, and his unhappiness that it had "dragged the negro into the war." The commander in chief gave a different version of the story. Two years later he told John Hay that Jesse Frémont had demanded the midnight audience and then "taxed me so violently with many things that I had to exercise all the awkward tact I have to avoid quarreling with her." The President also accused her of intimating "more than once" that the Frémonts' public support outweighed his. If crossed, "[t]he Pathfinder" could simply "set up for himself."[86]

The Blairs angrily accosted Jesse Frémont the next day, accusing her of alienating the chief executive and trying to undermine their family. They let slip that they had written to Lincoln, complaining about her husband's slipshod military skills and lack of control in Missouri. Although they had not been present at the meeting between Frémont and Lincoln, they wrote a for-publication account, featuring a raging Jesse, who "stamped her foot like a virago" when her unrealistic demands were not met. Jesse then wrote to the White House, asking for copies of the Blair correspondence relating to Missouri, as well as for a reply to her husband's missive. The President sent a placating answer but evaded her request. Instead, he sent a message through military channels to rescind Frémont's proclamation. Lincoln, who needed to act quickly in a delicate matter, believed he had good reasons for doing this, and not just because he was suspicious of Frémont's potential rivalry.[87]

Still, the version of the meeting Lincoln gave Hay was not accurate. The time on Jesse's note shows that it was the President, not she, who insisted on the midnight meeting; Lincoln exaggerated Frémont's intentions by claiming he was planning to set up a "bureau of Abolition"; and he erroneously placed Mrs. Frémont's confrontation with the Blairs before the White House meeting, making it appear she was motivated by a personal feud rather than genuine political differences over the proclamation. The competing stories form an arresting example of the way gender lines were drawn on these occasions. The lady voiced bitter resentment at unbending male authority and the disdainful attitude shown her abilities. The President's team fell back on the convenient stereotype of a shrewish woman, out of her depth and out of control.[88]

VI

Lincoln's impatience with women who challenged his opinions is perhaps understandable, given prevailing attitudes. After all, even Miss Leslie's *Behavior Book* noted in 1853 that it was "injudicious for ladies to attempt arguing with gentlemen on political or financial topics" because it would "not elevate them in the opinion of the masculine mind." More intriguing is the fact that Lincoln kept women who were actively working on his behalf at a distance. His ambivalence here is striking, for they played a large role in spurring the North to victory, by supplying the Army, tending the wounded, and invigorating morale. Yet Lincoln did little to encourage them, and he often seemed to look askance at feminine activities. When he did praise female war workers it was for cheering on the men, who, he stressed, were the ones actually saving the Union.[89]

An unprecedented number of women offered their services during the Civil War. Some eight thousand alone worked as nurses on the Union side, and countless others established hospitals and orphanages, guided slaves to freedom, or met in community circles to sew. Indeed, they were among the first to join the cause. Dorothea Dix, who was appointed to superintend female nurses, arrived at the scene on April 19, 1861, three hours after Union troops were fired upon in Baltimore; Mary Ann ("Mother") Bickerdyke began work in Cairo, Illinois, a few days later. Many women were motivated by helping their soldier sons or husbands. Those with abolitionist leanings viewed the conflict with missionary zeal, believing it would finally bring true liberty to the land. Still others felt the adrenaline rush of a righteous battle. Caught up in the martial spirit, Clara Barton admitted that "[t]he fight is in me and I will find a pretext."[90]

Although countless women found an outlet in rolling bandages or hemming blankets, others found only frustration in the traditional female roles of clothing, healing, or encouraging men. "A lonely, dull day—stitch, stitch, stitch," Caroline Healey Dall confided to her diary—and that moment decided to contribute with her intellect, as well as her needle. "It was the only time in my life that I ever thought I would rather be a man than a woman, that I might go and fight and perhaps die for my country and freedom," agreed author Lucy Larcom; she then added, with a sigh, "I had to content myself with knitting blue army socks and writing verses." The stories of Florence Nightingale, whose saga of hospital reform in the Crimean War had been published in 1858, caused many women to believe their highest mission was to tend the sick, inspiring their active involvement in hospital wards. A few score cast off convention completely to don a soldier's uniform and fight at the front. Another handful, like Elizabeth Van Lew of Richmond, faced daily danger spying for the Union.[91]

The outpouring of assistance, however well intentioned, was unofficial and uncoordinated. In some quarters it aroused more alarm than appreciation. When Dr. Elizabeth Blackwell, the first woman to receive a medical degree in America, tried to systemize a training program for nurses, she found herself sidelined by male physicians who were not enthusiastic about female volunteers and did not want advice from a woman whose credentials equaled their own. They "refused to have anything to do with the nurse education plan if 'that Miss Blackwell, were going to engineer the matter,'" she wrote, adding regretfully that "we kept in the background." Instead, a group of powerful New York doctors and businessmen created the United States Sanitary Commission (USSC) to advise on matters of soldiers' health, raise funds, and assist in procuring supplies and hiring personnel. Both Blackwell and the USSC organizers hoped to structure war efforts so that a stream of well-meaning amateurs would not inundate hospital corridors. The men involved were also eager to have a springboard to political influence, and the rivalry for access and recognition began early. Heeding the War Department, which viewed all outside activities as meddling, Lincoln was slow to encourage citizen contributions. Such interference, the President thought, might become "like a fifth wheel to the coach." Although Lincoln authorized the Sanitary Commission on June 19, 1861, it was only when Winfield Scott publicly acknowledged how much the citizens' relief efforts were needed that it was officially sanctioned.[92]

"United States Sanitary Commission: Our Heroines," wood engraving, *Harper's Weekly*, April 9, 1864

Dorothea Dix, nationally known for her work reforming insane asylums, was appointed to supervise the flood of volunteer nurses. She was earnest and hardworking, but completely inexperienced in this line of work. "Miss Dix, though in many respects an estimable & sensible woman is deficient in the power of organization, and has no idea of the details of Hospital management," observed Dr. Blackwell's sister Emily, herself a physician. "I think there cannot fail to be much confusion." It would prove to be an understatement. Dix directed affairs under a strict code of conduct, shunning nurses who looked for adventure (or seemed too attractive), in hopes of overturning the popular view that women serving the Army were wrongly motivated. The regimentation was well meant, but so harsh that it alienated doctors as well as nurses. (Jane Swisshelm, who worked for seven weeks at Washington's Campbell Military Hospital, described Dix as "a self sealing can of horror tied up with red tape.") In any case, the war's pressing needs proved too great to address with the modest corps Dix recruited. Freelancers—among them, Barton, Bickerdyke, and Sojourner Truth—either ignored or avoided her. There were problems as well with the USSC leaders, who found Dix a difficult personality and suspected she was responsible for the creation of a powerful rival organization, the Western Sanitary Commission. When these commissions began leveling criticism at the administration's ability to discipline the Army, and interfered in the selection of a new surgeon general, Secretary of War Edwin Stanton curtailed their activities. Ultimately Dix, too, was given a smaller portfolio.[93]

Dix struggled in her position, showing more doggedness than genius, but in many ways she had been given a near impossible task. All but a few army doctors disliked the presence of women in their wards, protesting loudly to the War Department. Some tolerated female laundresses and cooks, but most resented participation in medical matters. Lincoln made a few overtures on Dix's behalf to reluctant officers, but the appeals went unheeded and soon stopped. "No one knows, who did not watch the thing from the beginning, how much opposition, how much ill-will . . . these women nurses endured," wrote Georgeanna Woolsey in 1864. Woolsey, who worked on hospital ships during the Peninsula campaign, came to believe the abuse was a "cool calculation" on the part of surgeons to eliminate female nurses from the system. "Government had decided that women should be employed, and the army surgeons . . . determined to make their lives so unbearable that they should be forced in self-defence to leave."[94]

Nurses were ignored, physically molested, given prisonlike living quarters, and sometimes spat upon. The strongest simply forged ahead. Dr. Mary Walker, a maverick in trousers, was denied a surgeon's commission by Lincoln, who informed her that he was "sure it would injure the service" to "thrust" her among male doctors against their consent. She proceeded to set up a valuable surgery without his sanction.[95] USSC official Frederick Law Olmsted initially doubted female nurses could survive the hostility but came away a true believer after observing the ladies' "untiring industry, self-possession and tranquil cheerfulness." Some volunteers, like Bickerdyke, garnered support from grateful soldiers, helping them to override doctors who were deficient or corrupt. (When an irate surgeon tried to keep Bickerdyke in line by handing her a copy of army regulations, she turned the tables by memorizing it, later finding it "invaluable" for holding officers to account.) Her work, if an irritation to incompetent doctors, earned the respect of senior commanders, including Ulysses S. Grant.[96] Writing from St. Louis, surgeon Francis Bacon gave full flavor to the annoyance, frustration, but ultimate respect "strong-minded" hospital matrons could inspire:

> I reluctantly confess that I am subjugated and crushed by a woman who sings The Star-Spangled Banner copiously through all the wards of my hospital. . . . She weighs three hundred pounds. She comes every morning, early. She wears the Flag of our Country pinned across her heart. She comes into *my* room, my own office, unabashed by the fact that I am the Surgeon in charge, and . . . looks me in the eye with perfect calmness and intrepidity. She takes off her sunbonnet and mantilla and lays them upon my table, over my papers . . . and begins to exude small parcels from every pocket. . . . She nurses tenderly, and feeds and cries over the bad cases. Poor Martin Rosebush, a handsome, smooth-faced, good boy from New Hampshire, desperately wounded and delirious would start up with a cry of joy when she came, and died with his arms around her neck, calling her his mammy. . . . Of course I do not encourage the visits of this creature with the Flag of our Country and the National Anthem. On the contrary, they encourage me.[97]

Ineffective or opportunistic volunteers, the very sort Dix was trying to weed out, inevitably did appear, and some of the ladies' more naïve contributions became the stuff of waggish jokes. "Oh! Woman—thoughtful woman! The soldier thanks thee for sending him pies and cakes that turn sour before they leave New York," crooned humorist Orpheus C. Kerr.[98] But many made real contributions. African Americans were among them, working chiefly in kitchens, but also playing an active political role, by raising funds, supporting the U.S. Colored Troops, and trying to improve conditions for freedmen and -women. Some, like Harriet Tubman, heroically challenged the slaveholding establishment by leading bondmen to freedom or serving as Union Army scouts.[99] Women also used the power of the press to further the cause. "Pestilential" feminist writer Gail Hamilton, though deeply concerned about the "astounding incapacity" of Lincoln's leadership, used her pen to inspire stead-fastness and sacrifice on the home front. "The war cannot be finished by sheets and pillow-cases," she insisted, calling on her countrywomen to throw off self-pity and commit themselves to upholding the glories of republican government. Hamilton went on to write rousing tracts after debacles like the 1862 battle at Fredericksburg, rallying the nation with cries of "Courage!" when the President's words failed to inspire.[100] Annie Wittenmyer, a special agent for the Iowa Sanitary Commission, despaired of the filth and inappropriate food of army hospitals, but persevered to initiate diet kitchens that became models in both theaters of the war. Wittenmyer downplayed her influence by claiming the kitchens were just an extension of women's traditional role in food preparation—but also insisted that she and her staff be treated as professionals. Later she established the first orphanages for children of slain soldiers. Some field workers, like Barton, found that resistance to them evaporated in the chaos of battle, when need trumped prejudice. When male nurses flinched under artillery fire at Antietam, Barton aided surgeon James Dunn with the amputations. Dunn would sing her praise: "In my feeble estimation, General McClellan, with all his laurels, sinks into insignificance beside the true heroine of the age, the *angel of the battlefield*."[101]

The hardships under which civilians—men and women—labored were sometimes severe. Dix recorded that "this dreadful civil war has as a huge wild beast consumed my whole of life." She refused all remuneration for her work. Barton too worked for free, proudly noting that "[n]o soldier has eaten harder 'tack' or slept on barer ground or under more malarious damps than I have within these four years." Yet the effort also yielded valuable insights and experience. Women working directly in the field tested their courage and their capacity to endure privation in ways that had been unimaginable a few years earlier. Those serving organizations like the USSC learned to budget and raise funds, to strategize and direct operations. They also had to navigate daily relations with men who were not part of their family and find ways to deal with jealousy, sexual advances, and the male propensity to take credit for their work. Most management skills were new to them, and some unprecedented for a woman to perform. Many volunteers surprised themselves with their abilities.[102]

These activities also had a way of politicizing women. Instincts about effective governance were honed, and their lack of political clout was painfully underscored. Wartime work fed the mounting frustration that female citizens had been reduced to what one group termed "legal pauperism." In addition, it exposed many for the first time to African Americans and their plight. Clara

Barton was among those whose consciousness was kindled in this regard: by war's end she had moved from defending herself against workplace inequality to campaigning for civil liberties that would benefit women as well as freed people. Nevertheless, even when the war blurred traditional gender roles, it did not represent a revolution in the status of women, or an abrupt change in what they considered their duty as helpmates for men. Rarely did it radically change lives, though it did offer a glimpse of greater possibilities. Successful women like Mary Livermore and Jane Hoge, who shaped the Western Sanitary Commission's work despite a male governing council, understood their position was subordinate to government officials, surgeons, and board members, and found ways to accommodate to that reality. Only a few truly broke the shackles to pursue careers in medicine or philanthropy.[103]

Among the large lessons these trailblazers learned was that whatever their achievements, they could not necessarily count on public appreciation. Many Unionists hesitated to recognize the contribution women made to their cause, including President Lincoln. He occasionally praised Sanitary Commission efforts and individual civilian sacrifice, but the words came sporadically and often seemed halfhearted. In the early days of the war, Lincoln sanctioned both Dix and the USSC, but he quickly adopted the War Department's skepticism, disparaging what he called the "sentimental department of the army," and accusing commission members of trying to "run the machine." Thereafter, Lincoln kept his distance. His meetings with dedicated women like Livermore were not—as previously noted—calculated to encourage their zeal. Barton, Swisshelm, Josephine Griffings, and other "angels" he declined to meet at all. Dix also seems to have had little access to the White House—the only direct evidence of her being consulted was when the President wanted to procure a caregiver for his wife and Tad after Willie's tragic death. Lincoln was friendly to the nurse Dix sent, but she was, after all, taking responsibility for his family. In most cases, he delegated meetings with benevolent ladies to other officials.[104]

Lincoln also shied away from participating in commission activities and charitable events, and from publicly praising women. He sent a draft of the Emancipation Proclamation to auction at the female-organized Western Sanitary Fair but only when prodded by male friends. It was a fine contribution, but the gesture soured when he declined to acknowledge either the organizers or the $550,000 they had raised for his army. The President took note when the clergyman Edward Everett, a former secretary of state, gave a handsome accolade to women in the address he made alongside Lincoln at Gettysburg in November 1863. He later read Everett's tribute to a delegation of war workers. But his own words of praise came more slowly and with less certainty. Compare remarks given a few months later by former president Millard Fillmore and Lincoln, at two fund-raising fairs held on the same day. Fillmore beamed brightly about the "noble and praiseworthy exertions" of the ladies, commending Dix's leadership, and concluding, "I can truly say that I am proud of my countrywomen for what they have done, and for what they are doing to mitigate the evils of war." At a parallel event Lincoln refused to speak until an embarrassing drumbeat of applause forced him onstage; he then chastised the organizers for practicing "a little fraud" by asking him to address the crowd. Fearing he "might do both himself and the nation harm" by speaking, he said only that he hoped the affair would be a success.[105]

That event may have jolted the President into realizing that the ladies' contribution had grown far beyond a few socks knitted by loving hands to a multimillion-dollar effort, with national attention and the backing of leading citizens. In any case, he appeared more appreciative when pressed to speak at the fair's closing. "I have never studied the art of paying compliments to women," he remarked, "but I must say that if all that has been said by orators and poets since the creation of the world in praise of woman were applied to the women of America, it would not do them justice for their conduct during this war." He might have done well to repeat these gracious comments on later occasions. Instead he generally chose to frame women's efforts in the terms most comfortable to him and to the prewar language of the "spheres"—that the ladies were working to "reward" the noble men who were saving the country.[106]

Lincoln was generally more supportive of women actually employed by his administration. A small group of ladies, like Barton, had entered government offices during the 1850s, but the numbers increased greatly as wartime bureaucracies grew and men were needed at the front. Lincoln showed no signs of the discomfort with female workers his predecessor had. Women like Anna Dickinson staffed the U.S. Mint, or signed and cut the newly created greenbacks issued by the Treasury Department. Swisshelm held a post at the War Department. Others were hired in factories producing uniforms and haversacks, in post offices or arsenals, and sometimes as teachers for the newly freed slaves. They faced many of the difficulties hospital staff did. The working world was a male preserve, where men acted freely in ways not always acceptable to mixed society. These men frequently balked at the presence of women—or competition from them. Barton, who held down a job at the Patent Office while ministering to soldiers, had already experienced the "hazing" in these situations, with men lining up to spit tobacco juice on her as she entered the building or actively conspiring to undermine her credibility. Swisshelm had long supported working women, railing against "shutting her out of employments . . . [for] which she is amply qualified," as well as unequal pay and dangerous conditions. Now she voiced irritation at men's inability to accept female co-workers. "The idea of treating them as copyists and clerks, simply this and nothing more," she complained, seemed "beyond the mental caliber of almost any man."[107]

Lincoln took the side of female workers a number of times, recognizing the need for better wages and working conditions. Just why he did this is not clear, because his administration was a highly capitalistic one. Perhaps he was influenced by the pitiable women filling his office, who so poignantly represented the catastrophe of war. Perhaps something of his reverence for labor was stirred, or his belief in the need for fair compensation. Whatever the reason, Lincoln tried to help several women find government employment when the death of male relatives left them destitute, and he sometimes intervened if a woman's property was being unjustly requisitioned by the military. When seamstresses at the Philadelphia armory complained in 1864 that businessmen were raking immense fortunes from government contracts while their own wages had been cut, he asked Stanton to increase the salaries. It was a simple case of "equity," wrote the President "that the laboring women in our employment, should be paid at the least as much as they were at the beginning of the war." The seamstresses' pay was raised by 20 percent, and Lincoln promised to run the factories at full capacity. Unfortunately, conditions did not really change, nor did the episode indicate a directed, long-term policy by the President. In 1865 sewing women in Cincinnati again protested that they were "unable to sustain life" while contractors "fattened" on their work. This time the chief executive did not defend them.[108] Nonetheless, he had at least given a nod to women's right to a fair wage as well as to legitimate protest against discrimination. Perhaps the most visible support Lincoln gave to female laborers came in June 1864, after an explosion at the Washington arsenal killed twenty-one young women who were filling minié-ball cartridges. The funeral included a mile-long procession and representatives of every military branch, with Lincoln leading the cortege as chief mourner. "It was most appropriate that he should," wrote a member of his staff, "and will be appreciated by all our citizens, particularly the humble class to which the victims belonged." There is no record of his speaking eulogistic words; nonetheless, it was the most public tribute Lincoln would offer the women who contributed to his cause.[109]

VII

O ne organization Lincoln and his wife tried actively to avoid was the Women's National Loyal League. Founded by two of the most forward-leaning feminists, Elizabeth Cady Stanton and Susan Brownell Anthony, the Loyal League was an outgrowth of their social activism—a long history of fighting for African Americans, promoting temperance, and speaking out for women's equality. When the league was envisioned in 1863, its stated purpose was to rally greater civilian support for the Union cause. Anthony and Stanton were strongly dedicated to the war effort, and both had relatives (a son and two nephews in the Stanton family and Anthony's brother) fighting at the front. But the Loyal League had an agenda broader than that of a patriotic ladies' aid society. Committed feminists viewed it as a new political stage, from which they could call on Lincoln to produce clearer policies. They had resolved, said Anthony, "to make an opportunity for Woman to speak her thought on the War" and to ensure that the battle was not one of bullets and bayonets alone, but a concerted action toward universal freedom. As Stanton remarked, women who diligently sewed, bound wounds, and sent loved ones off to die deserved "an object equal to the sacrifice."[110]

Like many feminists, Stanton and Anthony had cut their activist teeth on the abolitionist cause. They were idealists—influenced, like other reformers, by evangelical Protestant teachings that encouraged God-fearing folk to fight for a more virtuous society. When Stanton had joined Lucretia Mott and like-minded women to hold the first women's rights conference at Seneca Falls, New York, in 1848, it was directly linked with the fight to overturn slavery. In their eyes there was glaring ethical inconsistency in a land devoted to liberty, yet denying freedom to four million people—and many believed women's condition was scarcely better than the bondmen's. "For although we have not the chains, the lash and the auction block, in their literal sense," wrote Elizabeth Buffum Chace, one of the pioneers, "there is enough that is unjust and degrading in the condition of women, to convince us that [it] is of far wider significance to the progress of all mankind than . . . the Anti-Slavery Struggle." The women's movement learned well from the robust organization of the abolitionists, honing tools of careful preparation, public visibility, and newspaper publicity for their fight. Men like Frederick Douglass, Wendell Phillips, and William Lloyd Garrison joined the coalition, and the issues broadened from legal parity to include prison reform, educational opportunity, and sexual relations. Lincoln was in sympathy with some of these views, but he did not like the abolitionists' inflexibility and absolutism. While the crusaders were fired by pure principle, and impatient with compromise, he advocated a practical approach, based on cautious advance. Radicals like Anthony took unyielding positions, forcing debate ever more to their side. Although the President did edge closer to emancipationist views over time, he also resented this pressure. Moreover, the zealots were broadly unpopular, especially the feminists. Lincoln evidently thought it best to keep well away from the "isms" of the reform movements.[111]

What these women were testing was whether democracy had fixed limits or could be expanded to include increasingly diverse groups of people. This had been debated since the dawn of America's experiment, with the question of race foremost among the issues. Women had tried to have their rights considered when the nation was created, but in the paternalistic spirit of the Revolutionary era it was widely believed their welfare, like children's, was *implied* by benevolent male oversight. The weak, the fearful, or the reactionary had sporadically tried to put fences around republican society, limiting who could enjoy its blessings and benefit from its protections. Catholics, immigrants, free blacks, and Jews had all been shunned at one time or another. Lincoln protested this, understanding that if the democratic circle was drawn ever smaller, it could ultimately exclude the majority it was designed to serve. If the Declaration of Independence guaranteed equality, he asked, when one began making exceptions, "I would like to know . . . where it will stop?" But he too defined inclusion narrowly, never embracing the concept of a truly pluralistic society. Frederick Douglass, who came to admire Lincoln, nonetheless noted that "in his interests, in his associations, in his habits of thought, and in his prejudices he was a white man," willing to sacrifice the rights of others to protect his own clan. Lincoln's friends agreed, describing him as bound by conservative structures and uncomfortable with change. "He loved to move on old roads," remarked William Herndon. Lincoln's long-term vision for Native Americans, freedmen, and women rarely extended further than the limited vista of the complacent masses.[112]

The feminists of his time wanted just the opposite: to test democracy's elasticity. They hoped to stretch the sense of inclusion, so that instead of being "protected" by laws administered with paternalistic "good-will," women played a role in forming those laws and defining national policy. They also wanted to mold public opinion, so that the war was seen as an opportunity to do more than just whip back the rebels. It was, as Stanton boldly wrote, a chance to "EDUCATE THIRTY MILLIONS OF PEOPLE INTO THE IDEA OF A TRUE REPUBLIC." This was the golden moment, she advised, to make democratic ideals a tangible reality. "Let none stand idle spectators now," Stanton and Anthony exclaimed; "every hour is big with destiny."[113]

Recognizing the opportunity to push forward emancipation, Stanton at first decided to let feminist concerns take a backseat to abolitionist activities. She canceled a women's rights convention scheduled for the spring of 1861, re-marking that the focus should now be to crush the "slaveocracy's power." An-thony did not agree and resented placing suffrage and other women's issues on hold. "I have not yet seen one good reason for the abandonment of all our meetings," she complained, "and am, as time lengthens, more and more ashamed and sad." But other feminists thought that with the slaves still in bondage, and the country distracted by military matters, it would look im-proper to push their own political agenda. "It is true, as you say, that we 'should not forget our principles, or fail to declare them because the majority do not or cannot recognize them,' " counseled Martha Coffin Wright, "but it is useless to speak if nobody will listen."[114]

By midwar, however, feminist leaders were convinced they could take a more visible role. They determined to hold a meeting, ostensibly to foster Northern morale and lobby for a constitutional amendment that would dis-mantle slavery completely. This led to the first Women's National Loyal League convention in May 1863. The Loyal League sincerely supported the Union, but its conferences looked remarkably like earlier women's suffrage assemblies. The same elected officers, similar resolutions, and a commitment to secure "the rights . . . of women to equal citizenship" were showcased. The meeting drew the predictable heckling from newsmen who noted the resemblance to those "funny" prewar conventions. One sarcastically quipped that the President should put these strong-viewed ladies in his cabinet, as the country "couldn't be worse any off." Statements from the league were quite serious, however, ear-nestly challenging women to "[f]orget conventionalisms; forget what the world will say, whether you are in your place or out of your place . . . looking only to suffering humanity, your own conscience, and God for approval." League members were also critical of Lincoln's leadership, which they thought errant.

They resolved to draw up a million-signature petition supporting full emancipation, something at odds with the President's program at the time. Under Anthony's direction, the women did gather some four hundred thousand signatures, which they persuaded Charles Sumner to present to the Senate.[115]

The following year the league went further, approving a platform that directly confronted a number of Lincoln's policies. It accused the administration of obscuring "light and liberality" by continuing to defend slavery in Union states like Kentucky, of underpaying female nurses, of pursuing a reconstruction policy that was lenient to slaveholders and negligent of black needs, and of failing to protect U.S. Colored Troops from outrages at rebel hands. All of this, noted their official statement, was "but added proof of its heartless character, or utter incapacity to conduct the war." Instead of rallying women to give unconditional support to the administration, the Loyal League rejected Lincoln's plea for "Unionism," voting instead to back only those who waged a war to establish equality as the cornerstone of government. The league also directly advocated suffrage for all who bore arms or paid taxes, and called on women to join fully in creating the structures of a freer nation. The day was past, wrote Stanton, when women needed "permission" to enter politics, or an "invitation" to participate in their own governance. This was a deep dive into public affairs, one that alarmed even the sympathetic Sumner, who cautioned the ladies against involvement in "the strife of politics" during an election year. But the stage had been set for a major leap forward in women's political influence. During the next months, the Women's National Loyal League would use all the power of its pens, its allies, and its public protests to try to unseat Abraham Lincoln.[116]

With or without the league's support, the election of 1864 was a difficult one for Lincoln. Many Americans were weary of war, sick of stalemate or outright disaster, and tired of pouring men into a directionless army. Unlike the feminists, much of the nation was skeptical about emancipation and fearful of a color-blind society. Military officers were also widely disgruntled. They formed their own caucus, called the Strong Band. This was a coalition between War Democrats and radical Republicans that worked to bring a bolder leader (they favored Benjamin Butler) into power. Lincoln was also challenged within his own party. The radical wing believed his limited political courage was retarding social progress as well as prolonging the war. Lincoln did not disdain the liberals (compared with the conservative Democrats, he said, "there could be no doubt which side we would choose"), but managing them had been a sore trial—one in which he did not always prevail. However well meaning his advocacy of compromise, attempts to be all things to all men frequently backfired, satisfying no one.[117]

Most of the complaints women had about Lincoln followed those of the radical faction. Like their male counterparts, progressive women criticized what they saw as halfway measures and short-distance vision, as well as the President's tendency to waste time by "forever pottering about details and calculating chances." Many saw him as a reluctant emancipator, a fear borne out by some tactless remarks Lincoln made to Sojourner Truth, who came to see him in 1864. Truth traveled far to greet the man who had freed her people, but when she thanked him, Lincoln bluntly told her that if Southerners had "behaved themselves" he would have liberated no one.[118] In addition, those working with freed people, like Frances Dana Gage and Josephine Griffings, shared Anna Dickinson's concern about Lincoln's reconstruction plan. "What judgments may be reserved for this Christian nation who snatch from the womb of Chattel Slavery a Race of Immortal Beings and throw them raw and naked into the jaws of starvation and the devouring blasts of winter," Griffings dramatically asked the President. Harriet Tubman, the "Moses" who led so many of her people out of bondage, agreed, angrily denouncing the lower pay given to U.S. Colored Troops as well as the chief executive's apparent disregard for the ex-slaves' welfare. She had no interest, stated Tubman, in meeting Mr. Lincoln.[119]

For her part, Elizabeth Cady Stanton saw Lincoln as "a dead weight on the people . . . at the very moment they needed a pillar of light to go before them in the wilderness." She and Anthony also protested the administration's "tendency to despotic rule," through the curtailment of civil liberties. Stanton's views were not changed by a conversation with the President in May 1864, during which he largely ignored her while telling stories to her husband. Even though she came away thinking Lincoln a "stronger & better man" than she had supposed, Stanton's main impression was still of a "wily" politician "making capital out of the blood of the nation." Vowing not to support him, she announced: "If Lincoln is reelected I shall immediately leave the country for the Figee Island."[120]

Outspoken as these pronouncements were, it was the Women's National Loyal League's *actions* in 1864 that were most striking. Not content with debate among themselves, they made public their disgruntlement with the administration. Elizabeth Cady Stanton and others had been proud to present ceremonial banners at torchlight parades in 1860, although their role was only slightly above that of stage decorations. Now they raised critical issues on na-tional platforms. Women like Dickinson and Swisshelm already had an audi-ence and used their word power to persuade the public that Lincoln was not the man for the job. The war would be prolonged under the present milk-toast policies, Swisshelm argued, and the nation's prestige would continue to fall. Dickinson's words were so strong that she was chastised by Republicans who feared she would severely impact the vote. Nonetheless, she held firm in her anti-Lincoln campaigning throughout the summer of 1864. "I think him the vilest scoundrel in the country," she stoutly declared, "& I would rather lose all the reputation I possess & sell apples & peanuts on the street, than say ought that would gain a vote for him." Authors like Gail Hamilton wrote anti-administration tracts, and Anna Ella Carroll used her political expertise to help the Democrats plot Lincoln's overthrow.[121.] Stanton also published bold diatribes in papers like the *Liberator* and the *National Anti-Slavery Stan-dard,* striking enough that they were reprinted around the nation. If her words pinched, she was unapologetic, asserting that women would "undoubtedly be a power in the coming Presidential campaign" and that it was their duty to speak forthrightly. An unprecedented number of people agreed with her. "Where is Anna Dickinson? Why don't she come to the rescue of her Uncle Abraham?" cried the *New Haven Courier.* "The men are all quitting him—the females should stick the closer."[122]

But the females took a further step back. Not content with rhetoric, An-thony and Stanton began to plan a populist movement that might overturn the renomination of Lincoln. What they had in mind was a liberal convention, Stanton told Jesse Frémont, that would embody "the right of the people to bring down a presidential platform, and chose a man who in word and action has proved himself great and grand enough to stand on it." It would be a real revo-lution, joined in Anthony, which would educate the people to shun candidates from the smoky back rooms and elect a leader directly. Their choice was Frémont, who still inspired them, despite the tarnished edges of his reputation.[123] It was a notion as idealistic as it was impractical; yet, as it happened, a good number of Republican men were also angling to put forward an alternative candidate. Ed-itors Theodore Tilton and Horace Greeley canvassed every Republican governor in the summer of 1864, asking them candidly if they would help overturn Lin-coln's nomination. They received remarkably similar replies from each man. Lincoln was "essentially lacking in the quality of leadership" needed to direct the country, wrote one; he had "disappointed the expectations of the people and has no hold on their affections," agreed another. But the governors would make no move to dislodge him, both for the party's sake and because it was too late to rally around a new man. An unprecedented meeting of the radicals, called to find another candidate, came to the same conclusion. Lincoln was inadequate but inevitable, wrote Massachusetts governor John Andrew. Charles Sumner echoed his fellow Bay Stater's words to Lydia Maria Child. He considered Lincoln's nomination a great mistake, the senator wrote, but he was not prepared to enter into "the darkness of the Presidential contest." Choosing Lincoln because he was the least objectionable candidate was like "self-deception," protested the feminists, but their plan to undercut his candidacy gradually disintegrated.[124]

What convinced many women to back off was the fear they might divide the electorate, pushing it into the arms of Democratic nominee George B. McClellan. Some began to give cautious support to the President, though real enthusiasm was rare. Caroline Healey Dall tried to answer Stanton's barbed critique by stating that as flawed as Lincoln was, he was improving and she would not second-guess him. Harriet Beecher Stowe, though so distressed about the war's direction that she was physically ill, also wrote on Lincoln's behalf, so as not to encourage the South to further defiance. He was not "a man who could dare and do," said Stowe, but she praised his presidential papers and allowed that he was perhaps the "safest" choice. Swisshelm also reluctantly backed off when faced with the prospect of McClellan as president. Dickinson was among the most immovable, vowing to remain a lone voice in the wilderness, until abolitionist leaders counseled her to relent or watch their program be undercut by the opposition. "I think," Tilton candidly told Dickinson, "that if you and I should do anything . . . to divide the Union party, and so break it with defeat, giving the government to the Copperheads, we would weep over it." Tilton would not praise Lincoln, for he did not admire him, the editor said, but neither would he desert the only acceptable party while the nation was in crisis. It was a painful personal struggle for the principled Dickinson. But the choices now were stark, and in the end she acquiesced. Carefully choosing her words, she told the public she could "support the party represented by Abraham Lincoln," but not the man. Stanton and Anthony were the last holdouts, but they were now isolated. When Stanton tried to keep dissent alive, the reformist Gerrit Smith, himself no administration admirer, told her he wondered "how sad you will be when you shall have defeated Lincoln & elected McClellan."[125]

Disillusioned, feminists accepted Lincoln's reelection on November 8 with resignation. "There was no enthusiasm for honest old Abe," sourly remarked Lydia Maria Child, marveling that the public would accept this man "notwithstanding the long, long drag upon their patience and their resources." Anna Dickinson almost immediately renewed her pointed criticism of Lincoln's reconstruction and racial policies. Others vowed to hold Republicans to their pledges, to renew their push for an emancipation amendment, and to simply ignore the President. But if male voters had chosen to march in place, women had broken new ground with their active participation in national affairs. Stanton was proud that she had tried "to lift the nation higher & that no word or thought or prayer of ours has been without its influence." Female activists had now moved significantly beyond "moral suasion" to hardheaded agendas, eye-catching public statements, and concrete political actions. Perhaps Lincoln took no notice, for as prolix and persistent as the feminists were, their ability to hinder him was limited while they could not vote. Yet, if the President missed the message it was too bad. For these women were doing nothing less than testing the "new birth of freedom" he himself had prescribed.[126]

VIII

Clara Barton was despondent on inauguration day, March 4, 1865. She had tried again to reach the President with her proposal to locate missing men but had once more been turned away. It was all most discouraging. Barton had supported this man for so long and now he would not even meet with her, leaving her frustrated that she had "*not one* request granted in all this year." She would go that evening to the inaugural ball, in a borrowed silk skirt, grandly escorted by Admiral David Farragut, but she was disenchanted with the festivities. Unwilling to force herself on a leader who ignored her work, she did not shake Lincoln's hand. In her diary Barton flew straight to the heart of why he so offended the nation's leading women: he failed to appreciate their contribution. "Remember that of all the anguish Our Heavenly Father calls us to endure," she mused, "none pierces more keenly or wounds more deeply—than the sting of ingratitude—"[127]

Barton's hurt may have been salved the next day after she read the inaugural address. Unconsciously or not, Lincoln's words recalled four years of arduous labor performed by thousands of women. The binding of wounds undertaken by Bickerdyke, Dix, and myriad others; caring for widows and orphans, pioneered by Annie Wittenmyer and the volunteers in freedmen's camps; the "firmness in the right" that had animated women like Stowe, Truth, Dickinson, and Stanton, who had never wavered from principle, despite resistance from party men and party machines; the "charity for all" shown by Barton in treating soldiers of both sides equally; even the reliance on God, about which Elizabeth Comstock had tried to persuade a skeptical Lincoln. The President's words never mentioned women by name or as a group, yet the power of what they had accomplished rang through the lines. He pledged to realize these goals in the future; women had been embracing them for years. Perhaps he was just oblivious—unaware that his eloquent purpose was borrowed from the "sentimental department" he had derided. Perhaps Lincoln was willfully obtuse; unable to admire what he refused to see. At best the inaugural's fine phrasing was a sideways glance at the ladies—a backhand tribute. But it mattered not. For there they stand, seven hundred cherished words, memorializing forever the influence, aspiration, and achievement of those feisty, fussing she-devils.[128]

Duff Green, photograph by Mathew Brady, c. 1860–65
LIBRARY OF CONGRESS

6

THE HOLLOW CROWN

The man on the wharf wore a baggy coat of rebel gray and carried a stick as tall and tough as he was. Some who saw him thought he looked scruffy and dangerous, but to others, Duff Green seemed almost a mystical apparition: a white-haired, wispy-bearded, sharp-eyed prophet come to warn that pride and defiance lingered in the smoldering ashes of the Confederate cause. It was April 5, 1865, two days after the fall of Richmond. Green intended to board Admiral David Dixon Porter's flagship, the USS *Malvern,* which was moored on the James River, downstream from the occupied city. He had a pass from the military governor allowing him through the lines, and he had a few words to say to the President of the United States, who was on the ship.[1]

Porter was concerned about the old man's "uneasy, restless look" and he was worried about that stick, which he called a "club . . . big enough to knock a house down." But Abraham Lincoln knew Duff Green and allowed him to enter the presidential cabin. Green, a Kentuckian, had lived and taught in Elizabethtown during the years that Lincoln's father did carpentry work there and was, in fact, related to the President by marriage (both Lincoln and the nephew of Green's wife, Ninian Edwards, married Todd sisters). When Lincoln was elected to Congress, he boarded at the Greens' lodging house on Capitol Hill. Although their politics increasingly diverged, the two men maintained a cordial friendship and shared an interest in promoting public works to develop the nation's potential.[2]

At a time when Lincoln was still learning the congressional ropes, Green was a near legendary figure in the capital, epitomizing the energy, opportunity—and sometimes the violence—of America's turbulent society. He had been by turns a surveyor; a lawyer; a representative to Missouri's 1820 constitutional convention, and to both houses of the state legislature; a brigadier in the mili-

USS *Malvern*, photograph taken near Hampton Roads, Virginia, December 1864
LIBRARY OF CONGRESS

tia; the owner and editor of several influential newspapers, including the *St. Louis Enquirer* and *United States Telegraph;* a member of Andrew Jackson's "kitchen cabinet"; and the special agent of President John Tyler in Europe and Mexico. Excited by the extraordinary chances to make money in America, Green also organized numerous industrial enterprises. He was an early Southern sectionalist, backing nullification in the 1830s and joining secret societies such as the Knights of the Golden Horseshoe, which hoped to extend Southern interests throughout the Caribbean basin. He shunned secession, however, and hoped to unify and develop his region within the structures of the United States.[3]

In politics Green could be as fiercely partisan as Lincoln, zealously backing John C. Calhoun and other Democrats, particularly as a newspaperman. His unrestrained editorials won applause from those sharing his views, as well as from advocates of a free press. But in the vitriolic politics of the day, the heated commentary sometimes brought on public clashes. In the late 1820s, Green attacked a rival from the *Daily National Intelligencer* on the Senate floor and reportedly gouged out his eyes. On another occasion, when James Watson Webb of the *New York Courier* challenged him, Green pulled a gun, forcing

Webb to run for his life into the Capitol. Most famously, he so incensed Congressman James Blair of South Carolina by repeatedly referring to the Union party as "Tories" that the 350-pound Blair assaulted him in the street, kicking him into the gutter and jumping on him until he had broken Green's arm, collarbone, and several ribs. After this incident, Green semiretired from the journalistic world and acquired his well-known stick. It was a prop he would employ with some drama, until at age seventy-four he finally broke it while beating a man who had insulted him in a railroad car.[4]

Green joined his ardent political agenda with an equally ambitious pursuit of entrepreneurial schemes. He gained exclusive contracting privileges for canal construction, and underwrote the rebuilding of Norfolk's Gosport shipyards, which the British had destroyed during the Revolution. Using his considerable influence, Green gained lucrative government contracts for the yard to produce naval vessels, among them the USS *Powhatan,* which Lincoln had attempted to use for the resupply of Fort Sumter. Once railroads became state-of-the-art technology, Green was indefatigable in their promotion. Believing Northern industrialists were wresting away the advantage in transportation, mining, and land development, he worked to expand competing Southern systems. In the 1850s he laid plans for a line that would link Washington and New Orleans via the rich valleys of Virginia and Tennessee, and another from Washington to Mobile, through Richmond, Raleigh, and Atlanta—essentially the routes still used today. From the state of Texas he obtained more than ten thousand acres of land and a loan of six thousand dollars per mile for a network of freight roads. Increasingly worried that Northern "fanatics" would wage an "unholy war" on slavery, Green saw economic expansion as the key to maintaining Southern power. Disunion was not the answer, he told the governor of Alabama. "Our only hope lies in this. . . . We must develop our resources and . . . increase the profits of labor by diminishing the expense of transporting its products to market. . . . Give us good Roads, and union & concert and we need fear no danger."[5]

Green particularly trained his eye toward the Pacific, hoping to strengthen the Southern states by joining their interests to the West. By the tense election year of 1860, he had formulated the most cogent scheme to date for a railroad stretching to the state of California. Working with the president of Mexico, Green obtained charters for a line linking Vera Cruz to the Pacific by way of Mexico City, which he planned to connect to his Texas roads, as well as to the New Orleans line. Approval for this project gave him capital to acquire mining rights and to attract further investment for the transcontinental venture.

On the eve of war, Green finally knit together a complicated coalition of states and individuals interested in supporting the project, with a holding company in Pennsylvania. The future looked bright as he envisioned a railroad that would extend the Southern way of life, increase trade and immigration, and link the region's ports to Europe and the mineral wealth of Mexico. Best of all, it could be constructed with cheap slave labor, something Northern investors understood to be a distinct advantage of the southerly route. It was "no small triumph to have devised the means of building the first road to the Pacific," Green justifiably boasted to his wife. The pearl of American promise was within reach; he had only to open the oyster.

Then Abraham Lincoln was elected president—on a platform that expressly threatened plans to extend Southern interests into the western territories.[6]

When Duff Green stepped aboard the *Malvern,* he meant to deliver a lecture and offer a proposal. His lecture addressed what he saw as Lincoln's chronic misunderstanding of the South—a perpetual tone deafness that had been present since before the inauguration. Depending on which version of the encounter is read, Green delivered his speech forthrightly, but politely; or with a kind of unleashed fury that had Porter calling for his sailors and Lincoln returning insults, his coarse hair standing on end "and his nostrils dilated like those of an excited race horse." Green was certainly capable of the capricious act, and Lincoln too could lose his cool with gusto. Still, it is hard to believe completely Porter's account of Green threatening with his stick, and accusing the President of playing the tyrant, with Lincoln responding that Green was nothing but a "political hyena" whose prejudices had unleashed the rebellion. Porter has the interview ending with the chief executive melodramatically shouting: "Miserable imposter! vile intruder! . . . Go, I tell you, and don't desecrate this national vessel another minute!" For his part, Green recalled that he took special care to be respectful, that Lincoln received him kindly, and that their conversation had been candid. Another eyewitness, former Supreme Court justice John Archibald Campbell, later wrote that he was present at the beginning of the interview and observed "no intemperate language, nor indecorous deportment on [Green's] part, or of exasperation on the part of the President." One of Lincoln's bodyguards claimed to have seen an angry Green, incensed at the "notorious crime of setting the niggers free," refusing to shake hands. None of these stories ring entirely true, since all were penned by participants who were under pressure, or looking for self-justification, when their accounts were written. Most likely the meeting was a tense one, with Green expressing himself in characteristically colorful style to a weary president who was out of patience with harangues from men he had now virtually vanquished.[7]

Nonetheless, Green had a point to make, and it was not a subtle one. Ultimately he wanted to know how Lincoln intended to deal with the collapsed Confederacy, but his immediate concern was the impression the President had left on a visit to Richmond the previous day. For several weeks Lincoln had been accompanying the Union Army and Navy in its final struggle to capture the rebel capital. His tour of the city, almost immediately after its capitulation, capped weeks of anxiety, as Lee's men fell back. The war was not yet over—Appomattox was four tense days away and Joe Johnston still stood his ground in the Carolinas—but it had become increasingly clear how the contest would end. Lincoln had witnessed sights both grisly and inspiring in recent weeks, and his mood seemed to swing between nervous apprehension and buoyancy over a victory now within grasp.[8]

Lincoln in Richmond, pencil, by Lambert Hollis, April 4, 1865
NATIONAL PORTRAIT GALLERY

Although he had been invited to the front by Grant, the top military men were also agitated. They had been handed additional responsibilities when Lincoln's demanding wife arrived, with young Tad in tow; but their main worry was for the President's safety. Lincoln had enjoyed the action scenes, and he had reportedly even teased Porter into making the *Malvern's* presence known, so it would flush out some rebel fire. In Richmond the commander in chief walked openly through the streets, while Porter called agitatedly for an escort, and Secretary of War Edwin Stanton wrung his hands back in Washington. Even the *New York Times,* which normally backed Lincoln, thought the exposure unwise. "If President LINCOLN has 'gone to the front,' or entered Richmond, he has departed widely from the discretion and good judgment which have hitherto marked his conduct," the editors opined. "He has no right to put [himself] at the mercy of any lingering desperado in Richmond, or of any stray ballet [*sic*] in the field, unless some special service can be rendered by his personal presence. It seems to as he might have left to Gen. GRANT the closing up of the great campaign."[9]

Prudent or not, Lincoln arrived in Richmond just hours after the Union cavalry galloped into the old city square and raised the Stars and Stripes above the seat of Confederate government. African American troops had been at the front of the procession, pride in their step, their exultant huzzahs filling the air. They found a city blanketed by a haze of red smoke so thick it blotted out the sun, with the populace reeling in stunned disbelief. Signs of defeat had been growing for weeks, but no one had really thought the Yankees could dislodge Lee. Now the highest officials had fled the capital, burning tobacco warehouses, detonating arsenals, and blowing up gunboats to keep them from Union hands. "The city was in a state of indescribable consternation," reported the French consul. "The silence which precedes great events was terrifying."[10] Then the fires spread through the town into business and residential districts, forcing many to take refuge with a few scanty possessions on the Capitol lawn. Boulevards and alleys were covered with pulverized glass from windows shattered by the explosions; and down the center of the streets ran long, smoldering piles of paper, "torn from the different departments' archives . . . from which soldiers in blue were picking out letters and documents that caught their fancy." Worse, the retreating army had smashed open stores of whiskey, meaning to destroy them before the liquor could enrage the invaders, and a rabble both white and black was scooping it from the gutters with pitchers and hands. In fact, wrote one Union occupier, "its contaminating influence came very near making me drunk, the air smell[ed] like the bung of a whiskey

keg."[11] Chaos, alcohol, and distress led to boisterous behavior, including looting and unearthly screaming. One shocked citizen described how a "gang of
drunken rioters dragged coffins sacked from undertakers, filled with spoils
from the speculators' shops," while howling madly. It was one of the most
chilling sights of the war, reported another eyewitness: "a city undergoing
pillage at the hands of its own mob, while the standards of an empire were
being taken from its capitol, and the tramp of a victorious enemy could be
heard at its gates." Through it all crowds of African Americans, of every age,
streamed into the city, loudly celebrating their liberation. One day later, on
April 4, the President of the United States waded into this pandemonium.[12]

It was an almost overwhelming day. Lincoln had come with Porter by
boat up the James River, through a landscape littered with destroyed rebel
ships and the carcasses of dead horses. Twice the group had to change boats to
pass by obstructions, and the presidential flotilla was partly conducted in row-
boats. A Union vessel under David Farragut's command had been caught in
the shoals and the group was grounded again when Porter tried to help his
comrade—an embarrassing moment for two admirals in the presence of their
commander in chief. Always there was the threat of undetected torpedoes in
the water. It was early afternoon before the party (which included Tad, celebrating his twelfth birthday that day) landed on a sandbar in a seedy section of
town and began clambering up a steep hill into the city. The sight must have
been extraordinary: smoking, half-crumbled façades; hot, sooty, choking air;
the detritus of a fallen nation. There was no one to greet the President, and
Porter, nervous for his safety, had only a few Marines to accompany him. Then,
suddenly, there was a shout from a group of African Americans who were re-
pairing a bridge close to the landing. Someone—likely a reporter named
Charles Coffin, who was standing nearby—told the group that the lanky man
in the long black coat and top hat, stepping off a modest launch, was Abraham
Lincoln.[13]

A spontaneous jubilation began, creating one of the most extraordinary
scenes in American history. As Lincoln and the small group climbed the hill
and walked through the devastated cityscape, black women and men joined a
growing throng. The city's newly freed people had been celebrating for days,
pouring into the streets to shout and sing and dance for joy at their emancipation and to salute the U.S. Colored Troops who occupied much of Richmond.
Part of the elation was that they were able to move freely in the city at all, for
among the fetters of bondage were restrictions on where slaves could go and
whom they could meet. "We uns kin go jist any whar—don't keer fur no

"President Lincoln riding through Richmond, April 4, amid the enthusiastic
cheers of the inhabitants," wood engraving,
Frank Leslie's Illustrated Newspaper, April 22, 1865

pass—go any whar yer want 'er," one overjoyed freedman told a journalist
from the *New York Herald,* who recorded the dialect. "Golly! de Kingdom
hab kum dis time fur sure." As the presidential party moved toward the former rebel capitol, the crowd grew, some turning handsprings, some praising
Lincoln as if he were Moses or the Messiah, many trying to touch his boots or
shake his hand. "They received him with many demonstrations that came
from the heart," noted a member of the Twenty-Ninth Connecticut, a U.S.
Colored Regiment, "thanking God that they had seen the day of their salvation, that freedom was theirs, that now they could live in this country, like
men and women, and go on their way rejoicing." George Bruce, a reporter
who described the unaffected outburst in his diary, called it the "wildest spectacle ever seen," with people throwing hats and clothing into the air, then

"throwing themselves flat upon the ground and remaining there for some seconds" in a "species of demonstration or worship." The sight of Lincoln, holding Tad's hand as he moved wearily up the hill in the center of the crowd, noted Bruce, was "one of the most remarkable in history." Porter, nearly frantic at the possibility of being crushed by the mob or becoming targets of an assassin, waved the flat of his sword "lustily" and was much relieved when they encountered General George Shepley, the newly appointed military governor, near Capitol Square.[14]

"President Lincoln visiting the late residence of Jefferson Davis in Richmond, April 4," wood engraving, *Frank Leslie's Illustrated Newspaper*, April 29, 1865

Shepley and other officers escorted Lincoln to their headquarters in the White House of the Confederacy, Jefferson Davis's former seat of power. An exhausted Lincoln sank into a chair—Davis's old desk chair, according to some—and consulted with the generals. A few prominent men who had not fled arrived to sound out the President on his plans for peace. Some witnesses reported that Lincoln wrote dispatches, toasted Union success with a sherry flip, and wandered over the house with boyish curiosity and glee. Others stated he addressed a crowd of former slaves in front of the mansion, telling them they were as free as he, and "had no master now but God." Exactly what transpired is not clear, but certainly Lincoln, who had been through a week of extreme tension, was awed by the magnitude of what he was witnessing, and emotionally worn out. Around 4:35 p.m. the *Malvern* arrived at Richmond's wharves and fired a thirty-five-gun salute, signaling to the citizenry that they had an extraordinary visitor. Lincoln and Porter then climbed into a small, two-seated military wagon, drawn by four horses, with Tad on his father's lap, and a clattering horse guard following. Moving briskly, they toured what was left of the once noble heart of the Confederacy, passing Thomas Crawford's heroic statue of George Washington, the elegant Capitol designed by Thomas Jefferson, the ghostly burnt mansions, the old slave auction rooms, and notorious Libby Prison. All the while, they were surrounded by a weeping, cheering, exultant African American crowd. At one point the President's party hastily retreated from an encounter with the sorry-looking funeral cortege of Confederate general A. P. Hill, who had been killed two days earlier near Petersburg. Sometime around 6:30 p.m. the entourage reached the wharf and boarded the *Malvern,* for the return trip to the Union base at the village of City Point.[15]

It had been a memorable, raucous, and risky day. What lingered was the image of those ecstatic freedmen and -women, so grateful for their liberation, and so hopeful of better prospects. A few working-class whites had joined the procession—what one stylish matron called "the low, lower, lowest of creation"—but for the most part the white population had remained purposefully absent from the scene. Many found the display of black enthusiasm distasteful or frightening. "I wish you could have witnessed Lincoln's triumphal entry into Richmond," sniffed Mary Custis Lee, who still believed her husband would be victorious. "He was surrounded by a crowd of blacks whooping & cheering like so many demons there was not a single respectable person to be seen." Some Richmonders were too overcome to enter the streets and "kept themselves away from a scene so painful," or they were too angry to acknowledge Lincoln with their presence. One woman reported remaining at home during the procession sobbing "Dixie" into her pillow; a minor bureaucrat, finding himself so agitated he could not write, went out to see what was happening, but "ran into so many Negroes and Negresses there that I couldn't stand it. I went home, heartbroken." The white population was wary but also curious, and they surreptitiously watched the scene from behind half-closed shutters or lowered blinds. One blue-coated cavalryman reported seeing as many as sixteen faces peering through a single window. "You know Lincoln came to Richmond Tuesday the 4th and was paraded through the streets," whispered an unreconstructed rebel. "The *'monkey show'* came right by here, but we wouldn't let them see us looking at them."[16] There *were* Northern sympathizers in Richmond, people like Elizabeth Van Lew, who had hoarded tiny flags and secretly sung "The Star-Spangled Banner," and even gathered intelligence for federal authorities. But no great contingent of closet Unionists came forth and the few who did only earned the scorn of their neighbors. Although the city was in desperate straits, there was little gratitude that an end to the long, dreadful ordeal had finally come. And virtually no respect was paid to the leader of the hated Yankees.[17]

Devastated by the collapse of their cherished hopes and smarting under the rebuke to their arrogant assumption of Southern fighting superiority, the white population also deeply resented the presence of so many black faces in blue uniform. Many thought the gesture unnecessary and impolitic, though even the most bitter admitted that the Union occupiers had conducted themselves well. (Federal soldiers had worked diligently to put out the fires, quickly establish order, and overall acted with discretion and courtesy.) What rankled was the *fact* of Lincoln's arrival in Richmond—a humiliating sign that Virginia was now under "the policy of the conquerors." From their perspective, the poky presidential contingent was little short of a triumphal tour by a despised tyrant.[18] Lincoln undoubtedly felt he was entering the city as a peacemaker—numerous accounts of his conversations at this time show him earnestly advising others to "judge not" and to seek a speedy route to reunion. Perhaps he was hoping his presence in the fallen capital would reassure the public that he meant conciliation, or even to win them over with his unpretentious manner.[19] But the spectacle of the small group struggling up the hill on foot, surrounded by a shrieking black mob, or dashing through the city with cavalrymen thrusting the public away with brandished bayonets only reinforced everything Southerners abhorred. A few who peered through those shuttered windows glimpsed only an old, tired man, but most saw the specter of their worst fears: military subjugation and uncontrolled bands of Negroes roaming the city, all at the hands of a undignified jokester. The sight of "these people in Richmond" had made him physically ill, wrote one man; another, who had escaped the city, but heard of Lincoln's visit from former governor "Extra Billy" Smith, mused: "I wonder how gentlemen can avail themselves of the misfortunes of the people they have been fighting, by such selfish & ungallant intrusions upon their private rights. . . . [I]t sickened my heart to think of the humiliation inflicted upon the people of my own state."[20]

Worse was the gossip about tactless conduct by the presidential party. Rumors of Lincoln's gleeful lounging in Davis's chair—or sleeping in his bed—were quickly whispered from person to person, as were reports of the "disgusting sight" of him familiarly shaking hands with black men or drinking toasts over the burning bier of the Confederacy. The "indelicate" visit of Mary Todd Lincoln and Julia Grant two days later only rubbed salt into the wound. "It is said that they took a collation at . . . our President's house!!" exclaimed a woman who had been one of the war's first refugees. "Ah! it is a bitter pill. I would that dear old house, with all its associations, so sacred to the Southerners . . . had shared in the general conflagration." Most of the stories were embellished, often with each retelling. Still, the evidence indicates that Lincoln had indeed indulged his curiosity to see the fallen Confederate capital; had put his feet up and his guard down while there; had risked his own safety, and that of his young son, and with it the stability of the government; and was in high spirits, perhaps understandably given the relief and excitement of the moment. Mrs. Lincoln, too, seemed less than discreet in her conduct, playfully asking friends if they would not like to "dine with us, in Jeff Davis' deserted banqueting hall?"[21] In the end it was not really important whether or not the tales were true—it was the perception that mattered, and at that moment it mattered greatly. A mighty war was ending and with it the collapse of an empire and a way of life. Just as Lincoln was contemplating what policies to pursue with the defeated rebels, Southerners were also deliberating their future course. The perception they got from Lincoln's excursion in Richmond was of an unwise victor, chuckling over his spoils in a most offensive manner. As always, humorist David Ross Locke, lampooning the visit a few days later, captured perfectly the tone of popular disgruntlement. "Linkin rides into Richmond! A Illinois railsplitter, a buffoon, a ape, a goriller, a smutty joker, sets hisself down in President Davis's cheer, and rites dispatches," cried his character Petroleum V. Nasby. "Where are the matrons uv Virginia? Did they not bare their buzzums and rush onto the Yankee bayonets . . . rather than see their city dishonored by the tread uv a conkerer's foot? Alars!" To many Southern minds, this sideshow would define their future reality.[22]

Duff Green had also heard the gossip from "Extra Billy" and General Shepley, an old friend, who had given him the pass to the *Malvern*. He was well aware of the way Richmond had reacted to Lincoln's visit. Porter maintained that this prompted Green's shipboard call, as well as how he addressed the President rudely, calling Lincoln a "Nero" who had come "to triumph over a poor conquered town, with only women and children in it; whose soldiers

have left it, and would rather starve than see your hateful presence here."
Whether Green attacked Lincoln as Porter insisted, or merely stated in his
pointed style that this was not the way to sway the hearts and minds of bitter
Confederates, is not clear. But Green admitted his purpose was to influence
Lincoln's thinking on postwar treatment of the South, and that he believed
the chief executive was veering dangerously from reality, particularly in the
treatment of ex-slaves. Lincoln, he maintained, was using his best wits to determine how to win over the former rebels, but acting in a manner that had
the opposite effect—and not for the first time.[23] It appears the President was
already aware of the unfortunate optic of his tour, however. He discussed it
with General Marsena Patrick about the time Green came on board; and with
the First Lady's favorite the Marquis de Chambrun and Charles Sumner, who
accompanied his wife to the town a few days later. The reception, with the
leading citizens "in total eclipse," had not been a good omen, he told the Marquis; and Sumner noted that "he saw with his own eyes at Richmond & Petersburg, that the *only people who showed themselves were negroes*. All the others
had fled or were retired in their houses." Both Chambrun and Sumner left
Lincoln's room admiring his goodwill, but concerned for his naïveté. "I am
very unhappy," Sumner confessed to Salmon Chase, now chief justice of the
Supreme Court, "for I see in the future strife, & uncertainty for my country."
The President, he worried, had not the disposition to make cogent plans and
"follow them logically & courageously."[24]

II

The brief encounter on the USS *Malvern* was not the first time Duff Green
had given Lincoln a prophesying message. In the nervous weeks following South Carolina's secession, Green had been sent by President James Buchanan to Illinois to invite the president-elect to come immediately to
Washington. Buchanan knew the two men were connected and hoped that
Green's forceful manner, and his own pledge that Lincoln would be treated
with honor, might persuade the president-elect to dispense with tradition and
party politics long enough to unite in a platform of peace. On December 28,
1860, Green had what he termed a "Special Interview" at the Lincoln home in
Springfield. He carried with him a copy of the recently passed Crittenden
Compromise, a last-ditch effort by Kentucky senator John Crittenden to
thwart war. The plan extended the line of the Missouri Compromise to the

Pacific Ocean, prohibiting slavery north of the 36°30' parallel, and addressed Southern concerns about enforcement of the Fugitive Slave Act. It also guaranteed that slavery would continue where it already existed. Hoping Lincoln would endorse Crittenden's work, Green tried to impress him with the urgency of the situation, as well as the intensity of Southern fears. Lincoln had been elected, he noted, by a minority vote from a single region. That rankled Southerners, who felt they had become a "subject province, conquered by the ballot-box." Dismissing abolitionists as little more than a honking gaggle of fanatics, Green recited the familiar pro-slavery arguments about paternal master-slave relations, topping it off with pseudo-biblical warnings against conflict between labor and capital, or among weak and strong states. Green spoke passionately, for, as he later noted, the moment was opportune, never to come again.[25]

But Lincoln was cautious. Green later stated that at first he responded positively to Buchanan's invitation, then backed away, saying he was obliged to wait in Springfield for a visit from hard-line Republican Benjamin Wade. Lincoln thought Crittenden's compromise might quiet agitation for the time being but believed slavery was only the current pretext in a power struggle that would quickly erupt again, over questions like the possible annexation of Mexico. The real issue, noted the president-elect, was one of "propagandism"— a war of words that had mushroomed on both sides until fears outpaced realities. He had been elected by his party, said Lincoln, and he intended to stick with it; but added that questions such as the Crittenden Compromise or any legislation prohibiting interference with slavery belonged with the people and the states. If such legislation should pass, "he would be inclined not only to acquiesce, but to give full force and effect to [the] will thus expressed." Green asked Lincoln to put his thoughts in a message that could be published and he did so, in a wordy letter drawing on party-platform language about the "inviolate" right of a state "to order and control its own domestic institutions." In the end, the president-elect shied away even from this qualified statement, adding an impossible condition that the document could not be published unless half the senators from the Deep South concurred with it in writing. Green returned home empty-handed. "I saw and had a frank conversation with Mr. Lincoln," he later reported to Jefferson Davis, "but found it impossible to convince him of the dangers of the impending crisis or the necessity of his intervention." To the president-elect, Green left a warning: "he alone could prevent a civil war, and that if he did not go [to Washington], upon his conscience must rest the blood that would be shed."[26]

Duff Green was hardly a disinterested emissary—he not only abhorred secession but had his own entrepreneurial projects at stake, which were destined to fail if the nation divided. However, he was not the only Unionist urging Lincoln to send the country a message that would allay panic. From both North and South, the president-elect was entreated to make a succinct declaration of his commitment to the nation as a whole, and his intention to uphold the principles that bound it together. The moment was unimaginably tricky, for the factions were so polarized that guarantees sought by one section only enflamed others. "The *eyes* of the whole nation will be upon you while unfortunately the *ears* of one half of it will be closed to any thing you say," Lincoln's close friend Joshua Speed advised him. "How to deal with the combustible material lying around you without setting fire to the edifice . . . of which you will be the chief custodian in is a difficult task." Some, like North Carolina Unionist John Gilmer, believed it was the Republicans' duty to defuse the crisis, and wanted Lincoln to lay out his program specifically, on sensitive points such as emancipation in Washington, D.C., or whether Congress had authority to interfere with slavery in the states. Others criticized Buchanan's mixed message regarding secession (he declared it nothing short of revolution, but believed he had no power to prevent it), urging Lincoln to speak firmly against the Fire-Eaters, quashing any notion that he would tolerate their challenge to national unity. When he did so, advised one supporter, the president-elect should mark his words with "the thunder of brevity."[27]

Montgomery Blair, seen as an uncompromising Republican, went so far as to query Supreme Court justice John A. Campbell about the precedent of a statement from the president-elect. Campbell, a Southerner who hesitated at secession, thought the measure would be extraordinary but not unconstitutional, and perhaps might forestall a tragedy based on misunderstanding. Republican power brokers William Seward and Thurlow Weed also saw that the stakes had changed since the election. Their party had won largely because of a three-way split among Democrats rather than a clear consensus of the voters, and the urgent questions were no longer those posed in the antislavery Republican platform, but the ones inherent in the nation's crumbling stability. They believed their party's job now was to pull back from brinkmanship and restore the Union. "I want to meet Disunion as Patriots rather than as partisans—as a People rather than as Republicans," Weed told Lincoln a few days after South Carolina seceded.[28] But the majority of the president-elect's compatriots urged him to hold fast to party and platform. A weak-kneed retreat from policies that were approved at the polls would look defensive at best, they argued, and might signal that the government was unable to defend its institutions, emboldening the South to make more aggressive demands. Moreover, there were legitimate ideological issues, which should not be compromised.[29] Congressman Samuel R. Curtis put the dilemma clearly:

> We cannot as republicans shrink back from the principles we have advocated and the people have approved. We might declare as we have done a thousand times that we have made no war on the South and will make none on their institutions . . . ; but for us to say as they desire that slaves are *property* and must be so regarded under the Constitution we cannot say it because we do not believe it[.] Neither can we say that slavery is a moral or political blessing because we do not believe it.[30]

For his part, Lincoln had made up his mind before the election that it was not only unseemly but useless to offer concessions. He probably knew through long political experience that his position was a weak one. He had been elected despite an unprecedented boycott of his candidacy in the South, and in that section he was considered illegitimate. Moreover, the Electoral College would not meet until mid-February, and until it pronounced him president he had no official status. Lincoln had long since come to the conclusion that Southerners were not listening to him; were, in fact, willfully deaf to protestations that he was a conservative man, with no intention of meddling in the internal affairs of slave states. He had said as much ten months earlier in his address at New York's Cooper Institute and he reiterated it the day before the election to a visitor who suggested he make an overture to honest Southern men who were genuinely alarmed. "There are no such men," Lincoln curtly told him, while his secretary took notes. "It is the trick by which the South breaks down every northern man." "Honest" men, he protested, would read his numerous public statements and see that they had nothing to fear. Repetition would change nothing. "Having told them these things ten times already, would they believe the eleventh declaration?" The president-elect told Duff Green that, in any case, he was personally more comfortable with silence—"whether that be wise or not"—and he preferred to watch and wait and let passions die down. It was as if he was back in the days of his youth, sizing up his wrestling opponent Jack Armstrong; taking care to avoid showing weakness; watching for the chance to disarm him—and hoping to find common ground to overcome animosity.[31]

But the situation was not as clear-cut as a young man's wrestling-ring show of strength. Lincoln was also concerned that compromise would alienate his supporters and send him to Washington "as powerless as a block of buckeye wood." He was bound by fundamental Republican ideals and goals and by the party's successful drive to promote policies that much of the North and West supported. It was, in fact, exactly what Southerners feared: a sectional party, representing the aspirations of modest farmers, craftsmen, and local businesses. The interests of these small-scale capitalists differed from those of ambitious entrepreneurs like Duff Green, Dixie's large agricultural enterprises, and even the Southern yeomen who were indirectly dependent on the plantation system. The issues were not limited to slavery, but ranged from tariffs to turnpikes; and many were intrinsically linked to Southern dreams and Southern identity. In general, Republicans supported free labor rather than the chattel arrangements that helped make the Gulf states so prosperous, but that did not mean the party was uniformly emancipationist. The 1860 platform upheld the right of states to control their own "domestic institutions" and, in any case, as *New York Tribune* editor Horace Greeley admitted, most Americans would "only swallow a little Anti-Slavery in a great deal of sweetening." Yet it was the issue of slavery's expansion that gave form and flavor to Republicanism—what Lincoln called "its active, life-giving principle."[32]

Within these terms, Lincoln was considered a moderate. He did not agree with abolitionists who thought the eradication of slavery was more important than maintaining the country's unity, nor did he side with those who believed every possible concession should be made in order to save the Union. His was a delicate dance between upholding old constitutional guarantees of state prerogatives and directly challenging slave-power aspirations. From the point of view of Southern interests, sectionalists arguably jumped the gun in assessing Lincoln. Had they stuck by the Union, instead of seceding, the uneasy coalition probably would have tottered on for a good while, probably to their advantage, for Lincoln, in 1860, was wedded only to the containment of slavery, not its abolition. The Republicans, however, had spent little energy canvassing the South and even moderates below the Mason-Dixon Line believed the party's trump card was the growing Northern population, which guaranteed a majority that could perpetually roll over and flatten Southern concerns. Moreover, the issues had long since crossed the bounds of rationality. A tide of emotionalism had engulfed the South, fostered by a handful of zealots who were skillful at raising the public temperature. Lincoln tried repeatedly to present himself as a conservative man, wedded to Revolutionary truths and obligated to the limitations of the Constitution, but he was unable to persuade Southerners of either his leadership capability or his goodwill. The words he used simply touched every raw Southern nerve.[33]

To this mix was added what was perhaps the least palatable ingredient for the South: a tang of moral superiority. The antislavery views expounded by key Republicans did not merely reflect pragmatic issues of law and economics, but humanitarian concerns that branded slave owners as callous, exploitative, or downright wicked. Left to themselves, only a handful of Southerners unconditionally defended their system; most were only too aware of its limitations, both practically and ethically. Yet few were able to imagine a post-emancipation society in which white and black citizens interacted freely. Burdened with what they considered impossible choices, many agreed with Northern moderates who hoped the system would die of its own accord, at some vague future date. Nevertheless, they did not want to be hectored by the Yankees, who they believed had their own moral failures, and whose rhetoric was putting them on the defensive. The momentum to overturn slavery, or at least revisit its legitimacy, pushed Southerners to develop an elaborate set of religious, economic, and racial justifications for human bondage, which they used not only to argue their position, but to convince themselves of its virtue. Lincoln was no radical; nonetheless, he had punctured this façade by expressing a view of the system that dismissed the middle ground. The words that propelled him to national recognition were absolutes, posing the great questions of the day in terms that allowed Southerners no option but to embrace slavery's eradication or admit wrongdoing.[34]

The president-elect had said the unsayable: that slavery was not just a national dilemma, to be solved nationally, but that it was evil, and that the South was responsible for its wickedness. "The Republican party think it wrong," Lincoln stated during his 1858 senate-race debates with Stephen A. Douglas; "we think it a moral, a social and a political wrong . . . that extends itself to the existence of the whole nation." He repeated the uncompromising image of right and wrong many times during the debates, and publicly thereafter. Lincoln ridiculed Douglas for claiming there was no moral issue at stake, scoffing that his opponent saw "this matter of keeping one-sixth of the population of the whole nation in a state of oppression and tyranny unequalled in the world . . . an exceedingly little thing—only equal to the question of the cranberry laws of Indiana."[35] Privately, Lincoln admitted he saw no way that the issue would be resolved peaceably; still, he proclaimed himself proud of his words. "It gave me a hearing on the great and durable question of the age, which I could have had in no other way," he told his friend Anson Henry. "I believe I have made some marks which will tell for the cause of civil liberty long after I am gone."[36]

He had once been careful to avoid blaming Southerners for their "peculiar institution," claiming that in a similar position Northern men would have felt and acted much the same. Once in full electioneering mode, however, candidate Lincoln began to chastise the region for close-mindedness, for exacerbating sectional differences, and for irresponsibly holding the nation hostage to threats of disunion. Claiming—incorrectly, as it happened—that the Declaration of Independence had been the work of men who wanted to dismantle slavery, Lincoln placed the North on the brighter side of history and the South outside the reach of reason. He capped it all with the pronouncement that "right makes might," a dubious assertion, that was seen below the Mason-Dixon Line as a thinly veiled threat. His words were at once courageous and rash: while Lincoln recognized slavery as a horrible blight in America's idealistic garden of liberty, he also taunted Southern extremists by making a direct hit to their pride. Perhaps Lincoln believed challenges to Southern principles would only be taken as just so much campaign rhetoric, yet he knew his speeches were being carried telegraphically across the country, and that they touched the South at its most vulnerable points. In a region where questions of honor were grounds for murder, the provocation could not be underestimated.[37]

One of the reasons Duff Green had traveled to Springfield was to offer the president-elect a chance to soften the hard-nosed verbiage, prove he was sensitive to Southern concerns, and underscore his intention to govern the country from a national, not sectional perspective. Green saw that mistrust of Lincoln stemmed from his own pronouncements, which had left the South with little room to maneuver. "We propose to measure Mr. Lincoln by his own standard," ran a typical comment in the *New Orleans Daily Crescent,* which also reprinted quotations from many of his antislavery speeches. The *Crescent* dismissed attempts by Northern newspapers to portray the president-elect as a "moderate, kindly-tempered, conservative man . . . [who] will make one of the best Presidents the South or the country ever had," concluding, "Will you walk into my parlor said the spider to the fly?" Green, knowing the danger, did not ask Lincoln to retract his words, but he did want him to play down some of the harsher messages, particularly his praise of John Brown, his moralistic Cooper Institute speech, and the 1858 address that declared "this government cannot endure, permanently half *slave* and half *free*." Lincoln's worshipful secretaries, John Nicolay and John Hay, later accused the old editor of trying to force their boss to accept personal responsibility for the growing rebellion, but Green told his family that the goal was quite the opposite: "to relieve him of that responsibility by satisfying the South that they had no reason to fear that he would make or countenance in others any attempt to emancipate their slaves." Green was also trying to reassure secessionists that Lincoln represented only a small faction even within his own party, and that the opposition majority in Congress could defend their interests more effectively if they stayed and voted their way out of the dilemma. He viewed the moment as one of "folly and delirium," he told Lincoln, but cautioned that no one should take lightly the power of the demagogues, or the determination of the Southern people to fight for their rights.[38]

Lincoln was disinclined to walk back his words, and in any case he was not convinced of the urgency of the moment. He thought many Southerners were simply reacting to a disappointing electoral loss or threatening secession to gain leverage. Reasonable men, he believed, would in time see him as benign, or even friendly to their concerns. He tenaciously held to the misguided assumption that, outside South Carolina, there were far more loyal citizens than secessionists. "There is much reason to believe that the Union men are the majority in many, if not in every other one, of the so-called seceded States," he would write. The president-elect appeared oblivious to the increasing danger of the situation, as hard-line disunionists seized the moment to strengthen their position before he actually made compromises that would soothe Southern anxieties. Lincoln was right in thinking that sophisticated men knew he had no intention of meddling with slavery in the Gulf states, but he underestimated how perfectly his electioneering had played into radical hands. His reluctance to offer reassurances that countered the radicals' inflated rhetoric simply handed them the advantage. Radical Southerners also wanted to move quickly to curtail Lincoln's power to dispense the kind of favors that might calm criticism. He was beginning to organize his cabinet, as well as look at key federal positions—post offices, custom houses, and land agencies. Secessionists wanted to leave the Union before a large number of Lincoln's followers were appointed to influential positions in Southern communities. Postmasters might propagandize; customs officials might hold local interests hostage to patronage; and strong personalities might even attract a Republican following. At the same time, the Fire-Eaters wanted to leave the Union before Lincoln could appoint moderate Southerners, a move that might appease those still on the fence about secession. Yet, even as anxious disunionists scrambled to maximize every moment, Lincoln, a lifelong temporizer, persisted in believing time was on *his* side, that the heated moment would cool, and that prudence would conquer passion. Duff Green left Springfield without the soothing presidential letter he sought, and the Fire-Eaters were left with an uncontested field. "O why does not Mr. Lincoln speak?" implored a Southerner who was desperate to stitch up the fragmented sections. "We are in fact drifting upon the rocks."³⁹

Lincoln thought any pronouncement, however soothing, would be "futile" since the South " 'has eyes but does not see, and ears but does not hear.' " Once he did speak out, however, he found Southerners were paying quite close attention. Lincoln broke his verbal fast in February 1861 as he made his way from Springfield to Washington, D.C., for the inauguration, which was to take place on March 4. It was a lengthy railway tour, covering more than nineteen hundred miles and lasting nearly two weeks. The new First Family was escorted by a clamorous company of political allies, military officers, and hangers-on. The train halted in dozens of towns and crossroads, where remarks were made to cheering crowds. The route was a northerly one, and the enthusiasm contrasted sharply with sobering events farther south. The threat of secession had now become a reality, as seven states withdrew from the Union, forming the Confederate States of America, just days before Lincoln embarked on the trip. In Washington, a peace conference had been called to resolve the situation, but members of the new Confederacy had declined to attend, and the careworn leaders, bereft of fresh ideas, were dubbed an "Old Gentleman's Club." The explosive political situation and fatigue of the journey put increasing pressure on the president-elect at an already tense moment.⁴⁰

Republican leaders had hoped the trip would lay down important political markers about the upcoming Lincoln government while rallying public support. But the president-elect's performance during these days was not one that inspired confidence. His speeches were often impromptu, rather than carefully worded, and sometimes deteriorated into flippancy or inappropriate language. He seemed uncertain of the right note to strike, now dismissing the emergency as an *"artificial"* crisis gotten up by politicians; then speaking of the situation in the gravest terms, hinting at violence, and vowing (with a deliberate stamp on the podium) "to put the foot down firmly" if need be. Whether the talk was tough or conciliatory, he kept on the defensive. Claiming there was little cause for worry, and no justification for the South's precipitous actions, he denied responsibility for the controversial policies that had triggered such an outsized response. If blood was to be shed, Lincoln maintained, "it shall be through no fault of mine."[41]

Those who came out to hear him liked the speeches. It could be argued that they were tailor-made to each situation, with more casual language for his comfortable western neighbors and harder lines aimed at prominent men of the East. But Lincoln seems not to have considered that the media age was already upon the nation, and what played popularly to dirt farmers in Peoria did not always sound good in press reports elsewhere. Serious Northern supporters such as Charles Francis Adams, a Massachusetts congressman and the son of the sixth president, who were looking for calm, cogent leadership, were dismayed by the drift of the president-elect's pronouncements. "His beginning is inauspicious," Adams remarked. "It indicates the absence of the heroic qualities which he most needs." Nervous Southerners, particularly those against secession, were even more distressed, for they were desperately hoping a strong hand would take hold of the national reins and guide them back home. "I am afraid Lincoln is a fool . . . if I may judge by a speech he made yesterday on his journey about 'Nobody is hurt' 'nobody is suffering' 'nothing is wrong,'" worried Dr. Charles Carter, a pro-Union cousin of Robert E. Lee:

> all this is sheer nonsense, because everybody about here is "hurt," and "suffering," and everything is "wrong" in the eyes of everyone except these robber republicans; who have ruined the country and now pretend that all is right, when 6 states are forming an independent government, and that they see nothing the matter; and at the same time cry out "no compromise," "Chicago Platform[,]" The "Union shall be preserved!"[42]

In addition, the unprecedented tour, with its look of a traveling circus, provided a spectacle that secessionist leaders, in no mood to be charitable, found easy to mock. "He no sooner compelled to break that silence, and to exhibit himself in public, than the delusion [of a man of ability] vanishes," wrote an editor in New Orleans, asserting that in silliness, duplicity, and ignorance "the speeches of Lincoln, on his way to the capital, have no equals in the history of any people, civilized or semi-civilized." Genteel Southerners, contrasting Lincoln's entourage with the more stately procession of Jefferson Davis, who made a similar whistle-stop trip to his inauguration, concluded that Lincoln was a vulgar upstart. "We are told not to speak evil of Dignities, but it is hard to realize he is a Dignity," scoffed one skeptical North Carolinian. "How glorious was the President elect on his tour, asking at Railway Stations for impudent girls who had written him about his whiskers & rewarding their impudence with a kiss! Faugh!" Lincoln had spoken at last; but his words were too late and too confused to calm passions or persuade critics; and his style only undercut his ability to instill confidence.[43]

Lincoln's meandering expedition was capped by an unfortunate incident on arrival. Security en route had been an issue from the start, and the presence of military officers and secret service men showed that threats against the incoming administration were not taken lightly. While in Pennsylvania, Lincoln's party was advised that an assassination plot had been uncovered by detective Allan Pinkerton. An ambush was allegedly planned for Baltimore, where there was a good deal of "secesh" sympathy, and where the entourage would have to change trains before continuing to Washington. The report was a serious one, and those responsible for Lincoln's security, including General Winfield Scott, took it seriously. The president-elect was reluctant to alter his plans, and only after coaxing agreed to arrive incognito, by a different train. There is every

Passage Through Baltimore, pencil, by Adalbert John Volck, 1861. Gift of Maxim Karolik for the M. and M. Karolik Collection of American Watercolors and Drawings, 1800–75
MUSEUM OF FINE ARTS, BOSTON

indication that it was a prudent move, aimed at deflecting either an escalation of tensions or an outright crime. The subterfuge might have been handled more elegantly, however. Lincoln's eccentric figure was difficult to disguise and he arrived dressed like a muffled-up scarecrow, reportedly wearing a soft "Kosuth" hat—which was made more ludicrous by the imaginative *New York Times* describing it as a Scotch-plaid cap and *Vanity Fair* showing the president-elect dancing the Highland fling. North and South tittered over reports of the disguise and seriously questioned the courage of a man who hid behind a cloak while traveling through the pro-slavery state of Maryland. (Mortified by the ridicule, Lincoln erred on the side of imprudence thereafter, with tragic results.) Among those who took advantage of the incident was humorist George Washington Harris, who wrote three stories featuring a backwoods character named Sut Lovingood, who claimed to have traveled in the procession as a bodyguard. Published in a New Orleans newspaper in 1861, and widely reprinted, Lovingood's description embellished Lincoln's costume, padding it with liquor bottles, and painted Abe's face red until "when I wer dun with him he looked like he'd been on a big drunk fur three weeks." Such reports, even tongue in cheek, fed the growing Southern caricature of Lincoln as an absurd bumbler, who not only was inept and cowardly, but had a fondness for mean whiskey. Worse, it appeared to be proof that the man was exactly what they most feared: an impostor who had sneaked into the presidency through the back door.[44]

THE MacLINCOLN HARRISBURG HIGHLAND FLING.

"The MacLincoln Harrisburg Highland Fling,"
wood engraving, *Vanity Fair*, March 9, 1861

"I went to Springfield," Duff Green told Lincoln, "to urge you to exert your influence to prevent the war." But could he, in fact, have halted the impending catastrophe? Historians have debated that critical issue with spirit, without coming to consensus. Some have seen Lincoln's actions during the secession winter as deliberate and canny; a ploy to remain on the defensive, forcing the South to initiate any hostile act. Others have seen him as reactive, stumbling into war without an overall strategy. His papers show him to be highly conflicted, claiming to sympathize with slaveholding regions and anxious to avoid bloodshed, but shunning compromise, which he thought would only leave the issues hanging. Lincoln was probably right that by the time he arrived in Washington nothing he could do or say would change the most intransigent Southern minds—in their rage they had become as deaf as the sea. Yet his inflexible silence was frightening, since it seemed to shut out the possibility of dialogue. Over time, there were signs that Lincoln was moving toward some concessions: he put two men from slave states in his cabinet, for example, and developed a paper that called for the repeal of laws interfering with the Fugitive Slave Act. However, he privately reiterated his rigid "right and wrong" interpretation of slavery to influential Southerners and never stepped back from opposition to the territorial expansion of slavery—and that was precisely what pricked Southerners the most. A conciliatory gesture, showing at least a willingness to forestall disaster, might profitably have been made. Its absence further hardened attitudes and placed him as the chief protagonist in a standoff. Others in his circle, such as secretary of state–designate William Seward, showed more determination to work with the South—particularly the border states—to resolve issues peaceably, but Lincoln undercut their efforts. By denying the crisis and eschewing compromise, rather than reassuring the public that he intended to be smarter than the problem, Lincoln placed himself in the worst possible position for conflict resolution.[45]

Lincoln's most important opportunity to reassure Southerners came at his inauguration on March 4, 1861. He had worked hard on the address, which he hoped would show both firmness and goodwill, softening the message at the encouragement of Seward and others who read the draft. The new president spoke of his constitutional duty to keep government functions, such as postal service and the collection of tariffs, running smoothly, and of his obligation to protect United States property—though he sidestepped the issue of "reclaiming" federal assets that had already been seized by the rebels. He also promised to keep "obnoxious strangers" from administrative positions in the South and expressed "no objection" to a constitutional amendment that would prohibit interference with slavery where it existed. But Lincoln also refused to admit that his "dissatisfied countrymen" had any legitimate grievances. Instead, he called secession "the essence of anarchy," asserted that the Union of states was "perpetual," and unequivocally placed responsibility for the rift on Southern shoulders.[46]

The address concluded on a lofty note, but the ceremony left many people with a sense of malaise. Security remained a concern, and the tight controls Scott placed throughout the city seemed the antithesis of a democratic celebration. "For the first time in the history of the United States it has been found necessary to conduct the President-elect to the Capitol surrounded by bayonets and with loaded cannon," wrote the daughter of a Union general, who thought the large military presence "detracted much" from the spirit of the day. She did not find Lincoln's words entirely reassuring. "On that sea of faces turned toward him I could read every variety of expression from exultation to despair"; and though the band hushed the crowd by playing "Dixie," she continued, "I knew positively that there was no hope for the South." In regions where many still favored a peaceful solution, newspapers put the best possible spin on the address. "It is not unfriendly to the South," maintained the loyalist *North Carolina Standard*. "It deprecates war, and bloodshed, and it pleads for the Union." In New York, the civic leader George Templeton Strong observed that "Southronizers" thought Lincoln's message was pacific and likely to avert confrontation. "Maybe so," wrote a skeptical Strong, "but I think there is a clank of metal in it." The clank was loud and clear to ardent separatists. In Charleston the *Mercury* announced that "'King Lincoln' O! low-born, despicable tyrant" had made a declaration of war. Sectional conflict "awaits only the signal gun," agreed the *Richmond Enquirer*. In Montgomery, Alabama, capital of the infant Confederacy and its new congress, Georgia representative T. R. R. Cobb snatched a copy of the inaugural address from the telegraph but candidly admitted that "it will not affect one man here, it matters not what it contains."[47]

Lincoln had hoped to set a determined tone, softened by conciliation, but stress fractures between the two halves of this policy became apparent in the weeks following his swearing in. He particularly wanted to avoid alarming border states like Virginia, Kentucky, and Tennessee, which had not yet joined the secession movement. In those areas, a burning question was whether Lincoln would try to *force* states back into the Union, and even those with the strongest loyalties balked at the idea of a "coerced" federation. "If the bond of the Union can only be maintained by the sword & bayonet," wrote an agonized Robert E. Lee, "its existence will lose all interest with me." Southerners were already suspicious of Republican motives, and Lincoln's inaugural pledge to protect government property sounded ominous. The question of whether to resupply—or in some cases reoccupy—forts that had been seized by zealous rebels became a pressing one just days into his presidency. At Charleston, where Fort Sumter's defenders were running out of food, and South Carolinians were blocking the harbor, the situation had become desperate. Lincoln tried to cut some creative deals—considering, among other things, the abandonment of the fort in exchange for a pledge that Virginia would remain in the Union.[48] But like Jefferson Davis and South Carolina governor Francis Pickens, he was a new man on the job; and although intensely nervous about the state of affairs, he was anxious not to appear weak. Under Seward's influence he approved the convoluted plan mentioned earlier that would have sent subsistence supplies, but no arms, to Sumter, and military reinforcements to another threatened post at Fort Pickens, Florida. It was a flawed operation, featuring the secretary of state planning an operation without the knowledge of either the war or navy secretary, and junior army men commanding ship movements, all of which was complicated by faulty communications and poor weather. The predictable result was that rebel forces opened fire on Fort Sumter. Lincoln's response was to call out seventy-five thousand militia, including troops from the border states, to protect government interests. With their fears that force would be used now realized, Virginians voted for secession rather than supply men to support what they considered "coercion," and three other states quickly followed. Lincoln, conscious of his inaugural pledges, and determined not to cede the moment to the rebels, countered by blockading Confederate ports. When a group of loyal Baltimoreans questioned his judgment, he forthrightly upheld his actions. "You would have me break my oath and surrender the Government without a blow. . . . I have no desire to invade the South; but I must have troops to defend this Capital."[49]

It had been a badly bungled job, though Lincoln would later gloss it over, presenting the loss of Fort Sumter as a clever ploy to make the Confederates fire the first shot. But his stated intent had been to avoid that shot, and to the South his actions put him squarely in the role of provocateur. Those hoping against hope for a peaceful resolution felt there was now no turning back. It was not just that Lincoln had called out troops to fight against fellow Americans, it was his manner of doing it that so incensed Southerners. Lincoln had refused to engage with Virginia's representatives in Washington, dismissing them with instructions to read his inaugural speech if they wanted to know his intentions, and they had learned of his call for troops from the newspaper.

Shocked and embarrassed, men like William Cabell Rives, who had worked hard to keep the Old Dominion from seceding, reluctantly admitted that "the times, & the nature of the contest, render it impossible for me to maintain a position of neutrality." His family, which had once pronounced the hotheads in Charleston "as capricious as monkeys," now watched in disbelief as Rives took a seat in the Confederate Congress. "I see nothing in Civil War to rejoice over let who may be victor," another prominent Virginia Unionist declared. "Yet I consider Lincoln's course utterly infamous, as well as wholly unwarranted. . . . His silence & stillness has been like a tiger's preparatory to his leap." Secretary of State Seward had also fostered bad will when he hinted unofficially about a brokered peace and withdrawal from Fort Sumter, causing many Southerners to feel they had been willfully misled. "*Your* President and Cabinet knew [Fort Sumter's] force and condition," a young Memphis rebel wrote hotly to his loyalist brother, "and after weeks of lying assurances of peace and evacuation of the Fort to get time to prepare to replenish it, the President issued his war proclamation, which he knew was . . . the signal for action." Caroline Plunkett, an ardent North Carolina Unionist who had once written that "[i]f I had a sheet of the largest size before me I could fill it with the one subject, my country, my country, my country," became physically ill when she read of Lincoln's proclamation and took to her bed in sorrow. She rose a converted woman. "I secede in my heart from the present administration, now that it has adopted coercive measures," Plunkett declared. She had resisted all family entreaties to drop her Union loyalty, she noted, "but Lincoln & his administration have now done it effectually & if I were a man I would lend all my aid to the Southern confederacy against them."[50]

III

Disaffection of the kind expressed by Caroline Plunkett was the last thing Lincoln had wanted to produce. It seemed a constant mystery to him that his policies—and indeed his person—alienated so many. The "good people of the South who will put themselves in the same temper and mood as you do," he had told Samuel Haycraft, a Kentucky friend, "will find no cause to complain of me." What he failed to realize was how few Southerners were in the same "temper and mood" as the pro-Republican Haycraft. In 1860, as in 1865, the thing Duff Green wanted to impress on Lincoln was that he was misreading the South and badly underestimating its commitment to the slave economy and to independence. As the secession movement gained force, Lincoln, still clinging to the idea that it would all end in "smoke," tried to convince Southerners that he sympathized with their concerns. In reality, he knew very little about the region, and was particularly naïve about the aspirations of cotton state demagogues like Barnwell Rhett of South Carolina, or Alabama's William Yancey.[51]

Born in Kentucky, of parents with Virginia lineage, Lincoln has sometimes been portrayed as a Southerner, or as having a special sensitivity to the tastes and inclinations of the region. He married into a prominent bluegrass family, avidly read the *Louisville Journal,* and revered Henry Clay, one of Kentucky's most accomplished politicians. He spent most of his life in parts of Indiana and Illinois that had a pronounced Southern accent, carried by migrants who crossed the Ohio River, bringing their habits and opinions with them. As a rising attorney, Lincoln had close friends and law partners who came from Kentucky stock, some of them retaining deep-seated social and racial views that reflected the hierarchical, pre-industrial prejudices of the Southern system. Laws that sanctioned quasi-bondage or the use of slave labor, or that excluded blacks, were well known in Illinois. (Some referred to the region as a kind of "breakwater" between the extremes of North and South, but abolitionist critics dismissed lower Illinois as a de facto slaveholding area.) Lincoln noted that he differed with his friends on many of these issues, though "not quite as much . . . as you may think." He had witnessed slavery firsthand, on visits to Kentucky and Missouri, and on two long flatboat journeys to New Orleans. While seeing slavery as ethically wrong and economically disadvantageous, he did not believe in racial equality and confessed he had no idea how to form a post-emancipation society. "When the southern people tell us they are no more responsible for the origin of slavery, than we . . . and that it is very difficult to get rid of it, in any satisfactory way, I can understand and appreciate the saying," Lincoln remarked in his famous Peoria speech of 1854. "I surely will not blame them for not doing what I should not know how to do myself."[52] Lincoln did do something about it; but just how to absorb blacks into the larger culture puzzled him for the rest of his life. Despite the fact that he professed affinity with Southern people and Southern manners, and on rare occasions defined himself by their terms, Lincoln also pointed to his Pennsylvania and New England roots when it was politically expedient. Most often he was considered a westerner—a "sturdy Sire of the Prairies"—as indeed was Henry Clay. Only those who mistrusted him, or thought him too tolerant of Dixie men and Dixie institutions, labeled Lincoln a Southerner.[53]

Lincoln may well have identified with his border region, but the South did not identify with him. Southerners saw him as a prototype of the fanatic Yankee: dangerous because he was tough and unsentimental, vulgar in manner and dress—"the kind who are always at corner stores, sitting on boxes, whittling sticks," concluded the Confederate gadfly and diarist Mary Boykin Chesnut. They did not share his vision of progress based on free labor, or the cries for universal suffrage and other means of leveling the society. Where Lincoln saw opportunity in programs such as homesteading, they saw little more than a chance for men to carve out lives of drudgery. This was not their ambition; it flew in the face of a strongly gentrified worldview. Their dream of upward mobility embraced ownership of land and slaves, luxury and leisure, and deference from those below, not a hardscrabble life on the frontier. That much of Southern reality bore no resemblance to this ideal did not matter: it was the *aspiration* that counted, the *chance* that yeomen could reach toward the aristocracy, and the *certainty* that someone was below—an African American—to keep them above the bottom rung. Eliminating that rung, by flooding the society with free black workers, only made the status of lower-class whites highly precarious. William Brownlow, a Tennessee Unionist, captured the power of antebellum fantasy when he asked a man in rebel uniform what "rights" he was fighting for. The reply was "the right to carry his negroes into the Territories," remarked Brownlow. "At the same time, the man never owned a negro in his life, and never was related, by consanguinity or affinity, to any one who did own a negro!" Although Southern yeomen were concerned about their wages and working conditions, and were more suspicious of disunion than firebrands above and below, they did not equate improving their lot with fundamentally altering the society. One of the problems Southerners had with Lincoln's program was that in a highly stratified world it seemed to lump everyone together, with policies that appeared disadvantageous to all but the slaves. As Mississippian J. Quitman Moore vehemently remarked, the Republican platform was "Radical, leveling, and revolutionary—intolerant, proscriptive, and arbitrary—violent, remorseless, and sanguinary." The result was a society that moved "constantly downward."[54]

Moreover, since the 1840s, middle-rank Southerners had believed there were advantages in capital controlling labor. The bustling economic expansion of the region, in railways and industry, supported this conviction. As the president of the Mississippi Central Railroad explained in 1855, "in ease of management, in economy of maintenance, in certainty of execution of work—in amount of labor performed—in absence of disturbance of riotous outbreaks, the slave is preferable to free labor." By 1861 more than fourteen thousand slaves were working on the railroad, many of them skilled blacksmiths, quarrymen, carpenters, and foremen. They held similar jobs in factories such as Richmond's Tredegar Iron Works. Only four Northern states exceeded their Southern counterparts in numbers of new railroad miles laid in the 1850s, and the remarkable growth of this industry was part of the justification for creating an independent nation. Lincoln never understood that the South had fundamentally changed its economic landscape, though Duff Green and others tried to enlighten him. It was no longer a pre-industrial agricultural sector, dominated by comparatively few plantation owners who controlled an assorted peasantry of gang laborers and subsistence-level poor whites, along with the political decision-making process. The Old Northwest, Lincoln's territory, was the South's only rival for burgeoning industry—the eastern states were already outpaced—and Southerners saw less to admire in Republican plans for national growth than did their Northern counterparts. Instead they worried that those plans would level off their progress and stifle their prospects.[55]

Added to this were genuine questions of political philosophy over the right of secession. Southerners certainly wanted to protect slavery, and they wanted to retain the stratified, class-driven society that rewarded a few and provided dreams to others. But they also wanted the liberty to choose their own brand of democracy, not have it dictated by the North. They did not believe the Yankees' "might" derived from "right," but from the larger population that gave them a lopsided advantage in representative government. Part of the drive to expand into the territories, to build railroads and extend their customs and laws, was to shore up their base of support—to augment the numbers, if you will. Without this, Southerners saw no way to enjoy a fair share of the government's power. The consequence they feared was continual humiliation at the hands of a sectional group that wanted to bully them into a republic that no longer represented Southern interests. A West Point man, posted to Texas at the time of its secession, advised his father that the debate was not just a public show of bravado, or a ploy to gain leverage—it represented a sincere concern about the tyranny of a majority. "I had expected to hear bluster and fanaticism, but was disappointed," wrote Lieutenant Edward Hartz. "[T]hey spoke with a conviction of injury which *must* be redressed." Southerners believed that fighting oppression was part of their birthright, the same impulse that had motivated separatists when the British crown restricted self-government in the colonies. Moreover, volunteer withdrawal from the Union had never been clearly barred by American statutes: the Constitution was silent on the issue. Northern as well as Southern states started threatening secession only a few years after the Revolution, and the legitimacy or illegitimacy of separation lay largely in the eye of the beholder. James Petigru, a distinguished South Carolina jurist noted for staking his personal integrity on supporting the Union in 1860, nonetheless maintained that the federal government had no power to extend its authority over the people of a state, even in cases of disunion. Men like Lincoln believed this self-contradictory aspect of American democracy could be resolved by public debate, regular exercise of the ballot, and a high degree of local autonomy on the fundamental issues of society. What worried the South was that the game was now rigged so that they could never win. Many Southerners had practical problems with secession—the expense, tensions, and spiraling fragmentation it could create. But nearly all believed they had a right to select their own kind of government. "Surely," argued a moderate, "it is contrary to the theory of our Government to subjugate a people who are unanimously opposed."[56]

Yet, somehow, Republicans were blind to Southern resolve. They ignored the warning signs and often treated serious statements with contempt or belittling humor. Northerners simply could not believe it possible for reasoning men "to take so wild and suicidal a course as that of the southern secessionists." The talk of disunion was simply the result of "Satanic Pride and Whiskey," declared jurist Francis Lieber. Yet Southerners were in deadly earnest. "The thought of coercing her, or more plainly of subduing her is simply madness," exclaimed the brother of Joseph Holt, a Lincoln ally who had successfully served as secretary of war in the last gasp of the Buchanan administration. "She can not be conquered until she has been made a desert, & the last defender has been put under the sod."[57] Duff Green was one of many men who tried to impress Lincoln with the idea that Southerners had "thrown their soul into the question," but Lincoln failed to take the point. William Tecumseh Sherman was shocked when he arrived from Louisiana in March 1861 to hear the new president lightly dismiss his warning that Southerners were preparing for war. Even at the end of the conflict Lincoln had a strange denial of Southern determination, believing a spontaneous movement for reunion was likely among the people if not within the Confederate government. What the South was loudly proclaiming, however, was something very different: that the issue had moved beyond discussion and no kind of peace could unite them. Now it was "war to the knife, and the knife to the hilt."[58]

Despite his intentions, Lincoln seemed to perpetually miss the point in his relations with the South. In addition, he personally commanded little respect in Dixie. He seemed to be an upstart and an awkward one at that. Southerners prided themselves on producing aristocratic leadership of Jefferson's or Madison's caliber, and even that up-by-the-bootstraps hustler Andrew Jackson had become a significant land and slave owner. By contrast, Lincoln was only a modest country lawyer with sporadic turns in public office. "Lincoln seems to me by his words & acts to be a nincompoop," opined a scion of the prestigious Tayloe family. "How low have we fallen that such should be the successor of Washington!" Another remarked that he would rather dwell "in hell without a fan" than be subjected to the lowborn Lincoln's governance. In addition, the new president was thought to have the physique and visage associated with poor whites, or with mulattoes. "The fact is he is a hideous half-civilized creature, of great length of figure—in color like a rotten pumpkin or Mississippi sediment," wrote a disdainful Francis R. Rives, the son of William Cabell Rives, despite his family's desire to cling to the Union. Worst of all, Lincoln had no background, no lineage—a striking deficit to Southerners. He had risen through *labor,* and some of it was labor with his *hands.* Up-country men found this as insufferable as the coastal aristocracy. Even a South Carolinian living in squalor saw reason to belittle Lincoln to a Northern visitor. When asked what made him so offensive, she said she had heard he chopped wood: "A 'Rail-splitter?' *Then he's a nigger, shore.*"[59] In reality, Southern society had been made up since colonial times of tooth-and-nail self-made men (including the vaunted Washington), but to give the appearance of striving was considered uncouth. The everyday myth was that ability, determination, and drive were secondary—that there was a pre-fixed hierarchy of place and privilege which eclipsed the idea that leadership was open to men of talent. Nobody thought raw ability could trump breeding; why, even the "darkies" had talent of sorts with their singing and cooking and dancing. A nation dependent on the unpredictability of talent was too crude, too frightening, to be contemplated. Even in the twenty-first century, the daughter of one of the South's best-connected families defined the foundation of a solid society as "bloodlines."[60]

Southern disdain for Lincoln only grew during the war. It was not a subtle kind of hatred, but overt, intense, and somehow gratifying to the rebellious population. His name blistered on their tongues, and the carefully honed image of "Honest Abe," as an unpretentious man of reason, never took hold below the Mason-Dixon Line. Lincoln bashing took a number of forms, but overall it fell into two categories. The first was a belief that he was an illegitimate ruler, unfairly elected, who not only was the architect of Yankee policy but was usurping more unwarranted power every day. The second revolved around his personal qualities: the popular image that he was a drunken, "underbred boor," a spineless fool, or "a dirty, cowardly & vulgar Black guard." Several of these ideas, particularly the notions of cowardice and inebriation, were far from the mark; but rumor trumped truth in popular passions, and the imagery stuck. A good "secesh" woman admitted that Southern newspapers no longer reported Lincoln's words straightforwardly. Instead, they "exhausted the vocabulary of coarse vituperation. 'Nigger thief,' 'slave driver,' were not uncommon words. . . . No opportunity for scornful allusion was lost."[61] Confederate soldiers used Lincoln effigies for target practice and passed around mocking caricatures to relieve anxiety in moments of defeat. Songs and ditties featuring a diabolical Lincoln made the rounds, with much chortling. A popular one, lisped even by children aged three or four, was sung to the tune of "The Bonnie Blue Flag."

> *Jeff Davis rides a white horse—*
> *Lincoln rides a mule!*
> *Jeff Davis is a gentleman!*
> *And Lincoln is a fool!*[62]

Children also learned about the Yankee leader in special textbooks, written to foster patriotic Southern feelings. Lincoln was pictured as the cause of the war, a mean wretch responsible for "the blood upon a hundred gory fields . . . and the faded glory of his nation's flag and honor." One Confederate revision of Webster's dictionary changed the definition of *despotism* from "the tyranny of an oppressive government" to "Despotism is a tyrannical, oppressive government. The administration of Abraham Lincoln is a despotism."[63]

A whole genre of plays roasting Lincoln sprang up, some going quite a bit beyond the bounds of dignity. Pieces like *The Royal Ape* took on not only Lincoln but his wife and cohorts, scathingly impeaching his morals as well as his wisdom. Even Southern critics frowned at scenes depicting the President and son Bob vying over the favors of a serving maid, but they posed no objection to the characterization of Lincoln as drunken, duped, and possibly mad. Some rebel skits allowed a bit of sympathy, such as *Ahab Lincoln: A Tragedy of the Potomac,* which portrayed him as a reluctant president, more sinned against than sinning.[64] Others are still remarkably funny, showing wit and a keen understanding of the real-life absurdity of many White House operations. *King*

Linkum the First, a musical composed by popular songwriter John Hill Hewitt, was notable among these. Its main character was the "last of his die-nasty, a long-drawn tyrant, uneasy in conscience, and addicted to rail-splitting." Many scenes ended with the characters announcing they were going to "take the oath"—a reference to Lincoln's policy of administering loyalty oaths both North and South—which in this burlesque indicated a swig from a near-to-hand whiskey bottle. Among the highlights was a revue number to the tune of "Vive la Companie" that captured precisely the farcical nature of Lincoln's appointees, with a chorus line of officers, from Scott, "used up like a duck with the croup," to Generals "Bolter" and the "Holey" Pope. Not surprisingly, the play was popular in Richmond and Augusta, Georgia, where it was performed at the height of Confederate military success.[65]

Added to this were scores of caricatures and satirical articles, as clever as anything in *Vanity Fair.* Bill Arp's *Side Show of the Southern Side of the War* was as quick to make a mockery of Lincoln's words as was Artemus Ward. *The Southern Illustrated News* facetiously suggested publishing a book of Lincoln's writings called *Gems from the Gorilla,* and some of the most memorable wartime cartoons came from its pages. To some extent the spoofs became formulaic, featuring bumbling Northerners, led by a president confounded by Southern skill and valor. Novelist John Esten Cooke's 1863

THE SOUTHERN ILLUSTRATED NEWS.

MASKS AND FACES.

King Abraham before and after issuing the EMANCIPATION PROCLAMATION.

"Masks and Faces: King Abraham before and after issuing the Emancipation Proclamation," wood engraving, *The Southern Illustrated News,* November 8, 1862

send-up of Lincoln's military skill was typical. Determined to take the field in person, "the Gorilla King" leads an army intent on booty, carrying guidons emblazed with the words "the war shall end in 90 days." Lincoln charges to the front, where . . . he makes a joke! "The thought of this 'Bufoon' having any authority" over men like Lee, wrote Cooke, made "the mind recoil in horror." Yet the composite image Confederate parodists drew of Lincoln remained more than a bit contradictory. "The Tyrant Lincoln," a bogus ruler, heavy-handed, determined, and cruel, was fused to "The Dictator of Doodle-land," a coarse simpleton under the influence of dangerous fanatics, beguiled by smutty humor and drink.[66]

All of this was comforting to the Confederate public, which badly wanted to escape not only the horrors of the war but responsibility for them. Increasingly, the conflict became personalized around Lincoln. *His* foolish vanity had impelled his run for office; *his* election had exacerbated divisions; *his* failure to mediate effectively had necessitated secession. "Lincoln's hirelings" and "Uncle Abe's ships" were what the South was fighting.[67] Some went so far as to hold him accountable for the disappearance of individual slaves and the destruction of property by the Union Army. "You damned old negro thief if you dont find the above described slave, you shall never be inaugurated President of the United States," threatened a Tennessee man. A devastated Louisianan, surveying the wreckage of her home, cried: "I stood in the parlor in silent amazement. . . . I could hardly believe that Abraham Lincoln's officers had really come so low down as to steal in such a wholesale manner."[68] Many believed, as well, that this Yankee upstart was personally liable for the shattering loss of life. From Bull Run to the bitter last days, Southern columnists pointed the finger of shame straight at the Northern president. "Abraham Lincoln is the murderer," declared the *Richmond Enquirer* when mourning the dead of the first battle. "We charge their blood upon him." After four years and Lincoln's reelection, the vilification had only intensified. At "Emperor Abraham's coronation," accused the *Petersburg Daily Express* in 1864, a sacred oath was taken by a man whose hands were "red with the slaughter of his fellow-beings." The loathing reached a crescendo at certain moments—after the Emancipation Proclamation, and during General Butler's administration in New Orleans and General Sherman's March to the Sea in Georgia. But the steady hum of hatred kept on during the long ordeal. Sermons and headlines, jokes and tunes and tintypes all proclaimed that the archenemy was Abraham Lincoln. In a land that often had trouble defining itself differently from the patriotic trappings it shared with the North, Confederates drew identity from their collective contempt for the Rail-splitter. If they did not always know who they were, Southerners were at least certain that they were not "Lincolnpoops."[69]

Although white Confederates were remarkably unified in their animosity toward Lincoln, feelings differed in the African American population. Black Southerners were generally far more positive in their attitudes, but they were not universally so, and their views contrast with white judgments in both range and nuance. There were a great many with feelings similar to the blissful crowd that ran after Lincoln in Richmond. They grasped their freedom lustily, "a shoutin' an' aprancin' an' a yellin' an' asingin'," as one participant described it. But there were others who proclaimed no "jubilo," and faced the news of liberation with uncertainty. A sizable group had worked diligently for emancipation and knew firsthand that the abolition of slavery was not the work of one Moses-like man, but the product of years of struggle, much of it by leaders of their own race.[70]

African American impressions of Lincoln were influenced by isolation and how much information could be obtained about politics and the war. Slaves were adept at keeping abreast of developments, whether climbing trees or crawling under floorboards to overhear white chitchat, or picking up the latest news when running errands in town. In some cases, one bondman's secret ability to read fed an entire community's information system. The slave "grapevine" was famously effective, so impressive that Union sympathizers such as Cyrena Stone and Elizabeth Van Lew, who gathered intelligence for federal forces, depended on it. "Most generally our reliable news is gathered from negroes," remarked Van Lew, "and they certainly show wisdom, discretion and prudence which is wonderful."[71] Despite the fact that many masters tried to mislead their slaves about events, some African Americans knew from the time of the 1860 election campaign that their owners feared Lincoln would disrupt the peculiar institution. One Kentucky slave testified that his master sold him when he heard about the Republican candidacy because he expected the system to crumble. "He said the next President would be an Abolitionist, and the colored people would be set free and he'd best sell me while he could get a good price," the man told General Lew Wallace. "I sent word to all the boys to pray for Lincoln to be elected and there was great joy when we heard the news." It was a patch of blue sky in the dark days of slavery, tangible hope that the long whispered promise of liberation might soon come true. "We black folks is going to be free—the Bible says so," a woman called Aunt Cherry confided to a sympathetic white ear, "and I think the time is might near."[72] After emancipation, masters often expressed surprise that their "contented" servants embraced freedom so readily, but in fact liberation had been the subject of heartfelt prayers for generations of slaves. With their future still uncertain, however, even those slaves who knew of the Emancipation Proclamation did not always reveal their elation but guardedly kept mum until the end of the conflict was at hand. Some even deceived their masters with professions of fear about Yankee intentions. "What's this Massa Lincoln is going to do to the poor nigger?" a Virginia slave disingenuously asked her mistress, all the time rejoicing over the news. "I hear he is going to cut 'em up awful bad." A Georgia woman noted no outward change in the demeanor of the black community, but another, more observant, mused: "who can tell of the wild joy that thrilled their hearts, when they felt that their chains were at last broken! Who can tell how many 'Praise de Lord!—Praise de Lords!' went up from cabin homes . . . winged to heaven silently, because they *dared* not be spoken."[73]

For such long suffering people, it was not surprising that Lincoln often took on a quasi-religious character. There were many who viewed him as a savior or liberator, with imagery formed by scriptural tradition and folkloric symbolism. A woman teaching freed people on the Sea Islands told of a man who mourned with her after the assassination: "Lincoln died for we, Christ died for we, and me believe him de same mans." For some, Lincoln actually became a charismatic figure, an apparition that embodied a variety of hopes and dreams, appearing at odd times to proclaim freedom on front porches or at kitchen tables, and vanishing just as quickly.[74] Others chose not to glorify Lincoln, or to see him as the principal architect of freedom, but as an instrument of God—and sometimes an unwilling one. "God's ahead ob Massa Linkum," opined Harriet Tubman, one of the great true liberators. "God won't let Massa Linkum, beat the South till he do de right ting." One woman thought of the sixteenth president as a kind of "medicine man" whom the Lord had "got into" and worked through. "Hear talk dat he been de one dat free de slaves, but whe' de power?" queried a South Carolinian, who was twelve when emancipation came. "De power been behind de throne, I say. . . . I believes it was intended from God for de slaves to be free en Abraham Lincoln was just de one what present de speech." Still, many were genuinely grateful that he had put a tangible structure on the long-held hope of freedom. After all, they had, as the old spiritual said, "Been in the Storm So Long."[75]

Other slaves envisioned Lincoln as a kind of super-master, stronger and more powerful than their owners and vested with the ability to intervene on the slaves' behalf. In this guise, blacks sometimes described Lincoln as a "friend," or guardian of their rights. African Americans petitioned the President for a variety of favors, in a manner not unlike the requests he received from other sectors of the society. But their needs differed, and they were often more desperate. A soldier in the U.S. Colored Troops named George Washington, for example, wrote to ask if Lincoln could not personally free his family from a harsh master in Kentucky (an area not covered by the Emancipation Proclamation). "If I had them I raise them up but I am here and if you will free me and hir and heir Children with me I Can take Cair of them," ran his epistle.[76] Lincoln's direct influence seemed more certain to these people than the workings of an impersonal bureaucracy. Indeed, in some cases, slaves viewed Lincoln as the embodiment of the government itself. In the Sea Islands there was a great fear that man and policy were intertwined so closely that one could not exist independently from the other. This was especially apparent after Lincoln's murder, when many ex-slaves feared a return to the status quo ante. A Northern teacher witnessed freed people anxiously questioning whether the "Government is dead" and if they must return to bondage. "They could not comprehend the matter at all—how Lincoln could die and the Government still live. It made them very quiet for a few days." Other workers in the area had similar experiences, and one described a particularly striking conversation. " 'I have lost a friend,' " a former slave quietly told her. " 'What friend?' she asked. 'They call him Sam,' he said; 'Uncle Sam, the best friend ever I had.' "[77]

Isolation, misinformation, and power plays among Union officers, federal officials, and local white authorities all contributed to the confusion of man and system. The closer African Americans were to the realities of power, however, the more focused their opinions about Lincoln became. Educated blacks, and those with access—through the Army, proximity to Washington, or, increasingly, through their own political exertions—held clear views about the pros and cons of Lincoln's governance. This segment of the population had few illusions about the President's quasi-sanctity, and they harbored no fantasies of personal salvation at his hands. "It must not be supposed that the blacks to a man are loyal to the old flag," wrote Thomas Morris Chester, an African American journalist who entered Richmond with the Union forces and, in a marvelous symbol of the world turned upside down, wrote his dispatches from the Speaker's chair in the Confederate Congress. Lincoln's hesitation, his enforcement of the Fugitive Slave Act, and similar setbacks had "induced many to cling to the cause of the South under protest," wrote Chester, "and suffer the evils they have than fly to others they know not of." Although the majority of blacks hoped for the restoration of the Union, and many were actively engaged in military or intelligence work, their grievances, Chester noted, were real.[78]

African Americans serving in the Union Army—some ninety-two thousand from Southern states—fought discrimination in treatment and pay, and thought Lincoln should more forthrightly tackle these issues. Sergeant George Stephens, a feisty freedman in the Fifty-Fourth Massachusetts Regiment who wrote for the *Weekly Anglo-African,* complained that he and his comrades were subjected to insults, assigned the most dangerous duties, and then rewarded with unequal compensation. "Now the plan is to inveigle the black man into the service by false pretenses, and then make him take half pay. . . . Does the Lincoln despotism think it can succeed? . . . Do you think that we will tamely submit like spaniels to every indignity?" he angrily queried. James Henry Gooding, another black soldier, echoed the sentiment: "Are we *Soldiers,* or are we LABOURERS[?]" he pointedly asked the President. The devotion of the U.S. Colored Troops had not flagged, Gooding maintained, despite "the evident apathy displayed in our behalf, but We feel as though, our Country spurned us." Gooding was joined by other protesters, who sent petitions with long lists of signatures to the White House, and in some cases refused to accept any pay at all until the discrepancy had been eliminated. Frederick Douglass, who was among those lobbying for equal pay, reported that Lincoln thought the discrepancy was necessary as a concession to those who opposed a black presence in the Army at all. (In 1864 Congress—which was generally ahead of the chief executive on such issues—passed provisions for equal compensation; retroactive pay to the time of enlistment was approved in March 1865.) Others complained that the President had dragged his feet in redressing a massacre of U.S. Colored Troops at Fort Pillow, Tennessee, in April 1864; and indeed it was only indirectly addressed by suspending prisoner exchanges until Confederate officials agreed to treat black captives equally under the laws of war.[79]

The limitations of the Emancipation Proclamation also concerned black leaders. There was widespread understanding that African American troops had transformed the war, and that the Emancipation Proclamation had fused liberation to the question of the nation's survival. Nonetheless, the partial jurisdiction of the proclamation, and the fact that it had been enacted as a military decree rather than the law of the land, gave blacks little faith that it would have any force once the war was over. "United States Emancipation is the fulmination of one man, by virtue of his military authority, who proposes to free the slaves of that portion of territory over which he has no control," railed a soldier on dangerous duty during the siege of Charleston, "while those portions of slave territory under control of the Union armies is exempted, and slavery receives as much protection as it ever did." It was at best a partial solution, as Lincoln himself acknowledged, and some prominent African Americans scorned it as the unlovely child of a reluctant emancipator, brought forth "by timid and heaven-doubting mid-wives."[80] Of equal interest was the absence of a policy to integrate fully liberated men and women into the society. The *New Orleans Tribune,* a bilingual newspaper run by an educated and enterprising group of free blacks, was particularly nervous about these points, sharply hammering the Lincoln administration to take action. The issue was an especially sticky one in Louisiana, where the occupying Union force was thought by many to have condoned a kind of semibondage, with bondmen returned to masters, a caste system enforced, and only marginal pay given to the ex-slaves. Noting that "the deep-rooted prejudice against this people still remains in all its pristine strength and vigor," and that emancipation had not truly been enacted anywhere, the *Tribune* charged Lincoln with suppressing movements for real equality in order to gain votes in his 1864 reelection campaign. Moving from specific matters to a general dissatisfaction with the President's leadership, the paper also lambasted him for faulty moral vision and for limp wartime policies that prolonged the conflict and made its outcomes doubtful. Lincoln, claimed the *Tribune,* "is now deluging the country with blood and continuing indefinitely the duration of the war, when bold, decisive, thorough-going measures would long since have ended it."[81]

One of the things that worried the *New Orleans Tribune* was the President's continued support for the colonization of emancipated African Americans. The issue irritated a great many, North and South, and some of the chief executive's comments gave real offense. Even as he was considering emancipation, Lincoln was also readying plans to deport freedmen and -women. It was his belief that American society would not tolerate a mix that included black people living with the same rights and privileges as whites. In August 1862 Lincoln met with a group of African Americans and proposed—in rather stark terms—that colonization was advantageous because of the natural animosity between the two races, which caused both races to suffer. In an unfortunate aside, he also told the black leaders that they were responsible for "our white men cutting each other's throats," and that "[b]ut for your race among us there could not be war"—which seemed to place the blame for slavery and its outcome on the victims. In addition, the President implied that their "selfish" unwillingness to be exiled was responsible for a lack of progress in their own society and would further retard American growth. When his comments reached the newspapers, he met a backlash from white as well as black leaders. The *Tribune* was among them, outraged that "instead of working to root out all those prejudices hitherto so little in harmony with the Declaration of Independence, politicians consecrate them anew to-day by paying homage to the prejudice of color." Other black leaders took on Lincoln's accusations directly. Among them was a lawyer who had lived and taught in Liberia, returning to the United States with the firm belief that colonization meant nothing but white prejudice. Appalled at the notion that African Americans were somehow responsible for the Civil War, he did not mince words in his rejoinder. "President of the United States, let me say . . . that the negro may be 'the bone of contention' in our present civil war . . . but he has not been its cause. . . . The white man's oppression of the negro, and not the negro himself, has brought upon the nation the leprosy under which it groans."[82]

Coupled with concerns about colonization was anxiety over the status of black people in a post-emancipation society. African Americans were desirous of true opportunity, not a de facto return to serfdom. Petitions were sent to the President and to such state legislatures as those of North Carolina, Tennessee, and Virginia, asking for help in starting new lives, and calling for a full and equal voice in postwar arrangements, including voting and holding office. In March 1864 a petition with one thousand signatures arrived in Washington from Louisiana, demanding suffrage rights, particularly for those whose attainments or wartime service merited special attention. Lincoln was impressed enough that he asked the provisional governor of the state to consider "whether some of the colored people may not be let in—as for instance, the very intelligent, and especially those who have fought gallantly in the ranks." While it seemed a step in the right direction, particularly for such a conservative chief executive, some protested that it might drive a wedge between lighter-skinned or better-educated freedmen and other members of the black community, creating a racial caste system. True equality was what the African American community sought, and, as the French edition of the *New Orleans Tribune* stated, while it sympathized with the difficulties of waging a national war, it did not intend to "cease protesting against all violations of our rights." When the limited suffrage measure was proposed formally in New Orleans, it was defeated, at least partially because of opposition by quadroons and other elites in the local colored population. "No system of gradual elevation is needed to make us men," argued J. R. Ingraham, who had served as a captain in the Union Army, and his words were roundly seconded by editors and politicians. By the close of the Civil War, the most educated, articulate, and prosperous African American community in the nation was largely alienated from the policies advocated by the Lincoln administration.[83]

Ultimately, the African Americans' dreams of equality would be disappointed. Lincoln remained skeptical about the extent to which newly freed people should participate in American society, and by December 1863 he had proposed reconstruction terms that were lenient to former slaveholders. He was also without a strategy for the economic well-being of freedmen, seeming to trust that an easy accommodation would be found between the humiliated and, in some cases, destitute masters and millions of former bondmen who were equally destitute, often illiterate, and without the political power to demand justice. Further confusion was created after General Sherman, in consultation with local black leaders, set aside some coastal areas of Georgia and South Carolina for the settlement of freedmen. Each family was to receive forty acres of land, and Sherman promised the Army would facilitate the loan of livestock to work it. Although the general's motives were not particularly pure—he basically wanted to rid his army of "surplus negroes, mules, and horses"—it nevertheless represented the pinnacle of opportunity for blacks to gain economic independence. Unfortunately, the short-lived experiment was later misconstrued to mean that every liberated family in the country would receive this allotment, and there was widespread disappointment when the promise of "forty acres and a mule" went unfulfilled. Ex-slaves instead had to fend for themselves, beginning a life without education or funds, or find themselves dependent on their past masters. "To set them free, and leave them without the necessary protection, at the mercy of their former owners, maddened by reason of their defeat, was indeed an oversight," remarked a preacher who had begun life in a slave cabin.[84] After his assassination, Lincoln quickly became a martyr in many black circles, but it is notable that over time a common feeling among former slaves was that the sixteenth president had left the job half done. "Lincoln got the praise for freeing us, but did he do it?" reflected Thomas Hall, of Raleigh, North Carolina. "He give us freedom without giving us any chance to live to ourselves and we still had to depend on the southern white man for work, food and clothing, and he held us through our necessity and want in a state of servitude but little better than slavery."[85]

Yet for all the imperfections in Lincoln's plan, and the disappointment when it became clear that no one was going to give African Americans a boost up, there was a lingering sense of that sweet, sweet first burst of freedom, when one old ex-slave went to the barn and jumped from straw stack to straw stack shouting "hallelujah," and Richmond streets were filled with singing and dancing and praising the Lord. Lincoln "upset the forms, laws, customs, and ceremonies of centuries" when he grasped hands in that raucous crowd, wrote a reporter who was present. "It was a . . . mortal wound to caste." A black woman who retained vivid memories of the moment concurred. "Uncle Abe made me a free agent. If you had yo hands tied and some one come and cut 'em aloose wouldn't you be glad?" she asked. "Dat's why I like Abe."[86]

IV

Reconstruction and the uncertainties of peace haunted whites as well as African Americans. They were foremost in the mind of Duff Green. Green's hope of harvesting riches from a transcontinental railway had been shattered in 1862, when secession cut him off from his Pennsylvania holding company. Seizing the opportunity, Green's fellow creditors reorganized the company, naming it Credit Mobilier of America, and moved the proposed route northward. Only one board member protested that Green, who was president of the corporation and owned 42,000 of its 50,000 shares, was not present. Undaunted, Green continued to hatch ambitious schemes for Southern industry. He exploited mineral resources and opened ironworks in Georgia and Tennessee, making everyday items such as nails and farm implements, as well as desperately needed military matériel. Always eager to squeeze the greatest profit from the least expenditure for labor, and creative in his choice of workers, Green experimented with imported labor for his rolling mills, as well as disabled soldiers, when slaves were not available.[87] But he was persistently hassled by the Davis government, which not only set unfair terms for the amount of production he was obliged to release to them but ignored a smart proposal he developed for streamlining Confederate banking systems. By 1864 Green realized he would never profit from the war and must have *peace* to realize his elaborate plans. He tried to contact both Lincoln and key figures in the Confederate cabinet to promote his ideas, but Lincoln never responded and he was rebuffed coldly in Richmond as well. He had a new project by the time he boarded the *Malvern* in April 1865 to converse with Lincoln: a way to turn the one remaining Southern asset—land—into capital. He believed his initiative would grow the banking system, energize Southerners to rebuild their society, and make a tidy sum for investors like him. What he proposed was that landholders could subscribe their real estate at 50 percent of value to a nearby branch of a new "federal" bank, and borrow from the association for 50 percent of their subscription. He also saw it as a way to harness the immense labor potential of free blacks who would be cut adrift with the demise of the plantation system. Green's idea was interesting and potentially workable. With an uncertain money supply, however, plus the slow return of rebellious areas to the Union, and the planters' reluctance to engage in speculation, this scheme too failed. Anticipating the importance of a secure political and financial backdrop for entrepreneurial efforts, what Green wanted to know from Lincoln on April 5 was just how he intended to foster normalcy, and how he envisioned such critical issues as reparations, civil legal structures, and the status of the ex-slaves.[88]

The *Malvern* was about to depart when Green boarded, but one of the men still aboard was John Archibald Campbell. Campbell's sharp, hawklike countenance had long been familiar to Lincoln, for he was a former justice of the United States Supreme Court, appointed from Alabama in 1853 by Franklin Pierce. A brilliant man, Campbell had graduated from college at fourteen and attended West Point with Jefferson Davis and Robert E. Lee. While on the court he used his position to uphold constitutional guarantees for slaveholders and protested that any restriction on slavery's expansion denied Southerners their due right to own and work human property. He voted with the majority on the Dred Scott case.[89] During the secession crisis, he remained in Washington, purportedly acting as a mediator while actually working in close association with the new Confederate government to broker a deal that would allow disunion, but retain strong, friendly ties with the North. His impression of Lincoln, formed during this time, was of a "light, inconsis-

Justice John Archibald Campbell, photograph by
Mathew Brady, c. 1860
LIBRARY OF CONGRESS

tent and variable" man, who waffled in his resolve, but cultivated the appearance of keeping his word. When his efforts to avoid war failed, Campbell resigned from the court. He was appointed assistant secretary of war by Jefferson Davis and was valued for his tireless work and judicious decision making. But he served under a series of lackluster Confederate appointees, and was feared or envied by many in Richmond's governing circle. As a result, Campbell experienced endless frustration and wielded little influence. He nevertheless refused to resign, feeling it would look like "desertion."[90]

For months Campbell had believed the Confederacy's days were numbered; now he thought the job at hand was to get the best deal possible for the South. "I had much conversation with Judge Campbell about . . . our prospects," wrote his subordinate Robert Garlick Hill Kean, who kept a diary of the Richmond bureaucracy's workings. "He thinks it will all end in reconstruction and that the only question now is the *manner of it*—whether the South shall be destroyed and subjugated or go back with honor and rights." Campbell had been among the Confederate representatives at the February 1865 Hampton Roads conference with Lincoln, an exercise he had hoped would end in an armistice and favorable adjustment of civil relations. When the talks broke down over whether the arrangement would be within "one common country" or between two sovereign nations, and whether peace would be based on laws of conquest or on civil conventions, Campbell sent a to-the-point assessment of Confederate prospects to Jefferson Davis. "The South may succumb, but it is not necessary that she should be destroyed," he argued. But Campbell's words only raised last-ditch resistance, increasing his alarm. "There is anarchy in the opinions of men here," he cautioned the South's secretary of war. When the Confederate government fled Richmond, Campbell purposely stayed behind to pick up the Hampton Roads discussion, though he claimed he had no authority to do so. As in 1861, he acted ex officio, believing he could play on Lincoln's impressibility and hoping, as Duff Green did, to get a sense of the President's reconstruction policy. His questions revolved around taxes, penalties, the right to representation in Congress, and whether an oath of allegiance would be required for Southerners. To that end, he called on Lincoln at the Confederate White House during the whirlwind visit to Richmond on April 4. Both men unofficially proffered some ideas; Lincoln told Campbell he would write his down and suggested they continue the conversation the next day.[91]

Even though his face was described by an observer as "full of disappointment and sadness," Campbell was actually in an exhilarated mood when he left Lincoln. The President had been far more forthcoming than he could have hoped, listening closely to the Alabaman's proposal that leading men be called together to cooperate in the rebuilding of social and political systems. That tone of openness and liberality was repeated aboard the *Malvern* the next morning, when Campbell, joined by prominent Richmond lawyer Gustavus Myers and Godfrey Weitzel, the commanding Union general, reopened the discussion. Asked his feeling about loyalty oaths, Lincoln reassured them he had "never attached much importance to the oaths of allegiance being required"—although it had been an integral part of his policy since 1863—then deferred the matter to Weitzel.[92] He also said he intended to be generous to former Confederates and was disinclined to confiscation or other forms of war reparation. While he gave no promise of amnesty, the President "told them he had the pardoning power and could save any repentant sinner from hanging." He had written out his requirements for peace, read them aloud, with running commentary on each issue, and then left the paper with Campbell. The indispensable points, Lincoln noted, were the acceptance of national authority throughout the former Confederate states, that no decisions or statements on the abolition of slavery be retracted, and that war would continue until all forces hostile to the Union were disbanded. He added that he truly desired to see an end to the conflict and "hoped in the Providence of God that there never would be another."[93]

Lincoln then told the group he was mulling over the idea of allowing the Virginia legislature to assemble for the purpose of recognizing federal authority and to recall Virginian forces from the field. He mistrusted intelligence that said Lee was on the verge of capitulation and thought the Confederate armies would obey an order from the legislature to disband. Campbell and Myers were enthusiastic about the idea, and the President followed up with an order to Weitzel to give safe passage to the legislature, provided it took no action hostile to the United States. The idea was surprising to say the least: Lincoln had steadfastly refused to recognize the authority of any Confederate assembly and had set up an alternative government in Virginia, with a separate legislature.[94] When he returned to Washington a few days later, the President met concern from his cabinet, who thought the move most unwise, as well as criticism from Congress and the press, which had already picked up the story. James Speed, the new attorney general (and brother of Lincoln's old friend Joshua Speed), and Secretary of State Seward thought its legality questionable, and War Secretary Stanton sputtered into one of his rages: his idea was to govern the South by martial law, not encourage a former rebel legislature to exercise power "after four years of trying to put it down." Navy Secretary Gideon Welles also cautioned the President against acting too hastily in his desire to bring about peace. Lincoln responded that his goal was to bring about reconciliation as quickly as possible and to treat the former rebels as fellow countrymen, who deserved respect, and to that end he was not going to "stickle about forms." He also believed the South was now so weak it had little ability to act with vigor, let alone defiance. But he had been surprised by the outcry—which included the *New York Times* bellowing that "this project contains several impracticable features"—and thought under the circumstances perhaps he should withdraw the order. He did so, rather defensively, on April 12, stating, with legal nicety, that he had never recalled the legislature, but the "gentlemen who have *acted* as the Legislature of Virginia," and that he had meant only to have them disband the troops and halt other support for the rebellion. Since Lee had now surrendered, those actions were now unnecessary. In the end, several people took the fall for the controversial plan, including Weitzel, even though it had been Lincoln's alone.[95]

The awkward to-and-fro over the Virginia legislature made it appear that Lincoln did not yet know exactly how he wanted to treat the defeated South. In fact, he had a very clear idea of the general parameters. He was inclined to be lenient to the overall population, he was avoiding nitpicking small points, and he wanted peace restored through civil, not military measures. To enforce policies "at the point of the bayonet," he insisted, would be both repugnant and counterproductive. The President envisioned no treason trials, even though he harbored little love for the generals and government officials who had fought against him. The best plan, one cabinet member recalled Lincoln saying—as he made a gesture, as if shooing sheep—was to "frighten them out of the country, open the gates, let down the bars, scare them off." Enough lives had already been sacrificed, he remarked. The President also wanted to give the returning states easy access to legal structures, and he designed his policy to facilitate restoration by building a small loyal nucleus, revamping constitutions, and holding popular elections. He was also adamant about not backing away from emancipation, especially his personal proclamations. He had, nonetheless, given Duff Green reason for encouragement when he hinted that states reentering the Union might block the Thirteenth Amendment, abolishing slavery in the United States, which had recently passed Congress and was awaiting ratification by the states. "If you wish to keep your slaves, vote against the amendments to the constitution," Green claims Lincoln remarked. Above all, Lincoln wanted the Union restored as soon as possible and was willing to make significant compromises to that end. By moving quickly, the President believed, he could avoid the reestablishment of old power structures in the former slaveholding states and begin the process of healing.[96]

What Lincoln wanted was reunification, not revenge, and he developed a program based on widespread amnesty, simple tests of allegiance, and reorganization of governmental bodies. The goal was to streamline reentry and put the Unionists in charge. What came to be known as the Ten-Percent Plan was proposed as early as December 1863 in the President's annual address to Congress. It recommended that former Confederate states could reenter the Union when 10 percent of the population (according to the 1860 census) took an oath of allegiance and agreed to accept the abolition of slavery. States could then elect delegates to revamp their constitutions and establish new state governments. All Southerners except high-ranking officials would be granted full pardons, and property rights (excepting slaveholdings) would be reinstated for anyone pledging future loyalty to the United States. The plan was at first greeted in the North with a good deal of enthusiasm, more as a war measure—to undercut Southern solidarity and animate Unionists—than as a postconflict framework for reunifying a nation that had undergone revolutionary change. Lincoln seemed to advocate keeping it purposefully loose to allow for vast differences in local structures, and to permit as much democratic involvement as possible. Undoubtedly the proposal was generous and well intentioned, but it was also disjointed and seemingly naïve about the competing agendas of both Northern and Southern political groups. The impracticality of its provisions became increasingly apparent as the experiment was adopted in various areas under Union occupation—notably, Louisiana, Arkansas, and Tennessee.[97]

Lincoln's program did not take hold for a variety of reasons, but chief among them was his optimism about its ease of accomplishment. Believing the South was not only weakened but innately desirous of reunion, he tried hard to make the transition as easy as possible. Yet reunion proved to be far trickier than anyone had imagined. Surrender might bring joy and relief to the victors, but the road back to normalcy was lengthy and pitted with strife. Guaranteeing the welfare of the newly liberated black population was a vexing problem; as Machiavelli had observed, "next to making free men slaves, the most difficult thing is to make slaves free." Added to this was the need to realign governmental structures; to overturn laws and customs that had stood for centuries; and to redefine questions of loyalty, patriotism, and trust. Property rights were often murky, and no one knew exactly how to handle the holdings of former rebels that had been confiscated, by either the Union or the Confederate government. Commerce had been nearly destroyed in some places. The South was bankrupt; and this was all made worse by instances of Yankee speculation, some of it by the Union Army, in the cotton trade and other Confederate industries. In some places the rampaging of two armies had so destroyed the landscape as to make it uninhabitable. There were prisoners of war to deal with, damages and reparations to be determined. Joseph Medill, editor of the *Chicago Tribune,* thought Southerners could simply be beaten into submission. ("Don't be in too much hurry for Peace," he advised Lincoln. "Don't *coax* the rebel chiefs but pound them a little more. When they are sufficiently whipped they will gladly accept *your terms,* and the peace then made will be enduring.") But the spirit of Dixie proved more resilient than Republican leaders had believed. The North had underestimated "the energy and enduring qualities of the Southern people who were slave-owners," mused Welles, two days after Lee's capitulation. "It was believed they were effeminate idlers, living on the toil and labor of others, who themselves could endure no hardship such as is indispensable to soldiers in the field." Experience, he noted, had corrected the misconception. Moreover, the Union was not just attempting to secure victory. It was vying for something far more perilous and precious: the resurrection of a nation.[98]

Among the challenges of fashioning a new order was the continued animosity toward emancipation, even among Southerners who had long supported returning to the Union. In most places it quickly became clear that Lincoln's vague oath—which pledged little beyond support of *future* federal policies—was not enough to make those policies stick, or to ensure stability. As he had in 1861, Lincoln miscalculated the fierce determination of Southerners to continue the slave system. Even liberals such as General Nathaniel Banks, head of the Department of the Gulf, realized that in most places military decrees alone could not coerce former rebels into embracing social elevation and political equality for former slaves. The Ten-Percent Plan met with a good deal of derision in the Confederacy, where it was viewed as a "crafty" scheme to create bogus governments supported by only a small minority of citizens.[99] As one outraged North Carolinian exclaimed, Lincoln had announced

a most anti-democratic doctrine when he declares that the vote of *one tenth* of the population shall be sufficient to send members to Congress & in Yankee eyes decide the status of the State—by no means *vox populi.* He creates . . . a dominant race! We are free it appears to live on an equality with the negro! The only thing required of Southern freemen & gentlemen is to give up their own rights & swear to protect the negro in those given him by Mr[.] Lincoln in his Proclamations, take him around the neck & from a slave make a master of him at Yankee bidding. He offers us pardon! Pardon for what? Forgiveness for what? Forgive us for having himself invaded our land, ravaged & desolated our homes . . . for having deluged our country with the blood of our brothers & sons, slain on their own soil & in defence of that soil? . . . Better learn State craft, Mr. Lincoln, before you attempt to practice *"King craft."*[100]

Others found the oath easily circumvented or meaningless. Southerners ignored it, or swore it to gain access to federal stores or to participate politically and thereby manipulate the process. Many were confused by what privileges the oath actually conferred, or what powers the new state governments would have vis-à-vis military authorities. Occupying generals in Louisiana thought it an empty gesture, highly offensive to the public, and not admissible in courts of law; one said it was capable only of "opening the door to perjury."[101] When Andrew Johnson was the military governor of Tennessee, he tried to give the loyalty test more bite, by requiring those wanting their rights reinstated to affirm they had *always* desired the defeat of the Confederacy and supported the abolition of slavery. Staunch Unionists and loyal skeptics alike protested the uneven application of the oath and the questionable process of rewriting legislation by a tiny, mistrusted minority, and in the end the Union coalition was badly ruptured. Lincoln did not interfere with Johnson's program, however. Under it, a handful of men from eastern Tennessee reorganized state structures to reflect the realities of victory but alienated a vast segment of the population.[102]

In Arkansas, more confusion reigned as rival conventions were called to refashion the state constitution, before loyalty oaths could be administered or proper elections held. Observers doubted whether the delegates represented anyone but themselves, but Lincoln ordered military officials to cooperate with the irregular body, disregarding what he considered a trivial legal point. The President told General Frederick Steele, the man in charge of Arkansas reconstruction, that as long as emancipation was respected, Steele would be able to "fix the rest." A year later citizens complained that Confederate officers were still recruiting throughout the state and no protection had been provided for loyalists. The motives of officials—both elected and appointed—were doubted. "We need some 'clearing up' measures," suggested one citizen. Although Lincoln tried to facilitate oath taking and encouraged Steele to maintain a strong presence, he stopped short of precisely delineating his policies or supporting Steele when the general was removed from command. At the time of the President's death, the status of Arkansas was still uncertain.[103]

Louisiana, the only Union-occupied state in the Deep South, had unusual visibility as a test case for postwar integration. With its complex society of prosperous free blacks, absentee planters, and bilingual culture, it harbored a sea of conundrums. Only a handful of whites chose to take the oath, raising serious questions about the legitimacy of elections held in early 1864. Had "the Devil (or Jeff Davis his agent on Earth) been *set up* as a *free state* man, and the soldiers and poor government employees, *ordered* to vote for *him*, the result would have been the same," cracked one who doubted the results. Tensions were high, as civil officials vied for power with the commanding officers, and free speech was curtailed. African Americans had their own concerns with programs instituted in occupied regions. It was unclear which slaves had been freed by Lincoln's Proclamation and which remained in slavery, and after centuries of bondage, ex-slaves were not certain just what liberation actually meant. The labor systems instituted under military authority uncomfortably resembled the old slave codes and no action was being taken for education or resettlement. As the *New Orleans Tribune* repeatedly declared, halfhearted steps toward civil equality, brought about without the participation or consent of blacks, only generated confusion and anger.[104] Even Unionists were divided. They quarreled over compensation for slave property, over the role reconstruction should play in the overthrow of the old aristocratic rule, and over the extent to which African Americans would participate in governance. As a New Orleans man advised the President, "people are *not* satisfied. They are indignant and anxious." Loyalists had faith in Lincoln, he wrote, and begged that he "not suffer a pretended State Government to be thrust upon them by such devices."[105]

Despite a barrage of criticism, Lincoln supported those elected under questionable circumstances in Louisiana. Skeptics saw his moves as an attempt to buy loyalty for his upcoming reelection bid—which it may partially have been. (A "fraudulent & illegal" government elected by a mere eleven thousand people, protested the ur-rebel Edmund Ruffin, was "to pass for the voice & will of the State" in the next presidential election, voting "for Lincoln of course.") But the President also wanted to harness the power of local leaders, as well as to keep as much flexibility as possible in reconstruction programs, so they would not break down under rigidity, or smack too much of dictatorship. He pocket vetoed a counterinitiative by radical leaders Benjamin Wade and Henry Winter Davis that would have required returning states to abolish slavery unequivocally and have 50 percent of their population swear an "ironclad oath" that they had never supported the Confederacy. Objecting to the idea that states needed to "rejoin" a Union he had never recognized as legitimately broken, Lincoln believed the measures would make reunification impossibly difficult.[106] The veto sparked a reaction from Wade and Davis, who publicly accused the President of "grave Executive usurpation" in his veto, then veered into general "outrage" at his policies. The Wade-Davis Manifesto, as it came to be called, was emblematic of the divisions Lincoln's reconstruction policy caused within his party and between government branches, as several leaders did not hesitate to tell him. "Too much blood & treasure have been spent to allow these states to come back again until they are really changed," vowed Charles Sumner. Although Sumner thought Lincoln might come round to the radicals' belief that blacks must participate in the creation of new local governments, the President surprised Congress and his cabinet by suggesting compensation for slaveholders, resurrecting the idea of colonizing ex-slaves, and dragging his feet on black rights. There "may be such a thing as overdoing it," wrote Welles of Lincoln's leniency toward the South; Chief Justice Salmon Chase also penned a worried note expressing "fear that our good President is so anxious for the restoration of the Union, that he will not care sufficiently about the basis of restoration."[107]

The South remained equally unconvinced of Lincoln's good intentions. In the absence of strict standards and clear, firm regulations, ex-Confederates derided or took advantage of what seemed to be an improbably lax structure for reunion. Federal officials complained that those elected under the new rules took office only to thwart progress or to allow military activities that continued to play into Confederate hands. However admirable the President's hope of charity for all, he stopped short of clearly delineating authority or setting up structures that could be understood and followed—even if unwillingly—by the conquered South. In the absence of a concerted policy, every one of his reconstruction experiments failed to attract broad support and not one state was brought back to the Union during his lifetime. In his eagerness to hurry up restoration, he either had not devised a sound strategy or had rushed the business into premature collapse.[108]

V

In tackling this daunting task, Lincoln was influenced by an assumption that had colored much of his strategy throughout the war years. This was the belief that a very large segment of Southern society had preferred to remain within the United States and to address its grievances through the tried-and-true channels of the federal Constitution. In many ways this was a touching personalization of the faith the sixteenth president felt in the United States, a loyalty he imagined was mirrored in Southern faces. But as Duff Green had told him in 1860, and tried to remind him again in April 1865, attachment to the Union was far more conditional than Lincoln believed. Even within the loyal population there were sharp divisions between those who wanted to cooperate at all costs, and those who had specific terms for remaining in the compact. Nor were the "conditionalists" of one mind; their requirements and expectations differed from region to region and among classes: former Whigs called for bridges to be built across the political gulf, while poorer whites hoped the federal government would strike a blow at the planter oligarchy, and Northern and European transplants reflected the ties and traditions of their homelands. Lincoln was correct in thinking that rabid secessionists represented only a strident minority in 1861, but they gained traction from the Unionists' failure to devise an alternative platform or a cohesive strategy.[109]

Unionist voices were also silenced by active hostility to them throughout the Confederacy, sometimes reaching violent proportions. "Submissionists" were forced into voting for secession, ambushed at the polls, and painted with tar or dye if they dared to cast a ballot in favor of the "Black Republican" government. At times, the "Tories" were threatened with lynching.[110] British journalist William Russell made an unofficial survey of Unionist harassment on a trip south in 1861, finding that vigilante committees had been formed to root out less-than-enthusiastic Confederates, and that tar and feathering as well as imprisonment were openly taking place. John A. Logan, later an important Union general, met a number of refugees in Washington who had been deported from the seceded states because of their opinions—their "property taken and they driven out penniless women & children on the charities of the people." When some Union sympathizers tried to hunker down and quietly continue their lives, they found their livestock stolen, sons impressed into the Confederate service, or themselves socially isolated. "The serpent has entered our Eden," worried a woman who had sought refuge in Arkansas. "If an incautious word betrays any want of sympathy with popular plans, one is 'traitorous,' 'ungrateful,' 'crazy.'"[111] Those who were allowed to express their opinions openly, such as former South Carolina attorney general James Petigru or Lee family cousins William Fanning Wickham and Edward Turner, did so by skating on the thin ice of their status. Even these men suffered threatening looks and backhanded taunts. "I . . . never concealed my sentiments, for which I was censored with great severity, by almost every one who heard them," acknowledged Wickham.[112]

Unionist sentiment was further eroded by policies that grated, even to those who hoped to reunite with the North. Federal actions that allowed confiscation of rebel property and abolished slavery were calculated to divide and demoralize Confederates. They had the same effect on the many loyalists who thought slavery justified, even if secession was not. Misconduct by occupying Union troops also estranged some, as did disappointment about the Army's inability to protect citizens against marauders. An army officer told Illinois senator Orville Hickman Browning that when he was first posted to Arkansas the majority of people were loyal and "if affairs had been properly managed" the state might well have returned to the Union, but plunder, irresponsible behavior, and punitive policies had taken their toll, so that "when he left there was not one Union man in ten thousand." Although such observations could not be taken entirely at face value—another Arkansan claimed that most of his fellow citizens still wanted to reclaim their national ties—undoubtedly Unionists were alienated by government actions that were ineffective or abusive.[113] Some Union-leaning areas rejoiced in the protection of federal troops, of course, and the cases of sheltering and feeding families that had suffered rebel vengeance were many. But others expressed disappointment when they were not protected, or when the course followed by blue-coated soldiers—such as commanding African American troops and controlling the sale of cotton and other commodities—did not conform to their ideas of rectitude. A Northern army man in Memphis observed that the Lincoln government's policies were having a demoralizing effect on otherwise accommodating citizens, and that "hundreds of influential men are rendered lukewarm, who would otherwise have the strongest incentives to use their influence in putting down the rebellion."[114]

Unfortunately, Lincoln himself was also a point of disgruntlement. Unionists found themselves apologizing for the awkward president or agreeing with their Confederate neighbors about his unimpressive performance. Even the unflappable James Petigru openly wondered that "such a man" should hold the job.[115] When they needed him most, during the secession cri-sis, loyalists had written again and again to urge Lincoln to give a statement or sign that would support their fragile position. And yet Lincoln had done nothing to bolster their cause. Evidently he held few conferences with signifi-cant Unionists during the war, and many complained that they waited in vain for a reply to their impassioned letters or were left lingering in the President's anteroom while he hobnobbed with weeping widows.[116] John Minor Botts, a distinguished Virginian whose unassailable loyalty twice caused him to be imprisoned by Confederate authorities, forcefully expressed the disappoint-ment of those hoping for a rallying spirit in the White House. Lincoln had passed over the highly qualified Botts for a cabinet post and had turned down suggestions that they confer. Much as he admired the President's self-taught shrewdness, wrote Botts, he had trouble identifying with his lackluster man-agement of Congress and the loose executive hold on army discipline, or with policies such as the Emancipation Proclamation, whose uneven application meant *his* property had been confiscated, while that of another Virginian, archrebel Henry Wise, was exempted. The Union Army had done as much destruction to his home as had the Confederates, Botts sadly noted, and as a result his appetite for playing an active role in the Lincoln administration had diminished. When appointed senator in the rump government Lincoln estab-lished for occupied Virginia, Botts declined the post.[117]

Some loyalists did hang on, and some even risked their lives and reputa-tions to aid the Union cause. Ardent supporters such as Elizabeth "Crazy Bet" Van Lew ran spy rings, passing information to the Union Army and shielding loyalists. Unionists worked in federal hospitals, steadfastly served in the Wash-ington bureaucracy, and published anti-Confederate newspapers. An impres-sive 100,000 white men from seceded states joined the Northern armed forces, as well as another 200,000 from border areas. Some of these, including Gen-eral George Thomas and Admirals David Farragut and David Dixon Porter, were among the most valiant men fighting for the Union. Added to the 150,000 Southern black troops, they totaled almost half of the 900,000 sol-diers who wore gray—and these were men the beleaguered Confederacy would have dearly loved to enfold. Others contributed by passive resistance: thwarting plans, wearing down officials, and circumventing regulations. They made an unquestionable difference in the final outcome; Lee, among others, cited halfhearted support and divisions within Dixie as a reason for the ulti-mate defeat of the Confederacy.[118]

Still, the dissenters were never quite able to do what the commander in chief really hoped they might—rise up in a massive counterrevolution. "Why did they not assert themselves?" cried an outraged Lincoln, complaining to a Louisiana Unionist of the "paralysis—the dead palsy" of those begging for government protection. "They are to touch neither a sail nor a pump, but to be merely passengers," the President railed, "dead-heads at that—to be carried snug and dry, throughout the storm, and safely landed right side up." Ward Hill Lamon, his burly confidant, was what the President had in mind: a Southerner (Lamon was born in Virginia) who proposed raising a thousand-man regiment to liberate his home county from the "thralldom" of secession. But like Lamon—who failed in his goal—most Unionists were too undirected to carry out such plans. When the time for reunification came, their fragmentation and lack of a cogent game plan, coupled with their neighbors' widespread hostility, made it unlikely that "Tories" would persuade the defeated public to accept Lincoln's reconstruction proposals.[119]

Lincoln tried to build easy off-ramps from the conflict, but his constructions were too shaky to last in most places. The Ten-Percent Plan toppled from its unrealistic assumptions; and his dream that Unionists would spring up to embrace the reunited nation was equally unstable. One place he built a durable structure was at Appomattox, where Northern generosity prevailed at the emotional surrender of Lee's skeletal force. Many contributed to that wonderful healing scene, when Grant and his generals "let 'em up easy," declining to crow over their hard-won victory. But the overarching ethos was pure Lincoln. This was his triumphal statement, not the ill-timed walk through Richmond, with its eerie mixture of darkened windows and frenetic joy. Of the many myths associated with the sixteenth president, the sympathy shown at Appomattox is unquestionably grounded in truth, and forever captures the poignancy of the war and the hope of rolling back its bitterness. *This* was the moment that made the man.

However, neither the soft landing at Appomattox nor the tragic assassination a few days later would vindicate Lincoln in the Southern mind. Most Confederates learned of the President's murder in nearly the same breath as the devastating news of Lee's capitulation, causing bewilderment and sometimes terror. Duff Green was among those who spread the news around Richmond, cautioning people to prudence, for John Wilkes Booth's violent act had enraged the North. His fear, that the entire South would be blamed for the crime, was not without justification. In the awful aftermath of the assassination, whatever charitable feelings may have existed for the defeated South quickly turned sour. "If our citizens should get hold of any one known to be in the slightest degree connected with the death of their adored President, I believe they would tear him to pieces!" exclaimed Benjamin French, Lincoln's commissioner of public buildings. "This awful murder has hardened all hearts against the rebels, & I fear mercy *will not* season justice."[120] Sensible Southerners understood that Booth's lawlessness would not "be productive of even temporary advantage," and even unrepentant foes like Davis and Lee condemned the act, though they stopped short of praising Lincoln. Some Southerners expressed regret because they suspected it would be more humiliating to live under the new president— tough Tennessee Unionist Andrew Johnson—than his predecessor. A few Confederate officials, such as Vice President Alexander Stephens, who had known Lincoln personally, were genuinely sorry about his death, and the loss of a man they believed would have tempered the harshness of defeat. In African American communities, concern over Lincoln's failure to devise a compassionate postbondage policy quickly turned round, as he was appropriated as a symbol of emancipation and martyrdom. Where federal troops were in control, citizens were careful to make appropriate expressions of sorrow, newspapers published editorials condemning Booth's rashness, and sermons expressed contrition over the waste of a good man's life. Just how sincere these manifestations were is difficult to gauge. In some places, such as New Orleans, public mourning was either required or essential for remaining in the good graces of the occupying forces. In others it was enforced with whippings or prison sentences.[121]

But for most ex-Confederates, the cup of sorrow was too full to be drained away by Booth's hideous act. Those writing in private, or beyond the Union Army's reach, expressed little grief, and some exalted at the grim news. There was hurrahing in the streets of Griffin, Georgia, and at Fort Delaware rebel prisoners danced until they were told to stop. In Texas, not a single newspaper condemned the President's murder and more than a few held it up as Divine Retribution. The diehards were predictably scathing. News of Lincoln's demise was the only "sweet drop" against "his howl of diabolical triumph against us," wrote a woman in Georgia. Edmund Ruffin, reading Easter sermons that likened Lincoln's death to the crucifixion, was "soon utterly disgusted by the servile sycophancy, the man-worship, of a low-bred & vulgar & illiterate buffoon, & the near approach to blasphemy, of these holy flatterers." In North Carolina, Catherine Edmonston merely asked "if Booth intended to turn assassin why, O why, did he delay it for so long?"[122]

More interesting are the circumspect reactions to the murder, for they revealed Southerners' lingering doubts about the President. An Episcopal minister in Richmond saw no symbolism in the Holy Week date of Lincoln's death; instead he harked back to 1861, noting it was "the anniversary of his proclamation calling out 75,000 men & really deciding that there should be a bloody, rather than a peaceful issue to the existing difficulties." Lizzie Hardin, a moderate Confederate from Kentucky, expressed it this way:

> Well, poor creature, I sincerely hope he was better prepared for death than we think he was. But for the sake of my country, I cannot but feel glad that he is dead. . . . The assassination was wrong, but to one who lives in the South . . . it seems a wrong for which there are many excuses. Little did Mr. Lincoln think when he told Western jokes . . . that his blood should flow with the torrent he was causing to be shed. And that there should fall upon him the divine anathema against the wicked, "Their sword also shall enter into their own heart."

In Louisiana, Sarah Morgan summed it up with mournful words: "Our Confederacy has gone with one crash—the report of the pistol fired at Lincoln. . . , I only pray never to be otherwise than what I am at this instant—a Rebel in heart and soul, and that all my life I may remember the cruel wrongs we have suffered."[123]

For these proud people, there was no contrition. There was no acknowledgment that Southerners might have brought destruction upon themselves or judged Northern commitment poorly, just as they had been poorly judged. They did not embrace Lincoln as a friend of Dixie, or even recognize him as a worthy foe. They only saw that "Coercion," "Emancipation," "Devastation," and, finally, "Subjugation"—all the fierce rallying cries of 1861—had befallen them. They had never believed that coarse western man when he pledged to avoid this scourge, even though, in truth, he had wanted badly to avert it. Now, at the end, every bone-marrow fear had come to pass. And all of it, however unwittingly, at Abraham Lincoln's hand.

Playbill for *Macbeth* at Grover's Theatre,
Washington, D.C., October 17, 1863. Printed on silk.
AMERICAN JEWISH HISTORICAL SOCIETY

7

EPILOGUE
TO THE HOLLOW CROWN:
Lincoln and Shakespeare

Four days after his heated interview with Duff Green, Lincoln sat aboard another boat, the *River Queen*, heading back to Washington. With him on deck were Senator Charles Sumner and the Marquis de Chambrun, who had accompanied his wife on her whirlwind tour of Richmond. At that very moment, Ulysses S. Grant was negotiating the final conditions of Lee's surrender at Appomattox, although the presidential party would not hear that news for several hours. As they steamed up the Potomac, the chief executive took a quarto volume from his pocket and began to read lines from Shakespeare. It was a favorite pastime, which charmed some and set others to nodding, as the President indulged himself, repeating beloved lines into the wee hours. This day he read for several hours, mainly passages from *Macbeth*, which he thought the best of the plays. "Treason has done his worst," recited Lincoln, from a scene after Duncan's death: "nor steel, nor poison, / Malice domestic . . . nothing / Can touch him further." He read the lines twice for emphasis. Those listening later thought the passages about Duncan's serene, eternal sleep prophesied the President's impending murder. There were other reasons Lincoln was drawn to these words, however. Without foreknowledge of the assassination, the lines seem more like a description of his tortured relation with the South's "malice domestic," and the terrible toll it had taken on him personally. The rebellion was very nearly exhausted, but he was not yet certain of the ending.[1]

Lincoln encountered William Shakespeare's majestic writing on sparsely filled bookshelves in the Indiana backcountry. He most likely saw it first in William Scott's *Lessons in Elocution,* a popular textbook, containing thoughtfully selected excerpts from the major tragedies and history plays. These texts remained Lincoln favorites. He regarded Scott's book highly enough to purchase a copy in Springfield and to borrow it from the Library of Congress during his presidency. He publicly praised many of the passages or committed them to memory, including Claudius's soliloquy from *Hamlet.*[2] The enduring image of Lincoln relaxing at the theater is perhaps overblown; he attended performances less often than portrayed and remarked to more than one person that he would rather read the scripts than watch players onstage. Still, we know that as president he saw *Henry IV, Part 1* and *The Merry Wives of Windsor,* and friends claimed to have accompanied him to *The Merchant of Venice* and *King Lear.* On October 17, 1863, Lincoln, his wife, and their son Tad attended a benefit performance of *Macbeth* for the United States Sanitary Commission at Grover's Theatre in Washington. He liked to critique the performances, held a spirited discussion with actor James Hackett about lines from *Hamlet* and *Henry IV,* and showed considerable insight into the meaning behind some of Shakespeare's notable speeches. (He did not always get it right: Lincoln believed the stirring opening of *Richard III*—"Now is the winter of our discontent / Made glorious summer. . . ."—should be spoken with bitter cynicism, for he held that Richard was a traitor, intending from the start to undermine his brother Edward, an interpretation rigorous historians have now persuasively overturned.) He read his favorite works many times, lingering over the beautiful words, and scrutinizing nuances in the stories. By his own admission, the plays that galvanized him were "Lear, Richard Third, Henry Eighth, Hamlet, and especially Macbeth." Others mentioned his passion for *Richard II, Henry VI,* and portions of *King John.* His interest in these dramas went beyond mere entertainment. For Lincoln, Shakespeare was not a shallow amusement but a route to deeper understanding of power, politics, and human folly.[3]

The words themselves were part of the enjoyment, and Lincoln freely appropriated language from these plays. He could use Saxon expressions like "wen" with effect, and paraphrased or copied Shakespearean lines such as "cancel and tear to pieces" or "the heavens are hung in black." Even the famous opening to the Gettysburg Address, "Four score and seven years ago," was arguably borrowed from the Bard of Avon.[4] At times one can feel Shakespeare's rhythm and wordplay in Lincoln's writing, and at least one acquaintance from his New Salem days thought Lincoln's natural skepticism and sense of irony were sharpened by the plays. It also seems likely that the sixteenth president appreciated—or identified with—Shakespeare's modest educational base and ability to juggle low comedy, probing intellect, and lofty lyricism. His love of dramas that featured Falstaff's clowning yet moved to trenchant issues of loyalty and leadership probably reflected this. Nonetheless, clear reflections of the great poet are hard to see in Lincoln's evolution as a writer. The nine volumes of Lincoln papers show a gradual development from early, self-conscious prose that struggled to impress, through the sharp logic of his prewar debates, and finally to a handful of masterly, poetically drawn works. Two of these, the Gettysburg Address and the Second Inaugural, have rightly earned literary laurels. (A third that is often cited, the poignant letter to Mrs. Bixby, who had "laid such a costly sacrifice upon the altar of freedom," was likely written by Lincoln's private secretary, John Hay.)[5] Lincoln could also agilely employ clear, decisive prose to sway opinion or silence public rage—as in his August 1862 letter to Horace Greeley. Other works contain some famously felicitous turns of phrase, such as his 1862 admonition that "the fiery trial through which we pass, will light us down, in honor or dishonor, to the latest generation."[6] But the vast majority of his papers are banal or workmanlike, unusually so for the expressive nineteenth century. In some cases they are so clumsily phrased as to be obtuse. There is also little to indicate Lincoln possessed Shakespeare's *sustained* genius. The soaring words of the Second Inaugural, for example, were followed by a rambling and defensive speech made a month later, just after Lee's surrender. Those remarks, essentially a reaction to Salmon Chase's criticism of his reconstruction agenda, unfortunately were Lincoln's last public words. The audience, hoping for a ringing victory address, wandered away from the podium, bored and disappointed.[7]

What strikes one most about Lincoln's interest in Shakespeare are his identification with character and circumstance, and the almost startling pertinence of the tragedies for the challenges of his presidency. The histories are so apt, and so starkly descriptive of Lincoln's impasse with the South, that an essay could easily be written by tacking quotations together like beads on a string. It is hard to believe that his preference for these works, especially during his presidency, was a coincidence. Lincoln admitted he read little for recreation beyond Shakespeare, and it was not *Love's Labour's Lost* that he chose. The midnight revelries, amusing mix-ups, and sweet sonnets of the lighter works were passed over for the full tragedies—the tales of insurrection, treachery, and knife-sharp political contests—the very story of his own struggle with factionalism and strife. How could he not identify with the Bishop of Carlisle's prediction in *Richard II* that "if you raise this house against this house, / It will the woefullest division prove"; or McDuff's lament that internal strife colored every day with terror as "each new morn / New widows howl, new orphans cry, new sorrows / Strike heaven on the face."[8] How could a president so unfairly smeared with loose talk and exaggerated characterizations not take comfort in a play that opened with the "blunt monster" "Rumor" as a character in its own right? Lincoln must have understood Ross precisely when he cried to Lady McDuff that "cruel are the times . . ."

> *when we hold rumour*
> *From what we fear, yet know not what we fear,*
> *But float upon a wild and violent sea. . . .*[9]

The heavy burden of power is also a theme of these plays. Shakespeare's rulers cannot sleep, as Lincoln could not, and mistrust and disappointment thwart their finely devised plans. Henry IV, "so shaken . . . so wan with care" that he had little time to "pant," let alone devise "new broils," must have seemed sadly familiar to Lincoln. Like Henry, he believed (largely erroneously) that his cabinet was disloyal, and knew that the war was exhausting his acuity. Then there was the irony of a ruler like Richard II, who, though legitimate, lost his authority because of ineptitude. This could not have been lost on someone like Lincoln as he watched his own managerial incompetence erode public confidence. Although well meaning, Richard was also seen as a thief, stealing the inheritance of his rival Bolingbroke, much as Southerners viewed Lincoln as robbing them of the future they had grounded in slavery. Lincoln liked the way Shakespeare used plays within plays to portray the perfidy of would-be allies, whose loyalty was determined by their own advantage, or to show the multiple roles a head of state must adopt to satisfy the fickle public. "Thus play I in one person many people / And none contented," muses Richard II, likening his rule to a prison, where everyone is suspect and every act potentially treasonous. This was the isolation of power, which Lincoln felt keenly.[10] Lincoln also knew the humiliation of being considered an impostor, a pretender to a position that should never have been his. When a segment of *Henry IV, Part 1,* in which Hal and Falstaff mockingly play at being king, was omitted from a production Lincoln attended in Washington, he protested. Shakespeare meant it as a comic interlude, but a revealing one, with the "monarch" sitting on a false throne, crowned with cushions. Hal struts like the spoiled prince he is, while Falstaff pleads that even though he acts the buffoon, he is kind and true and wants to be taken seriously. James Hackett, to whom Lincoln made his complaint, missed the point, thinking Shakespeare meant it as a device to mimic Henry. Instead, the scene was actually designed to reveal the folly of bogus rulers, by alternating Hal's adolescent hubris with the lurching, leering "false staff"—a jester pretending to power without the wisdom or presence to rule—the very image Lincoln projected to the South.[11]

Sleeplessness and anxiety in Shakespeare's kings reflect disease and decay in the state—a blight caused by the accession of anyone not strong and tough enough to defend his realm. But if the government was ill, what was the sickness? Passion, jealousy, treachery, and greed were all subjects of Shakespeare's tragedies. In the plays Lincoln loved, ambition and the struggle for power were most often the maladies. This struck a chord with the sixteenth president, whose outsized personal aspiration—akin to Macbeth's "vaulting ambition"—had been apparent from his youth. A number of people who knew him in Indiana, including cousins who lived with the family, recalled that even as a boy he proclaimed he would someday be president of the United States, using the boast to taunt his father and others who wondered where his aversion to labor and sarcastic wit were taking him.[12] One of Lincoln's earliest writings shows his admiration, an attribute he thought placed men in the company of lions and eagles. "Towering genius disdains a beaten path," he proclaimed. "It thirsts and burns for distinction." His own thirst did not abate with the years. Instead, as he admitted, it was like the persistent sting of a horsefly on his neck. "No man knows what that *gnawing* is," he commented, "till he has had it." He was quick to qualify his yearning, saying he would never let it interfere with the greater good. Yet in the same breath he did his best to undermine rival political parties and cast doubts on alternative candidates for office. Lincoln tried to understand his craving for public acclaim and at times deprecated it. But, as his law partner William Herndon noted, it never abated. "He was," remarked Herndon, "the most ambitious man I ever saw or expect to see."[13]

What Shakespeare cautioned was that ambition could prove a bad master as well as a good servant. Those who sought their goals ruthlessly, or took power without heeding consequences, were destined to wear a hollow crown: void of legitimacy, empty of glory. The passages Lincoln read over and over were those that described the self-induced hell of rulers who usurped authority, only to find themselves impotent and unfulfilled. "Nought's had, all's spent / Where our desire is got without content," moaned Lady Macbeth. It was a powerful thought to a man who faced daily frustration with a half-nation that would not recognize his leadership. Lincoln was particularly taken with the speech of Claudius in the third act of *Hamlet,* in which the king had murderously seized the "wicked prize" of crown and consort only to face horrific consequences with no way to redress or atone for them.[14] Then there was Richard II, a man who told his devastating tale with sorrow, summing it up in a speech that affected Lincoln strongly. "The terrible outburst of grief and despair into which Richard falls in the third act had a peculiar fascination for him," recalled John Hay. "I have heard him read it at Springfield, at the White House, and at the Soldiers' Home." It was a story of what it was to rule a kingdom and then lose it; to have won the right to lead and have it disappear, at least partly by personal incompetence; of a crown so hollow it encircled nothing but a mocking death's head. *Henry IV, Part 2* also speaks of the transience of power, of the crown as a "troublesome bedfellow." Henry had bested Richard by questionable means, but he is emotionally shattered by the victory and now must guard his position carefully, because his hold on power is fragile. "Where is the crown? who took it from my pillow?" he anxiously cries, seeing his once coveted realm, now "sick with civil blows," disintegrating into rebellion. He is not only forced to watch the dismantling of his country but to face responsibility for it. No matter how he tries to rationalize his problematic ascension to power, Henry cannot redeem himself, either by a show of force or by avoiding bloodshed. A secretary who went with Lincoln to see this play was surprised that the President laughed so little at Falstaff's slapstick, and "appeared even gloomy, although intent upon the play," closely studying the characters. Henry's despair must have seemed profoundly familiar to Lincoln. He knew just how precarious a king's position was when he faced either triumph or disaster. There were no other options.[15]

Like Macbeth, all of these men have the blood of ambition on their hands, blood that cannot be wished or washed away. Claudius wails that his "cursed hand" was covered with "brother's blood," and rants: "Is there not rain enough in the sweet heavens / To wash it white as snow?" Sin and irresponsibility have cast these characters into a state of perpetual guilt, robbing them of sleep. This was what Lincoln emphasized to his fellow travelers on the *River Queen,* when he played out the envy Macbeth felt for Duncan's sweet rest. "How true" it was, Lincoln reportedly said, that once a questionable goal was achieved, the "tortured perpetrator came to envy the sleep of his victim."[16] Just how close to Lincoln's bone such passages rubbed is hard to know. Publicly, he often tried to deny responsibility for the war, describing events in the passive tense ("And the war came"), or blaming Southern demagogues, the long suffering slaves, or even God for the misfortune. But on some level he must have known that the war had been very much about him personally: about his provocative words, his audacity in running for president without executive or military experience, and his uncertain performance in the crisis of 1861. It was clearly perceived this way in the South and in much of the North as well. "Mr. Lincoln's election precipitated the rebellion," wrote Hugh McCulloch, whom Lincoln appointed treasury secretary, adding that it had forced the issues of slavery and states' rights to be resolved "sooner than had been expected and in a different way" than many statesmen desired. Whether Lincoln was trying to understand, expiate, or atone for his role by studying Shakespeare's historical tragedies is not certain. That he perused them with such intent, however, indicates a notable willingness to come to terms with the colossal ego that formed a part of his character.[17]

There on the *River Queen,* steaming away from the conquered rebel capital, Lincoln reflected on the costliness of even just ambition. This was not an easy thing to do: as Macbeth observed, "To know my deed / 'Twere best not know myself." Lincoln could be self-effacing at times, but despite his historical reputation he was not a humble man. Yet he had been humbled by the South's defiance, by his inability to close the war swiftly and efficiently, and by the staggering bloodshed stemming from his easy assertion that the "house divided" could not long stand. Of the terrible consequences his ascent to power produced, the most personal for Lincoln was the way inner peace eluded him. This was the trauma of King Lear who so abused the authority of his position that he lost his realm, his family—and even his sanity. It was the agony of Macbeth, who found that the word "amen" stuck in his throat, just when he "had most need of blessing"; and the shattering inner knowledge of Richard III, who groaned that "no soul shall pity me / Nay, wherefore should they, since that I myself / Find in myself no pity to myself?" Instead of being exhilarated by the power he had acquired, Lincoln was chastened by his inability to exercise it effectively. "Now I don't know what the soul is," he reportedly said, "but whatever it is, I know that it can humble itself." The deep furrows in Lincoln's face, the late-night hand wringing in the War Department telegraph office, and even the beautiful words of the Gettysburg Address, with its plea that the great democratic experiment not perish from the

Earth, all bespeak a man who, like Henry IV, had to face his outsized aspirations, and stand by, while the nation he had hoped to lead disintegrated before him.[18]

The grail of legitimate authority and respect had been so tantalizingly close. Yet he never completely grasped it, for he was killed before the final reunion of the nation. And we are left soberly to imagine the kind of desperation Abraham Lincoln must have felt, knowing that for all his aspiration, he was never, within his lifetime, truly president of the entire United States.

Abbreviations

AL	Abraham Lincoln
ALP-LC	Abraham Lincoln Papers, Library of Congress, Washington, D.C.
C.N.	Cherokee Nation
CU	Columbia University, Butler Library, Rare Book and Manuscript Library, New York, N.Y.
CW	*The Collected Works of Abraham Lincoln.* Edited by Roy P. Basler. 9 vols. New Brunswick, N.J.: Rutgers University Press, 1953.
DU	Duke University, David M. Rubenstein Rare Book and Manuscript Library, Durham, N.C.
GU	Georgetown University, Booth Family Center for Special Collections, Washington, D.C.
HI	*Herndon's Informants: Letters, Interviews and Statements About Abraham Lincoln.* Edited by Douglas L. Wilson and Rodney O. Davis. Urbana: University of Illinois Press, 1998.
HL	The Huntington Library, San Marino, Calif.
HU	Harvard University, Cambridge, Mass.
ILPL	Abraham Lincoln Presidential Library, Springfield, Ill.
JALA	*Journal of the Abraham Lincoln Association*
LC	Library of Congress, Washington, D.C.
MoC*	Museum of the Confederacy, Eleanor S. Brockenbrough Library, Richmond, Va.
MTL	Mary Todd Lincoln
NARA	National Archives and Records Administration, Washington, D.C.
NYHS	New-York Historical Society, New York, N.Y.
OR	*The War of the Rebellion: A Compilation of the Official Records of the Union and Confederate Armies.* Prepared Under the Direction of the Secretary of War. 70 vols. Washington, D.C.: Government Printing Office, 1880–1901.

*These holdings have now been moved to the VHS.

SHC-UNC	Southern Historical Collection, University of North Carolina, Chapel Hill, N.C.
UR	University of Rochester, Rush Rhees Library, Rochester, N.Y.
USAHEC	United States Army Heritage and Education Center, Carlisle, Pa.
UVa	University of Virginia, Albert and Shirley Small Special Collections Library, Charlottesville, Va.
VHS	Virginia Historical Society, Richmond, Va.
WHH	William H. Herndon

Notes

INTRODUCTION

1. John J. Leary Jr., *Talks with T.R. from the Diaries of John J. Leary, Jr.* (Boston: Houghton Mifflin, 1920), viii.
2. Clinton quoted in Ryan Lizza, "The Second Term: What Will Obama Do Now That He's Reëlected?" *The New Yorker,* June 18, 2012.
3. From the Diary of Adam Gurowski, January 20, 1863, *Diary from November 18, 1862 to October 18, 1863* (New York: Carleton, 1864), 99–100.
4. AL, "Annual Message to Congress," December 1, 1862, *CW,* 5:537; AL, "First Debate with Stephen A. Douglas, Ottawa, Ill.," August 21, 1858, ibid., 3:16.
5. Stuart Jeffries, "Mario Vargas Llosa: A Life in Writing," *The Guardian,* June 15, 2013.
6. From the Diary of Adam Gurowski, April 14, 1865, *Diary 1863–'64–'65* (Washington, D.C.: Morrison, 1866), 398–99.
7. Robert G. Ingersoll in Allen Thorndike Rice, ed., *Reminiscences of Abraham Lincoln by Distinguished Men of His Time* (New York: North American Review, 1888), 307–8; Stephen Greenblatt, *The Swerve: How the World Became Modern* (New York: W. W. Norton, 2011), 11–12.
8. Douglas L. Wilson, *Honor's Voice: The Transformation of Abraham Lincoln* (New York: Alfred A. Knopf, 1998); Douglas L. Wilson, *Lincoln Before Washington: New Perspectives on the Illinois Years* (Urbana: University of Illinois Press, 1997).
9. AL, "Second Inaugural Address, March 4, 1865," *CW,* 8:332.
10. Frederick Douglass, *The Frederick Douglass Papers. Series One: Speeches, Debates, and Interviews,* ed. John W. Blassingame et al. (New Haven: Yale University Press, 1979–1992), 4:436.

CHAPTER 1. A WARY HANDSHAKE

1. Diary of Benjamin B. French, February 24, 1861, Benjamin B. French Family Papers, LC; Diary of Elizabeth Virginia Lomax, March 12 and 31, 1861, Lomax Family Papers, VHS; George Mason to Samuel Cooper, Spring Bank, Va., March 10, 1861, Cooper Family Papers, VHS; entry of March 12, 1861, in *The Diary of George Templeton Strong,* ed. Allan Nevins and Milton Halsey Thomas (New York: Macmillan, 1952), 3:109; "Deplorable State of Affairs at Washington," *New York Herald,* March 13, 1861.
2. Descriptions vary as to the number of officers in attendance (from fourteen to two hundred). Samuel P. Heintzelman, a precise engineer who attended the meeting, noted in his diary that seventy-eight officers were present: Heintzelman Diary, March 13, 1861, Samuel Peter Heintzelman Papers, LC; also Gideon Welles to Edgar T. Welles, Washington, D.C., March 13, 1861, Gideon Welles Papers, LC; "From Washington," *Alexandria* [Va.] *Gazette,* March 13, 1861; "Affairs of the Nation," *New York Times,* March 13, 1861; Albert Gallatin Riddle, *Recollections of War Times: Reminiscences of Men and Events in Washington 1860–1865* (London: G. P. Putnam, 1895), 11.

3. The author is grateful to the White House Historical Association for providing several images of the East Room from this time; a contemporary depiction of its shabbiness can be found in William O. Stoddard, *Inside the White House in War Times: Memories and Reports of Lincoln's Secretary,* ed. Michael Burlingame (Lincoln: University of Nebraska Press, 2000), 5. The description of the officers' uniform is in "Uniform and Dress of the Army of the United States," n.d. (c. 1856), RG 94, NARA. The quotations are from Riddle, *Recollections of War Times,* 11, and John Caldwell Tidball, "Washington 1861," John Caldwell Tidball Manuscripts, LC.

4. The Confederate Constitution can be found at www.avolon.law.yale.edu/19th_century/csa .asp; Joseph Holt to AL, War Department, March 9, 1861, ALP-LC; correspondence between Confederate commissioners, William Seward, and Judge John Campbell, Washington, D.C., March 12, 1861, ALP-LC; Commissioners to Robert Toombs, March 12, 1861, in John G. Nicolay and John Hay, *Abraham Lincoln: A History* (New York: Century, 1886–1890), 3:403–7; see also Heintzelman Diary, March 7, 1861, Heintzelman Papers, LC; Eric Foner, *The Fiery Trial: Abraham Lincoln and American Slavery* (New York: W. W. Norton, 2010), 160; L. E. Chittenden, *Personal Reminiscences, 1840–1890* (New York: Richmond, Croscup, 1893), 90–91; John G. Nicolay, Notes on Situation 1861, n.d. [c. 1880], John G. Nicolay Papers, LC.

5. Tidball, "Washington 1861," Tidball Manuscripts, LC; Joseph Holt and Winfield Scott to AL, War Department, March 5, 1861, ALP-LC. Two thoughtful accounts of the Fort Sumter crisis are Russell McClintock, *Lincoln and the Decision for War: The Northern Response to Secession* (Chapel Hill: University of North Carolina Press, 2008), and William W. Freehling, *The Road to Disunion,* vol. 2, *Secessionists Triumphant, 1854–1861* (New York: Oxford University Press, 2007).

6. AL, "Address to the Ohio Legislature, Columbus," February 13, 1861, *CW,* 4:204; AL, "Speech at Pittsburgh," February 15, 1861, ibid., 4:211; AL, "Address to the New Jersey General Assembly," February 1861, ibid., 4:237; Montgomery Blair to Martin Van Buren, Washington, D.C., April 29, 1861, Martin Van Buren Papers, LC; Francis P. Blair to Van Buren, Silver Springs, Md., May 1, 1861, Van Buren Papers, LC; Robert Anderson to "dear friend," Fort Sumter, S.C., March 11, 1861, Samuel Wylie Crawford Papers, LC.

7. Nelson D. Lankford, *Cry Havoc! The Crooked Road to Civil War, 1861* (New York: Viking, 2007), 34–35; Anderson to "dear friend," March 11, 1861, Crawford Papers, LC; James Buchanan to Joseph Holt, Wheatland, March 16, 1861, Joseph Holt Papers, LC; William Butler to Lyman Trumbull, March 14, 1861, quoted in McClintock, *Lincoln and the Decision for War,* 222. Lincoln's 1861 deliberations on peace and war are discussed in more detail in chapter 6.

8. For varied responses to the inaugural address, see Diary of Francis O. French, March 4, 1861, French Papers, LC; Edwin Greble to Sue [Greble], March 4, 1861, Edwin Greble Papers, LC; Diary of Mrs. Eugene McLean, March 4, 1861, quoted in "When the States Seceded," *Harper's Monthly Magazine,* January 28, 1914, 286; Charles Brown Fleet to Fred [Fleet], Columbian College, March 5, 1861, in Betsy Fleet and John D. P. Fuller, eds., *Green Mount: A Virginia Plantation Family During the Civil War; Being the Journal of Benjamin Robert Fleet and Letters of His Family* (Lexington: University of Kentucky Press, 1962), 49–50; [Homo], "Letter from Washington," *Alexandria* [Va.] *Gazette,* March 5, 1861; "Mr. Lincoln's Inaugural Address," *Milledgeville* [Ga.] *Southern Federal Union,* March 12, 1861; Lankford, *Cry Havoc!,* 25–29. See also *New York Times,* March 14, 1861, quoted in Lankford, *Cry Havoc!,* 24; AL, "First Inaugural Address," *CW,* 4:249–71. There is an insightful analysis in Douglas L. Wilson, *Lincoln's Sword: The Presidency and the Power of Words* (New York: Vintage, 2006), 42–70.

9. William T. H. Brooks to father, Fort Clark, Tex., March 15, [18]61, William T. H. Brooks Papers, USAHEC; David Dixon Porter, "Journal of Occurrences During the War of the Rebellion," n.d. [c. 1865], David D. Porter Family Papers, LC; Journal of Samuel Wylie Crawford, March 6 and 8, 1861, Crawford Papers, LC; Crawford to brother, Fort Sumter, S.C., March 7, 1861, Crawford Papers, LC. See also Heintzelman Diary, March 5, 1861, Heintzelman Papers, LC. For a longer description of the inaugural's impact on Southerners, see chapter 6.

10. James M. McPherson, *Tried by War: Abraham Lincoln as Commander in Chief* (New York: Penguin Press, 2008), 14–15; Sam Ward to [Samuel L. M.] Barlow, Washington, D.C., March 31, 1861, Samuel L. M. Barlow Papers, HL; A. K. McClure, *Abraham Lincoln and Men of War-Times* (Philadelphia: Times Publishing, 1892), 293; Stoddard, *Inside the White House*, 3; AL, quoted July 3, 1861, in *The Diary of Orville Hickman Browning, 1850–1864*, ed. Theodore Calvin Pease and James G. Randall (Springfield: Illinois State Historical Society, 1925), 1:476.

11. William H. L. Wallace to Ann [Wallace], Washington, D.C., March 9, 1861, in Harry E. Pratt, ed., *Concerning Mr. Lincoln, in Which Abraham Lincoln Is Pictured as He Appeared to Letter Writers of His Time* (Springfield, Ill.: The Abraham Lincoln Association, 1944), 70–71; Gideon Welles Diary, March 8, 1861, Welles Papers, LC; Porter, "Journal of Occurrences," n.d. [c. 1865], Porter Papers, LC.

12. For a lengthier description of AL during the Black Hawk War, see chapter 4. Detailed descriptions of the war can be found in Patrick J. Jung, *The Black Hawk War of 1832* (Norman: University of Oklahoma Press, 2007); and Cecil Eby, "*That Disgraceful Affair*": *The Black Hawk War* (New York: W. W. Norton, 1973).

13. Statements of John T. Stuart and George M. Harrison in *HI*, 64, 327–28, and 554; Noah Brooks, "Personal Reminiscences of Lincoln," *Scribner's Monthly*, February 1878, 563; Jung, *Black Hawk War*, 88–89; AL, "Speech in the House of Representatives on the Presidential Question," July 27, 1848, *CW*, 1:509–10; AL, "Speech at Bath, Ill.," August 16, 1858, ibid., 2:543.

14. For AL's pride in his captaincy, see AL to Jesse W. Fell, Springfield, Ill., December 20, 1859, *CW*, 3:512. His command is discussed in Benjamin F. Irwin to WHH, September 22, 1866, *HI*, 353; David M. Pantier to WHH, Petersburg, Ill., July 21, 1865, *HI*, 78; Jung, *Black Hawk War*, 79–80; Eby, "*That Disgraceful Affair*," 107–8; William H. Herndon and Jesse W. Weik, *Herndon's Lincoln*, ed. Douglas L. Wilson and Rodney O. Davis (Galesburg, Ill.: Knox College Lincoln Studies Center, 2006), 70–71; Ida M. Tarbell, *The Life of Abraham Lincoln* (New York: Macmillan, 1920), 1:76–77. For the general lack of discipline, see Report of William Orr to John Y. Sawyer, n.d. [c. July 1, 1832], in Ellen M. Whitney, ed., *The Black Hawk War, 1831–1832* (Springfield: Illinois State Historical Library, 1970–1978), 2:727–28. AL's problems as commander in chief are discussed in Elizabeth Brown Pryor, " 'The Grand Old Duke of York': How Abraham Lincoln Lost the Confidence of His Military Command," forthcoming.

15. AL, "The War with Mexico," January 12, 1848, *CW*, 1:439; AL, "Speech to Springfield Scott Club," August 14 and 26, 1852, ibid., 2:149–50; see also Gerald J. Prokopowicz, " 'If I Had Gone Up There, I Could Have Whipped Them Myself': Lincoln's Military Fantasies," in *The Lincoln Forum: Rediscovering Abraham Lincoln*, ed. John Y. Simon and Harold Holzer (New York: Fordham University Press, 2002), 77–92.

16. Constitution of the United States of America, article 2, section 2, paragraphs 1 and 2, in Johnny H. Killian, George A. Costello, and Kenneth R. Thomas, eds., *The Constitution of the United States of America: Analysis and Interpretation* (Washington, D.C.: Government Printing Office, 2004), 459–91; McPherson, *Tried by War*, 4–5; Mark E. Neely Jr., "War and Partisanship: What Lincoln Learned from James K. Polk," *Journal of the Illinois State Historical Society* 74, no. 3 (Autumn 1981): 209–10; David M. Potter, *The Impending Crisis, 1848–1861* (New York: Harper Torchbooks, 1976), 95; Fergus M. Bordewich, *America's Great Debate: Henry Clay, Stephen A. Douglas, and the Compromise That Preserved the Union* (New York: Simon & Schuster, 2012), 131–33; AL, "The War with Mexico," January 12, 1848, *CW*, 1:431–42.

17. AL to Governor Andrew Curtin, Harrisburg, Pa., February 22, 1861, *CW*, 4:243; Dorothy Schaffter and Dorothy M. Mathews, *The Powers of the President as Commander in Chief of the Army and Navy of the United States* (Washington, D.C.: Government Printing Office, 1956), 17–18 and 31; AL, "Message to Congress," July 4, 1861, *CW*, 4:421–41. The quotation is from AL to Baltimore Committee, April 22, 1861, ibid., 4:341.

18. Erasmus D. Keyes, *Fifty Years' Observation of Men and Events, Civil and Military* (New York: Charles Scribner's Sons, 1884), 348. For Lincoln's wavering on his appointment of

Cameron, see AL to Cameron, Springfield, Ill., December 31, 1860, and January 3, 1861, Simon Cameron Papers, LC. For petitions to AL promoting or denouncing Cameron, see Joseph Medill to Charles Ray, Washington, D.C., January 13, 1861; Elihu B. Washburne to Ray, Washington, D.C., January 13, 1861; Herman Kreismann to Ray, Washington, D.C., January 16, 1861; Horace White to "doctor" [Charles Ray], Washington, D.C., n.d. [January 1861], all in Charles H. Ray Papers, HL; see also *CW,* 4:165–68; WHH to Lyman Trumbull, Springfield, Ill., January 27, 1861, Lyman Trumbull Papers, LC. For Fogg's quotation, see George C. Fogg to AL, Washington, D.C., February 5, 1861, ALP-LC. For Cameron's admission that he knew nothing of military matters, see undated entry for November 1861 in Adam Gurowski, *Diary from March 4, 1861 to November 12, 1862* (Boston: Lee & Shepard, 1862), 117. For an assessment of Cameron's qualifications, see A. Howard Meneely, *The War Department, 1861: A Study in Mobilization and Administration* (New York: Columbia University Press, 1928), 83–84.

19. Diary of Ethan Allen Hitchcock, October 4, 1861, copy in William A. Croffut Papers, LC; Orville Hickman Browning to AL, Chicago, January 19, 1861, ALP-LC; T. S. Bell to Joseph Holt, Louisville, January 19, 1861 (quoting *New York Tribune*), Holt Papers, LC; S. S. English to Joseph Holt, Louisville, March 2, 1861, Holt Papers, LC; Jos. Sagar to Joseph Holt, Richmond, March 6, 1861, Holt Papers, LC; AL to Holt, Executive Mansion, March 12, 1861, Holt Papers, LC; correspondence of Robert Holt and Joseph Holt, 1860–1861, Holt Papers, LC. See also the biography of Holt by Elizabeth D. Leonard, *Lincoln's Forgotten Ally: Judge Advocate General Joseph Holt of Kentucky* (Chapel Hill: University of North Carolina Press, 2011).

20. Robert V. Bruce, *Lincoln and the Tools of War* (Indianapolis: Bobbs-Merrill, 1956), 49; Simon Cameron, "Vindication of the Administration of the War Department," n.d. [c. 1865], Cameron Papers, LC; Diary of Ethan Allen Hitchcock, August 29 and October 4, 1861, Croffut Papers, LC; Horace Gray to [Henry] Dawes, Boston, August 26, 1861, Henry Dawes Papers, LC; "Sutler Outrage by Secretary of War," *New York Tribune,* undated clipping in J. H. Jordan to AL, Cincinnati, July 4, 1861, ALP-LC; William C. Davis, *Lincoln's Men: How President Lincoln Became Father to an Army and a Nation* (New York: Free Press, 1999), 52; "Conversation with the President," October 2, 1861, Nicolay Papers, LC.

21. William T. Sherman to brother [John Sherman], Lancaster, Pa., March 9, 1861, and to Thomas Ewing Jr., St. Louis, April 26, 1861, both in William Tecumseh Sherman, *Sherman's Civil War: Selected Correspondence of William T. Sherman, 1860–1865,* ed. Brooks D. Simpson and Jean V. Berlin (Chapel Hill: University of North Carolina Press, 1999), 61–62 and 75. See also Sherman to brother, St. Louis, April 18, 1861, William Tecumseh Sherman Papers, LC; William Tecumseh Sherman to John Sherman, April 22, 1861, in William Tecumseh Sherman, *Memoirs of General William T. Sherman* (New York: D. Appleton, 1875), 1:168. Sherman's diary indicates he was in Washington only on March 6–7, 1861, and he must have met Lincoln at that time. See also Rachel Sherman Thorndike, ed., *The Sherman Letters: Correspondence Between General and Senator Sherman from 1837 to 1891* (London: Sampson, Low, Marston, 1894), 108–9.

22. Two excellent biographies of Scott are Charles Winslow Elliott, *Winfield Scott: The Soldier and the Man* (New York: Macmillan, 1937), and Allan Peskin, *Winfield Scott and the Profession of Arms* (Kent, Ohio: Kent State University Press, 2003). For Scott's personal grandeur, see William Woods Averell, *Ten Years in the Saddle: The Memoir of William Woods Averell,* ed. Edward K. Eckert and Nicholas J. Amato (San Rafael, Calif.: Presidio Press, 1978), 242; John P. Usher, *President Lincoln's Cabinet* (Omaha: Nelson H. Loomis, 1925), 21–22. For Scott's bias toward Southerners, see James B. Fry, *Military Miscellanies* (New York: Brentano's, 1889), 482–83; Keyes, *Fifty Years' Observation,* 134, 318, 319, and 328. Keyes expressed his bitterness on the issue to president-elect Lincoln even before the conflict began: see Erasmus D. Keyes to AL, New York, November 26, 1860, Civil War Letters 1861–1865, NYHS.

23. Winfield Scott, *General Regulations for the Army; or, Military Institutes* (Philadelphia: M. Carey & Sons, 1821). For differing views of Scott's abilities and infirmities at the time of

the secession crisis, see Elihu B. Washburne to AL, Washington, D.C., December 17, 1860, ALP-LC; Diary of Virginia Woodbury Fox, March 9, 1861, Levi Woodbury Papers, LC.

24. Winfield Scott, "Views," October 29, 1860, manuscript copy in Wyndham Robertson Papers, VHS; marginal notes indicate Scott sent copies to Buchanan, Secretary of War John Floyd, Virginia governor John Letcher, Richmond banker William H. MacFarland, Unionist William Cabell Rives, Col. Francis H. Smith (the head of the Virginia Military Institute), and Kentucky congressman John J. Crittenden. See also the dispatches of Rudolph Schleiden in Ralph Haswell Lutz, "Rudolph Schleiden and the Visit to Richmond, April 25, 1861," *Annual Report of the American Historical Association for the Year 1915,* 210. For "I lived there once," see Elihu B. Washburne to AL, Washington, D.C., December 17, 1860, ALP-LC; for "a *firm* man," see Diary of Mary Boykin Chesnut, November 8, 1861, in *Mary Chesnut's Civil War,* ed. C. Van Woodward (New Haven: Yale University Press, 1981), 232.

25. Peskin, *Winfield Scott,* 233–41; Scott, "Views," October 29, 1860, Robertson Papers, VHS; Scott to John B. Floyd, New York, October 30, 1860 ("all dangers and difficulties"), ALP-LC; Scott to Secretary of War, Washington, D.C., December 28, 1860, Crawford Papers, LC; Scott to Hon. J.J. Crittenden, New York, November 12, 1860 ("*silence* . . . may be fatal"), John J. Crittenden Papers, LC.

26. Heintzelman Diary, March 13, 1861, Heintzelman Papers, LC.

27. For the number of officers in the capital, see "From Washington," *Alexandria* [Va.] *Gazette,* March 13, 1861. The best sources on the military in 1861 are Meneely, *War Department,* and George T. Ness Jr., *The Regular Army on the Eve of the Civil War* (Baltimore: Toomey Press, 1990). George Washington is quoted in Meneely, *War Department,* 14, and the standing army figures are from Ness, *Regular Army,* 1–5. See also Charles P. Stone, "Washington on the Eve of the War," in *Battles and Leaders of the Civil War,* ed. Robert Underwood Johnson and Clarence Clough Buell (New York: Century, 1887–1888), 1:7n; Fred Albert Shannon, *The Organization and Administration of the Union Army, 1861–1865* (Cleveland: Arthur H. Clark, 1928), 1:28; Jefferson Davis to John B. Floyd, December 13, 1860, RG 94, NARA.

28. For conditions and regulations in the Army in 1861, see William B. Skelton, *An American Profession of Arms: The Army Officer Corps, 1784–1861* (Lawrence: University Press of Kansas, 1992), 193–200 and 283–90; Ness, *Regular Army,* 1–5 and 19–46; Meneeley, *War Department,* 108–9; James B. Fry to "general" [James S. Wadsworth], Arlington, Va., August 12, 1861, Wadsworth Family Papers, LC; L. E. Chittenden, *Recollections of President Lincoln and His Administration* (New York: Harper & Brothers, 1891), 152 and 169–70; Henry Adams, *The Education of Henry Adams* (Washington: Privately published, 1907), 90–93. For the "dis-g-u-s-t" at the situation felt by one star officer—Robert E. Lee—see Elizabeth Brown Pryor, *Reading the Man: A Portrait of Robert E. Lee Through His Private Letters* (New York: Viking, 2007), 184–86.

29. For West Point's superior scientific credentials, see Skelton, *American Profession of Arms;* Todd Shallat, *Structures in the Stream: Water, Science and the Rise of the U.S. Army Corps of Engineers* (Austin: University of Texas Press, 1994); Edward M. Coffman, *The Old Army: A Portrait of the American Army in Peacetime, 1784–1898* (Oxford, U.K.: Oxford University Press, 1986); Russell F. Weigley, *Towards an American Army: Military Thought from Washington to Marshall* (New York: Columbia University Press, 1962). See also "William Buel Franklin," in George Washington Cullum, *Biographical Register of the Officers and Graduates of the U.S. Military Academy at West Point, N.Y.* (Boston: Houghton Mifflin, 1891), 2:152–53; "Montgomery C. Meigs," ibid., 1:631–32; Remarks of Mrs. Philip Rounseville Alger [Meigs's granddaughter], Annapolis, Md., 1957, Montgomery C. Meigs Papers, LC.

30. Army operations during the Mexican War are well laid out in Richard Bruce Winders, *Mr. Polk's Army: The American Military Experience in the Mexican War* (College Station: Texas A&M University Press, 1997). For Scott's "head-work," see Winfield Scott, *Memoirs of Lieut.-General Winfield Scott, L.L.D., Written by Himself* (New York: Sheldon, 1864), 2:428. The Duke of Wellington is quoted in Frederic D. Schwarz, "The Halls of Montezuma," *American Heritage* 48, no. 5 (September 1997): 106.

31. Ness, *Regular Army,* 3; Meneely, *War Department,* 28–30 and 49–52; Diary of Elizabeth
 Virginia Lomax, December 7, 1860, Lomax Papers, VHS; James A. Hardie to William T.
 Sherman, Fort Vancouver, February 28, 1861, W. T. Sherman Papers, LC; C[admus] M.
 Wilcox to George B. McClellan, Santa Fe, March 24, 1861, George B. McClellan Papers,
 LC; Diary of William Howard Russell, April 2, 1861 in William Howard Russell, *My Diary
 North and South* (Boston: Burnham, 1863), 5; Gideon Welles to Gustavus Fox, Hartford,
 December 5, 1870, Woodbury Papers, LC; Simon Cameron, Remarks on Return to
 Harrisburg, n.d. [c. 1864], Cameron Papers, LC; Statement of Henry Wilson in *Congressio-
 nal Globe,* 36th Cong., 1st sess., 1861:2794.
32. Meneely, *War Department,* 29–49. See also Alfred Mordecai to G. B. Lamar, Watervliet
 Arsenal, N.Y., December 2, 1860; G. B. Lamar to Major A. Mordecai, New York, Decem-
 ber 3, 1860; John E. Wool to Maj. A[lfred] Mordecai, Head Quarters, Dept. of the East,
 Troy, N.Y., December 27, 1860; George T. Balch to John E. Wool, Watervliet Arsenal, N.Y.,
 December 27 and 28, 1860; John E. Wool to Winfield Scott, Washington, D.C., February
 25, 1861; Alfred Mordecai to sister, Watervliet Arsenal, N.Y., November 24, 1860 ("chafe of
 public affairs"), all Alfred Mordecai Papers, LC.
33. Bernard Bee to [Henry] Heth, Fort Laramie, Nebraska Territory, January 4, 1861, MoC;
 Joseph E. J[ohnston] to George B. McClellan, Washington, D.C., December 3, 1860,
 McClellan Papers, LC; Jeanne T. Heidler, "'Embarrassing Situation': David E. Twiggs and
 the Surrender of the United States Forces in Texas, 1861," in *Lone Star Blue and Gray: Essays
 on Texas in the Civil War,* ed. Ralph A. Wooster (Austin: Texas State Historical Association,
 1995), 35–36; Walter L. Buenger, *Secession and the Union in Texas* (Austin: University of
 Texas Press, 1984), 154.
34. David E. Twiggs to Scott, December 13, 1860, *OR,* I, 1:579; Col George W. Lay for
 Winfield Scott to Twiggs, December 28, 1860, ibid. I, 1:579; Twiggs to L[orenzo] Thomas,
 December 27, 1860, ibid., I, 1:579; Twiggs to Thomas, January 2 and 7, 1861, ibid., I,
 1:590; Twiggs to Scott, January 15, 1861, ibid., I, 1:581; Twiggs to Thomas, January 18,
 1861, ibid., I, 1:581; Sam Houston to Gen. D[avid] E. Twiggs, Austin, January 20, 1861, in
 The Writings of Sam Houston, 1813–1861, ed. Amelia W. Williams and Eugene C. Barker
 (Austin: University of Texas Press, 1938–1943), 8:284–85; Twiggs to Houston, San
 Antonio, January 22, 1861, in ibid., 8:285; Ben McCulloch to John H. Reagan, San
 Antonio, February 25, 1861 ("an insult to the commissioners"), *OR,* I, 1:609.
35. William T. H. Brooks to father, March 15, 1861, Brooks Papers, USAHEC; Edward L.
 Hartz to father, Camp Hudson, Tex., March 11, 1861, Edward L. Hartz Papers, LC; David
 E. Twiggs to James Buchanan, East Pascagoula, Miss., March 30, 1861, Edwin M. Stanton
 Papers, LC.
36. Heintzelman Diary, February 25, March 2 and 25, 1861, Heintzelman Papers, LC; Samuel
 Wylie Crawford to brother, Fort Sumter, S.C., March 14 and 15, 1861, Crawford Papers,
 LC; John E. Wool to Sarah [Wool], Washington, D.C., February 28, 1861, John E. Wool
 Papers, New York State Library, Albany, N.Y.
37. Samuel Cooper to Alfred Mordecai, Montgomery, Ala., April 1, 1861, Mordecai Papers,
 LC; "Samuel Cooper" in Cullum, *Biographical Register,* 1:150–51; "Ambrose Hill," ibid.,
 2:314; "John Withers," ibid., 2:388–89; "Julius P. Garesché," ibid., 2:81–82; James I.
 Robertson Jr., *General A. P. Hill: The Story of a Confederate Warrior* (New York: Random
 House, 1987), 33–34.
38. Louis Garesché, *Biography of Lieut. Col. Julius P. Garesché, Assistant Adjutant-General, U.S.
 Army* (Philadelphia: J. B. Lippincott, 1887), 350–52 and 357–58; Army Register 1861, kept
 by Garesché, Julius J. Garesché Papers, LC. The percentage of defections is taken from
 Wayne Wei-Siang Hsieh, *West Pointers and the Civil War: The Old Army in War and Peace*
 (Chapel Hill: University of North Carolina Press, 2009), 91–92. Meneely states that a total
 of 313 men resigned from the Army (*War Department,* 106). Skelton gives a smaller
 percentage, but his numbers do not include those who left but chose not to fight on either
 side; his source is Francis B. Heitman, *Historical Register and Dictionary of the United States
 Army from Its Organization, September 29, 1789, to March 2, 1903* (Washington, D.C.:
 Government Printing Office, 1903), which is less complete and accurate than calculations

based on Cullum, which Hsieh and Meneely used—see Skelton, *American Profession of Arms*, 355. See also carte de visite of Julius P. Garesché, n.d. [c. 1861–1862]; William J. Easton to A. J. P. Garesché, St. Louis, April 23, 1863; William Rosecrans to Maj. A. J. Dallas, San Francisco, January 21, 1880, all Julius Garesché Papers, GU; and Dr. Homer Pittard, "The Strange Death of Julius Peter Garesché," at www.latinamericanstudies.org /civil-war.

39. Winfield Scott, *Rules and Regulations for the Field Exercise and Manoeuvres of Infantry* (Philadelphia: Anthony Finley, 1824), 247; Charles P. Stone, "Washington in March and April, 1861," *Magazine of American History*, July 1885, 3; Samuel Du Pont to Commander Andrew Hull, January 25, 1861, and Samuel Du Pont to Henry Winter Davis, Louviers, February 17, 1861, both in *Samuel Francis Du Pont: A Selection from His Civil War Letters*, ed. John D. Hayes (Ithaca, N.Y.: Cornell University Press, 1969), 1:32. See also William S. Dudley, *Going South: U.S. Navy Officer Resignations and Dismissals on the Eve of the Civil War* (Washington, D.C.: Naval Historical Foundation, 1981), 4 and 11. A copy of Navy Department orders striking men from the rolls is in Gideon Welles to Thomas Locke Harrison, Navy Department, July 26, 1861, John M. McCalla Papers, DU. For an example of someone who tried to have his honor reestablished after dismissal, see Fitzhugh Lee to Dr. S. Glasgow, November 18, 1894, Edmund Jennings Lee Papers, VHS. John Bankhead Magruder's brother George Magruder, who resigned but did not fight for either side, was another who attempted, unsuccessfully, to have his honorable status reinstated in the Navy.

40. Copies of the army form letters accepting resignations can be found in the Mordecai Papers, LC, and the James Ewell Brown Stuart Papers, VHS. For disgruntlement at the casual acceptance of resignations, see Porter, "Journal of Occurrences," n.d. [c. 1865], Porter Papers, LC; see also *Diary of George Templeton Strong*, April 27, 1861, 3:135–36; "Look to the Army," *New York Times*, March 7, 1861; "Resignation of Major Mordecai," *Albany Evening Journal*, n.d. [May 1861], photostats, Mordecai Papers, LC.

41. Averell, *Ten Years in the Saddle*, 245 ("gradually receded"); Gideon Welles to wife, Washington, D.C., April 20, 1861, Welles Papers, LC; "Narrative," in Gideon Welles, *Diary of Gideon Welles: Secretary of the Navy Under Lincoln and Johnson*, ed. Howard K. Beale (New York: W. W. Norton, 1960), 1:5; Cameron, "Remarks on Return to Harrisburg," n.d. [c. 1864], Cameron Papers, LC; John A. Dahlgren quoted in Bruce, *Lincoln and the Tools of War*, 6; Dabney Herndon Maury, *Recollections of a Virginian in the Mexican, Indian, and Civil Wars* (New York: Charles Scribner's Sons, 1894), 128–29; William Farrar Smith, *Autobiography of Major General William F. Smith, 1861–1864*, ed. Herbert M. Schiller (Dayton, Ohio: Morningside, 1990), 29; Heintzelman Diary, March 13, 1861, Heintzelman Papers, LC; Diary of Mrs. Eugene McLean, January 1, 1861, in McLean, "When the States Seceded," 283–84.

42. Henry L. Wayne to J. E. B. Stuart, Milledgeville, Ga., April 12, 1861, Stuart Papers, VHS; Averell, *Ten Years in the Saddle*, 235.

43. Stephen N. Siciliano, "Major General William Farrar Smith: Critic of Defeat and Engineer of Victory," PhD diss., College of William and Mary, 1984, 45–46; G. W. Custis Lee to "Mac" [James B. McPherson], Engineer Department, November 19, 1860, James B. McPherson Papers, LC; John Wool to Thurlow Weed, January 20, 1861, in Samuel Rezneck, "The Civil War Role 1861–1863 of a Veteran New York Officer Major-General John E. Wool (1784–1869)," *New York History* 44, no. 3 (July 1963): 255n.

44. William B. Skelton, "Officers and Politicians: The Origins of Army Politics in the United States Before the Civil War," *Armed Forces and Society* 6, no. 1 (Fall 1979): 22–48; Heintzelman Diary, February 22, 1861, Heintzelman Papers, LC; Edward Hartz to father, Camp Hudson, Tex., December 15, 1860, Hartz Papers, LC; Quotations: Garesché, *Biography of Julius Garesché*, 350–51; Edward L. Hartz to father, Camp Hudson, Tex., March 11, 1861, Hartz Papers, LC ; J. H. Bailey to John P. Hawkins, Jefferson Barracks, St. Louis, March 14, 1861, Hawkins-Canby-Speed Family Papers, USAHEC; Samuel Wylie Crawford to brother, Fort Sumter, S.C., January 17, 1861, Crawford Papers, LC; Samuel Wylie Crawford to "AS," March 19, 1861, Crawford Papers, LC.

45. The two naval officers in Pensacola were Commander Ebenezer Ferrand and Lt. Francis B.

Renshaw: see Dudley, *Going South,* 5–6; see also J[ohn] G. Nicolay, Memorandum of Conversation with Joseph Holt, April 2, 1874, Nicolay Papers, LC; John E. Wool to AL, Head Quarters Dept. of the East, Troy, N.Y., January 11, 1861, ALP-LC.

46. For concerns about Scott, see Elihu B. Washburne to AL, December 17, 1860, ALP-LC; Lyman Trumbull to AL, Senate Chamber, January 3, 1861, ALP-LC; see also Jesse W. Weik, "How Lincoln Was Convinced of General Scott's Loyalty," *The Century Magazine,* February 1911, 593–94; Keyes Diary, March 29, 1861, in Keyes, *Fifty Years' Observation,* 61 and 377–78; Charles P. Stone, "A Dinner with General Scott," *Magazine of American History,* June 1884, 528–29 (Scott quotation on 529); Mary Custis Lee to Charles Marshall, n.d. [February 1871], Mary Custis Lee Papers, VHS; Peskin, *Winfield Scott,* 86–88 and 233–36.

47. Peskin, *Winfield Scott,* 233–36; Nannie Rodgers Macomb to Montgomery C. Meigs, January 6, 1861, Meigs Papers, LC; Diary of Virginia Woodbury Fox, March 9, 1861, Woodbury Papers, LC.

48. Peskin, *Winfield Scott,* 239; AL to Winfield Scott, copy in hand of John Nicolay, March 9, 1861, ALP-LC; Scott to Robert Anderson, Washington, D.C., March 11, 1861, ALP-LC; Scott to AL, Washington, D.C., March 12, 1861, ALP-LC.

49. For a "narrative" of the cabinet meetings, see Welles, *Diary of Gideon Wells,* 1:3–6; *Diary of Edward Bates,* March 9, 1861, Edward Bates Papers, LC; Nicolay and Hay, *Abraham Lincoln,* 3:392–93; see also Francis P. Blair to Montgomery Blair, Silver Spring, Md., March 12, 1861, ALP-LC; memorandum of A. D. Bache, Washington, D.C., March 7 and 8, 1861, Crawford Papers, LC. For contradictory advice about Fort Sumter, see Ethan Allen Hitchcock to Winfield Scott, St. Louis, March 7, 1861, Ethan Allen Hitchcock Papers, LC; James Watson Webb to AL, Washington, D.C., March 12, 1861, ALP-LC; Alexander Rives to William H. Seward, Washington, D.C., March 9, 1861, William H. Seward Papers, UR; Henry Dana Ward to William H. Seward, New York, March 9, 1861, Seward Papers, UR. "Is Democracy a Failure?" appeared in the *New York Times* on March 14, 1861.

50. John A. Dahlgren to T. R. Westherook [?], Washington, D.C., January 18, 1861, John Adolphus Bernard Dahlgren Papers, LC; Fitz John Porter to Samuel Cooper, Report on Fort Moultrie, November 11, 1860, Civil War Letters 1861–1865, NYHS; Porter's record shows he left Washington on special assignment on February 15, 1861, but returned before March 30: see "Fitz-John Porter" in Cullum, *Biographical Register,* 2:219–30.

51. "Don Carlos Buell" in Cullum, *Biographical Register,* 2:219–30; for Buell's grasp of the situation, see Averell, *Ten Years in the Saddle,* 244; Stephen D. Engle, *Don Carlos Buell: Most Promising of All* (Chapel Hill: University of North Carolina Press, 1999), 58–63. See also Francis W. Pickens to D. F. Jamison, Executive Department, December 28, 1860; Orders of F[rancis] Pickens, December 28–29, 1860, and January 1–2, 1861; F[rancis] W. Pickens to Maj. Gen. Schierle, Head Quarters, December 31, 1860, all Crawford Papers, LC. And see John B. Floyd to President [Buchanan], War Department, December 29, 1860, John B. Floyd Papers, VHS; Memorandum of John G. Nicolay, December 22, 1860, Nicolay Papers, LC. The quotation about Hill is from Crawford Diary, March 25 and April 4, 1861, Crawford Papers, LC.

52. David Hunter to AL, Fort Leavenworth, Kans., October 20 and December 18, 1860, ALP-LC; David Hunter to AL, Washington, D.C., March 4, 1861, ALP-LC; John Pope to AL, Cincinnati, January 27, 1861, ALP-LC; George W. Hazzard to AL, Cincinnati, October 21 and December 24, 1860, ALP-LC; Edwin V. Sumner to AL, St. Louis, December 17, 1860, ALP-LC; E[rasmus] D. Keyes to AL, New York, November 26, 1860, Erasmus D. Keyes Correspondence, NYHS.

53. *Diary of Orville Hickman Browning,* February 11, 1861, 1:453–54.

54. AL proposed Ellsworth for both chief clerk of the War Department and inspector general of the militia, with oversight of a newly created bureau. Orlando B. Willcox, *Forgotten Valor: The Memoirs, Journals and Civil War Letters of Orlando B. Willcox,* ed. Robert Garth Scott (Kent, Ohio: Kent State University Press, 1999), 270–71; Isaac Hill Bromley: "Historic Moments: The Nomination of Lincoln," *Scribner's Magazine,* November 1893, 648; AL to Simon Cameron, March 5, 1861, Cameron Papers, LC; AL, "Draft of a Proposed Order to

Establish a Militia Bureau," March 18, 1861, *CW,* 4:291; AL to Edward Bates, Washington, D.C., March 18, 1861, ibid., 4:291; Herman Kreismann to Charles Ray, January 16, 1861, Ray Papers, HL; AL quoted in Elmer Ellsworth to Mrs. Charles H. Spofford, Washington, D.C., March 22, 1861, in Don E. Fehrenbacher and Virginia Fehrenbacher, eds., *Recollected Words of Abraham Lincoln* (Stanford, Calif.: Stanford University Press, 1996), 151. See also Alexander H. Britton to uncle [John Morris], Washington, D.C., May 6, 1861, Alexander H. Britton Correspondence, NYHS; Frank E. Brownell, "Ellsworth's Career: *Philadelphia Weekly Times,* June 18, 1881," in Peter Cozzens and Robert I. Girardi, eds., *The New Annals of the Civil War* (Mechanicsburg, Pa.: Stackpole, 2004), 3–11; "C. Augustus" [Artemus Ward], "Progress of Mr. Lincoln," *Vanity Fair,* March 2, 1861.

55. David Herbert Donald, *Lincoln* (New York: Simon & Schuster, 1995), 254–55 and 273; Winfield Scott, Memo to AL, May 1, 1861, ALP-LC; Diary of Frank Vizetelly, May 25, 1861, quoted in www.emergingcivilwar.com/2012/04/04/drawing-the-war-part-3-frank -vizetelly; Willcox, *Forgotten Valor,* 269–72; Brownell, "Ellsworth's Career," 11.

56. *New York Herald,* May 25, 1861; C. M. Butler to wife, Washington, D.C., n.d. [May 27, 1861], C. M. Butler Correspondence, ILPL; David Detzer, "Fateful Encounter: Jim Jackson and Elmer Ellsworth," *North and South* 9, no. 3 (June 2006): 43–44. Overviews of Ellsworth's actions can be found in Brownell, "Ellsworth's Career," and Charles A. Ingraham, *Elmer E. Ellsworth and the Zouaves of '61* (Chicago: University of Chicago Press, 1925). For the way professionals handled these situations, see S. F. Du Pont to Sophie [Du Pont], Port Royal, S.C., May 29, 1862, in *Samuel Francis Du Pont,* 2:78. Du Pont's men encountered a South Carolina woman hoisting a rebel flag above the town hall; one officer "felt much instigated to . . . pull it down, but was restrained lest it might bring on a fight and he be compelled to shell the town."

57. Printed invitation to Miss Mary E. Edwards, Inaugural Ball of Zachary Taylor, March 1849, Decatur House Papers, LC.

58. Douglas Southall Freeman, *R. E. Lee: A Biography* (New York: Charles Scribner's Sons, 1934–1935), 1:417. For Lee's charisma, see Pryor, *Reading the Man,* chapter 12.

59. R. E. Lee to Agnes Lee, San Antonio, November 7, 1860, Nancy Astor Papers, Museum of English Rural Life, University of Reading, Reading, U.K. For Lee's unsettled state of mind, see, e.g., Heintzelman Diary, March 5, 1861, Heintzelman Papers, LC; Diary of William Oliver Webster, March 18, 1861, private collection.

60. For details of Lee's ambivalence and the division of his family, see Pryor, *Reading the Man,* chapter 17; Elizabeth Brown Pryor, " 'Thou Knowest Not the Time of Thy Visitation': A Newly Discovered Letter Reveals Robert E. Lee's Lonely Struggle with Disunion," *Virginia Magazine of History and Biography* 119, no. 3 (September 2011): 277–96. See also Williams C. Wickham to Winfield Scott, Richmond, March 11, 1861, ALP-LC; Worthington G. Snethen to AL, Baltimore, December 13, 1860, ALP-LC; "Richard Bland Lee," in Cullum, *Biographical Register,* 1:160–61; Mary Custis Lee to Charles Marshall, n.d. [February 1871], Mary Custis Lee Papers, VHS.

61. For Lee's stance on slavery see Pryor, *Reading the Man,* chapters 9 and 16. For his ideas on secession, see ibid., 285–97; Pryor, " 'Thou Knowest Not' "; Heintzelman Diary, March 5, 1861, Heintzelman Papers, LC. The Lee quotations in this paragraph are from, respectively, R. E. Lee to "dear son," San Antonio, December 14, 1860, Robert E. Lee Papers, DU; Cornelius Walker Diary, March 26, 1861, MoC; and Lee to Agnes Lee, Fort Mason, Tex., January 29, 1861, Lee Family Papers, VHS; see also Ness, *Regular Army,* 9. No overtures from the Confederate government to Lee have been found, but so many were directed to other Southern officers it would be surprising if he had not been approached. Examples include W. H. Hardee to Alfred Mordecai, Montgomery, Ala., March 4, 1861, Mordecai Papers, LC; George Thomas to Gov. John Letcher, New York Hotel, March 12, 1861, online at www.virginiamemory.com.

62. "Narrative," in Welles, *Diary of Gideon Welles,* 1:6 and 39. Examples of Virginians lobbying the administration include Alexander Rives to William H. Seward, Washington, D.C., March 9, 1861, Seward Papers, UR; Benjamin Ogle Tayloe to Seward, Washington, D.C., March 13, 1861, Seward Papers, UR; statement of Charles H. Morehead, October 9, 1862,

in David Rankin Barbee and Milledge L. Bonham Jr., eds., "Fort Sumter Again," *Mississippi Valley Historical Review* 28, no. 1 (June 1941): 64–71; entry of October 22, 1861, in John Hay, *Inside Lincoln's White House: The Complete Civil War Diary of John Hay,* ed. Michael Burlingame and John R. Turner Ettlinger (Carbondale: Southern Illinois University Press, 1997), 28; Lucius E. Chittenden, "President Lincoln and His Administration at the Commencement of the War," n.d. [c. 1865], Lucius E. Chittenden Manuscripts, HL. An overview of AL's overtures to Virginians can be found in Michael Burlingame, *Abraham Lincoln: A Life* (Baltimore: Johns Hopkins University Press, 2008), 2:119–23. The quotation is from AL to Montgomery Blair, March 13, 1861, *CW,* 4:282.

63. Scott quoted in Howell Cobb, "Reminiscences of Washington," Cameron Papers, LC; "Robert E. Lee," in Cullum, *Biographical Register,* 1:421; Mary C. Lee to "Rooney," n.d., enclosed with R. E. Lee to same, March 27, 1861, George Bolling Lee Papers, VHS.

64. Sam Houston to Sam Houston Jr., Austin, November 7, 1860, in *Writings of Sam Houston,* 8:184–85; Sam Houston to Thomas L. Rosser, Austin, November 17, 1860, in ibid., 8:199; see also Houston to John B. Floyd, Austin, November 28, 1860, in ibid., 8:204–5; Houston to "old friend," excerpt, *Southern Intelligencer,* February 20, 1861, ibid., 8:264. The last statement was excerpted more fully in *Alexandria* [Va.] *Gazette,* March 6, 1861.

65. William H. Seward to AL, Sunday evening, [March 1861], ALP-LC, reported that Lander was in Washington and that Seward would bring him to meet the President that evening. Notes to this letter state that this was written on March 24. However Lander was in Austin by March 29 and could not possibly have reached Texas in such a short time. Given that it was written on a Sunday, the note must have been sent on March 10: see F. W. Lander to Col. C. A. Waite, Austin, March 29, 1861, *OR,* I, 1:551–52. Houston's account is in Sam Houston to Editor, *Civilian and Galveston Gazette,* September 16, 1861, quoted in Joy Leland, ed., *Frederick West Lander: A Biographical Sketch (1822–1862)* (Reno, Nev.: Desert Research Institute, 1993), 195–97. Discussion of proposed size of force in Howard C. Westwood, "President Lincoln's Overture to Sam Houston," *The Southwestern Historical Quarterly* 88, no. 2 (October 1984): 143–44. Scott's order to entrench Union men is in Scott to Col. Carlos A. Waite, March 19, 1861, *OR,* I, 1:589 and 599. For Houston's meeting with advisers and his rejection of the offer, see, A. W. Terrell, "Recollections of General Sam Houston," *The Southwestern Historical Quarterly* 16, no. 2 (April 1912): 134–35; Charles A. Culberson, "General Sam Houston and Secession," *Scribner's Magazine,* May 1906, 586–87. The best overviews are in Llerena B. Friend, *Sam Houston: The Great Designer* (Austin: University of Texas Press, 1954), 351–57; Westwood, "President Lincoln's Overture." Houston's public statement of March 6, 1861, "To the People of Texas," can be found in *Writings of Sam Houston,* 8:277.

66. Diary of Erasmus Keyes, March 22, 1861, in Keyes, *Fifty Years' Observation,* 420; Fitz John Porter to A[lbert] S. Johnston, April 8, 1861, copy in Fitz-John Porter Papers, LC; Charles P. Roland, *Albert Sidney Johnston: Soldier of Three Republics* (Austin: University of Texas Press, 1964), 244–50; Brian McGinty, "I Will Call a Traitor a Traitor," *Civil War Times Illustrated* 20, no. 3 (June 1981): 28–30 (Johnston quoted on 29).

67. Lee had, in fact, known Houston since his cadet days at West Point. For their association and the high regard in which Lee was held, see Albert M. Lea to R. E. Lee, Austin, February 18, 1860, Mary Custis Lee Papers, VHS; Lea to Sam Houston, Austin, February 18, 1860, Mary Custis Lee Papers, VHS; R. E. Lee to Albert M. Lea, San Antonio, March 1, 1860, Texas State Library, Austin, Tex.

68. Every full colonel from Virginia but Lee remained with the Union Army, as did ten out of thirteen from the South as a whole. See Wayne Wei-Siang Hsieh, " 'I Owe Virginia Little, My Country Much': Robert E. Lee, the United States Regular Army and Unconditional Unionism," in Edward L. Ayers, Gary Gallagher, and Andrew Torget, eds., *Crucible of the Civil War: Virginia from Secession to Commemoration* (Charlottesville: University of Virginia Press, 2006), 36–49; "Lundsford Lindsay Lomax," in Cullum, *Biographical Register,* 2:654; William Marvel, *Mr. Lincoln Goes to War* (Boston: Houghton Mifflin Harcourt, 2006), 12. The Lomax quotation is from Lansford Lindsay Lomax to "Billy," Washington, D.C., April 21, 1861, Lomax Papers, VHS. For praise of Charles Read Collins—"he was superb &

admirable, both in person & character"—see Edward Porter Alexander, *Fighting for the Confederacy: The Personal Recollections of General Edward Porter Alexander,* ed. Gary W. Gallagher (Chapel Hill: University of North Carolina Press, 1989), 366; see also "Charles Read Collins," in Cullum, *Biographical Register,* 2:716. For angst in the Mordecai family, see Alfred Mordecai Jr. to father [Alfred Mordecai], West Point, N.Y., April 28, 1861, and extensive correspondence of March through May 1861, Mordecai Papers, LC; see also "Alfred Mordecai, Jr.," in Cullum, *Biographical Register,* 1:299–301.

69. Caroline Mordecai Plunkett to Alfred Mordecai, Richmond, March 11, 1861, Mordecai Papers, LC; Cobb, "Reminiscences," Cameron Papers, LC; Peter Johnston to Joseph Johnston, Richmond, March 10, 1861, Joseph E. Johnston Papers, Earl Gregg Swem Library, College of William and Mary, Williamsburg, Va.; J. E. Johnston to Col. T[homas] Gantt, Washington, D.C., June 23, 1888, Johnston Papers, Swem Library, College of William and Mary. See also Craig Symonds, *Joseph E. Johnston: A Civil War Biography* (New York: W. W. Norton, 1992), 93–96.

70. For financial concerns see entry of September 2, 1861, in *Mary Chesnut's Civil War,* 187; Alexander Dallas Boche to Alfred Mordecai, Washington, D.C., January 4, 1861, Mordecai Papers, LC; see also Pryor, "'Thou Knowest Not,'" 293n; Diary of Elizabeth Virginia Lomax, February 8, 1861, Lomax Papers, VHS.

71. For Lee's disloyalty (as well as that of Johnston and Magruder) as an impulse to the suspension of the writ of habeas corpus, see AL to Erastus Corning and Others, [June 12], 1863, *CW,* 6:265; see also "John B. Magruder," in Cullum, *Biographical Register,* 1:455–56; Stephen W. Sears, *George B. McClellan: The Young Napoleon* (New York: Ticknor & Fields, 1988), 175; Thomas M. Settles, *John Bankhead Magruder: A Military Reappraisal* (Baton Rouge: Louisiana State University Press, 2009), 113–15; Gilbert E. Govan and James W. Livingood, *A Different Valor: The Story of General Joseph E. Johnston, C.S.A.* (Indianapolis: Bobbs-Merrill, 1956), 27–28. Lincoln pointedly refused to protect Lee property (even with its Mount Vernon connections), quickly agreed to the proposal of turning the Lees' home at Arlington into a cemetery that would preclude the return of the family, and was particularly irate when he found that Lee's son Rooney, taken prisoner in 1863, was being treated with leniency. See Journal of Horace Green, June 17, 1862, in Horace Green, "Lincoln Breaks McClellan's Promise," *The Century Magazine,* February 1911, 594–95; M[ontgomery] C. Meigs to Edwin M. Stanton, Washington, D.C., June 15, 1864, Records of Office of the Quartermaster General, NARA; Remarks of Mrs. Alger, 1957, Meigs Papers, LC; Reminiscence of Benjamin F. Butler, in Allen Thorndike Rice, ed., *Reminiscences of Abraham Lincoln by Distinguished Men of His Time* (New York: North American Review, 1888), 145.

72. John B. Magruder to James Lyons, Fort Clark, Tex., January 24 and August 25, 1856, in John Bankhead Magruder, *The Presidential Contest of 1856 in Three Letters* (Washington, D.C.: Privately published, 1857), 2–15; *Washington Evening Star,* March 26, 1861.

73. Settles, *John Bankhead Magruder,* 113–15; Bruce, *Lincoln and the Tools of War,* 16; Allan Magruder Statement in [John B. Baldwin], *Interview Between President Lincoln and Col. John B. Baldwin, April 4th, 1861: Statements and Evidence* (Staunton, Va.: Spectator Job Office, 1866).

74. Settles, *John Bankhead Magruder,* 113–14; entry of April 21, 1861, Hay, *Inside Lincoln's White House,* 5; James Lyons to Jefferson Davis, Dagger's Springs, July 31, 1878, in *Jefferson Davis, Constitutionalist: His Letters, Papers, and Speeches,* ed. Dunbar Rowland (Jackson: Mississippi Department of Archives and History, 1923), 8:216; Rebecca R. J. Pomeroy to Mary [?], Indiana Hospital, Washington, D.C., March 27, 1862, typescript, Rebecca R. J. Pomeroy Letters, Schlesinger Library, HU; AL quoted in Samuel D. Sturgis to Editor, *Philadelphia Evening Telegraph,* June 12, 1870, in Fehrenbacher and Fehrenbacher, *Recollected Words,* 431–32.

75. Tidball, "Washington in 1861," Tidball Manuscripts, LC.

76. Samuel Du Pont to William Whetten, Port Royal, S.C., December 28, 1861, in *Samuel Francis Du Pont,* 1:293; T. W. Higginson, "Regular and Volunteer Officers," *Atlantic Monthly,* September 1864, 349–50; Potter, *The Impending Crisis,* 95.

77. Robert Colby to AL, New York, May 18, 1861, ALP-LC.

78. Several historians have intimated that AL seriously studied military science, but there is no evidence that he consulted more than one book. See Gerald J. Prokopowicz, *Did Lincoln Own Slaves? And Other Frequently Asked Questions About Abraham Lincoln* (New York: Pantheon, 2008), 127n; comment on Halleck's work in John F. Marszalek, *Commander of All Lincoln's Armies: A Life of Henry W. Halleck* (Cambridge: Harvard University Press, 2004), 44–46; also David Homer Bates, *Lincoln in the Telegraph Office: Recollections of the United States Military Telegraph Corps During the Civil War* (New York: Century, 1907), 122. For AL's continued awkwardness at formal military gatherings, see, e.g., entries of April 6, 8, and 9, 1863, in Marsena Rudolph Patrick, *Inside Lincoln's Army: The Diary of Marsena Rudolph Patrick, Provost Marshal General, Army of the Potomac,* ed. David S. Sparks (New York: Thomas Yoseloff, 1964), 231–32; Stearns E. Tyler to wife, April 6 [1863], Stearns E. Tyler Letters, UVa; Adam H. Pickel to brother, April 12, 1863, Adam H. Pickel Correspondence, ILPL; Journal of Samuel Clear, March 23, 1865, in *The Civil War Notebook of Daniel Chisholm: A Chronicle of Daily Life in the Union Army, 1864–1865,* ed. W. Springer Menge and J. August Shimrak (New York: Ballantine, 1989), 70; Col. August V. Kautz to Isabelle Savage, Headqrs. 1st Div. Army of the James, March 29, 1865, August V. Kautz Papers, ILPL.

79. John G. Nicolay to General [C. B.] Fisk, Washington, D.C., August 14, 1864, Nicolay Papers, LC; Elihu B. Washburne to AL, Siller's Plantation, [Fort Gibson], May 1, 1863, ALP-LC; Ethan Allen Hitchcock to Mary Mann, Washington, D.C., July 14, 1864, Hitchcock Papers, LC; Peter Welsh to wife, camp near Falmouth, Mass., April 10, 1863, in Peter Welsh, *Irish Green and Union Blue: The Civil War Letters of Peter Welsh, Color Sergeant, 28th Regiment Massachusetts Volunteers,* ed. Lawrence Frederick Kohl with Margaret Cossé Richard (New York: Fordham University Press, 1986), 84; *Diary of George Templeton Strong,* September 24, 1862, 3:259; AL to Joseph Hooker, Washington, D.C., April 15, 1863, *CW,* 6:175; Meigs, "Conduct of the War," 292; Frederick Law Olmsted to Henry Whitney Bellows, Washington, D.C., September 21, 1862, in *The Papers of Frederick Law Olmsted,* ed. Charles E. Beveridge et al. (Baltimore: Johns Hopkins University Press, 1977–2015), 4:426; George Meade to [wife], camp opposite Fredericksburg, Va., May 23, 1862, in *The Life and Letters of George Gordon Meade: Major-General United States Army,* ed. George Gordon Meade Jr. (New York: Charles Scribner's Sons, 1913), 1:267; entry of July 14, 1863, Hay, *Inside Lincoln's White House,* 62. A longer discussion of AL's struggle to project authority is in Pryor, " 'Grand Old Duke of York.' "

80. Donald, *Lincoln,* 288–90; William Seward to AL, Washington, D.C., April 1, 1861, ALP-LC; AL to Seward, April 1, 1861, *CW,* 4:316–17; "Narrative," in Welles, *Diary of Gideon Welles,* 1:21; Montgomery Blair to Martin Van Buren, April 29, 1861, Van Buren Papers, LC; Francis P. Blair to Van Buren, May 1, 1861, Van Buren Papers, LC; Franklin Pierce to Martin Van Buren, Concord, N.H., April 16, 1861, Van Buren Papers, LC.

81. John Hay to WHH, Paris, September 5, 1866, *HI,* 331–32; Diary of Ethan Allen Hitchcock, May 24, 1863, Croffut Papers, LC; see also Chester G. Hearn, *Lincoln, the Cabinet, and the Generals* (Baton Rouge: Louisiana State University Press, 2010), ix and xi. For the need to establish a proper war council, see, e.g., Samuel F. Du Pont to Henry Winter Davis, Astor House, October 8, 1861, in *Samuel Francis Du Pont,* 1:162–64; entry of December 31, 1861, in Edward Bates, *The Diary of Edward Bates, 1859–1866,* ed., Howard K. Beale (Washington, D.C.: Government Printing Office, 1933), 218–19; Herman Haupt to AL, Washington, D.C., December 22, 1861, Stanton Papers, LC; AL to Edwin M. Stanton, Washington, D.C., January 22, 1862, *CW,* 5:108. The quotation is from Edwin D. Mansfield to E. A. Hitchcock, May 26, 1862, Hitchcock Papers, LC. For a longer discussion of AL's stylistic problems, see Francis V. Greene, "Lincoln as Commander-in-Chief," *Scribner's Magazine,* July 1909, 107 and 109; Pryor, " 'Grand Old Duke of York.' "

82. AL admitted his discomfort with the military in AL to William S. Rosecrans, March 17, 1863, *CW,* 6:139. See also Michael Burlingame, "Surrogate Father Abraham" in *The Inner World of Abraham Lincoln* (Urbana: University of Illinois Press, 1994), 73–91; Propkopowicz, "If I Had Gone Up There," 88–91; Thomas J. Goss, *The War Within the Union High Command: Politics and Generalship During the Civil War* (Lawrence: University Press of

Kansas, 2003), 206. The colonel's quotation is from Alvin C. Voris to wife, Suffolk, Va., December 10, 1862, typescript, Alvin Coe Voris Papers, VHS.

83. Montgomery C. Meigs, "General M. C. Meigs on the Conduct of the Civil War," *American Historical Review* 26, no. 2 (January 1921): 286; Gustavus V. Fox to M[ontgomery] Blair, *Baltic,* at sea, April 17, 1861, in Gustavus Vasa Fox, *Confidential Correspondence of Gustavus Vasa Fox, Assistant Secretary of the Navy, 1861–1865,* ed. Robert Means Thompson and Richard Wainwright (New York: Naval History Society/De Vinne Press, 1918–1919), 1:33–36; Fox, "Result of G. V. Fox's Plan for Reinforcing Fort Sumter; in His Own Writing," ibid., 1:40–41; Montgomery Blair to Martin Van Buren, Washington, D.C., April 29, 1861, Van Buren Papers, LC; AL to Capt. G. V. Fox, Washington, D.C., May 1, 1861 ("accident, for which"), *CW,* 4:350–51; Tom Ewing [?] to brother [W. T. Sherman], Washington, D.C., April 24, 1861 ("blown his trumpet"), W. T. Sherman Papers, LC. For accounts of this remarkable mess-up, see Diary of Montgomery Meigs, March 29 through April 6, 1861, in Meigs, "On the Conduct of the Civil War," 299–302 and 286; Francis P. Blair to Martin Van Buren, May 1, 1861, Van Buren Papers, LC; "Narrative," in Welles, *Diary of Gideon Welles,* 1:21–28 and 35–41; Gideon Welles, "Fort Sumter," *The Galaxy,* November 1870, 624–30; "Admiral [David Dixon] Porter's Statement," March 11, 1873, Crawford Papers, LC. An overview is in Craig L. Symonds, *Lincoln and His Admirals* (New York: Oxford University Press, 2008), 15–34.

84. For AL's haphazard method of consultation and "administration," see "Narrative," in Welles, *Diary of Gideon Welles,* 1:62–67; *Diary of Edward Bates,* January 10, 1862, 223. For the chronic irregular correspondence of Chase, Blair, and others, see, e.g., Salmon P. Chase to George B. McClellan, Washington, D.C., July 7, 1861, in Salmon P. Chase, *The Salmon P. Chase Papers,* ed. John Niven et al. (Kent, Ohio: Kent State University Press, 1993–1998), 3:74–75; Chase to Bradford R. Wood, Washington, D.C., March 28, 1862, ibid., 3:152–53; Chase to David Hunter, Washington, D.C., February 14, 1863, ibid., 3:381; Chase Diary, August 2, 1862, ibid., 1:355–56; Frank P. Blair to "dear judge" [Montgomery Blair], St. Louis, August 21 and 29, and September 1, 1861, Blair Family Papers, LC; *Diary of Edward Bates,* February 26, 1863, 280–81. The source for the quotation is James H. Wilson to U. S. Grant, February 25, 1864, in Ulysses S. Grant, *The Papers of Ulysses S. Grant,* ed. John Y. Simon et al. (Carbondale: Southern Illinois University Press, 1967–2012), 10:141–42n.

85. Hundreds of such irregular letters are available; the examples here are George W. Hazzard to John G. Nicolay, Ft. McHenry, July 6, 1861, ALP-LC; William Nelson to Salmon P. Chase, Shiloe [*sic*], April 10, 1862, in *Chase Papers,* 3:168–69; Malcolm Ives to James Gordon Bennett, Washington, D.C., January 15, 1862 (example of speaking to the press), James Gordon Bennett Papers, LC; Fitz John Porter to "dear friend" [Manton Marble], near Yorktown, April 26, and n.p., August 10, 1862, both Manton Marble Papers, LC; Edward A. Miller, *Lincoln's Abolitionist General: The Biography of David Hunter* (Columbia: University of South Carolina Press, 1997), 123–24 and 131–32; *OR,* I, 14:448–49; Henry W. Halleck to Francis Lieber, Washington, D.C., June 6, 1863, Francis Lieber Papers, HL; Samuel Curtis to AL, Benton Barracks, October 12, 1861, ALP-LC. See also entry of July 24, 1861, Russell, *My Diary,* 475–76. For one of many examples of McClellan's disrespectful attitude, see McClellan to wife [Mary Ellen McClellan], Coal Harbor, Va., May 25 [1862], in George B. McClellan, *The Civil War Papers of George B. McClellan: Selected Correspondence, 1860–1865,* ed. Stephen W. Sears (New York: Ticknor & Fields, 1989), 275.

86. Winfield Scott to George B. McClellan, Washington, D.C., May 21, 1861, McClellan Papers, LC; Winfield Scott to S[imon] Cameron, Washington, D.C., August 9, 1861, ALP-LC; Scott to Cameron, October 15, 1861, copy in Stanton Papers, LC; *OR,* II, pt. 3:4; William D. Kelley, *Lincoln and Stanton: A Study of the War Administration of 1861 and 1862 with Special Consideration of Some Recent Statements of Gen. Geo. B. McClellan* (New York: G. P. Putnam's Sons, 1885), 4; *Diary of Edward Bates,* January 10, 1862, and February, 26, 1863, 223 and 280. See also Skelton, *American Profession of Arms,* 284.

87. *Diary of Edward Bates,* February 20, 1863, and June 13–16, 1864, 280, 376–77, and 386; Dispatch of Henry Villard, December 16, 1860, in Henry Villard, *Lincoln on the Eve of '61: A Journalist's Story,* ed. Harold G. Villard and Oswald Garrison Villard (Westport, Conn.:

Greenwood Press, 1974), 39; Chase Diary, October 11, 1862, *Chase Papers,* 1:420; entry of December 24, 1864, Welles, *Diary of Gideon Welles,* 2:207; Symonds, *Lincoln and His Admirals,* xi–xiii; Greene, "Lincoln as Commander-in-Chief," 107 and 109.

88. Dudley, *Going South,* 4 and 11; Lankford, *Cry Havoc!,* 71–72.

89. AL to William S. Rosecrans, March 17, 1863, *CW,* 6:139; McClintock, *Lincoln and the Decision for War,* 192–93; General Order No. 7, Adjutant General's Office, March 20, 1861, Garesché Papers, GU.

90. Meigs, "On the Conduct of the Civil War"; AL to Winfield Scott (note in John Hay's hand), June 5, 1861, *CW,* 4:394. Russell F. Weigley, *Quartermaster General of the Union Army: A Biography of M. C. Meigs* (New York: Columbia University Press, 1959), is well done.

91. The issue of picking leaders is discussed at greater length in Pryor, "'Grand Old Duke of York.'" See also W. T. Sherman to brother [John Sherman], camp near Vicksburg, January 25, 1863, in Sherman, *Selected Correspondence,* 375; Sherman to Thomas Ewing Sr., St. Louis, June 3, 1861, ibid., 97; Sherman to brother [John Sherman], St. Louis, June 8, 1861, ibid., 100; Sherman to brother [John Sherman], Lancaster, Pa., December 29 and 30, 1863, ibid., 578–80; Sherman to brother [John or C. T. Sherman?], St. Louis, April 18, 1861, W. T. Sherman Papers, LC. For Meigs distancing himself from White House politics, see Meigs Diary, 1861–1865, Meigs Papers, LC.

92. Upholding AL's choices are Archer Jones, who denied he ever promoted generals for political reasons; Herman Hattaway, who donned him with nearly omniscient foresight; Mark Neely, who added that the President had a "clear-sighted unwillingness to allow partisan concerns to interfere with decisions critical to the army"; James McPherson, who defended the frequently disastrous appointments as "the best possible at the time"—or actually the product of bungling by Halleck (himself a Lincoln appointee); and Craig Symonds, who apologized that Lincoln's decisions were "the product of political necessity" and stated that he was willing to reverse them when necessary—although the inept Halleck, Banks, Dahlgren, Sigel, Butler, and myriad others were allowed to continue destroying campaigns and wasting lives until the end of the war. See Brooks D. Simpson, "Lincoln and His Political Generals," *JALA* 21, no. 1 (Winter 2000): 65; Mark E. Neely Jr., *The Last Best Hope of Earth: Abraham Lincoln and the Promise of America* (Cambridge: Harvard University Press, 1993), 61–62 and 90; McPherson, *Tried by War,* 5–13 and 266; Craig L. Symonds, "Men, Machines, and Old Abe: Lincoln and the Civil War Navy," in Simon and Holzer, *The Lincoln Forum,* 50. Others assessing AL's methodology as commander in chief have found that at best there was only marginal political advantage to his political appointments, that politics and preference polarized the Army and dictated the pace of the war, and that much of AL's tactical failure came from faulty commissions. Simpson has neatly laid out the grave cost of the political mistakes: see Simpson, "Lincoln and His Political Generals," 63–77; see also David Work, *Lincoln's Political Generals* (Urbana: University of Illinois Press, 2009), 31 and 227–34; Goss, *War Within the Union High Command,* 48, 77, and 105.

93. On Baker and the unfortunate affair at Ball's Bluff, see the meticulous William F. Howard, *The Battle of Ball's Bluff: The Leesburg Affair, October 21, 1861* (Lynchburg, Va.: Privately published, 1994); Dahlgren's promotion and its unfortunate aftermath are discussed in entries of October 9, 1862, and June 23, 1863, Welles, *Diary of Gideon Welles,* 1:163–64 and 341; see George Boweryem to Sydney Howard Gay, Morris Island, S.C., October 9 and 13, 1863, Sydney Howard Gay Family Papers, CU. For a good overview, see Robert J. Schneller Jr., *A Quest for Glory: A Biography of Rear Admiral John A. Dahlgren* (Annapolis, Md.: Naval Institute Press, 1996), 180–97, 229–42, and 279–82. One of many examples of disgruntlement at Pope's promotion can be found in the entry for June 27, 1862, in David Hunter Strother, *A Virginia Yankee in the Civil War: The Diaries of David Hunter Strother,* ed. Cecil D. Eby Jr. (Chapel Hill: University of North Carolina Press, 1961), 63. For Lincoln's political reasons for picking Hooker, despite his awareness of Hooker's character flaws, see Henry J. Raymond, "Extracts from the Journal of Henry J. Raymond," *Scribner's Monthly,* February 1880, 704–5 (entry for January 24, 1863); and *Diary of Orville Hickman Browning,* January 26, 1863, 1:619; the phrase "glib and oily art" is from *King Lear* (a

Lincoln favorite), act I, sc. 1. Farragut's reaction is in his letter to Samuel Du Pont, April 20, 1863, *Samuel Francis Du Pont,* 3:49; for Garesché's, see Garesché, *Biography of Julius Garesché,* 365–66.

94. Goss, *War Within the Union High Command,* 105–7; Work, *Lincoln's Political Generals,* 230–33. A detailed discussion of army reaction to Stanton and Halleck is in Pryor, " 'Grand Old Duke of York.' " For Bank's nonperformance, see William Baker to Sydney Howard Gay, New Orleans, April 15, 1864, Gay Papers, CU; T. Harry Williams, *Lincoln and His Generals* (New York: Vintage, 2011), 190, 228–29, and 309. The quotation on McClernand comes from Charles A. Dana to Edwin M. Stanton, behind Vicksburg, June 22, 1863, Stanton Papers, LC. AL's general acquiescence to the demands of the radicals is discussed in Bruce Tap, *Over Lincoln's Shoulder: The Committee on the Conduct of the War* (Lawrence: University Press of Kansas, 1998); T. Harry Williams, *Lincoln and the Radicals* (Madison: University of Wisconsin Press, 1965).

95. George [John G.] Nicolay to Therena [Bates], Washington, D.C., December 28, 1862, Nicolay Papers, LC; Philip Kearny to [Cortland] Parker, Williamsburg Road, May 27, 1862, typescript, Philip Kearny Papers, LC; George Thomas to Andrew Johnson, Dickens, Tenn., August 16, 1862, George H. Thomas Manuscripts, HL; John Reynolds quoted in Jeffry D. Wert, *The Sword of Lincoln: The Army of the Potomac* (New York: Simon & Schuster, 2005), 257; W. T. Sherman to brother [John Sherman], Vicksburg, May 29, 1863, Sherman, *Selected Correspondence,* 474.

96. For Garfield's battlefield prowess and AL's attempt to co-opt him politically, see William Dennison to Edwin M. Stanton, Columbus, November 4, 1863, Stanton Papers, LC; James A. Garfield to Henry Hopkins, n.d. [c. December 1863], in Theodore Clarke Smith, *The Life and Letters of James Abram Garfield* (New Haven: Yale University Press, 1925), 1:355–56; James A. Garfield, account of campaigns in Kentucky and Tennessee, n.d. [1864], John Roberts Gilmore Papers, Johns Hopkins University, Special Collections, Milton S. Eisenhower Library, Baltimore, Md. For "stupidity and weakness," see Allan Peskin, *Garfield* (Kent, Ohio: Kent State University Press, 1978), 153. Alpheus Williams comments on the "low, groveling lick-spittle subserving [*sic*]" manner needed to receive a promotion in a letter to his daughter written near the Chattahoochee River, Ga., on July 15, 1864, in Alpheus S. Williams, *From the Cannon's Mouth: The Civil War Letters of General Alpheus S. Williams,* ed. Milo M. Quaife (Detroit: Wayne State University Press, 1959), 332. Baldy Smith's remark is in W. F. Smith to Montgomery Blair, August 23, 1863, in Siciliano, "Major General William Farrar Smith," 205–6; see also 183–85. See also AL to Carl Schurz, Washington, D.C., November 10, 1862, *CW,* 5:494.

97. Henry Halleck to John M. Schofield, Washington, D.C., September 20, 1862, in *OR,* I, 13:654. AL discussed his military appointments with Carl Schurz, November 10, 1862, *CW,* 5:494–95; and AL to John M. Schofield, May 27, 1863, *CW,* 6:234. See also David Farragut to wife [Virginia Farragut], USFS *Hartford,* May 7, 1864, David Glasgow Farragut Papers, HL.

98. Simpson, "Lincoln and His Political Generals"; Goss, *War Within the Union High Command,* 207–11, gives a somewhat more upbeat assessment of political generals than does Work, *Lincoln's Political Generals,* 228–33, which is more detailed.

99. For AL's reluctance to shed blood, see his reply to Gov. Andrew J. Curtain at Harrisburg, Pa., February 22, 1861, *CW,* 4:243. For claims that he excelled as commander or improved over time, see Herman Hattaway and Archer Jones, *How the North Won: A Military History of the Civil War* (Urbana: University of Illinois Press, 1983), 689 and 695; see also Williams, *Lincoln and His Generals,* 7; Frank J. Williams, "Abraham Lincoln and the Changing Role of Commander in Chief," in *Lincoln Reshapes the Presidency,* ed. Charles E. Hubbard (Macon, Ga.: Mercer University Press, 2003), 26 and 28; McPherson, *Tried by War,* 5–13 and 266–67; Symonds, *Lincoln and His Admirals,* 36; John F. Marszalek, *Lincoln and the Military* (Carbondale: Southern Illinois University Press, 2014), 110–13. For AL's lack of improvement over time and officers' assessment of his performance, see Pryor, " 'Grand Old Duke of York.' "

CHAPTER 2. PFUNNY PFACE

1. The flag raising took place on June 29, 1861—see *Daily National Intelligencer,* July 1, 1861. For a description of the South Lawn and atmosphere of military concerts, see entry for April 27, 1861, in John Hay, *Inside Lincoln's White House: The Complete War Diary of John Hay,* ed. Michael Burlingame and John R. Turner Ettlinger (Carbondale: Southern Illinois University Press, 1997), 13. For Lincoln's pensive mood, see N. P. Willis to Ida Tarbell, n.d., quoted in Ida M. Tarbell, *The Life of Abraham Lincoln* (New York: Macmillan, 1920), 2:51–52.

2. *Daily National Intelligencer,* July 1, 1861; Benjamin P. Thomas, *Abraham Lincoln: A Biography* (New York: Alfred A. Knopf, 1952), 270.

3. *Daily National Intelligencer,* July 1, 1861; Tarbell, *Life of Lincoln,* 2:51–52; Dorothy Schaffter and Dorothy M. Mathews, *The Powers of the President as Commander in Chief of the Army and Navy of the United States* (Washington, D.C.: Government Printing Office, 1956), 17; Edward S. Corwin, *Total War and the Constitution* (New York: Alfred A. Knopf, 1947), 16–19.

4. Tarbell, *Life of Lincoln,* 2:51–52; *Daily National Intelligencer,* July 1, 1861; B[enjamin] B. French to Ellen M. French, Washington, D.C., June 30, 1861, Benjamin B. French Family Papers, LC; *Chicago Tribune,* June 30 [?], 1861 (the author is grateful to Michael Burlingame for providing the *Tribune* reference). A sketch of the scene by Alfred R. Waud is owned by the Library of Congress's Prints and Photograph Division (DRAW/US-Waud, no. 291).

5. *Daily National Intelligencer,* July 1, 1861; AL, "Speech at Lafayette, Ind.," February 11, 1861, *CW,* 4:192; AL, "Speech at Flag Raising Before Independence Hall, Philadelphia," February 22, 1861, ibid., 4:241; AL, "Remarks at Flag Raising at the Post Office," May 22, 1861, quoted in *Daily National Intelligencer,* May 23, 1861. A similar but slightly less interesting version of the later speech is found in *CW,* 4:382–83. Ken Burns's documentary *The Civil War* quotes Lincoln as saying that he would "rather be assassinated than see a single star removed from the American flag," but this author found no such authenticated statement; the closest is the speech given at Independence Hall on February 22, 1861, in which AL says he would almost rather be assassinated on the spot than give up the principles embodied in the Declaration of Independence (*CW,* 4:240). For slogans on patriotic envelopes, see Steven R. Boyd, *Patriotic Envelopes of the Civil War: The Iconography of Union and Confederate Covers* (Baton Rouge: Louisiana State University Press, 2010).

6. Entry of June 29, 1861, Horatio Nelson Taft Diary, LC; *Chicago Tribune,* June 30 [?], 1861. The quotations are from B[enjamin] B. French to Ellen M. French, Washington, D.C., June 30, 1861, French Papers, LC; [Charles Farrar Browne], "Artemus Ward on the Crisis," *Vanity Fair,* January 26, 1861.

7. "Remarks of A. Lincoln at Flag Raising at South Front of the Treasury Building," July 4, 1861, unnamed newspaper quoted in Allen C. Clark, "Abraham Lincoln in the National Capital," *Records of the Columbia Historical Society* 27 (1925): 26 (the statement does not appear in *CW*); entry of June 29, 1861, Taft Diary, LC; *Chicago Tribune,* June 30 [?], 1861; Benjamin B. French to Ellen M. French, Washington, D.C., June 30, 1861, French Papers, LC; *Daily National Intelligencer,* July 1, 1861.

8. *Daily National Intelligencer,* July 1, 1861; Benjamin Brown French, *From the Diary and Correspondence of Benjamin Brown French,* ed. Amos Tuck French (New York: Privately published, 1904); Benjamin Brown French, *Witness to the Young Republic: A Yankee's Journal, 1828–1870,* ed. Donald B. Cole and John J. McDonough (Hanover, N.H.: University Press of New England, 1989).

9. MTL to Josiah G. Holland, Chicago, December 4, 1865, in Justin G. Turner and Linda Levitt Turner, eds., *Mary Todd Lincoln: Her Life and Letters* (New York: Alfred A. Knopf, 1972), 293.

10. John Henry Brown to John M. Read, Springfield, Ill., August 16, 1860, Read Family Papers, LC; Robert Gould Shaw to Effie [Josephine Shaw], Washington, D.C., April 30, 1861, in Robert Gould Shaw, *Blue-Eyed Child of Fortune: The Civil War Letters of Colonel*

Robert Gould Shaw, ed. Russell Duncan (Athens: University of Georgia Press, 1992), 88; Edward Dicey, *Spectator of America,* ed. Herbert Mitgang (Chicago: Quadrangle, 1971), 95; Reminiscence of Benjamin Perley Poore, n.d. [c. 1888], in Allen Thorndike Rice, ed., *Reminiscences of Abraham Lincoln by Distinguished Men of His Time* (New York: North American Review, 1888), 230–31. For AL at the punch line, see Henry Villard, *Memoirs of Henry Villard, Journalist and Financier, 1835–1900* (Boston: Houghton Mifflin, 1904), 1:143.

11.   Diary of Benjamin B. French, September 4, 1861, French Papers, LC; Noah Brooks, *Washington in Lincoln's Time,* ed. Herbert Mitgang (New York: Rinehart, 1958), 260; Reminiscence of Donn Piatt, n.d. [c. 1888], in Rice, *Reminiscences of Lincoln,* 480; AL to Mary Speed, Bloomington, Ill., September 27, 1841 (on tooth loss), *CW,* 1:260–61; John H. Littlefield to WHH, Washington, D.C., December 13, 1866, *HI,* 514. See also entry of October 23, 1861, in *The Diary of George Templeton Strong,* ed. Allan Nevins and Milton Halsey Thomas (New York: Macmillan, 1952), 3:188; Reminiscence of James B. Fry, n.d. [c. 1888], in Rice, *Reminiscences of Lincoln,* 389; Henry C. Whitney, *Life on the Circuit with Lincoln* (Boston: Estes & Lauriat, 1892), 171–72.

12.   WHH interview with Dennis F. Hanks, Chicago, June 13, 1865, *HI,* 37; William G. Greene to WHH, Tallula, Ill., December 20, 1865, ibid., 145; Joseph Gillespie to WHH, Edwardsville, Ill., December 8, 1866, ibid., 508; AL, "Speech in the Illinois Legislature Concerning the Surveyor of Schuyler County," January 6, 1835, *CW,* 1:31; WHH interview with S. T. Johnson, Indiana, September 14, 1835, *HI,* 118; Elizabeth Crawford to WHH, n.p., January 4, 1866, ibid., 151–52; AL to Sangamo Journal (the "Rebecca Letter"), Lost Townships, August 27, 1842, *CW,* 1:291–97; AL, "Memorandum of Duel Instructions to Elias H. Merryman," September 19, 1841, ibid., 1:300. For a discussion of the Shields episode, see Douglas L. Wilson, *Honor's Voice: The Transformation of Abraham Lincoln* (New York: Alfred A. Knopf, 1998), 265–76. The quip about McClellan, from November 1862, is often quoted with various wording—see Charles Lincoln Van Doren and Robert McHenry, eds., *Webster's Guide to American History: A Chronological, Geographical and Biographical Survey and Compendium* (Springfield, Mass.: G. & C. Merriam, 1971), 233.

13.   Joseph Gillespie to WHH, Edwardsville, Ill., January 31, 1866, *HI,* 181–82; Constance Rourke, *American Humor: A Study of the National Character* (New York: Harcourt, Brace, 1931), 152–56; T. G. Onstot quoted in Benjamin Thomas, *"Lincoln's Humor" and Other Essays,* ed. Michael Burlingame (Urbana: University of Illinois Press, 2002), 4; Whitney, *Life on the Circuit,* 185; Noah Brooks, "Personal Reminiscences of Lincoln," *Scribner's Monthly,* March 1878, 680; Albert B. Chandler, unpublished reminiscences from journal entries, c. 1892, Albert B. Chandler Papers, USAHEC.

14.   Brooks, *Washington in Lincoln's Time,* 255–59; Thomas D. Jones, "A Sculptor's Recollections of Lincoln," in Rufus Rockwell Wilson, ed., *Lincoln Among His Friends: A Sheaf of Intimate Memories* (Caldwell, Idaho: Caxton Printers, 1942), 261–62; dispatch of Henry Villard, *New York Herald,* February 20, 1861, quoted in Don E. Fehrenbacher and Virginia Fehrenbacher, eds., *Recollected Words of Abraham Lincoln* (Stanford, Calif.: Stanford University Press, 1996), 456–57; Diary of Fanny Seward, January 20, 1862, William H. Seward Papers, UR; Samuel F. Du Pont to Sophie [Du Pont], USS *Wabash,* Port Royal, S.C., April 25, 1863, in Samuel Francis Du Pont, *Samuel Francis Du Pont: A Selection from His Civil War Letters,* ed. John D. Hayes (Ithaca, N.Y.: Cornell University Press, 1969), 3:60; undated entry from July or August 1863, Hay, *Inside Lincoln's White House,* 78.

15.   Reminiscence of Elihu B. Washburne, n.d. [c. 1888], in Rice, *Reminiscences of Lincoln,* 13; P. D. Gurley reminiscences in Ervin Chapman, ed., *Latest Light on Abraham Lincoln and War-Time Memories* (New York: Fleming H. Revel, 1917), 2:502; Silas W. Burt, "Lincoln on His Own Storytelling," *The Century Magazine,* February 1907, 502.

16.   P. M. Zall, ed., *Abe Lincoln Laughing: Humorous Anecdotes from Original Sources by and About Abraham Lincoln* (Berkeley: University of California Press, 1982); Alexander K. McClure, *"Abe" Lincoln's Yarns and Stories* (Chicago: Henry Neal, 1904). McClure's "close" relationship with Lincoln is in question; John Hay referred to him as one of the "professional liars" who had "written several volumes of reminiscences of Lincoln with whom I

really think he never had two hours' conversation in his life": John Hay to Charles Francis Adams, December 19, 1903, quoted in John Hay, *Lincoln and the Civil War in the Diaries and Letters of John Hay*, ed. Tyler Dennett (1939; repr., Westport, Conn.: Negro Universities Press, 1972), 136. See also John Forney in Charles M. Segal, ed., *Conversations with Lincoln* (New York: G. P. Putnam's Sons, 1961), 272; Reminiscence of George Julian, n.d. [c. 1888], in Rice, *Reminiscences of Lincoln*, 54; Brooks, *Washington in Lincoln's Time*, 256.

17. Joseph Gillespie to WHH, January 31 and December 8, 1866, *HI*, 181–82 and 508; Whitney, *Life on the Circuit*, 177; Egbert L. Viele, "A Trip with Lincoln, Chase and Stanton," *Scribner's Monthly*, October 1878, 816 (Viele wrote another piece containing the same story, with slight variations, for *The Independent Lincoln Number*, April 4, 1895, copy in John G. Nicolay Papers, LC); entry of December 31, 1863, Hay, *Inside Lincoln's White House*, 135. The New York politician Chauncey DePew, n.d. [c. 1888], is quoted in Rice, *Reminiscences of Lincoln*, 434.

18. Entry of July 18, 1863, and addendum for July–August 1863, Hay, *Inside Lincoln's White House*, 64 and 76; *Diary of George Templeton Strong*, December 13, 1862, 3:278; A. J. Blucker to James Gordon Bennett, July 14, 1862, James Gordon Bennett Papers, LC.

19. Abner Ellis, statement for WHH, n.d. [January 1866], *HI*, 173; Henry Whitney to WHH, June 23 and September 17, 1887, ibid., 442 and 617; WHH interview with H. E. Drummer, n.p., n.d. [c. 1865–1866], ibid., 644; Nathaniel Hawthorne's excised remarks in Rufus Rockwell Wilson, ed., *Intimate Memories of Lincoln* (Elmira, N.Y.: Primavera Press, 1945), 466. Hawthorne later wrote of his decision to edit his remarks in "Our Whispering Gallery, IV," *Atlantic Monthly*, April 1871, 512. See also Walt Whitman to Nat and Fred Gray, Washington, D.C., March 19, 1863, in Walt Whitman, *Walt Whitman's Civil War*, ed. Walter Lowenfels (New York: Alfred A. Knopf, 1961), 174; Reminiscence of Hugh McCulloch, n.d. [c. 1888], in Rice, *Reminiscences of Lincoln*, 417.

20. General Ethan Allen did not actually visit England after the Revolution. However, he did conduct negotiations with the British in Quebec. The Lincoln anecdotes in this paragraph are from WHH interview with Christopher C. Brown, n.p., n.d. [c. 1865–1866], *HI*, 438; Abner Ellis, statement for WHH, n.d. [January 1866], ibid., 174; John B. Weber to WHH, Pawnee, Ill., November 5, 1866, ibid., 396 (a similar story to Ellis's); Chandler, unpublished reminiscences, Chandler Papers, USAHEC.

21. Leonard Swett to WHH, Chicago, January 17, 1866, *HI*, 165–66; Abram Bergen, "Personal Recollections of Abraham Lincoln as a Lawyer," *The American Lawyer* 5 (May 1897): 213; Thomas, "Lincoln's Humor," 12; David Donald quoted in Zall, *Abe Lincoln Laughing*, 7.

22. WHH interview with Richard M. Lawrence, n.p., June 23, 1888, *HI*, 715–16; entry of April 30, 1864, Hay, *Inside Lincoln's White House*, 194; entry of January 11, 1862, Taft Diary, LC; Diary of Benjamin B. French, May 4, 1862, and March 23, 1864, French Papers, LC; Diary of Virginia Woodbury Fox, March 3, 1863, Levi Woodbury Papers, LC; Dicey, *Spectator of America*, 92–95. For the performances of Tom Thumb and Hermann the Prestidigitateur, see George [John G.] Nicolay to Therena Bates, Washington, D.C., November 24, 1861, Nicolay Papers, LC; Journal of Samuel Heintzelman, November 25, 1861, Samuel Peter Heintzelman Papers, LC; Diary of Virginia Woodbury Fox, February 13, 1863, Woodbury Papers, LC; Diary of Benjamin B. French, November 24, 1861, French Papers, LC.

23. Joshua Speed to WHH, Louisville, December 6, 1866, *HI*, 499; WHH to [Jesse] Weik, Springfield, Ill., November 17, 1885, and December 22, 1888, Herndon-Weik Collection, LC; Charles A. Dana, "Reminiscences of Men and Events of the Civil War: IX. The End of the War," *McClure's Magazine*, August 1898, 381.

24. For discussions of Lincoln's mercurial moods, see Joshua Wolf Shenk, *Lincoln's Melancholy: How Depression Challenged a President and Fueled His Greatness* (Boston: Houghton Mifflin, 2005); Norbert Hirschhorn, Robert G. Feldman, and Ian Greaves, "Abraham Lincoln's Blue Pills: Did Our 16th President Suffer from Mercury Poisoning?" *Perspectives in Biology and Medicine* 44, no. 3 (Summer 2001): 315–32; Michael Burlingame, "Melancholy Dript from Him as He Walked," in *The Inner World of Abraham Lincoln* (Urbana: University of

Illinois Press, 1994), 92–122; Seymour Fisher and Rhoda L. Fisher, *Pretend the World Is Funny and Forever: A Psychological Analysis of Comedians, Clowns, and Actors* (Hillsdale, N.J.: Lawrence Erlbaum, 1981). In his poem "Lincoln," James Whitcomb Riley wrote, "And yet there stirred within his breast / A fateful pulse that, like a roll / Of drums, made high above the rest / A tumult in his soul."

25. For AL's magnetic appeal in his early years, see, e.g., WHH interview with Dennis F. Hanks, June 13, 1865, *HI*, 42; Abner Y. Ellis, statement for WHH, Moro, Ill., January 23, 1866, ibid., 171; WHH interview with James H. Matheny, n.p., n.d. [November 1866], ibid., 431–32; Joseph Gillespie to WHH, January 31 and December 8, 1866, ibid., 181 and 508; Jason Duncan to WHH, n.d. [c. late 1866–early 1867], ibid., 541; Henry C. Whitney, statement for WHH, n.d. [c. 1887], ibid., 648. See also John J. Duff, *A. Lincoln, Prairie Lawyer* (New York: Rinehart, 1960), 18; Wilson, *Honor's Voice*, chapters 1 and 2.

26. WHH interview with Dennis F. Hanks, June 13, 1865, *HI*, 37; Bergen, "Personal Recollections of Abraham Lincoln as a Lawyer," 213; Duff, *A. Lincoln, Prairie Lawyer*, 59–60.

27. William Howard Russell, *My Diary North and South* (Boston: Burnham, 1863), 43–44; Reminiscence of Titian J. Coffey, n.d. [c. 1888], in Rice, *Reminiscences of Lincoln*, 235; Ward Hill Lamon, *Recollections of Abraham Lincoln, 1847–1865*, ed. Dorothy Lamon Teillard (Washington, D.C.: Privately published, 1911), 124.

28. Silas Burt claimed that these words were Lincoln's, recorded just after speaking with him: Silas Burt, "Lincoln on His Own Story Telling," in Wilson, *Lincoln Among His Friends*, 333; AL, "Speech on the Sub-Treasury," December [26], 1839, *CW*, 1:177–78; AL, "First Debate with Stephen A. Douglas, Ottawa, Ill.," August 21, 1858, ibid., 3:29; AL, "Speech at Hartford, Conn.," March 5, 1860, ibid., 4:10–11; Brooks, *Washington in Lincoln's Time*, 264–65.

29. George B. McClellan to wife [Mary Ellen McClellan], n.p. [Washington, D.C.], October 16, 1861, in George B. McClellan, *The Civil War Papers of George B. McClellan: Selected Correspondence, 1860–1865*, ed. Stephen W. Sears (New York: Ticknor & Fields, 1989), 107; Horace Greeley, "Lincoln to Hodges," *New York Tribune*, April 29, 1864; Henry Dawes, statement on Abraham Lincoln, n.d., Henry Dawes Papers, LC.

30. AL, "The Presidential Question," July 27, 1848, *CW*, 1:509, quoting Shakespeare's Sonnet 94; Robert Bray, "'The Power to Hurt': Lincoln's Early Use of Satire and Invective," *JALA* 16, no. 1 (1995): 39–58; Wilson, *Honor's Voice*, 300–303; Douglas L. Wilson, "Abraham Lincoln Versus Peter Cartwright," in *Lincoln Before Washington: New Perspectives on the Illinois Years* (Urbana: University of Illinois Press, 1997), 55–73.

31. Judge [David] Davis, n.d., note in Nicolay Papers, LC; AL, "'A House Divided' Speech," Springfield, Ill., June 16, 1858, *CW*, 2:467; Stephen A. Douglas, c. 1858, from untitled newspaper story, in Zall, *Abe Lincoln Laughing*, 4–5; Noah Brooks, "The President's Last Story," February 22, 1865, in Noah Brooks, *Lincoln Observed: Civil War Dispatches of Noah Brooks*, ed. Michael Burlingame (Baltimore: Johns Hopkins University Press, 1998), 163–64; Noah Brooks, "Personal Reminiscences," *Scribner's Monthly*, February 1878, 564; Brooks, *Washington in Lincoln's Time*, 263; John Nicolay to E. Stafford, Springfield, Ill., March 17, 1860, Nicolay Papers, LC.

32. WHH to Jesse Weik, Springfield, Ill., February 9, 1887, Herndon-Weik Collection, LC; WHH notes for Jesse Weik, "A new & good one," n.d., Herndon-Weik Collection, LC; Leonard Swett to WHH, Chicago, July 17, 1866, Herndon-Weik Collection, LC; entries of November 29, 1862, and April 22, 1865, in Orville Hickman Browning, *The Diary of Orville Hickman Browning, 1850–1864*, ed. Theodore Calvin Pease and James G. Randall (Springfield: Illinois State Historical Society, 1925), 1:588–89 and 2:25; Shenk, *Lincoln's Melancholy*, 116–17; Martinette Hardin quoted in Wilson, *Honor's Voice*, 180–81; AL, "Remarks at Pittsburgh," February 14, 1861, *CW*, 4:209.

33. *Diary of George Templeton Strong*, October 23, 1861, 3:188; Villard, *Memoirs of Henry Villard*, 1:152; Benjamin B. French to brother [Henry F. French], Washington, D.C., March 6, 1861, French Papers, LC; Reminiscence of R. E. Fenton, n.d. [c. 1888], in Rice, *Reminiscences of Lincoln*, 70–71; WHH quoted in Zall, *Abe Lincoln Laughing*, 5; John Hay to John Nicolay, September 11, 1863, in Hay, *Lincoln and the Civil War*, 91. Some Euro-

pean journalists agreed with Hay's assessment: see *The Times* [London], September 17, 1863. See also WHH to C. O. Poole, Springfield, Ill., January 9, 1886, Herndon-Weik Collection, LC.

34. For Lincoln's application in perfecting the English language, see Chandler, unpublished reminiscences, Chandler Papers, USAHEC; Brooks, "Personal Reminiscences," 565–67; WHH, notes on "Lincoln Individuality," n.d., Herndon-Weik Collection, LC; Douglas L. Wilson, *Lincoln's Sword: The Presidency and the Power of Words* (New York: Vintage, 2006); AL, "Remarks at Opening of Patent Office Fair" [Sanitary Commission Fair], February 22, 1864, *CW*, 7:197–98; see also AL, "Response to a Serenade," April 10, 1865, ibid., 8:394.

35. Dispatch from Henry Villard, January 26, 1861, in Henry Villard, *Lincoln on the Eve of '61: A Journalist's Story,* ed. Harold G. Villard and Oswald Garrison Villard (Westport, Conn.: Greenwood Press, 1974), 55; Reminiscence of Henry Ward Beecher, n.d. [c. 1888], in Rice, *Reminiscences of Lincoln,* 249–50; Diary of Charles Wainwright, January 19, 1862, in Charles S. Wainwright, *A Diary of Battle: The Personal Journals of Colonel Charles S. Wainwright, 1861–1865,* ed. Allan Nevins (New York: Harcourt, Brace & World, 1962), 10; WHH, "Analysis of the Character of Abraham Lincoln," [December 12], 1865, William Henry Herndon Papers, HL; George B. McClellan to wife [Mary Ellen McClellan], Washington, D.C., November 17, 1861, in McClellan, *The Civil War Papers,* 135–36; Francis Donaldson to Jacob Donaldson, March 3, 1864, in William C. Davis, *Lincoln's Men: How President Lincoln Became Father to an Army and a Nation* (New York: Free Press, 1999), 133–34; entry of March 27, 1861, Russell, *My Diary,* 37–38; Nathaniel Hawthorne for *Atlantic Monthly,* July 1862, in Wilson, *Intimate Memories,* 465; James A. Garfield to Crete [Lucretia Garfield], Columbus, February 17, 1861, in John Shaw, ed., *Crete and James: Personal Letters of Lucretia and James Garfield* (East Lansing: Michigan State University Press, 1994), 107; James A. Garfield to Burke Aaron Hinsdale, Columbus, February 17, 1861, in Mary L. Hinsdale, ed., *Garfield–Hinsdale Letters: Correspondence Between James Abram Garfield and Burke Aaron Hinsdale* (Ann Arbor: University of Michigan Press, 1949), 56–57; *Diary of George Templeton Strong,* January 29, 1862, 3:204.

36. For AL's ability to "whistle off" ridicule, see WHH, "Lincoln's Ambition—selfishness—Envy—Jealousy &c," n.d. (on letterhead marked "188"), Herndon-Weik Collection, LC; Enoch Huggins to Joseph Huggins, Orange Prairie, Ill., July 26, 1858, in Harry E. Pratt, ed., *Concerning Mr. Lincoln, in Which Abraham Lincoln Is Pictured as He Appeared to Letter Writers of His Time* (Springfield, Ill.: The Abraham Lincoln Association, 1944), 18; AL, "Speech at Springfield, Ill.," July 17, 1858, *CW*, 2:506; William H. Crook, "Lincoln as I Knew Him," *Harper's Monthly Magazine,* June 1907, 47; John J. Pullen, *Comic Relief: The Life and Laughter of Artemus Ward, 1834–1867* (Hamden, Conn.: Archon, 1983), 4 and 32; "Shaky," *Vanity Fair,* June 9, 1860, reproduced in Rufus Rockwell Wilson, *Lincoln in Caricature: 165 Posters, Cartoons and Drawings for the Press* (Elmira, N.Y.: Primavera Press, 1945), 4, pl. 1; two-faced Lincoln as "Honest old Abe on the Stump, Springfield 1858," reproduced in ibid., 40–41, pl. 20; *Chicago Tribune,* December 3, 1863, quoted in Hay, *Inside Lincoln's White House,* 327–28, n299.

37. For AL's sensitivity, see WHH to [Jesse] Weik, Springfield, Ill., January 7, 1886, Herndon-Weik Collection, LC; Rice, *Reminiscences of Lincoln,* xxviii; *Diary of Orville Hickman Browning,* December 18, 1862, 1:600–601. AL's smutty rhyme "The Chronicles of Reuben" is in J. W. Wartmann to WHH, Rockport, Ind., July 21, 1865, *HI,* 79; Elizabeth Crawford to WHH, January 4, 1866, ibid., 152. For AL's early public writings, see AL and Mr. Talbott, "First Reply to James Adams," September 6, 1837, *CW,* 1:95; AL, "Second Reply to Adams," October 18, 1837, ibid., 1:105. AL's touchiness about his 1861 arrival in Washington is evident in AL, "Draft Fragment of Speech for Baltimore Sanitary Fair," [April 1864], ibid., 7:303; see also Gerald J. Prokopowicz, *Did Lincoln Own Slaves? And Other Frequently Asked Questions About Abraham Lincoln* (New York: Pantheon, 2008), 78–79; "Movements of Mr. Lincoln," *Vanity Fair,* March 9, 1861; *Harper's Weekly,* January 31, 1863; AL to Reverdy Johnson, Washington, D.C., July 16, 1862, *CW,* 5:342–43; AL, "Reply to Emancipation Memorial Presented by Chicago Christians of All Denominations," September 13, 1862, ibid., 5:421; AL to Carl Schurz, Washington, D.C., November 10 and

24, 1862, ibid., 5:493–95 and 509; Carl Schurz, *The Reminiscences of Carl Schurz* (New York: McClure, 1907), 2:395–96; Herman Haupt, *Reminiscences of General Herman Haupt* (Milwaukee: Wright & Joys, 1901), 298. The author found many dozen contemporary accounts of such incidents. For an example of AL's finely worded nonconfrontation policy, see AL to James M. Cutts Jr., Washington, D.C., October 26, 1863, *CW,* 6:538.

38. *Illinois State Register,* November 23, 1839, quoted in Zall, *Abe Lincoln Laughing,* 4; entry of September 3, 1861, Russell, *My Diary,* 523; William Thompson Lusk to mother, Meridian Hill, September 6, 1862, and Falmouth, Mass., December 16, 1862, both in William Thompson Lusk, *War Letters of William Thompson Lusk, Captain, Assistant Adjutant-General, United States Volunteers, 1861–1863* (New York: Privately published, 1911), 188–89 and 244–45; entry of January 4, 1863, Wainwright, *A Diary of Battle,* 156; Charles S. Morehead, speech delivered to the Southern Club in Liverpool, England, October 9, 1862, in David Rankin Barbee and Milledge L. Bonham Jr., eds., "Fort Sumter Again," *Mississippi Valley Historical Review* 28, no. 1 (June 1941): 71; undated entry [January 1862], Adam Gurowski, *Diary from March 4, 1861 to November 12, 1862* (Boston: Lee & Shepard, 1862), 144.

39. George B. McClellan to wife [Mary Ellen McClellan], November 17, 1861, in McClellan, *The Civil War Papers,* 135–36; Diary of Salmon P. Chase, September 23, 1863, in Salmon P. Chase, *The Salmon P. Chase Papers,* ed. John Niven et al. (Kent, Ohio: Kent State University Press, 1993–1998), 1:452; Edwin M. Stanton to Charles A. Dana, January 24, 1862, Charles A. Dana Papers, LC. See also Charles A. Dana, *Recollections of the Civil War with the Leaders at Washington and in the Field in the Sixties* (New York: D. Appleton, 1902), 261–62; Benjamin B. French to Pamela French, Washington, D.C., n.d. [early August] 1864, French Papers, LC.

40. For AL's willingness to have his picture taken, see Mark E. Neely Jr. and Harold Holzer, *The Lincoln Family Album* (New York: Doubleday, 1990), 60; see also Stephen Hess and Sandy Northrop, *Drawn and Quartered: The History of American Political Cartoons* (Montgomery, Ala.: Elliott & Clark, 1996), 38 and 45–47; Roger Penn Cuff, "The American Editorial Cartoon—A Critical Historical Sketch," *Journal of Educational Sociology* 19, no. 2 (October 1945): 87–96. The *New York Herald* article, "The Great Crime—Abraham Lincoln's Place in History," appeared on April 17, 1865.

41. James E. Combs and Dan Nimmo, *The Comedy of Democracy* (Westport, Conn.: Praeger, 1996), 15–17, 48–49, 108–9, and 122; Hess and Northrop, *Drawn and Quartered,* 30; Jon Grinspan, "'Sorrowfully Amusing': The Popular Comedy of the Civil War," *Journal of the Civil War Era* 1, no. 3 (September 2011): 313–38; William F. Fry, "The Power of Political Humor," *The Journal of Popular Culture* 10, no. 1 (Summer 1976): 231; William Shepard Walsh, *Abraham Lincoln and the London Punch: Cartoons, Comments and Poems, Published in the London Charivari, During the American Civil War (1861–1865)* (New York: Moffat, Yard, 1909); Howard Lessoff, *The Civil War with "Punch"* (Wendell, N.C.: Broadfoot, 1984); Gary Bunker, *From Rail-splitter to Icon: Lincoln's Images in Illustrated Periodicals, 1860–1865* (Kent, Ohio: Kent State University Press, 2001).

42. Joseph Medill to AL, Chicago, June 19, 1860, ALP-LC; AL, "Memorandum Concerning the *New York Herald,*" c. February 28, 1863, *CW,* 6:120. For more on Bennett, see Robert S. Harper, *Lincoln and the Press* (New York: McGraw-Hill, 1951), 319–24.

43. David Kunzle, "200 Years of the Great American Freedom to Complain," *Art in America* 65, no. 2 (March–April 1977): 99–105; H. L. Mencken, *A Mencken Chrestomathy* (New York: Alfred A. Knopf, 1949), 622. For lampooning Buchanan, see issues of *Vanity Fair,* November 1860 through March 1861.

44. Diary of Henry J. Raymond, January 22, 1863, in Henry J. Raymond, "Extracts from the Journal of Henry J. Raymond," *Scribner's Monthly,* January 1880, 424; *New York Herald,* February 19, 1864; Brooks, "Personal Reminiscences," 567. The wood engraving in *Harper's Weekly* of January 3, 1863, was based on Alfred. R. Waud's drawing, which depicts Uncle Sam rather than Columbia confronting Lincoln: Prints and Photographs Division (DRAW/ US-Waud, no. 63), LC. For the *New York World* episode, see Harper, *Lincoln and the Press,* 305–8; Lamon, *Recollections,* 144–49; AL, "Memorandum Concerning Ward H. Lamon

and the Antietam Episode," c. September 12, 1864, *CW,* 7:548–49; Harper found that the source for the story was fictitious, but Lincoln did not entirely deny the events. For accounts of AL's rudeness, merriment, and ribald storytelling during that visit, see notation by Stephen Minot Weld, *War Diary and Letters of Stephen Minot Weld, 1861–1865* (Cambridge: Riverside Press, 1912), 83n; entries of October 1 and 3, 1862, Wainwright, *A Diary of Battle,* 109–10.

45. For comic publications of the era, see Alice Fahs, *The Imagined Civil War: Popular Literature of the North and South, 1861–1865* (Chapel Hill: University of North Carolina Press, 2001), 204–5; Grinspan, "Popular Comedy of the Civil War."

46. James T. Nardin, "Civil War Humor: The War in *Vanity Fair,*" *Civil War History* 2, no. 3 (September 1956): 67–85; the antiproclamation song is reprinted on 75. See also *Vanity Fair,* January 4, 1862; James R. Gilmore, *Personal Recollections of Abraham Lincoln and the Civil War* (Boston: L. C. Page, 1898), 67; F. B. Carpenter, *Six Months at the White House with Abraham Lincoln* (New York: Hurd & Houghton, 1866), 150.

47. Browne quoted in C. C. Ruthrauff, "Artemus Ward at Cleveland," *Scribner's Monthly,* October 1878, 791; Melville Landon, "Travelling with Artemus Ward," *The Galaxy,* September 1871, 443; Artemus Ward [Charles Farrar Browne], *The Complete Works of Artemus Ward* (New York: G. W. Dillingham, 1898), 72 and 186. See also Robert E. Abrams, "Charles Farrar Browne (Artemus Ward)," in *Dictionary of Literary Biography, XI: American Humorists, 1800–1950,* ed. Stanley Trachtenberg (Detroit: Gale, 1982), 1:60–68; John Q. Reed, "Civil War Humor: Artemus Ward," *Civil War History* 2, no. 3 (September 1956): 87–101.

48. Reed, "Artemus Ward," 100–101; Don C. Seitz, *Artemus Ward (Charles Farrar Browne): A Biography and Bibliography* (New York: Harper Brothers, 1919), 115–16; *Vanity Fair,* January 4, April 26, and July 5, 1862; Artemus Ward [Charles Farrar Browne], *His Book* (New York: Carleton, 1862), 34–35.

49. Chase Diary, September 22, 1862, *Chase Papers,* 1:393. Stanton's comments are in Seitz, *Artemus Ward,* 113–14. "Artemus Ward and the President," *New York Herald,* February 3, 1863, is quoted in Pullen, *Comic Relief,* 65–66.

50. Orpheus C. Kerr [Robert Henry Newell], *Orpheus C. Kerr Papers: First Series* (New York: Blakeman & Mason, 1863), 9; Frederick Seward to mother, March 21, 1861, Seward Papers, UR; Michael Butler, "Robert Henry Newell (Orpheus C. Kerr)," in *Dictionary of Literary Biography, XI,* 2:350–54 ("graceful door-hinge" on 351–52); *Diary of George Templeton Strong,* February 17, 1863, 3:300. Among those who mentioned AL's attraction to Orpheus C. Kerr are George Alfred Townsend, *The Life, Crime and Capture of John Wilkes Booth with a Full Sketch of the Conspiracy of which He Was the Leader and the Pursuit, Trial and Execution of His Accomplices* (New York: Dick and Fitzgerald, 1865), 58; Reminiscence of David Ross Locke, n.d. [c. 1888], in Rice, *Reminiscences of Lincoln,* 448.

51. Kerr, *Orpheus C. Kerr Papers;* Butler, "Robert Henry Newell," 350–51; Ellen Bremner, "Civil War Humor: Orpheus C. Kerr," *Civil War History* 2, no. 3 (September 1956): 122–28.

52. The best study of Locke is John M. Harrison, *The Man Who Made Nasby, David Ross Locke* (Chapel Hill: University of North Carolina Press, 1969); Locke's use of language is discussed on 100. See also [David Ross Locke], "The Return of Vallandigham," in *The Struggles (Social, Financial and Political) of Petroleum V. Nasby* (Boston: Lee & Shepard, 1888), 124; [David Ross Locke], "Shows Why He Should Not Be Drafted," in *The Nasby Papers* (Indianapolis: C. O. Perrine, 1864), 9 (other Nasbyisms can be found on 3–4, 5, and 30); Fahs, *Imagined Civil War,* 213.

53. Locke, "Masked Traitors," *Bucyrus* [Ohio] *Journal,* August 16, 1861, quoted in Harrison, *Man Who Made Nasby,* 61. Locke is quoted in Harrison, *Man Who Made Nasby,* 97 and 100; I have paraphrased Harrison's commentary, 101. See also Richard Carwardine, "Just Laughter: The Moral Springs of Lincoln's Humor," paper delivered at Lincoln Forum, 2009, and Richard Carwardine, *Lincoln's Just Laughter: Humour and Ethics in the Civil War Union* (London: The British Library, 2014; www.bl.uk/ecclescentre).

54. Reminiscence of David Ross Locke, n.d. [c. 1888], in Rice, *Reminiscences of Lincoln,* 447–49; Carwardine, *Lincoln's Just Laughter;* entry of October 11, 1864, Hay, *Inside*

Lincoln's White House, 239; entry of February 7, 1865, Welles, *Diary of Gideon Welles,* 2:238; Carpenter, *Six Months at the White House,* 150–51; Harrison, *Man Who Made Nasby,* 112–13; Charles Sumner, Introduction to Locke, *Struggles,* 14–15. Instances of Lincoln reading *Nasby* aloud can be found in Brooks, *Washington in Lincoln's Time,* 105–6.

55. Sumner, Introduction to Locke, *Struggles,* 13.

56. "SNB" to AL, n.d. [summer 1863], Edwin W. Stanton Papers, LC; A. G. Frick to AL, February 14, 1861, quoted in Harold Holzer, *Lincoln, President-Elect: Abraham Lincoln and the Great Secession Winter 1860–1861* (New York: Simon & Schuster, 2008), 327; "What Will Come of Re-Electing Lincoln," *The Old Guard,* September 1864, quoted in Frank L. Klement, *Lincoln's Critics: The Copperheads of the North* (Shippensburg, Pa.: White Mane, 1999), 200; Pomeroy's epithet in *La Crosse* [Wisc.] *Democrat,* August 24, 1864, quoted in ibid., 135.

57. Klement, *Lincoln's Critics,* 136–39; Harrison, *Man Who Made Nasby,* 86–87; Carwardine, *Lincoln's Just Laughter.*

58. Locke, *Nasby Papers,* 41; Edward Lyulph Stanley to "Kate," Philadelphia, April 10, 1864, Edward Lyulph Stanley Papers, Cambridge University Library: Royal Commonwealth Society Library, Cambridge, U.K.

59. Horatio Seymour to AL, Albany, August 3 and 7, 1863, ALP-LC; AL to Seymour, August 7, 1863, *CW,* 6:370; William F. Havemeyer to AL, New York, August 4, 1863, ALP-LC; *West Chester* [Pa.] *Jeffersonian,* July 24, 1864, quoted in Ray H. Abrams, "*The Jeffersonian,* Copperhead Newspaper," *Pennsylvania Magazine of History and Biography* 57, no. 3 (July 1933): 279; Klement, *Lincoln's Critics,* 4–15 and 50–51; Jennifer L. Weber, *Copperheads: The Rise and Fall of Lincoln's Opponents in the North* (New York: Oxford University Press, 2006), 9, 52–53, and 77–78. For public concerns about corruption, see Michael Thomas Smith, *The Enemy Within: Fears of Corruption in the Civil War North* (Charlottesville: University of Virginia Press, 2011), 30–33.

60. Joel H. Silbey, *A Respectable Minority: The Democratic Party in the Civil War Era, 1860–1868* (New York: W. W. Norton, 1977), ix–x and 69–70; Melinda Lawson, *Patriot Fires: Forging a New American Nationalism in the Civil War North* (Lawrence: University Press of Kansas, 2002), 67–69, 71–72, and 83–85; Richard Carwardine, *Lincoln: A Life of Purpose and Power* (New York: Alfred A. Knopf, 2006), 167; Weber, *Copperheads,* 3; Charles H. Coleman, "The Use of the Term 'Copperhead' During the Civil War," *Mississippi Valley Historical Review* 25, no. 2 (September 1938): 263–64; George Partridge to [Henry] Dawes, St. Louis, January 27, 1863, Dawes Papers, LC; entry of August 17, 1863, in Adam Gurowski, *Diary from November 18, 1862 to October 18, 1863* (New York: Carleton, 1864), 302.

61. Jane Swisshelm to *St. Cloud* [Minn.] *Democrat,* February 9, 1863, in Jane Grey Swisshelm, *Crusader and Feminist: Letters of Jane Grey Swisshelm, 1858–1865,* ed. Arthur J. Larsen (Westport, Conn.: Hyperion Press, 1976), 173; Robert Churchill, "Liberty, Conscription, and Delusions of Grandeur: The Sons of Liberty Conspiracy of 1863–64," *Prologue* 30, no. 4 (Winter 1998): 297–300; W. Holmes to AL, Du Quoin, Ill., January 22, 1863, ALP-LC; Henry B. Carrington to AL and Edwin M. Stanton, Indianapolis, January 14 and March 19, 1863, both ALP-LC; F. P. Freese to Edwin M. Stanton, Philadelphia, March 23, 1863, Stanton Papers, LC; William S. Rosecrans to AL, St. Louis, June 14 and 22, 1864, ALP-LC; *CW,* 7:386–87n; entry of June 17, 1864, Hay, *Inside Lincoln's White House,* 204–8 ("malice" and "puerility" on 207). For a report on plot to overtake prisons, see *OR,* II, 8:684–89.

62. Weber, *Copperheads,* 10 and 216–17; Klement, *Lincoln's Critics,* 18; Churchill, "Liberty, Conscription, and Delusions of Grandeur," 297–300; Heintzelman Diary, October 20, 1864, Heintzelman Papers, LC.

63. Letters of John Jackson Kenley, July–August 1863, in author's possession; Oliver P. Morton to Edwin M. Stanton, Indianapolis, June 25, 1862, ALP-LC; W. R. Halloway to John G. Nicolay, Indianapolis, January 2, 1863, ALP-LC. The Democratic effort in Illinois resulted in prohibiting blacks from settling in the state: see Weber, *Copperheads,* 48–49. See also R. E. Lee to Jefferson Davis, opposite Williamsport, June 25, 1863, R. E. Lee Letterbook #4, Lee Family Papers, VHS.

64. Lawson, *Patriot Fires,* 71–72; diary of William B. Pratt quoted in Glenn C. Altschuler and

Stuart M. Blumin, *Rude Republic: Americans and Their Politics in the Nineteenth Century* (Princeton, N.J.: Princeton University Press, 2000), 17–50 and ("war Republicans") 157; Diary of Charles Mason, 1861–1865, typescript, Remey Family Papers, LC; John C. Gray Jr. to John C. Ropes, Maryland Heights, Md., October 15–20, 1862, in Worthington Chauncey Ford, ed., *War Letters, 1862–1865, of John Chipman Gray and John Codman Ropes* (Boston: Houghton Mifflin, 1927), 6.

65. Locke, *Struggles,* 92; ministers quoted in Carwardine, *Lincoln's Just Laughter,* 8.
66. Mark E. Neely Jr., *The Fate of Liberty: Abraham Lincoln and Civil Liberties* (New York: Oxford University Press, 1991), 196–98, 211, and 215; George B. Loring to Gen. B. F. Butler, Salem, Mass., August 6, 1861, in Benjamin F. Bulter, *Private and Official Correspondence of Gen. Benjamin F. Butler During the Period of the Civil War,* ed. Jesse Ames Marshall (N.p.: Privately published, 1917), 1:192; Charles Sumner to Francis Lieber, Boston, September 17, 1861, in Charles Sumner, *The Selected Letters of Charles Sumner,* ed. Beverly Wilson Palmer (Boston: Northeastern University Press, 1990), 2:79.
67. Locke, *Nasby Papers,* 42–43; Locke, *Struggles,* 48; Carwardine, *Lincoln: A Life of Purpose,* 255–57; AL, "Message to Congress in Special Session," July 4, 1861, *CW,* 4:421–41; AL to Erastus Corning and Others, Washington, D.C., [June 12], 1863, ibid., 6:260–69; AL to James C. Conkling, Washington, D.C., August 26, 1863, ibid., 6:406–10 (quotation on 410). The writ of habeas corpus is protected in U.S. Constitution, article 1, sect. 9.
68. Neely, *Fate of Liberty,* 12–13 and 27–28; Weber, *Copperheads,* 65–66; Resolution of Connecticut Assembly, December 2, 1862, ALP-LC; AL, "Proclamation Suspending the Writ of Habeas Corpus," September 24, 1862, *CW,* 5:436–37; opinion of Chief Justice Walter H. Lowrie in *Hodgson v. Millward,* February 1863, quoted in Abrams, "*The Jeffersonian,*" 275; entry of September 25, 1862, in David Hunter Strother, *A Virginia Yankee in the Civil War: The Diaries of David Hunter Strother,* ed. Cecil D. Eby Jr. (Chapel Hill: University of North Carolina Press, 1961), 118–19; John C. Gray to John C. Ropes, Fort Gaines, Ala., August 21, 1864, in Ford, *War Letters,* 377; Edward Bates to AL, Washington, D.C., July 5, 1861, ALP-LC; Edward Bates to AL, Washington, D.C., November 21, 1861, ALP-LC; for "lukewarmness," see Edward Bates to AL, Washington, D.C., May 20, 1863, ALP-LC.
69. *Diary of Orville Hickman Browning,* November 12, 1862, and May 17 and 23, 1863, 1:585 and 630–31. On the closing of the Baltimore newspaper, see Joshua M. Bosley and James R. Brewer to AL, Baltimore, October 5, 1864, ALP-LC; Reverdy Johnson to AL, Baltimore, October 6, 1864, ALP-LC; W. Kimmel and Joshua M. Bosley to AL, Washington, D.C., October 8, 1864, ALP-LC; Henry Wilson to AL, Natick, Mass., October 13, 1864 ("the stopage"), ALP-LC. For the Louisianan Sarah Morgan: see entry of July 10, 1862, in her *The Civil War Diary of a Southern Woman,* ed. Charles East (New York: Simon & Schuster, 1991), 160. The Confederate War Department employee was John B. Jones: see his *A Rebel War Clerk's Diary at the Confederate States Capital,* ed. Howard Swiggett (New York: Old Hickory Bookshop, 1935), 1:159.
70. Brooks, *Washington in Lincoln's Time,* 105–6. The Nasby piece so admired by AL was "On Negro Emigration," in Locke, *Nasby Papers,* 4.
71. Amasa Converse to son, [Philadelphia], August 23, 1861, ALP-LC; Amasa Converse to AL, Philadelphia, August 28, 1861, ALP-LC; Edward Lyulph Stanley to "mamma," New Orleans, May 27, 1864, Stanley Papers, Cambridge University Library; Neely, *Fate of Liberty,* 32–50; Anonymous ["T. Blank"] to Montgomery Blair, St. Louis, September 25, 1861, ALP-LC; Samuel T. Glover to Montgomery Blair, St. Louis, May 27, 1864, ALP-LC; Jeremiah T. Boyle to AL, Louisville, July 2, 1864, ALP-LC; Rufus K. Williams to AL, Louisville, July 8, 1864, ALP-LC. See also Harper, *Lincoln and the Press,* 290–302; AL, "Order for Draft of 300,000 Men," Washington, D.C., May 17, 1864, *CW,* 7:344. For examples of protests, see editorial, *New York World,* May 24, 1864, Manton Marble Papers, LC; Sydney H. Gay et al. to AL, May 19, 1864, ALP-LC.
72. Entry of July 10, 1861, Russell, *My Diary,* 399; Sydney Howard Gay to Adams S. Hill, New York, May 14, 1863, Sydney Howard Gay Family Papers, CU; Joseph Medill to John G. Nicolay, Niagara Falls, N.Y., May 17, [1863], Nicolay Papers, LC; W. Kimmel and Joshua

M. Bosley to AL, Washington, D.C., October 8, 1864, ALP-LC; Abrams, *"The Jefferso-nian,"* 270–76; William Russ Jr., "Franklin Weirick: 'Copperhead' of Central Pennsylva-nia," *Pennsylvania History: A Journal of Mid-Atlantic Studies* 5, no. 4 (October 1938): 246–56 (quotation on 248–49).

73. AL to John M. Schofield, Washington, D.C., May 27, 1863, *CW,* 6:234; AL to Charles Drake and Others, Washington, D.C., October 5, 1863, ibid., 6:500–501. For the Richard Carmichael case, see George Vickers to William Price, Chester Town, Md., June 3, 1862, ALP-LC; John A. Dix to Edward M. Stanton, Fort Monroe, June 25, 1862, ALP-LC; George Vickers to AL, Chester Town, Md., June 30, 1862, ALP-LC; AL to John W. Crisfield, Washington, D.C., June 26, 1862, *CW,* 5:285; see also the excellent paper by Brandon P. Righi, "'A Power Unknown to Our Laws': A Study of the Effect of Federal Policies on Border State Unionism in Kent County, Maryland 1861–1865," senior honors thesis, Washington College. n.d. [c. 2007], www.revcollege.washcoll.edu. For election and other civil violations, see, e.g., Mason Diary, November 2, 1864, Remey Papers, LC; George R. Dennis to Montgomery Blair, Frederick, Md., July 21, 1864, ALP-LC; Augustus W. Bradford to AL, Annapolis, Md., November 3, 1863, ALP-LC; John W. Crisfield to Montgomery Blair, Princess Anne [Co., Md.], November 8, 1863, ALP-LC; Augustus W. Bradford to Thomas G. Pratt et al., Annapolis, Md., November 22, 1863, ALP-LC. The folder in ALP-LC for November 16–21, 1863, contains numerous complaints about the conduct of elections. See also W. B. Campbell et al. to AL, n.d. [c. Oct. 1864], *CW,* 8:58–63n (AL quoted on 58). For AL replies, see AL to Bradford, November 2, 1863, ibid., 6:556–57 and 557–58n; AL to Blair, November 11, 1863, ibid., 7:9.

74. In Missouri Lincoln revoked Frémont's proclamation, ignored Schofield's actions, and questioned the wisdom of Rosecrans, but did not order the latter to reverse his decision. For William Rosecrans's order—Special Orders No. 61, of March 7, 1864—see William M. Leftwich, *Martyrdom in Missouri: A History of Religious Proscription, the Seizure of Churches, and the Persecution of Ministers of the Gospel, in the State of Missouri During the Late Civil War* (St. Louis: Southwestern, 1870), 2:64–66; Rev. A. P. Forman to Edward Bates, Hannibal, Mo., March 15, 1864, ALP-LC; AL to John C. Frémont, Washington, D.C., September 2 and 11, 1861, *CW,* 4:506 and 517–18; AL to Rosecrans, April 4, 1864, ibid., 7:283–84. See also Neely, *Fate of Liberty,* 32–50; Michael Fellman, *Inside War: The Guerrilla Conflict in Missouri During the American Civil War* (New York: Oxford University Press, 1989), 89–97 and 112–27.

75. Mark W. Delahay to AL, n.d. [June–July 1863], ALP-LC; AL to James H. Lane, Executive Mansion, July 17, 1863, *CW,* 5:334; Albert Castel, "The Jayhawkers and Copperheads of Kansas," *Civil War History* 5, no. 3 (September 1959): 283–93; AL to Thomas C. Fletcher, Washington, D.C., February 20, 1865, *CW,* 8:308.

76. James M. Ashley to AL, Toledo, June 23, 1863, ALP-LC; General Orders No. 38, *OR,* I, 23, pt. 2:237. For discussion of the Vallandigham case, see Michael Burlingame, *Abraham Lincoln: A Life* (Baltimore: Johns Hopkins University Press, 2008), 2:505–8; Frank L. Klement, "Clement L. Vallandigham's Exile in the Confederacy, May 25–June 17, 1863," *Journal of Southern History* 31, no. 2 (May 1965): 149–62; entry of June 17, 1864, Hay, *Inside Lincoln's White House,* 207–8; AL to John Brough and Samuel P. Heintzelman, Washington, D.C., June 20, 1864, *CW,* 7:402.

77. Craig D. Tenney, "To Suppress or Not to Suppress: Abraham Lincoln and the *Chicago Times,*" *Civil War History* 27, no. 3 (September 1981): 248–59; Stanton's final order of June 4, 1863, to Burnside, under direction of AL, is on 257n. See also General Orders No. 84, June 1, 1863, *OR,* I, 23, pt. 2:381; Citizens of Chicago to AL, Chicago, June 3, 1863, *OR,* I, 23, pt. 2:385; Isaac N. Arnold and Lyman Trumbull to AL, Chicago, June 3, 1863, ALP-LC; N. H. McLean, General Orders No. 91, June 4, 1863, *OR,* I, 23, pt. 2:386; AL to Edwin Stanton, June 4, 1864, *OR,* III, 3:252; E. D. Townsend to Burnside, June 4, 1864, *OR,* III, 3:252; entry of June 3, 1863, Welles, *Diary of Gideon Welles,* 321–22; Burlingame, *Abraham Lincoln,* 2:507.

78. "Cooking the Hell-Broth," *The Old Guard,* June 1864, 140; "Keep on the Track," *Vanity Fair,* November 22, 1862; *Diary of George Templeton Strong,* September 6, 1864, 3:83.

79. Although Locke remained a loyal Republican, he thought AL was too amiable in his prosecution of the war, overly concerned with the defense of Washington, and obsessive in his mistrust of Democratic-leaning generals. He was dismayed by the President's insensitivity in 1862, when a White House ball was held while the troops suffered in the field, writing an editorial called "The Dance of Death." See also chapter 5. Neither was he averse to placing the blame for Union failures squarely on the commander in chief, particularly after the debacles at Manassas and Fredericksburg. See Harrison, *Man Who Made Nasby,* 55–56; Locke's editorials in *Bucyrus* [Ohio] *Journal* and *Findlay* [Ohio] *Jeffersonian* are in ibid., 57–58, 87–90, 93–94, and 118. See also "An Interview with the President," in Locke, *Struggles,* 94–95; Kerr, *Orpheus C. Kerr Papers,* 377.

80. AL to Isaac Arnold, Washington, D.C., May 25, 1864, *CW,* 7:361. Examples of extraordinary actions by earlier presidents include: Washington proclaimed the doctrine of neutrality on his own; Adams sidestepped the Congress to send commissioners to France to end a quasi-war with that country; Jefferson, in theory a strict constructionist, inaugurated war with the Barbary pirates; when France looked like it was going to renege on its debt in 1831, Jackson ordered the Navy to prepare for active service; Polk ordered Zachary Taylor across the Nueces River and precipitated the Mexican War, presenting it to Congress as a fait accompli—see Schaffter and Mathews, *Powers of the President,* 35–36. See also James G. Randall, *Constitutional Problems Under Lincoln* (Urbana: University of Illinois Press, 1951), 120–21.

81. AL, "Speech to One Hundred Sixty-Fourth Ohio Regiment," August 18, 1864, *CW,* 7:504–5; AL, "Response to a Serenade," October 19, 1864, ibid., 8:52–53; AL to Benjamin Butler, Washington, D.C., August 9, 1864, ibid., 7:487–88; AL, "Address at Sanitary Fair, Baltimore," April 18, 1864, ibid., 7:301–2; AL to Albert G. Hodges, Washington, D.C., April 4, 1864, ibid., 7:281.

82. Neely, *Fate of Liberty,* 69–71; *Diary of Edward Bates,* September 14, 1863, 306–7; Chase Diary, September 14, 1863, *Chase Papers,* 1:441–42; AL to Erastus Corning and Others, [June 12], 1863, *CW,* 6:260–69 (quotation on 263). Michael Burlingame's commentary in *Abraham Lincoln,* 2:508, is very helpful, as is Neely, *Fate of Liberty,* 196–99.

83. Erastus Corning to AL, Albany, N.Y., June 30, 1863, ALP-LC.

84. AL, "Response to Serenade," n.d. [November 10, 1864], *CW,* 8:100–101; entry of June 1, 1864, Welles, *Diary of Gideon Welles,* 2:43.

85. Henry Hayward to sister, Dumfries, Va., March 1, 1863, in Ambrose Henry Hayward, *Last to Leave the Field: The Life and Letters of First Sergeant Ambrose Henry Hayward, 28th Pennsylvania Volunteer Infantry,* ed. Timothy J. Orr (Knoxville: University of Tennessee Press, 2011), 132; Peter B. Lee to John G. Nicolay, camp near Murfreesboro, Tenn., March 26, 1863, Nicolay Papers, LC.

86. Horatio Seymour artfully dodged the President's attempts to engage him in conversation and remained a powerful, credible spokesperson for the Peace Democrats. Saying that he would meet with anyone who acted "within the scope of their Constitutional powers," he essentially foreclosed the opportunity of an interview. When Fernando Wood, a savvy but slippery opponent, approached Lincoln with plans to negotiate for peace, or to calm domestic nerves through an amnesty, he was met with suspicion. Lincoln also appears to have ignored those who recommended he build bridges by conceding a few points to the Copperheads or by showing more appreciation for the thousands of Democrats who were loyally serving in the Army. See Weber, *Copperheads,* 10 and 117; Neely, *Fate of Liberty,* 192–93 and 209–10; Silbey, *A Respectable Minority;* AL to Horatio Seymour, Washington, D.C., March 23, 1863, *CW,* 6:145–46; Horatio Seymour to AL, Albany, N.Y., April 14, 1863, ALP-LC; Fernando Wood to AL, New York, September 12, 1862, ALP-LC; Wood to AL, Washington, D.C., April 29, 1864, ALP-LC; Memorandum of John G. Nicolay, December 14, 1863, Nicolay Papers, LC; entry of June 17, 1864, Hay, *Inside Lincoln's White House,* 208; see also Samuel M. Shaw to Thurlow Weed, Cooperstown, N.Y., February 15, 1863, ALP-LC.

87. Washington C. Cassell to AL, Franklin, Ind., March 4, 1864, ALP-LC; Reverdy Johnson to the Committee on the Arrangements for the Meeting Held in New York on 17 September 1864, copy in *The Liberator,* October 21, 1864, David Rankin Barbee Papers, GU; entry of March 5, 1863, Taft Diary, LC.

88. John T. Hanks to AL, Canyon Vill[e], Ore., February 25, 1864, ALP-LC (series II).
89. For more on the stance of the *New York World* during the four years of Lincoln's presidency, see Harper, *Lincoln and the Press*, 289–90 and 305–8.
90. The letters Townsend filed with the *World* in 1865 were collected and published as a book later that year, see Townsend, *The Life, Crime and Capture of John Wilkes Booth*, 58.

CHAPTER 3. TWO EMANCIPATORS MEET

1. This chapter is an expanded version of Elizabeth Brown Pryor, "Brief Encounter: A New York Cavalryman's Striking Conversation with Abraham Lincoln," *JALA* 30, no. 2 (Summer 2009): 1–24. Lucien Waters's letter to his brother Lemuel of August 12, 1862, which describes this meeting, can be found in full at the end of this chapter.

2. Lucien P. Waters to parents, Camp Relief, Washington, D.C., April 2, 1862, and Waters to Lemuel Waters, Camp Relief, Washington, D.C., August 12, 1862, both in Lucien P. Waters Papers, NYHS. Many complained of the heat in the summer of 1862 and drought conditions were recorded in numerous areas around Washington, D.C. The temperature did not climb to the degree Waters felt it did, but did hover above 90 degrees for weeks. See, e.g., John Hay to J. G. Nicolay, Washington, D.C., August 11, 1862, in John Hay, *Lincoln and the Civil War in the Diaries and Letters of John Hay*, ed. Tyler Dennett (1939; repr., Westport, Conn.: Negro Universities Press, 1972), 43; Clara Barton to Mary Norton, Washington, D.C., July 4, 1862, Mary Norton Papers, DU; Diary of Chauncy Pond Joslin, July 5–August 9, 1862, at www.cpjoslincivilwar.org; *Daily National Intelligencer*, July 31 and August 7, 1862.

3. Seventh Decennial Census of the United States (1850), Ward 12, New York, NARA; Lucian [*sic*] P. Waters Certificate of Service, Adjutant General's Office, March 31, 1917, Civil War Pension Records, RG 94, NARA (Waters is also at times referred to as "Lucius" in these and other records); Waters to the Committee for the Relief of the Contrabands at Port Royal and Elsewhere, Plainfield, N.J., February 21, 1862, Waters Papers, NYHS. Waters must have either attended or read about the meeting the American Missionary Association held at the Cooper Institute on February 20, 1862, to jump-start the work with the freedmen, because his letter offering to volunteer is dated the following day. See also Willie Lee Rose, *Rehearsal for Reconstruction* (New York: Vintage, 1967), 41.

4. Waters to parents, March 20, 1861, Waters Papers, NYHS; Waters to the Committee for the Relief of the Contrabands, February 21, 1862, Waters Papers, NYHS; Waters to parents, Port Tobacco, Md., June 18 and July 13, 1862, both Waters Papers, NYHS.

5. Thomas West Smith, *The Story of a Cavalry Regiment: "Scott's 900" Eleventh New York Cavalry, from the St. Lawrence River to the Gulf of Mexico, 1861–1865* (Chicago: Veteran Association of the Regiment, 1897); Henry Murray Calvert, *Reminiscences of a Boy in Blue, 1862–1865* (New York: G. P. Putnam's Sons, 1920), 25. The regimental history is at www.civilwar.nps.gov/cwss/regiments.cfm.

6. Waters Certificate of Service, NARA; Calvert, *Reminiscences of a Boy in Blue*, 60; Smith, *Story of a Cavalry Regiment*, 11–12; Waters to parents, Camp Relief, Washington, D.C., May 11, 1862, Waters Papers, NYHS.

7. Smith, *Story of a Cavalry Regiment*, 11 and 15–16; Calvert, *Reminiscences of a Boy in Blue*, 19; Waters to parents, Camp Relief, Washington, D.C., n.d. [Spring 1862], Waters Papers, NYHS; Waters to parents, Camp Relief, Washington, D.C., May 10, 1862, Waters Papers, NYHS; In February 1863 he was made Acting Battalion Sergeant. Waters's duties increased in August 1863, when he was given charge of all teams and teamsters as wagon master of the regiment: Waters to parents, Camp Relief, Washington, D.C., August 25, 1863, Waters Papers, NYHS; Waters Pension Records, NARA.

8. Calvert, *Reminiscences of a Boy in Blue*, 18; Smith, *Story of a Cavalry Regiment*, 25; Walt Whitman, "Abraham Lincoln," no. 45, August 12, 1863, in Walt Whitman, *Memoranda During the War and Death of Abraham Lincoln*, ed. Roy P. Basler (Bloomington: Indiana

University Press, 1962), 6–7; Joseph Hopkins Twichell quoted in Gerald J. Prokopowicz, *Did Lincoln Own Slaves? And Other Frequently Asked Questions About Abraham Lincoln* (New York: Pantheon, 2008), 142; Matthew Pinsker, *Lincoln's Sanctuary: Abraham Lincoln and the Soldiers' Home* (New York: Oxford University Press, 2003), 15 and 50. Pinsker calculated that AL began receiving the escort in late summer 1862, but Waters's letters indicate that it had already started by June of that year.

9. Pinsker, *Lincoln's Sanctuary*, 60; Smith, *Story of a Cavalry Regiment*, 25; and F. B. Carpenter, *Six Months at the White House with Abraham Lincoln* (New York: Hurd & Houghton, 1866), 64–67. On AL's mock disguise, see chapter 6.

10. Waters to parents, July 13, 1862, Waters Papers, NYHS; Calvert, *Reminiscences of a Boy in Blue,* 20–21.

11. Waters to parents, July 13, 1862, Waters Papers, NYHS; Waters to parents, Camp Relief, Washington, D.C., October 7, 1862, Waters Papers, NYHS; Smith, *Story of a Cavalry Regiment*, 22–24, 32, 45, and 70–71; Calvert, *Reminiscences of a Boy in Blue,* 82–83.

12. Eric Foner, *The Fiery Trial: Abraham Lincoln and American Slavery* (New York: W. W. Norton, 2010), 170, 175, and 194–95.

13. Waters to parents, Camp Relief, Washington, D.C., June 18, 1862, Waters Papers, NYHS; Waters to parents, July 13, 1862, Waters Papers, NYHS; Smith, *Story of a Cavalry Regiment,* 23; Calvert, *Reminiscences of a Boy in Blue,* 48–49.

14. W. A. Gorman to Henry Wilson, Washington, D.C., December 22, 1861, Henry Wilson Papers, LC; [Joseph K.] Mansfield to wife, Newports News [*sic*], Va., May 23, 1862, Joseph K. Mansfield Papers, United States Military Academy, West Point, N.Y.; Mansfield to wife, Suffolk, Va., June 15, 1862, Mansfield Papers, U.S. Military Academy.

15. Benjamin Quarles, *Lincoln and the Negro* (New York: Da Capo, 1962), 70–71 and 78; Statement of James H. Haight, in Smith, *Story of a Cavalry Regiment*, 267; Waters to parents, June 18, 1862, Waters Papers, NYHS; Waters to parents, Chapel Point, Md., November 15, 1862, Waters Papers, NYHS.

16. Allen C. Guelzo, *Lincoln's Emancipation Proclamation: The End of Slavery in America* (New York: Simon & Schuster, 2004), 3–5 and 29–38; Foner, *The Fiery Trial,* 201–2; Orville Hickman Browning, *The Diary of Orville Hickman Browning, 1850–1864,* ed. Theodore Calvin Pease and James G. Randall (Springfield: Illinois State Historical Society, 1925), 1:555.

17. Waters to parents, Camp Relief, Washington, D.C., August 5, 1862, Waters Papers, NYHS; Waters to parents, Chapel Point, Md., December 10, 1862, Waters Papers, NYHS. See also Calvert, *Reminiscences of a Boy in Blue,* 48–49; Smith, *Story of a Cavalry Regiment,* 23.

18. For a look at the variety of attitudes that motivated Northern soldiers, see Chandra Manning, *What This Cruel War Was Over: Soldiers, Slavery and the Civil War* (New York: Alfred A. Knopf, 2007); Smith, *Story of a Cavalry Regiment,* 267; Calvert, *Reminiscences of a Boy in Blue,* 196–98. The Waters quotations are from his letters to, respectively, parents, August 5, 1862, "Bro. Lemuel," August 12, 1862, and "Bro. James," Chapel Point, Md., November 15, 1862, all Waters Papers, NYHS.

19. Waters to parents, July 13, 1862; Waters to parents, August 5, 1862; Waters to parents, November 15, 1862; and Waters to parents, Chapel Point, Md., February 10, 1863, all Waters Papers, NYHS; AL, "Address on Colonization to a Deputation of Negroes," August 14, 1862, *CW,* 5:370–75; Waters's notation on back of [John Brent] to Waters, Washington, D.C., December 6, 1862, Waters Papers, NYHS.

20. Waters to parents, August 5, 1862; Waters to parents, November 15, 1862; Waters to parents, Chapel Point, Md., December 10, 1862; and Waters to parents, February 10, 1863, all Waters Papers, NYHS. For examples of Waters's later work on behalf of ex-slaves, see Waters, fragment of letter or report on condition of freedmen in Louisiana, July [1864], Waters Papers, NYHS; Report, Camp of 11th N.Y. Vol. Cav., Manning's Plantation, July 28, 1864, Waters Papers, NYHS.

21. Waters to parents, June 18, 1862, Waters Papers, NYHS.

22. Waters to parents, Camp Relief, Washington, D.C., July 21, 1862; Waters to "Bro. Lemuel," August 12, 1862, both Waters Papers, NYHS.

23. Waters to parents, Camp Relief, Washington, D.C., July 31, 1862; Waters to parents, August 5, 1862; and Waters to "Bro. Lemuel," August 12, 1862, all Waters Papers, NYHS. Many people described AL's reluctance to turn away those who wished to speak to him—see, e.g., Joshua Speed to WHH, Louisville, January 12, 1866, *HI*, 156; John Hay to WHH, Paris, September 5, 1866, ibid., 331; Henry Wilson to WHH, Natick, Mass., May 30, 1867, ibid., 561–62; Carpenter, *Six Months at the White House,* 281.

24. An almost identical description of AL perched on the White House steps is found in Reminiscence of Donn Piatt, n.d. [c. 1888], in Allen Thorndike Rice, ed., *Reminiscences of Abraham Lincoln by Distinguished Men of His Time* (New York: North American Review, 1888), 491: "Arriving at the entrance to the White House . . . The President sat down upon the steps of the porch, and continued his study of the protest. I have him photographed on my mind, as he sat there, and a strange picture he presented. His long, slender legs were drawn up until his knees were level with his chin, while his long arms held the paper, which he studied regardless of the crowd before him." See also the undated statement of John Hanks to WHH, *HI*, 142; William G. Greene to WHH, Tallula, Ill., November 27, 1865, ibid., 455; Henry Villard, *Memoirs of Henry Villard, Journalist and Financier, 1835–1900* (Boston: Houghton Mifflin, 1904), 1:143; Conversation with Hamilton Fish, March 6, 1874, in John G. Nicolay, *An Oral History of Abraham Lincoln: John G. Nicolay's Interviews and Essays,* ed. Michael Burlingame (Carbondale: Southern Illinois University Press, 1996), 52; statements of S. P. Kase and Frederick Douglass in Doris Kearns Goodwin, *Team of Rivals: The Political Genius of Abraham Lincoln* (New York: Simon & Schuster, 2005), 509 and 551.

25. Waters to "Bro. Lemuel," August 12, 1862, Waters Papers, NYHS.

26. Ibid. Waters's placement of the exclamation points outside the quotation marks after Lincoln's words seems to indicate that the emphasis was on his reaction, not AL's tone of voice. See also Donn Piatt, n.d. [c. 1888], in Rice, *Reminiscences of Lincoln,* 495–97.

27. Francis Carpenter, who spent several months with AL living in the White House, was one who excused Lincoln's rough edges: see his *Six Months at the White House,* 80–81. For "a very high temper," see Conversation with S. T. Logan at Springfield, July 6, 1875, in Nicolay, *Oral History,* 36. Pierce's quotation is from Edward L. Pierce to WHH, Milton, Mass., September 15, 1889, Herndon-Weik Collection, LC. In a later statement for publication, Pierce cleaned up AL's language, though it is doubtful that the cleansed word choice would have offended him as the interview apparently did, or caused him to search for a reason for AL's "temper" (see *HI,* 684).

28. Conversation with Hon. M. S. Wilkinson, May 23, 1876, in John G. Nicolay Papers, LC; John G. Nicolay and John Hay, *Abraham Lincoln: A History* (New York: Century, 1886–1890), 6:154; Michael Burlingame, *The Inner World of Abraham Lincoln* (Urbana: University of Illinois Press, 1994), 207 ("utterly tired out"); Edward Lillie Pierce, *Enfranchisement and Citizenship: Addresses and Papers,* ed. A. W. Stevens (Boston: Roberts Brothers, 1896), 87; Horace Maynard to Andrew Johnson, Washington, D.C., June 7, 1862, in *The Papers of Andrew Johnson,* ed. Leroy P. Graf and Ralph W. Haskins (Knoxville: University of Tennessee Press, 1967–2000), 5:452; Samuel Giles Buckingham, *The Life of William A. Buckingham, the War Governor of Connecticut* (Springfield, Mass.: W. F. Adams, 1894), 261–62 (the author is grateful to Michael Burlingame for pointing out this source).

29. AL's most succinct statement of his conflicted views about slavery and the Constitution is found in his letter to Albert G. Hodges, Washington, D.C., April 4, 1864, *CW,* 7:281–82. The story of AL's conflict over emancipation is also well told in Guelzo, *Lincoln's Emancipation Proclamation;* Douglas L. Wilson, *Lincoln's Sword: The Presidency and the Power of Words* (New York: Vintage, 2006), 105–61; Richard J. Carwardine, *Lincoln* (Harlow, U.K.: Pearson Longman, 2003), 203–20. AL's concerns about the border states can be found in AL to Orville H. Browning, Washington, D.C., September 22, 1861, *CW,* 4:532; AL, "Remarks to a Deputation of Western Gentlemen," August 4, 1862, ibid., 5:356–57. For "I

have God on my side," see Lowell H. Harrison, *Lincoln of Kentucky* (Lexington: University Press of Kentucky, 2000), 135.

30. AL, "Speech at Chicago, Ill.," July 10, 1858, *CW,* 2:501; AL, "Remarks to a Committee of Reformed Presbyterian Synod," July 17, 1862, ibid., 5:327; Leonard Swett to WHH, Chicago, January 17, 1866, *HI,* 162; Joseph Gillespie to WHH, Edwardsville, Ill., December 8, 1866, ibid., 507.

31. Lincoln quoted in Carpenter, *Six Months at the White House,* 77.

32. Gillespie to WHH, December 8, 1866, *HI,* 507.

33. Wendell Phillips quoted in Guelzo, *Lincoln's Emancipation Proclamation,* 25–26; Charles Sumner to John Andrew, Washington, D.C., May 20, 1862, in Charles Sumner, *The Selected Letters of Charles Sumner,* ed. Beverly Wilson Palmer (Boston: Northeastern University Press, 1990), 2:115; *CW,* 5:278–79, 327, and 356–57; Horace Greeley, "The Prayer of Twenty Millions," *New York Tribune,* August 20, 1862; Elizabeth Todd Grimsley, "Six Months in the White House," *Journal of the Illinois State Historical Society* 19, nos. 3–4 (October 1926–January 1927): 60.

34. AL to John C. Frémont, Washington, D.C., September 2, 1861, *CW,* 4:506; AL, "Proclamation Revoking General Hunter's Order of Military Emancipation of 9 May 1862," ibid., 5:222–24; Quarles, *Lincoln and the Negro,* 71. For "One old chap," see Dillard C. Donnohue interview with Jesse W. Weik, February 13, 1887, *HI,* 602.

35. Horace Maynard to AL, House of Representatives, July 16, 1862, ALP-LC; Joshua Speed to AL, Cin[cinnati], September 1, 1861, ALP-LC; Henry Wilson, *History of the Antislavery Measures of the Thirty-Seventh and Thirty-Eighth United-States Congresses, 1861–64* (Boston: Walker, Wise, 1864), 83, 122, and 143; *Daily National Intelligencer,* July 22, 28, 29, 30, and 31, and August 6 and 11, 1862.

36. Wilson, *History of the Antislavery Measures,* 79–202; Bruce Tap, "Joint Committee on the Conduct of the War (1861–1865)," in *Encyclopedia of the American Civil War,* ed. David S. Heidler and Jeanne T. Heidler (Santa Barbara, Calif.: ABC-CLIO, 2000; online at www .civilwarhome.com); *Diary of Orville Hickman Browning,* July 14, 15, and 21, 1862, 1:558–61; Charles Sumner quoted in entry of June 28, 1862, ibid., 1:558; AL quoted in Burlingame, *Inner World,* 176.

37. *Diary of Orville Hickman Browning,* July 14, 1862, 1:558. For a good overview of AL's concerns over the second Confiscation Act, see Matthew Pinsker, "Lincoln's Summer of Emancipation," in *Lincoln and Freedom: Slavery, Emancipation and the Thirteenth Amendment,* ed. Harold Holzer and Sara Vaughn Gabbard (Carbondale: Southern Illinois University Press, 2007), 79–99. On AL's pique at Congress, a relevant conversation was recollected by Secretary of the Interior John P. Usher; it concluded with AL exploding, "Then I am to be bullied by Congress am I? I'll be d——d if I will": John Nicolay notes, conversation with Hon. J. P. Usher, Washington, D.C., October 8, 1878, Nicolay Papers, LC.

38. Unbound diary notes of Edward Bates, July 15, 1862, Edward Bates Papers, LC; Salmon P. Chase to AL, Washington, D.C., May 16, 1862, ALP-LC; Salmon P. Chase to Benjamin P. Butler, Washington, D.C., June 24, 1862, in Benjamin F. Butler, *Private and Official Correspondence of Gen. Benjamin F. Butler During the Period of the Civil War,* ed. Jesse Ames Marshall (N.p.: Privately published, 1917), 1:633; John Sherman to Gov. [Salmon P.] Chase, Mansfield, Ohio, August 3, 1862, in Salmon P. Chase, *The Salmon P. Chase Papers,* ed. John Niven et al. (Kent, Ohio: Kent State University Press, 1993–1998), 3:240–41; Robert Dale Owen to Edwin M. Stanton, July 23, 1862, ALP-LC.

39. Nicolay notes on conversation with Swett, March 14, 1878, Nicolay Papers, LC; Sherman to Chase, August 3, 1862, in *Chase Papers,* 3:240–41.

40. Owen to Stanton, July 23, 1862, ALP-LC; Waters to "Bro. Lemuel," August 12, 1862, Waters Papers, NYHS; AL, "Address to Union Meeting in Washington," August 6, 1862, *CW,* 5:359.

41. John L. Scripps to AL, Chicago, September 23, 1861, ALP-LC; George Bancroft to AL, New York, November 15, 1861, ALP-LC; AL to George Bancroft, Washington, D.C., November 18, 1861, ALP-LC.

42. AL on Blondin quoted in "Conversation with Hon. T. Lyle Dickey, Washington," October

20, 1876, in Burlingame, *Oral History,* 49. A variant of this story is found in Burlingame, *Inner World,* 178.

43. Adam Gurowski's precise counterpoint to the Blondin analogy reads: "O, could I only win confidence in Mr. Lincoln, it would be one of the most cheerful days and events in my life. Perhaps, elephant-like, Mr. Lincoln slowly, cautiously but surely feels his way across a bridge leading over a precipice. Perhaps so; only his slowness is marked with blood and disasters": Adam Gurowski, *Diary from November 18, 1862 to October 18, 1863* (New York: Carleton, 1864), 153.

44. John G. Nicolay, notes on conversation with M. Morrill of Me., September 20, 1878, Nicolay Papers, LC. Another who spoke of AL's "balancing" was George W. Julian, n.d. [c. 1888], in Rice, *Reminiscences of Lincoln,* 49. See also AL to Zachariah Chandler, November 20, 1863, *CW,* 7:24, where he writes, "I hope to 'stand firm' enough to not go backward, yet not go forward fast enough to wreck the country's cause."

45. William E. Channing, *Slavery* (Boston: James Munroe, 1835); entry of April 27, 1861, in Hay, *Lincoln and the Civil War,* 12; Sumner to Andrew, in Sumner, *Selected Letters,* 2:115; Salmon P. Chase to AL, Washington, D.C., May 16, 1862, ALP-LC; *Diary of Orville Hickman Browning,* July 21, 1862, 1:561–62; Owen to Stanton, July 23, 1862, ALP-LC. Owen, like AL, hoped that compensation would accompany any property seizure.

46. "George" [John G.] Nicolay to Therena [Bates], Washington, D.C., July 13, 1862, Nicolay Papers, LC; Chase Diary, July 21 and 22, 1862, *Chase Papers,* 1:348–51; Gideon Welles, *Diary of Gideon Welles: Secretary of the Navy Under Lincoln and Johnson,* ed. Howard K. Beale (New York: W. W. Norton, 1960), 1:70–71; Carpenter, *Six Months at the White House,* 20–21; *New York Times,* July 17, 1862.

47. Chase Diary, July 21 and 22, 1862, *Chase Papers,* 1:348–51; Chase to Richard C. Parsons, Washington, D.C., July 20, 1862, 3:231 ("these measures"); Edwin M. Stanton, "The Cabinet on Emancipation," memo dated July 22, 1862, Edwin M. Stanton Papers, LC; Montgomery Blair to AL, draft letter, Post Office Dept., July 23, 1862, Blair Family Papers, LC; Carpenter, *Six Months at the White House,* 20–22. For a good summary of the evolution and timing of the proclamation, see Foner, *The Fiery Trial,* 206–47.

48. Conversation with Leonard Swett, March 14, 1878, in Burlingame, *Oral History,* 58–59; AL quoted in Carpenter, *Six Months at the White House,* 281. In the original, "public opinion baths" is emphasized by Carpenter. See also AL, "Speech at Peoria, Ill.," October 16, 1854, reported in *Peoria Journal,* October 21, 23, 24, 25, 26, 27, and 28, 1854, *CW,* 2:256; AL, "First Debate with Stephen A. Douglas, Ottawa, Ill.," August 21, 1858, ibid., 3:28; Bates Notebook, page marked "1862" in Notebook for 1863–66, Edward Bates Papers, LC.

49. Entry of July 8, 1864, Hay, *Lincoln and the Civil War,* 206–7; John Hay to WHH, Paris, September 5, 1866, *HI,* 331; Henry Wilson to WHH, Natick, Mass., May 30, 1867, ibid., 561–62.

50. Adam Gurowski, *Diary 1863-'64-'65* (Washington, D.C.: Morrison, 1866), December 6, 1863, 40; entry of February 26, 1863, in Edward Bates, *The Diary of Edward Bates, 1859–1866,* ed. Howard K. Beale (Washington, D.C.: Government Printing Office, 1933), 279–80; Bates Notebook, page marked "1862" in Notebook for 1863–66, Bates Papers, LC; Donn Piatt, n.d. [c. 1888], in Rice, *Reminiscences of Lincoln,* 482; Mary Mann to S. P. Chase, Concord, Mass., April 26, 1862, in *Chase Papers,* 3:185. For examples of grudging admiration for Gurowski, see entry of August 9, 1864, Welles, *Diary of Gideon Welles,* 2:100; P. H. Watson [assistant secretary of war] to Count A. Gurowski, Washington, D.C., March 22, 1863, Adam Gurowski Papers, LC; Henry Wilson to Count [Gurowski], Washington, D.C., July 17, 1863, Gurowski Papers, LC.

51. David Herbert Donald, "Sixteenth President Wrote His Own Book on Leadership," in *Lincoln in the Times: The Life of Abraham Lincoln as Originally Reported in the New York Times,* ed. David Herbert Donald and Harold Holzer (New York: St. Martin's, 2005), 5–6. For a discussion of AL's frequently manipulative political style, see LaWanda Cox, "Lincoln and Black Freedom," in *The Historian's Lincoln: Pseudohistory, Psychohistory, and History,* ed. Gabor S. Boritt (Urbana: University of Illinois Press, 1988), 175–96.

52. AL to Cuthbert Bullitt, Washington, D.C., July 28, 1862, *CW,* 5:344–46; Reminiscence of George S. Boutwell, n.d. [c. 1888], in Rice, *Reminiscences of Lincoln,* 124–25.

53. For a discussion of AL's reply to Horace Greeley, see Wilson, *Lincoln's Sword,* 143–61. Once he hit upon it, AL used the public letter format to good effect on a number of occasions: see, e.g., AL to Erastus Corning and Others, Washington, D.C., [June 12], 1863, *CW,* 6:260–69.

54. Edward L. Pierce quoted in Rose, *Rehearsal for Reconstruction,* 35. AL's writings on colonization and amalgamation are extensive. Among the most important are "Eulogy on Henry Clay," July 6, 1852, *CW,* 2:127–32; "Outline for a Speech to the Colonization Society," January 4, 1855 [?], ibid., 2:298–99; "Speech at Springfield, Ill.," June 26, 1857, ibid., 2:403–9; "First Debate with Douglas," August 21, 1858, ibid., 3:14–30; "Speech at Columbus, Ohio," September 16, 1859, ibid., 3:401–25; "Appeal to Border State Representatives to Favor Compensated Emancipation," July 12, 1862, ibid., 5:317–19; "Address on Colonization to a Deputation of Negroes," August 14, 1862, ibid., 5:370–75; "Annual Message to Congress," December 1, 1862, ibid., 5:518–37; see also Reminiscence of Cassius M. Clay, n.d. [c. 1888], in Rice, *Reminiscences of Lincoln,* 297. Lengthy discussions of AL's complex beliefs about colonization are in Foner, *The Fiery Trial;* Michael Burlingame, *Abraham Lincoln: A Life* (Baltimore: Johns Hopkins University Press, 2008), 2:382–96. See also Paul J. Scheips, "Lincoln and the Chiriqui Colonization Project," *Journal of Negro History* 37 (July 1952): 418–53; Michael Vorenberg, "Abraham Lincoln and the Politics of Black Colonization," *JALA* 14, no. 2 (Summer 1993): 22–45.

55. AL, "Address on Colonization to a Deputation of Negroes," August 14, 1862, *CW,* 5:370–75; Burlingame, *Abraham Lincoln,* 2:382–96.

56. Burlingame, *Abraham Lincoln,* 2:382–96. Lerone Bennett Jr.'s discussion of colonization, though highly politicized, cites well-documented testimony for AL's sincere promotion of the idea: Lerone Bennett Jr., *Forced into Glory: Abraham Lincoln's White Dream* (Chicago: Johnson Publishing, 2000), 381–87 and 456–60. A good discussion of the debate among historians over the politics of this meeting is in Phillip Shaw Paludan, "Lincoln and Colonization: Policy or Propaganda?" *JALA* 25, no. 1 (Winter 2004): 23–37. The quotations are from, respectively, Chase Diary, August 15, 1862, *Chase Papers,* 1:362; Foner, *The Fiery Trial,* 225; and *Harper's Weekly,* September 6, 1862.

57. Calvert, *Reminiscences of a Boy in Blue;* Smith, *Story of a Cavalry Regiment;* Waters, notation on back of [John Brent] to Waters, December 6, 1862, Waters Papers, NYHS; Waters, fragment of letter or report, July [1864], quotation note added on July 18, [1864], Waters Papers, NYHS.

58. Foner, *The Fiery Trial,* 258–61.

59. Bennett, *Forced into Glory,* 54 and 103–6; [David Ross Locke], *The Nasby Papers* (Indianapolis: C. O. Perrine, 1864), 31. See also Carpenter, *Six Months at the White House,* 37, 80, and 159; Quarles, *Lincoln and the Negro,* 16. For AL's delight in Petroleum V. Nasby see, e.g., entry of October 11, 1864, in John Hay, *Inside Lincoln's White House: The Complete Civil War Diary of John Hay,* ed. Michael Burlingame and John R. Turner Ettlinger (Carbondale: Southern Illinois University Press, 1997), 239; Leonard Swett to WHH, Chicago (revised letter), January 17, 1866, in Herndon and Weik, *Herndon's Lincoln,* 45n. See also chapter 2.

60. AL, "Speech at Ottawa, Ill.," August 21, 1858, *CW,* 3:20 and 27; AL, "Speech at Carlinsville, Ill.," August 31, 1858, ibid., 3:77; AL, "Speech at Clinton, Ill.," September 2, 1858, ibid., 3:81; AL, "Speech at Paris, Ill.," September 7, 1858, ibid., 3:91; AL, "Speech at Edwardsville, Ill.," September 11, 1858, ibid., 3:94; AL, "Speech at Council Bluffs, Iowa," August 13, 1859, ibid., 3:396; AL, "Speech at Clinton, Ill.," October 14, 1859, ibid., 3:487; AL, "Speech at Hartford, Conn.," March 5, 1860, ibid., 4:4–5. At Council Bluffs, AL used the same phrase Waters recorded, stating that he intended to speak "about the 'eternal Negro.'"

61. See sources in nn. 26–27, above; see also Carpenter, *Six Months at the White House,* 80 and 104; Leonard Swett to WHH, Chicago, August 30, 1887, Herndon-Weik Collection, LC; WHH to [Jesse] Weik, Spfyd, Ill., October 22, 1887, Herndon-Weik Collection, LC; Allen

C. Guelzo, *Lincoln and Douglas: The Debates That Defined America* (New York: Simon & Schuster, 2008), 113; Phillip Shaw Paludan, "Greeley, Colonization, and a 'Deputation of Negroes': Three Considerations on Lincoln and Race," in *Lincoln Emancipated: The President and the Politics of Race,* ed. Brian R. Dirck (DeKalb: Northern Illinois University Press, 2007), 29–30; Bennett, *Forced into Glory,* 96–97, citing Carl Sandburg and Paul Angle.

62. Jabari Asim, *The N Word: Who Can Say It, Who Shouldn't and Why* (Boston: Houghton Mifflin, 2007), 10–11; Hosea Easton quoted in Randall Kennedy, *Nigger: The Strange Career of a Troublesome Word* (New York: Pantheon, 2002), 5; Seward quoted in *New York Tribune,* March 7, 1854.

63. AL quoted in Paludan, "Greeley, Colonization," 31; Benjamin Wade to wife, December 29, 1851, Benjamin Wade Papers, LC. Other antislavery men who employed the word "nigger" now and again were John Hay, in entry of April 25, 1861, Hay, *Lincoln and the Civil War,* 11; Benjamin French, in his letter to Frank [Francis O. French], Washington, D.C., April 14, 1861, Benjamin B. French Family Papers, LC; entry from September 5, 1863, in Gurowski, *Diary from November 18, 1862,* 314. Even Lucien Waters sometimes used it, though in quotation marks: see Waters to "Bro. James," November 15, 1862, Waters Papers, NYHS.

64. See n. 27.

65. AL had a field day with Douglas's tale of the crocodile and the Negro, using it in many addresses; one example is his speech at Hartford, Conn., March 5, 1860, *CW,* 4:4. The mockery of the New England Democrat is in ibid., 4:7.

66. AL to Albert G. Hodges, Washington, D.C., April 4, 1864, *CW,* 7:281–82.

67. For Lee's complex racial attitudes, see Elizabeth Brown Pryor, *Reading the Man: A Portrait of Robert E. Lee Through His Private Letters* (New York: Viking, 2007), chapters 8, 9, and 16. See also Hans L. Trefousse, "Ben Wade and the Negro," *Ohio Historical Quarterly* 68, no. 2 (April 1959): 161–76.

68. WHH interview with Joshua F. Speed, n.d. [1865–1866], *HI,* 477.

69. Waters to "Bro. Lemuel," August 12, 1862, Waters Papers, NYHS.

70. For the anxious discussion of troop numbers see, e.g., August Belmont to Thurlow Weed, Newport, July 20, 1862, in Thurlow Weed Barnes, *The Life of Thurlow Weed Including His Autobiography and a Memoir* (Boston: Houghton Mifflin, 1883–1884), 2:420–22; AL's concern about the size of his force and slow Union enlistments is mentioned in Earl Schenck Miers, ed., *Lincoln Day by Day: A Chronology* (Washington, D.C.: Lincoln Sesquicentennial Commission, 1960), entry for August 8, 1862, 3:132; "War Department," *Daily National Intelligencer,* August 5, 1862; "An Important Order," *Daily National Intelligencer,* August 9, 1862; Waters to parents, July 21, 1862, Waters Papers, NYHS; AL to Edwin Stanton, Washington, D.C., July 22, 1862, Stanton Papers, LC; Reminiscence of Joshua B. Fry, n.d. [c. 1888], in Rice, *Reminiscences of Lincoln,* 392–93; Waters Certificate of Service, RG 94, NARA.

71. James Oakes, *The Radical and the Republican: Frederick Douglass, Abraham Lincoln, and the Triumph of Antislavery Politics* (New York: W. W. Norton, 2007), 229–45; Foner, *The Fiery Trial,* 291–98.

72. Eleventh New York Volunteer Cavalry Regimental History, www.civilwar.nps.gov/cwss /regiments.cfm; Calvert, *Reminiscences of a Boy in Blue;* Smith, *Story of a Cavalry Regiment;* Waters to parents, August 25, 1863, in Lucien P. Waters, Pension File, RG 94, NARA; Waters to father and mother, Baton Rouge, La., November 13, 1864, Waters Papers, NYHS; Waters's report of condition of freedmen in Louisiana, fragment, n.d. [1864], Waters Papers, NYHS; Waters Certificate of Service, RG 94, NARA; Application for pension by Mary G. Waters, testimony of Sarah B. Bertholf, September 17, 1918, Pension File, RG 94, NARA.

73. Waters almost certainly means *canaille,* defined in the 1862 edition of Noah Webster's *American Dictionary of the English Language* as "the lowest class of people; the rabble; the vulgar."

CHAPTER 4. OF FATHERS AND SONS

1. An excellent short biography of Ross is found in the introduction to John Ross, *The Papers of Chief John Ross*, ed. Gary E. Moulton (Norman: University of Oklahoma Press, 1985). For a longer study, see Gary E. Moulton, *John Ross, Cherokee Chief* (Athens: University of Georgia Press, 1978). See also Ely Parker to sister, November 21, 1863, in Laurence M. Hauptman, *The Iroquois in the Civil War: From Battlefield to Reservation* (Syracuse, N.Y.: Syracuse University Press, 1993), 54 and 56.
2. Robert V. Remini, *The Life of Andrew Jackson* (New York: Harper & Row, 1988), 216.
3. Moulton, Introduction to *Ross Papers*, 1:6–10; Kenny A. Franks, *Stand Watie and the Agony of the Cherokee Nation* (Memphis: Memphis State University Press, 1979), 91–94.
4. Moulton, *John Ross*, 155 and 159; rival notions of Cherokee nationhood are discussed in Troy Smith, "Nations Colliding: The Civil War Comes to Indian Territory," *Civil War History* 59, no. 3 (September 2013): 279–319; James M. Bell to Caroline Bell, Skullyville, C.N., May 16, 1863, quoted in *Cherokee Cavaliers: Forty Years of Cherokee History as Told in the Correspondence of the Ridge-Watie-Boudinot Family*, ed. Edward Everett Dale and Gaston Litton (Norman: University of Oklahoma Press, 1939), 123.
5. Moulton, Introduction to *Ross Papers*, 1:9–10.
6. John Ross to Mary B. Ross, Washington, D.C., May 1, 1860, in *Ross Papers*, 2:441–42; John Ross to Henry M. Rector, Tahlequah, C.N., February 22, 1861, ibid., 2:465; William Seward quoted in Francis Paul Prucha, *The Great Father: The United States Government and the American Indians* (Lincoln: University of Nebraska Press, 1984), 1:417.
7. John Ross to J. S. Dunham, Tahlequah, C.N., February 1, 1861, in *Ross Papers*, 2:458; Ross to J. R. Kannady, Park Hill, C.N., May 17, 1861, ibid., 2:468–69; Ross, Proclamation, Park Hill, C.N., May 17, 1861, ibid., 2: 469–70. See also Edward Clark to Jefferson Davis, Austin, May 15, 1861, *OR*, IV, 1:322–25; James E. Harrison, James Bourland, and Charles A. Hamilton to Edward Clark, n.d. [c. May 15, 1861], ibid., IV, 1:322–25.
8. John Ross to AL, Lawrenceville, N.J., September 16, 1862, ALP-LC; David A. Nichols, "Lincoln and the Indians," in *The Historian's Lincoln: Pseudohistory, Psychohistory, and History*, ed. Gabor S. Boritt (Urbana: University of Illinois Press, 1988), 149–50; Theda Perdue, "The Civil War in Indian Territory," in *American Indians and the Civil War*, ed. Robert K. Sutton and John A. Latschar (Washington, D.C.: National Park Service, 2013), 92; AL, "Annual Message to Congress," December 3, 1861, *CW*, 5:46.
9. Perdue, "Civil War in Indian Territory," 88–93; Prucha, *The Great Father*, 1:415–19; Moulton, *John Ross*, 167–68.
10. Theda Perdue, *Slavery and the Evolution of Cherokee Society, 1540–1866* (Knoxville: University of Tennessee Press, 1979), 129–30; Robert Lipscomb Duncan, *Reluctant General: The Life and Times of Albert Pike* (New York: E. P. Dutton, 1961), 172–74; John Ross to John B. Ogden, Park Hill, C.N., February 28, 1861, in *Ross Papers*, 2:466.
11. Moulton, *John Ross*, 170–73 (Ross quoted on 172–73); F[ielding] Johnson to William P. Dole, Delaware Agency, Kans., October 11, 1861, ALP-LC; George A. Cutler to William P. Dole, Topeka, October 21, 1861, ALP-LC; Prucha, *The Great Father*, 1:419; John Ross, Annual Message, Tahlequah, C.N., October 9, 1861, in *Ross Papers*, 2:493; the CSA treaty can be found in *OR*, IV, 1:669–87.
12. Harry Lemley, ed., "Letters of Henry M. Rector and J. P. Kannaday to John Ross of the Cherokee Nation," *Chronicles of Oklahoma* 42, no. 3 (Autumn 1964): 328; Wiley Britton, "Union and Confederate Indians in the Civil War," in *Battles and Leaders of the Civil War*, ed. Robert Underwood Johnson and Charles Clough Buell (New York: Century, 1887–1888), 1:335–36; Muriel H. Wright, "Colonel Cooper's Civil War Report on the Battle of Round Mountain," *Chronicles of Oklahoma* 39, no. 4 (Winter 1961–1962): 352–97; Moulton, *John Ross*, 173–74; John Ross to Jefferson Davis, Park Hill, C.N., May 10, 1862, in *Ross Papers*, 2:512–13.
13. David Hunter to Lorenzo Thomas, Leavenworth, Kans., November 27, 1861, ALP-LC; Diary of Samuel R. Curtis, January 19, 1862, Samuel R. Curtis Papers, ILPL; Minutes of War Board, March 21, 1862, Edwin M. Stanton Papers, LC. Only one case of scalping by

Indian soldiers was officially confirmed: see Britton, "Union and Confederate Indians," 1:336. See also Perdue, "Civil War in Indian Territory," 96; AL to Edwin M. Stanton, January 31, 1862, CW, 5:115–16; AL to David Hunter and James Lane, February 10, 1862, ibid., 5:131; AL to Henry W. Halleck, April 4, 1862, ibid., 5:180; Nichols, "Lincoln and the Indians," 150–53 (Lane quoted on 152).

14. Prucha, The Great Father, 1:424–26; S. C. Gwynne, Empire of the Summer Moon: Quanah Parker and the Rise and Fall of the Comanches, the Most Powerful Indian Tribe in American History (New York: Scribner, 2010), 211; Coffin quoted in Perdue, "Civil War in Indian Territory," 97; Col. William F. Cloud to Cherokee Nation, Park Hill, C.N., August 3, 1862, ALP-LC.

15. James G. Blunt to AL, Fort Scott, August 13, 1862, ALP-LC; Mark W. Delahay to AL, Leavenworth City, Kans., August 21, 1862, ALP-LC; John Ross to AL, September 16, 1862, in Ross Papers, 2:516–18.

16. Diary of Salmon P. Chase, August 3, 1862, in Salmon P. Chase, The Salmon P. Chase Papers, ed. John Niven et al. (Kent, Ohio: Kent State University Press, 1993–1998), 1:357.

17. For AL's struggle over the Emancipation Proclamation, see chapter 3. See also AL to Horace Greeley, August 22, 1862, CW, 5:388–89; Edward S. Corwin, Total War and the Constitution (New York: Alfred A. Knopf, 1947), 16–17.

18. John Ross to AL, September 16, 1862, in Ross Papers, 2:516–18; AL to Ross, September 25, 1862, CW, 5:439.

19. Ross to William P. Dole, Washington, D.C., October 13, 1862, in Ross Papers, 2:519–20; Ross to Edwin M. Stanton, Philadelphia, November 8, 1862, ibid., 2:520–21; William P. Dole, "Report of the Commissioner of Indian Affairs, November 27, 1861," in Report of the Commissioner of Indian Affairs, Accompanying the Annual Report of the Secretary of the Interior for the Year 1861 (Washington, D.C.: Government Printing Office, 1861), 10; Caleb B. Smith to AL, September 29, 1862, ALP-LC; AL to Samuel R. Curtis, October 10, 1862, CW, 5:456; Curtis to AL, St. Louis, October 10, 1862, OR, I, 13:723.

20. White Catcher et al. to John Ross, Head Quarters Blunt's Division, December 2, 1862, in Ross Papers, 2:522–23; Huckleberry Downing et al. to Ross, Post Neosho, Mo., January 8, 1863, in ibid., 2:527–29. For an assessment of AL's slow reaction to Ross's predicament, see Introduction of Richard W. Etulain, ed., Lincoln Looks West: From the Mississippi to the Pacific (Carbondale: Southern Illinois University Press, 2010), 31–32.

21. Jane Swisshelm to St. Cloud [Minn.] Democrat, Washington, D.C., March 26, 1864, in Jane Grey Swisshelm, Crusader and Feminist: Letters of Jane Grey Swisshelm, 1858–1865, ed. Arthur J. Larsen (Westport, Conn.: Hyperion Press, 1976), 270.

22. Mrs. H. R. Schoolcraft to MTL, Washington, D.C., April 6, 1861, Henry Rowe Schoolcraft Papers, LC; entry of April 30, 1861, in John Hay, Inside Lincoln's White House: The Complete Civil War Diary of John Hay, ed. Michael Burlingame and John R. Turner Ettlinger (Carbondale: Southern Illinois University Press, 1997), 14; entry of February 28, 1863, Horatio Nelson Taft Diary, LC; William P. Dole to AL, July 8, 1864, ALP-LC; Marquis Adolphe de Chambrun to wife, [Washington, D.C.], March 10, [1865], in Marquis Adolphe de Chambrun, Impressions of Lincoln and the Civil War: A Foreigner's Account, trans. General Aldebert de Chambrun (New York: Random House, 1952), 40–43.

23. Texts of early 1850s treaties with the Plains Indians in Charles J. Kappler, ed., Indian Affairs: Laws and Treaties (Washington, D.C.: Government Printing Office, 1904), 2:594–96, 598–602, and 608–14; Ernest Wallace and E. Adamson Hoebel, The Comanches: Lords of the South Plains (Norman: University of Oklahoma Press, 1986), 305–6; Edmund Jefferson Danziger Jr., Indians and Bureaucrats: Administering the Reservation Policy During the Civil War (Urbana: University of Illinois Press, 1974), 24–37.

24. For photographs of Indians at the White House, see Peter B. Kunhardt Jr., Philip B. Kunhardt III, and Peter W. Kunhardt, P. T. Barnum: America's Greatest Showman (New York: Alfred A. Knopf, 1995), 178–79; Washington Daily Morning Chronicle, March 28, 1863, CW, 6:152–53n; B[enjamin] B. French to Frank [Francis O. French], Washington, D.C., March 27, 1863, Benjamin B. French Family Papers, LC; Diary of Benjamin French, March 28, 1863, French Papers, LC; "Our Indian Relations," Daily National Intelligencer,

undated clipping in French Papers, LC. For an embellished recollection, see Albert Rhodes, "A Reminiscence of Abraham Lincoln," *St. Nicholas Magazine,* November 1876, 8–10.

25. Kunhardt, Kunhardt, and Kunhardt, *P. T. Barnum,* 176; "'Big Injuns' at the White House," *Lawrence* [Kans.] *Republican,* April 9, 1863, reprinted from the *Missouri Democrat,* in Herbert Mitgang, ed., *Lincoln as They Saw Him* (New York: Rinehart, 1956), 338–39; *Daily National Intelligencer,* undated clipping in French Papers, LC; Rhodes, "A Reminiscence," 8–10; *Washington Daily Morning Chronicle,* March 28, 1863, *CW,* 6:152n.

26. AL, "Speech to Indians," March 27, 1863, *CW,* 6:151–52; *Washington Daily Morning Chronicle,* March 28, 1863, ibid., 6:152n; "'Big Injuns' at the White House," Mitgang, *Lincoln as They Saw Him,* 338–39; Rhodes, "A Reminiscence," 10.

27. Dee Brown, *Bury My Heart at Wounded Knee: An Indian History of the American West* (New York: Bantam, 1972), 69–70; Gwynne, *Empire of the Summer Moon,* 218. The medals can be seen in photographs in Kunhardt, Kunhardt, and Kunhardt, *P. T. Barnum,* 178–79; see also *Boston Gazette,* April 23, 1863, in Don E. Fehrenbacher and Virginia Fehrenbacher, eds., *Recollected Words of Abraham Lincoln* (Stanford, Calif.: Stanford University Press, 1996), 10; [John] George [Nicolay] to Terena [Bates], Washington, D.C., April 9, 1863, John G. Nicolay Papers, LC; Diary of Fanny Seward, March 28, 1863, William H. Seward Papers, UR; "'Big Injuns' at the White House," Mitgang, *Lincoln as They Saw Him,* 339.

28. Fred Kaplan, *Lincoln: The Biography of a Writer* (New York: Harper Perennial, 2010), 343–44; P. T. Barnum, *Struggles and Triumphs, or, Forty Years' Recollections* (Hartford: J. B. Burr, 1869), 573–78.

29. For Indian receptions/shows similar to the March 1863 event, see, e.g., Marquis de Chambrun to wife, March 10, [1865], in *Impressions of Lincoln and the Civil War,* 40–43; John Nicolay, "Indian Tales," Miscellaneous Notes, Nicolay Papers, LC; John G. Nicolay, "Hole-in-the-Day," *Harper's New Monthly Magazine,* January 26, 1863, 186–91 (quotations on 187 and 191); Louis Agassiz to Edwin M. Stanton, Washington, D.C., January 20, 1865, Edwin M. Stanton Papers, LC; John Hay to George [Nicolay], August 11 and 29, 1862, typescripts, Tyler Dennett Papers, LC. Michael Burlingame transcribes the text somewhat differently in *At Lincoln's Side: John Hay's Civil War Correspondence and Selected Writings* (Carbondale: Southern Illinois University Press, 2000), 25.

30. AL, "Annual Message to Congress," December 1, 1862, *CW,* 5:527; AL, "Annual Message to Congress," December 8, 1863, ibid., 7:47–48; Daniel Walker Howe, *What Hath God Wrought: The Transformation of America, 1815–1848* (New York: Oxford University Press, 2007), 247–48 and 251; see also Daniel Walker Howe, *The Political Culture of the American Whigs* (Chicago: University of Chicago Press, 1979), 274; David Hackett Fischer and James C. Kelly, *Bound Away: Virginia and the Westward Movement* (Charlottesville: University Press of Virginia, 2000), 70; John Quincy Adams is quoted in Lynn Hudson Parsons, "'A Perpetual Harrow upon My Feelings': John Quincy Adams and the American Indian," *New England Quarterly* 46, no. 3 (September 1973): 339; Henry Clay, Address to the Colonization Society of Kentucky, [Washington, D.C.], *Daily National Intelligencer,* January 12, 1830.

31. AL, "Communication to the People of Sangamo County," March 2, 1832, *CW,* 1:8; AL, "Speech at Worcester, Mass.," September 12, 1848, ibid., 2:4; AL, "Second Lecture on Discoveries and Inventions," [February 11, 1859], ibid., 3:358 and 360; AL, "Fragment of a Tariff Discussion," [December 1, 1847], ibid., 1:412 (emphasis is AL's); Eric Foner, *Free Soil, Free Labor, Free Men: The Ideology of the Republican Party Before the Civil War* (New York: Oxford University Press, 1970), 11–39. Examples of AL's promotion of upward mobility include AL, "Annual Message to Congress," December 3, 1861, *CW,* 5:52–53; AL, "Speech to One Hundred Sixty-Sixth Ohio Regiment," August 22, 1864, ibid., 7:512.

32. AL, "Speech in the House of Representatives Against the War with Mexico," January 12, 1848, *CW,* 1:431–41; AL, "Speech at Worcester, Mass.," September 12, 1848, ibid., 2:4; AL to Joshua Speed, August 24, 1855, ibid., 2:323; AL, "Speech at New Haven," March 6, 1860, ibid., 4:24–25; "AL and Stephen Douglas, Debate at Alton, Ill.," October 15, 1858, ibid., 3:301; Dorothy Ross, "Lincoln and Ethics of Emancipation: Universalism, Nationalism, Exceptionalism," *Journal of American History* 96, no. 2 (September 2009): 390–92;

Gabor S. Boritt, "Lincoln and the Economics of the American Dream," in *The Historian's Lincoln,* 91–94 and 99.

33. Danziger, *Indians and Bureaucrats,* 2–5, 9–10, and 13; George E. Tinker, *Missionary Conquest: The Gospel and Native American Cultural Genocide* (Minneapolis: Fortress Press, 1993), 4–9 and 12–16; Robert J. Conley, *The Cherokee Nation: A History* (Albuquerque: University of New Mexico Press, 2005), 7; Alexis de Tocqueville, *Democracy in America,* ed. and trans. Harvey C. Mansfield and Delba Winthrop (Chicago: University of Chicago Press, 2000), 314.

34. AL, "Address at the Cooper Institute," New York, February 27, 1860, *CW,* 3:550.

35. Fischer, *Bound Away,* 126; Richard F. Nation, *At Home in the Hoosier Hills: Agriculture, Politics, and Religion in Southern Indiana, 1810–1870* (Bloomington: Indiana University Press, 2005), 8–13.

36. Scott Berg speculates that the Indians were Shawnee who had recently lost tribal members at white hands and were following their custom of replacing them with white hostages: see Berg, *38 Nooses: Lincoln, Little Crow, and the Beginning of the Frontier's End* (New York: Pantheon, 2012), xi. Louis A. Warren did the pioneering research on the Lincoln ancestry from court, county, and church records. When the author rechecked about two-thirds of the sources cited by Warren, all checked out; see Louis A. Warren, "Abraham Lincoln, Senior, Grandfather of the President," *Filson Club History Quarterly* 5, no. 3 (July 1931): 148–49; AL to Jesse Lincoln, Springfield, Ill., April 1, 1854, *CW,* 2:217; AL, "Autobiography for Jesse W. Fell, Springfield, Ill.," December 20, 1859, ibid., 3:511; Louis Austin Warren, *Lincoln's Parentage and Childhood: A History of the Kentucky Lincolns Supported by Documentary Evidence* (New York: Century, 1926), 62–68; Louis A. Warren, *Lincoln's Youth: Indiana Years Seven to Twenty-One, 1816–1830* (New York: Appleton, Century, Crofts, 1959), 32–33; William E. Bartelt, *"There I Grew Up": Remembering Abraham Lincoln's Indiana Youth* (Indianapolis: Indiana Historical Society, 2008), 6; Jean H. Baker, *Mary Todd Lincoln: A Biography* (New York: W. W. Norton, 1987), 65.

37. Herman Melville, *The Confidence-Man: His Masquerade,* ed. Hershel Parker (New York: W. W. Norton, 1971), 126–27.

38. Warren, "Abraham Lincoln, Senior," 137–44; William E. Barton, *The Lincolns in Their Old Kentucky Home: An Address Delivered Before the Filson Club, Louisville, Kentucky, December 4, 1922* (Berea, Ky.: Berea College Press, 1923), 17–18. On the Quaker heritage, see AL, "Autobiography for Fell," *CW,* 3:511; AL, "Autobiography Written for John L. Scripps," n.d. [June 1860], ibid., 4:61; A. H. Chapman, statement for WHH, September 8, 1865, *HI,* 95. An examination of records in Berks County shows that when AL's great-grandfather wed Anne Boone (a cousin of the frontiersman Daniel Boone), she was censured by the local Friends meeting for marrying outside the Quaker community, indicating the Lincolns were not part of the Society of Friends. Mordecai Lincoln House, Nomination for National Register of Historic Places, August 8, 1988, link available through "Mordecai Lincoln House," www.en.wikipedia.org/wiki/Mordecai_Lincoln_House. For the Mordecai Lincoln house in Kentucky, see www.parks.ky.gov/parks/recreationparks/lincoln-homes.

39. AL, "Autobiography for Scripps," *CW,* 4:61–62; AL, "Communication to the People of Sangamo County," March 2, 1832, ibid.,1:8; AL, "Eulogy on Henry Clay," July 6, 1852, ibid., 2:124; Warren, *Lincoln's Parentage,* 164–65; Roy P. Basler, introduction to John Locke Scripps, *Life of Abraham Lincoln,* ed. Roy P. Basler and Lloyd A. Dunlap (Bloomington: Indiana University Press, 1961), 31n; WHH interview with Nathaniel Grigsby, Gentryville, Ind., September 12, 1865, *HI,* 111; WHH interview with William Wood, September 15, 1865, ibid., 123; WHH interview with Elizabeth Crawford, September 16, 1865, ibid., 126; John Y. Simon, *House Divided: Lincoln and His Father* (Fort Wayne, Ind.: Louis A. Warren Lincoln Library and Museum, 1987), 5–6.

40. Boritt, "Economics of the American Dream," 93–94; Nation, *Home in the Hoosier Hills,* 8–11, 82–83, and 86; Minute Book of Little Pigeon Creek Baptist Church, 1816–1840, Spencer County, Indiana, ILPL; WHH interview with Dennis F. Hanks, Chicago, June 13, 1865, *HI,* 37; WHH interview with Grigsby, September 12, 1865, ibid., 111; WHH interview with David Turnham, Elizabeth [now Dale], Ind., September 15, 1865, ibid., 121.

41. Nation, *Home in the Hoosier Hills*, 24, 29–30, and 78–86; Arthur E. Morgan, interview with Dr. LeGrand, n.d., Arthur E. Morgan Papers, LC; Arthur E. Morgan, "New Light on Lincoln's Boyhood," *Atlantic Monthly*, February 1920, 208 and 212–13; WHH interview with Dennis F. Hanks, June 13, 1865, *HI*, 37; WHH interview with Grigsby, September 12, 1865, ibid., 111.

42. Michael Burlingame contends that the rough treatment AL received at the hands of his father caused him to sympathize with the plight of slaves: see "'I Used to Be a Slave': The Origins of Lincoln's Hatred of Slavery," in Michael Burlingame, *The Inner World of Abraham Lincoln* (Urbana: University of Illinois Press, 1994), 20–56; for alternative views, see WHH interview with John Hanks, Decatur, Ill., May 25, 1865, *HI*, 5. On patterns of fatherhood, see Nation, *Home in the Hoosier Hills*, 32–36; Stephen M. Frank, *Life with Father: Parenthood and Masculinity in the Nineteenth-Century North* (Baltimore: Johns Hopkins University Press, 1998), 9–15 and 140–46; Bernard Wishy, *The Child and the Republic: The Dawn of Modern American Child Nurture* (Philadelphia: University of Pennsylvania Press, 1968), 11–14; Philip Greven, *The Protestant Temperament: Patterns of Child-Rearing, Religious Experience and the Self in Early America* (New York: Alfred A. Knopf, 1977), 32–43 and 339–41; Robert L. Griswold, *Fatherhood in America: A History* (New York: Basic Books, 1993), 11–14. For AL feeling that he was not in bondage, see his "Speech at Indianapolis," September 19, 1859, *CW*, 3:468. For AL's disinclination to work and tendency to interrupt, see WHH interview with Dennis F. Hanks, June 13, 1865, *HI*, 39; WHH interview with Nathaniel Grigsby, Lincoln Farm, September 14, 1865, ibid., 118; WHH interview with Anna Caroline Gentry, Rockport, Ind., September 17, 1865, ibid., 131; see also Replies to Queries to Dr. LeGrand, n.d., Morgan Papers, LC; Morgan, "New Light on Lincoln's Boyhood," 213–16; AL to Jesse W. Fell, Springfield, Ill., December 20, 1859, *CW*, 3:511. By "cipherin," AL meant arithmetic: see AL to Fell, December 20, 1859, ibid., 3:511; Leonard Swett, "Mr. Lincoln's Story of His Own Life," in Allen Thorndike Rice, ed., *Reminiscences of Abraham Lincoln by Distinguished Men of His Time* (New York: North American Review, 1888), 458. Pictures of a cupboard fashioned by Thomas Lincoln and a spice cabinet supposedly by AL are in Bartelt, *"There I Grew Up,"* 147 and 189.

43. For lecturing his father on financial affairs and lack of support, see AL to Thomas Lincoln and John D. Johnston, Washington, D.C., December 24, 1848, *CW*, 2:15–16; Simon, "Divided House," 12–14. Letters requesting AL to come to his father's bedside and expressing Thomas Lincoln's affection are Augustus H. Chapman to AL, Charleston, Ill., May 24, 1849, and John D. Johnston to AL, Char[leston, Ill.], May 25, 1849, both ALP-LC; the terse reply is AL to John D. Johnston, Springfield, Ill., January 12, 1851, *CW*, 2:96–97.

44. Anthony F. C. Wallace, "Prelude to Disaster: The Course of Indian-White Relations Which Led to the Black Hawk War of 1832," introduction to Ellen M. Whitney, ed., *The Black Hawk War, 1831–1832* (Springfield: Illinois State Historical Library, 1970–1978), 1:3–4 and 10–21; Treaty with the Sauk and Fox, 1804, in Kappler, *Laws and Treaties*, 2:74 and 76.

45. Black Hawk, *The Life of Ma-ka-tai-me-she-kia-kiak or Black Hawk Embracing the Tradition of His Nation* (Cincinnati: J. B. Patterson, 1831), 89. The credibility of Black Hawk's autobiography has been questioned, but Donald Jackson believes it largely authentic, though containing some overly elaborate translations: see Donald Jackson, ed., *Black Hawk: An Autobiography* (Urbana: University of Illinois Press, 1964), 24–30. See also Memorandum of Talks Between Edmund P. Gaines and the Sauk, [Rock Island, June 4, 5, and 7, 1831], in Whitney, *Black Hawk War*, 2:28.

46. Wallace, "Prelude to Disaster," 27–30 and 39–45; George A. McCall to father, Rock Island, June 16, 1831, in George A. McCall, *Letters from the Frontier: Written During a Period of Thirty Years' Service in the Army of the United States* (Philadelphia: Lippincott, 1868), 225–26; George Y. Cutler to Stephen B. Munn, Hancock County, Ill., June 9, 1831, in Whitney, *Black Hawk War*, 2:37–38.

47. Citizens of Rock River to John Reynolds, April 30, 1831, in Whitney, *Black Hawk War*, 2:3; Horatio Newhall to brother [Isaac Newhall], fragment, September 18, 1831, Horatio Newhall Papers, ILPL; Horatio Newhall to brother [Isaac Newhall], Galena, Ill., April 29,

1832, Newhall Papers, ILPL; George A. McCall to father, Steamer *Winnebago*, July 5, 1831, in McCall, *Letters from the Frontier*, 240–41; John Reynolds to William Clark, Belleville, May 26, 1831, in Whitney, *Black Hawk War*, 2:13. For Black Hawk's repeated statement of his peaceful intentions, see Felix St. Vrain to William Clark, St. Louis, May 28, 1831, in ibid., 2:21; Edmund P. Gaines to [?], Rock Island, June 20, 1831, in ibid., 2:63.

48. John R. Herndon to WHH, Quincy, May 28, 1865, Herndon-Weik Collection, LC; William H. Herndon and Jesse W. Weik, *Herndon's Lincoln*, ed. Douglas L. Wilson and Rodney O. Davis (Galesburg, Ill.: Knox College Lincoln Studies Center, 2006), 70; WHH interview with Royal Clary [Roil A. Clary], [October 1866], *HI*, 371. In "Lincoln in the Black Hawk War," *Bulletin of the Abraham Lincoln Association* 54 (December 1938): 4, Harry E. Pratt gives the date of AL's muster as April 19, 1832; however, the official muster roll shows it was April 21: see Whitney, *Black Hawk War*, 1:176.

49. William Cullen Bryant and an unidentified soldier quoted in Dr. Wayne C. Temple, *Lincoln's Arms, Dress and Military Duty During and After the Black Hawk War* (Springfield: State of Illinois Military and Naval Department, 1981), 10–11; Asher Edgerton to brother, Quincy, Ill., May 28, 1832, Asher Edgerton Correspondence, ILPL; Report of William Orr to John Y. Sawyer, n.p., [c. June 21, 1832], in Whitney, *Black Hawk War*, 2:641; Benjamin F. Irwin to WHH, September 22, 1866, *HI*, 353.

50. For AL's pride in his captaincy, see AL to Fell, December 20, 1859, *CW*, 3:512. For his ability at sports and idolization, see Irwin to WHH, September 22, 1866, *HI*, 353. For questions about the vote and AL's disciplinary problems, see David M. Pantier to WHH, Petersburg, Ill., July 21, 1865, ibid., 78. See also Patrick J. Jung, *The Black Hawk War of 1832* (Norman: University of Oklahoma Press, 2007), 79–80; Cecil Eby, *"That Disgraceful Affair": The Black Hawk War* (New York: W. W. Norton, 1973), 17–18 (Zachary Taylor quoted on 17); Herndon and Weik, *Herndon's Lincoln*, 70–71; Ida M. Tarbell, *The Life of Abraham Lincoln* (New York: Macmillan, 1920), 1:76–77. Eby rightly notes that many of the disparaging memoirs of AL as captain came after the Civil War and were gathered by a pro-Southern antiquarian. Because of the number and consistency of the remarks, however, Eby believed they must be considered seriously; see also J. Snyder to Frank Stevens, April 1, 1916, Frank Stevens Collection, ILPL. For general lack of discipline, see Report of Orr to Sawyer, [c. July 1, 1832], in Whitney, *Black Hawk War*, 2:727–28.

51. Wilson and Davis, *Herndon's Lincoln*, 73; Robert Anderson to E[lihu] B. Washburne, Tours, France, May 10, 1870, photostat, ILPL; *CW*, 1:10n; George M. Harrison to WHH, n.d. [c. 1865], in Whitney, *Black Hawk War*, 2:1327n.

52. AL, "Speech at Bath, Ill.," August 16, 1858, *CW*, 1:543; AL, "Speech in House of Representatives," July 27, 1848, ibid., 1:509–10; Jung, *Black Hawk War*, 108–9 and 129; Report of Orr to Sawyer, [c. July 1, 1832], in Whitney, *Black Hawk War*, 2:724.

53. Zachary Taylor to Quartermaster General Thomas Sidney Jesup, December 4, 1832, quoted in the introduction to Jackson, *Black Hawk*, 23; Noah Brooks, "Personal Reminiscences of Lincoln," *Scribner's Monthly*, February 1878, 563; Jung, *Black Hawk War*, 88–89. AL's presence after the engagement at Stillman's Run has sometimes been disputed; for others corroborating AL's recollection, see Asher Edgerton to brother, May 28, 1832, Edgerton Correspondence, ILPL; Report of Orr to Sawyer, [c. July 1, 1832], in Whitney, *Black Hawk War*, 2:724–25; George W. Harrison to WHH, n.d. [c. late summer 1866], *HI*, 328; see also Scott D. Dyar, "Stillman's Run: Militia's Foulest Hour," *Military History* 22, no. 1 (March 2006): 38–44.

54. Wallace, "Prelude to Disaster," 2–3, 10–11, and 51; Charles E. Rosenberg, *The Cholera Years: The United States in 1832, 1849 and 1866* (Chicago: University of Chicago Press, 1987), 36; Lewis Cass to Winfield Scott, Detroit, September 4, 1832, Lewis Cass Correspondence, ILPL; Beverley W. Bond Jr., *The Civilization of the Old Northwest: A Study of Political, Social, and Economic Development, 1788–1812* (New York: Macmillan, 1934), 245–47; Eby, *"That Disgraceful Affair,"* 23; Report of Orr to Sawyer, [c. July 1, 1832], in Whitney, *Black Hawk War*, 2:727.

55. Introduction to Jackson, *Black Hawk*, 1–3 and 7–15; Black Hawk, *The Life*, 154–55; Eby, *"That Disgraceful Affair,"* 267 and (Black Hawk quote) 277. James Westhall Ford's triple

portrait, *Wabokieshiek (Known as The Prophet), Black Hawk and His Son Nasheaskuk,* was one of three pictures he painted in 1833 in Richmond; Black Hawk is depicted in the contemporary European dress President Andrew Jackson forced him to wear.

56. AL, "Speech in House of Representatives," July 27, 1848, *CW,* 1:509–10; AL, "Speech at Bath, Ill.," August 16, 1858, ibid., 1:543; John Ross to Henry Meigs, Washington, D.C., January 26 and 27, 1864, in *Ross Papers,* 2:554–55.

57. Stephen R. Riggs, *Tah'-koo Wah-Kań or The Gospel Among the Dakotas* (Boston: Congregational Publishing Society, 1869); Bishop Henry Whipple, "My Life Among the Indians," *North American Review* 150, no. 401 (April 1890): 432; William Welsh, *Journal of the Rev. S. D. Hinman, Missionary to the Santee Sioux Indians and Taopi* (Philadelphia: McCalla & Stavely, 1869), x and 40; Danziger, *Indians and Bureaucrats,* 96–98; Prucha, *The Great Father,* 1:438–39; John G. Nicolay, "The Sioux War," *Continental Monthly,* February 1863, 195–97; George A. S. Crooker to AL, St. Paul, October 7, 1862, ALP-LC; treaty texts in Kappler, *Laws and Treaties,* 2:594–96 and 781–85.

58. [Robert I. Holcombe], "A Sioux Story of War: Chief Big Eagle's Story of the Sioux Outbreak of 1862," *Collections of the Minnesota Historical Society* 6 (1894): 384–86 and 388. Two translators present at the time Big Eagle gave this interview reported him to be frank and nonpolemical. See also Thomas J. Galbraith to Clark W. Thompson, January 27, 1863, in *Report of the Commissioner of Indian Affairs, October 13, 1863* (Washington, D.C.: Government Printing Office, 1864), 266–301; Hank H. Cox, *Lincoln and the Sioux Uprising of 1862* (Nashville: Cumberland House, 2005), 162–63; Tinker, *Missionary Conquest,* 102–3 and 108–10; Joseph R. Brown to [Henry B.] Whipple, Fort Abercrombie, January 26, 1864, in Joseph R. Brown and Samuel P. Hinman, *Missionary Paper by the Bishop Seabury Mission, Number Thirty: Letters on the Indian System* (Faribault, Minn.: Central Republican Book & Job Office, 1864), 6–9.

59. "A Sioux Story of War," 384–85; Danziger, *Indians and Bureaucrats,* 102; Galbraith quoted in Mark Diedrich, "Chief Hole-in-the-Day and the 1862 Chippewa Disturbance: A Reappraisal," *Minnesota History* 50, no. 5 (Spring 1987): 195 (see also 198–200); George E. H. Day to AL, St. Anthony, Minn., January 1, 1862, ALP-LC.

60. Janet Youngholm, "Violence and the Dakota War of 1862," in Sutton and Latschar, *American Indians and the Civil War,* 41–42 (Bishop Whipple to AL, March 6, 1862, quoted on 42); Hinman, *Journal,* x; George A. S. Crooker to AL, St. Paul, October 7, 1862, ALP-LC; John Hay to "dear sir" [John G. Nicolay], Washington, D.C., August 29, 1862, typescript, Dennett Papers, LC. A slightly different reading of the text is in Burlingame, *At Lincoln's Side,* 25.

61. Whipple, "My Life Among the Indians," 432; AL to Whipple, Washington, D.C., March 27, 1862, in Prucha, *The Great Father,* 1:440 and 470; Diedrich, "Chief Hole-in-the-Day," 197–98; "A Sioux Story of War," 386–87 and 388–90; Danziger, *Indians and Bureaucrats,* 102–3; Crooker to AL, October 7, 1862, ALP-LC.

62. Good overviews of the uprising are found in Prucha, *The Great Father,* 1:440–44; Youngholm, "Violence and the Dakota War," 35–36; Cox, *Lincoln and the Sioux,* 51–53; Robert M. Utley, *Frontiersmen in Blue: The United States Army and the Indian, 1848–1865* (New York: Macmillan, 1967), 264–72; *Vanity Fair,* September 13, 1862.

63. Cox, *Lincoln and the Sioux,* 51–53; Nicolay, "The Sioux War," 201–2; AL, "Annual Address to Congress," December 1, 1862, *CW,* 5:525; Nichols, "Lincoln and the Indians," 154–55; a longer version of Nichols's assessment is in his *Lincoln and the Indians: Civil War Policy and Politics* (Columbia: University of Missouri Press, 1978), 65–93. For friendly chiefs' attempts to rescue white captives, see Wabashaw to [Henry] Sibley, and Maya-wakan to Sibley, both September 14, 1862; Ma-za-ku-ta-ma-ne to Sibley, Red Iron's Village, September 15, 1862; Tatanka Najin (Standing Buffalo) to Sibley, September 19, 1862; Ma-za-ku-ta-ma-ne, Taopee, and Wake-Wan-Wa to Sibley, Red Iron's Village, September 24, 1862, all in Isaac V. D. Heard, *History of the Sioux War and Massacres of 1862 and 1863* (New York: Harper Brothers, 1865), 163–65.

64. Thaddeus Williams to AL, St. Paul, November 22, 1862, and Jane Swisshelm, *St. Cloud* [Minn.] *Democrat,* November 13, 1862, both quoted in Berg, *38 Nooses,* 209 (see also

217–18); George A. S. Crooker to William H. Seward, St. Paul, October 8, 1862, ALP-LC; Salmon P. Chase to AL, n.d. [December 1862], ALP-LC; Protestant Episcopal Church to AL, November 20, 1862, ALP-LC; H[enry] B. Whipple, *Missionary Paper by the Bishop Seabury Mission, Number Twenty-Four: An Appeal for the Red Man* (Faribault, Minn.: Central Republican Book & Job Office, 1863), 2–8 (quotation on 2–3); Henry B. Whipple to cousin [Henry Halleck], Faribault, Minn., December 19, 1862, James W. Eldridge Collection, HL.

65. Nichols, "Lincoln and the Indians," 154; John Nicolay to John Hay, Fort Ripley, September 1, 1862, Nicolay Papers, LC; Nicolay, "Hole-in-the-Day," 189–90; Elmo Richardson and Alan W. Farley, *John Palmer Usher: Lincoln's Secretary of the Interior* (Lawrence: University Press of Kansas, 1960), 20–21; Usher's report in Berg, *38 Nooses,* 260–61; Diedrich, "Chief Hole-in-the-Day," 201. Pope's attitude toward Native Americans is addressed in Richard N. Ellis, *General Pope and U.S. Indian Policy* (Albuquerque: University of New Mexico Press, 1970), 7–11.

66. Nichols, "Lincoln and the Indians," 155–57; William P. Dole to Caleb B. Smith, Office of Indian Affairs, November 10, 1862, ALP-LC; AL to John Pope, telegram, November 10, 1862, *CW,* 5:493; Pope to AL, telegram, St. Paul, November 24, 1862, ALP-LC; Jane L. Williamson to Stephen R. Riggs, Travers des Sioux, November 14, 1862, ALP-LC; AL to Joseph Holt, Washington, D.C., December 1, 1862, *CW,* 5:537–38; Holt to AL, Judge Advocate General's office, December 1, 1862, ALP-LC; AL to the Senate, December 11, 1862, *CW,* 5:551; Henry H. Sibley to AL, telegram, St. Paul, December 15, 1862, ALP-LC.

67. Nichols, "Lincoln and the Indians," 157–58 (Lincoln quoted on 158); Thomas S. Williamson to AL, Washington, D.C., April 27, 1864, ALP-LC; John Peck and M. N. Adams to AL, Winnebago City, Minn., April 30, 1864, ALP-LC; AL, "Order for Discharge of Big Eagle," Washington, D.C., November 19, 1864, *CW,* 8:116; Big Eagle quoted in "Big Eagle's Story," 399.

68. Joseph R. Brown to [Henry B.] Whipple, Fort Abercrombie, January 26, 1864, and Samuel D. Hinman to [Henry B.] Whipple, Fort Thompson, January 15, 1864, both in Brown and Hinman, *Missionary Paper Number Thirty,* 9 and 15–17; Danziger, *Indians and Bureaucrats,* 112–24; entry of October 14, 1862, in Gideon Welles, *Diary of Gideon Welles: Secretary of the Navy Under Lincoln and Johnson,* ed. Howard K. Beale (New York: W. W. Norton, 1960), 1:171; Testimony of S. C. Hayes, September 2, 1865, Joint Special Committee, Senate Report No. 156, 39th Cong., 2nd sess.; Hinman, *Journal,* 5; Robert W. Furnas to William P. Dole, December 19, 1864, Office of Indian Affairs, Letters Received, Winnebago Agency, RG 75, NARA; *St. Paul Union,* November 22, 1863, quoted in Youngholm, "Violence and the Dakota War," 44; Sibley quoted in ibid., 43 (see also 46–47).

69. Samuel D. Hinman to [Henry B.] Whipple, Fort Thompson, January 15, 1864, in Brown and Hinman, *Missionary Paper Number Thirty,* 15–17; Danziger, *Indians and Bureaucrats,* 123–30; Hinman, *Journal,* 5, 9, 15, and, for quotations, 30 and 34.

70. Diedrich, "Chief Hole-in-the-Day," 200–201; Thomas Galbraith to Clark Thompson, January 27, 1863, in *Report of the Commissioner of Indian Affairs, 1863;* William P. Dole to Ely S. Parker, March 12, 1862, in Harry Kelsey, "William P. Dole and Mr. Lincoln's Indian Policy," *Journal of the West* 10, no. 3 (July 1971): 486.

71. Laurence M. Hauptman, *Between Two Fires: American Indians in the Civil War* (New York: Free Press, 1995), x (see also 145–61); Hauptman, *The Iroquois,* 18–19; John Ross to Edwin M. Stanton, Philadelphia, November 8, 1862, in *Ross Papers,* 2:520–21; James G. Blunt, Notes on Civil War Operations, Washington, D.C., April 3, 1866, in "General Blunt's Account of His Civil War Experiences," *Kansas Historical Quarterly* 1, no. 3 (May 1932): 222–23; *Detroit Free Press,* May 14, 1861, quoted in Eric Hemenway and Sammye Meadows, "Soldiers in the Shadows: Company K, 1st Michigan Sharpshooters," in Sutton and Latschar, *American Indians and the Civil War,* 53.

72. William P. Dole to Ely S. Parker, March 12, 1862, quoted in Kelsey, "William P. Dole and Mr. Lincoln's Indian Policy," 486; Hauptman, *Between Two Fires,* 126–45. For the Pamunkey Indians, see Brendan Wolfe, "Indians in Virginia," at www.encyclopedia virginia.org/Indians_in_Virginia. See also Hemenway and Meadows, "Soldiers in the Shadows," 55–63 (Lt. William H. Randall quoted on 60); Wiley Britton, *The Union Indian*

Brigade in the Civil War (Kansas City, Mo.: Franklin Hudson, 1922), 10–11; Russell Horton, "Unwanted in a White Man's War: The Civil War Service of the Green Bay Tribes," *Wisconsin Magazine of History* 88, no. 2 (Winter 2004–2005): 21–22; Hauptman, *The Iroquois,* 59–62.

73. Blunt, "General Blunt's Account," 224; *Report of the Commissioner of Indian Affairs, November 16, 1864* (Washington, D.C.: Government Printing Office, 1865), 43; Hemenway and Meadows, "Soldiers in the Shadows," 61; Hauptman, *The Iroquois,* 67–80, 151; Horton, "Unwanted in a White Man's War," 24–26; Britton, "Union and Confederate Indians," 1:336; Elisha Stockwell Jr., *Private Elisha Stockwell Jr. Sees the Civil War,* ed. Byron R. Abernathy (Norman: University of Oklahoma Press, 1985), 74–75 and 79–80; Nicolay, "Chief Hole-in-the-Day," 188.

74. John Ross to AL, September 16, 1862, in *Ross Papers,* 2:516–18; Ross to William P. Dole, Philadelphia, April 2, 1863, in ibid., 2:534–35; Hauptman, *Between Two Fires,* 92 and 131–33; Hemenway and Meadows, "Soldiers in the Shadows," 50–52 (Gaminoodhich quoted on 52); Jo Ann P. Schedler, "Wisconsin American Indians in the Civil War," in Sutton and Latschar, *American Indians and the Civil War,* 71–73.

75. Hoseca X Maria, Ke-Had-a-Wah, Buffalo Hump, Te-Nah, Geo. Washington, and Jim Pockmark to John Jumper, Wichita Agency, December 15, 1861, in Annie Heloise Abel, *The American Indian as Participant in the Civil War* (Cleveland: Arthur H. Clark, 1919), 64–65; Hauptman, *Between Two Fires,* 87–89 and 102; Smith, "Nations Colliding," 279–82; Perdue, *Slavery and the Evolution of Cherokee Society,* 129–30.

76. Jefferson Davis to Howell Cobb, March 12, 1861, at www.avalon.law.yale.edu/19th _century/csa_m031261.asp; Hauptman, *Between Two Fires,* 79 and 87–88; Britton, "Union and Confederate Indians," 1:336; Albert Pike to Jefferson Davis, September 20, 1862, *OR,* I, 13:820–21 and 823. See also Moty Kanard et al. to Jefferson Davis, Creek Nation, August 17, 1863; Stand Watie to S. S. Scott, C.N., August 8, 1863; Stand Watie to Governor of Choctaw and Chickasaw Nations, C.N., August 9, 1863; E. Kirby-Smith to Stand Watie, September 8, 1863, all *OR,* I, 22, pt. 2: 999–1000 and 1104–8; Jefferson Davis to Watie, February 22, 1864, *OR,* I, 34, pt. 3:824–25; Franks, *Stand Watie,* 141–55 and 158.

77. James M. Bell to Caroline Bell, Boggy Deport, September 2, 1863, in Dale and Litton, *Cherokee Cavaliers,* 136–37; W[illia]m Steele to S[amuel] Cooper, Doaksville, C.N., December 19, 1863, *OR,* I, 22, pt. 2:1100–1101; Steele to E. Kirby Smith, June 24, 1863, *OR,* I, pt. 2: 884.

78. Franks, *Stand Watie,* 139, 145–46, 155–58, and 174–77; Stand Watie to Governor of Creek Nation, C.N., August 9, 1863, *OR,* I, 22, pt. 2: 1105–6; Bruce S. Allardice and Lawrence Lee Hewitt, eds., *Kentuckians in Gray: Confederate Generals and Field Officers of the Bluegrass State* (Lexington: University Press of Kentucky, 2008), 101; Hauptman, *Between Two Fires,* 103 and 108.

79. David G. Taylor, "Thomas Ewing, Jr., and the Origins of the Kansas Pacific Railway Company," *Kansas Historical Quarterly* 42, no. 2 (Summer 1976): 155; Republican National Platform, Chicago, 1860, in *Tribune Almanac for the Years 1838–1868, Inclusive* (New York: New York Tribune, 1868), 30–31; Edgar Conkling to AL, Cincinnati, November 14, 1861, ALP-LC; Samuel Hallett & Co. to AL, New York, May 7, 1863 ("the productive wealth"), ALP-LC; AL, "Speech to Germans at Cincinnati," February 12, 1861, *CW,* 4:202–3; AL, "Annual Address to Congress," December 1, 1862 , ibid., 5:526; AL, "Annual Address to Congress," December 8, 1863, ibid., 7:46–48.

80. Taylor, "Thomas Ewing, Jr.," 155–60; Anna Heloise Abel, "Indian Reservations in Kansas and the Extinguishment of Their Title," *Transactions of the Kansas State Historical Society* 8 (1903–1904): 88–90; Richard White, *Railroaded: The Transcontinentals and the Making of Modern America* (New York: W. W. Norton, 2011), 25.

81. Taylor, "Thomas Ewing, Jr.," 161–63; Abel, "Indian Reservations in Kansas," 89–90; S. N. Simpson to Caleb B. Smith, Lawrence, Kans., April 8, 1861, Thomas Ewing Family Papers, LC; J. W. Wright to AL, Washington, D.C., May 29, 1861, Ewing Papers, LC; R. G. Corwin to [Thomas] Ewing Jr., Delaware Mission, July 11, 1861, Ewing Papers, LC;

Archibald Williams to AL, Leavenworth, Kans., July 2, 1861, ALP-LC; H. Craig Miner
and William E. Unrau, *The End of Indian Kansas: A Study of Cultural Revolution, 1854–
1871* (Lawrence: Regent's Press of Kansas, 1978), 29–31.
82. Thomas Ewing Jr. to Orville H. Browning, draft, Leavenworth, Kans., July 1, 1861; H. G.
Faut to Thomas Ewing Sr., Washington, D.C., July 10, 1861; Fielding Johnson to H. B.
Branch, Delaware Agency, July 10, 1861; A. C. Wilder to [Thomas] Ewing Jr., Washington,
D.C., July 16 and 18, 1861; Thomas Ewing Jr. to father [Thomas Ewing Sr.], Leavenworth,
Kans., September 12, 1861, all Ewing Papers, LC. See also AL, "Order for Issue of Bonds
for Use of Delaware Indians," June 10, 1861, *CW,* 4:400–402; AL, "Designation of
William P. Dole to Present Treaty to the Delaware Indians," Washington, D.C., August 7,
1861, ibid., 4:476–77; Taylor, "Thomas Ewing, Jr.," 163; Paul Wallace Gates, *Fifty Million
Acres: Conflicts over Kansas Land Policy, 1854–1890* (Ithaca, N.Y.: Cornell University Press,
1954), 118–20.
83. Ronald D. Smith, *Thomas Ewing, Jr.: Frontier Lawyer and Civil War General* (Columbia:
University of Missouri Press, 2008), 130–31; Mark Delahay to [Thomas Ewing], n.d.
[October 1861], Ewing Papers, LC; Thomas Ewing Jr. to Ellen [Ewing Sherman], Lawrence,
Kans., September 4, 1861, Ewing Papers, LC; Thomas Ewing Jr. to father [Thomas Ewing],
Leavenworth, Kans., September 12, 1861, Ewing Papers, LC; Miner and Unrau, *The End of
Indian Kansas,* 34–35.
84. Richardson and Farley, *John Palmer Usher,* 50–51; Taylor, "Thomas Ewing, Jr.," 166–67;
Thomas Ewing Jr. to Genl. J. Stone, Leavenworth, Kans., December 27, 1861, Ewing
Papers, LC; Gates, *Fifty Million Acres,* 121–22 and 139.
85. The 1861 treaty is in Kappler, *Laws and Treaties,* 2:814–24. See also Taylor, "Thomas
Ewing, Jr.," 167–77; Miner and Unrau, *The End of Indian Kansas,* 34–38; John Ross to
James Steele, Washington, D.C., June 8, 1864, in *Ross Papers,* 2:586; Petition to the Senate
and House of Representatives, Washington, D.C., February 18, 1865, in ibid., 2:624–27.
86. Nichols, "Lincoln and the Indians," 164; AL, "Speech to Germans at Cincinnati," February
12, 1861, *CW,* 4:202; AL, "Annual Message to Congress," December 8, 1863, ibid.,
7:46–48; AL, "Annual Message to Congress," December 6, 1864, ibid., 8:146; Gates, *Fifty
Million Acres,* 7–47; Foner, *Free Soil, Free Labor, Free Men,* 28–33; White, *Railroaded,* xvii,
17–26.
87. H. B. Branch to Gen. F[rank] P. Blair, St. Joseph, Mo., December 6, 1862, Blair Family
Papers, LC; Abel, "Indian Reservations in Kansas," 100–109; White, *Railroaded,* 25. The
Potawatomi, Ottawa, and Kickapoo treaties are in Kappler, *Laws and Treaties,* 2:824–28,
830–33, and 835–39. See also Miner and Unrau, *The End of Indian Kansas,* 65–78; Alfred
R. Elder to AL, Olympia, December 18, 1862, ALP-LC; James Short to AL, January 17,
1864, ALP-LC; Anson G. Henry to Col. Wallace, Olympia, October 24, 1861, ALP-LC;
Anson G. Henry to William P. Dole, October 28, 1861, ALP-LC; New Mexico Territory
Legislature to AL, Santa Fe, January 23, 1863, ALP-LC; Noah Brooks, "Superintendent of
Indian Affairs in Northern California," September 26, 1863, in *Lincoln Observed: The Civil
War Dispatches of Noah Brooks,* ed. Michael Burlingame (Baltimore: Johns Hopkins
University Press, 1998), 62–63; Reminiscence of John Conness, n.d. [c. 1888], in Rice,
Reminiscences of Lincoln, 567–68.
88. For detailed discussions of the Indian system, see Danziger, *Indians and Bureaucrats;*
Nichols, *Lincoln and the Indians,* 5–24. On the patronage system and patterns of corruption, see Mark Wahlgren Summers, *The Era of Good Stealings* (New York: Oxford University Press, 1993), 16–18, 20, and 22–23. On the low caliber of administration appointees,
see Prucha, *The Great Father,* 1:467; Samuel D. Hinman to [Henry B.] Whipple, Fort
Thompson, January 15, 1864, in Brown and Hinman, *Missionary Paper Number Thirty,*
15–17; Whipple, "My Life Among the Indians," 433.
89. Danziger, *Indians and Bureaucrats,* 14–16; Richardson and Farley, *John Palmer Usher,* 18
and 48–51; *Report of the Commissioner of Indian Affairs, November 26, 1862* (Washington,
D.C.: Government Printing Office, 1863), 11–12; *Report of the Commissioner of Indian
Affairs 1864,* 3–8; AL, "Annual Address to Congress," December 1, 1862, *CW,* 5:525
and 526.

90. Robert E. Lee to Mary Custis Lee, Fort Brown, Tex., January 24, 1857, Lee Papers, DU; Samuel R. Curtis to Henry Halleck, Fort Leavenworth, Kans., January 12, 1865, *OR*, I, 48, pt. 1:502–3; Ellis, *General Pope and U.S. Indian Policy*, 33–42; Pope to Henry Sibley, September 28, 1862, quoted in Danziger, *Indians and Bureaucrats*, 106; Utley, *Frontiersmen in Blue*, 215–18.

91. George A. McCall, Report to the Secretary of War, Santa Fe, July 15, 1850, in *Letters from the Frontier*, 512–17; Carleton quoted in *Condition of the Indian Tribes: Report of the Joint Special Committee Appointed Under Joint Resolution, March 3, 1865* (Washington, D.C.: Government Printing Office, 1867), 134; Prucha, *The Great Father*, 1:447–52.

92. Prucha, *The Great Father*, 1:452–57; Utley, *Frontiersmen in Blue*, 237–47; James Wilson, *The Earth Shall Weep: A History of Native America* (New York: Atlantic Monthly Press, 1999), 269–70.

93. Brigham Dwaine Madsen, *Encounter with the Northwestern Shoshoni at Bear River in 1863: Battle or Massacre?* (Ogden, Utah: Weber State College Press, 1984), 3–25; a Native American interpretation of the event, containing some inaccuracies, is found in Mae Timbimboo Parry, edited by Robert K. Sutton, "The Bear River Massacre," in Sutton and Latschar, *American Indians and the Civil War*, 112–31.

94. Stan Hoig, *The Sand Creek Massacre* (Norman: University of Oklahoma Press, 1961), 51–93; John G. Nicolay to William P. Dole, Washington, D.C., November 10, 1863, copy in scrapbook, Nicolay Papers, LC; John Evans to Edwin M. Stanton (with endorsement by AL), Washington, D.C., December 14, 1863, ALP-LC; Testimony of Gov. John Evans, March 15, 1865, Maj. Gen. Samuel R. Curtis to Maj. Gen. Henry Halleck, August 8, 1864, and Halleck to Curtis, September 3, 1864, all in "Massacre of Cheyenne Indians," in *Report of the Joint Committee on the Conduct of the War at the Second Session Thirty-Eighth Congress* (Washington, D.C.: Government Printing Office, 1865), 3:32–43, 62–63, and 66.

95. Gwynne, *Empire of the Summer Moon*, 220; Testimony of Lt. Cramer, July 27, 1865, in *Condition of the Indian Tribes*, 74. Cramer's testimony quotes Chivington more circumspectly than later descriptions, including Gwynne's. Etualin, *Lincoln Looks West*, 43, says AL appointed Evans because he was a Methodist. However, AL was no lover of Methodists and his real motive was to anchor Colorado for the Republicans. See also Danziger, *Indians and Bureaucrats*, 39–45; Testimony of Maj. Scott Anthony, March 14, 1865, in "Massacre of Cheyenne Indians," 16–29.

96. Captain O. H. P. Baxter to William B. Thom, Pueblo, February 11, 1910, in "Battle of Sand Creek," *New York Times*, June 3, 1915; Maj. E. W. Wynkoop to "sir," Fort Lyon, Col. Terr., January 15, 1865, Testimony of Lt. James Cannon, January 16, 1865, and *Rocky Mountain News* editorial, n.d., all in "Massacre of Cheyenne Indians," 81–84, 88–89, and 56–59; Diary of John Dailey, November 29, 1864, quoted on Sand Creek Massacre National Historic Site Web site, www.nps.gov/sand/historyculture; Silas S. Soule to Ned [Wynkoop], Fort Lyon, Colo., December 14, 1864, Sand Creek Web site; Joe A. Cramer to Major [Edward Wynkoop], Fort Lyon, Colo., December 19, 1864, Sand Creek Web site. For Chivington quote, see Gwynne, *Empire of the Summer Moon*, 221. See also John Nicolay to William P. Dole, November 10, 1863, Nicolay Papers, LC. The National Park Service estimates Indian deaths at around 200, while eyewitness figures range from 70 to 137; Chivington lost 24 men. A discussion of the statistics is at www.en/wikipededia.org/wiki/ Sand_Creek_massacre.

97. The casual procedures of the investigation have caused some to question its utility, but the recent rediscovery of diaries and letters written at the time reaffirm the validity of most accounts. For thoughtful, though somewhat outdated, discussions of the Joint Committee's investigation, see Raymond G. Carey, "The Puzzle of Sand Creek," *Colorado Magazine* 41, no. 4 (Fall 1964): 279–98; Michael A. Sievers, "Sands of Sand Creek Historiography," *Colorado Magazine* 49, no. 2 (Spring 1972): 116–42. The contemporary documents are found on the Sand Creek Massacre National Historic Site Web site, www.nps.gov/sand /historyculture. Questions have also arisen about the underlying causes of the brutality. Some have speculated that it resulted from callousness built from the years of the Civil War.

But those studying the actions closely have found that similar atrocities were not practiced by the Union Army against white Southerners off the battlefield. Violence of the kind seen at Sand Creek, it seems, was as ethnically motivated by the white tribe as the most ferocious acts of the Native Americans: see Mark E. Neely Jr., *The Civil War and the Limits of Destruction* (Cambridge: Harvard University Press, 2007), 140–50; and Mark Grimsley, "'Rebels' and 'Redskins': U.S. Military Conduct Toward White Southerners and Native Americans in Comparative Perspective," in *Civilians in the Path of War*, ed. Mark Grimsley and Clifford J. Rogers (Lincoln: University of Nebraska Press, 2002), 137–62. For transcripts of the investigation, see *Condition of the Indian Tribes*. Wade is quoted in "Massacre of Cheyenne Indians," v. See also "Gen. McCook and the Sand Creek Massacre," *Ohio Statesman,* August 22, 1865.

98. No response by AL to the Sand Creek massacre was found in any archive. Anson G. Henry to wife, Washington, D.C., March 13, 1865, Anson Henry Papers, ILPL; Black Kettle quoted in Hoig, *Sand Creek Massacre,* 174. For a historiographical discussion of the lingering memory of the massacre, see Ari Kelman, *A Misplaced Massacre: Struggling over the Memory of Sand Creek* (Cambridge: Harvard University Press, 2013).

99. AL, "Annual Address to Congress," December 1, 1862, *CW,* 5:526; AL, "Annual Address to Congress," December 8, 1863, ibid., 7:48; AL, "Annual Address to Congress," December 6, 1864, ibid., 8:146–47; AL to William Windom, n.p., March 30, 1864, ibid., 7:275; Whipple, "My Life Among the Indians," 438. Whipple gives several slightly different accounts of the meetings with AL and Stanton in his *Lights and Shadows of a Long Episcopate: Being Reminiscences and Recollections of the Right Reverend Henry Benjamin Whipple, DD., LL.D., Bishop of Minnesota* (New York: Macmillan, 1899), 136–37 and 144; and *Missionary Paper Number Twenty-Four,* 8, in which he quotes administration officials as saying, "'Bishop, every word you say of this Indian system is true; the nation knows it. It is useless; you will not be heard. Your faith is only like that of the man that stood on the bank of the river waiting for the water to run by, that he might cross over dry shod.'" See also Jane Swisshelm to Will[iam B. Mitchell], Washington, D.C., March 19, 1863, in Swisshelm, *Crusader and Feminist,* 191–93; Nichols, "Lincoln and the Indians," 163–65. For an apologist view, see Hans L. Trefousse, "Commentary on Nichols," in Boritt, *The Historian's Lincoln,* 170–74. For a discussion of how AL spent time on trivial issues, see chapter 3 of this book, as well as Elizabeth Brown Pryor, "'The Grand Old Duke of York': How Abraham Lincoln Lost the Confidence of His Military Command," forthcoming.

100. *Report of the Commissioner of Indian Affairs 1861,* 11; Hinman, *Journal,* January 19, 1869, 29–30; Henry Dawes, "The Indian," speech, n.d. [c. 1868], Henry Dawes Papers, LC.

101. Lewis Downing to John Ross and Evan Jones, C.N., n.d. [c. October 18, 1864]; John Ross to AL, Philadelphia, November 7, 1864; John Ross to Mary B. Ross, Washington, D.C., February 28, 1865, all in *Ross Papers,* 2:612–14 and 614–15. See also Perdue, "Civil War in Indian Territory," 104–6.

102. Elliott West, "Conclusion," in Sutton and Latschar, *American Indians and the Civil War,* 180–84; Jeffery S. King, "'Do Not Execute Chief Pocatello': President Lincoln Acts to Save the Shoshoni Chief," *Utah Historical Quarterly* 53, no. 3 (Summer 1985): 237–47. The *Congressional Globe* is filled with Indian debates in addition to the discussions in *Condition of the Indian Tribes:* see, e.g., Senate Debate, 38th Cong., 1st sess., June 10–11, 1864, 2846–51.

103. Among those addressing this aspect of AL's leadership are James MacGregor Burns, *Presidential Government: The Crucible of Leadership* (Boston: Houghton Mifflin, 1965), 37–45; David Herbert Donald, "Introduction: Sixteenth President Wrote His Own Book on Leadership," in *Lincoln in the Times: The Life of Abraham Lincoln as Originally Reported in the New York Times,* ed. David Herbert Donald and Harold Holzer (New York: St. Martin's, 2005), 4–5. The quotations are from AL, "Speech at Cincinnati—Omitted Portion," September 17, 1859, *CW,* 9:44.

CHAPTER 5. HELL-CATS

1. Isabella Beecher Hooker to John Hooker, December 2, 1862, quoted in Barbara A. White, *The Beecher Sisters* (New Haven: Yale University Press, 2003), 91–93; Annie Fields, "Days with Mrs. Stowe," *Atlantic Monthly*, August 1896, 145–46. For AL not listening closely, see Noah Brooks, *Washington in Lincoln's Time*, ed. Herbert Mitgang (New York: Rinehart, 1958), 69.

2. Harriet Beecher Stowe to Duchess of Argyll, Andover, July 31, [1862], in Annie Fields, ed., *Life and Letters of Harriet Beecher Stowe* (Cambridge: Riverside Press, 1897), 271–72; Harriet Beecher Stowe, "Prayer," *The Independent*, August 28, 1862, in Joan D. Hedrick, *Harriet Beecher Stowe: A Life* (New York: Oxford University Press, 1994), 303 [incorrectly cited in that volume's notes]; AL to Horace Greeley, August 22, 1862, *CW*, 5:388.

3. Harriet Beecher Stowe to Calvin Stowe, November 16, 1862, in Barbara A. White, *Visits with Lincoln: Abolitionists Meet the President at the White House* (Lanham, Md.: Lexington, 2011), 44; Harriet Beecher Stowe to Henry Ward Beecher, November 2, 1862, in Hedrick, *Stowe*, 305; Harriet Beecher Stowe to [James Thomas] Fields, Hartford, November 13, 1862, James T. Fields Papers, HL.

4. Later biographies state that Stowe's brother Charles accompanied the party, and a biography written by Charles and his son Lyman fifty years after the fact claimed that AL greeted the gifted author with the words "So you're the little woman who wrote the book that made this great war! Sit down, please," see Charles Edward Stowe and Lyman Beecher Stowe, *Harriet Beecher Stowe: The Story of Her Life* (Boston: Houghton Mifflin, 1911), 203. This has become a standard quip of Lincoln lore and there is even a statue of the meeting at the Lincoln Financial Sculpture Walk in Hartford, Conn., but documents from the time show it to have been unlikely. Isabella Beecher Hooker makes it clear that Wilson was only briefly present, and that otherwise the women were alone; and the fact that AL did not recognize Stowe makes such an opening remark implausible. Isabella Beecher Hooker to John Hooker, December 2, 1862, in White, *Beecher Sisters*, 93. F. Lauriston Bullard's "Abraham Lincoln and Harriet Beecher Stowe," *Lincoln Herald*, 49 (June 1946): 11–14, also contains material inconsistent with the documentary evidence. Barbara A. White did the spade work uncovering these discrepancies—see White, *Visits with Lincoln*, 49 and 59n; and also Daniel R. Vollaro, "Lincoln, Stowe, and the 'Little Woman/Great War' Story: The Making, and Breaking, of a Great American Anecdote," *JALA* 30, no. 1 (Winter 2009): 18–34.

5. Isabella Beecher Hooker to John Hooker, December 2, 1862, in White, *Beecher Sisters*, 93; Fields, "Days with Mrs. Stowe," 145–46; Harriet Beecher Stowe to [James Thomas] Fields, Washington, D.C., November 27, 1862, James T. Fields Papers, HL; Isabella Beecher Hooker to John [Hooker], November 20, [1862], in White, *Visits with Lincoln*, 44; Hatty Stowe to Eliza [Stowe], Washington, D.C., December 3, 1862, Beecher-Stowe Family Papers, Schlesinger Library, HU.

6. For biographical information on Swisshelm, see Sylvia D. Hoffert, *Jane Grey Swisshelm: An Unconventional Life, 1815–1884* (Chapel Hill: University of North Carolina Press, 2004); a shorter discussion is in the introduction to Jane Grey Swisshelm, *Crusader and Feminist: Letters of Jane Grey Swisshelm, 1858–1865*, ed. Arthur J. Larsen (Westport, Conn.: Hyperion Press, 1976), 1–28. Descriptions of Swisshelm can be found in entry of February 21, 1863, Horatio Nelson Taft Diary, LC; "Pen Portraits on the Floor of the House," *Chicago Tribune*, December 23, 1863, in Hoffert, *Swisshelm*, 103. For Swisshelm's retorts, see Jane Grey Swisshelm, *Half a Century* (Chicago: Jansen, McClurg, 1880), 114.

7. Hoffert, *Swisshelm*, 104–6; "Pen Portraits on the Floor of the House," in ibid., 103; Swisshelm, *Half a Century*, 234.

8. Jane Swisshelm to Will[iam] A. Mitchell, Washington, D.C., February 9 and 14, 1863, in Swisshelm, *Crusader and Feminist*, 173 and 180; Swisshelm, *Half a Century*, 236.

9. Elizabeth Cady Stanton, Susan B. Anthony, Matilda Joslyn Gage, and Ida Husted Harper, eds., *History of Woman Suffrage* (Rochester, N.Y.: Susan B. Anthony and New York: National American Woman Suffrage Association, 1887–1922), 2:41; Anna Dickinson to William Lloyd Garrison, Phila[delphia], March 16, 1862, Anna Dickinson Papers, LC;

William Lloyd Garrison to Anna Dickinson, Boston, March 22, 1862, Dickinson Papers, LC; Anna Dickinson to Susan E. Dickinson, Boston, April 28, 1862, Dickinson Papers, LC. For Dickinson's early years and work as a lecturer, see J. Matthew Gallman, *America's Joan of Arc: The Life of Anna Elizabeth Dickinson* (New York: Oxford University Press, 2006), 17–35; Melanie Susan Gustafson, *Women and the Republican Party, 1854–1924* (Urbana: University of Illinois Press, 2001), 24–25.

10. Gallman, *America's Joan of Arc,* 31; *Philadelphia Evening Bulletin,* undated clipping, and "A Lady Stump-Speaker," both in Dickinson's scrapbook, Dickinson Papers, LC; Diary of Nathan Daniels, January 17, 1864, Nathan Daniels Diaries, LC; White, *Visits with Lincoln,* 85; Mary Elizabeth Massey, *Bonnet Brigades: American Women and the Civil War* (New York: Alfred A. Knopf, 1966), 154; Gustafson, *Women and the Republican Party,* 27–29; Nina Silber, *Daughters of the Union: Northern Women Fight the Civil War* (Cambridge: Harvard University Press, 2005), 145; J. W. Batterson to Republican State Central Committee, Hartford, April 15, 1863, Dickinson Papers, LC. A dated look at the impact of Dickinson's lecturing is in James Harvey Young, "Anna Elizabeth Dickinson and the Civil War: For and Against Lincoln," *Mississippi Valley Historical Review* 31, no. 1 (June 1944): 59–80.

11. "The National Crisis," March 6, 1862, and Anna Dickinson to sister, Boston, May 27, 1862, both Dickinson Papers, LC; William D. Kelley, Anna E. Dickinson, and Frederick Douglass, *Addresses of Hon. W. D. Kelley, Miss Anna E. Dickinson, and Mr. Frederick Douglass at a Mass Meeting Held at National Hall, Philadelphia, 6 July 1863 for the Promotion of Colored Enlistments* (Philadelphia: Commission for United States Colored Troops, 1863).

12. White, *Visits with Lincoln,* 86–88 and 95n; description of speech in Diary of Nathan Daniels, January 19, 1864, Daniels Diaries, LC; AL, "Annual Message to Congress," December 8, 1863, *CW,* 7:36–53; "The Perils of the Hour," copy in Dickinson Papers, LC; Young, "Dickinson and the Civil War," 69; Henry Dawes to "my own priceless beauty" [Electra Dawes], Washington, D.C., January 17, 1864, Henry Dawes Papers, LC.

13. Young, "Dickinson and the Civil War," 69–70; Gallman, *America's Joan of Arc,* 37; Giraud Chester, *Embattled Maiden: The Life of Anna Dickinson* (New York: G. P. Putnam, 1951), 76–77; *Daily National Republican,* January 18, 1864: Charles D. Warner to Anna Dickinson, Hartford, January 19, 1864, Dickinson Papers, LC.

14. Gallman, *America's Joan of Arc,* 39; Chester, *Embattled Maiden,* 80; *Boston Daily Courier,* April 28, 1864, clipping in Dickinson Papers, LC.

15. William D. Kelley to [James] McKim, Washington, D.C., May 1, 1864, and James McKim to [William Lloyd] Garrison, Philadelphia, May 3, 1864, both Anti-Slavery Collection, Boston Public Library, Boston, Mass. For Dickinson's excitable nature, see Anne Gilbert to Anna Dickinson, Oxford, January 7, 1861, Dickinson Papers, LC; William D. Kelley to Anna Dickinson, Washington, D.C., July 24, 1864, Dickinson Papers, LC; Chester, *Embattled Maiden,* 80–81; White, *Visits with Lincoln,* 89–90. For a discussion of similar male encounters with AL, see chapter 2.

16. Clara Barton to Henry Wilson, Washington, D.C., September 29 and December 19, 1865, Clara Barton Papers, LC; Elizabeth Brown Pryor, *Clara Barton, Professional Angel* (Philadelphia: University of Pennsylvania Press, 1987), 73 and 76; Clara Barton to Captain Denny, n.d. [1861–1862], Barton Papers, LC.

17. Barton's wartime work is discussed in Pryor, *Clara Barton,* 73–137; a longer treatment is in Stephen B. Oates, *A Woman of Valor: Clara Barton and the Civil War* (New York: Free Press, 1994). See also entry of May 24, 1865 ("I am told"), Taft Diary, Taft Papers, LC; Clara Barton's statement about her motivation to help others was made at a conference c. 1886, cited in Percy H. Epler, *The Life of Clara Barton* (New York: Macmillan, 1915), 32.

18. Clara Barton to Thad[deus] W. Meighan, Hilton Head, S.C., June 24, 1863, Barton Papers, LC; Clara Barton to Ladies Relief Committee of Worcester, Mass., December 16, 1861, Clara Barton Papers, American Antiquarian Society, Worcester, Mass.; Barton to Stephen Barton Jr., North Oxford, March 1, 1862, Barton Papers, LC; Barton to Frances D. Gage, copy in Barton Journal, May 1, 1864, Barton Papers, LC.

19. Description of Barton in Alvin C. Voris to wife, Petersburg, Va., August 26, 1864, typescript, Alvin Coe Voris Papers, VHS. Barton's clothing is described in Clara [Barton] to Amelia Barton, Hilton Head, S.C., September 17, 1863, Clara Barton Papers, HL. See also Clara Barton Diary, February 27 and March 2, 1865, Barton Papers, LC.
20. Clara Barton Petition to AL, n.d. [February 1865]; W. G. Washburn to AL, Washington, D.C., February 28, 1865; [Ethan Allen] Hitchcock to Clara Barton, Washington, D.C., February 28, 1865; H[enry] Wilson to AL, Washington, D.C., February 28, 1865, all Barton Papers, LC. For Wilson's consultations with Barton, see Barton to Wilson, January 28, 1863, and March 9 and October 29, 1865, Barton Papers, LC; Barton Diary, January 29 and February 26, 1865, Barton Papers, LC. Barton's work with missing men is described in Pryor, *Clara Barton*, 134–46; Oates, *Woman of Valor*, 300–369; see also Drew Gilpin Faust, *This Republic of Suffering: Death and the American Civil War* (New York: Alfred A. Knopf, 2008), 211–49.
21. For a description of Barton's string of rejections, see Barton Diary, February 26 through March 4, 1865, Barton Papers, LC; the quotation is from the entry of February 27.
22. AL's endorsement, "As it is a matter pertaining to prisoners Gen. Hitchcock is authorized to do as he thinks fit in this matter of Miss Barton," is in Ethan Allen Hitchcock to Clara Barton, February 28, 1865, Barton Papers, LC. A promoter of Barton's work in the early twentieth century quoted another note from AL that gave clearer backing, but the document has never been found and that author's work is unreliable in many other ways: see AL, "To the Friends of Missing Persons," n.d., *CW*, 8:423; Corra Bacon-Foster, *Clara Barton, Humanitarian* (Washington, D.C.: Columbia Historical Society, 1918), 19. Roy P. Basler apparently believed AL held productive interviews with both Barton and Swisshelm. However, their papers make it clear the President did not meet them officially: see Basler, "Lincoln, Blacks, and Women," in *The Public and the Private Lincoln,* ed. Cullom Davis et al. (Carbondale: Southern Illinois University Press, 1979), 45.
23. Edward Bates to Miss [Anna] Carroll, September 21, 1861, and Anna Ella Carroll, request for reimbursement, Misc. Doc. 58 (HR, 45th Cong., 2nd sess.), in Sarah Ellen Blackwell, *A Military Genius: Life of Anna Ella Carroll of Maryland* (Washington, D.C.: Judd & Detweiler, 1891), 41–42 and 125; Anna Ella Carroll, "The War Powers of the General Government" (Washington, D.C.: Henry Polkinhorn, 1861); Anna Ella Carroll to AL, n.p., August 14, 1862, ALP-LC; AL to Anna E. Carroll, August 19, 1862, *CW*, 5:381; Janet L. Coryell, *Neither Heroine nor Fool: Anna Ella Carroll of Maryland* (Kent, Ohio: Kent State University Press, 1990), 57 and 79–80. Documents relating to the promise of government funds are in Blackwell, *A Military Genius;* see also Basler, "Lincoln, Blacks, and Women," 45–47.
24. Mrs. A. H. [Jane Currie] Hoge, *The Boys in Blue; or Heroes of the "Rank and File"* (New York: E. B. Treat, 1867), 83; Mary A. Livermore, *My Story of the War* (Hartford: A. D. Worthington, 1889), 554–60; Julia Ward Howe, "The Civil War," unpublished manuscript, January 24, 1906, Howe Family Papers, Schlesinger Library, HU.
25. Gail Hamilton (Mary Abigail Dodge) to mother, Meriden, Conn., March 20, 1861, in Gail Hamilton, *Gail Hamilton's Life in Letters,* ed. H. Augusta Dodge (Boston: Lee & Shepard, 1901), 1:315; Cordelia A. P. Harvey, "A Wisconsin Woman's Picture of President Lincoln," *Wisconsin Magazine of History* 1, no. 3 (March 1918): 233–55. AL's awkward interactions with women are also discussed in Michael Burlingame, *The Inner World of Abraham Lincoln* (Urbana: University of Illinois Press, 1994), 126–33.
26. Reminiscence of William D. Kelley, n.d. [c. 1888], in Allen Thorndike Rice, ed., *Reminiscences of Abraham Lincoln by Distinguished Men of His Time* (New York: North American Review, 1888), 284–85.
27. Mary P. Ryan, *Women in Public: Between Banners and Ballots, 1825–1880* (Baltimore: Johns Hopkins University Press, 1990), 3–18 and 52; Richard J. Carwardine, *Evangelicals and Politics in Antebellum America* (New Haven: Yale University Press, 1993), 32; Jo Freeman, *A Room at a Time: How Women Entered Party Politics* (Lanham, Md.: Rowman & Littlefield, 2000), 28; Gustafson, *Women and the Republican Party,* 1–2; Bruce Dorsey, *Reforming Men and Women: Gender in the Antebellum City* (Ithaca, N.Y.: Cornell University Press, 2002), 32–33.

28. Gustafson, *Women and the Republican Party*, 10–12; Elizabeth Varon, "Tippecanoe and the Ladies, Too," *Journal of American History* 82, no. 2 (September 1995): 495–503; Carwardine, *Evangelicals and Politics*, 33–34.

29. Rebecca Edwards, *Angels in the Machinery: Gender in American Party Politics from the Civil War to the Progressive Era* (New York: Oxford University Press, 1997), 16, 18, and 28; H. Preston James, "Political Pageantry in the Campaign of 1860 in Illinois," *Abraham Lincoln Quarterly* 4, no. 7 (September 1947): 313–47.

30. Douglas L. Wilson, *Honor's Voice: The Transformation of Abraham Lincoln* (New York: Alfred A. Knopf, 1998), 213–15; John Nicolay, interview with S[tephen] T. Logan, Springfield, Ill., July 6, 1875, in John G. Nicolay, *An Oral History of Abraham Lincoln: John G. Nicolay's Interviews and Essays*, ed. Michael Burlingame (Carbondale: Southern Illinois University Press, 1996), 39; Mary Todd to Mercy Ann Levering, Springfield, Ill., December [15?], 1840, in Justin G. Turner and Linda Levitt Turner, eds., *Mary Todd Lincoln: Her Life and Letters* (New York: Alfred A. Knopf, 1972), 21; Henry Clay quoted in Edwards, *Angels in the Machinery*, 14.

31. Massey, *Bonnet Brigades*, 17–24; Lydia Maria Child to Sarah Shaw, Wayland, August 3, 1856, in Lydia Maria Child, *Selected Letters, 1817–1880*, ed. Milton Meltzer and Patricia G. Holland (Amherst: University of Massachusetts Press, 1982), 290.

32. Silber, *Daughters of the Union*, 45; Coryell, *Neither Heroine nor Fool*, xiii–xiv; "Isola" quoted in Lori D. Ginzberg, " 'Moral Suasion Is Moral Balderdash': Women, Politics, and Moral Activism in the 1850s," *Journal of American History* 73, no. 3 (December 1986): 601.

33. Isabella Beecher Hooker to John Hooker, November 25, 1862, quoted in White, *Beecher Sisters*, 93; Sarah Smith (Martyn) quoted in Ginzberg, " 'Moral Suasion Is Moral Balderdash,' " 608.

34. Henry Ward Beecher, "Women's Influence in Politics: Address Delivered at the Cooper Institute, New York, 2 February 1860" (Boston: R. F. Wallcut, 1860).

35. Diary entry of February 11, 1861, in Caroline Healey Dall, *Daughter of Boston: The Extraordinary Diary of a Nineteenth-Century Woman*, ed. Helen R. Deese (Boston: Beacon Press, 2005), 302; Julia Ward Howe to Charles Sumner, [Philadelphia], February 23, 1864, Howe Family Papers, Houghton Library, HU; *Geneva* [N.Y.] *Gazette*, March 1, 1864, quoted in Mary Elizabeth Massey, *Women in the Civil War* (Lincoln: University of Nebraska Press, 1994), 153–54; [David Ross Locke], "The Struggles of a Conservative with the Woman Question," in *The Struggles (Social, Financial and Political) of Petroleum V. Nasby* (Boston: Lee & Shepard, 1888), 660–86; Artemus Ward [Charles Farrar Browne], *His Book* (New York: Carleton, 1862), 49–53 and 119–22; *Vanity Fair*, May 30, 1863, 85–86.

36. An example of denying strong-mindedness is in Rhoda E. White to AL, New York, December 15, 1860, ALP-LC; see also MTL to James Gordon Bennett, October 4, 1862, in Turner and Turner, *Life and Letters*, 138.

37. AL to Andrew McCallen, Springfield, Ill., June 19, 1858, *CW*, 2:469; he reiterates this sentiment in a letter to Henry Wilson, Springfield, Ill., September 1, 1860, ibid., 4:109.

38. AL to Editor of the *Sangamo Journal*, New Salem, Ill., June 13, 1836, *CW*, 1:48; for a variety of commentary on this remark, see Basler, "Lincoln, Blacks, and Women," 41; Richard N. Current, *The Lincoln Nobody Knows* (New York: McGraw-Hill, 1958), 33; Gerald J. Prokopowicz, *Did Lincoln Own Slaves? And Other Frequently Asked Questions About Abraham Lincoln* (New York: Pantheon, 2008), 181.

39. Wilson, *Honor's Voice*, 71; Earl Schenck Miers, ed., *Lincoln Day by Day* (Washington, D.C.: Lincoln Sesquicentennial Commission, 1960), 2:186; AL, "Speech at Springfield," July 17, 1858, *CW*, 2:520; WHH to Jesse Weik, Springfield, Ill., February 11, 1887, Herndon-Weik Collection, LC; "An Unpublished Letter from Lincoln's Law Partner," *The Independent*, April 4, 1895. AL's secretary John Nicolay confirmed that he never heard AL support women's rights: see memo in Nicolay's hand to Mr. Gilder, n.d., John G. Nicolay Papers, LC.

40. Wilson, *Honor's Voice*, 102–3; Miers, *Day by Day*, 2:20–21, 53, and 98. There are numerous examples of AL taking the part of women suffering from deprivation caused by war: see, e.g., AL to James F. Simmons, May 21, 1862, *CW*, 5:228; AL to Montgomery Blair, July

24, 1863, ibid., 6:346; AL to John D. Defrees, November 12, 1863, ibid., 7:12; see also AL to Charles Sumner, May 19, 1864, ibid., 9:243.

41. No contemporary description exists for Nancy Hanks Lincoln (sometimes called Nancy Sparrow, a name used after her mother began living with Henry Sparrow). For recollections see, e.g., WHH interviews with John Hanks, Decatur, Ill., May 25, 1865, and n.d. [1865–1866], *HI,* 5 and 37; WHH interview with Dennis F. Hanks, Chicago, June 13, 1865, ibid., 454; for the relative quote, see WHH interview with Nathaniel Grigsby, Gentryville, Ind., September 12, 1865, ibid., 113.

42. AL, quoted in WHH to Ward Hill Lamon, March 6, 1870 ("a brilliant woman"), Ward Hill Lamon Papers, HL; AL to Mrs. Orville Browning, April 1, 1838 ("weather-beaten"), *CW,* 1:118. There is a possibility that AL was describing his stepmother in this latter passage, but another description of his mother also mentions dental problems: see James K. Rardin to Jesse Weik, Chicago, March 9, 1888, *HI,* 652. Lloyd Ostendorf's 1963 imagining of Nancy Hanks Lincoln can be found at www.nps.gov/albi/learn/historyculture/nancy -hanks-lincoln; Dennis Hanks, a cousin on her side, does indeed show a marked likeness to the sixteenth president. On Nancy Lincoln's death, see Nathaniel Grigsby to WHH, Gentryville, Ind., September 4, 1865, and A. H. Chapman, Statement, c. September 8, 1865, *HI,* 93 and 97–98.

43. Louis A. Warren, *Lincoln's Youth: Indiana Years Seven to Twenty-One, 1816–1830* (New York: Appleton, Century, Crofts, 1959), 9–10; WHH interview with Elizabeth Crawford, September 16, 1865, *HI,* 126; WHH interview with John Hanks, n.d. [1865–1866], ibid., 456; John Hanks to Jesse Weik, Linkville, Ore., June 12, 1887, ibid., 615.

44. William E. Bartelt, *"There I Grew Up": Remembering Abraham Lincoln's Indiana Youth* (Indianapolis: Indiana Historical Society, 2008), 36; Grigsby to WHH, September 12, 1865, *HI,* 114; WHH interview with Nathaniel Grigsby, Silas Richardson, Nancy Richardson, and John Romine, Lincoln Farm, September 14, 1865, ibid., 118; WHH interview with Crawford, September 16, 1865, ibid., 127; WHH interview with Green Taylor, September 16, 1865, ibid., 130; Samuel Kercheval to Jesse Weik, Rockport, December 2, 1887, ibid., 645. See also Wilson, *Honor's Voice,* 295.

45. WHH to Jesse Weik, Springfield, Ill., October 8, 1881, Herndon-Weik Collection, LC; Warren, *Lincoln's Youth,* 60–66; WHH interview with Sarah Bush Lincoln, September 8, 1865, *HI,* 106–9; Harriet Chapman to WHH, Charleston, Ill., December 17, 1865, ibid., 144; WHH interview with Crawford, September 16, 1865, ibid., 126; Bartelt, *"There I Grew Up,"* 64. Another photograph of Sarah Bush Johnston Lincoln was identified in 2003 in the Stephenson County Historical Society, Freeport, Ill.

46. AL to John D. Johnston, Springfield, Ill., November 25, 1851, *CW,* 2:113; John J. Hall to AL, October 18, 1864, ALP-LC; Harriet Chapman to AL, Charleston, Ill., January 17, 1865, ALP-LC; WHH interview with Sarah Bush Lincoln, September 8, 1865, *HI,* 106–9.

47. The trauma of childhood loss is examined in Sigmund Freud, "Mourning and Melancholia" (1917), in James Strachey, ed., *The Standard Edition of the Complete Psychological Works of Sigmund Freud* (London: Hogarth, 1957), 14 and 239–58; George H. Pollack, "Mourning and Adaptation," *International Journal of Psycho-Analysis* 42 (1961); Alicia F. Lieberman, "Separation in Infancy and Early Childhood: Contributions of Attachment Theory and Psychoanalysis," and Janice L. Krupnick and Frederic Solomon, "Death of a Parent or Sibling During Childhood," both in Jonathan Bloom-Feshbach and Sally Bloom-Feshbach, eds., *The Psychology of Separation and Loss* (San Francisco: Jossey Bass, 1987), 345–65; John Bowlby, *The Making and Breaking of Affectional Bonds* (London: Tavistock, 1979); Alicia F. Lieberman et al., eds., *Losing a Parent to Death in the Early Years: Guidelines for the Treatment of Traumatic Bereavement in Infancy and Early Childhood* (Washington, D.C.: Zero to Three, 2003). They postulate that such loss can cause a boy to cling to and yet try to dominate the surviving parent or suffer a sharp fear of dependence. During mourning, young children may reproach themselves, believing they contributed to the death, and guilty feelings may arise from this. There may be rage or despair in the face of abandonment and those who internalize these feelings may later suffer depression, feelings of inadequacy, or physical illness, sometimes masked by an outer shell of equanimity.

48. AL to Fanny McCullough, December 23, 1862, *CW,* 6:16–17; William Knox, "Mortality," online at www.poets.org; AL to Andrew Johnston, Tremont, April 18, 1846, *CW,* 1:377–79; Lawrence Weldon, notes for speech, August 1, 1865, *HI,* 88. AL's depression is discussed in Burlingame, *Inner World,* 92–122; Joshua Wolf Shenk, *Lincoln's Melancholy: How Depression Challenged a President and Fueled His Greatness* (Boston: Houghton Mifflin, 2005).

49. WHH's description of the conversation about Nancy Hanks's legitimacy is in Wilson, *Honor's Voice,* 12–13. See also David Herbert Donald, *Lincoln* (New York: Simon & Schuster, 1995), 20 and 603n; Prokopowicz, *Did Lincoln Own Slaves?,* 6–8; Richard N. Collins to WHH, Cincinnati, August 19, 1867, *HI,* 198–99; Alfred M. Brown to Jesse Weik, [Elizabethtown, Ky.], March 23, 1887, ibid., 567; Dennis Hanks to WHH, Charleston, Ill., February 10, 1866, ibid., 612; Henry C. Whitney to WHH, Chicago, August 29, 1887, ibid., 635.

50. Wilson, *Honor's Voice,* 110; conversation with O. H. Browning, Springfield, Ill., June 17, 1875, and with William Butler, Springfield, Ill., June 13, 1875, in Nicolay, *An Oral History of Abraham Lincoln,* 1–7 and 18–19; Anson Henry to wife, Washington, D.C., February 8, 1865, Anson Henry Papers, ILPL. On avoiding girls, see WHH interview with N. W. Branson, Petersburg, Ill., August 3, 1865, *HI,* 91; WHH interview with Anna Caroline Gentry, Rockport, Ill., September 17, 1865, ibid., 131. "Too frivolous" from statement of John Hanks in Burlingame, *Inner World,* 123.

51. Burlingame, *Inner World,* 123–24; Mrs. Samuel Chowning quoted in John Y. Simon, *House Divided: Lincoln and His Father* (Fort Wayne, Ind.: Louis A. Warren Lincoln Library and Museum, 1987); AL, "Speech in Illinois Legislature, Concerning Apportionment," [January 9, 1841?], *CW,* 1:228; Reminiscence of Samuel R. Weed, c. 1882, in Don E. Fehrenbacher and Virginia Fehrenbacher, eds., *Recollected Words of Abraham Lincoln* (Stanford, Calif.: Stanford University Press, 1996), 460. For more on AL's self-deprecation, see chapter 2.

52. Statement of Abner Ellis, January 23, 1866, *HI,* 170; Henry Clay Whitney, *Life on the Circuit with Lincoln* (Boston: Estes & Lauriat, 1892), 37; WHH interview with Elizabeth Todd Edwards, n.d. [1865–1866], *HI,* 443; Mary Owens Vineyard to WHH, Weston, Mo., May 23 and July 22, 1866, ibid., 256 and 262.

53. WHH, "Analysis of the Character of Abraham Lincoln," December 26, 1865, William Henry Herndon Papers, HL; Replies to Queries by Dr. Le Grand, n.d., Arthur E. Morgan Papers LC; see also Arthur E. Morgan, "New Light on Lincoln's Boyhood," *Atlantic Monthly,* February 1920, 216; Henry Villard, "Recollections of Lincoln," *Atlantic Monthly,* February 1904, 165–74.

54. AL to Mary Owens, Springfield, Ill., May 7 and August 16, 1837, *CW,* 1:78–79 and 95; AL to Mrs. Orville H. Browning, April 1, 1838, ibid., 1:117–19; WHH interview with John Lightfoot, September 13, 1887, *HI,* 639; Sarah Rickard Barret to WHH, Connors, Kans., August 3, 1888, ibid., 663–64. See also Fred Kaplan, *Lincoln: The Biography of a Writer* (New York: Harper Perennial, 2010), 39; Current, *The Lincoln Nobody Knows,* 41; Catherine Clinton, *Mrs. Lincoln: A Life* (New York: Harper, 2009), 42.

55. A sensitive discussion of AL's relation with Anne Rutledge is in Wilson, *Honor's Voice,* 106–7 and 114–26 (Robert Rutledge quoted on 118); see also Donald, *Lincoln,* 55–57; Sarah Rutledge Saunders to Mary Saunders, enclosure in J. R. Saunders to Mary Saunders, Sisquoc, Calif., May 14, 1914, ILPL. In his afterword to C. A. Tripp, *The Intimate World of Abraham Lincoln,* ed. Lewis Gannett (New York: Free Press, 2005), 236–37, Michael Burlingame argues strongly against Tripp's skepticism about the romance, as well as the questions raised in Lewis Gannett, "'Overwhelming Evidence' of a Lincoln–Ann Rutledge Romance?: Reexamining Rutledge Family Reminiscences," *JALA* 26, no. 1 (Winter 2005): 28–41.

56. Tripp, *Intimate World,* is a lengthy psychological assessment of AL's purported homosexuality; Jean Baker proposes in the introduction he was bisexual, xxii; for AL's friendship with Derickson, see 2–17. Matthew Pinsker believes that the stories about Derickson, though based on fact, were inflated by gossip: see Pinsker, *Lincoln's Sanctuary: Abraham Lincoln and the Soldiers' Home* (New York: Oxford University Press, 2003), 84–87. See also Current, *The Lincoln Nobody Knows,* 32. "What stuff!" is from Diary of Virginia Woodbury Fox, November 16, 1862, Levi Woodbury Papers, LC.

57. Statement of Abner Ellis, January 23, 1866, *HI,* 171; WHH interview with David Davis, September 20, [1866], ibid., 350; WHH interview with Joshua Speed, January 5, 1889, ibid., 719; Burlingame, "Afterword," in Tripp, *Intimate World,* 229–30; WHH to Jesse Weik, Springfield, Ill., December 10, 1885, and January 23, 1890, Herndon-Weik Collection, LC; Wilson, *Honor's Voice,* 127–29.

58. On changing concepts of manliness, see Gail Bederman, *Manliness and Civilization: A Cultural History of Gender and Race in the United States, 1880–1917* (Chicago: University of Chicago Press, 1995), 5–8 and 16–18; Michael Kimmel, *Manhood in America: A Cultural History* (New York: Free Press, 1996), 18, 22–23, and 33; Wilson, *Honor's Voice,* 295; WHH interview with Dennis F. Hanks, June 13, 1865 (source for Thomas Lincoln's whipping a bully), *HI,* 37; A. H. Chapman Statement, ante September 8, 1865, ibid., 96.

59. Charles E. Rosenberg, "Sexuality, Class and Role in 19th-Century America," *American Quarterly* 25, no. 2 (May 1973): 137–39 and 143–45; Kimmel, *Manhood in America,* 25–28, 39–45, 52, and 60; Wilson, *Honor's Voice,* 296–98; Stephen M. Frank, *Life with Father: Parenthood and Masculinity in the Nineteenth-Century American North* (Baltimore: Johns Hopkins University Press, 1998), 3–4.

60. WHH to Jesse Weik, December 10, 1885, and "Notes on Lincoln and Mary Todd," n.d. [post-1880], both Herndon-Weik Collection, LC [incorrectly transcribed in *The Hidden Lincoln: From the Letters and Papers of William H. Herndon,* ed. Emanuel Hertz (New York: Blue Ribbon, 1940), 111–12]; Jean H. Baker, *Mary Todd Lincoln: A Biography* (New York: W. W. Norton, 1987), 37; WHH interview with Edwards, [c. 1865–1866], *HI,* 443.

61. James Conkling quoted in Wilson, *Honor's Voice,* 219–20; WHH interview with Edwards, [c. 1865–1866], *HI,* 443. My interpretation of the Todd-Lincoln relationship is largely drawn from Wilson's account, 215–31, which painstakingly examines the fragmented evidence.

62. AL to John T. Stuart, Springfield, Ill., January 20 and 23, 1841, *CW,* 1:228 and 229; Joshua Speed to WHH, Louisville, November 30, 1866, *HI,* 430; WHH interview with Edwards, [c. 1865–1866], ibid., 443; WHH interview with Joshua Speed, [c. 1865–1866], ibid., 475. See also Jane D. Bell to Ann Bell, January 27, 1841, in Wilson, *Honor's Voice,* 237.

63. AL to Joshua F. Speed, Springfield, Ill., March 24, 1843, *CW,* 1:319; see also AL to Samuel D. Marshall, Springfield, Ill., November 11, 1842, ibid., 1:303. For Speed's similar doubts about marriage, see AL to Joshua F. Speed, Springfield, Ill., October 5, 1842, ibid., 1:305; Wilson, *Honor's Voice,* 233–64, 284–86, and 291, offers an insightful account of the marriage; a sympathetic treatment is in Daniel Mark Epstein, *The Lincolns: Portrait of a Marriage* (New York: Ballantine, 2008); a more critical view is in Michael Burlingame, "Honest Abe, Dishonest Mary," *Bulletin of the 54th Annual Meeting of the Lincoln Fellowship of Wisconsin* 50 (April 1994).

64. MTL to AL, New York, November 2, [1862], in Turner and Turner, *Life and Letters,* 139–40; MTL to Mary Jane Welles, near Chicago, July 11, 1865, ibid., 257. For AL's correspondence with his wife, see the letters of April 16, June 12, and July 2, 1848, *CW,* 1:465, 477, and 495; excerpt, [Exeter, N.H.], n.d. [March 4, 1860], ibid., 3:555; letters of June 9, August 8, and September 21, 22, and 24, 1863, ibid., 6:256, 371–72, 471, 474, and 478; letter of April 28, 1864, ibid., 7:320; telegrams of December 21, 1864, and April 2, 1865, ibid., 8:174 and 382. See also WHH to [Joseph Smith] Fowler, Springfield, Ill., October 30, 1888, Ethan Allen Hitchcock Papers, LC. For "as a business," see AL to Mrs. M. J. Green, Springfield, Ill., September 22, 1860, *CW,* 4:118. Ideas about the marriage bond also gleaned from the interview with Damián Szifrón in Larry Rohter, "The Making of 'Wild Tales' an Oscar Nominee," *New York Times,* February 15, 2015.

65. Douglas L. Wilson, "William H. Herndon and Mary Todd Lincoln," *JALA* 22, no. 2 (Summer 2001); WHH interview with James Gourley, *HI,* 452–53. The baby carriage incident is in Katherine Helm, *The True Story of Mary, Wife of Lincoln* (New York: Harper Brothers, 1928), 113. For a who-struck-whom recitation of the Lincolns' home life, with a pro-AL emphasis, see Burlingame, "The Lincolns' Marriage," in *Inner World,* 268–355; for more sympathetic accounts of MTL's trials with AL, see Clinton, *Mrs. Lincoln,* 74, 105, and

125; Emily Todd Helm, "Mary Todd Lincoln: Reminiscences and Letters of the Wife of President Lincoln," *McClure's Magazine,* September 1898, 479; David Donald, "Herndon and Mrs. Lincoln," in *Lincoln Reconsidered: Essays on the Civil War Era,* 2nd ed. (New York: Alfred A. Knopf, 1972), 50–56. The WHH quotation is in Wilson, "William H. Herndon and Mary Todd Lincoln."

66. Clinton, *Mrs. Lincoln,* 74 and 105; Katheryn Kish Sklar, "Victorian Women and Domestic Life: Mary Todd Lincoln, Elizabeth Cady Stanton and Harriet Beecher Stowe," in Davis, *The Public and the Private Lincoln,* 30–34; WHH to Fowler, October 30, 1888, Hitchcock Papers, LC; Whitney, *Life on the Circuit,* 97; Mark E. Neely Jr., *The Last Best Hope of Earth: Abraham Lincoln and the Promise of America* (Cambridge: Harvard University Press, 1993), 32–33; AL to MTL, April 16 and June 12, 1848, *CW,* 1:465–66 and 477–78; Henry C. Bowen, "Recollection of Abraham Lincoln," in William Hayes Ward, ed., *Abraham Lincoln: Tributes from His Associates, Reminiscences of Soldiers, Statesmen and Citizens* (New York: Thomas Y. Crowell, 1895), 32.

67. Elizabeth Todd Edwards to Julia [Edwards], Andover, February 10, [1861], Elizabeth Todd Edwards Correspondence, LC; Herman Kreismann to Charles Ray, Washington, D.C., January 16, 1861, Charles H. Ray Papers, HL; for a closer look at the pre-inauguration period, see chapter 6.

68. Diary of William Howard Russell, March 28 and 30, 1861, in William Howard Russell, *My Diary North and South* (Boston: Burnham, 1863), 41–42 and quotation on 54. For criticism, see Lydia Maria Child to [Sarah Blake Sturgis], Wayland, November 24, 1861, Lydia Maria Child Correspondence, LC; Benjamin B. French to Pamela [French], Washington, D.C., December 24, 1861, Benjamin B. French Family Papers, LC. The often quoted quip "flub dubs . . ." is sometimes put in italics, but those do not appear in the original manuscript. For example, see the entry of December 16, 1861, in Benjamin Brown French, *Witness to the Young Republic: A Yankee's Journal, 1828–1870,* ed. Donald B. Cole and John J. McDonough (Hanover, N.H.: University Press of New England, 1989), 382.

69. Examples of MTL's many freelance political letters are MTL to David Davis, New York, January 17, 1861 [*sic;* likely 1862]; MTL to Simon Cameron, March 29, [1861]; MTL to Montgomery Meigs, October 4, 1861; MTL to Edwin D. Morgan, New York, November 13, 1862; MTL to Charles Sumner, November 20, 1864; and MTL to Simon Draper, January 26, 1865, all in Turner and Turner, *Life and Letters,* 74, 83, 107–8, 142, 191, and 199. See also Margaret Leech, *Reveille in Washington, 1860–1865* (New York: Harper Brothers, 1941), 290; entry of September 27, 1861, Taft Diary, LC. The Wikoff affair is discussed in Epstein, *The Lincolns,* 339–42 and 353–56; Henry M. Smith to Eds. [*Chicago*] *Tribune,* n.d. [November 1861], Ray Papers, HL. AL's papers show no response to his wife's efforts to influence affairs, and no action taken, although some historians have projected that he chastised or stopped confiding in MTL: Turner and Turner, *Life and Letters,* 183.

70. Diary of Benjamin B. French, September 7 and December 18, 1861, French Papers, LC; French to Pamela [French], Washington, D.C., December 24, 1861, French Papers, LC; George Bancroft to wife, Washington, D.C., December 12 and 15, 1861, George Bancroft Papers, Cornell University, Ithaca, N.Y.; John Sedgwick to sister, n.p. [Headquarters Sixth Army Corps], April 12, 1863, in John Sedgwick, *Correspondence of John Sedgwick, Major-General,* ed. Henry D. Sedgwick (New York: Printed for Carl and Ellen Battille Stoeckel by De Vinne Press, 1902–1903), 2:90; see also Maria Lydig Daly Diary, July 14, 1863, in *Diary of a Union Lady,* ed. Harold Earl Hammond (New York: Funk & Wagnalls, 1962), 248. For an example of the insinuations against MTL, see entry of September 11, 1862, in *The Diary of George Templeton Strong,* ed. Allan Nevins and Milton Halsey Thomas (New York: Macmillan, 1952), 3:255; entry of November 3, 1861, *Russell, My Diary,* 322. The contemporary accounts of MTL used for this chapter reveal a three-to-one favorable impression of her.

71. Kathleen L. Endres, "The Women's Press in the Civil War: A Portrait of Patriotism, Propaganda, and Prodding," *Civil War History* 30, no. 1 (March 1984): 36. For Hermann and the Tom Thumb receptions, see George B. McClellan to wife [Mary Ellen McClellan], [Washington, D.C.], November 21, [1861], in George B. McClellan, *The Civil War Papers of*

George B. McClellan: Selected Correspondence, 1860–1865, ed. Stephen W. Sears (New York: Ticknor & Fields, 1989), 137; Diary of Benjamin B. French, November 24, 1861, French Papers, LC; Diary of Virginia Woodbury Fox, February 13, 1863, Woodbury Papers, LC; Leech, *Reveille in Washington,* 297; Henry Dawes to Ella [Dawes], January 29, 1862, Dawes Papers, LC; unidentified newspaper clipping, February 5, 1862 ("A dancing-party"), enclosed in Henry Dawes to Ella Dawes, February 13, 1862, Dawes Papers, LC; *Frank Leslie's Illustrated Newspaper,* February 22, 1862, 216–17.

72. Description of Willie Lincoln's illness and death in Doris Kearns Goodwin, *Team of Rivals: The Political Genius of Abraham Lincoln* (New York: Simon & Schuster, 2005), 415–23; Rebecca R. J. Pomeroy to Mary [?], Indiana Hospital, Washington, D.C., March 27, 1862, typescript, Rebecca R. J. Pomeroy Letters, Schlesinger Library, HU; Anson G. Henry to wife, Washington, D.C., May 8, 1865, Henry Papers, ILPL; MTL to Mrs. [Julia] Sprigg, Washington, D.C., May 29, 1862, Mary Todd Lincoln Papers, LC. For details of AL's poor military interventions in the spring of 1862, see Elizabeth Brown Pryor, " 'The Grand Old Duke of York': How Abraham Lincoln Lost the Confidence of His Military Command," forthcoming.

73. For MTL's possible use of morphine, see WHH to Fowler, Springfield, Ill., October 30, 1888, Hitchcock Papers, LC; Wilson, "Herndon and Mary Todd Lincoln"; "Diary" of Emily Todd Helm, n.d. [various entries c. post-October 1863], in Helm, *True Story of Mary,* 224–27, quotations on 224–25; see also 201–3. For "I do not believe," see Julia Taft Bayne, *Tad Lincoln's Father* (Boston: Little, Brown, 1931), 205.

74. "Diary" of Emily Todd Helm, n.d., in Helm, *True Story of Mary,* 222; Rebecca R. J. Pomeroy to Mary [?], March 27, 1862, Pomeroy Letters, Schlesinger Library, HU; Frederick Law Olmsted to Henry Whitney Bellows, Washington, D.C., September 21, 1862, in Frederick Law Olmsted, *The Papers of Frederick Law Olmsted,* ed. Charles E. Beveridge et al. (Baltimore: Johns Hopkins University Press, 1977–2015), 4:426; Isabella Beecher Hooker to John Hooker, December 2, 1862, quoted in White, *Beecher Sisters,* 93; entry of June 5, 1863, in Adam Gurowski, *Diary from November 18, 1862 to October 18, 1863* (New York: Carleton, 1864), 241–42; Charles W. Reed's drawing of *Lincoln's Midnight Thinky,* MSS Collection, Manuscript Reading Room, LC.

75. Turner and Turner, *Life and Letters,* 41; John Hay to John G. Nicolay, April 5, 1862, in Burlingame, *Inner World,* 326n; Charles A. Dana, "Reminiscences of Men and Events of the Civil War: I. From the 'Tribune' to the War Department," *McClure's Magazine,* November 1897, 21–22; S. D. Cox to [Manton] Marble, House of Representatives, May 20, 1864, Manton Marble Papers, LC. For the episode at the military review, see John S. Barnes, "With Lincoln from Washington to Richmond in 1865," *Appleton's Magazine,* May 1907, 517–19 and 523–24; Adam Badeau, *Grant in Peace: From Appomattox to Mount McGregor: A Personal Memoir* (Hartford: S. S. Scranton, 1887), 356–65; Julia Dent Grant, *The Personal Memoirs of Julia Dent Grant (Mrs. Ulysses S. Grant),* ed. John Y. Simon (Carbondale: Southern Illinois University Press, 1988), 146–47. Henry Adams described Badeau as alcoholic, "vicious, narrow . . . and vindictive" and Grant also ultimately dismissed him; *The Education of Henry Adams* (Washington, D.C.: Privately published, 1907), 229.

76. Elizabeth Cady Stanton to Gerrit Smith, New York, May 6, 1863 [*sic;* 1864], Elizabeth Cady Stanton and Susan B. Anthony Papers, Schlesinger Library, HU; Pinsker, *Lincoln's Sanctuary,* 12 and 131; Clinton, *Mrs. Lincoln,* 219 and 223; Mark E. Neely Jr. and R. Gerald McMurtry, *The Insanity File: The Case of Mary Todd Lincoln* (Carbondale: Southern Illinois University Press, 1986), 3–5. AL's financial methods are detailed in Harry E. Pratt, *The Personal Finances of Abraham Lincoln* (Springfield, Ill.: The Abraham Lincoln Association, 1943); Epstein, *The Lincolns,* 382. For accusations of stealing and further aberrations, see Burlingame, "Honest Abraham, Dishonest Mary."

77. Turner and Turner, *Life and Letters;* Baker, *Mary Todd Lincoln,* 240; Thomas F. Schwartz and Kim M. Bauer, eds., "Unpublished Mary Todd Lincoln," *JALA* 17, no. 2 (Summer 1996): 1–21.

78. William O. Stoddard, *Inside the White House in War Times: Memories and Reports of Lincoln's Secretary,* ed. Michael Burlingame (Lincoln: University of Nebraska Press, 2000),

185; Henry Wilson to AL, Washington, D.C., February 28, 1865, Barton Papers, LC; W. G. Washburn to AL, February 28, 1865, Barton Papers, LC; Julia Ward Howe, "The Civil War," January 24, 1906, Howe Papers, Schlesinger Library, HU; Hoge, *Boys in Blue,* 82 and 235; Gallman, *America's Joan of Arc,* 39; Seward quoted in John Hay to J. G. Nicolay, Washington, D.C., September 24, 1864, in John Hay, *Lincoln and the Civil War in the Diaries and Letters of John Hay,* ed. Tyler Dennett (1939; repr., Westport, Conn.: Negro Universities Press, 1972), 207–8; statement of James A. Briggs in *Belleville* [Ill.] *Advocate,* June 8, 1866, quoted in Burlingame, "Afterword," in Tripp, *Intimate World,* 229.

79. Anna Ella Carroll to AL, April 15, 1862, Anna Ellen Carroll Papers, Maryland Historical Society, Baltimore, Md.; Lydia Sayer Hasbrouck to AL, Middletown, N.Y., March 8, 1861, ALP-LC; Lydia Maria Child, "Mrs. L. Maria Child to the President of the United States," *National Anti-Slavery Standard,* September 6, 1862, quoted in Lyde Cullen Sizer, *The Political Work of Northern Women Writers and the Civil War, 1850–1872* (Chapel Hill: University of North Carolina Press, 2000), 104; Mary A. Livermore to AL, Chicago, October 11, 1863, ALP-LC; Mrs. A. H. Hoge and Mrs. D. P. Livermore to AL, Chicago, October 21, 1863, ALP-LC; Isaac Arnold to AL, Chicago, October 21, 1863, ALP-LC. For more on AL's dislike of criticism, see Pryor, "'The Grand Old Duke of York.'"

80. Women's wartime situation in Sizer, *Political Work of Northern Women Writers,* 84–86, 90–91, and 113; Lois Bryan Adams for *Detroit Advertiser* and *New York Tribune,* January 2, 1865, in Lois Bryan Adams, *Letter from Washington, 1863–1865,* ed. Evelyn Leasher (Detroit: Wayne State University Press, 1999), 224–25. For women asking the impossible, see Diary of August Laugel, January 7, 1865, in Fehrenbacher and Fehrenbacher, *Recollected Words,* 294. For evidence of AL treating women kindly, see *American and Commercial Advertiser,* March 23, 1865, in Charles M. Segal, ed., *Conversations with Lincoln* (New York: G. P. Putnam's Sons, 1961), 377; AL to Montgomery Blair, July 24, 1863, *CW,* 6:346; for claims that he universally did so, see Stoddard, *Inside the White House,* 186; Helen Nicolay in Burlingame, *Inner World,* 126 and 130–31; AL, "Memo on Gabriel R. Paul," August 23, 1862, *CW,* 5:390–91.

81. On flirtatious advances, see Diary of Virginia Woodbury Fox, December 7, 1862, Woodbury Papers, LC; Burlingame, "Afterword," in Tripp, *Intimate World,* 229–30. Jane Speed quotation in her letter to AL, Louisville, October 26, 1864, ALP-LC.

82. Seward quoted in Donn Piatt, *Memories of the Men Who Saved the Union* (New York: Belford, Clarke, 1887), 37.

83. Electra Dawes to husband [Henry L. Dawes], North Adams, Mass., December 8, 1861, Dawes Papers, LC; A. Y. Ellis to WHH, December 6, 1866, typescript, David Rankin Barbee Papers, GU; Neely, *Last Best Hope,* 149; Diary of Virginia Woodbury Fox, December 12, 1861, Woodbury Papers, LC; Maunsell B. Field, *Memories of Many Men and of Some Women* (New York: Harper & Brothers, 1874), 312.

84. White, *Visits with Lincoln,* 14; W. T. Sherman to Lorenzo Thomas, Louisville, October 22, 1861, in William Tecumseh Sherman, *Memoirs of General William T. Sherman* (New York: D. Appleton, 1875), 1:204–5; Ellen Ewing Sherman to AL, Lancaster, Ohio, January 9, 1862, ALP-LC; Ellen Ewing Sherman to brother [Thomas Ewing Jr.], Lancaster, Ohio, December 30, 1861, Thomas Ewing Family Papers, LC; Michael Fellman, "Lincoln and Sherman," in Gabor Boritt, ed., *Lincoln's Generals* (New York: Oxford University Press, 1994), 135–38; Ellen Ewing Sherman to "Cump" [William T. Sherman], Washington, D.C., January 29 and February 4, 1862, both William Tecumseh Sherman Family Papers, University of Notre Dame Archives, Notre Dame, Ind. Another example of such a petition is in Catharine M. Dix to AL, New York, December 18, [1864], ALP-LC.

85. Frank P. Blair to "dear judge" [Montgomery Blair], September 6, 1861, Blair Family Papers, LC; Francis P. Blair Sr. to Jessie Benton Frémont, Silver Spring, Md., August 13, 1861, ALP-LC; White, *Visits with Lincoln,* 2–7; AL to John C. Frémont, September 2, 1861, *CW,* 4:506.

86. Jesse B. Frémont to President [AL], September 10 and 12, 1861, both ALP-LC; entry of December 9, 1863, in John Hay, *Inside Lincoln's White House: The Complete Civil War Diary of John Hay,* ed. Michael Burlingame and John R. Turner Ettlinger (Carbondale: Southern

Illinois University Press, 1997), 123; John G. Nicolay and John Hay, *Abraham Lincoln: A History* (New York: Century, 1886–1890), 4:415; Jessie Benton Frémont, "Great Events: The Lincoln Interview," c. 1891, in *The Letters of Jessie Benton Frémont*, ed. Pamela Herr and Mary Lee Spence (Urbana: University of Illinois Press, 1993), 264–69.

87. White, *Visits with Lincoln*, 9–13; AL to John C. Frémont, September 11, 1861, *CW*, 4:517–18; AL to Mrs. John C. Frémont, September 12, 1861, ibid., 4:519; AL to Orville H. Browning, September 22, 1861, ibid., 4:531–33; entry of December 9, 1863, Hay, *Inside Lincoln's White House*, 123; Francis P. Blair's version of the story is in Blair to Elizabeth Blair Lee, September 17–18, 1861, quoted in Pamela Herr, *Jesse Benton Frémont: A Biography* (New York: Franklin Watts, 1987), 340–41.

88. Entry of December 9, 1863, Hay, *Inside Lincoln's White House*, 123; Jesse Frémont to President [AL], September 10, 1861, ALP-LC; White, *Visits with Lincoln*, 9–12. After the September 1861 meeting, Jesse Frémont continued to exert her influence on Republican politics. Although she occasionally attended White House levees, she still saw AL as a "dictator," of "sly, slimy nature," and spread rumors of the Blairs' alcoholism and their intrigues—to some extent true—in Missouri. For his part, AL tolerated the inconsistent John Frémont for a while, then marginalized him. The President accepted Frémont's resignation when the general objected to the command of John Pope, and AL declined to reinstate Frémont: see Jesse B. Frémont to Thomas Starr King, December 29, 1861, and October 16, [1863], in *Letters of Jessie Benton Frémont*, 303–4 and 356; Jesse B. Frémont to [George Washington] Julian, Wheeling [W. Va.], May 25, 1862, Joshua R. Giddings and George W. Julian Papers, LC.

89. Eliza Leslie, *The Behavior Book: A Manual for Ladies* (Philadelphia: Willis P. Hazard, 1853), 197.

90. Sizer, *Political Work of Northern Women Writers*, 170; Dorothea Dix to Annie Heath, Washington, D.C., April 20, 1861, Dorothea Lynde Dix Papers, Houghton Library, HU; Lillie B. Chace to "friend" [Anna Dickinson], Cherry Lawn, June 17, 1861, Dickinson Papers, LC; Clara Barton to Fanny Childs, Washington, D.C., January 7, 1862, Barton Papers, LC.

91. Entry of February 20, 1862, Dall, *Daughter of Boston*, 214; Lucy Larcom quoted in Judith Harper, ed., *Women During the Civil War: An Encyclopedia* (New York: Routledge, 2004), 235. For female soldiers, see DeAnne Blanton and Lauren M. Cook, *They Fought Like Demons: Women Soldiers in the American Civil War* (Baton Rouge: Louisiana State University Press, 2002). Van Lew's activities are described in Elizabeth R. Varon, *Southern Lady, Yankee Spy: The True Story of Elizabeth Van Lew, A Union Agent in the Heart of the Confederacy* (New York: Oxford University Press, 2003); Van Lew's rather disjointed diary appears in her *A Yankee Spy in Richmond: The Civil War Diary of "Crazy Bet" Van Lew*, ed. David D. Ryan (Mechanicsburg, Pa.: Stackpole, 1996).

92. Elizabeth [Blackwell] to Barbara [Bodichon], June 5, 1861, Elizabeth Blackwell Correspondence, CU; Silber, *Daughters of the Union*, 176–77; William Quentin Maxwell, *Lincoln's Fifth Wheel: The Political History of the United States Sanitary Commission* (New York: Longmans, Green, 1956), 2–8 (AL quoted on 8); Winfield Scott to "the loyal women of America," Washington, D.C., October 1, 1861 (with endorsement by AL of September 30, 1861), in *New York Tribune*, October 7, 1861, 7.

93. Entry of April 19, 1861, Hay, *Inside the White House*, 3; Simon Cameron, Circular on Dix's role, n.d. [April 23, 1861], Dix Papers, Houghton Library, HU; AL, "Order Regarding Miss Dix" (in another hand, but signed and dated by AL), July 26, 1861, Dix Papers, Houghton Library, HU; Emily Blackwell to Barbara [Bodichon], New York, June 1 and 11, 1861, Blackwell Correspondence, CU; William A. Hammond, Surgeon General's Circulars No. 7 and 8, July 14, 1862, copy in Dix Papers, Houghton Library, HU; Swisshelm quoted in Cornelia Hancock to Sarah [?], City Point, Va., July 7, 1864, in Cornelia Hancock, *South After Gettysburg: Letters of Cornelia Hancock from the Army of the Potomac, 1863–1868*, ed. Henrietta Stratton Jaquette (New York: Thomas Y. Crowell, 1956), 131; *Diary of George Templeton Strong*, August 2, 1861, 3:173–74; Frederick Law Olmsted, Report on the Demoralization of Volunteers, September 5, 1861, in Olmsted, *Papers of Olmsted*, 4:153–54;

Thomas J. Brown, *Dorothea Dix: New England Reformer* (Cambridge: Harvard University Press, 1998), 278–86, 310–11, and 315–20.

94. Judith Ann Giesberg, *Civil War Sisterhood: The U.S. Sanitary Commission and Women's Politics in Transition* (Boston: Northeastern University Press, 2000), 43–50; AL to Medical Director at Winchester, Va., March 30, 1862, *CW,* 9:127–28; Georgeanna Woolsey, 1864, quoted in *Letters of a Family During the War for the Union, 1861–1865,* ed. Georgeanna Woolsey Bacon (N.p.: Privately published, c. 1899), 1:142.

95. AL to Mary Walker, January 16, 1864, Walker Papers, Syracuse University, Syracuse, N.Y., quoted in Elizabeth D. Leonard, *Yankee Women: Gender Battles in the Civil War* (New York: W. W. Norton, 1994), 130; see also 112–14 and 129. This letter to Walker is not contained in *CW.*

96. Frederick Law Olmsted to Henry Whitney Bellow, Washington, D.C., September 25, 1861, in Olmsted, *Papers of Olmsted,* 4:202–3; Olmsted to Henry Whitney Bellow, USS *Ocean Queen,* May 7, 1862, ibid., 4:322; Olmsted to Henry Whitney Bellow, White House [Plantation], Va., June 2, 1862, ibid., 4:353; Olmsted to John Foster Jenkins, Floating Hospital, May 25 and 29, [1862], ibid., 4:363–64 and ("untiring industry") 322. For Bickerdyke, see the draft of a memoir, written after 1893, in Mary Ann Bickerdyke Papers, LC.

97. Francis Bacon to Georgeanna Woolsey, [St. Louis], July 6, 1863, in Bacon, *Letters of a Family,* 2:522–23.

98. Orpheus C. Kerr [Robert Henry Newell], October 6, 1861, *Orpheus C. Kerr Papers: First Series* (New York: Blakeman & Mason, 1863), 110.

99. Jane E. Schultz, "Seldom Thanked, Never Praised and Scarcely Recognized: Gender and Racism in Civil War Hospitals," *Civil War History* 48, no. 3 (September 2002): 220–36; Kate Clifford Larson, *Bound for the Promised Land: Harriet Tubman, Portrait of an American Hero* (New York: Ballantine, 2004), 196, 223–24, and 368n; Rosa Belle Holt, "A Heroine in Ebony," *Chautauquan* 23 (July 1896): 459–62; Tubman interview in *Boston Commonwealth,* July 1863, quoted in Sizer, *Political Work of Northern Women Writers,* 141; Silber, *Daughters of the Union,* 167; Margaret Washington, *Sojourner Truth's America* (Urbana: University of Illinois Press, 2009), 316–20.

100. Randall Stewart, "'Pestiferous Gail Hamilton,' James T. Fields, and the Hawthornes," *New England Quarterly* 17, no. 3 (September 1944): 418; Mary Abigail Dodge (Gail Hamilton) to Mr. Wood, Great Falls, N.H., September 6 and October 25, 1862, both Mary Abigail Dodge Papers, UVa; Gail Hamilton, "A Call to My Country-Women," *Atlantic Monthly,* March 1863, 345–49; Gail Hamilton, "Tracts for Our Time: Courage!" *Congregationalist,* January 27, 1862 [*sic;* 1863]; Sizer, *Political Work of Northern Women Writers,* 121.

101. Leonard, *Yankee Women,* 60–75 and 101–3; Edwin M. Stanton directive [concerning Wittenmyer], Washington, D.C., July 25, 1862, photostat, Annie Wittenmyer Letters, LC; AL, "Order Concerning Mrs. Annie Wittenmyer," October 20, 1864, *CW,* 8:54; Dr. James Dunn to wife, printed in *Pittsburgh Christian Union,* July 4, 1896, Barton Papers, LC.

102. Dorothea Dix to William Rathbone, November 28, [1861], and Dorothea Dix to Annie [Heath], Washington, D.C., March 16, 1863, both Dix Papers, Houghton Library, HU; Dix to Cameron, January 12, 1862, in Brown, *Dix,* 305; Silber, *Daughters of the Union,* 160–61, 192–93, and 203, Barton quoted on 201.

103. "Woman's Rights Convention," unidentified clipping, February 7–8, 1861, Stanton and Anthony Papers, Schlesinger Library, HU; Glenn C. Altschuler and Stuart M. Blumin, *Rude Republic: Americans and Their Politics in the Nineteenth Century* (Princeton, N.J.: Princeton University Press, 2000), 162–67; Hoge, *Boys in Blue,* 333; Giesberg, *Civil War Sisterhood,* 126–28. For Barton's politicization, see Pryor, *Clara Barton,* 120–22.

104. Samuel F. Du Pont to H. W. Davis, October 25, 1862, in Samuel Francis Du Pont, *Samuel Francis Du Pont: A Selection from His Civil War Letters,* ed. John D. Hayes (Ithaca, N.Y.: Cornell University Press, 1969), 2:253n; *Diary of George Templeton Strong,* October 23, 1861, and April 25, 1863, 3:188 and 314–15; Rebecca R. J. Pomeroy to Mary [?], March 27, 1862, Pomeroy Letters, Schlesinger Library, HU; AL to Dorothea Dix, Washington, D.C., May 4, 1862, *CW,* 9:132. AL's passing off benevolent women to others is ubiquitous, but

see, e.g., Jane Swisshelm to Will[iam] A. Mitchell, Washington, D.C., February 9 and 14, 1863, in Swisshelm, *Crusader and Feminist,* 173 and 180; AL to Ethan A[llen] Hitchcock, n.p., March 13, 1865, *CW,* 9:283.

105. Chicago Sanitary Commission to AL, October 11, 1863, ALP-LC; Mary A. Livermore to AL, Chicago, October 11 and 21, 1863, ALP-LC; Isaac Arnold to AL, Chicago, October 21, 1863, ALP-LC; Mrs. A. H. Hoge and Mrs. D. P. Livermore to AL, Chicago, November 26, 1863, ALP-LC. Instead of thanking the women for their magnificent effort, AL thanked a man who had donated a gold watch to the fair: see AL to James H. Hoes, December 17, 1863, *CW,* 7:75. See also AL to Edward Everett, November 20, 1863, ibid., 7:24; AL, "Reply to Philadelphia Delegation," [Washington, D.C.], January 24, 1864, ibid., 8:236; Address of Edward Everett, Gettysburg, Pa., November 19, 1863, at voicesof democracy.umd.edu/everett-gettysburg-address-speech-text; Millard Fillmore, Address at Opening of Christian Commission Fair, Buffalo, February 22, 1864, *Millard Fillmore Papers,* ed. Frank H. Severance (Buffalo: Buffalo Historical Society, 1907), 2:89–90; Lois Bryan Adams, "Opening of the Great Fair at the Patent Office," Washington, D.C., February 23, 1864, *Letter from Washington,* 84; AL, "Remarks at Opening of Patent Office Fair," February 22, 1864, *CW,* 7:197–98.

106. AL, "Remarks at Closing of Sanitary Fair," March 18, 1864, *CW,* 7:253–54; AL, "Address at Sanitary Fair, Baltimore," April 18, 1864, ibid., 7:301. See also AL to Mrs. Sarah B. Meconkey, May 9, 1864, ibid., 7:333.

107. Pryor, *Clara Barton,* 56–61; Gallman, *America's Joan of Arc,* 17; Hoffert, *Swisshelm,* 81–83; Jane Swisshelm to editor, *St. Cloud* [Minn.] *Democrat,* Washington, D.C., November 13, 1865, in Swisshelm, *Crusader and Feminist,* 307–8.

108. AL to Montgomery Blair, July 24, 1863, *CW,* 6:346; AL to Joseph J. Reynolds, January 20, 1865, ibid., 8:228–29; AL to Edwin M. Stanton, n.p., July 27, 1864, ibid., 7:466–67; J. Andrews Harris to AL, Philadelphia, January 23, 1865, ALP-LC; Neely, *Last Best Hope,* 148–50; Sizer, *Political Work of Northern Women Writers,* 119.

109. Benjamin B. French to brother [Henry F. French], Washington, D.C., June 19, 1864, French Papers, LC; *Washington Star,* June 20, 1864.

110. The Women's National Loyal League was known by various names, including the Union Loyal League and National Women's Loyal League. The term used here is the one used by Stanton and Anthony. Mary Ellen French to Pamela French, Washington, D.C., June 6, 1864, French Papers, LC; Gustafson, *Women and Republicans,* 26; Susan B. Anthony to Amelia Bloomer, New York, April 10, 1863, Stanton and Anthony Papers, Schlesinger Library, HU; Susan B. Anthony to Amy Kirby Post, New York, April 13, 1863, in Ann D. Gordon, ed., *The Selected Papers of Elizabeth Cady Stanton and Susan B. Anthony* (New Brunswick, N.J.: Rutgers University Press, 1997–2013), 1:481; Susan B. Anthony to Samuel May Jr., New York, September 21, 1863, ibid., 1:500. For "an object equal," see Ryan, *Women in Public,* 152–53.

111. For Stanton and Anthony's background with the abolitionist movement, see Lori D. Ginzberg, *Elizabeth Cady Stanton: An American Life* (New York: Hill & Wang, 2009), 26–27, 36–41, 46–47, 77, and 93–94; Sue Davis, *The Political Thought of Elizabeth Cady Stanton: Women's Rights and the American Political Tradition* (New York: New York University Press, 2008), 6–7 and 119–21; see also Daniel Walker Howe, *What Hath God Wrought: The Transformation of America, 1815–1848* (New York: Oxford University Press, 2007), 849 and 853; Carwardine, *Evangelicals and Politics,* 34; Elizabeth Buffum Chace, *Anti-Slavery Reminiscences* (Central Falls, R.I.: E .L. Freeman & Son, 1891), 46–47; Eric Foner, *The Fiery Trial: Abraham Lincoln and American Slavery* (New York: W. W. Norton, 2010), 30–31; *Boston Daily Courier,* April 28, 1864.

112. For a nuanced discussion of the interplay of Stanton's liberal and republican philosophies, see Davis, *Political Thought,* 13–21; Jeanne Munn Bracken, ed., *Women in the American Revolution* (Boston: History Compass, 2009); Cokie Roberts, *Founding Mothers: The Women Who Raised Our Nation* (New York: William Morrow, 2004). See also AL, "Speech at Chicago," July 10, 1858, *CW,* 2:500; Frederick Douglass, Oration in Memory of AL, April 14, 1876, at www.usf.edu/lit2go/184/a-lincoln-anthology; WHH to Jesse Weik,

Springfield, Ill., January 27, 1888, Herndon-Weik Collection, LC; WHH to Weik, fragment, n.d. [c. 1888], Herndon-Weik Collection, LC. AL's attitude toward freedmen and Native Americans is explored in chapters 3 and 4.

113. Handbill for Women's National Loyal League, n.d. [1864], copy in Dickinson Papers, LC; "Call for Meeting of the Loyal Women of the North," in Stanton, Anthony, Gage, and Harper, eds., *History of Woman Suffrage*, 2:53n.

114. Susan B. Anthony to Wendell Phillips, Seneca Falls, N.Y., April 29, 1861, Stanton and Anthony Papers, Schlesinger Library, HU; Susan B. Anthony to Mrs. [Martha Coffin] Wright, Rochester, N.Y., May 28, 1861, typescript, Sophia Smith Collection, HL; Martha Coffin Wright to Susan B. Anthony, Philadelphia, March 31, 1862, Stanton and Anthony Papers, Schlesinger Library, HU.

115. Ryan, *Women in Public*, 152–53; Massey, *Bonnet Brigades*, 164–65; "The Strong Woman's League," *Vanity Fair*, May 30, 1863; *Proceedings of Meeting of Loyal Women of the Republic*, New York, May 14, 1863, 7.

116. "Anniversary of the Women's National League," *National Anti-Slavery Standard*, May 28, 1864; Massey, *Bonnet Brigades*, 165–66; E[lizabeth] Cady Stanton to Caroline H. Dall, New York, May 7, 1864, in "Mrs. E. Cady Stanton to Mrs. Dall," *The Liberator*, June 3, 1864, clipping in Stanton and Anthony Papers, Schlesinger Library, HU; Sizer, *Political Work of Northern Women Writers*, 110.

117. Michael C. C. Adams, *Fighting for Defeat: Union Military Failure in the East, 1861–1865* (Lincoln: University of Nebraska Press, 1992), 108. For activities of the Strong Band, see Diary of Nathan Daniels, March 15 and June 6–8, 1864, Daniels Diaries, LC; David E. Long, *The Jewel of Liberty: Abraham Lincoln's Re-election and the End of Slavery* (Mechanicsburg, Pa.: Stackpole, 1994), 1–20. AL is quoted in entry of December 10, 1863, Hay, *Inside Lincoln's White House*, 125; see also Bruce Tap, *Over Lincoln's Shoulder: The Committee on the Conduct of the War* (Lawrence: University Press of Kansas, 1998).

118. Lydia Maria Child to Gerrit Smith, Wayland, July 23, 1864, in Child, *Selected Letters*, 445; for "forever pottering," see Lydia Maria Child to Charles Sumner, Wayland, July 31, 1864, Lydia Maria Child Correspondence, LC. The tenor of AL's meeting with Sojourner Truth has been the subject of some debate. Truth commented that AL treated her with kindness, even though she recorded—through a white transcriber—his remarks about being compelled to emancipation by the deeds of the South. Truth was accompanied by Lucy Colman, a staunch feminist and abolitionist, who later claimed they had been kept waiting and treated with disdain. Several historians have seized on this as proof of AL's unsympathetic view of African Americans, and his reluctance to liberate them. At the time, however, Colman wrote a letter in which she gave a softer view of the meeting, stating that it was highly awkward, but that AL greeted them cordially. In this letter Colman praised the candor of his remarks regarding emancipation: see Testimony of Sojourner Truth, October 29, 1864, in Segal, *Conversations with Lincoln*, 345–47; Lucy Colman to Editor, *National Anti-Slavery Standard*, November 26, 1864, quoted in Washington, *Sojourner Truth's America*, 313; Lucy N. Colman, *Reminiscences* (Buffalo: H. L. Green, 1891), 65–66. Discussion of the meeting is found in Washington, *Sojourner Truth's America*, 311–16; White, *Visits with Lincoln*, 113–27; Nell Irvin Painter, *Sojourner Truth: A Life, A Symbol* (New York: W. W. Norton, 1996), 200–207; Carlton Mabee, "Sojourner Truth and President Lincoln," *New England Quarterly* 61, no. 4 (December 1988): 519–29.

119. Frances D. Gage to Clara Barton, St. Louis, May 7, 1864, private collection; Josephine S. Griffings to AL, Burlington, Iowa, September 24, 1864, ALP-LC; Holt, "A Heroine in Ebony," 223–24; Larson, *Bound for the Promised Land*, 368n.

120. "Mrs. E. Cady Stanton to Mrs. Dall," Stanton and Anthony Papers, Schlesinger Library, HU; Elizabeth Cady Stanton to Gerrit Smith, New York, May 6 and June 2, [1864], and Elizabeth Cady Stanton to Wendell Phillips, New York, June 6, 1864, all Stanton and Anthony Papers, Schlesinger Library, HU. See also Susan B. Anthony to Charles Sumner, New York, March 16, 1864, in Gordon, *Selected Papers of Stanton and Anthony*, 1:513.

121. Elizabeth Cady Stanton to "Nellie" [Ellen Dwight Eaton], n.d. [September 9, 1860], Stanton and Anthony Papers, Schlesinger Library, HU; Elizabeth Cady Stanton, Speech to

"Wide Awakes," September 10, 1860, Stanton and Anthony Papers, Schlesinger Library, HU; Jane Swisshelm to editor, *St. Cloud* [Minn.] *Democrat,* Washington, D.C., March 26 and September 28, 1864, in Swisshelm, *Crusader and Feminist,* 272–74; William D. Kelley to "my dear child" [Anna Dickinson], West Philad[elphia], July 24, 1864, Dickinson Papers, LC; Anna E. Dickinson to "dear friend" [Elizabeth Cady Stanton], Philadelphia, July 12, 1864, Ida Husted Harper Collection, HL; Gail Hamilton (Mary Abigail Dodge) to [?] (possibly diary entry), March 6 and 17, 1863, in Hamilton, *Life in Letters,* 1:342–44; diary of Charles Mason, July 24, 1864, Remey Family Papers, LC.

122. "Mrs. E. Cady Stanton to Mrs. Dall," Stanton and Anthony Papers, Schlesinger Library, HU; E[lizabeth] Cady Stanton to Caroline Wells Dall, New York, c. April 14, 1864, Stanton and Anthony Papers, Schlesinger Library, HU; *New Haven Courier,* reprinted in *Boston Courier,* September 1, 1864.

123. Elizabeth Cady Stanton to Jesse Benton Frémont, New York, n.d. [May 4, 1864]; Elizabeth Cady Stanton to William Lloyd Garrison, New York, April 22, 1864; Elizabeth Cady Stanton to Wendell Phillips, New York, May 6, 1864; Elizabeth Cady Stanton to Gerrit Smith, New York, June 2, [1864]; Susan B. Anthony to Elizabeth Cady Stanton, Rochester, N.Y., June 3, 1864, all Stanton and Anthony Papers, Schlesinger Library, HU.

124. Letters to and from Theodore Tilton and Horace Greeley, September 1864, Theodore Tilton Papers, NYHS; the three quotations are taken from, respectively, William A. Buckingham to Horace Greeley, Norwich, [Conn.], September 3, 1864; Joseph A. Gilmore to Theodore Tilton, Concord, September 5, 1864; John A. Andrews to Horace Greeley, Boston, September 3, 1864. See also Long, *Jewel of Liberty,* 193–94; Charles Sumner to Lydia Maria Child, Boston, August 7, 1864, *Selected Letters of Charles Sumner,* 2:249; Lillie B. Chace to Anna [Dickinson], Valley Falls, September 19, 1864, Dickinson Papers, LC.

125. Harriet Beecher Stowe to "dear friend" [Annie Fields], n.p., November 29, 1864, Fields Papers, HL; Harriet Beecher Stowe, "Abraham Lincoln," *Littell's Living Age,* February 6, 1864, in Herbert Mitgang, ed., *Lincoln as They Saw Him* (New York: Rinehart, 1956), 376–78; Caroline H. Dall to Editor, *National Anti-Slavery Standard,* May 7, 1864; Gustafson, *Women and the Republican Party,* 32–33; Jane Swisshelm to editor, *St. Cloud* [Minn.] *Democrat,* Washington, D.C., October 22, 1864, in Swisshelm, *Crusader and Feminist,* 277–78; Theodore Tilton to Annie [Dickinson], New York, July 13, 1864, Dickinson Papers, LC; Gerrit Smith to E[lizabeth] Cady Stanton, Peterboro, August 20, 1864, Stanton and Anthony Papers, Schlesinger Library, HU.

126. Lydia Maria Child to Eliza Scudder, Wayland, November 14, 1864, Child Correspondence, LC; Gustafson, *Women and the Republican Party,* 32–33; Elizabeth Cady Stanton to "friend" [Wendell Phillips], [New York], [November 6, 1864], Stanton and Anthony Papers, Schlesinger Library, HU; Wendell Phillips to Elizabeth Cady Stanton, November 10, [1864], in Gordon, *Selected Papers of Stanton and Anthony,* 1:533.

127. Clara Barton to Will [Childs], Washington, D.C., April 25, 1861, Barton Papers, LC; Barton, undated lecture notes, [c. 1865–1867], Barton Papers, LC; Barton Diary, March 2–8, 1865, Barton Papers, LC.

128. AL, "Second Inaugural Address," March 4, 1865, *CW,* 8:332–33 (a nice overview of the Second Inaugural is in Harold Holzer, "Multiple Threads to Bind Up a Divided Nation," *Wall Street Journal,* February 28, 2015); Sizer, *Political Work of Northern Women Writers,* 163; Silber, *Daughters of the Union,* 203.

CHAPTER 6. THE HOLLOW CROWN

1. Margaret Green Calhoun to Patr[ick] Calhoun, n.d. [c. 1885], copy, Duff Green Papers, SHC-UNC, attests that when Green met AL he was wearing the same clothes and carrying the stick he is shown with in Mathew Brady's photograph; the letter also describes Green's friendship with General George Shepley, the provost marshal who gave him the pass. Porter wrote several versions of this encounter, the most believable of which was in his "Journal of Occurrences During the War of the Rebellion," n.d. [c. 1865], David D. Porter Family

Papers, LC. As time went on, Porter embellished the story: see "Lincoln at Richmond: Admiral Porter Recalls Some Striking Scenes," *New York Tribune,* January 18, 1885; David D. Porter, "President Lincoln's Entry into Richmond After the Evacuation of That Place by the Confederates," *Belford's Magazine,* September–October 1890, 585–96 and 649–58. Porter claimed the more exaggerated versions were based on facts recorded at the time: see ibid., and Porter to I. T. Headley, Annapolis, Md., October 16, 186[5], letterpress copy, Porter Papers, LC.

2. Porter, "Journal of Occurrences," n.d. [c. 1865], Porter Papers, LC; Ben E. Green, notes for response to Porter's *Tribune* article, c. 1885, Green Papers, SHC-UNC; Ben E. Green, "Buchanan, Lincoln, and Duff Green," *The Century Magazine,* June 1889, 317–18; Mark A. Lause, *A Secret Society History of the Civil War* (Urbana: University of Illinois Press, 2011), 93; "Duff Green," *American National Biography,* online at anb.org.

3. Fletcher Green, "Duff Green, Industrial Promoter," *Journal of Southern History* 2, no. 1 (February 1936): 29–30; Fletcher M. Green, "Duff Green, Militant Journalist of the Old School," *American Historical Review* 52, no. 2 (January 1947): 250–52; Lause, *A Secret Society History,* 123.

4. Green, "Militant Journalist," 250–52; Margaret Green Calhoun to Patr[ick] Calhoun, n.d. [c. 1885], Green Papers, SHC-UNC.

5. Green, "Duff Green, Industrial Promoter," 30–35, quotation on 30–31.

6. Ibid., 34–37; Green to Lucretia Green, November 8, 1859, quoted in ibid., 37; William G. Thomas, *The Iron Way: Railroads, the Civil War, and the Making of Modern America* (New Haven: Yale University Press, 2011), 200–201.

7. Porter, "President Lincoln's Entry into Richmond," 655; Duff Green, *Facts and Suggestions, Biographical, Historical, Financial and Political* (New York: Richardson, 1866), 232; Margaret Green Calhoun to Patr[ick] Calhoun, n.d. [c. 1885], Green Papers, SHC-UNC; John A. Campbell to Ben E. Green, Baltimore, April 7, 1885, Green Papers, SHC-UNC; William H. Crook, "Lincoln's Last Day," *Harper's Monthly Magazine,* September 1907, 522. Porter was trying to justify his earlier reminiscences, which had been criticized for their extravagant embroidery; Green was hoping to rally sympathy for treating the South with leniency; Crook's account was written forty-two years after the fact and it is not altogether clear that he was actually at the meeting; and Campbell has been accused of a series of traitorous activities, and for misrepresenting his own role in the days after Richmond's fall. A few of the many examples of AL colorfully losing his temper are: Horace White to Joseph Medill, Washington, D.C., March 3, 1862, Charles H. Ray Papers, HL; Horace White to Charles H. Ray, Washington, D.C., March 3, 1862, Ray Papers, HL; Herman Haupt, *Reminiscences of General Herman Haupt* (Milwaukee: Wright & Joys, 1901), 298.

8. There are many accounts of the war's final weeks, but most are questionable, written long after the events. Among the most credible is George T. Dudley, "Lincoln in Richmond: True Version of the War President's Famous Visit," *National Tribune* [Washington, D.C.], October 1, 1896, 1–2; Dudley, a member of Lincoln's party, took care not to embellish the story. Also useful are Green, *Facts and Suggestions,* 232; Porter, "Lincoln's Entry into Richmond," 653–54; John S. Barnes, "With Lincoln from Washington to Richmond in 1865," *Appleton's Magazine,* May 1907, 515–24. For AL's buoyancy, see entry of March 27, 1865, in Marsena Rudolph Patrick, *Inside Lincoln's Army: The Diary of Marsena Rudolph Patrick, Provost Marshal General, Army of the Potomac,* ed. David S. Sparks (New York: Thomas Yoseloff, 1964), 483; J. R. Hamilton to William Swinton, City Point, Va., March 28, 1865, VHS; MTL to Abram Wakeman, Washington, D.C., April 4, 1865, in Justin G. Turner and Linda Levitt Turner, eds., *Mary Todd Lincoln: Her Life and Letters* (New York: Alfred A. Knopf, 1972), 212–13.

9. Ulysses S. Grant to AL, City Point, Va., March 20, 1865, ALP-LC; Edwin M. Stanton to AL, telegram, Washington, D.C., April 3, 1865, ALP-LC; "The President's Visit to Richmond," *New York Times,* April 4, 1865.

10. Entry of April 3, 1865, in Michael Bedout Chesson and Leslie Jean Roberts, eds., *Exile in Richmond: The Confederate Journal of Henri Garidel* (Charlottesville: University Press of

Virginia, 2001), 367–68; Arthur R. Henry, "Report on the Fall of Richmond Filed with the *New York Tribune,* April 3, 1865," VHS. The report was published in the *New York Tribune,* April 5, 1865, 1. Emmie Sublett to Emile, Waverly Place, April 27, 1865, Emmie Sublett Correspondence, MoC; Lelian M. Cook Diary, April [3], 1865, in *Richmond News Leader,* April 3, 1935; Fannie Taylor Dickinson Diary, April 4, 1865, typescript, VHS; Susan M. Hoge to "dear friend" [Elizabeth H. Howard], Richmond, October 28, [1865], Hoge Family Papers, VHS; Alfred Paul to Drouyn de Lhuys, Richmond, April 11, 1865, in Warren F. Spencer, "A French View of the Fall of Richmond: Alfred Paul's Report to Drouyn de Lhuys, April 11, 1865," *Virginia Magazine of History and Biography* 73, no. 2 (April 1965): 181–82.

11. Constance Cary to mother and brother, [Richmond], April 4, 1865, in Constance Cary Harrison, *Refugitta of Richmond: The Wartime Recollections, Grave and Gay, of Constance Cary Harrison,* ed. Nathaniel Cheairs Hughes Jr. and S. Kittrell Rushing (Knoxville: University of Tennessee Press, 2011), 155; Emma Mordecai to Edward [Mordecai], Richmond, April 5, 1865, Mordecai Family Correspondence, MoC; entry of April 3, 1865, in John B. Jones, *A Rebel War Clerk's Diary at the Confederate States Capital,* ed. Howard Swiggett (New York: Old Hickory Bookshop, 1935), 2:647–49; Diary of Levi Graybill, April 3, 1865, Levi S. Graybill Papers, HL.

12. Constance Cary to mother and brother, April 4, 1865, in Harrison, *Refugitta,* 158; Edward M. Boykin, *The Falling Flag: Evacuation of Richmond, Retreat and Surrender at Appomattox* (New York: E. J. Hale, 1874), 12–13. An excellent overview of Richmond's fall is in Nelson Lankford, *Richmond Burning: The Last Days of the Confederate Capital* (New York: Viking, 2002).

13. The author is extremely grateful to Park Ranger Mike Gorman of Richmond National Battlefield Park for sharing his interpretive notes and his exhaustive research on AL's visit to Richmond. Most of the accounts of this visit are impressionistic and contradictory, and Gorman's work has established the best information to date (many accounts have AL arriving at Rockett's Landing, rather than aground on a sandbar, for example). Charles Coffin's report for the *Boston Journal,* April 10, 1865, and his review of the day's events in Coffin to Thomas Nast, Boston, July 19, 1866, copy in Gorman notes, along with Dudley, "Lincoln in Richmond," are the most accurate sources. See also Marquis Adolphe de Chambrun to wife, [Washington, D.C.], April 10, [1865], in Marquis Adolphe de Chambrun, *Impressions of Lincoln and the Civil War: A Foreigner's Account,* trans. General Aldebert de Chambrun (New York: Random House, 1952), 74; USS *Malvern* Logbook, April 4, 1865, NARA (copy in Gorman notes).

14. "To Richmond and Back: Why, How, What," *New York Tribune,* April 10, 1865; Charles Coffin, "Late Scenes in Richmond," *Atlantic Monthly,* June 1865, 755; Henry, "Report of Fall of Richmond" for Porter, "Journal of Occurrences," n.d. [c. 1865], Porter Papers, LC; Gorman notes; Alexander H. Newton, *Out of the Briars: An Autobiography and Sketch of the Twenty-Ninth Connecticut Volunteers,* excerpted in Donald Yacovone, ed., *Freedom's Journey: African American Voices of the Civil War* (Chicago: Lawrence Hill, 2004), 376–77; George A. Bruce, diary notes, April 4, 1865, enclosed in Bruce to John Nicolay, January 1, 1887, John G. Nicolay Papers, LC.

15. Dudley, "Lincoln in Richmond"; Godfrey Weitzel, *Richmond Occupied: Entry of the United States Forces into Richmond, Va., April 3, 1865, Calling Together of the Virginia Legislature and Revocation of the Same,* ed. Louis H. Manarin (Richmond: Richmond Civil War Centennial Committee, 1965), 52–56; Lelian M. Cook Diary, April 4, 1865, *Richmond News Leader,* April 3, 1935; entry of April 4, 1865, in Jones, *A Rebel War Clerk's Diary,* 2:469–70; Thomas Thatcher Graves, "The Occupation," in Robert Underwood Johnson and Clarence Clough Buell, eds., *Battles and Leaders of the Civil War* (New York: Century, 1887–1888), 4:726–28; Deckbook, USS *Malvern,* April 4, 1865, *Official Records of the Union and Confederate Navies in the War of the Rebellion* (Washington, D.C: Government Printing Office, 1894–1922), I, 12:176, Constance Cary to Burton Harrison, [Richmond], [c. April 5–6, 1865], in Harrison, *Refugitta,* 161; Bruce, diary notes, April 4, 1865, enclosed in Bruce to Nicolay, January 1, 1887, Nicolay Papers, LC.

16. Mary Custis Lee to Louisa [Snowden], Richmond, April 16, [1865], Society of Lees of
Virginia Collection, Kate Waller Barrett Branch, Alexandria Public Library, Alexandria,
Va.; [Judith White Brockenbrough McGuire], *Diary of a Southern Refugee, During the War,
by a Lady of Virginia* (New York: E. J. Hale, 1867), 350; Emma Mordecai to Edward
[Mordecai], Richmond, April 5, 1865, Mordecai Correspondence, MoC; Constance Cary
to Burton Harrison, [Richmond], [c. April 5–6, 1865], in Harrison, *Refugitta,* 161; entry of
April 4, 1865, in Chesson and Roberts, *Exile in Richmond,* 370; Emmie Sublett to Emilie,
April 29, 1865, Sublett Correspondence, MoC.

17. Marquis Adolphe de Chambrun to wife, April 10, [1865], in de Chambrun, *Impressions,* 75
and 77; Diary of Levi Graybill, April 3, 1865, Graybill Papers, HL; Dickinson Diary, April
5, 1865, VHS.

18. Entries of April 4–6, 1865, in Jones, *A Rebel War Clerk's Diary,* 2:469–72; entries of April
4, 5, and 7, 1865, Diary of Clara Shafer, UVa; Noah Brooks, "The President at Richmond,"
April 6, 1865, in Michael Burlingame, ed., *Lincoln Observed: Civil War Dispatches of Noah
Brooks* (Baltimore: Johns Hopkins University Press, 1998), 180–81.

19. Charles Sumner to Salmon P. Chase, Washington, D.C., April 10, 1865, in Charles
Sumner, *The Selected Letters of Charles Sumner,* ed. Beverly Wilson Palmer (Boston:
Northeastern University Press, 1990), 2:282; Charles Sumner to the Duchess of Argyll,
April 24, 1865, ibid., 2:295; Marquis Adolphe de Chambrun, "Personal Recollections of
Mr. Lincoln," *Scribner's Magazine,* January 1893, 32–33.

20. "Agnes" [?] to Mrs. Roger Pryor, Richmond, April 5, 1865, in Mrs. Roger A. Pryor [Sara
Agnes Rice], *Reminiscences of Peace and War* (New York: Macmillan, 1905), 357; entry of
April 6, 1865, in Chesson and Roberts, *Exile in Richmond,* 372–73; Christopher Q.
Tompkins, "The Occupation of Richmond, April 1865: The Memorandum of Events of
Colonel Christopher Q. Tompkins," ed. William M. E. Rachal, *Virginia Magazine of
History and Biography* 73, no. 2 (April 1965): 194 and 195–96.

21. Entry of April 6, 1865, in Chesson and Roberts, *Exile in Richmond,* 372–73; Tompkins,
"Memorandum," 194; entry of April 6, 1865, in McGuire, *Diary of a Southern Refugee,* 350;
Dickinson Diary, April 4, 1865, VHS. For the Lincolns' high spirits at the time, see
statement of James Harlan, n.d., in Katherine Helm, *The True Story of Mary, Wife of Lincoln*
(New York: Harper Brothers, 1928), 252; MTL to Abram Wakeman, Washington, D.C.,
April 4, 1865, in Turner and Turner, *Life and Letters,* 213.

22. "The Fall of Richmond and Lee's Surrender, Saint's Rest . . . April the 10th 1865," in
[David Ross Locke], *The Struggles (Social, Financial and Political) of Petroleum V. Nasby*
(Boston: Lee & Shepard, 1888), 170.

23. Porter, "Lincoln's Entry into Richmond," 653–54; Green, *Facts and Suggestions,* 232;
Margaret Green Calhoun to Patr[ick] Calhoun, n.d. [c. 1885], Green Papers, SHC-UNC.

24. Entry of April 5, 1865, Patrick, *Diary of Marsena Rudolph Patrick,* 488; Charles Sumner to
Salmon P. Chase, Washington, D.C., April 10 and 12, 1865, in Sumner, *Selected Letters,*
2:282 and (quotations) 283; Chambrun, "Personal Recollections," 28.

25. Duff Green to James Buchanan, December 28, 1860, in Charles M. Segal, ed., *Conversa-
tions with Lincoln* (New York: G. P. Putnam's Sons, 1961), 62–63; Green to AL, Richmond,
January 2, 1865, typescript, Green Papers, SHC-UNC; "Interview of Duff Green with Mr.
Lincoln on the Crisis," *New York Herald,* January 6 [*sic;* 8], 1865, in Green, *Facts and
Suggestions,* 226–31.

26. Green, "Buchanan, Lincoln, and Duff Green," 318; Green to Buchanan, December 28,
1860, in Segal, *Conversations,* 62–63; AL to Duff Green, and AL to Lyman Trumbull, both
Springfield, Ill., December 28, 1860, *CW,* 4:162–63; Edward D. Baker to AL, Lafayette,
n.d. [later stamped c. December 31, 1860], ALP-LC; Green to President [Jefferson Davis],
Richmond, January 15, 1864, Green Papers, SHC-UNC; Green to Jefferson Davis, May
26, 1862 [?], in John G. Nicolay and John Hay, *Abraham Lincoln: A History* (New York:
Century, 1886–1890), 3:286.

27. Joshua Speed to AL, Louisville, November 14, 1860, ALP-LC; Thomas Corwin to AL, and
John Gilmer to AL, both House of Representatives, December 10, 1860, ALP-LC; William
Hunt to AL, Philadelphia, December 13, 1860, ALP-LC; Diary of Samuel R. Curtis,

December 5, 1860, Samuel R. Curtis Papers, ILPL; William J. Cooper, *We Have the War upon Us: The Onset of the Civil War, November 1860–April 1861* (New York: Alfred A. Knopf, 2012), 177.

28. Montgomery Blair to AL, Washington, D.C., December 14, 1860, ALP-LC; Thurlow Weed to AL, New York, December 11, [1860], ALP-LC; William S. Thayer to Bancroft Davis, Washington, D.C., February 4, [1861], J. C. Bancroft Davis Papers, LC; Cooper, *We Have the War upon Us*, 78–79.

29. There are scores of such letters: see, e.g., Gideon Welles to AL, Hartford, November 12, 1860, Gideon Welles Papers, HL; Carl Schurz to AL, Manchester, N.H., December 18, [18]60, ALP-LC.

30. Curtis Diary, December 5, 1860, Curtis Papers, ILPL.

31. AL, "Address at Cooper Institute," February 27, 1860, *CW,* 3:522–50; AL, "Remarks at Monongahela House, Pittsburgh," February 14, 1861, ibid., 4:209. For an examination of AL as a wrestler, see Douglas L. Wilson, *Honor's Voice: The Transformation of Abraham Lincoln* (New York: Alfred A. Knopf, 1998), 19–51.

32. John G. Nicolay Memorandum, November 5, 1860, Nicolay Papers, LC; AL, "Remarks at Monongahela House, Pittsburgh," February 14, 1861, *CW,* 4:209; AL, "Speech at Beloit, Wis.," October 1, 1859, ibid., 3:482; Eric Foner, *Free Soil, Free Labor, Free Men: The Ideology of the Republican Party Before the Civil War* (New York: Oxford University Press, 1970), 205–8, 224–25, and 313–17, Greeley quoted on 213.

33. Robert W. Johannsen, *Lincoln, the South, and Slavery: The Political Dimension* (Baton Rouge: Louisiana State University Press, 1991), 107–8. Dated, but still thought-provoking on the subject of emotionalism is Avery Craven, *The Repressible Conflict, 1830–1861* (Baton Rouge: Louisiana State University Press, 1939), 63–97.

34. Foner, *Free Soil*, 313–17; Drew Gilpin Faust, "Introduction," in Drew Gilpin Faust, ed., *The Ideology of Slavery: Proslavery Thought in the Antebellum South, 1830–1860* (Baton Rouge: Louisiana State University Press, 1981), 9–17. For one community's reaction to increasingly harsh Northern rhetoric, see Elizabeth Brown Pryor, *Reading the Man: A Portrait of Robert E. Lee Through His Private Letters* (New York: Viking, 2007), 150–54.

35. AL, "Debate at Quincy, Ill.," October 13, 1858, *CW,* 3:254. AL reiterated this idea at, among other places, Alton, October 15, 1858, ibid., 3:312–13; Cooper Institute, February 27, 1860, ibid., 3:549–50; Hartford, March 5, 1860, ibid., 4:8. For "this matter of keeping," see AL, "Speech at Chicago," July 10, 1858, ibid., 2:493.

36. AL to George Robertson, Springfield, Ill., August 15, 1855, *CW,* 2:318; AL to Anson G. Henry, Springfield, Ill., November 19, 1858, ibid., 3:339.

37. AL, "Speech at Bloomington, Ill.," September 12, 1854, *CW,* 2:230; AL, "Speech at Peoria," October 16, 1854, ibid., 2:255; AL, "Address at Cooper Institute," February 27, 1860, ibid., 3:522–50; AL, "Debate at Galesburg," October 7, 1858, ibid., 3:221. See also Cooper, *We Have the War upon Us,* 16; John Burt, *Lincoln's Tragic Pragmatism: Lincoln, Douglas, and Moral Conflict* (Cambridge: Harvard University Press, 2013), 608–21.

38. Green, *Facts and Suggestions,* 231; "The President-Elect," *New Orleans Daily Crescent,* November 12, 1860, in Dwight Lowell Dumond, ed., *Southern Editorials on Secession* (New York: Century, 1931), 229–31; Edward Bates to Wyndham Robertson, St. Louis, November 3, 1860, Wyndham Robertson Papers, VHS; Green, "Buchanan, Lincoln, and Duff Green," 317–18; AL, "Speech at Springfield," June 16, 1858, *CW,* 2:461; AL, "Speech at Elwood, Kans.," December 3, 1859, ibid., 3:496; John G. Nicolay and John Hay, "The President-Elect at Springfield," *The Century Magazine,* November 1887, 87.

39. Cooper, *We Have the War upon Us,* 31–32; William W. Freehling, *The Road to Disunion* (New York: Oxford University Press, 2007), 2:218 and 441; AL, "Message to Congress," July 4, 1861, *CW,* 4:437; L. S. Hardee [?] to Geo[rge] W. Julian, Milan, Ind., October 18, 1860, Joshua R. Giddings and George W. Julian Papers, LC; W[illia]m Stickney to AL, Washington, D.C., December 10, 1860, ALP-LC.

40. Henry Villard, Dispatch, December 11, 1860, in Henry Villard, *Lincoln on the Eve of '61: A Journalist's Story,* ed. Harold G. Villard and Oswald Garrison Villard (Westport, Conn.: Greenwood Press, 1974), 34. A detailed description of the trip is in Harold Holzer, *Lincoln,*

President-Elect: Abraham Lincoln and the Great Secession Winter 1860–1861 (New York: Simon & Schuster, 2008), 305–90.

41. David Herbert Donald, *Lincoln* (New York: Simon & Schuster, 1995), 273–77; David M. Potter, *Lincoln and His Party in the Secession Crisis* (New Haven: Yale University Press, 1942), 317; Kenneth M. Stampp, "Lincoln and the Strategy of Defense in the Crisis of 1861," *Journal of Southern History* 11, no. 3 (August 1945): 309–11; Burt, *Lincoln's Tragic Pragmatism,* 628–29; AL, "Speech at Pittsburgh," February 15, 1861, *CW,* 4:211; AL, "Speech at Bates House, Indianapolis," February 11, 1861, ibid., 4:194–95; AL, "Speech at Steubenville, Ohio," February 14, 1861, ibid., 4:207. The quotations in this paragraph are from, respectively, AL, "Address to the New Jersey General Assembly, Trenton," February 21, 1861, ibid., 4:237; AL, "Address to the Pennsylvania General Assembly, Harrisburg," February 22, 1861, ibid., 4:245; Michael Burlingame, *Abraham Lincoln: A Life* (Baltimore: Johns Hopkins University Press, 2008), 2:30.

42. Charles Francis Adams quoted in Holzer, *Lincoln, President-Elect,* 339; Charles Carter to [William] Overton Winston, Philadelphia, February 16, 1861, Winston Family Papers, VHS. The number of Confederate States Carter gives is correct, for at the time he wrote Texas had voted to secede but not yet joined the Confederacy.

43. Donald, *Lincoln,* 274; *New Orleans Daily Delta,* February 26, 1861, quoted in Michael Davis, *The Image of Lincoln in the South* (Knoxville: University of Tennessee Press, 1971), 28–29 (see also 35); entry of March 4, 1861, in Catherine Ann Devereux Edmondston, *Journal of a Secesh Lady: The Diary of Catherine Ann Devereux Edmondston, 1860–1866,* ed. Beth Gilbert Crabtree and James W. Patton (Raleigh: North Carolina Department of Cultural Resources, 1979), 39–40.

44. Donald, *Lincoln,* 277–79; Curtis Diary, February 23, 1861, Curtis Papers, ILPL; Davis, *Image of Lincoln,* 31–34; *New York Times,* February 28, 1861; *Vanity Fair,* March 9, 1861; George Washington Harris, *Sut Lovingood Travels with Old Abe Lincoln* (Chicago: Black Cat Press, 1937), 34.

45. Green, *Facts and Suggestions,* 232. For a sampling of views, see Allan Nevins, *The Emergence of Lincoln,* vol. 2, *Prologue to Civil War, 1859–1861* (New York: Scribner, 1950); David M. Potter, *The Impending Crisis, 1848–1861* (New York: Harper Torchbooks, 1976); Stampp, "Lincoln and the Strategy of Defense," 297–323; Russell McClintock, *Lincoln and the Decision for War: The Northern Response to Secession* (Chapel Hill: University of North Carolina Press, 2008); William J. Cooper, *We Have War upon Us;* Freehling, *The Road to Disunion;* Burt, *Lincoln's Tragic Pragmatism.* See also AL, "Resolutions Drawn Up for Senate Committee," [December 20, 1860], *CW,* 4:156–57; AL to Elihu B. Washburne, Springfield, Ill., December 13 and 21, 1860, ibid., 4:151 and 159; conversation with D. M. Smith, Sp[ringfield], July 8, 1875, in John G. Nicolay, *An Oral History of Abraham Lincoln: John G. Nicolay's Interviews and Essays,* ed. Michael Burlingame (Carbondale: Southern Illinois University Press, 1996), 17–18; AL to Alexander Stephens, Springfield, Ill., December 22, 1860, *CW,* 4:160.

46. AL, "First Inaugural Address," March 4, 1861, *CW,* 4:262–71; Douglas L. Wilson, *Lincoln's Sword: The Presidency and the Power of Words* (New York: Vintage, 2006), 42–70; Davis, *Image of Lincoln,* 36.

47. Diary of Mrs. Eugene McLean, March 4, 1861, excerpted in "When the States Seceded," *Harper's Monthly Magazine,* January 1914, 286; entry of March 5, 1861, in *The Diary of George Templeton Strong,* ed. Allan Nevins and Milton Halsey (New York: Macmillan, 1952), 3:106; *Charleston Mercury,* March 9, 1861; *Richmond Enquirer,* March 5, 1861; *North Carolina Standard,* March 9, 1861. T. R. R. Cobb is quoted in Davis, *Image of Lincoln,* 37.

48. Robert E. Lee to Agnes [Lee], Fort Mason, Tex., January 29, 1861, Lee Family Papers, VHS; Charles S. Morehead to John J. Crittenden, Washington, D.C., February 23, 1862, John J. Crittenden Papers, LC; Statement of Charles S. Morehead, October 9, 1862, in David Rankin Barbee and Milledge L. Bonham Jr., eds., "Fort Sumter Again," *Mississippi Valley Historical Review* 28, no. 1 (June 1941): 63–73. For an excellent overview of sources on the Sumter-for-Virginia deal, see Burlingame, *Abraham Lincoln,* 2:119–21.

49. Both McClintock, *Lincoln and the Decision for War,* and Cooper, *We Have the War upon Us,*

deal extensively with the Fort Sumter crisis, from different perspectives. See also the comments in chapter 1. The most complete manuscript sources are in the Samuel Wylie Crawford Papers, LC; see also AL, "Proclamation Calling Militia," April 15, 1861, *CW,* 4:331–32; AL, "Proclamation of a Blockade," April 19, 1861, ibid., 4:338–39; AL, "Reply to Baltimore Committee," April 22, 1861, ibid., 4:341.

50. George Alexander Magruder to "friend" [Samuel F. Du Pont], Washington, D.C., April 22, 1861, in Samuel Francis Du Pont, *Samuel Francis Du Pont: A Selection from His Civil War Letters,* ed. John D. Hayes (Ithaca, N.Y.: Cornell University Press, 1969), 1:59; Judith Walker Rives to son, Castle Hill, Va., March 15, 1861, William Cabell Rives Family Papers, LC; William C. Rives to John Janney, Castle Hill, Va., May 1, 1861, Rives Papers, LC; William C. Rives to son [William C. Rives Jr.], Castle Hill, Va., May 6, 1861, Rives Papers, LC; Wyndham Robertson to Frank Robertson, Richmond, April 13 [?; blotted, but between April 12 and 17], 1861, Robertson Papers, VHS; James Wickersham to brother, Memphis, May 8, 1861, Civil War Letters 1861–1865, NYHS; Emma Mordecai to Nell, Richmond, April 21, 1861, Mordecai Family Papers, SHC-UNC; Caroline Mordecai Plunkett to Alfred Mordecai, Richmond, March 11, 1861, Mordecai Papers, LC; Emma Hays to Sara [Mordecai], Richmond, April 21, 1861, Mordecai Papers, LC; Caroline M. Plunkett to Alfred Mordecai, Richmond, April 18, 1861, Mordecai Papers, LC.

51. AL to Samuel Haycraft, Springfield, Ill., November 13, 1860, *CW,* 4:139; Davis, *Image of Lincoln,* 16–18; Ben E. Green, undated notes on Lincoln-Green meeting, Green Papers, SHC-UNC.

52. J. G. Randall attempts to show AL's special affinity with the South in *Lincoln and the South* (Baton Rouge: Louisiana State University Press, 1946), 23 and 26–27; the connection is also made in Ward Hill Lamon, *Recollections of Abraham Lincoln, 1847–1865,* ed. Dorothy Lamon Teillard (Washington, D.C.: Privately published, 1911), 69. AL's ties to Kentucky are detailed in William H. Townsend, *Lincoln and the Bluegrass: Slavery and Civil War in Kentucky* (Lexington: University of Kentucky Press, 1955); Eric Foner, *The Fiery Trial: Abraham Lincoln and American Slavery* (New York: W. W. Norton, 2010), 6–8; AL to Joshua Speed, Springfield, Ill., August 24, 1855, *CW,* 2:320; AL, "Speech at Peoria," October 16, 1864, ibid., 2:255.

53. Richard Nelson Current, "Lincoln the Southerner," in *Speaking of Abraham Lincoln: The Man and His Meaning for Our Times* (Urbana: University of Illinois Press, 1983), 148–49, 153–56, and 161–62; AL, "Fragment of Speech for Kentucky," [c. February 12, 1861], *CW,* 4:200; Lucius E. Chittenden, "President Lincoln and His Administration at the Commencement of the War," n.d. [c. 1865], Lucius E. Chittenden Manuscripts, HL. For mistrust of AL, see Diary of Salmon P. Chase, October 11, 1862, in Salmon P. Chase, *The Salmon P. Chase Papers,* ed. John Niven et al. (Kent, Ohio: Kent State University Press, 1993–1998), 1:420; Fisher A. Hildreth to [Benjamin] Butler, Lowell, Mass., March 24, 1864, in Benjamin F. Butler, *Private and Official Correspondence of Gen. Benjamin F. Butler During the Period of the Civil War,* ed. Jesse Ames Marshall (N.p.: Privately published, 1917), 3:574–75.

54. Diary of Mary Boykin Chesnut, March 11, 1861, in *Mary Chesnut's Civil War,* ed. C. Van Woodward (New Haven: Yale University Press, 1981), 25; Jonathan Daniel Wells, *The Origins of the Southern Middle Class, 1800–1861* (Chapel Hill: University of North Carolina Press, 2004), 188–90, 202–3, and 222; William Gannaway Brownlow, *Sketches of the Rise, Progress, and Decline of Secession* (Philadelphia: G. W. Childs, 1862), 273–74; Michael T. Bernath, *Confederate Minds: The Struggle for Intellectual Independence in the Civil War South* (Chapel Hill: University of North Carolina Press, 2010), 43.

55. Wells, *Origins of the Southern Middle Class,* 181–88; Thomas, *The Iron Way,* 17–36 (quotation on 22); Green, *Facts and Suggestions,* 228–31.

56. For an overview of secessionist viewpoints, see Holzer, *Lincoln, President-Elect,* and David C. Keehn, *Knights of the Golden Circle: Secret Empire, Southern Secession, Civil War* (Baton Rouge: Louisiana State University Press, 2013). See also James L. Petigru to "Willie" [Carson], Charleston, S.C., March 2, 1861, James L. Petigru Papers, LC; Edward Hartz to father, Camp Hudson, Tex., December 15, 1860, Edward L. Hartz Papers, LC. Secession's

practical problems are discussed in Robert E. Lee to Agnes Lee, San Antonio, November 7, 1860, Nancy Astor Papers, Museum of English Rural Life, Reading University, Reading, U.K. The moderate is Robert War Johnson; his letter to Joseph Holt of January 16, 1861, is quoted in Elizabeth D. Leonard, *Lincoln's Forgotten Ally: Judge Advocate General Joseph Holt of Kentucky* (Chapel Hill: University of North Carolina Press, 2011), 117.

57. Henry Adams, *The Great Secession Winter of 1860–61 and Other Essays by Henry Adams,* ed. George Hochfield (New York: Sagamore Press, 1958), 3–4; Maria Lydig Daly Diary, November 24, 1861, in *Diary of a Union Lady,* ed. Harold Earl Hammond (New York: Funk & Wagnalls, 1962), 82; David M. Potter, *Lincoln and His Party in the Secession Crisis* (New Haven: Yale University Press, 1942), 6–19; Robert S. Holt to Joseph Holt, Yazoo City, Miss., January 10, 1861, Joseph Holt Papers, LC.

58. Green, *Facts and Suggestions,* 227–30. Numerous pleas for AL to take Southern determination seriously are in ALP-LC: see, e.g., Richard W. Thompson to AL, Washington, D.C., December 25, 1860. See also William H. Russell to [Bancroft] Davis, Cairo, June 22, 1861, Davis Papers, LC; William Tecumseh Sherman, *Memoirs of General William T. Sherman* (New York: D. Appleton, 1875), 1:167–68; entry of February 6, 1865, Richard Launcelot Maury Diary, VHS.

59. Edward Tayloe to B[enjamin] O. Tayloe, Washington, D.C., March 9, 1861, William H. Seward Papers, UR; Flora Darling to [R. J.] Walker, Southampton, Eng., March 8, 1861, in Flora Adams Darling, *Mrs. Darling's Letters or Memories of the Civil War* (New York: John Lovell, 1883), 42; Francis R. Rives to Will[iam C. Rives], New York, March 13, 1861, Rives Papers, LC; James R. Gilmore, ed., *Among the Pines or South in Secession Time by Edmund Kirke* (New York: J. R. Gilmore, 1862), 75.

60. Freehling, *Road to Disunion,* 2:372.

61. Entry of April 17, 1861, in Edmondston, *Journal of a Secesh Lady,* 51; George Mason to Samuel Cooper, Spring Bank, Va., March 10, 1861, Cooper Family Papers, VHS; Davis, *Image of Lincoln,* 63–66; Mrs. Pryor, *Reminiscences of Peace and War,* 97.

62. Recollection of Esther King Casey, Birmingham, June 4, 1937, in George P. Rawick, ed., *The American Slave: A Composite Autobiography* (Westport, Conn.: Greenwood Press, 1972–1981), 6.1:56; Arthur James Lyon Fremantle, *Three Months in the Southern States, April–June, 1863* (New York: John Bradburn, 1864), 279; "The Devil's Visit to 'Old Abe,'" *Southern Confederacy,* September 27, 1861, in Martin Abbott, "President Lincoln in Confederate Caricature," *Journal of the Illinois State Historical Society* 51, no. 3 (Autumn 1958): 312–13—this song shows up in many places, see, e.g., entry of October 8, 1863, in Edmondston, *Journal of a Secesh Lady,* 476. See also Recollection of George Wood, June 1, 1937, Rawick, *The American Slave,* 3.4:250.

63. Bernath, *Confederate Minds,* 200–203.

64. [William Russell Smith], *The Royal Ape: A Dramatic Poem* (Richmond: West & Johnson, 1863); criticism of *The Royal Ape* in Introduction to John Hill Hewitt, *King Linkum the First: As Performed at the Concert Hall Augusta, Georgia, February 23, 1863,* ed. Richard Barksdale Harwell (Atlanta: Emory University, 1947), 7; Davis, *Image of Lincoln,* 71–72.

65. Hewitt, *King Linkum,* 8–12, 21–22, and 25–26.

66. [Charles Henry Smith], *Bill Arp, So Called: A Side Show of the Southern Side of the War* (New York: Metropolitan Records Office, 1866); Mark E. Neely Jr., Harold Holzer, and Gabor S. Boritt, *The Confederate Image: Prints of the Lost Cause* (Chapel Hill: University of North Carolina Press, 1987), 44–45 and 95–96; "Lincoln on the Lyre," *The Southern Illustrated News,* February 7, 1863; "The Times," *The Southern Illustrated News,* March 14, 1863; Richard Barksdale Harwell, "John Esten Cooke, Civil War Correspondent," *Journal of Southern History* 19, no. 4 (November 1953): 501–16.

67. For examples of "personalizing" the war, see Robert S. Hudson to AL, Yazoo County, Miss., November 3, 1860, ALP-LC; J. H. Woods to AL, Lebanon, Tenn., January 14, 1861, ALP-LC; Thomas Smith Taylor to sister, Fairfax Station, Va., September 15, 1861, in Thomas Smith Taylor, *Letters Home: Three Years Under General Lee in the 6th Alabama,* ed. Harlan Eugene Cross Jr. (Fairfax, Va.: History4All, 2010), 10; James A. Graham to Augustus W. Graham, Fort Macon, November 20, 1861, in Max R. Williams and Joseph

Grégoire de Roulhac Hamilton, eds., *The Papers of William Alexander Graham* (Raleigh: North Carolina Office of Archives and History, 1957–1992), 5:310.

68. J. B. Long to AL, Jackson, Tenn., January 18, 1861, ALP-LC; entries of August 25 and 28, 1862, in Sarah Morgan, *The Civil War Diary of a Southern Woman*, ed. Charles East (New York: Simon & Schuster, 1991), 232–40, quotation on 258.

69. *Richmond Enquirer*, July 25, 1861, quoted in Don. E. Fehrenbacher, "The Anti-Lincoln Tradition," *JALA* 4, no. 1 (1982), at www.quod.lib.umich.edu/j/jala (no page numbers online); "Inauguration Day," *Petersburg* [Va.] *Daily Express*, March 4, 1865, in Herbert Mitgang, ed., *Lincoln as They Saw Him* (New York: Rinehart, 1956), 436–37. On AL and Confederate identity, see Drew Gilpin Faust, *The Creation of Confederate Nationalism: Ideology and Identity in the Civil War South* (Baton Rouge: Louisiana State University Press, 1988), 1–21.

70. Bell Irvin Wiley, *Southern Negroes, 1861–1865* (New Haven: Yale University Press, 1938), 12–13; Narrative of Moble Hopson in Charles L. Perdue Jr., Thomas E. Barden, and Robert K. Phillips, eds., *Weevils in the Wheat: Interviews with Virginia Ex-Slaves* (Charlottesville: University Press of Virginia, 1976), 145–46. The scarcity of African American contemporary accounts necessitates the use of narratives, as imperfect as they are; I have tried to use as a guide John W. Blassingame, "Using the Testimony of Ex-Slaves: Approaches and Problems," *Journal of Southern History* 41, no. 4 (November 1975): 473–92.

71. Wiley, *Southern Negroes,* 14–18; Booker T. Washington, *Up from Slavery: An Autobiography* (New York: Doubleday, Page, 1901), 7–8; Elizabeth Hyde Botume, *First Days Amongst the Contrabands* (Boston: Lee & Shepard, 1893), 6–7; Interview with Hanna Fambro, Cuyahoga Co., Ohio, n.d., in Rawick, *American Slave,* Sup. 1.5:341; diary of Cyrena Stone, [May 21, 1864], in Thomas G. Dyer, *Secret Yankees: The Union Circle in Confederate Atlanta* (Baltimore: Johns Hopkins University Press, 1999), 308; entry of May 14, 1864, in Elizabeth Van Lew, *A Yankee Spy in Richmond: The Civil War Diary of "Crazy Bet" Van Lew,* ed. David D. Ryan (Mechanicsburg, Pa.: Stackpole, 1996), 94.

72. Washington, *Up from Slavery,* 7–8; Narrative of Louis Meadow, Lee Co., Ala., n.d., in Rawick, *American Slave,* Sup. 1.1:255; Lew Wallace to [?], Paducah, Ky., December 22, 1861, Lew and Susan Wallace Papers, Indiana Historical Society, Indianapolis, Ind.; diary of Cyrena Stone, n.d. [c. June 7, 1864], in Dyer, *Secret Yankees,* 316.

73. Leon F. Litwack, *Been in the Storm So Long: The Aftermath of Slavery* (New York: Vintage, 1980), 4–5 and 17–20; entry of April 23, 1865, *Mary Chesnut's Civil War,* 794; diary of Cyrena Stone, [January 20, 1864], in Dyer, *Secret Yankees,* 286.

74. Laura Towne to [?], n.p., April 29, 1865, in Laura M. Towne, *Letters and Diary of Laura M. Towne: Written from the Sea Islands of South Carolina, 1862–1884,* ed. Rupert Sargent Holland (Cambridge: Riverside Press, 1912), 162. "Visitation" stories are legion; some samples are Elizabeth Thomas interview, *Washington Star,* July 11, 1903; Charlie Davenport Narrative, Adams Co., Miss., n.d. [c. 1937], in Rawick, *American Slave,* Sup. 1.7:562; Bob Maynard, Weleetka, Okla., n.d. [c. 1937], ibid., Sup. 7.1:225.

75. Harriet Tubman, quoted in Lydia Maria Child to John G. Whittier, January 21, 1862, in Lydia Maria Child, *Letters of Lydia Maria Child with a Biographical Introduction by John G. Whittier* (Boston: Houghton Mifflin, 1883), 161; George E. Stephens, *A Voice of Thunder: The Civil War Letters of George E. Stephens,* ed. Donald Yacovone (Urbana: University of Illinois Press, 1997), 18. For "medicine man," see Hannah Crasson, slave near Raleigh, n.d. [c. 1937], in Rawlins, *American Slave,* 14.1:193. For "Hear talk," see Sallie Paul, Marion, S.C., November 1937, ibid., 3.3:247. See also Litwack, *Been in the Storm,* epigraph page.

76. Gregory P. Downs, *Declarations of Dependence: The Long Reconstruction of Practical Politics in the South, 1861–1908* (Chapel Hill: University of North Carolina Press, 2011), 70–73 and 94; George Washington to AL, Taylors Barracks [Louisville], December 4, 1864, in Ira Berlin et al., eds., *Freedom: A Documentary History of Emancipation, 1861–1867,* series 1, vol. 1, *The Destruction of Slavery* (Cambridge, U.K.: Cambridge University Press, 1985), 384; see also Annie Davis to AL, Belair, August 25, 1864, ibid., 608.

77. "TER" to "CPW," St. Helena, May 6, 1865, in Elizabeth Ware Pearson, ed., *Letters from Port Royal, Written at the Time of the Civil War (1862–1868)* (Boston: W. B. Clarke, 1906),

310–11; Laura Towne to [?], April 29, 1865, in Towne, *Letters and Diary,* 162. See also Botume, *Days Amongst the Contrabands,* 173 and 178.

78. Dispatch of Thomas Morris Chester, before Richmond, February 3, 1865, in R. J. M. Blackett, ed., *Thomas Morris Chester, Black Civil War Correspondent: His Dispatches from the Virginia Front* (Baton Rouge: Louisiana State University Press, 1989), 249–50; Ervin L. Jordan Jr., *Black Confederates and Afro-Yankees in Civil War Virginia* (Charlottesville: University Press of Virginia, 1995), 265–68 and 289–384. For other examples of African American intelligence work, see Claim of Sylvanus T. Brown, Charles City Co., Va., March 14, 1879, Southern Claims Commission, NARA; Ryan, *A Yankee Spy in Richmond,* 109.

79. Jordan, *Black Confederates and Afro-Yankees,* 289; George E. Stephens to *Weekly Anglo-African,* Morris Island, S.C., August 1, 1864, in Donald Yacovone, ed., *Freedom's Journey: African American Voices of the Civil War* (Chicago: Lawrence Hill, 2004), 165–66; James Henry Gooding to AL, Morris Island, S.C., September 28, 1863, in ibid., 154; Anonymous ["Hagar"] to AL (endorsed by AL), [June 16, 1864], ALP-LC; James Oakes, *The Radical and the Republican: Frederick Douglass, Abraham Lincoln, and the Triumph of Antislavery Politics* (New York: W. W. Norton, 2007), 214–16; Foner, *The Fiery Trial,* 253–55.

80. George E. Stephens to [Robert Hamilton], Morris Island, S.C., August 1, 1864, in *A Voice Like Thunder,* xi–xii and 17–19, quotations on 19 and 324.

81. *New Orleans Tribune,* August 9, 11, 13, and 25, 1864, quotations from issues of August 11 and 25, 1864; James M. McPherson, ed., *The Negro's Civil War: How American Negroes Felt and Acted During the War for the Union* (New York: Pantheon, 1965), 128–29; Eric Foner, *Reconstruction: America's Unfinished Revolution, 1863–1877* (New York: Harper & Row, 1988), 63–65.

82. AL, "Address on Colonization to a Deputation of Negroes," August 14, 1862, *CW,* 5:370–75 and 370–71n; "ESP" to [?], n.p. [Sea Islands, S.C.], October 5, 1862, in Pearson, *Letters from Port Royal,* 91; *L'Union* translated in *New Orleans Tribune,* August 13, 1864; George B. Vashon to AL, September 1862, reprinted in *Douglass' Monthly,* October 1862, and quoted in Yacovone, *Freedom's Journey,* 41–43. For a longer discussion of the colonization issue, see chapter 3.

83. Letter to Union Convention, Nashville, January 9, 1865, in Edward L. Ayers and Bradley C. Mittendorf, eds., *The Oxford Book of the American South: Testimony, Memory, and Fiction* (New York: Oxford University Press, 1997), 194–99; Petition to AL, c. May 14, 1864, and Petition to AL, c. March 12, 1864, both in McPherson, *The Negro's Civil War,* 275–84; AL to Michael Hahn, March 13, 1864, *CW,* 7:243; "La Population de Couleur et les Yankees," *La Tribune de la Nouvelle-Orléans* (French edition of *New Orleans Tribune*), August 4, 1864; Speech of Capt. J. R. Ingraham, c. March 18, 1865, in McPherson, *The Negro's Civil War,* 130; Foner, *Reconstruction,* 566.

84. *New Orleans Tribune,* July 28, August 9, 11, and 13, and November 18, 1864, and March 29, 1865; Foner, *Reconstruction,* 70–71; William W. Freehling, *The South vs. the South: How Anti-Confederate Southerners Shaped the Course of the Civil War* (New York: Oxford University Press, 2001), 165–66; Peter Randolph, *From Slave Cabin to the Pulpit: The Autobiography of Rev. Peter Randolph; The Southern Question Illustrated and Sketches of Slave Life* (Boston: James H. Earle, 1893), 69 and 135.

85. For quick turnaround in black views after the assassination, see *New Orleans Tribune,* April 20, 1865; Thomas Hall testimony, Raleigh, N.C., September 10, 1937, in Rawlins, *American Slave,* 14.1:361. An informal count of positive and negative postwar views of AL expressed in Rawlins revealed that 54 percent of ex-slaves who mentioned AL had a positive view, 39 percent had a negative one, and 6.6 percent expressed indifference.

86. Wiley, *Southern Negroes,* 22–23; Coffin, "Late Scenes in Richmond," 755; Mary Barnes, Charles Co., Md., n.d. [1937], in Rawlins, *American Slave,* Sup. 2–1.9:300.

87. Green, "Industrial Pioneer," 37–38; "Inside Views of Dixie, by the Northern Spy Duff Green," *New York Times,* May 1, 1864; William Prezter, " 'The British, Duff Green, the Rats and the Devil': Custom, Capitalism, and Conflict in the Washington Printing Trade, 1834–36," *Labor History* 27, no. 1 (Winter 1985): 5–30.

88. Duff Green to AL, Richmond, January 20, 1864, ALP-LC; Green, *Facts and Suggestions,* 232; Green, "Industrial Pioneer," 39–41; "Inside Views of Dixie."

89. For Campbell's presence at the Green-Lincoln interview, see Green, *Facts and Suggestions,* 232; John A. Campbell to Ben E. Green, Baltimore, April 7, 1885, Green Papers, SHC-UNC. See also "John Archibald Campbell," www.encyclopediaofalabama.org.

90. John A. Campbell to [Jefferson Davis], Washington, D.C., April 3, 23, and 28, 1861, copies in Nicolay Papers, LC (quotation from April 3); entries of December 13, 1862, and August 13 and November 15, 1863, in Robert Garlick Hill Kean, *Inside the Confederate Government: The Diary of Robert Garlick Hill Kean,* ed. Edward Younger (New York: Oxford University Press, 1957), 33, 93–94, and 122–23.

91. Entries of December 25, 1864, and March 23, 1865, in Kean, *Inside the Confederate Government,* 182 and 202; John Archibald Campbell, *Reminiscences and Documents Relating to the Civil War During the Year 1865* (Baltimore: John Murphy, 1887), 3–19; for "There is anarchy," see Campbell to John Breckinridge, March 5, 1865, ibid., 31. See also John A. Campbell to [Godfrey] Weitzel, Richmond, April 7, 1865, copy in Edwin M. Stanton Papers, LC; Lankford, *Richmond Burning,* 201–2.

92. Lankford, *Richmond Burning,* 203; Memorandum of Gustavus A. Myers, Richmond, April 5, 1865, Holt Papers, LC (a slightly different copy is in Myers Family Papers, VHS); AL, "Proclamation of Amnesty and Reconstruction," December 8, 1863, *CW,* 7:53–56; AL to Nathaniel P. Banks, January 31, 1864, ibid., 7:161–62.

93. John A. Campbell to Horace Greeley, Richmond, April 26, 1865, in "Papers of Hon. John A. Campbell," *Southern Historical Society Papers* 42 (1917): 61–65; Charles H. Dana to Edwin M. Stanton, Richmond, March 5, 1865, Stanton Papers, LC; AL to John A. Campbell, [April 5, 1865], *CW,* 8:386–87.

94. Myers Memorandum, April 5, 1865, Holt Papers, LC; J[ohn] A. Campbell to Lt. Gen. R. Taylor, April 11, 1865, copy in Stanton Papers, LC; AL to Godfrey Weitzel, City Point, Va., April 6, 1865, *CW,* 8:389.

95. John A. Campbell to Lt. Gen. R. Taylor, April 11, 1865, Stanton Papers, LC; Weitzel, *Richmond Occupied,* 56–58; entry of April 13, 1865, in Gideon Welles, *Diary of Gideon Welles: Secretary of the Navy Under Lincoln and Johnson,* ed. Howard K. Beale (New York: W. W. Norton, 1960), 2:279–80; *New York Times,* April 10, 1865; "A Revisal of Belligerent Rights," *New York Times,* April 12, 1865; Gideon Welles, "Lincoln and Johnson: Their Plan of Reconstruction and the Resumption of National Authority," *The Galaxy,* April 1872, 524 and 526–27; AL to Godfrey Weitzel, Washington, D.C., April 12, 1865, *CW,* 8:406–7. For congressional outrage, see Recollections of George Julian in T. Harry Williams, *Lincoln and the Radicals* (Madison: University of Wisconsin Press, 1965), 372. Stanton is quoted in Memoranda Book of Isham Haynie, April 14, 1865, Isham Nicholas Haynie Papers, ILPL.

96. AL to Whom It May Concern [Horace Greeley], July 18, 1864, *CW,* 7:451; AL to George F. Shepley, November 21, 1862, ibid., 5:504; Welles, "Plan of Reconstruction," 526; Green, *Facts and Suggestions,* 232; Michael P. Riccards, *The Ferocious Engine of Democracy: A History of the American Presidency* (New York: Madison, 1997), 1:275–76 and 278. Blocking the amendment was indeed technically possible, if all Southern states voted against it, denying the three-quarters needed for it to enter into law; Alexander Stephens maintained that a similar opening was given to him at the Hampton Roads Conference—see Donald, *Lincoln,* 558.

97. AL, "Annual Message to Congress," December 8, 1863, *CW,* 7:50–52; AL, "Proclamation of Amnesty and Reconstruction," December 8, 1863, ibid., 7:53–56; Foner, *Reconstruction,* 35–37 and 62; Carwardine, *Lincoln,* 235–39; Mark E. Neely Jr., *The Last Best Hope of Earth: Abraham Lincoln and the Promise of America* (Cambridge: Harvard University Press, 1993), 179–81.

98. Machiavelli, *Discourses,* III.8—on March 13, 1862, Salmon P. Chase recorded that the Rev. Dr. [Richard] Fuller of Baltimore had thus quoted Machiavelli, *Chase Papers,* 1:331; J. B. Henderson to Gen. John M. Schofield, St. Louis, September 4, 1863, John B. Schofield Papers, LC; Joseph Medill to AL, Washington, D.C., January 15, 1865, ALP-LC; entry of April 7, 1865, Welles, *Diary of Gideon Welles,* 2:277–78.

99. Neely, *Last Best Hope,* 179–81; entry of December 14, 1863, Kean, *Inside the Confederate Government,* 127.

100. Entry of December 20, 1863, in Edmonston, *Journal of a Secesh Lady,* 508–9.

101. Dr. Henderson to George D. Blakey, Louisville, June 18, 1864, ALP-LC; John S. Brien to AL, Nashville, January 30, 1864, ALP-LC; Myers Memorandum, April 5, 1865, Holt Papers, LC.

102. "Reconstruction in Tennessee," *New York Times,* February 2, 1864; Edwin H. Ewing to AL, Murfreesboro, Tenn., January 23, 1864, ALP-LC; Horace Maynard to AL, Nashville, February 2, 1864, ALP-LC; AL to Maynard, February 13, 1864, *CW,* 7:183; William C. Harris, *With Charity for All: Lincoln and the Restoration of the Union* (Lexington: University Press of Kentucky, 1997), 212–28; Foner, *Reconstruction,* 43–45.

103. AL to Frederick Steele, January 27 and 30, 1864, *CW,* 7:154–55 and 161; Donald, *Lincoln,* 484; T. M. Jacks to AL (endorsed by AL), Washington, D.C., January 13, 1865, ALP-LC; Harris, *With Charity for All,* 197–211.

104. D. Christie to AL, New Orleans, February 28, 1864, ALP-LC; P. M. Lapice to George F. Shepley, New Orleans, December 15, 1862, George F. Shepley Papers, Maine Historical Society, Portland, Me.; George H. Hepworth, *The Whip, Hoe, and Sword; or The Gulf-Department in '63* (Boston: Walker, Wise, 1864), 27–28; Harris, *With Charity for All,* 182–84; Foner, *Reconstruction,* 47–50; *La Tribune de la Nouvelle-Orléans,* July 28 and August 11, 1864.

105. Foner, *Reconstruction,* 47–50; Nathaniel P. Banks to AL, New Orleans, December 16, 1863, January 22 and February 12, 1864, all ALP-LC; Thomas S. Bacon to AL, n.p., February 5, 1864, ALP-LC.

106. Entry of September 22, 1864, in Edmund Ruffin, *The Diary of Edmund Ruffin,* ed. William Kaufman Scarborough (Baton Rouge: Louisiana State University Press, 1972–1989), 3:573; AL, "Proclamation Concerning Reconstruction," July 8, 1864, *CW,* 7:433–34; AL to Whom It May Concern [Greeley], July 18, 1864, ibid., 7:451; Donald, *Lincoln,* 510–11; entry for July 4, 1864, in John Hay, *Inside Lincoln's White House: The Complete Civil War Diary of John Hay,* ed. Michael Burlingame and John R. Turner Ettlinger (Carbondale: Southern Illinois University Press, 1997), 217–19.

107. Donald, *Lincoln,* 524; Charles Sumner to John Bright, Washington, D.C., March 27, 1865, in Sumner, *Selected Letters,* 2:279; AL to the Senate and House of Representatives, n.d. [February 5, 1865], *CW,* 8:260–61; entry of February 6, 1865, Welles, *Diary of Gideon Welles,* 2:237; Salmon P. Chase to Jas R. Gilmore, Washington, D.C., February 23, 1865, John Roberts Gilmore Papers, Johns Hopkins University, Special Collections, Milton S. Eisenhower Library, Baltimore, Md.

108. Edward Lyulph Stanley to "mamma," Quebec [Parish, La.], July 17, 1864, Edward Lyulph Stanley Papers, Cambridge University Library: Royal Commonwealth Society Library, Cambridge, U.K.; Michael Hahn to AL (endorsed by AL), New Orleans, September 24, 1864, ALP-LC; William O. Stoddard to AL, Little Rock, January 16, 1865, ALP-LC; Foner, *Reconstruction,* 73–74.

109. AL, "Message to Congress in Special Session," July 4, 1861, *CW,* 4:437; Freehling, *Road to Disunion,* 2:453–66 and 506; Stephen V. Ash, *When the Yankees Came: Conflict and Chaos in the Occupied South, 1861–1865* (Chapel Hill: University of North Carolina Press, 1995), 109–10; Carl N. Degler, *The Other South: Southern Dissenters in the Nineteenth Century* (New York: Harper & Row, 1974), 168–69; Dale Baum, *The Shattering of Texas Unionism: Politics in the Lone Star State During the Civil War Era* (Baton Rouge: Louisiana State University Press, 1998), 82–83.

110. John W. Palmer to W[illiam] G. Brownlow, Unionville, S.C., October 4, 1860, in Brown- low, *Sketches of the Rise,* 65–66; *Alexandria* [Va.] *Gazette,* November 9, 1860; Hiram Cockrell to Ward Hill Lamon, Fairfax Court House, Va., January 15, 1861, Ward Hill Lamon Papers, HL; Claim of Abraham Garber, Harrisonburg, Va., October 25, 1871, in David A. Rodes, Norman R. Wenger, and Emmert F. Bittinger, eds., *Unionists and the Civil War Experience in the Shenandoah Valley* (Rockport, Me.: Penobscot Press, 2003–2012), 1:90.

111. Diary of William Howard Russell, April 15, 17, and 25 and May 6, 11, and 27, 1861, in William Howard Russell, *My Diary North and South* (Boston: Burnham, 1863), 94, 100, 136–37, 171, 190, and 239; John A. Logan to wife [Mary Logan], Washington, D.C., July 16, 1861, John A. Logan Family Papers, LC; unidentified diary, March 11, 1862, in G. W. Cable, ed., "War Diary of a Union Woman in the South," *The Century Magazine* 38, no. 6 (October 1889): 936.

112. Entry of April 25, 1861, Russell, *My Diary*, 136–37; William Fanning Wickham to Dr. Charles Carter, near Hanover C'House, April 25, 1865, Wickham Family Papers, VHS; Claim of Edward C. Turner, Kinloch, Fauquier County, Va., March 1876, Southern Claims Commission Records, NARA.

113. Entry of October 14, 1862, in *The Diary of Orville Hickman Browning, 1850–1864*, ed. Theodore Calvin Pease and James G. Randall (Springfield: Illinois State Historical Society, 1925), 1:578; Isaac Murphy to AL, St. Louis, February 17, 1863, ALP-LC; Charles P. Bertrand to AL, Little Rock, October 19, 1863, ALP-LC; Ash, *When the Yankees Came,* 111, 113, 116, and 118–19.

114. Ash, *When the Yankees Came,* 110–16; William W. Gallaher to AL, Memphis, February 9, 1863, ALP-LC.

115. Unionist letters decrying AL are legion, e.g., Wyndham Robertson to Frank Robertson, Richmond, c. April 12–17, 1861, Robertson Papers, VHS; Hector Green to Johnnie [Green], Henderson, [Ky.], May 12, 1861, Green Family Papers, Filson Historical Society, Louisville, Ky.; [Gov. Thomas E. Bramlette] to AL, fragment, Frankfort, Ky., September 15, 1864, Abraham Lincoln Papers, DU; James L. Petigru to [Alfred] Hugar, White Sulphur Springs, Va., September 5, 1860, copy, Petigru Papers, LC.

116. R. B. Smith et al. to AL, Ringgold, Ga., December 17, 1860, ALP-LC; Unionist pleas for direct contact with AL are plentiful, e.g., Thomas Brown to Ward Hill Lamon, Washington, D.C., February 5, 1862, Lamon Papers, HL; Amos Young to AL, Washington, D.C., March 20, 1862, ALP-LC.

117. James W. Jones to AL, Harrison County, [Va.], December 11, 1860, ALP-LC; Elizabeth R. Varon, *Southern Lady, Yankee Spy: The True Story of Elizabeth Van Lew, A Union Agent in the Heart of the Confederacy* (New York: Oxford University Press, 2003), 71; entry of November 19, 1863, in Elisha Hunt Rhodes, *All for the Union: The Civil War Diary and Letters of Elisha Hunt Rhodes,* ed. Robert Hunt Rhodes (New York: Vintage, 1985), 125; John B. Fry to AL, Washington, D.C., September 29, 1863, ALP-LC; John M. Botts to John B. Fry, Auburn, Va., January 22, 1864, ALP-LC.

118. In *The South vs. the South,* Freehling gives a detailed discussion of pro-Union Southerners' contribution to the Northern effort (statistics on xiii); Ash, *When the Yankees Came,* 128–31; Varon, *Southern Lady, Yankee Spy,* 78–82 and 158–59; entry of September 18, 1862, in Frances Peter, *A Union Woman in Civil War Kentucky: The Diary of Frances Peter,* ed. John David Smith and William Cooper Jr. (Lexington: University Press of Kentucky, 2000), 33–34; Elizabeth Brown Pryor, "Robert E. Lee and the Full Mobilization of the South," *North and South* 10, no. 4 (November–December 2007): 61–70.

119. AL to Cuthbert Bullitt, July 28, 1862, *CW,* 5:344–45; Ward H. Lamon to AL, Washington, D.C., May 27, 1861, ALP-LC.

120. Entry of April 17, 1865, in Jones, *A Rebel War Clerk's Diary,* 2:479; Margaret Green Calhoun to Patr[ick] Calhoun, n.d. [c. 1885], Green Papers, SHC-UNC; Benjamin B. French to Frank [Francis O. French], Washington, D.C., April 30, 1865, Benjamin B. French Family Papers, LC.

121. Thomas M. Cook, "The Rebellion: Views of General Lee," *New York Herald,* April 29, 1865; William Parker Miles to Mrs. William Mason Smith, Anderson, S.C., April 24, 1865, in Daniel E. Huger Smith, Alice R. Huger Smith, and Arney R. Childs, eds., *Mason Smith Family Letters, 1860–1868* (Columbia: University of South Carolina Press, 1950), 200; Martin Abbott, "Southern Reaction to Lincoln's Assassination," *Abraham Lincoln Quarterly* 7, no. 3 (September 1952): 112–14, 117, and 119–20.

122. Entry of April 20, 1865, in Kate Cumming, *Kate: The Journal of a Confederate Nurse,* ed. Richard Barksdale Harwell (Baton Rouge: Louisiana State University Press, 1959), 275;

Abbott, "Southern Reaction to Lincoln's Assassination," 114 and 116; *Houston Telegraph,* April 26, 1865, and *Dallas Herald,* May 4, 1865, in Ralph W. Steen, "Texas Newspapers and Lincoln," *The Southwestern Historical Quarterly* 51, no. 3 (January 1948): 201–2; entry of April 23, 1865, in Ellen Renshaw House, *A Very Violent Rebel: The Civil War Diary of Ellen Renshaw House,* ed. Daniel E. Sutherland (Knoxville: University of Tennessee Press, 1996), 162; Caroline S. Jones to Mary Jones, Augusta, Ga., April 30, 1865, in Robert Manson Myers, ed., *The Children of Pride: A True Story of Georgia and the Civil War* (New Haven: Yale University Press, 1972), 1268; entry of April 21, 1865, in *The Diary of Edmund Ruffin,* 3:859–60; entry of April 23, 1865, in Edmonston, *Journal of a Secesh Lady,* 702.

123. Entry of April 17, 1865, Cornelius Walker Diary, MoC; entries of April 22 and 26, 1865, in Lizzie Hardin, *The Private War of Lizzie Hardin,* ed. G. Glenn Clift (Frankfort: Kentucky Historical Society, 1963), 233–35; entry of June 15, 1865, in Morgan, *Civil War Diary,* 611.

CHAPTER 7. EPILOGUE TO THE HOLLOW CROWN: LINCOLN AND SHAKESPEARE

1. Charles Sumner, *The Promise of the Declaration of Independence: Eulogy on Abraham Lincoln, Delivered Before the Municipal Authorities of the City of Boston, June 1, 1865* (Boston: J. E. Farwell, 1865), 45; Marquis Adolphe de Chambrun, *Impressions of Lincoln and the Civil War: A Foreigner's Account,* trans. General Aldebert de Chambrun (New York: Random House, 1952), 83; Marquis Adolphe de Chambrun, "Personal Recollections of Mr. Lincoln," *Scribner's Magazine,* January 1893, 35; *Macbeth,* act III, sc. 2 (all Shakespeare quotations are from www.shakespeare.mit.edu); AL to James H. Hackett, August 17, 1863, *CW,* 6:392. For appreciation of AL's readings, see F. B. Carpenter, *Six Months at the White House with Abraham Lincoln* (New York: Hurd & Houghton, 1866), 52. For "nodding off," see entry of August 23, 1863, in John Hay, *Inside Lincoln's White House: The Complete Civil War Diary of John Hay,* ed. Michael Burlingame and John R. Turner Ettlinger (Carbondale: Southern Illinois University Press, 1997), 76.

2. R. Gerald McMurtry, "Lincoln Knew Shakespeare," *Indiana Magazine of History* 31, no. 4 (December 1935): 265–70; *Hamlet,* act III, sc. 3; AL to James H. Hackett, August 17, 1863, *CW,* 6:392; Carpenter, *Six Months at the White House,* 49–51.

3. Douglas L. Wilson, "His Hour upon the Stage," *The American Scholar,* Winter 2012, online at www.theamericanscholar.org; entries of August 13 and December 18, 1863, Hay, *Inside Lincoln's White House,* 76 and 127–28; Noah Brooks, "Personal Reminiscences of Lincoln," *Scribner's Monthly,* March 1878, 675; Carpenter, *Six Months at the White House,* 49–51; *Daily National Republican* (Washington, D.C.), October 19, 1863; AL to James H. Hackett, August 17, 1863, *CW,* 6:392; William O. Stoddard, *Inside the White House in War Times: Memories and Reports of Lincoln's Secretary,* ed. Michael Burlingame (Lincoln: University of Nebraska Press, 2000), 188.

4. AL, "Remarks to a Committee of Reformed Presbyterian Synod," July 17, 1862, *CW,* 5:327; AL, "Speech at Great Central Sanitary Fair," June 16, 1864, ibid., 7:394; *Macbeth,* act II, sc. 4, and act III, sc. 2.

5. Ward H. Lamon, *The Life of Abraham Lincoln: From His Birth to His Inauguration as President* (Boston: James R. Osgood, 1872), 146; Robert Berkelman, "Lincoln's Interest in Shakespeare," *Shakespeare Quarterly* 2, no. 4 (October 1951): 310–11; Michael Burlingame, "The Trouble with the Bixby Letter," *American Heritage* 50, no. 4 (July–August 1999): 64–67; Jason Emerson, "America's Most Famous Letter," *American Heritage* 57, no. 1 (February–March 2006): 41–49.

6. AL, "Annual Message to Congress," December 1, 1862, *CW,* 5:537; AL to Horace Greeley, August 22, 1862, ibid., 5:388–89; Berkelman, "Lincoln's Interest in Shakespeare," 310–11. An analysis of influences on AL's writing and his use of words and cadence can be found in Ronald C. White Jr., *The Eloquent President: A Portrait of Lincoln Through His Words* (New York: Random House, 2005). See also Douglas L. Wilson, *Lincoln's Sword: The Presidency and the Power of Words* (New York: Vintage, 2006).

7. Salmon P. Chase to AL, Baltimore, April 11 and 12, 1865, ALP-LC; AL, "Last Public Address," April 11, 1865, *CW,* 8:399–405; David Herbert Donald, *Lincoln* (New York: Simon & Schuster, 1995), 582–85.

8. *Richard II,* act IV, sc. 1; *Macbeth,* act IV, sc. 3.

9. *Henry IV, Part 2,* act I, sc. 1; *Macbeth,* act IV, sc. 2.

10. For more on AL's managerial problems, see Elizabeth Brown Pryor, " 'The Grand Old Duke of York': How Abraham Lincoln Lost the Confidence of His Military Command," forthcoming; *Henry IV, Part 1,* act I, sc. 1; *Richard II,* act V, sc. 5.

11. Entry of December 13, 1863, Hay, *Inside Lincoln's White House,* 127–28; *Henry IV, Part 1,* act II, sc. 4.

12. Notes on Interview with Dr. LeGrand, n.d., Arthur E. Morgan Papers, LC; Address of William Fortune, Princeton, Ind., November 12, 1925, in Bess V. Ehrmann, *The Missing Chapter in the Life of Abraham Lincoln* (Chicago: Walter M. Hill, 1938), 64.

13. AL, "Address Before the Young Men's Lyceum," January 27, 1838, *CW,* 1:114; AL to Richard M. Corwine, Springfield, Ill., April 6, 1860, ibid., 4:36; AL to Lyman Trumbull, Springfield, Ill., April 29, 1860, ibid., 4:45; Reminiscence of Henry J. Raymond, in Don E. Fehrenbacher and Virginia Fehrenbacher, eds., *Recollected Words of Abraham Lincoln* (Stanford, Calif.: Stanford University Press, 1996), 375–76; Reminiscence of James B. Fry, n.d. [c. 1888], in Allen Thorndike Rice, ed., *Reminiscences of Abraham Lincoln by Distinguished Men of His Time* (New York: North American Review, 1888), 390; WHH, "Analysis of the Character of Abraham Lincoln," December 26, 1865, William Henry Herndon Papers, HL.

14. *Macbeth,* act III, sc. 2; *Hamlet,* act III, sc. 3; AL to James H. Hackett, August 17, 1863, *CW,* 6:392; Carpenter, *Six Months at the White House,* 50–51.

15. *Richard II,* act III, sc. 2; John Hay, "Life in the White House in the Time of Lincoln," in *Addresses of John Hay* (New York: Century, 1907), 334; *Henry IV, Part 2,* act IV, sc. 5; William Stoddard quoted in Wilson, "His Hour upon the Stage."

16. *Hamlet,* act III, sc. 3; insomnia passages in *Macbeth,* act II, sc. 1 and 2, and act III, sc. 2; *Henry IV, Part 1,* act II, sc. 3; *Henry IV, Part 2,* act III, sc. 1; Chambrun, "Personal Recollections," 35.

17. AL, "Second Inaugural Address," March 4, 1865, *CW,* 8:332; AL, "Address on Colonization to a Deputation of Negroes," August 14, 1862, ibid., 5:372; AL, "Speech at Great Central Sanitary Fair," June 16, 1864, ibid., 7:395; Reminiscence of Hugh McCulloch, n.d. [c. 1888], in Rice, *Reminiscences of Lincoln,* 411. For other Northerners holding AL accountable for the war, see, e.g., Maria Lydig Daly Diary, September 11, 1862, in *Diary of a Union Lady,* ed. Harold Earl Hammond (New York: Funk & Wagnalls, 1962), 170; Carl Schurz to AL, November 20, 1862, Centreville, Va., ALP-LC. Donald, *Lincoln,* 566, believes AL had shifted his responsibility "to a Higher Power," but other historians disagree: see, e.g., Richard Hofstadter, *The American Political Tradition and the Men Who Made It* (New York: Alfred A. Knopf, 1948), 133–34.

18. Michael Knox Beran, "Lincoln, *Macbeth,* and the Moral Imagination," *Humanitas* 11, no. 2 (1998), www.nhnet.org/beran, informed much of this and the previous paragraph; AL's humility was more oriented to a recognition of the insignificance of mankind in a universal sense than deference in interpersonal relations. See John Hay to WHH, Paris, September 5, 1866, *HI,* 332; William Pitt Fessenden to J. M. Forbes, Portland, November 13, 1862, in John Murray Forbes, *Letters and Recollections of John Murray Forbes,* ed. Sarah Forbes Hughes (Boston: Houghton Mifflin, 1899), 1:337; WHH, "Analysis of the Character of Abraham Lincoln," December 26, 1865, HL. The quotations are from *Macbeth,* act II, sc. 2; *Richard III,* act V, sc. 3; AL, "Gettysburg Address," November 19, 1863, *CW,* 7:20–21; Hofstadter, *American Political Tradition,* 133.

Bibliography

PRIMARY SOURCES (ARCHIVES)

Abraham Lincoln Presidential Library, Springfield, Ill.

Robert Anderson Memoirs (Black Hawk War)
H. Barber Correspondence
Black Hawk War Collection
Ambrose Burnside Correspondence
C. M. Butler Correspondence
John Caldwell Correspondence
John Archibald Campbell Papers
William Campbell Correspondence
Thomas Carney Correspondence
Lewis Cass Correspondence
Salmon P. Chase Correspondence
Chiriqui Colonization Collection
Samuel R. Curtis Papers
Charles Dresser Correspondence
Asher Edgerton Correspondence
Ulysses S. Grant Papers (Elihu B. Washburne Correspondence)
Duff Green Correspondence
Isham Nicholas Haynie Papers
Anson Henry Papers
August V. Kautz Papers
John A. Logan Papers
John A. McClernand Papers
Minute Book of Little Pigeon Creek Baptist Church, 1816–1840, Spencer County, Indiana
John J. Mudd Correspondence
Horatio Newhall Papers
Richard J. Oglesby Papers
Lewis B. Parsons Papers
Adam H. Pickel Correspondence
Frank Stevens Collection
Lyman Trumbull Papers
Richard Halsted Ward Papers

E. D. Webster Correspondence
James Harrison Wilson Papers

Alexandria Public Library, Kate Waller Barrett Branch, Alexandria, Va.

Eaches, Fendall, Tackett Collection
Society of Lees of Virginia Collection

Allen County [Ind.] Public Library

Lincoln Financial Foundation Collection

American Antiquarian Society, Worcester, Mass.

Clara Barton Papers
Abby Kelley Foster Papers

Boston Public Library, Boston, Mass.

Anti-Slavery Collection

Boston University, Boston, Mass.

John C. Ropes Papers, Military Historical Society of Massachusetts Collection

Cambridge University Library: Royal Commonwealth Society Library, Cambridge, U.K.

Edward Lyulph Stanley Papers

College of William and Mary, Earl Gregg Swem Library, Williamsburg, Va.

Joseph E. Johnston Papers
Robert E. Lee Papers

Columbia University Butler Library, Rare Book and Manuscript Library, New York, N.Y.

Elizabeth Blackwell Correspondence
Charles C. Cotton Diaries
John A. Dix Papers
Sydney Howard Gay Family Papers
John Wesley Hill Papers
Kelley Family Papers
Richard Yates Papers

Cornell University, Ithaca, N.Y.

George Bancroft Papers

Duke University, David M. Rubenstein Rare Book and Manuscript Library, Durham, N.C.

Robert E. Lee Papers
Abraham Lincoln Papers
John M. McCalla Papers
Mary Norton Papers
Hanson A. Risley Papers
William S. Stryker Manuscripts

Filson Historical Society, Louisville, Ky.

Don Carlos Buell Papers
Dow Family Papers
Green Family Papers
Hill Family Correspondence
Jones Family Papers
Kincheloe-Eskridge Family Papers
Speed Family Papers
Richard Yates Papers

Franklin and Marshall College, Lancaster, Pa.

Letters of John Fulton Reynolds

Georgetown University, Booth Family Center for Special Collections, Washington, D.C.

David Rankin Barbee Papers
Julius Garesché Papers

Gettysburg College, Musselman Library, Gettysburg, Pa.

Collection of Patriotic Envelopes
John C. Tidball Papers

Harvard University, Arthur and Elizabeth Schlesinger Library on the History of Women in America, Radcliffe Institute, Cambridge, Mass.

Beecher-Stowe Family Papers
Antoinette Brown Blackwell Papers
Howe Family Papers
Rebecca R. J. Pomeroy Letters
Elizabeth Cady Stanton and Susan B. Anthony Papers

Harvard University, Houghton Library, Cambridge, Mass.

Dorothea Lynde Dix Papers
Howe Family Papers
Howe Family Additional Papers
Julia Ward Howe Papers
Julia Ward Howe Papers Relating to "Battle Hymn of the Republic"
Charles Sumner Papers
Fannie Garrison Villard Papers
Henry Villard Papers

The Huntington Library, San Marino, Calif.

Anthony Family Papers
Samuel L. M. Barlow Papers
Clara Barton Papers
Marvin Henry Bovee Papers
Joseph M. Chambers Correspondence
Lucius E. Chittenden Manuscripts
Civil War Collection
Joel Barber Clough Letters
Samuel Ryan Curtis Papers
James W. Eldridge Collection
David Glasgow Farragut Papers
James T. Fields Papers
William Given Correspondence
Levi S. Graybill Papers
Charles G. Halpine Papers
Ida Husted Harper Collection
William Henry Herndon Papers
Joseph E. Johnston Papers
Ward Hill Lamon Papers
Lee Family Papers
Francis Lieber Papers
Lincoln Collection
George A. Magruder Pocket Notebook
Maury Family Papers (Brock Collection)
George A. McCall Papers
David Dixon Porter Papers
Charles H. Ray Papers
Warren E. Sawyer Letters
William Tecumseh Sherman Papers
Sophia Smith Collection
George H. Thomas Manuscripts
E. D. Townsend Papers
Gideon Welles Papers
A[nsel] Whedon Letter

Indiana Historical Society, Indianapolis, Ind.

Lew and Susan Wallace Papers

Johns Hopkins University, Special Collections, Milton S. Eisenhower Library, Baltimore, Md.

John Roberts Gilmore Papers

Library of Congress, Washington, D.C.

John Emerson Anderson Manuscript
Susan B. Anthony Papers
John C. Babcock Papers
Orra B. Bailey Papers
Nathaniel Prentiss Banks Papers
Clara Barton Papers
Edward Bates Papers
James Gordon Bennett Papers
Mary Ann Bickerdyke Papers
Jeremiah S. Black Papers
Blackwell Family Papers
Blair Family Papers
Charles H. Boyce Manuscript
Simon Cameron Papers
Edwin Carr Correspondence
Joshua Lawrence Chamberlain Papers
Lydia Maria Child Correspondence
Cyrus B. Comstock Papers
Samuel Wylie Crawford Papers
John J. Crittenden Papers
William A. Croffut Papers
John Adolphus Bernard Dahlgren Papers
Charles A. Dana Papers
Nathan Daniels Diaries
J. C. Bancroft Davis Papers
Henry Dawes Papers
Decatur House Papers
Tyler Dennett Papers
Anna Dickinson Papers
James Dodd Doolittle Papers
Elizabeth Todd Edwards Correspondence
Thomas Ewing Family Papers
Hamilton Fish Papers
Andrew Hull Foote Papers
Douglas Southall Freeman Papers
Benjamin B. French Family Papers

Julius P. Garesché Papers
James A. Garfield Papers
Joshua R. Giddings and George W. Julian Papers
Edwin Greble Papers
Adam Gurowski Papers
Henry W. Halleck Papers
Winfield Scott Hancock Papers
John Marshall Harlan Papers
Edward L. Hartz Papers
Esther Hill Hawks Papers
Samuel Peter Heintzelman Papers
Herndon-Weik Collection of Lincolniana
Ethan Allen Hitchcock Papers
Joseph Holt Papers
Emil Hurja Collection
Samuel Jones Papers
Philip Kearny Papers
Frederick West Lander Papers
Francis Lieber Correspondence
Abraham Lincoln Papers
Mary Todd Lincoln Papers
John A. Logan Family Papers
Joseph K. F. Mansfield Papers
Manton Marble Papers
Mathew Fontaine Maury Papers
George B. McClellan Papers
James B. McPherson Papers
Montgomery C. Meigs Papers
James Burtis Merwin Papers
Alfred Mordecai Papers
Arthur E. Morgan Papers
Martha Elizabeth Wright Morris Diary
John G. Nicolay Papers
Catherine Oliphant Papers
James L. Petigru Papers
David D. Porter Family Papers
Fitz-John Porter Papers
Read Family Papers
Charles Wellington Reed Papers
Remey Family Papers
William Cabell Rives Family Papers
Almon F. Rockwell Papers
Rodgers Family Papers
Rodgers Family Papers—Naval Historical Foundation Collection
John B. Schofield Papers
Henry Rowe Schoolcraft Papers

Carl Schurz Papers
Winfield Scott Papers
Philip H. Sheridan Papers
John Sherman Papers
William Tecumseh Sherman Papers
Edwin M. Stanton Papers
Elizabeth Cady Stanton Papers
Horatio Nelson Taft Diary
John Caldwell Tidball Manuscripts
Samuel Treat Correspondence
Lyman Trumbull Papers
Martin Van Buren Papers
Benjamin Wade Papers
Wadsworth Family Papers
Elihu B. Washburne Papers
Gideon Welles Papers
John Hill Wheeler Diary
Cadmus M. Wilcox Papers
Charles Wilkes Papers
Henry Wilson Papers
Annie Wittenmyer Letters
Levi Woodbury Papers

Library of Virginia, Richmond, Va.

Executive Papers of the Commonwealth of Virginia
Gravely Family Papers
Duff Green Papers
Special Collections—Broadsides
Alexander H. H. Stuart to F. S. Wood Letter

Maine Historical Society, Portland, Me.

Joshua Chamberlain Papers
George F. Shepley Papers

Maryland Historical Society, Baltimore, Md.

Anna Ellen Carroll Papers
Carroll-Cradock-Jensen Papers
Joseph Eggleston Johnston Papers
McLane-Fisher Papers

Massachusetts Historical Society, Boston, Mass.

William Lloyd Garrison Papers
Winthrop Family Papers

Museum of the Confederacy, Eleanor S. Brockenbrough Library, Richmond, Va.

Note: As of 2017, the contents of this archive have been transferred to the Virginia Historical Society.
Lelia M. Cook Diary
D. H. Hill Correspondence
Fitzhugh Lee Correspondence
Isabel Maury Correspondence [Maury Family Papers]
Ben McCulloch Papers
Mordecai Family Correspondence
Emmie Sublett Correspondence
Vertical Files: Richmond 1865
Cornelius Walker Diary

Museum of English Rural Life, University of Reading, Reading, U.K.

Nancy Astor Papers

National Archives and Records Administration, Washington, D.C.

Censes of the United States
Military Service and Pension Records
Records of the Commissioner of Indian Affairs (RG 77)
Southern Claims Commission Records (RG 217)
Joseph Totten Confidential Letter Book

New-York Historical Society, New York, N.Y.

Alexander H. Britton Correspondence
William H. Christian Correspondence
Civil War Letters, 1861–1865
Erasmus D. Keyes Correspondence
Oscar C. Lewis Correspondence
John Pope Correspondence
Theodore Tilton Papers
Lucien P. Waters Papers

New York State Library, Albany, N.Y.

John E. Wool Papers

Online

Diary and Letters of Chauncey Pond Joslin, Washington, D.C.: www.cpjoslincivilwar.org

Texas State Library, Austin, Tex.

Official Documents, 1858–1861

United States Army Heritage and Education Center, Carlisle, Pa.

William T. H. Brooks Papers
Albert B. Chandler Papers
Sylvester Churchill Papers
Civil War Times Illustrated Collection
Hawkins-Canby-Speed Family Papers
Albert J. Myer Papers
Smith-Kirby-Webster-Black-Danner Family Papers

United States Military Academy, West Point, N.Y.

Alexander Bowman Papers
William W. Burns Papers
Joseph K. Mansfield Papers
John C. Tidball Papers

University of California, Los Angeles, Special Collections, Los Angeles, Calif.

William S. Rosecrans Papers

University of North Carolina, Southern Historical Collection, Chapel Hill, N.C.

Duff Green Papers
Mordecai Family Papers

University of Notre Dame Archives, Notre Dame, Ind.

Thomas Ewing Family Papers
William Tecumseh Sherman Family Papers

University of Rochester, Rush Rhees Library, Rochester, N.Y.

William H. Seward Papers

University of Virginia, Albert and Shirley Small Special Collections Library, Charlottesville, Va.

Lydia Maria Francis Child Papers
Mary Abigail Dodge [Gail Hamilton] Papers
John H. Gilmer Letters
Diary of Clara Shafer
Stearns E. Tyler Letters

Virginia Historical Society, Richmond, Va.

John Lyddall Bacon Letter
Cornelius Hart Carlton Diary
Clarke Family Papers

Giles B. Cooke Papers
Cooper Family Papers
Crenshaw Family Papers
Caroline Keen Hill Davis Diary
Fannie Taylor Dickinson Diary
John B. Floyd Papers
Thomas Green Papers
J. R. Hamilton to William Swinton Letter
Arthur R. Henry Report
Hoge Family Papers
Lee Family Papers
Edmund Jennings Lee Papers
George Bolling Lee Papers
Mary Custis Lee Papers
Emmeline Crump Lightfoot Narrative
Lomax Family Papers
Lucas Family Papers
Mason Family Papers
Richard Lancelot Maury Diary
Berkeley Minor Affidavit
Minor Family Papers
John Kirkwood Mitchell Papers
Myers Family Papers
Nash Family Papers
Read Family Papers
Wyndham Robertson Papers
Robinson Family Papers
James Ewell Brown Stuart Papers
Helen Marie Taylor Collection
Tyler Family Papers
Alvin Coe Voris Papers
Wickham Family Papers
Margaret Brown Wight Diary
B. H. Wilkins Manuscripts
Winston Family Papers
George Albert Zabriskie Papers

PRIMARY SOURCES (PUBLISHED)

Adams, Henry. "The Great Secession Winter of 1860–61." In *The Great Secession Winter of 1860–61 and Other Essays by Henry Adams.* Edited by George Hochfield, 1–31. Written 1861, first published 1909. Reprint, New York: Sagamore Press, 1958.
Adams, John R. *Memorial and Letters.* Cambridge: Privately published, 1890.
Adams, Lois Bryan. *Letter from Washington, 1863–1865.* Edited by Evelyn Leasher. Detroit: Wayne State University Press, 1999.

Alcott, Louisa May. *The Journals of Louisa May Alcott.* Edited by Joel Myerson, Daniel Shealy, and Madeleine B. Stern. Boston: Little, Brown, 1989.

Ames, Blanche Butler, comp. *Chronicles from the Nineteenth Century: Family Letters of Blanche Butler and Adelbert Ames, Married July 21st 1870.* 2 vols. N.p.: Privately published, 1957.

Anonymous. *Diary of Count Kangaroosky, April 1, 1862.* N.p.: Unknown publisher, 1862.

Ayers, Edward L., and Bradley C. Mittendorf, eds. *The Oxford Book of the American South: Testimony, Memory, and Fiction.* New York: Oxford University Press, 1997.

Bacon, Georgeanna Woolsey, ed. *Letters of a Family During the War for the Union, 1861–1865.* 2 vols. N.p.: Privately published, c. 1899.

Barbee, David Rankin, and Milledge L. Bonham Jr., eds. "Fort Sumter Again." *Mississippi Valley Historical Review* 28, no. 1 (June 1941): 63–73.

Barnum, P. T. *Selected Letters of P. T. Barnum.* Edited by A. H. Saxon. New York: Columbia University Press, 1983.

Bates, Edward. *The Diary of Edward Bates, 1859–1866.* Edited by Howard K. Beale. Washington, D.C.: Government Printing Office, 1933.

Beecher, Henry Ward. "Women's Influence in Politics: Address Delivered at the Cooper Institute, New York, 2 February 1860." Boston: R. F. Wallcut, 1860.

Berlin, Ira, Barbara J. Fields, Thavolia Glymph, Joseph F. Reidy, and Leslie S. Rowland, eds. *Freedom: A Documentary History of Emancipation, 1861–1867: Selected from the Holdings of the National Archives of the United States.* Series 1, vol. 1, *The Destruction of Slavery.* Cambridge, U.K.: Cambridge University Press, 1985.

Blassingame, John W., ed. *Slave Testimony: Two Centuries of Letters, Speeches, Interviews, and Autobiographies.* Baton Rouge: Louisiana State University Press, 1977.

Bogue, Allan G., ed. "William Parker Cutler's Congressional Diary of 1862–63." *Civil War History* 33, no. 4 (December 1987): 315–30.

Botts, Edward Nichols (Wilfred W. Black, ed.). "Civil War Letters of E. N. Botts, Virginia, 1862." *Virginia Magazine of History and Biography* 69, no. 2 (April 1961): 194–209.

Brewster, Charles Harvey. *When This Cruel War Is Over: The Civil War Letters of Charles Harvey Brewster.* Edited by David W. Blight. Amherst: University of Massachusetts Press, 1992.

Brooke, John M. *Ironclads and the Big Guns of the Confederacy: The Journal and Letters of John M. Brooke.* Edited by George M. Brook Jr. Columbia: University of South Carolina Press, 2002.

Brooks, Noah. *Lincoln Observed: Civil War Dispatches of Noah Brooks.* Edited by Michael Burlingame. Baltimore: Johns Hopkins University Press, 1998.

Brown, Joseph R., and Samuel P. Hinman. *Missionary Paper by the Bishop Seabury Mission, Number Thirty: Letters on the Indian System.* Faribault, Minn.: Central Republican Book & Job Office, 1864.

Browne, Henry R., and Symmes E. Browne. *From the Fresh Water Navy, 1861–64: The Letters of Acting Master's Mate Henry R. Browne and Acting Ensign Symmes E. Browne.* Edited by John D. Milligan. Annapolis, Md.: United States Naval Institute, 1970.

Browning, Orville Hickman. *The Diary of Orville Hickman Browning, 1850–1864.* Edited by Theodore Calvin Pease and James G. Randall. 2 vols. Springfield: Illinois State Historical Society, 1925.

Brownlow, William Gannaway. *Sketches of the Rise, Progress, and Decline of Secession.* Philadelphia: G. W. Childs, 1862.

Buchanan, John C. (George M. Blackburn, ed.). "The Negro as Viewed by a Michigan Civil War Soldier: Letters of John C. Buchanan." *Michigan History* 47, no. 1 (March 1963): 75–84.

Butler, Benjamin F. *Private and Official Correspondence of Gen. Benjamin F. Butler During the Period of the Civil War.* Edited by Jesse Ames Marshall. 5 vols. N.p.: Privately published, 1917.

Cable, G. W., ed. "War Diary of a Union Woman in the South." *The Century Magazine,* October 1889, 931–46.

Campbell, John A. "Evacuation Echoes: Assistant-Secretary of War Campbell's Interview with Mr. Lincoln." *Southern Historical Society Papers* 24 (1896): 351–53.

———. "Papers of Hon. John A. Campbell." *Southern Historical Society Papers* 42 (1917): 3–81.

Chamberlain, Joshua L. *A Life in Letters: The Previously Unpublished Letters of a Great Leader of the Civil War.* Edited by Thomas Desjardin. Harrisburg, Pa.: The National Civil War Museum, 2012.

———. *Through Blood and Fire: Selected Civil War Papers of General Joshua Chamberlain.* Edited by Mark Nesbett. Mechanicsburg, Pa.: Stackpole, 1996.

Chamberlayne, C. G., ed. "Abraham Lincoln in Richmond: Memorandum of Gustavus A. Myers." *Virginia Magazine of History and Biography* 41, no. 4 (October 1933): 318–22.

Chambrun, Marquis Adolphe de. *Impressions of Lincoln and the Civil War: A Foreigner's Account.* Translated by General Aldebert de Chambrun. New York: Random House, 1952.

Channing, William E. *Slavery.* Boston: James Munroe, 1835.

Chase, Salmon P. *Inside Lincoln's Cabinet: The Civil War Diaries of Salmon P. Chase.* Edited by David Donald. New York: Longman's Green, 1954.

———. *The Salmon P. Chase Papers.* Edited by John Niven et al. 5 vols. Kent, Ohio: Kent State University Press, 1993–1998.

Chesnut, Mary Boykin. *Mary Chesnut's Civil War.* Edited by C. Van Woodward. New Haven: Yale University Press, 1981.

Chester, Thomas Morris. *Thomas Morris Chester, Black Civil War Correspondent: His Dispatches from the Virginia Front.* Edited by R. J. M. Blackett. Baton Rouge: Louisiana State University Press, 1989.

Child, Lydia Maria. *Letters of Lydia Maria Child with a Biographical Introduction by John G. Whittier.* Boston: Houghton Mifflin, 1883.

———. *Selected Letters, 1817–1880.* Edited by Milton Meltzer and Patricia G. Holland. Amherst: University of Massachusetts Press, 1982.

Chisholm, Daniel. *The Civil War Notebook of Daniel Chisholm: A Chronicle of Daily Life in the Union Army, 1864–1865.* Edited by W. Springer Menge and J. August Shimrak. New York: Ballantine, 1989.

Coffin, Charles. "Late Scenes in Richmond." *Atlantic Monthly,* June 1865, 753–55.

Colton, Kenneth E., ed. "Frontier War Problems: The Letters of Samuel Ryan Curtis." *The Annals of Iowa* 24, no. 4 (April 1943): 298–315.

———. " 'The Irrepressible Conflict of 1861': The Letters of Samuel Ryan Curtis." *The Annals of Iowa* 24, no. 1 (July 1942): 14–58.

———. "With Fremont in Missouri in 1861: The Letters of Samuel Ryan Curtis." *The Annals of Iowa* 24, no. 2 (October 1942): 105–67.

Comstock, Elizabeth L. *Life and Letters of Elizabeth L. Comstock.* Compiled by Caroline Hare. Philadelphia: John C. Winston, 1895.

Conolly, Thomas. *An Irishman in Dixie: Thomas Conolly's Diary of the Fall of the Confederacy.* Edited by Nelson D. Lankford. Columbia: University of South Carolina Press, 1988.

Cook, Lelian M. "Diary, 2–18 April, 1865." *Richmond News Leader,* April 3, 1935.

Cumming, Kate. *Kate: The Journal of a Confederate Nurse.* Edited by Richard Barksdale Harwell. Baton Rouge: Louisiana State University Press, 1959.

Dale, Edward Everett, and Gaston Litton, eds. *Cherokee Cavaliers: Forty Years of Cherokee History as Told in the Correspondence of the Ridge-Watie-Boudinot Family.* Norman: University of Oklahoma Press, 1939.

Dall, Caroline Healey. *Daughter of Boston: The Extraordinary Diary of a Nineteenth-Century Woman.* Edited by Helen R. Deese. Boston: Beacon Press, 2005.

Daly, Maria Lydig. *Diary of a Union Lady.* Edited by Harold Earl Hammond. New York: Funk & Wagnalls, 1962.

Darling, Flora Adams. *Mrs. Darling's Letters or Memories of the Civil War.* New York: John Lovell, 1883.

Davis, Jefferson. *Jefferson Davis, Constitutionalist: His Letters, Papers, and Speeches.* Edited by Dunbar Rowland. 10 vols. Jackson: Mississippi Department of Archives and History, 1923.

De Tocqueville, Alexis. *Democracy in America.* Edited and translated by Harvey Mansfield and Delba Winthrop. Chicago: University of Chicago Press, 2000.

Dicey, Edward. *Spectator of America.* Edited by Herbert Mitgang. Chicago: Quadrangle, 1971.

Douglass, Frederick. *The Frederick Douglass Papers. Series One: Speeches, Debates, and Interviews.* Edited by John W. Blassingame et al. 5 vols. New Haven: Yale University Press, 1979–1992.

Drayton, Percival. *Naval Letters from Captain Percival Drayton, 1861–1865.* Edited by Gertrude L. Hoyt. New York: New York Public Library, 1906.

Dumond, Dwight Lowell, ed. *Southern Editorials on Secession.* New York: Century, 1931.

Du Pont, Samuel Francis. *Samuel Francis Du Pont: A Selection from His Civil War Letters.* Edited by John D. Hayes. 3 vols. Ithaca, N.Y.: Cornell University Press, 1969.

Edmondston, Catherine Ann Devereux. *Journal of a Secesh Lady: The Diary of Catherine Ann Devereux Edmondston, 1860–1866.* Edited by Beth Gilbert Crabtree and James W. Patton. Raleigh: North Carolina Department of Cultural Resources, 1979.

Edwards, Whit, ed. *The Prairie Was on Fire: Eyewitness Accounts of the Civil War in the Indian Territory.* Oklahoma City: Oklahoma Historical Society, 2001.

Emerson, Ralph Waldo. *The Journals and Miscellaneous Notebooks of Ralph Waldo Emerson.* Edited by William H. Gilman et al. 16 vols. Cambridge: Belknap Press, 1960–1982.

Farragut, Loyall, ed. *The Life of David Glasgow Farragut, First Admiral of the United States Navy, Embodying His Journal and Letters.* New York: D. Appleton, 1879.

Faust, Drew Gilpin, ed. *The Ideology of Slavery: Proslavery Thought in the Antebellum South, 1830–1860.* Baton Rouge: Louisiana State University Press, 1981.

"Federal Generals and a Good Press." *American Historical Review* 39, no. 2 (January 1934): 284–97.

Fields, Annie, ed. *Life and Letters of Harriet Beecher Stowe.* Cambridge: Riverside Press, 1897.

Fillmore, Millard. *Millard Fillmore Papers.* Edited by Frank H. Severance. 2 vols. Buffalo: Buffalo Historical Society, 1907.

Fleet, Betsy, and John D. P. Fuller, eds. *Green Mount: A Virginia Plantation Family During the Civil War; Being the Journal of Benjamin Robert Fleet and Letters of His Family.* Lexington: University of Kentucky Press, 1962.

Floyd, Elbert F., ed. "Insights into the Personal Friendship and Patronage of Abraham Lincoln and Anson Gordon Henry, M.D.: Letters from Dr. Henry to His Wife, Eliza." *Journal of the Illinois State Historical Society* 98, no. 4 (Winter 2005–2006): 218–53.

Forbes, John Murray. *Letters and Recollections of John Murray Forbes.* Edited by Sarah Forbes Hughes. 2 vols. Boston: Houghton Mifflin, 1899.

Ford, Worthington Chauncey, ed. *A Cycle of Adams Letters, 1861–1865.* 2 vols. Boston: Houghton Mifflin, 1920.

———. *War Letters, 1862–1865, of John Chipman Gray and John Codman Ropes.* Boston: Houghton Mifflin, 1927.

Forten, Charlotte. "Life on the Sea Islands." *Atlantic Monthly,* May–June 1864, 587–96 and 666–76.

Fox, Gustavus Vasa. *Confidential Correspondence of Gustavus Vasa Fox, Assistant Secretary of the Navy, 1861–1865.* Edited by Robert Means Thompson and Richard Wainwright. 2 vols. New York: Naval History Society/De Vinne Press, 1918–1919.

Fremantle, Arthur James Lyon. *Three Months in the Southern States, April–June, 1863.* New York: John Bradburn, 1864.

Frémont, Jessie Benton. *The Letters of Jessie Benton Frémont.* Edited by Pamela Herr and Mary Lee Spence. Urbana: University of Illinois Press, 1993.

French, Benjamin Brown. *From the Diary and Correspondence of Benjamin Brown French.* Edited by Amos Tuck French. New York: Privately published, 1904.

———. *Witness to the Young Republic: A Yankee's Journal, 1828–1870.* Edited by Donald B. Cole and John J. McDonough. Hanover, N.H.: University Press of New England, 1989.

Garfield, James A. *The Wild Life of the Army: Civil War Letters of James A. Garfield.* Edited by Frederick D. Williams. Lansing: Michigan State University Press, 1964.

Garidel, Henri. *Exile in Richmond: The Confederate Journal of Henri Garidel.* Edited by Michael Bedout Chesson and Leslie Jean Roberts. Charlottesville: University Press of Virginia, 2001.

Garrison, William Lloyd. *The Letters of William Lloyd Garrison.* Edited by Walter M. Merrill. 6 vols. Cambridge: Belknap Press, 1971–1981.

Gilmore, James R., ed. *Among the Pines or South in Secession Time by Edmund Kirke.* New York: J. R. Gilmore, 1862.

Gordon, Ann D., ed. *The Selected Papers of Elizabeth Cady Stanton and Susan B. Anthony.* 6 vols. New Brunswick, N.J.: Rutgers University Press, 1997–2013.

Grant, Ulysses S. *The Papers of Ulysses S. Grant.* Edited by John Y. Simon et al. 32 vols. Carbondale: Southern Illinois University Press, 1967–2012.

Green, Duff. *Facts and Suggestions, Biographical, Historical, Financial and Political.* New York: Richardson, 1866.

Greenhow, Rose O'Neal. *My Imprisonment and the First Year of Abolition Rule at Washington.* London: Richard Bentley, 1863.

Gurowski, Adam. *Diary from March 4, 1861 to November 12, 1862.* Boston: Lee & Shepard, 1862.

———. *Diary from November 18, 1862 to October 18, 1863.* New York: Carleton, 1864.

———. *Diary 1863–'64–'65.* Washington, D.C.: Morrison, 1866.

Halleck, Henry. *Elements of War and Science.* New York: D. Appleton, 1846.

Halliwell, James Orchard. *Tarlton's Jests and News out of Purgatory.* London: Shakespeare Society, 1844.

[Halpine, Charles G.]. *The Life and Adventures, Songs, Services and Speeches of Private Miles O'Reilly.* New York: Carleton, 1864.

Hamilton, Gail [Mary Abigail Dodge]. "A Call to My Country-Women." *Atlantic Monthly,* March 1863, 345–49.

————. *Gail Hamilton's Life in Letters.* Edited by H. Augusta Dodge. 2 vols. Boston: Lee & Shepard, 1901.

————. "Lights Among the Shadows of Our Civil War." In *Country Living and Country Thinking,* 366–461. Boston: Ticknor & Fields, 1862.

————. "Men and Women." In *Country Living and Country Thinking,* 80–205. Boston: Ticknor & Fields, 1862.

————. *Skirmishes and Sketches.* Boston: Ticknor & Fields, 1865.

————. "A Spasm of Sense." *Atlantic Monthly,* April 1863, 407–19.

————. "Tracts for Our Time: Courage!" *Congregationalist,* January 27, 1862 [*sic;* 1863].

Hancock, Cornelia. *South After Gettysburg: Letters of Cornelia Hancock from the Army of the Potomac, 1863–1868.* Edited by Henrietta Stratton Jaquette. New York: Thomas Y. Crowell, 1956.

Hardin, Lizzie. *The Private War of Lizzie Hardin: A Kentucky Confederate Girl's Diary of the Civil War in Kentucky, Virginia, Tennessee, Alabama, and Georgia.* Edited by G. Glenn Clift. Frankfort: Kentucky Historical Society, 1963.

Harris, George Washington. *Sut Lovingood Travels with Old Abe Lincoln.* Chicago: Black Cat Press, 1937.

Hawks, Esther Hill. *A Woman Doctor's Civil War: Esther Hill Hawks Diary.* Edited by Gerald Schwartz. Columbia: University of South Carolina Press, 1984.

Hawthorne, Nathaniel. "Our Whispering Gallery, IV." *Atlantic Monthly,* April 1871, 505–12.

Hay, John. *At Lincoln's Side: John Hay's Civil War Correspondence and Selected Writings.* Edited by Michael Burlingame. Carbondale: Southern Illinois University Press, 2000.

————. *Inside Lincoln's White House: The Complete Civil War Diary of John Hay.* Edited by Michael Burlingame and John R. Turner Ettlinger. Carbondale: Southern Illinois University Press, 1997.

————. *Lincoln and the Civil War in the Diaries and Letters of John Hay.* Edited by Tyler Dennett. 1939. Reprint, Westport, Conn.: Negro Universities Press, 1972.

Hayward, Ambrose Henry. *Last to Leave the Field: The Life and Letters of First Sergeant Ambrose Henry Hayward, 28th Pennsylvania Volunteer Infantry.* Edited by Timothy J. Orr. Knoxville: University of Tennessee Press, 2011.

Hedrick, John A. *Letters from a North Carolina Unionist: John A. Hedrick to Benjamin S. Hedrick, 1862–1865.* Edited by Judkin Browning and Michael Thomas Smith. Raleigh: North Carolina Department of Cultural Resources, 2001.

Hepworth, George H. *The Whip, Hoe, and Sword; or The Gulf-Department in '63.* Boston: Walker, Wise, 1864.

Herndon, William H., and Jesse W. Weik. *Herndon's Lincoln.* Edited by Douglas L. Wilson and Rodney O. Davis. Galesburg, Ill.: Knox College Lincoln Studies Center, 2006.

Hertz, Emanuel, ed. *The Hidden Lincoln: From the Letters and Papers of William H. Herndon.* New York: Blue Ribbon, 1940.

Hewitt, John Hill. *King Linkum the First: As Performed at the Concert Hall Augusta, Georgia, February 23, 1863.* Edited by Richard Barksdale Harwell. Atlanta: Emory University, 1947.

Higginson, Thomas Wentworth. *The Complete Civil War Journal and Selected Letters of Thomas Wentworth Higginson.* Edited by Christopher Looby. Chicago: University of Chicago Press, 2000.

————. "Regular and Volunteer Officers." *Atlantic Monthly,* September 1864, 348–57.

Hinsdale, Mary L., ed. *Garfield–Hinsdale Letters: Correspondence Between James Abram Garfield and Burke Aaron Hinsdale*. Ann Arbor: University of Michigan Press, 1949.

Hitchcock, Ethan Allen. *Fifty Years in Camp and Field: Diary of Major-General Ethan Allen Hitchcock, U.S.A.* Edited by William A. Croffut. New York: G. P. Putnam's Sons, 1909.

Holmes, Sarah Katherine (Stone). *Brokenburn: The Journal of Kate Stone, 1861–1868.* Edited by John G. Anderson. Baton Rouge: Louisiana State University Press, 1972.

Hopley, Catherine Cooper. *Life in the South: From the Commencement of the War by a Blockaded British Subject.* 2 vols. London: Chapman & Hall, 1863.

Horrocks, James. *My Dear Parents: An Englishman's Letters Home from the American Civil War.* Edited by A. S. Lewis. London: Victor Gollancz, 1982.

House, Ellen Renshaw. *A Very Violent Rebel: The Civil War Diary of Ellen Renshaw House.* Edited by Daniel E. Sutherland. Knoxville: University of Tennessee Press, 1996.

Houston, Sam. *The Writings of Sam Houston, 1813–1863.* Edited by Amelia W. Williams and Eugene C. Barker. 8 vols. Austin: University of Texas Press, 1938–1943.

Howells, W. D. *Selected Letters.* Edited by George Arms, Richard H. Ballinger, Christoph K. Lohmann, and John K. Reeves. 6 vols. Boston: Twayne, 1979–1983.

Hubbell, Jay B., ed. "The War Diary of John Esten Cooke." *Journal of Southern History* 7, no. 4. (November 1941): 526–40.

Hudson, Anna Ridgely. "A Girl of the Sixties: Excerpts from the Journal of Anna Ridgely." *Journal of the Illinois State Historical Society* 22, no. 3 (October 1929): 401–46.

Johnson, Andrew. *The Papers of Andrew Johnson.* Edited by Leroy P. Graf and Ralph W. Haskins. 16 vols. Knoxville: University of Tennessee Press, 1967–2000.

Jones, John B. *A Rebel War Clerk's Diary at the Confederate States Capital.* Edited by Howard Swiggett. 2 vols. New York: Old Hickory Bookshop, 1935.

Kean, Robert Garlick Hill. *Inside the Confederate Government: The Diary of Robert Garlick Hill Kean.* Edited by Edward Younger. New York: Oxford University Press, 1957.

Kelley, William D., Anna E. Dickinson, and Frederick Douglass. *Addresses of Hon. W. D. Kelley, Miss Anna E. Dickinson, and Mr. Frederick Douglass at a Mass Meeting Held at National Hall, Philadelphia, 6 July 1863 for the Promotion of Colored Enlistments.* Philadelphia: Commission for United States Colored Troops, 1863.

Kerr, Orpheus C. [Robert Henry Newell]. *Orpheus C. Kerr Papers: First Series.* New York: Blakeman & Mason, 1863.

———. *Orpheus C. Kerr Papers: Second Series.* New York: Carleton, 1863.

Lamson, Roswell H. *Lamson of the Gettysburg: The Civil War Letters of Lieutenant Roswell H. Lamson, U.S. Navy.* Edited by James M. McPherson and Patricia McPherson. New York: Oxford University Press, 1997.

Lee, Elizabeth Blair. *Wartime Washington: The Civil War Letters of Elizabeth Blair Lee.* Edited by Virginia Jeans Laas. Urbana: University of Illinois Press, 1991.

Lemley, Harry, ed. "Letters of Henry M. Rector and J. P. Kannaday to John Ross of the Cherokee Nation." *Chronicles of Oklahoma* 42, no. 3 (Autumn 1964): 320–29.

Leslie, Eliza. *The Behavior Book: A Manual for Ladies.* Philadelphia: Willis P. Hazard, 1853.

"Letter from Hon. Jas. Lyons" [to Col. Allen B. Magruder]. White Sulphur Springs, Greenbrier County, Va., August 23, 1875. (Pamphlet at VHS.)

Leyda, Jay, ed. *The Melville Log: A Documentary Life of Herman Melville, 1819–1891.* 2 vols. New York: Harcourt Brace, 1951.

Lieber, Francis. *The Life and Letters of Francis Lieber*. Edited by Thomas Sergeant Perry. Boston: James R. Osgood, 1882.

Lincoln, Abraham. *Abraham Lincoln: Complete Works, Comprising His Speeches, Letters, State Papers, and Miscellaneous Writings*. Edited by John G. Nicolay and John Hay. 2 vols. New York: Century, 1894.

———. *The Collected Works of Abraham Lincoln*. Edited by Roy P. Basler. 9 vols. New Brunswick, N.J.: Rutgers University Press, 1953.

[Locke, David Ross]. *The Nasby Papers*. Indianapolis: C. O. Perrine, 1864.

——— . *The Struggles (Social, Financial and Political) of Petroleum V. Nasby*. Boston: Lee & Shepard, 1888.

Longfellow, Henry Wadsworth. *The Letters of Henry Wadsworth Longfellow*. Edited by Andrew Hilen. 6 vols. Cambridge: Belknap Press, 1966–1982.

Lusk, William Thompson. *War Letters of William Thompson Lusk, Captain, Assistant Adjutant-General, United States Volunteers, 1861–1863*. New York: Privately published, 1911.

Lyman, Colonel Theodore. *With Grant and Meade from the Wilderness to Appomattox*. Edited by George R. Agassiz. Lincoln: University of Nebraska Press, 1994.

Lytle, William Haines. *For Honor Glory and Union: The Mexican and Civil War Letters of Brig. Gen. William Haines Lytle*. Edited by Ruth C. Carter. Lexington: University Press of Kentucky, 1999.

Magruder, John Bankhead. *The Presidential Contest of 1856 in Three Letters*. Washington, D.C.: Privately published, 1857.

McAllister, Robert. *The Civil War Letters of General Robert McAllister*. Edited by James I. Robertson Jr. New Brunswick, N.J.: Rutgers University Press, 1965.

McCall, George A. *Letters from the Frontier: Written During a Period of Thirty Years' Service in the Army of the United States*. Philadelphia: Lippincott, 1868.

McClellan, George B. *The Civil War Papers of George B. McClellan: Selected Correspondence 1860–1865*. Edited by Stephen W. Sears. New York: Ticknor & Fields, 1989.

[McGuire, Judith White Brockenbrough]. *Diary of a Southern Refugee, During the War, by a Lady of Virginia*. New York: E. J. Hale, 1867.

Meade, George Gordon, Jr., ed. *The Life and Letters of George Gordon Meade, Major-General United States Army*. 2 vols. New York: Charles Scribner's Sons, 1913.

Melville, Herman. *The Confidence-Man: His Masquerade*. Edited by Hershel Parker. New York: W. W. Norton, 1971.

Mitgang, Herbert, ed. *Lincoln as They Saw Him*. New York: Rinehart, 1956.

Morgan, Sarah. *The Civil War Diary of a Southern Woman*. Edited by Charles East. New York: Simon & Schuster, 1991.

Mott, Lucretia Coffin. *Selected Letters of Lucretia Coffin Mott*. Edited by Beverly Wilson Palmer. Urbana: University of Illinois Press, 2002.

Myers, Robert Manson, ed. *The Children of Pride: A True Story of Georgia and the Civil War*. New Haven: Yale University Press, 1972.

Naglee, Henry Morris. *A Chapter from the Secret History of the War*. Philadelphia: Unknown publisher, 1864.

Nicolay, John G. "Hole-in-the-Day." *Harper's New Monthly Magazine,* January 26, 1863, 186–91.

———. "The Sioux War." *Continental Monthly,* February 1863, 195–204.

Olmsted, Frederick Law. *The Papers of Frederick Law Olmsted.* Edited by Charles E. Beveridge et al. 9 vols. Baltimore: Johns Hopkins University Press, 1977–2015.

Patrick, Marsena Rudolph. *Inside Lincoln's Army: The Diary of Marsena Rudolph Patrick, Provost Marshal General, Army of the Potomac.* Edited by David S. Sparks. New York: Thomas Yoseloff, 1964.

Patrick, Robert. *The Secret Diary of Robert Patrick, 1861–1865.* Edited by F. Jay Taylor. Baton Rouge: Louisiana State University Press, 1959.

Pearson, Elizabeth Ware, ed. *Letters from Port Royal, Written at the Time of the Civil War (1862–1868).* Boston: W. B. Clarke, 1906.

Peskin, Allan, ed. "Two White House Visits: Congressman James H. Campbell Prods President Lincoln and 'Shares a Dish of Gossip with the First Lady.'" *Lincoln Herald* 94, no. 4 (Winter 1992): 157–58.

Peter, Frances. *A Union Woman in Civil War Kentucky: The Diary of Frances Peter.* Edited by John David Smith and William Cooper Jr. Lexington: University Press of Kentucky, 2000.

Pierce, Edward Lillie. *Enfranchisement and Citizenship: Addresses and Papers.* Edited by A. W. Stevens. Boston: Roberts Brothers, 1896.

Pratt, Harry E., ed. *Concerning Mr. Lincoln, in Which Abraham Lincoln Is Pictured as He Appeared to Letter Writers of His Time.* Springfield, Ill.: The Abraham Lincoln Association, 1944.

Rankin, David C. "Political Parades and American Democracy: Jean-Charles Houzeau on Lincoln's 1864 Reelection Campaign." *Civil War History* 30, no. 4 (December 1984): 324–29.

Ravenel, Henry William. *The Private Journal of Henry William Ravenel, 1859–1887.* Edited by Arney Robinson Childs. Columbia: University of South Carolina Press, 1947.

Raymond, Henry J. "Extracts from the Journal of Henry J. Raymond." *Scribner's Monthly,* January and February 1880, 419–24 and 703–10.

Reed, Charles Wellington. *"A Grand Terrible Dramma": From Gettysburg to Petersburg: The Civil War Letters of Charles Wellington Reed.* Edited by Eric A. Campbell. New York: Fordham University Press, 2000.

Reid, Harvey. *The View from Headquarters: Civil War Letters of Harvey Reid.* Edited by Frank L. Byrne. Madison: State Historical Society of Wisconsin, 1965.

Rhodes, Elisha Hunt. *All for the Union: The Civil War Diary and Letters of Elisha Hunt Rhodes.* Edited by Robert Hunt Rhodes. New York: Vintage, 1985.

Ropes, Hannah. *Civil War Nurse: The Diary and Letters of Hannah Ropes.* Edited by John R. Brumgardt. Knoxville: University of Tennessee Press, 1980.

Rose, Ernestine L. *Mistress of Herself: Speeches and Letters of Ernestine L. Rose, Early Women's Rights Leader.* Edited by Paula Doress-Worters. New York: Feminist Press at the City University of New York, 2007.

Ross, John. *The Papers of Chief John Ross.* Edited by Gary E. Moulton. 2 vols. Norman: University of Oklahoma Press, 1985.

Ruffin, Edmund. *The Diary of Edmund Ruffin.* Edited by William Kaufman Scarborough. 3 vols. Baton Rouge: Louisiana State University Press, 1972–1989.

Russell, William Howard. *My Diary North and South.* Boston: Burnham, 1863.

Schurz, Carl. *Intimate Letters of Carl Schurz, 1841–1869.* Edited by Joseph Schafer. Madison: State Historical Society of Wisconsin, 1928.

Schwartz, Thomas F., and Kim Bauer, eds. "Unpublished Mary Todd Lincoln." *JALA* 17, no. 2 (Summer 1996): 1–21.

Schwartz, Thomas F., and Anne V. Shaughnessy, eds. "Unpublished Mary Lincoln Letters." *JALA* 11, no. 1 (1990): 34–40.

Sedgwick, John. *Correspondence of John Sedgwick, Major-General.* Edited by Henry D. Sedgwick. 2 vols. New York: Printed for Carl and Ellen Battille Stoeckel by De Vinne Press, 1902–1903.

Segal, Charles M., ed. *Conversations with Lincoln.* New York: G. P. Putnam's Sons, 1961.

Seitz, Don C., ed. "Artemus Ward Letters." *American Collector* 3, no. 5 (February 1927): 195–98.

Shaw, John, ed. *Crete and James: Personal Letters of Lucretia and James Garfield.* East Lansing: Michigan State University Press, 1994.

Shaw, Robert Gould. *Blue-Eyed Child of Fortune: The Civil War Letters of Colonel Robert Gould Shaw.* Edited by Russell Duncan. Athens: University of Georgia Press, 1992.

Sherman, William Tecumseh. *Home Letters of General Sherman.* Edited by M. A. DeWolfe Howe. New York: Charles Scribner's Sons, 1909.

———. *Sherman's Civil War: Selected Correspondence of William T. Sherman, 1860–1865.* Edited by Brooks D. Simpson and Jean V. Berlin. Chapel Hill: University of North Carolina Press, 1999.

[Smith, Charles Henry]. *Bill Arp, So Called: A Side Show of the Southern Side of the War.* New York: Metropolitan Records Office, 1866.

Smith, Daniel E. Huger, Alice R. Huger Smith, and Arney R. Childs, eds. *Mason Smith Family Letters, 1860–1868.* Columbia: University of South Carolina Press, 1950.

[Smith, William Russell]. *The Royal Ape: A Dramatic Poem.* Richmond: West & Johnston, 1863.

Snyder, Charles M., ed. *The Lady and the President: The Letters of Dorothea Dix and Millard Fillmore.* Lexington: University Press of Kentucky, 1975.

Spencer, Warren F. "A French View of the Fall of Richmond: Alfred Paul's Report to Drouyn de Lhuys, April 11, 1865." *Virginia Magazine of History and Biography* 73, no. 2 (April 1965): 178–88.

Stanton, Elizabeth Cady. *Elizabeth Cady Stanton as Revealed in Her Letters, Diary and Reminiscences.* Edited by Theodore Stanton and Harriot Stanton Blatch. New York: Harper & Brothers, 1922.

Steedman, Charles. *Memoir and Correspondence of Charles Steedman, Rear Admiral, United States Navy; with His Autobiography and Private Journals, 1811–1890.* Edited by Amos Lawrence Mason. Cambridge: Privately published, 1912.

Stephens, George E. *A Voice of Thunder: The Civil War Letters of George E. Stephens.* Edited by Donald Yacovone. Urbana: University of Illinois Press, 1997.

Stockwell, Elisha, Jr. *Private Elisha Stockwell Jr. Sees the Civil War.* Edited by Byron R. Abernathy. Norman: University of Oklahoma Press, 1985.

[Stone, Cyrena A.]. "Miss Abbey's Diary." In *Secret Yankees: The Union Circle in Confederate Atlanta.* Edited by Thomas G. Dyer, 283–328. Baltimore: Johns Hopkins University Press, 1999.

Stone, Lucy, and Antoinette Brown Blackwell. *Friends and Sisters: Letters Between Lucy Stone and Antoinette Brown Blackwell, 1846–93.* Edited by Carol Lasser and Marlene Deahl Merrill. Urbana: University of Illinois Press, 1987.

Stone, Lucy, and Henry B. Blackwell. *Loving Warriors: Selected Letters of Lucy Stone and Henry B. Blackwell, 1853 to 1893.* Edited by Leslie Wheeler. New York: Dial, 1981.

Strong, George Templeton. *The Diary of George Templeton Strong.* Edited by Allan Nevins and Milton Halsey Thomas. 4 vols. New York: Macmillan, 1952.

Strother, David Hunter. *A Virginia Yankee in the Civil War: The Diaries of David Hunter Strother.* Edited by Cecil D. Eby Jr. Chapel Hill: University of North Carolina Press, 1961.

Sumner, Charles. *The Promise of the Declaration of Independence: Eulogy on Abraham Lincoln, Delivered Before the Municipal Authorities of the City of Boston, June 1, 1865.* Boston: J. E. Farwell, 1865.

———. *The Selected Letters of Charles Sumner.* Edited by Beverly Wilson Palmer. 2 vols. Boston: Northeastern University Press, 1990.

Swisshelm, Jane Grey. *Crusader and Feminist: Letters of Jane Grey Swisshelm, 1858–1865.* Edited by Arthur J. Larsen. Westport, Conn.: Hyperion Press, 1976.

———. *Half a Century.* Chicago: Jansen, McClurg, 1880.

Tapert, Annette, ed. *The Brothers' War: Civil War Letters to Their Loved Ones from the Blue and Gray.* New York: Vintage, 1988.

Taylor, Thomas Smith. *Letters Home: Three Years Under General Lee in the 6th Alabama.* Edited by Harlan Eugene Cross Jr. Fairfax, Va.: History4All, 2010.

Thorndike, Rachel Sherman, ed. *The Sherman Letters: Correspondence Between General and Senator Sherman from 1837 to 1891.* London: Sampson, Low, Marston, 1894.

Ticknor, George. *Life, Letters, and Journals of George Ticknor.* 2 vols. Boston: James R. Osgood, 1877.

Tompkins, Christopher Q. "The Occupation of Richmond, April 1865: The Memorandum of Events of Colonel Christopher Q. Tompkins." Edited by William M. E. Rachal. *Virginia Magazine of History and Biography* 73, no. 2 (April 1965): 189–98.

Towne, Laura M. *Letters and Diary of Laura M. Towne: Written from the Sea Islands of South Carolina, 1862–1884.* Edited by Rupert Sargent Holland. Cambridge: Riverside Press, 1912.

Townsend, George Alfred. *The Life, Crime and Capture of John Wilkes Booth with a Full Sketch of the Conspiracy of which He Was the Leader and the Pursuit, Trial and Execution of His Accomplices.* New York: Dick and Fitzgerald, 1865.

Trobriand, Régis de. *Four Years with the Army of the Potomac.* Boston: Ticknor, 1889.

Turner, Arlin. "Elizabeth Peabody Visits Lincoln, February 1865." *New England Quarterly* 48, no. 1 (March 1975): 116–24.

Turner, Justin G., and Linda Levitt Turner, eds. *Mary Todd Lincoln: Her Life and Letters.* New York: Alfred A. Knopf, 1972.

Van Lew, Elizabeth. *A Yankee Spy in Richmond: The Civil War Diary of "Crazy Bet" Van Lew.* Edited by David D. Ryan. Mechanicsburg, Pa.: Stackpole, 1996.

Villard, Henry. *Lincoln on the Eve of '61: A Journalist's Story.* Edited by Harold G. Villard and Oswald Garrison Villard. Westport, Conn.: Greenwood Press, 1974.

Voris, Alvin C. *A Citizen-Soldier's Civil War: The Letters of Brevet Major General Alvin C. Voris.* Edited by Jerome Mushkat. DeKalb: Northern Illinois University Press, 2002.

Wadsworth, James S., and George Bancroft. *Words of Wisdom from War Democrats: Letters of Hon. James Wadsworth, Late Senator from Erie County, and Hon. George Bancroft, the Historian.* New York: Privately published, 1862.

Wainwright, Charles S. *A Diary of Battle: The Personal Journals of Colonel Charles S. Wainwright, 1861–1865.* Edited by Allan Nevins. New York: Harcourt, Brace & World, 1962.

Wallace, Isabel. *Life and Letters of General W. H. L. Wallace.* Chicago: R. R. Donnelley & Sons, 1909.

Ward, Artemus [Browne, Charles Farrar]. *The Complete Works of Artemus Ward.* New York: G. W. Dillingham, 1898.

———. *The Complete Works of Artemus Ward.* New York: Burt Franklin, 1970.

———. *His Book*. New York: Carleton, 1862.

Weld, Stephen Minot. *War Diary and Letters of Stephen Minot Weld, 1861–1865*. Cambridge: Riverside Press, 1912.

Welles, Gideon. *Diary of Gideon Welles: Secretary of the Navy Under Lincoln and Johnson*. Edited by Howard K. Beale. 3 vols. New York: W. W. Norton, 1960.

Welsh, Peter. *Irish Green and Union Blue: The Civil War Letters of Peter Welsh, Color Sergeant, 28th Regiment Massachusetts Volunteers*. Edited by Lawrence Frederick Kohl with Margaret Cossé Richard. New York: Fordham University Press, 1986.

Welsh, William. *Journal of the Rev. S. D. Hinman, Missionary to the Santee Sioux Indians and Taopi*. Philadelphia: McCalla & Stavely, 1869.

Whipple, H[enry] B. *Missionary Paper by the Bishop Seabury Mission, Number Twenty-Four: An Appeal for the Red Man*. Faribault, Minn.: Central Republican Book & Job Office, 1863.

Whiting, William. *War Powers of the President and the Legislative Powers of Congress in Relation to Rebellion, Treason and Slavery*. Boston: John L. Shorey, 1863.

Whitman, Walt. *Memoranda During the War and Death of Abraham Lincoln*. Edited by Roy P. Basler. Bloomington: Indiana University Press, 1962.

———. Walt *Whitman's Civil War*. Edited by Walter Lowenfels. New York: Alfred A. Knopf, 1961.

Whitney, Ellen M., ed. *The Black Hawk War, 1831–1832*. 2 vols. Springfield: Illinois State Historical Library, 1970–1978.

Wight, Margaret. *A Refugee at Hanover Tavern: The Civil War Diary of Margaret Wight*. Edited by Shirley A. Haas and Dale Paige Talley. Charleston, S.C.: History Press, 2013.

Willcox, Orlando B. *Forgotten Valor: The Memoirs, Journals, and Civil War Letters of Orlando B. Willcox*. Edited by Robert Garth Scott. Kent, Ohio: Kent State University Press, 1999.

Williams, Alpheus S. *From the Cannon's Mouth: The Civil War Letters of General Alpheus S. Williams*. Edited by Milo M. Quaife. Detroit: Wayne State University Press, 1959.

Williams, Max R., and Joseph Grégoire de Roulhac Hamilton, eds. *The Papers of William Alexander Graham*. 8 vols. Raleigh: North Carolina Office of Archives and History, 1957–1992.

Wilson, Douglas L., and Rodney O. Davis, eds. *Herndon's Informants: Letters, Interviews and Statements About Abraham Lincoln*. Urbana: University of Illinois Press, 1998.

Wilson, Henry. *History of the Antislavery Measures of the Thirty-Seventh and Thirty-Eighth United-States Congresses, 1861–64*. Boston: Walker, Wise, 1864.

Winthrop, Robert C. "The Fall of Richmond: Speech Made at Faneuil Hall, Boston, 4 April 1865." In *Addresses and Speeches on Various Occasions from 1852 to 1867*, 658–60. Boston: Little, Brown, 1867.

Wood, Alice Davis, ed. *Dorothea Dix and Dr. Francis T. Stribling: An Intense Friendship Letters: 1849–1874*. Bloomington, Ind.: Xlibris, 2008.

Yacovone, Donald, ed. *Freedom's Journey: African American Voices of the Civil War*. Chicago: Lawrence Hill, 2004.

GOVERNMENT AND PUBLIC DOCUMENTS

Carroll, Anna Ella. "The War Powers of the General Government." Washington, D.C.: Henry Polkinhorn, 1861.

Condition of the Indian Tribes: Report of the Joint Special Committee Appointed Under Joint Resolution, March 3, 1865. Washington, D.C.: Government Printing Office, 1867.

Congressional Globe, 36th–39th Congresses.

Cullum, George Washington. *Biographical Register of the Officers and Graduates of the U.S. Military Academy at West Point, N.Y.* 3 vols. Boston: Houghton Mifflin, 1891.

Hardee, W. J. *Rifle and Light Infantry Tactics: For the Exercise and Maneuvers of Troops When Acting as Light Infantry or Riflemen.* Washington, D.C.: War Department, 1855.

Heitman, Francis B. *Historical Register and Dictionary of the United States Army from Its Organization, September 29, 1789, to March 2, 1903.* 2 vols. Washington, D.C.: Government Printing Office, 1903.

Kappler, Charles J., ed. *Indian Affairs: Laws and Treaties.* 4 vols. Washington, D.C.: Government Printing Office, 1904.

Killian, Johnny H., George A. Costello, and Kenneth R. Thomas, eds. *The Constitution of the United States of America: Analysis and Interpretation.* Washington, D.C.: Government Printing Office, 2004.

Official Records of the Union and Confederate Navies in the War of the Rebellion. Washington, D.C.: Government Printing Office, 1894–1922.

Prucha, Francis Paul, ed. *Documents of United States Indian Policy.* Lincoln: University of Nebraska Press, 1975.

Report of the Commissioner of Indian Affairs, Accompanying the Annual Report of the Secretary of the Interior for the Year 1861. Washington, D.C.: Government Printing Office, 1861.

Report of the Commissioner of Indian Affairs, November 26, 1862. Washington, D.C.: Government Printing Office, 1863.

Report of the Commissioner of Indian Affairs, October 13, 1863. Washington, D.C.: Government Printing Office, 1864.

Report of the Commissioner of Indian Affairs, November 16, 1864. Washington, D.C.: Government Printing Office, 1865.

Report of the Joint Committee on the Conduct of the War at the Second Session Thirty-Eighth Congress, 3 vols. Washington, D.C.: Government Printing Office, 1865.

Rodes, David A., Norman R. Wenger, and Emmert F. Bittinger, eds. *Unionists and the Civil War Experience in the Shenandoah Valley.* 6 vols. Rockport, Me.: Penobscot Press, 2003–2012.

Schaffter, Dorothy, and Dorothy M. Mathews. *The Powers of the President as Commander in Chief of the Army and Navy of the United States.* Washington, D.C.: Government Printing Office, 1956.

Scott, Winfield. *General Regulations for the Army; or, Military Institutes.* Philadelphia: M. Carey & Sons, 1821.

———. *Rules and Regulations for the Field Exercise and Manoeuvres of Infantry.* Philadelphia: Anthony Finley, 1824.

———. *To the Loyal Women of America.* Washington, D.C.: United States Sanitary Commission, 1861.

The War of the Rebellion: A Compilation of the Official Records of the Union and Confederate Armies. Prepared Under the Direction of the Secretary of War. 70 vols. Washington, D.C.: Government Printing Office, 1880–1901.

CONTEMPORARY PERIODICALS

Alexandria [Va.] *Gazette*
Boston Daily Courier
Charleston Mercury
Chicago Times
Chicago Tribune
Daily National Intelligencer [Washington, D.C.]
Daily National Republican [Washington, D.C.]
Detroit Free Press
Geneva [N.Y.] *Gazette*
Harper's New Monthly Magazine
Harper's Weekly
Journal of Commerce
La Crosse [Wisc.] *Democrat*
Liberator
Milledgeville [Ga.] *Southern Federal Union*
National Anti-Slavery Standard
New Haven Courier
New Orleans Daily Crescent
New Orleans Daily Delta
New Orleans Tribune (French co-edition, *La Tribune de la Nouvelle-Orléans*)
New York Evening Post
New York Times
New York Tribune
New York World
North Carolina Standard
The Old Guard
Petersburg Daily Express
Philadelphia Pennsylvanian
Punch
Richmond Enquirer
Sacramento Bee
St. Cloud [Minn.] *Democrat*
Selinsgrove Times
The Southern Illustrated News
The Times [London]
Vanity Fair
Washington Evening Star
Washington Morning Chronicle

AUTOBIOGRAPHIES AND MEMOIRS

Adams, Henry. *The Education of Henry Adams.* Washington, D.C.: Privately published, 1907.
Alexander, Edward Porter. *Fighting for the Confederacy: The Personal Recollections of General*

Edward Porter Alexander. Edited by Gary W. Gallagher. Chapel Hill: University of North Carolina Press, 1989.

Averell, William Woods. *Ten Years in the Saddle: The Memoir of William Woods Averell.* Edited by Edward K. Eckert and Nicholas J. Amato. San Rafael, Calif.: Presidio Press, 1978.

Badeau, Adam. *Grant in Peace: From Appomattox to Mount McGregor: A Personal Memoir.* Hartford: S. S. Scranton, 1887.

[Baldwin, John B.]. *Interview Between President Lincoln and Col. John B. Baldwin, April 4th, 1861: Statements and Evidence.* Staunton, Va.: Spectator Job Office, 1866.

Barnes, John S. "With Lincoln from Washington to Richmond in 1865." *Appleton's Magazine,* May 1907, 515–24.

Barnes, Thurlow Weed. *The Life of Thurlow Weed Including His Autobiography and a Memoir.* 2 vols. Boston: Houghton Mifflin, 1883–1884.

Barnum, P. T. *Struggles and Triumphs, or, Forty Years' Recollections.* Hartford: J. B. Burr, 1869.

Bates, David Homer. *Lincoln in the Telegraph Office: Recollections of the United States Military Telegraph Corps During the Civil War.* New York: Century, 1907.

Bayne, Julia Taft. *Tad Lincoln's Father.* Boston: Little, Brown, 1931.

Bergen, Abram. "Personal Recollections of Abraham Lincoln as a Lawyer." *The American Lawyer* 5 (May 1897): 212–15.

Black Hawk. *The Life of Ma-ka-tai-me-she-kia-kiak or Black Hawk Embracing the Tradition of His Nation.* Cincinnati: J. B. Patterson, 1831.

Bloomer, D. C. *Life and Writings of Amelia Bloomer.* Boston: Arena Publishing, 1895.

Blunt, James G. "General Blunt's Account of His Civil War Experiences." *Kansas Historical Quarterly* 1, no. 3 (May 1932): 211–65.

Botume, Elizabeth Hyde. *First Days Amongst the Contrabands.* Boston: Lee & Shepard, 1893.

Boyd, Belle. *Belle Boyd in Camp and Prison.* 2 vols. London: Saunders, Otley, 1865.

Boykin, Edward M. *The Falling Flag: Evacuation of Richmond, Retreat and Surrender at Appomattox.* New York: E. J. Hale, 1874.

Britton, Wiley. "Union and Confederate Indians in the Civil War." In *Battles and Leaders of the Civil War.* Edited by Robert Underwood Johnson and Clarence Clough Buell, 1:335–36. 4 vols. New York: Century, 1887–1888.

———. *The Union Indian Brigade in the Civil War.* Kansas City, Mo.: Franklin Hudson, 1922.

Bromley, Isaac Hill. "Historic Moments: The Nomination of Lincoln." *Scribner's Magazine,* November 1893, 645–56.

Brooks, Noah. "Personal Reminiscences of Lincoln." *Scribner's Monthly,* February and March 1878, 561–69 and 673–81.

———. *Washington in Lincoln's Time.* Edited by Herbert Mitgang. New York: Rinehart, 1958.

Brownell, Frank E. "Ellsworth's Career: *Philadelphia Weekly Times,* June 18, 1881." In *The New Annals of the Civil War,* edited by Peter Cozzens and Robert I. Girardi, 2–17. Mechanicsburg, Pa.: Stackpole, 2004.

Calvert, Henry Murray. *Reminiscences of a Boy in Blue, 1862–1865.* New York: G. P. Putnam's Sons, 1920.

Campbell, John A. *Recollections of the Evacuation of Richmond, April 2d 1865.* Baltimore: John Murphy, 1880.

———. *Reminiscences and Documents Relating to the Civil War During the Year 1865.* Baltimore: John Murphy, 1887.

———. "A View of the Confederacy from the Inside." *The Century Magazine,* October 1889, 950–54.

Carpenter, F. B. *Six Months at the White House with Abraham Lincoln.* New York: Hurd & Houghton, 1866.

Chace, Elizabeth Buffum. *Anti-Slavery Reminiscences.* Central Falls, R.I.: E. L. Freeman & Son, 1891.

Chambrun, Marquis Adolphe de. "Personal Recollections of Mr. Lincoln." *Scribner's Magazine,* January 1893, 26–38.

Chapman, Ervin, ed. *Latest Light on Abraham Lincoln and War-Time Memories.* 2 vols. New York: Fleming H. Revel, 1917.

Chittenden, L. E. *Personal Reminiscences, 1840–1890: Including Some Not Hitherto Published of Lincoln and the War.* New York: Richmond, Croscup, 1893.

———. *Recollections of President Lincoln and His Administration.* New York: Harper & Brothers, 1891.

Clark, Allen C. "Abraham Lincoln in the National Capital." *Records of the Columbia Historical Society* 27 (1925): 1–174.

Colman, Lucy N. *Reminiscences.* Buffalo: H. L. Green, 1891.

Conway, Moncure D. "Personal Recollections of President Lincoln." *The Fortnightly Review* 1, no. 1 (May 1865): 56–65.

Cox, Jacob Dolson. *Military Reminiscences of the Civil War.* 2 vols. New York: Charles Scribner's Sons, 1900.

Cozzens, Peter, ed. *Battles and Leaders of the Civil War.* Vol. 5. Urbana: University of Illinois Press, 2002. (Contains John Hay, "Life in the White House with President Lincoln," 104–13; John B. Magruder, "War in 1861: The First Battle of the War; Big Bethel," 34–40.)

———, ed. *Battles and Leaders of the Civil War.* Vol. 6. Urbana: University of Illinois Press, 2004.

Cozzens, Peter, and Robert I. Girardi, eds. *The New Annals of the Civil War.* Mechanicsburg, Pa.: Stackpole, 2004.

Crawford, Samuel Wylie. *The Genesis of the Civil War: The Story of Sumter, 1860–1861.* New York: C. L. Webster, 1889.

Crook, William H. "Lincoln as I Knew Him." *Harper's Monthly Magazine,* June 1907, 41–48.

———. "Lincoln's Last Day." *Harper's Monthly Magazine,* September 1907, 519–30.

Dabney, Rev. R. L. "Memoir of a Narrative Received of Colonel John B. Baldwin, of Staunton, Touching on the Origin of the War." *Southern Historical Society Papers* 1, no. 6 (June 1876): 443–55.

Dana, Charles A. *Recollections of the Civil War with the Leaders at Washington and in the Field in the Sixties.* New York: D. Appleton, 1902.

———. "Reminiscences of Men and Events of the Civil War: I. From the 'Tribune' to the War Department." *McClure's Magazine,* November 1897, 20–31.

———. "Reminiscences of Men and Events of the Civil War: IX. The End of the War." *McClure's Magazine,* August 1898, 380–92.

Dawes, Henry L. "Washington the Winter Before the War." *Atlantic Monthly,* August 1893, 160–67.

Dudley, George T. "Lincoln in Richmond: True Version of the War President's Famous Visit." *National Tribune* [Washington, D.C.], October 1, 1896, 1–2.

Eytinge, Rose. *The Memories of Rose Eytinge: Being Recollections and Observations of Men, Women, and Events During Half a Century.* New York: Frederick A. Stokes, 1905.

Fehrenbacher, Don E., and Virginia Fehrenbacher, eds. *Recollected Words of Abraham Lincoln.* Stanford, Calif.: Stanford University Press, 1996.

Field, Maunsell B. *Memories of Many Men and of Some Women: Being Personal Recollections of Emperors, Kings, Queens, Princes, Presidents, Statesmen, Authors, and Artists at Home and Abroad During the Last Thirty Years.* New York: Harper & Brothers, 1874.

Fields, Annie. "Days with Mrs. Stowe." *Atlantic Monthly,* August 1896, 145–56.

Fry, James B. *Army Sacrifices; or Briefs from Official Pigeon-holes.* New York: D. Van Nostrand, 1879.

———. *Military Miscellanies.* New York: Brentano's, 1889.

Gilmore, James R. *Personal Recollections of Abraham Lincoln and the Civil War.* Boston: L. C. Page, 1898.

Grant, Julia Dent. *The Personal Memoirs of Julia Dent Grant (Mrs. Ulysses S. Grant).* Edited by John Y. Simon. Carbondale: Southern Illinois University Press, 1988.

Grant, Ulysses S. *Personal Memoirs of U. S. Grant.* Edited by E. B. Long. New York: Da Capo, 1982.

Green, Ben E. "Buchanan, Lincoln, and Duff Green." *The Century Magazine,* June 1889, 317–18.

Grimsley, Elizabeth Todd. "Six Months in the White House." *Journal of the Illinois State Historical Society* 19, nos. 3–4 (October 1926–January 1927): 43–73.

Harrison, Constance Cary. *Refugitta of Richmond: The Wartime Recollections, Grave and Gay, of Constance Cary Harrison.* Edited by Nathaniel Cheairs Hughes Jr. and S. Kittrell Rushing. Knoxville: University of Tennessee Press, 2011.

Harvey, Cordelia A. P. "A Wisconsin Woman's Picture of President Lincoln." *Wisconsin Magazine of History* 1, no. 3 (March 1918): 233–55.

Haupt, Herman. *Reminiscences of General Herman Haupt.* Milwaukee: Wright & Joys, 1901.

Hay, John. "Life in the White House in the Time of Lincoln." In *Addresses of John Hay.* New York: Century, 1907.

Haynes, Captain Dennis E. *A Thrilling Narrative: The Memoir of a Southern Unionist.* Edited by Arthur W. Bergeron Jr. Fayetteville: University of Arkansas Press, 2006.

Helm, Emily Todd. "Mary Todd Lincoln: Reminiscences and Letters of the Wife of President Lincoln." *McClure's Magazine,* September 1898, 476–80.

Herndon, William H. "Analysis of the Character of Abraham Lincoln." *Abraham Lincoln Quarterly* 1, nos. 7 and 8 (September and December 1941): 343–83 and 403–41.

Hoge, Mrs. A. H. [Jane Currie]. *The Boys in Blue; or Heroes of the "Rank and File."* New York: E. B. Treat, 1867.

[Holcombe, Robert I.]. "A Sioux Story of War: Chief Big Eagle's Story of the Sioux Outbreak of 1862." *Collections of the Minnesota Historical Society* 6 (1894): 382–400.

Howard, J. Q. *The Life of Abraham Lincoln with Extracts from His Speeches.* Columbus: Follet, Foster, 1860.

Howe, Julia Ward. *Reminiscences, 1819–1899.* Boston: Houghton Mifflin, 1899.

Howells, W. D. *Life of Lincoln: This Campaign Biography Corrected by the Hand of Abraham Lincoln in the Summer of 1860.* Bloomington: Indiana University Press, 1960.

Jackson, Donald, ed. *Black Hawk: An Autobiography.* Urbana: University of Illinois Press, 1964.

Johnson, Robert Underwood, and Clarence Clough Buell, eds. *Battles and Leaders of the Civil War.* 4 vols. New York: Century, 1887–1888.

Johnston, Joseph E. *Narrative of Military Operations Directed During the Late War Between the States.* New York: D. Appleton, 1874.

Keckley, Elizabeth. *Behind the Scenes, or, Thirty Years a Slave and Four Years in the White House.* New York: G. W. Carleton, 1868.

Keyes, Erasmus D. *Fifty Years' Observation of Men and Events, Civil and Military.* New York: Charles Scribner's Sons, 1884.

Lamon, Ward Hill. *Recollections of Abraham Lincoln, 1847–1865.* Edited by Dorothy Lamon Teillard. Washington, D.C.: Privately published, 1911.

Lawley, Francis. "The Last Six Days of Secessia." *Fortnightly Review* 2, no. 1 (August 1865): 1–11.

Leary, John J., Jr. *Talks with T.R. from the Diaries of John J. Leary, Jr.* Boston: Houghton Mifflin, 1920.

Livermore, Mary A. *My Story of the War: A Woman's Narrative of Four Years Personal Experience as Nurse in the Union Army and Relief Work at Home, in Hospitals, Camps, and at the Front During the War of the Rebellion.* Hartford: A. D. Worthington, 1889.

Magruder, Allan B. "A Piece of Secret History: President Lincoln and the Virginia Convention of 1861." *Atlantic Monthly* 35, no. 210 (April 1875): 438–45.

Maury, Dabney Herndon. *Recollections of a Virginian in the Mexican, Indian, and Civil Wars.* New York: Charles Scribner's Sons, 1894.

McClure, A. K. *Abraham Lincoln and Men of War-Times: Some Personal Recollections of War and Politics During the Lincoln Administration.* Philadelphia: Times Publishing, 1892.

McLean, Mrs. Eugene [Margaret Sumner McLean]. "A Northern Woman in the Confederacy." *Harper's Monthly Magazine,* February 1914, 440–51.

———. "When the States Seceded." *Harper's Monthly Magazine,* January 1914, 282–88.

McPherson, James M., ed. *The Negro's Civil War: How American Negroes Felt and Acted During the War for the Union.* New York: Pantheon, 1965.

Meigs, Montgomery C. "General M. C. Meigs on the Conduct of the Civil War." *American Historical Review* 26, no. 2 (January 1921): 285–303.

———. "Memoranda on the Life of Lincoln: Lincoln's Visit to Richmond." *The Century Magazine,* June 1890, 307.

Miller, Morris S. *Memoir of the Services of Morris S. Miller.* N.p.: Unknown publisher, 1860.

Nicolay, John G. "Lincoln's Personal Appearance." *The Century Magazine,* October 1891, 932–38.

———. *An Oral History of Abraham Lincoln: John G. Nicolay's Interviews and Essays.* Edited by Michael Burlingame. Carbondale: Southern Illinois University Press, 1996.

Ostendorf, Lloyd, and Walter Olesky, eds. *Lincoln's Unknown Private Life: An Oral History by His Black Housekeeper Mariah Vance, 1850–1860.* Mamaroneck, N.Y.: Hastings House, 1995.

Perdue, Charles L., Jr., Thomas E. Barden, and Robert K. Phillips, eds. *Weevils in the Wheat: Interviews with Virginia Ex-Slaves.* Charlottesville: University Press of Virginia, 1976.

Piatt, Donn. *Memories of the Men Who Saved the Union.* New York: Belford, Clarke, 1887.

Porter, David Dixon. *Incidents and Anecdotes of the Civil War.* New York: D. Appleton, 1885.

———. "President Lincoln's Entry into Richmond After the Evacuation of That Place by the Confederates." *Belford's Magazine,* September–October 1890, 585–96 and 649–58.

Pryor, Mrs. Roger A. [Sara Agnes Rice]. *Reminiscences of Peace and War.* New York: Macmillan, 1905.

Putnam, Sallie Brock [A Richmond Lady]. *Richmond During the War: Four Years of Personal Observation.* New York: G. W. Carleton, 1867.

Radford, Victoria, ed. *Meeting Mr. Lincoln: Firsthand Recollections of Abraham Lincoln by People, Great and Small, Who Met the President.* Chicago: Ivan R. Dee, 1998.

Randolph, Peter. *From Slave Cabin to the Pulpit: The Autobiography of Rev. Peter Randolph; The Southern Question Illustrated and Sketches of Slave Life.* Boston: James H. Earle, 1893.

Rawick, George P., ed. *The American Slave: A Composite Autobiography.* 41 vols. Westport,
Conn.: Greenwood Press, 1972–1981.

Rhodes, Albert. "A Reminiscence of Abraham Lincoln." *St. Nicholas Magazine,* November 1876,
8–10.

Rice, Allen Thorndike, ed. *Reminiscences of Abraham Lincoln by Distinguished Men of His Time.*
New York: North American Review, 1888.

Riddle, Albert Gallatin. *Recollections of War Times: Reminiscences of Men and Events in Washington 1860–1865.* London: G. P. Putnam, 1895.

Riggs, Stephen R. *Tah'-koo Wah-Kaṅ or The Gospel Among the Dakotas.* Boston: Congregational
Publishing Society, 1869.

Robinson, William H. *From Log Cabin to the Pulpit or Fifteen Years in Slavery.* N.p.: Privately
published, c. 1907.

Schofield, John M. *Forty-Six Years in the Army.* New York: Century, 1897.

Schurz, Carl. *The Reminiscences of Carl Schurz.* 3 vols. New York: McClure, 1907.

Scott, Winfield. *Memoirs of Lieut.-General Winfield Scott, L.L.D., Written by Himself.* 2 vols.
New York: Sheldon, 1864.

Seward, Frederick W. *Reminiscences of a War-Time Statesman and Diplomat, 1830–1915.* New
York: G. P. Putnam's Sons, 1916.

Sheridan, Philip Henry. *Personal Memoirs of P. H. Sheridan, General United States Army.* 2 vols.
New York: Charles L. Webster, 1888.

Sherman, William Tecumseh. *Memoirs of General William T. Sherman.* 2 vols. New York:
D. Appleton, 1875.

Singleton, William Henry. *Recollections of My Slavery Days.* Peekskill, N.Y.: Highland Democrat,
1922.

Smith, Thomas West. *The Story of a Cavalry Regiment: "Scott's 900" Eleventh New York Cavalry,
from the St. Lawrence River to the Gulf of Mexico, 1861–1865.* Chicago: Veteran Association
of the Regiment, 1897.

Smith, William Farrar. *The Autobiography of Major General William F. Smith, 1861–1864.*
Edited by Herbert M. Schiller. Dayton, Ohio: Morningside, 1990.

Stanton, Elizabeth Cady. *Eighty Years and More (1815–1897): Reminiscences.* New York:
European Publishing, 1898.

Stanton, Elizabeth Cady, Susan B. Anthony, Matilda Joslyn Gage, and Ida Husted Harper, eds.
History of Woman Suffrage. 6 vols. Rochester, N.Y.: Susan B. Anthony (vols. 1–4) and New
York: National American Woman Suffrage Association (vols. 5–6), 1887–1922.

Stoddard, William O. *Inside the White House in War Times: Memories and Reports of Lincoln's
Secretary.* Edited by Michael Burlingame. Lincoln: University of Nebraska Press, 2000.

Stone, Charles P. "A Dinner with General Scott." *Magazine of American History,* June 1884, 528–32.

———. "Washington in March and April, 1861." *Magazine of American History,* July 1885, 1–21.

———. "Washington on the Eve of the War." In *Battles and Leaders of the Civil War.* Edited by
Robert Underwood Johnson and Clarence Clough Buell, 1:7–25. 4 vols. New York: Century,
1887–1888.

Stowe, Harriet Beecher. *Men of Our Times or Leading Patriots of the Day, Including Biographical
Sketches and Anecdotes.* Hartford: Hartford Publishing, 1868.

Swinton, William. *Campaigns of the Army of the Potomac; a Critical History of Operations in
Virginia, Maryland and Pennsylvania, from the Commencement to the Close of the War.* New
York: C. B. Richardson, 1866.

Taylor, Susie King. *A Black Woman's Civil War Memoirs: Reminiscences of My Life in the 33rd U.S. Colored Troops, Late 1st South Carolina Volunteers.* Edited by Patricia W. Romero. New York: Markus Wiener, 1988.

Terrell, A. W. "Recollections of General Sam Houston." *The Southwestern Historical Quarterly* 16, no. 2 (April 1912): 113–36.

Townsend, E. D. *Anecdotes of the Civil War in the United States.* New York: D. Appleton, 1884.

Usher, John P. *President Lincoln's Cabinet.* Omaha: Nelson H. Loomis, 1925.

Viele, Egbert L. "A Trip with Lincoln, Chase and Stanton." *Scribner's Monthly,* October 1878, 813–22.

Villard, Henry. *Memoirs of Henry Villard, Journalist and Financier, 1835–1900.* 2 vols. Boston: Houghton Mifflin, 1904.

———. "Recollections of Lincoln." *Atlantic Monthly,* February 1904, 165–74.

Wallace, Lew. *Lew Wallace: An Autobiography.* 2 vols. New York: Harper & Brothers, 1906.

Ward, William Hayes, ed. *Abraham Lincoln: Tributes from His Associates, Reminiscences of Soldiers, Statesmen and Citizens.* New York: Thomas Y. Crowell, 1895.

Washington, Booker T. *Up from Slavery: An Autobiography.* New York: Doubleday, Page, 1901.

Weik, Jesse W. "How Lincoln Was Convinced of General Scott's Loyalty." *The Century Magazine,* February 1911, 593–94.

Weitzel, Godfrey. *Richmond Occupied: Entry of the United States Forces into Richmond, Va., April 3, 1865, Calling Together of the Virginia Legislature and Revocation of the Same* [from *Philadelphia Weekly Times,* August 27, 1881]. Edited by Louis H. Manarin. Richmond: Richmond Civil War Centennial Committee, 1965.

Welles, Gideon. "Fort Sumter." *The Galaxy,* November 1870, 613–37.

———. "Lincoln and Johnson: Their Plan of Reconstruction and the Resumption of National Authority." *The Galaxy,* April and May 1872, 520–32 and 663–73.

Whipple, Henry B. *Lights and Shadows of a Long Episcopate: Being Reminiscences and Recollections of the Right Reverend Henry Benjamin Whipple, D.D., LL.D., Bishop of Minnesota.* New York: Macmillan, 1899.

———. "My Life Among the Indians." *North American Review* 150, no. 401 (April 1890): 432–39.

Whitney, Henry Clay. *Life on the Circuit with Lincoln with Sketches of Generals Grant, Sherman and McClellan, Judge Davis, Leonard Swett and Other Contemporaries.* Boston: Estes & Lauriat, 1892.

Wilkes, Charles. *Autobiography of Rear Admiral Charles Wilkes, U.S. Navy, 1798–1877.* Edited by William James Morgan, David B. Tyler, Joye L. Leonhart, and Mary F. Loughlin. Washington, D.C.: Department of the Navy, 1978.

Wilkins, B. H. *"War Boy": A True Story of the Civil War and Re-Construction Days.* Tullahoma, Tenn.: Wilson Bros., 1990.

Wilson, Rufus Rockwell, ed. *Intimate Memories of Lincoln.* Elmira, N.Y.: Primavera Press, 1945.

———. *Lincoln Among His Friends: A Sheaf of Intimate Memories.* Caldwell, Idaho: Caxton Printers, 1942. (Contains Alfred Taylor Bledsoe, "Review of Lamon's *Life of Lincoln,*" 462–93; Silas W. Burt, "Lincoln on His Own Story Telling," 328–36; Anna Byers-Jennings, "A Missouri Girl Visits with Lincoln," 374–78; Schuyler Hamilton, "Why Lincoln Discarded His Linen Duster," 315–19; Thomas D. Jones, "A Sculptor's Recollections of Lincoln," 255–66.)

Winchell, J. M. "Three Interviews with President Lincoln." *The Galaxy,* July 1873, 33–41.

SECONDARY SOURCES

Abbott, Martin. "President Lincoln in Confederate Caricature." *Journal of the Illinois State Historical Society* 51, no. 3 (Autumn 1958): 306–19.

———. "Southern Reaction to Lincoln's Assassination." *Abraham Lincoln Quarterly* 7, no. 3 (September 1952): 111–27.

Abel, Annie Heloise. *The American Indian as Participant in the Civil War.* Cleveland: Arthur H. Clark, 1919.

———. "Indian Reservations in Kansas and the Extinguishment of Their Title." *Transactions of the Kansas State Historical Society* 8 (1903–1904): 72–109.

Abrams, Ray H. "*The Jeffersonian,* Copperhead Newspaper." *Pennsylvania Magazine of History and Biography* 57, no. 3 (July 1933): 260–83.

Abrams, Robert E. "Charles Farrar Browne (Artemus Ward)." In *Dictionary of Literary Biography, XI: American Humorists, 1800–1950,* 1:60–68. Edited by Stanley Trachtenberg. 2 vols. Detroit: Gale, 1982.

Adams, Michael C. C. *Fighting for Defeat: Union Military Failure in the East, 1861–1865.* Lincoln: University of Nebraska Press, 1992.

Allardice, Bruce S., and Lawrence Lee Hewitt, eds. *Kentuckians in Gray: Confederate Generals and Field Officers of the Bluegrass State.* Lexington: University Press of Kentucky, 2008.

Altschuler, Glenn C., and Stuart M. Blumin. *Rude Republic: Americans and Their Politics in the Nineteenth Century.* Princeton, N.J.: Princeton University Press, 2000.

Ambrose, Stephen E. *Halleck: Lincoln's Chief of Staff.* Baton Rouge: Louisiana State University Press, 1962.

Ash, Stephen V. *When the Yankees Came: Conflict and Chaos in the Occupied South, 1861–1865.* Chapel Hill: University of North Carolina Press, 1995.

Asim, Jabari. *The N Word: Who Can Say It, Who Shouldn't and Why.* Boston: Houghton Mifflin, 2007.

Bacon-Foster, Corra. *Clara Barton, Humanitarian.* Washington, D.C.: Columbia Historical Society, 1918.

Baker, Jean H. *Mary Todd Lincoln: A Biography.* New York: W. W. Norton, 1987.

Bartelt, William E. *"There I Grew Up": Remembering Abraham Lincoln's Indiana Youth.* Indianapolis: Indiana Historical Society, 2008.

Barton, William E. *The Lincolns in Their Old Kentucky Home: An Address Delivered Before the Filson Club, Louisville, Kentucky, December 4, 1922.* Berea, Ky.: Berea College Press, 1923.

Baum, Dale. *The Shattering of Texas Unionism: Politics in the Lone Star State During the Civil War Era.* Baton Rouge: Louisiana State University Press, 1998.

Bederman, Gail. *Manliness and Civilization: A Cultural History of Gender and Race in the United States, 1880–1917.* Chicago: University of Chicago Press, 1995.

Belko, W. Stephen. *The Invincible Duff Green: Whig of the West.* Columbia: University of Missouri Press, 2006.

Bennett, Lerone, Jr. *Forced into Glory: Abraham Lincoln's White Dream.* Chicago: Johnson Publishing, 2000.

Beran, Michael Knox. "Lincoln, *Macbeth,* and the Moral Imagination." *Humanitas* 11, no. 2 (1998): 4–21.

Berg, Scott W. *38 Nooses: Lincoln, Little Crow, and the Beginning of the Frontier's End.* New York: Pantheon, 2012.

Beringer, Richard E., Herman Hattaway, Archer Jones, and William N. Still Jr. *Why the South Lost the Civil War*. Athens: University of Georgia Press, 1986.

Berkelman, Robert. "Lincoln's Interest in Shakespeare." *Shakespeare Quarterly* 2, no. 4 (October 1951): 303–12.

Bernath, Michael T. *Confederate Minds: The Struggle for Intellectual Independence in the Civil War South*. Chapel Hill: University of North Carolina Press, 2010.

Bingham, Emily. *Mordecai: An Early American Family*. New York: Hill & Wang, 2003.

Blackman, Ann. *Wild Rose: Rose O'Neal Greenhow, Civil War Spy*. New York: Random House, 2005.

Blackwell, Sarah Ellen. *A Military Genius: Life of Anna Ella Carroll of Maryland*. Washington, D.C.: Judd & Detweiler, 1891.

Blanton, DeAnne, and Lauren M. Cook. *They Fought Like Demons: Women Soldiers in the American Civil War*. Baton Rouge: Louisiana State University Press, 2002.

Blassingame, John W. "Using the Testimony of Ex-Slaves: Approaches and Problems." *Journal of Southern History* 41, no. 4 (November 1975): 473–92.

Bond, Beverley W., Jr. *The Civilization of the Old Northwest: A Study of Political, Social, and Economic Development, 1788–1812*. New York: Macmillan, 1934.

Bordewich, Fergus M. *America's Great Debate: Henry Clay, Stephen A. Douglas, and the Compromise That Preserved the Union*. New York: Simon & Schuster, 2012.

Boritt, G. S. *Lincoln and the Economics of the American Dream*. Urbana: University of Illinois Press, 1994.

Boritt, Gabor S., ed. *The Historian's Lincoln: Pseudohistory, Psychohistory, and History*. Urbana: University of Illinois Press, 1988. (Contains Gabor S. Boritt, "Lincoln and the Economics of the American Dream," 87–106; M. E. Bradford, "Commentary on Boritt," 107–15; LaWanda Cox, "Lincoln and Black Freedom," 175–96; David A. Nichols, "Lincoln and the Indians," 149–69; Hans L. Trefousse, "Commentary on Nichols," 170–74.)

———. *Lincoln's Generals*. New York: Oxford University Press, 1994. (Contains Michael Fellman, "Lincoln and Sherman," 121–60; Mark E. Neely Jr., "Wilderness and the Cult of Manliness: Hooker, Lincoln, and Defeat," 51–78; Stephen W. Sears, "Lincoln and McClellan," 1–50; John Y. Simon, "Grant, Lincoln, and Unconditional Surrender," 161–98.)

Boyd, Steven R. *Patriotic Envelopes of the Civil War: The Iconography of Union and Confederate Covers*. Baton Rouge: Louisiana State University Press, 2010.

Bracken, Jeanne Munn, ed. *Women in the American Revolution*. Boston: History Compass, 2009.

Bray, Robert. "'The Power to Hurt': Lincoln's Early Use of Satire and Invective." *JALA* 16, no. 1 (1995): 39–58.

Bremner, Ellen. "Civil War Humor: Orpheus C. Kerr." *Civil War History* 2, no. 3 (September 1956): 121–29.

Brown, Dee. *Bury My Heart at Wounded Knee: An Indian History of the American West*. New York: Bantam, 1972.

Brown, Thomas J. *Dorothea Dix: New England Reformer*. Cambridge: Harvard University Press, 1998.

Bruce, Robert V. *Lincoln and the Tools of War*. Indianapolis: Bobbs-Merrill, 1956.

Buckingham, Samuel Giles. *The Life of William A. Buckingham, the War Governor of Connecticut*. Springfield, Mass.: W. F. Adams, 1894.

Buenger, Walter L. *Secession and the Union in Texas*. Austin: University of Texas Press, 1984.

Bullard, F. Lauriston. "Abraham Lincoln and Harriet Beecher Stowe." *Lincoln Herald* 49 (June 1946): 11–14.

Bunker, Gary. *From Rail-splitter to Icon: Lincoln's Image in Illustrated Periodicals, 1860–1865.* Kent, Ohio: Kent State University Press, 2001.

Burlingame, Michael. *Abraham Lincoln: A Life.* 2 vols. Baltimore: Johns Hopkins University Press, 2008.

———. "Honest Abe, Dishonest Mary." *Bulletin of the 54th Annual Meeting of the Lincoln Fellowship of Wisconsin* 50 (April 1994).

———. *The Inner World of Abraham Lincoln.* Urbana: University of Illinois Press, 1994.

———. "The Trouble with the Bixby Letter." *American Heritage* 50, no. 4 (July–August 1999): 64–67.

Burns, James MacGregor. *Leadership.* New York: Harper & Row, 1978.

———. *Presidential Government: The Crucible of Leadership.* Boston: Houghton Mifflin, 1965.

Burt, John. *Lincoln's Tragic Pragmatism: Lincoln, Douglas, and Moral Conflict.* Cambridge: Harvard University Press, 2013.

Burt, Silas W. "Lincoln on His Own Storytelling." *The Century Magazine,* February 1907, 499–502.

Butler, Michael. "Robert Henry Newell (Orpheus C. Kerr)." In *Dictionary of Literary Biography, XI: American Humorists, 1800–1950,* 2:350–54. Edited by Stanley Trachtenberg. 2 vols. Detroit: Gale, 1982.

Bynum, Victoria E. *The Long Shadow of the Civil War: Southern Dissent and Its Legacies.* Chapel Hill: University of North Carolina Press, 2010.

Cain, Marvin R. *Lincoln's Attorney General: Edward Bates of Missouri.* Columbia: University of Missouri Press, 1965.

Carey, Raymond G. "The Puzzle of Sand Creek." *Colorado Magazine* 41, no. 4 (Fall 1964): 279–98.

Carwardine, Richard J. *Evangelicals and Politics in Antebellum America.* New Haven: Yale University Press, 1993.

———. "Just Laughter: The Moral Springs of Lincoln's Humor." Paper presented at Lincoln Forum, 2009.

———. *Lincoln.* Harlow, U.K.: Pearson Longman, 2003.

———. *Lincoln: A Life of Purpose and Power.* New York: Alfred A. Knopf, 2006.

———. *Lincoln's Just Laughter: Humour and Ethics in the Civil War Union.* London: The British Library, 2014; online at www.bl.uk/ecclescentre.

Castel, Albert. "The Jayhawkers and Copperheads of Kansas." *Civil War History* 5, no. 3 (September 1959): 283–93.

Chester, Giraud. *Embattled Maiden: The Life of Anna Dickinson.* New York: G. P. Putnam, 1951.

Churchill, Franklin Hunter. *Sketch of Bvt. Brigadier General Sylvester Churchill . . . with Notes and Appendices.* New York: W. McDonald, 1888.

Churchill, Robert. "Liberty, Conscription, and Delusions of Grandeur: The Sons of Liberty Conspiracy of 1863–64." *Prologue* 30, no. 4 (Winter 1998): 295–303.

Clinton, Catherine. *Harriet Tubman: Road to Freedom.* New York: Little, Brown, 2004.

———. *Mrs. Lincoln: A Life.* New York: Harper, 2009.

Clinton, Catherine, and Nina Silber, eds. *Battle Scars: Gender and Sexuality in the American Civil War.* Oxford: Oxford University Press, 2006. (Contains Elizabeth D. Leonard, "Mary Walker, Mary Surratt, and Some Thoughts on Gender in the Civil War," 104–19.)

Coffman, Edward M. *The Old Army: A Portrait of the American Army in Peacetime, 1784–1898.* Oxford, U.K.: Oxford University Press, 1986.

Coleman, Charles H. "The Use of the Term 'Copperhead' During the Civil War." *Mississippi Valley Historical Review* 25, no. 2 (September 1938): 263–64.

Combs, James E., and Dan Nimmo. *The Comedy of Democracy*. Westport, Conn.: Praeger, 1996.

Conley, Robert J. *The Cherokee Nation: A History*. Albuquerque: University of New Mexico Press, 2005.

Connelly, Thomas, and Barbara L. Bellows. *God and General Longstreet: The Lost Cause and the Southern Mind*. Baton Rouge: Louisiana State University Press, 1982.

Conwell, Russell H. *Why Lincoln Laughed*. New York: Harper Brothers, 1922.

Cooper, William J. *We Have the War upon Us: The Onset of the Civil War, November 1860–April 1861*. New York: Alfred A. Knopf, 2012.

Corwin, Edward S. *Total War and the Constitution*. New York: Alfred A. Knopf, 1947.

Coryell, Janet L. *Neither Heroine nor Fool: Anna Ella Carroll of Maryland*. Kent, Ohio: Kent State University Press, 1990.

Coultrap-McQuinn, Susan. "Legacy Profile: Gail Hamilton (1833–1896)." *Legacy* 4, no. 2 (Fall 1987): 53–58.

Cox, Hank H. *Lincoln and the Sioux Uprising of 1862*. Nashville: Cumberland House, 2005.

Cozzens, Peter. *General John Pope: A Life for the Nation*. Urbana: University of Illinois Press, 2000.

Cramer, Janet M. "For Women and the War: A Cultural Analysis of the Mayflower, 1861–1864." In *The Civil War and the Press*. Edited by David B. Sacksman, S. Kittrell Rushing, and Debra Reddin van Tuyll, 209–26. New Brunswick, N.J.: Transaction Publishers, 2000.

Craven, Avery. "Lee's Dilemma." *Virginia Magazine of History and Biography* 69, no. 2 (April 1961): 131–48.

———. *The Repressible Conflict, 1830–1861*. Baton Rouge: Louisiana State University Press, 1939.

Crofts, Daniel. *A Secession Crisis Enigma: William Henry Hurlbert and "The Diary of a Public Man."* Baton Rouge: Louisiana State University Press, 2010.

Cuff, Roger Penn. "The American Editorial Cartoon—A Critical Historical Sketch." *Journal of Educational Sociology* 19, no. 2 (October 1945): 87–96.

Culberson, Charles A. "General Sam Houston and Secession." *Scribner's Magazine*, May 1906, 584–91.

Current, Richard Nelson. *Lincoln's Loyalists: Union Soldiers from the Confederacy*. Boston: Northeastern University Press, 1992.

———. *The Lincoln Nobody Knows*. New York: McGraw-Hill, 1958.

———. *Speaking of Abraham Lincoln: The Man and His Meaning for Our Times*. Urbana: University of Illinois Press, 1983.

———. *Unity, Ethnicity and Abraham Lincoln*. Fort Wayne, Ind.: Louis A. Warren Lincoln Library and Museum, 1978.

Danziger, Edmund Jefferson, Jr. *Indians and Bureaucrats: Administering the Reservation Policy During the Civil War*. Urbana: University of Illinois Press, 1974.

Davis, Cullom, Charles B. Strozier, Rebecca Monroe Veach, and Geoffrey C. Ward, eds. *The Public and the Private Lincoln: Contemporary Perspectives*. Carbondale: Southern Illinois University Press, 1979. (Contains Roy B. Basler, "Lincoln, Blacks, and Women," 38–53; Katheryn Kish Sklar, "Victorian Women and Domestic Life: Mary Todd Lincoln, Elizabeth Cady Stanton and Harriet Beecher Stowe," 20–37.)

Davis, Michael. *The Image of Lincoln in the South*. Knoxville: University of Tennessee Press, 1971.

Davis, Sue. *The Political Thought of Elizabeth Cady Stanton: Women's Rights and the American Political Tradition*. New York: New York University Press, 2008.

Davis, William C. *Lincoln's Men: How President Lincoln Became Father to an Army and a Nation*. New York: Free Press, 1999.

Degler, Carl N. *The Other South: Southern Dissenters in the Nineteenth Century*. New York: Harper & Row, 1974.

Dennett, Tyler. *John Hay: From Poetry to Politics*. New York: Dodd, Mead, 1933.

Detzer, David. "Fateful Encounter: Jim Jackson and Elmer Ellsworth." *North and South* 9, no. 3 (June 2006): 36–47.

Diedrich, Mark. "Chief Hole-in-the-Day and the 1862 Chippewa Disturbance: A Reappraisal." *Minnesota History* 50, no. 5 (Spring 1987): 194–203.

Dirck, Brian R., ed. *Lincoln Emancipated: The President and the Politics of Race*. DeKalb: Northern Illinois University Press, 2007.

Donald, David Herbert. *Lincoln*. New York: Simon & Schuster, 1995.

——— *Lincoln Reconsidered: Essays on the Civil War Era*. 2nd ed. New York: Alfred A. Knopf, 1972.

Donald, David Herbert, and Harold Holzer, eds. *Lincoln in the Times: The Life of Abraham Lincoln as Originally Reported in the New York Times*. New York: St. Martin's, 2005.

Dorsey, Bruce. *Reforming Men and Women: Gender in the Antebellum City*. Ithaca, N.Y.: Cornell University Press, 2002.

Downs, Alan Craig. "'Gone Past All Redemption'? The Early Years of General Joseph Eggleston Johnston." PhD diss., University of North Carolina, 1991.

Downs, Gregory P. *Declarations of Dependence: The Long Reconstruction of Practical Politics in the South, 1861–1908*. Chapel Hill: University of North Carolina Press, 2011.

Dudley, William S. *Going South: U.S. Navy Officer Resignations and Dismissals on the Eve of the Civil War*. Washington, D.C.: Naval Historical Foundation, 1981.

Duff, John J. *A. Lincoln, Prairie Lawyer*. New York: Rinehart, 1960.

Duncan, Robert Lipscomb. *Reluctant General: The Life and Times of Albert Pike*. New York: E. P. Dutton, 1961.

Dyar, Scott D. "Stillman's Run: Militia's Foulest Hour." *Military History* 22, no. 1 (March 2006): 38–44.

Dyer, Thomas G. *Secret Yankees: The Union Circle in Confederate Atlanta*. Baltimore: Johns Hopkins University Press, 1999.

Eby, Cecil. *"That Disgraceful Affair": The Black Hawk War*. New York: W. W. Norton, 1973.

Edwards, Rebecca. *Angels in the Machinery: Gender in American Party Politics from the Civil War to the Progressive Era*. New York: Oxford University Press, 1997.

Ehrmann, Bess V. *The Missing Chapter in the Life of Abraham Lincoln: A Number of Articles, Episodes, Photographs, Pen and Ink Sketches, Concerning the Life of Abraham Lincoln in Spencer County, Indiana, Between 1816–1830 and 1844*. Chicago: Walter M. Hill, 1938.

Ellerton, Nerida F., and M. A. Clements. *Abraham Lincoln's Cyphering Book and Ten Other Extraordinary Cyphering Books*. Cham, Switz.: Springer, 2014.

Elliott, Charles Winslow. *Winfield Scott: The Soldier and the Man*. New York: Macmillan, 1937.

Ellis, Richard N. *General John Pope and U.S. Indian Policy*. Albuquerque: University of New Mexico Press, 1970.

Emerson, Jason. "America's Most Famous Letter." *American Heritage* 57, no. 1 (February–March 2006): 41–49.

Endres, Kathleen L. "The Women's Press in the Civil War: A Portrait of Patriotism, Propaganda, and Prodding." *Civil War History* 30, no. 1 (March 1984): 31–53.

Engle, Stephen D. *Don Carlos Buell: Most Promising of All.* Chapel Hill: University of North Carolina Press, 1999.

Epler, Percy H. *The Life of Clara Barton.* New York: Macmillan, 1915.

Epstein, Daniel Mark. *The Lincolns: Portrait of a Marriage.* New York: Ballantine, 2008.

Etulain, Richard W., ed. *Lincoln Looks West: From the Mississippi to the Pacific.* Carbondale: Southern Illinois University Press, 2010.

Fahs, Alice. *The Imagined Civil War: Popular Literature of the North and South, 1861–1865.* Chapel Hill: University of North Carolina Press, 2001.

Faust, Drew Gilpin. *The Creation of Confederate Nationalism: Ideology and Identity in the Civil War South.* Baton Rouge: Louisiana State University Press, 1988.

———. *This Republic of Suffering: Death and the American Civil War.* New York: Alfred A. Knopf, 2008.

Fehrenbacher, Don E. "The Anti-Lincoln Tradition." *JALA* 4, no. 1 (1982): 6–28.

———. "Lincoln's Wartime Leadership: The First Hundred Days." *JALA* 9, no. 1 (1987): 2–18.

Fellman, Michael. *Citizen Sherman: A Life of William Tecumseh Sherman.* New York: Random House, 1995.

———. *Inside War: The Guerrilla Conflict in Missouri During the American Civil War.* New York: Oxford University Press, 1989.

Fischer, David Hackett, and James C. Kelly. *Bound Away: Virginia and the Westward Movement.* Charlottesville: University Press of Virginia, 2000.

Fischer, LeRoy Henry. *Lincoln's Gadfly, Adam Gurowski.* Norman: University of Oklahoma Press, 1964.

Fisher, Seymour, and Rhoda L. Fisher. *Pretend the World Is Funny and Forever: A Psychological Analysis of Comedians, Clowns, and Actors.* Hillsdale, N.J.: Lawrence Erlbaum, 1981.

Foner, Eric. *The Fiery Trial: Abraham Lincoln and American Slavery.* New York: W. W. Norton, 2010.

———. *Free Soil, Free Labor, Free Men: The Ideology of the Republican Party Before the Civil War.* New York: Oxford University Press, 1970.

———. *Reconstruction: America's Unfinished Revolution, 1863–1877.* New York: Harper & Row, 1988.

Foner, Eric, ed. *Our Lincoln: New Perspectives on Lincoln and His World.* New York: W. W. Norton, 2008. (Contains Catherine Clinton, "Abraham Lincoln: The Family That Made Him, the Family He Made," 249–66; Eric Foner, "Lincoln and Colonization," 135–66; James Oakes, "Natural Rights, Citizenship Rights, States' Rights, and Black Rights: Another Look at Lincoln and Race," 109–34; Sean Wilentz, "Abraham Lincoln and Jacksonian Democracy," 62–78.)

Foreman, Amanda. *A World on Fire: An Epic History of Two Nations Divided.* New York: Allen Lane, 2010.

Frank, Stephen M. *Life with Father: Parenthood and Masculinity in the Nineteenth-Century American North.* Baltimore: Johns Hopkins University Press, 1998.

Franks, Kenny A. "The Confederate States and the Five Civilized Tribes." *Journal of the West* 12, no. 3 (July 1973): 439–54.

———. *Stand Watie and the Agony of the Cherokee Nation.* Memphis: Memphis State University Press, 1979.

Frederickson, George M. *Big Enough to Be Inconsistent: Abraham Lincoln Confronts Slavery and Race*. Cambridge: Harvard University Press, 2008.

Freehling, William W. *The Road to Disunion*. Vol. 1, *Secessionists at Bay, 1776–1854*. New York: Oxford University Press, 1990.

———. *The Road to Disunion*. Vol. 2, *Secessionists Triumphant, 1854–1861*. New York: Oxford University Press, 2007.

———. *The South vs. the South: How Anti-Confederate Southerners Shaped the Course of the Civil War*. New York: Oxford University Press, 2001.

Freeman, Douglas Southall. *R. E. Lee: A Biography*. 4 vols. New York: Charles Scribner's Sons, 1934–1935.

Freeman, Jo. *A Room at a Time: How Women Entered Party Politics*. Lanham, Md.: Rowman & Littlefield, 2000.

Friend, Llerena B. *Sam Houston: The Great Designer*. Austin: University of Texas Press, 1954.

Fry, William F. "The Power of Political Humor." *The Journal of Popular Culture* 10, no. 1 (Summer 1976): 227–31.

Gallman, J. Matthew. *America's Joan of Arc: The Life of Anna Elizabeth Dickinson*. New York: Oxford University Press, 2006.

Gannett, Lewis. "'Overwhelming Evidence' of a Lincoln–Ann Rutledge Romance?: Reexamining Rutledge Family Reminiscences." *JALA* 26, no. 1 (Winter 2005): 28–41.

Gannon, Barbara A. *The Won Cause: White and Black Comradeship in the Grand Army of the Republic*. Chapel Hill: University of North Carolina Press, 2011.

Garesché, Louis. *Biography of Lieut. Col. Julius P. Garesché, Assistant Adjutant-General, U.S. Army*. Philadelphia: J. B. Lippincott, 1887.

Gates, Henry Louis, Jr., ed. *Lincoln on Race and Slavery*. Princeton, N.J.: Princeton University Press, 2009.

Gates, Paul Wallace. *Fifty Million Acres: Conflicts over Kansas Land Policy, 1854–1890*. Ithaca, N.Y.: Cornell University Press, 1954.

Genovese, Eugene B. *Roll, Jordan, Roll: The World the Slaves Made*. New York: Pantheon, 1974.

George, Joseph, Jr. "'Abraham Africanus I': President Lincoln Through the Eyes of a Copperhead Editor." *Civil War History* 14, no. 3 (September 1968): 226–39.

Giesberg, Judith Ann. *Civil War Sisterhood: The U.S. Sanitary Commission and Women's Politics in Transition*. Boston: Northeastern University Press, 2000.

Ginzberg, Lori D. *Elizabeth Cady Stanton: An American Life*. New York: Hill & Wang, 2009.

———. "'Moral Suasion Is Moral Balderdash': Women, Politics, and Social Activism in the 1850s." *Journal of American History* 73, no. 3 (December 1986): 601–22.

Glatthaar, Joseph T. *Partners in Command: The Relationship Between Leaders in the Civil War*. New York: Free Press, 1994.

Goodwin, Doris Kearns. *Team of Rivals: The Political Genius of Abraham Lincoln*. New York: Simon & Schuster, 2005.

Gordon, Julian. "Abraham Lincoln in His Relations to Women." *The Cosmopolitan*, December 1894, 205–10.

Goss, Thomas J. *The War Within the Union High Command: Politics and Generalship During the Civil War*. Lawrence: University Press of Kansas, 2003.

Govan, Gilbert E., and James W. Livingood. *A Different Valor: The Story of General Joseph E. Johnston, C.S.A.* Indianapolis: Bobbs-Merrill, 1956.

Green, Fletcher. "Duff Green, Industrial Promoter." *Journal of Southern History* 2, no. 1 (February 1936): 29–42.

————. "Duff Green, Militant Journalist of the Old School." *American Historical Review* 52, no. 2 (January 1947): 247–64.

Green, Horace. "Lincoln Breaks McClellan's Promise." *The Century Magazine,* February 1911, 594–96.

Greenbie, Sydney, and Majorie Barstow Greenbie. *Anna Ella Carroll and Abraham Lincoln: A Biography.* Tampa: University of Tampa Press, 1952.

Greene, Francis V. "Lincoln as Commander-in-Chief." *Scribner's Magazine,* July 1909, 104–15.

Greven, Philip. *The Protestant Temperament: Patterns of Child-Rearing, Religious Experience and the Self in Early America.* New York: Alfred A. Knopf, 1977.

Grimsley, Mark, and Clifford J. Rogers, eds. *Civilians in the Path of War.* Lincoln: University of Nebraska Press, 2002.

Grinspan, Jon. "'Sorrowfully Amusing': The Popular Comedy of the Civil War." *Journal of the Civil War Era* 1, no. 3 (September 2011): 313–38.

Griswold, Robert L. *Fatherhood in America: A History.* New York: Basic Books, 1993.

Guelzo, Allen C. *Lincoln and Douglas: The Debates That Defined America.* New York: Simon & Schuster, 2008.

————. *Lincoln's Emancipation Proclamation: The End of Slavery in America.* New York: Simon & Schuster, 2004.

Gunderson, Robert Gray. *Old Gentlemen's Convention: The Washington Peace Conference of 1861.* Madison: University of Wisconsin Press, 1961.

Gustafson, Melanie Susan. *Women and the Republican Party, 1854–1924.* Urbana: University of Illinois Press, 2001.

Gwynne, S. C. *Empire of the Summer Moon: Quanah Parker and the Rise and Fall of the Comanches, the Most Powerful Indian Tribe in American History.* New York: Scribner, 2010.

Hagerman, Edward. "The Professionalization of George B. McClellan and Early Civil War Field Command." *Civil War History* 21 (June 1975): 113–35.

Hamilton, Joseph Grégoire de Roulhac. "Lincoln and the South." *The Sewanee Review* 17 (April 1909): 128–38.

Hanchett, William. *Irish: Charles G. Halpine in Civil War America.* Syracuse, N.Y.: Syracuse University Press, 1970.

Harper, Judith, ed. *Women During the Civil War: An Encyclopedia.* New York: Routledge, 2004.

Harper, Robert S. *Lincoln and the Press.* New York: McGraw-Hill, 1951.

Harris, William C. "The Southern Unionist Critique of the Civil War." *Civil War History* 31, no. 1 (March 1985): 39–56.

————. *With Charity for All: Lincoln and the Restoration of the Union.* Lexington: University Press of Kentucky, 1997.

Harrison, John M. *The Man Who Made Nasby, David Ross Locke.* Chapel Hill: University of North Carolina Press, 1969.

Harrison, Lowell H. *Lincoln of Kentucky.* Lexington: University Press of Kentucky, 2000.

Harwell, Richard Barksdale. "John Esten Cooke, Civil War Correspondent." *Journal of Southern History* 19, no. 4 (November 1953): 501–16.

Hattaway, Herman. "Lincoln's Presidential Example in Dealing with the Military." *JALA* 7, no. 1 (1985): 18–29.

Hattaway, Herman, and Archer Jones. *How the North Won: A Military History of the Civil War.* Urbana: University of Illinois Press, 1983.

———. "Lincoln as Military Strategist." *Civil War History* 26, no. 4 (December 1980): 293–303.

Hauptman, Laurence M. *Between Two Fires: American Indians in the Civil War.* New York: Free Press, 1995.

———. *The Iroquois in the Civil War: From Battlefield to Reservation.* Syracuse, N.Y.: Syracuse University Press, 1993.

Heard, Isaac V. D. *History of the Sioux War and Massacres of 1862 and 1863.* New York: Harper Brothers, 1865.

Hearn, Chester G. *Lincoln, the Cabinet, and the Generals.* Baton Rouge: Louisiana State University Press, 2010.

Hedrick, Joan D. *Harriet Beecher Stowe: A Life.* New York: Oxford University Press, 1994.

Heidler, Jeanne T. "'Embarrassing Situation': David E. Twiggs and the Surrender of the United States Forces in Texas, 1861." In *Lone Star Blue and Gray: Essays on Texas in the Civil War.* Edited by Ralph A. Wooster, 29–46. Austin: Texas State Historical Association, 1995.

Helm, Katherine. *The True Story of Mary, Wife of Lincoln.* New York: Harper Brothers, 1928.

Hennessy, John J. *Return to Bull Run: The Campaign and Battle of Second Manassas.* Norman: University of Oklahoma Press, 1993.

Herr, Pamela. *Jesse Benton Frémont: A Biography.* New York: Franklin Watts, 1987.

Hess, Stephen, and Sandy Northrop. *Drawn and Quartered: The History of American Political Cartoons.* Montgomery, Ala.: Elliott & Clark, 1996.

Hirschhorn, Norbert, Robert G. Feldman, and Ian Greaves. "Abraham Lincoln's Blue Pills: Did Our 16th President Suffer from Mercury Poisoning?" *Perspectives in Biology and Medicine* 44, no. 3 (Summer 2001): 315–32.

Hoehling, A. A., and Mary Hoehling. *The Day Richmond Died.* San Diego: A. S. Barnes, 1981.

Hoffert, Sylvia D. *Jane Grey Swisshelm: An Unconventional Life, 1815–1884.* Chapel Hill: University of North Carolina Press, 2004.

Hofstadter, Richard. *The American Political Tradition and the Men Who Made It.* New York: Alfred A. Knopf, 1948.

Hoig, Stan. *The Sand Creek Massacre.* Norman: University of Oklahoma Press, 1961.

Holland, J. G. *The Life of Abraham Lincoln.* Springfield, Mass.: Gurdon Bill, 1866.

Holt, Rosa Belle. "A Heroine in Ebony." *Chautauquan* 23 (July 1896): 459–62.

Holzer, Harold. *Lincoln, President-Elect: Abraham Lincoln and the Great Secession Winter 1860–1861.* New York: Simon & Schuster, 2008.

Holzer, Harold, and Sara Vaughn Gabbard, eds. *Lincoln and Freedom: Slavery, Emancipation, and the Thirteenth Amendment.* Carbondale: Southern Illinois University Press, 2007. (Contains James Oliver Horton, "Slavery During Lincoln's Lifetime," 7–19; Phillip Shaw Paludan, "Lincoln and the Limits of Constitutional Authority," 37–47; Matthew Pinsker, "Lincoln's Summer of Emancipation," 79–99.)

Horton, Russell. "Unwanted in a White Man's War: The Civil War Service of the Green Bay Tribes." *Wisconsin Magazine of History* 88, no. 2 (Winter 2004–2005): 18–27.

Howard, William F. *The Battle of Ball's Bluff: The Leesburg Affair, October 21, 1861.* Lynchburg, Va.: Privately published, 1994.

Howe, Daniel Walker. *The Political Culture of the American Whigs.* Chicago: University of Chicago Press, 1979.

————. *What Hath God Wrought: The Transformation of America, 1815–1848*. New York: Oxford University Press, 2007.

Hoxie, R. Gordon. "The Office of Commander in Chief: An Historical and Projective View." *Presidential Studies Quarterly* 6, no. 4 (Fall 1976): 10–36.

Hsieh, Wayne Wei-Siang. "'I Owe Virginia Little, My Country Much': Robert E. Lee, the United States Regular Army and Unconditional Unionism." In *Crucible of the Civil War: Virginia from Secession to Commemoration*. Edited by Edward L. Ayers, Gary Gallagher, and Andrew Torget, 35–57. Charlottesville: University of Virginia Press, 2006.

————. *West Pointers and the Civil War: The Old Army in War and Peace*. Chapel Hill: University of North Carolina Press, 2009.

Hulbert, Matthew C. "How to Remember 'This Damnable Guerilla Warfare': Four Vignettes from Civil War Missouri." *Civil War History* 59, no. 2 (June 2013): 143–68.

Huntington, Samuel P. *The Soldier and the State: Theory and Politics of Civil-Military Relations*. Cambridge: Belknap Press, 1957.

Ingraham, Charles A. *Elmer E. Ellsworth and the Zouaves of '61*. Chicago: University of Chicago Press, 1925.

Inscoe, John C., and Robert C. Kenzer, eds. *Enemies of the Country: New Perspectives on Unionists in the Civil War South*. Athens: University of Georgia Press, 2001. (Contains Jonathan M. Berkey, "Fighting the Devil with Fire: David Hunter Strother's Private Civil War," 18–36; Robert Tracy McKenzie, "Prudent Silence and Strict Neutrality: The Parameters of Unionism in Parson Brownlow's Knoxville, 1860–1863," 73–96; William Warren Rogers Jr., "Safety Lies Only in Silence," 172–87.)

James, H. Preston. "Political Pageantry in the Campaign of 1860 in Illinois." *Abraham Lincoln Quarterly* 4, no. 7 (September 1947): 313–47.

Johannsen, Robert W. *Lincoln, the South, and Slavery: The Political Dimension*. Baton Rouge: Louisiana State University Press, 1991.

Johnson, Ludwell H. "Jefferson Davis and Abraham Lincoln as War Presidents: Nothing Succeeds Like Success." *Civil War History* 27, no. 1 (March 1981): 49–63.

————. "Lincoln and Equal Rights: The Authenticity of the Wadsworth Letter." *Journal of Southern History* 32, no. 1 (February 1966): 83–87.

Jordan, Ervin L., Jr. *Black Confederates and Afro-Yankees in Civil War Virginia*. Charlottesville: University Press of Virginia, 1995.

Jordan, Philip D. "Humor of the Backwoods, 1820–1840." *Mississippi Valley Historical Review* 25, no. 1 (June 1938): 25–38.

Jung, Patrick J. *The Black Hawk War of 1832*. Norman: University of Oklahoma Press, 2007.

Kaplan, Fred. *Lincoln: The Biography of a Writer*. New York: Harper Perennial, 2010.

Keehn, David C. *Knights of the Golden Circle: Secret Empire, Southern Secession, Civil War*. Baton Rouge: Louisiana State University Press, 2013.

Keller, Christian B. "Pennsylvania and Virginia Germans During the Civil War: A Brief History and Comparative Analysis." *Virginia Magazine of History and Biography* 109, no. 1 (2001): 37–86.

Kelley, William D. *Lincoln and Stanton: A Study of the War Administration of 1861 and 1862 with Special Consideration of Some Recent Statements of Gen. Geo. B. McClellan*. New York: G. P. Putnam's Sons, 1885.

Kelman, Ari. *A Misplaced Massacre: Struggling over the Memory of Sand Creek*. Cambridge: Harvard University Press, 2013.

Kelsey, Harry. "William P. Dole and Mr. Lincoln's Indian Policy." *Journal of the West* 10, no. 3 (July 1971): 484–92.

Kennedy, Randall. *Nigger: The Strange Career of a Troublesome Word*. New York: Pantheon, 2002.

Kimmel, Michael. *Manhood in America: A Cultural History*. New York: Free Press, 1996.

King, Jeffery S. " 'Do Not Execute Chief Pocatello': President Lincoln Acts to Save the Shoshoni Chief." *Utah Historical Quarterly* 53, no. 3 (Summer 1985): 237–47.

Klein, Maury. *Days of Defiance: Sumter, Secession, and the Coming of the Civil War*. New York: Alfred A. Knopf, 1997.

Klement, Frank L. "Clement L. Vallandigham's Exile in the Confederacy, May 25–June 17, 1863." *Journal of Southern History* 31, no. 2 (May 1965): 149–62.

———. *Lincoln's Critics: The Copperheads of the North*. Shippensburg, Pa.: White Mane, 1999.

Krick, Robert K. *Lee's Colonels: A Biographical Register of the Field Officers of the Army of Northern Virginia*. 5th ed. Wilmington N.C.: Broadfoot, 2009.

Kunhardt, Peter B., Jr., Philip B. Kunhardt III, and Peter W. Kunhardt. *P. T. Barnum: America's Greatest Showman*. New York: Alfred A. Knopf, 1995.

Kunhardt, Philip B., III, Peter W. Kunhardt, and Peter B. Kunhardt Jr. *Looking for Lincoln: The Making of an American Icon*. New York: Alfred A. Knopf, 2008.

Kunzle, David. "200 Years of the Great American Freedom to Complain." *Art in America* 65, no. 2 (March–April 1977): 99–105.

Lamb, Brian, and Susan Swain, eds. *Abraham Lincoln: Great American Historians on Our Sixteenth President*. New York: Public Affairs, 2008.

Lamon, Ward H. *The Life of Abraham Lincoln: From His Birth to His Inauguration as President*. Boston: James R. Osgood, 1872.

Landon, Melville. "Travelling with Artemus Ward." *The Galaxy*, September 1871, 442–45.

Lankford, Nelson D. *Cry Havoc! The Crooked Road to Civil War, 1861*. New York: Viking, 2007.

———. *Richmond Burning: The Last Days of the Confederate Capital*. New York: Viking, 2002.

Larsen, Lawrence H. "Draft Riot in Wisconsin, 1862." *Civil War History* 7, no. 4 (December 1961): 421–27.

Larson, Kate Clifford. *Bound for the Promised Land: Harriet Tubman, Portrait of an American Hero*. New York: Ballantine, 2004.

Laskin, Elisabeth Lauterbach. "Good Old Rebels: Soldiering in the Army of Northern Virginia, 1862–1865." PhD diss., Harvard University, 2003.

Lause, Mark A. *A Secret Society History of the Civil War*. Urbana: University of Illinois Press, 2011.

Lawson, Melinda. *Patriot Fires: Forging a New American Nationalism in the Civil War North*. Lawrence: University Press of Kansas, 2002.

Leahy, Christopher J. "Playing Her Greatest Role: Priscilla Cooper Tyler and the Politics of the White House Social Scene, 1841–44." *Virginia Magazine of History and Biography* 120, no. 3 (Autumn 2012): 236–69.

Leech, Margaret. *Reveille in Washington, 1860–1865*. New York: Harper Brothers, 1941.

Leftwich, William M. *Martyrdom in Missouri: A History of Religious Proscription, the Seizure of Churches, and the Persecution of Ministers of the Gospel, in the State of Missouri During the Late Civil War*. 2 vols. St. Louis: Southwestern, 1870.

Leland, Joy, ed. *Frederick West Lander: A Biographical Sketch (1822–1862)*. Reno, Nev.: Desert Research Institute, 1993.

Leonard, Elizabeth D. *Lincoln's Forgotten Ally: Judge Advocate General Joseph Holt of Kentucky.* Chapel Hill: University of North Carolina Press, 2011.

———. *Yankee Women: Gender Battles in the Civil War.* New York: W. W. Norton, 1994.

Lessoff, Howard. *The Civil War with "Punch."* Wendell, N.C.: Broadfoot, 1984.

Litwack, Leon F. *Been in the Storm So Long: The Aftermath of Slavery.* New York: Vintage, 1980.

Long, David E. *The Jewel of Liberty: Abraham Lincoln's Re-election and the End of Slavery.* Mechanicsburg, Pa.: Stackpole, 1994.

Lowry, Thomas. *Don't Shoot That Boy! Abraham Lincoln and Military Justice.* Mason City, Iowa: Savas, 1999.

Lutz, Alma. *Created Equal: A Biography of Elizabeth Cady Stanton, 1815–1902.* New York: John Day, 1940.

Lutz, Ralph Haswell. "Rudolph Schleiden and the Visit to Richmond, April 25, 1861." *Annual Report of the American Historical Association for the Year 1915,* 207–16.

Mabee, Carlton. "Sojourner Truth and President Lincoln." *New England Quarterly* 61, no. 4 (December 1988): 519–29.

Madsen, Brigham Dwaine. *Encounter with the Northwestern Shoshoni at Bear River in 1863: Battle or Massacre?* Ogden, Utah: Weber State College Press, 1984.

———. *The Shoshoni Frontier and the Bear River Massacre.* Salt Lake City: University of Utah Press, 1983.

Maher, Edward R., Jr. "Sam Houston and Secession." *The Southwestern Historical Quarterly* 55, no. 4 (April 1952): 448–58.

Manning, Chandra. *What This Cruel War Was Over: Soldiers, Slavery and the Civil War.* New York: Alfred A. Knopf, 2007.

Marszalek, John F. *Commander of All Lincoln's Armies: A Life of Henry W. Halleck.* Cambridge: Harvard University Press, 2004.

———. *Lincoln and the Military.* Carbondale: Southern Illinois University Press, 2014.

Marvel, William. *Mr. Lincoln Goes to War.* Boston: Houghton Mifflin Harcourt, 2006.

Mason, Virginia. *The Public Life and Diplomatic Correspondence of James M. Mason with Some Personal History.* New York: Neale, 1906.

Massey, Mary Elizabeth. *Bonnet Brigades: American Women and the Civil War.* New York: Alfred A. Knopf, 1966.

———. *Women in the Civil War.* Lincoln: University of Nebraska Press, 1994.

Maurice, Sir Frederick. "Lincoln as a Strategist." *The Forum* 75, no. 2 (February 1926): 161–69.

Maxwell, William Quentin. *Lincoln's Fifth Wheel: The Political History of the United States Sanitary Commission.* New York: Longmans, Green, 1956.

McClintock, Russell. *Lincoln and the Decision for War: The Northern Response to Secession.* Chapel Hill: University of North Carolina Press, 2008.

McClure, Alexander K. *"Abe" Lincoln's Yarns and Stories: The Complete Collection of the Funny and Witty Anecdotes That Made Lincoln Famous as America's Greatest Storyteller.* Chicago: Henry Neal, 1904.

McGinty, Brian. "I Will Call a Traitor a Traitor." *Civil War Times Illustrated* 20, no. 3 (June 1981): 24–30.

McMurtry, R. Gerald. "Lincoln Knew Shakespeare." *Indiana Magazine of History* 31, no. 4 (December 1935): 265–77.

McPhee, John. "Elicitation." *The New Yorker,* April 7, 2014, 50–57.

McPherson, James M. *This Mighty Scourge: Perspectives on the Civil War.* New York: Oxford University Press, 2007.

———. *Tried by War: Abraham Lincoln as Commander in Chief.* New York: Penguin Press, 2008.

Mencken, H. L. *A Mencken Chrestomathy.* New York: Alfred A. Knopf, 1949.

Meneely, A. Howard. *The War Department, 1861: A Study in Mobilization and Administration.* New York: Columbia University Press, 1928.

Miers, Earl Schenck, ed. *Lincoln Day by Day: A Chronology 1809–1865.* 3 vols. Washington, D.C.: Lincoln Sesquicentennial Commission, 1960.

Miller, David W. *Second Only to Grant: Quartermaster-General Montgomery C. Meigs.* Shippensburg, Pa.: White Mane, 2000.

Miller, Edward A. *Lincoln's Abolitionist General: The Biography of David Hunter.* Columbia: University of South Carolina Press, 1997.

Miller, William Lee. "Lincoln's Profound and Benign Americanism, or Nationalism Without Malice." *JALA* 22, no. 1 (Winter 2001): 1–13.

Miner, H. Craig, and William E. Unrau. *The End of Indian Kansas: A Study of Cultural Revolution, 1854–1871.* Lawrence: Regent's Press of Kansas, 1978.

Moore, Wilton P. "The Provost Marshal Goes to War." *Civil War History* 5, no. 1 (March 1959): 62–71.

Morgan, Arthur E. "New Light on Lincoln's Boyhood." *Atlantic Monthly,* February 1920, 208–17.

Moulton, Gary E. "John Ross and W. P. Dole: A Case Study of Lincoln's Indian Policy." *Journal of the West* 12, no. 3 (July 1973): 414–23.

———. *John Ross, Cherokee Chief.* Athens: University of Georgia Press, 1978.

Munkres, Robert L. "Indian-White Contact Before 1870: Cultural Factors in Conflict." *Journal of the West* 10, no. 3 (July 1971): 439–73.

Nardin, James T. "Civil War Humor: The War in *Vanity Fair.*" *Civil War History* 2, no. 3 (September 1956): 67–85.

Nation, Richard F. *At Home in the Hoosier Hills: Agriculture, Politics, and Religion in Southern Indiana, 1810–1870.* Bloomington: Indiana University Press, 2005.

Neely, Mark E., Jr. *The Civil War and the Limits of Destruction.* Cambridge: Harvard University Press, 2007.

———. *The Fate of Liberty: Abraham Lincoln and Civil Liberties.* New York: Oxford University Press, 1991.

———. *The Last Best Hope of Earth: Abraham Lincoln and the Promise of America.* Cambridge: Harvard University Press, 1993.

———. "War and Partisanship: What Lincoln Learned from James K. Polk." *Journal of the Illinois State Historical Society* 74, no. 3 (Autumn 1981): 199–216.

Neely, Mark E., Jr., and Harold Holzer. *The Lincoln Family Album.* New York: Doubleday, 1990.

Neely, Mark E., Jr., and R. Gerald McMurtry. *The Insanity File: The Case of Mary Todd Lincoln.* Carbondale: Southern Illinois University Press, 1986.

Neely, Mark E., Jr., Harold Holzer, and Gabor S. Boritt. *The Confederate Image: Prints of the Lost Cause.* Chapel Hill: University of North Carolina Press, 1987.

Ness, George T., Jr. *The Regular Army on the Eve of the Civil War.* Baltimore: Toomey Press, 1990.

Nevins, Allan. *The Emergence of Lincoln.* Vol. 2, *Prologue to Civil War, 1859–1861.* New York: Scribner, 1950.

Nichols, David A. *Lincoln and the Indians: Civil War Policy and Politics.* Columbia: University of Missouri Press, 1978.

Nicolay, Helen. *Personal Traits of Abraham Lincoln.* New York: Century, 1919.

Nicolay, John G., and John Hay. *Abraham Lincoln: A History.* 10 vols. New York: Century, 1886–1890.

———. "The President-Elect at Springfield." *The Century Magazine,* November 1887, 64–87.

Oakes, James. *The Radical and the Republican: Frederick Douglass, Abraham Lincoln, and the Triumph of Antislavery Politics.* New York: W. W. Norton, 2007.

Oates, Stephen B. *A Woman of Valor: Clara Barton and the Civil War.* New York: Free Press, 1994.

———. *With Malice Toward None: The Life of Abraham Lincoln.* New York: Harper & Row, 1977.

Orrmont, Arthur. *Mr. Lincoln's Master Spy: Lafayette Baker.* New York: Julian Messner, 1966.

Page, Jake. *In the Hands of the Great Spirit: The 20,000-Year History of American Indians.* New York: Free Press, 2003.

Painter, Nell Irvin. *Sojourner Truth: A Life, A Symbol.* New York: W. W. Norton, 1996.

Paludan, Phillip Shaw. "Greeley, Colonization, and a 'Deputation of Negroes': Three Considerations on Lincoln and Race." In *Lincoln Emancipated: The President and the Politics of Race.* Edited by Brian R. Dirck, 29–46. DeKalb: Northern Illinois University Press, 2007.

———. "Lincoln and Colonization: Policy or Propaganda?" *JALA* 25, no. 1 (Winter 2004): 23–37.

———. *The Presidency of Abraham Lincoln.* Lawrence: University Press of Kansas, 1994.

Parsons, Lynn Hudson. "'A Perpetual Harrow upon My Feelings': John Quincy Adams and the American Indian." *New England Quarterly* 46, no. 3 (September 1973): 339–79.

Paschal, George W. "The Last Years of Sam Houston." *Harper's New Monthly Magazine,* April 1866, 630–34.

Patrick, Rembert W. *The Fall of Richmond.* Baton Rouge: Louisiana State University Press, 1960.

Perdue, Theda. *Slavery and the Evolution of Cherokee Society, 1540–1866.* Knoxville: University of Tennessee Press, 1979.

Peskin, Allan. *Garfield.* Kent, Ohio: Kent State University Press, 1978.

———. *Winfield Scott and the Profession of Arms.* Kent, Ohio: Kent State University Press, 2003.

Pinsker, Matthew. *Lincoln's Sanctuary: Abraham Lincoln and the Soldiers' Home.* New York: Oxford University Press, 2003.

Potter, David M. *The Impending Crisis, 1848–1861.* New York: Harper Torchbooks, 1976.

———. *Lincoln and His Party in the Secession Crisis.* New Haven: Yale University Press, 1942.

Pratt, Harry E. "Lincoln in the Black Hawk War." *Bulletin of the Abraham Lincoln Association* 54 (December 1938): 3–13.

———. *The Personal Finances of Abraham Lincoln.* Springfield, Ill.: The Abraham Lincoln Association, 1943.

Prezter, William. "'The British, Duff Green, the Rats and the Devil': Custom, Capitalism, and Conflict in the Washington Printing Trade, 1834–36." *Labor History* 27, no. 1 (Winter 1985): 5–30.

Prokopowicz, Gerald J. *Did Lincoln Own Slaves? And Other Frequently Asked Questions About Abraham Lincoln.* New York: Pantheon, 2008.

Prucha, Francis Paul. *The Great Father: The United States Government and the American Indians.* 2 vols. Lincoln: University of Nebraska Press, 1984.

Pryor, Elizabeth Brown. "Brief Encounter: A New York Cavalryman's Striking Conversation with Abraham Lincoln." *JALA* 30, no. 2 (Summer 2009): 1–24.

———. *Clara Barton, Professional Angel*. Philadelphia: University of Pennsylvania Press, 1987.

———. "'The Grand Old Duke of York': How Abraham Lincoln Lost the Confidence of His Military Command." Forthcoming.

———. *Reading the Man: A Portrait of Robert E. Lee Through His Private Letters*. New York: Viking, 2007.

———. "Robert E. Lee and the Full Mobilization of the South." *North and South* 10, no. 4 (November–December 2007): 61–70.

———. "'Thou Knowest Not the Time of Thy Visitation': A Newly Discovered Letter Reveals Robert E. Lee's Lonely Struggle with Disunion." *Virginia Magazine of History and Biography* 119, no. 3 (September 2011): 277–96.

Pullen, John J. *Comic Relief: The Life and Laughter of Artemus Ward, 1834–1867*. Hamden, Conn.: Archon, 1983.

Quarles, Benjamin. *Lincoln and the Negro*. New York: Da Capo, 1962.

Rafuse, Ethan S. "General McClellan and the Politicians Revisited." *Parameters* 43 (Summer 2012): 71–85.

Randall, James G. *Constitutional Problems Under Lincoln*. Urbana: University of Illinois Press, 1951.

———. *Lincoln and the South*. Baton Rouge: Louisiana State University Press, 1946.

———. *Lincoln, the Liberal Statesman*. New York: Dodd, Mead, 1947. (Contains "The Unpopular Mr. Lincoln," 65–87; "Lincoln the Liberal Statesman," 88–117; "The Rule of Law Under Lincoln," 118–34.)

Randall, Ruth Painter. *Mary Todd Lincoln: Biography of a Marriage*. Boston: Little, Brown, 1953.

Rawley, James A. "Isaac Newton Arnold, Lincoln's Friend and Biographer." *JALA* 19, no. 1 (Winter 1998): 39–56.

Reck, W. Emerson. *A. Lincoln, His Last 24 Hours*. Jefferson, N.C.: McFarland, 1987.

Reed, Gerald Alexander. "The Ross-Waitie Conflict: Factionalism in the Cherokee Nation, 1839–1865." PhD diss., University of Oklahoma, 1967.

Reed, John Q. "Civil War Humor: Artemus Ward." *Civil War History* 2, no. 3 (September 1956): 87–101.

Reed, Michael. "The Evolution of Joint Operations During the Civil War." Master's thesis, U.S. Army Command and General Staff College. Fort Leavenworth, Kans., 2009.

Reed, Rowena. *Combined Operations in the Civil War*. Annapolis, Md.: Naval Institute Press, 1978.

Remini, Robert V. *The Life of Andrew Jackson*. New York: Harper & Row, 1988.

Reynolds, David S. *Mightier than the Sword: Uncle Tom's Cabin and the Battle for America*. New York: W. W. Norton, 2011.

Rezneck, Samuel. "The Civil War Role 1861–1863 of a Veteran New York Officer Major-General John E. Wool (1784–1869)." *New York History* 44, no. 3 (July 1963): 237–58.

Riccards, Michael P. *The Ferocious Engine of Democracy: A History of the American Presidency*. 2 vols. New York: Madison, 1997.

Richardson, Elmo, and Alan W. Farley. *John Palmer Usher: Lincoln's Secretary of the Interior*. Lawrence: University Press of Kansas, 1960.

Righi, Brandon P. "'A Power Unknown to Our Laws': A Study of the Effect of Federal Policies on Border State Unionism in Kent County, Maryland 1861–1865." Senior honors thesis, Washington College, c. 2007; www.revcollege.washcoll.edu.

Roberts, Cokie. *Founding Mothers: The Women Who Raised Our Nation*. New York: William Morrow, 2004.

Robertson, James I., Jr. *General A. P. Hill: The Story of a Confederate Warrior*. New York: Random House, 1987.

Roland, Charles P. *Albert Sidney Johnston: Soldier of Three Republics*. Austin: University of Texas Press, 1964.

Rose, Willie Lee. *Rehearsal for Reconstruction: The Port Royal Experiment*. New York: Vintage, 1967.

Rosenberg, Charles E. *The Cholera Years: The United States in 1832, 1849 and 1866*. Chicago: University of Chicago Press, 1987.

———. "Sexuality, Class and Role in 19th-Century America." *American Quarterly* 25, no. 2 (May 1973): 131–53.

Ross, Dorothy. "Lincoln and Ethics of Emancipation: Universalism, Nationalism, Exceptionalism." *Journal of American History* 96, no. 2 (September 2009): 379–99.

Rourke, Constance. *American Humor: A Study of the National Character*. New York: Harcourt, Brace, 1931.

Rowland, Dunbar. *Jefferson Davis, Constitutionalist*. 10 vols. Jackson: Mississippi Department of Archives and History, 1923.

Royster, Charles. *The Destructive War: William Tecumseh Sherman, Stonewall Jackson, and the Americans*. New York: Alfred A. Knopf, 1991.

Russ, William, Jr. "Franklin Weirick: 'Copperhead' of Central Pennsylvania." *Pennsylvania History: A Journal of Mid-Atlantic Studies* 5, no. 4 (October 1938): 245–56.

Ruthrauff, C. C. "Artemus Ward at Cleveland." *Scribner's Monthly*, October 1878, 785–91.

Ryan, Mary P. *Women in Public: Between Banners and Ballots, 1825–1880*. Baltimore: Johns Hopkins University Press, 1990.

Scheips, Paul J. "Lincoln and the Chiriqui Colonization Project." *Journal of Negro History* 37 (July 1952): 418–53.

Schneller, Robert J., Jr. *A Quest for Glory: A Biography of Rear Admiral John A. Dahlgren*. Annapolis, Md.: Naval Institute Press, 1996.

Schultz, Jane E. "Seldom Thanked, Never Praised and Scarcely Recognized: Gender and Racism in Civil War Hospitals." *Civil War History* 48, no. 3 (September 2002): 220–36.

Schutz, Walter J., and Walter N. Trenerry. *Abandoned by Lincoln: A Military Biography of General John Pope*. Urbana: University of Illinois Press, 1990.

Schwarz, Frederic D. "The Halls of Montezuma." *American Heritage* 48, no. 5 (September 1997): 105–6.

Scripps, John Locke. *Life of Abraham Lincoln*. Edited by Roy P. Basler and Lloyd A. Dunlap. Bloomington: Indiana University Press, 1961.

Sears, Stephen W. *George B. McClellan: The Young Napoleon*. New York: Ticknor & Fields, 1988.

———. *To the Gates of Richmond: The Peninsula Campaign*. New York: Ticknor & Fields, 1992.

Seitz, Don C. *Artemus Ward (Charles Farrar Browne): A Biography and Bibliography*. New York: Harper Brothers, 1919.

Settles, Thomas M. *John Bankhead Magruder: A Military Reappraisal*. Baton Rouge: Louisiana State University Press, 2009.

Shallat, Todd. *Structures in the Stream: Water, Science and the Rise of the U.S. Army Corps of Engineers*. Austin: University of Texas Press, 1994.

Shankman, Arnold. "Converse, the *Christian Observer*, and Civil War Censorship." *Journal of Presbyterian History* 52, no. 3 (Fall 1974): 227–44.

Shannon, Fred Albert. *The Organization and Administration of the Union Army, 1861–1865*. 2 vols. Cleveland: Arthur H. Clark, 1928.

Sheehan-Dean, Aaron. *Why Confederates Fought: Family and Nation in Civil War Virginia.* Chapel Hill: University of North Carolina Press, 2007.

Shenk, Joshua Wolf. *Lincoln's Melancholy: How Depression Challenged a President and Fueled His Greatness.* Boston: Houghton Mifflin, 2005.

Siciliano, Stephen N. "Major General William Farrar Smith: Critic of Defeat and Engineer of Victory." PhD diss., College of William and Mary, 1984.

"Side-lights on Lincoln." *The Century Magazine,* February 1911, 589–99.

Sievers, Michael A. "Sands of Sand Creek Historiography." *Colorado Magazine* 49, no. 2 (Spring 1972): 116–42.

Silber, Nina. *Daughters of the Union: Northern Women Fight the Civil War.* Cambridge: Harvard University Press, 2005.

Silbey, Joel H. *A Respectable Minority: The Democratic Party in the Civil War Era, 1860–1868.* New York: W. W. Norton, 1977.

Simon, John Y. *House Divided: Lincoln and His Father.* Fort Wayne, Ind.: Louis A. Warren Lincoln Library and Museum, 1987.

———. *The Union Forever: Lincoln, Grant, and the Civil War.* Edited by Glenn W. LaFantasie. Lexington: University Press of Kentucky, 2012.

Simon, John Y., and Harold Holzer, eds. *The Lincoln Forum: Rediscovering Abraham Lincoln.* New York: Fordham University Press, 2002. (Contains James McPherson, "Lincoln as Commander in Chief," 11–15; Gerald J. Prokopowicz, "'If I Had Gone Up There, I Could Have Whipped Them Myself': Lincoln's Military Fantasies," 77–92; John Y. Simon, "Commander in Chief Lincoln and General Grant," 16–33; Craig L. Symonds, "Men, Machines, and Old Abe: Lincoln and the Civil War Navy," 48–64; Frank J. Williams, "'A Matter of Profound Wonder': The Women in Lincoln's Life," 112–21.)

Simpson, Brooks D. "Lincoln and His Political Generals." *JALA* 21, no. 1 (Winter 2000): 63–77.

———. *Ulysses S. Grant: Triumph over Adversity, 1822–1865.* Boston: Houghton Mifflin, 2000.

Sizer, Lyde Cullen. *The Political Work of Northern Women Writers and the Civil War, 1850–1872.* Chapel Hill: University of North Carolina Press, 2000.

Skelton, William B. *An American Profession of Arms: The Army Officer Corps, 1784–1861.* Lawrence: University Press of Kansas, 1992.

———. "Officers and Politicians: The Origins of Army Politics in the United States Before the Civil War." *Armed Forces and Society* 6, no. 1 (Fall 1979): 22–48.

Smith, Michael Thomas. *The Enemy Within: Fears of Corruption in the Civil War North.* Charlottesville: University of Virginia Press, 2011.

Smith, Ronald D. *Thomas Ewing, Jr.: Frontier Lawyer and Civil War General.* Columbia: University of Missouri Press, 2008.

Smith, Theodore Clarke. *The Life and Letters of James Abram Garfield.* 2 vols. New Haven: Yale University Press, 1925.

Smith, Troy. "Nations Colliding: The Civil War Comes to Indian Territory." *Civil War History* 59, no. 3 (September 2013): 279–319.

Smith, William Earnest. *The Francis Preston Blair Family in Politics.* 2 vols. New York: Macmillan, 1933.

Stampp, Kenneth M. "Lincoln and the Strategy of Defense in the Crisis of 1861." *Journal of Southern History* 11, no. 3 (August 1945): 297–323.

Starr, Stephen Z. *The Union Cavalry in the Civil War.* 3 vols. Baton Rouge: Louisiana State University Press, 1979–1985.

Steen, Ralph W. "Texas Newspapers and Lincoln." *The Southwestern Historical Quarterly* 51, no. 3 (January 1948): 199–212.

Steinberg, Theodore. *Slide Mountain or the Folly of Owning Nature.* Berkeley: University of California Press, 1995.

Stewart, Randall. " 'Pestiferous Gail Hamilton,' James T. Fields, and the Hawthornes." *New England Quarterly* 17, no. 3 (September 1944): 418–23.

Stowe, Charles Edward, and Lyman Beecher Stowe. *Harriet Beecher Stowe: The Story of Her Life.* Boston: Houghton Mifflin, 1911.

Stuart, Meriwether. "Colonel Ulric Dahlgren and Richmond's Union Underground, April 1864." *Virginia Magazine of History and Biography* 72, no. 2 (April 1964): 153–204.

Summers, Mark Wahlgren. *The Era of Good Stealings.* New York: Oxford University Press, 1993.

Sutherland, Daniel E. "Abraham Lincoln, John Pope, and the Origins of Total War." *Journal of Military History* 56, no. 4 (October 1992): 567–86.

———, ed. *Guerrillas, Unionists, and Violence on the Confederate Home Front.* Fayetteville: University of Arkansas Press, 1999.

Sutton, Robert K., and John A. Latschar, eds. *American Indians and the Civil War.* Washington, D.C.: National Park Service, 2013.

Symonds, Craig L. *Joseph E. Johnston: A Civil War Biography.* New York: W. W. Norton, 1992.

———. *Lincoln and His Admirals.* New York: Oxford University Press, 2008.

Symonds, Craig L., ed. *Union Combined Operations in the Civil War.* New York: Fordham University Press, 2010. (Contains Craig L. Symonds, "Introduction," 2–9; Edward H. Wiser, "Union Combined Operations in the Civil War: Lessons Learned, Lessons Forgotten," 135–49.)

Taaffe, Stephen R. *Commanding Lincoln's Navy: The Union Naval Leadership During the Civil War.* Annapolis, Md.: Naval Institute Press, 2009.

———. *Commanding the Army of the Potomac.* Lawrence: University Press of Kansas, 2006.

Tagg, Larry. *The Unpopular Mr. Lincoln: The Story of America's Most Reviled President.* New York: Savas Beatie, 2009.

Tandy, Jeannette. *Crackerbox Philosophers in American Humor and Satire.* New York: Columbia University Press, 1925.

Tap, Bruce. "Joint Committee on the Conduct of the War (1861–1865)." In *Encyclopedia of the American Civil War.* Edited by David S. Heidler and Jeanne T. Heidler. 5 vols. Santa Barbara, Calif.: ABC-CLIO, 2000; online at www.civilwarhome.com.

———. *Over Lincoln's Shoulder: The Committee on the Conduct of the War.* Lawrence: University Press of Kansas, 1998.

Tarbell, Ida M. *The Early Life of Abraham Lincoln.* New York: S. S. McClure, 1896.

———. *The Life of Abraham Lincoln,* 2 vols. New York: Macmillan, 1920.

Taylor, David G. "Thomas Ewing, Jr., and the Origins of the Kansas Pacific Railway Company." *Kansas Historical Quarterly* 42, no. 2 (Summer 1976): 155–77.

Temple, Dr. Wayne C. *Lincoln's Arms, Dress and Military Duty During and After the Black Hawk War.* Springfield: State of Illinois Military and Naval Department, 1981.

Tenney, Craig D. "To Suppress or Not to Suppress: Abraham Lincoln and the Chicago *Times*." *Civil War History* 27, no. 3 (September 1981): 248–59.

Thomas, Benjamin P. *Abraham Lincoln: A Biography.* New York: Alfred A. Knopf, 1952.

———. *"Lincoln's Humor" and Other Essays.* Edited by Michael Burlingame. Urbana: University of Illinois Press, 2002.

Thomas, Benjamin, and Harold M. Hyman. *Stanton: The Life and Times of Lincoln's Secretary of War.* New York: Alfred A. Knopf, 1962.

Thomas, William G. *The Iron Way: Railroads, the Civil War, and the Making of Modern America.* New Haven: Yale University Press, 2011.

Tidball, Eugene C. *"No Disgrace to My Country": The Life of John C. Tidball.* Kent, Ohio: Kent State University Press, 2002.

Tiffany, Francis. *Life of Dorothea Lynde Dix.* Boston: Houghton Mifflin, 1890.

Tinker, George E. *Missionary Conquest: The Gospel and Native American Cultural Genocide.* Minneapolis: Fortress Press, 1993.

Townsend, William H. *Lincoln and the Bluegrass: Slavery and Civil War in Kentucky.* Lexington: University of Kentucky Press, 1955.

Trefousse, Hans L. "Ben Wade and the Negro." *Ohio Historical Quarterly* 68, no. 2 (April 1959): 161–76.

Tripp, C. A. *The Intimate World of Abraham Lincoln.* Edited by Lewis Gannett. New York: Free Press, 2005.

Trulock, Alice Rains. *In the Hands of Providence: Joshua L. Chamberlain and the American Civil War.* Chapel Hill: University of North Carolina Press, 1992.

Utley, Robert M. *Frontiersmen in Blue: The United States Army and the Indian, 1848–1865.* New York: Macmillan, 1967.

VandeCreek, Drew E. "Native American Relations." Online at http://lincoln.lib.niu/native american.html.

Van Deusen, Glyndon Garlock. *William Henry Seward.* New York: Oxford University Press, 1867.

Van Doren, Charles Lincoln, and Robert McHenry, eds. *Webster's Guide to American History: A Chronological, Geographical and Biographical Survey and Compendium.* Springfield, Mass.: G. & C. Merriam, 1971.

Van Dyke, John C. "Lincoln's Reading and Modesty." *The Century Magazine,* February 1911, 597–98.

Varon, Elizabeth R. *Southern Lady, Yankee Spy: The True Story of Elizabeth Van Lew, A Union Agent in the Heart of the Confederacy.* New York: Oxford University Press, 2003.

———. "Tippecanoe and the Ladies, Too: White Women and Party Politics in Antebellum Virginia." *Journal of American History* 82, no. 2 (September 1995): 494–521.

Venet, Wendy Hamand. "The Emergence of a Suffragist: Mary Livermore, Civil War Activism, and the Moral Power of Women." *Civil War History* 48, no. 2 (June 2002): 143–64.

Voigt, David Quentin. " 'Too Pitchy to Touch': Abraham Lincoln and Editor Bennett." *Abraham Lincoln Quarterly* 6, no. 3 (September 1950): 139–60.

Vollaro, Daniel R. "Lincoln, Stowe, and the 'Little Woman/Great War' Story: The Making, and Breaking, of a Great American Anecdote." *JALA* 30, no. 1 (Winter 2009): 18–34.

Vorenberg, Michael. "Abraham Lincoln and the Politics of Black Colonization." *JALA* 14, no. 2 (Summer 1993): 22–45.

Wallace, Anthony F. C. "Prelude to Disaster: The Course of Indian-White Relations Which Led to the Black Hawk War of 1832." In *The Black Hawk War, 1831–1832.* Edited by Ellen M. Whitney, 1:1–51. 4 vols. Springfield: Illinois State Historical Library, 1970–1978.

Wallace, Ernest, and E. Adamson Hoebel. *The Comanches: Lords of the South Plains.* Norman: University of Oklahoma Press, 1986.

Walsh, William Shepard. *Abraham Lincoln and the London Punch: Cartoons, Comments and Poems, Published in the London Charivari During the American Civil War (1861–1865)*. New York: Moffat, Yard, 1909.

Warren, Louis A. "Abraham Lincoln, Senior, Grandfather of the President." *Filson Club History Quarterly* 5, no. 3 (July 1931): 136–52.

———. *Lincoln's Parentage and Childhood: A History of the Kentucky Lincolns Supported by Documentary Evidence*. New York: Century, 1926.

———. *Lincoln's Youth: Indiana Years Seven to Twenty-One, 1816–1830*. New York: Appleton, Century, Crofts, 1959.

Washington, Margaret. *Sojourner Truth's America*. Urbana: University of Illinois Press, 2009.

Weber, Jennifer L. *Copperheads: The Rise and Fall of Lincoln's Opponents in the North*. New York: Oxford University Press, 2006.

Weigley, Russell F. *Quartermaster General of the Union Army: A Biography of M. C. Meigs*. New York: Columbia University Press, 1959.

———. *Towards an American Army: Military Thought from Washington to Marshall*. New York: Columbia University Press, 1962.

Wells, Jonathan Daniel. *The Origins of the Southern Middle Class, 1800–1861*. Chapel Hill: University of North Carolina Press, 2004.

Wert, Jeffry D. *General James Longstreet: The Confederacy's Most Controversial Soldier*. New York: Simon & Schuster, 1999.

———. *The Sword of Lincoln: The Army of the Potomac*. New York: Simon & Schuster, 2005.

Westwood, Howard C. "President Lincoln's Overture to Sam Houston." *The Southwestern Historical Quarterly* 88, no. 2 (October 1984): 125–44.

White, Barbara A. *The Beecher Sisters*. New Haven: Yale University Press, 2003.

———. *Visits with Lincoln: Abolitionists Meet the President at the White House*. Lanham, Md.: Lexington, 2011.

White, Richard. *Railroaded: The Transcontinentals and the Making of Modern America*. New York: W. W. Norton, 2011.

White, Ronald C., Jr. *The Eloquent President: A Portrait of Lincoln Through His Words*. New York: Random House, 2005.

Wiley, Bell Irvin. *Southern Negroes, 1861–1865*. New Haven: Yale University Press, 1938.

Williams, Frank J. "Abraham Lincoln and the Changing Role of Commander in Chief." In *Lincoln Reshapes the Presidency*. Edited by Charles E. Hubbard, 9–29. Macon, Ga.: Mercer University Press, 2003.

Williams, Kenneth P. *Lincoln Finds a General: A Military Study of the Civil War*. 5 vols. New York: Macmillan, 1949–1959.

Williams, T. Harry. "Abraham Lincoln—Principle and Pragmatism in Politics: A Review Article." *Mississippi Valley Historical Review* 40, no. 1 (June 1953): 89–106.

———. *Lincoln and His Generals*. New York: Vintage, 2011.

———. *Lincoln and the Radicals*. Madison: University of Wisconsin Press, 1965.

Wilson, Douglas L. "His Hour upon the Stage." *The American Scholar*, Winter 2012; www.theamericanscholar.org.

———. *Honor's Voice: The Transformation of Abraham Lincoln*. New York: Alfred A. Knopf, 1998.

———. *Lincoln Before Washington: New Perspectives on the Illinois Years*. Urbana: University of Illinois Press, 1997.

————. *Lincoln's Sword: The Presidency and the Power of Words.* New York: Vintage, 2006.

————. "William H. Herndon and Mary Todd Lincoln." *JALA* 22, no. 2 (Summer 2001): 1–26.

Wilson, Edmund. *Patriotic Gore: Studies in the Literature of the American Civil War.* New York: Farrar, Straus and Giroux, 1962.

Wilson, James. *The Earth Shall Weep: A History of Native America.* New York: Atlantic Monthly Press, 1999.

Wilson, Rufus Rockwell. *Lincoln in Caricature: 165 Posters, Cartoons and Drawings for the Press.* Elmira, N.Y.: Primavera Press, 1945.

Winders, Richard Bruce. *Mr. Polk's Army: The American Military Experience in the Mexican War.* College Station: Texas A&M University Press, 1997.

Wisehart, M. K. *Sam Houston: American Giant.* Washington, D.C.: Robert B. Luce, 1962.

Wishy, Bernard. *The Child and the Republic: The Dawn of Modern American Child Nurture.* Philadelphia: University of Pennsylvania Press, 1968.

Wolfe, Brendan. "Indians in Virginia." Online at www.encyclopediavirginia.org/Indians_in _Virginia.

Work, David. *Lincoln's Political Generals.* Urbana: University of Illinois Press, 2009.

Wright, Muriel H. "Colonel Cooper's Civil War Report on the Battle of Round Mountain." *Chronicles of Oklahoma* 39, no. 4 (Winter 1961–1962): 352–97.

Young, James Harvey. "Anna Elizabeth Dickinson and the Civil War: For and Against Lincoln." *Mississippi Valley Historical Review* 31, no. 1 (June 1944): 59–80.

Young, Robert W. *Senator James Murray Mason: Defender of the Old South.* Knoxville: University of Tennessee Press, 1998.

Zall, P. M., ed. *Abe Lincoln Laughing: Humorous Anecdotes from Original Sources by and About Abraham Lincoln.* Berkeley: University of California Press, 1982.

Illustration Credits

Index

Page numbers in italics refer to illustrations.

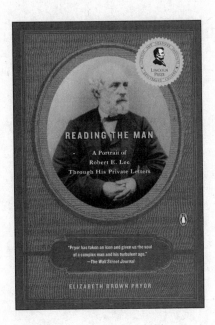